~ Colonial Latin America

～ *Colonial Latin America*

A Documentary History

Edited by

KENNETH MILLS
Princeton University

WILLIAM B. TAYLOR
University of California, Berkeley

and

SANDRA LAUDERDALE GRAHAM
Santa Fe, New Mexico

A Scholarly Resources Inc. Imprint
Wilmington, Delaware

© 2002 by Scholarly Resources Inc.
All rights reserved
First published 2002
Printed and bound in the United States of America

Scholarly Resources Inc.
104 Greenhill Avenue
Wilmington, DE 19805-1897
www.scholarly.com

Library of Congress Cataloging-in-Publication Data

Colonial Latin America : a documentary history / edited by Kenneth Mills, William B. Taylor, and Sandra Lauderdale Graham.
    p.   cm.
    Includes index.
    ISBN 0-8420-2996-6 (alk. paper) — ISBN 0-8420-2997-4 (pbk. : alk. paper)
    1. Latin America—History—To 1830. 2. Latin America—History—To 1830—Sources.
I. Mills, Kenneth (Kenneth R.) II. Taylor, William B. III. Lauderdale Graham, Sandra, 1943–

F1412.C642 2002
980'.01—dc21

2002066960

✌ ACKNOWLEDGMENTS

The editors express their special thanks to the following people, places, and institutions who have helped make this project a pleasure.

Sandra Lauderdale Graham thanks Alida Metcalf for generously contributing the priest's will from her research in Santa Anna de Parnaíba; Neusa Esteves for kindly supplying an eleventh-hour transcription of the freed woman's will; and Laura de Mello e Souza for bringing to light the account of the Pamplona expedition. These friends and colleagues, along with Guilherme Neves, offered good counsel throughout the preparation of these selections. Russ Lohse assisted often and always graciously. Alice Davis, head of interlibrary loan services at the Santa Fe Public Library, retrieved numerous hard-to-find sources with remarkable speed. Helga von Sydow helped to make possible our cover by kindly translating essential information from German. And once again the Allá Bookstore in Santa Fe supplied unexpected resources.

William Taylor is indebted to E. William Jowdy for his generous interest and bracing criticism of many introductions to selections. He also thanks Thomas B. F. Cummins for collaborating on short notice on an appraisal of the enigmatic portrait of the three gentlemen from Esmeraldas; Karin E. Taylor for redrawing the plan of the Huejotzingo altarpiece and sending her father off to read Italo Calvino; Daniel Slive for advice about colonial engravings; and James Early for sharing slides from his splendid collection on colonial Mexican architecture. The Edmund and Louise Kahn Chair fund at Southern Methodist University helped cover editorial costs.

Kenneth Mills thanks Roger Highfield for the way he speaks about the place of primary sources in teaching; Elizabeth Mills for her timely criticism and suggestions; Meri Clark, Karen Caplan, Peter Lake, Peter Brown, Robert Connor, and J. Paul Hunter, among others, for criticism, advice, and encouragement along the way. He is grateful for support of this project from the National Humanities Center and the John Carter Brown Library at Brown University as well as the University Committee for Research in the Humanities and Social Sciences, the Program in Latin American Studies, and the Department of History, all at Princeton University. John Blazejewski, Richard Hurley, and Andrew Reisberg expertly photographed a number of the previously published images. Fergus Bremmer has generously shared his computing skills. Margaret Case's careful eye helped the contents of this book's first edition, but both that beginning and this revised second edition owe most to the editorial creativity and expertise of Linda Pote Musumeci of Scholarly Resources. Richard Hopper of SR has also been supportive of the project from the start.

Finally, the three editors acknowledge the students in their respective classes who, usually without knowing it, have partaken of a number of teaching experiments and contributed both to what appears in, and what has been shed from, this book.

✑ CONTENTS

Editors' Note   xi
List of Illustrations   xiii
Reference Maps
    Map 1. The Iberian Peninsula   xv
    Map 2. The West African Coast and "Atlantic Mediterranean"   xvi
    Map 3. Brazil   xvii
    Map 4. New Spain and the Caribbean Basin   xviii
    Map 5. Peru   xix
    Map 6. The Pajonal on Peru's Tarma Frontier   xx
Introduction—Texts and Images for Colonial History   xxi

PART I   *Old Worlds and the Time of Discoveries*

1. *The Ancestors of the People Called Indians*
   A View from Huarochirí, Peru (ca. 1598–1608)   3

2. *The Inka's Tunics (fifteenth to sixteenth centuries)*   14

3. *The Lords and Holy Men of Tenochtitlan Reply to the Franciscans, 1524 (1564)*   19

4. *The Aztec Stone of the Five Eras (late fifteenth century)*   23

5. *Coexistence in the Medieval Spanish Kingdoms (ninth to twelfth centuries)*   27

6. *A Pope Rewards "So Salutary and Laudable a Work" (1455)*   34

7. *"There Can Easily Be Stamped Upon Them Whatever Belief We Wish to
   Give Them"*
   The First Letter from Brazil (1500)   43

8. *Orders Given to "the Twelve" (1523)*   59

9. *Francisco de Vitoria "On the Evangelization of Unbelievers," Salamanca,
   Spain (1534–35)*   65

10/6

10. *Two Woodcuts Accompanying a 1509 German Translation of Amerigo Vespucci's Letter to Pietro Soderini* (1504)	78
11. *Christoph Weiditz's Drawing of an Indian Woman of Mexico* (1529)	84
12. *Christoph Weiditz's Drawing of a Morisco Woman and Her Daughter at Home* (1529)	87

PART II   *The Americas as New Worlds for All?*

13. *The Jesuit and the Bishop, Bahia, Brazil* (1552–53)   93

14. *Fray Pedro de Gante's Letter to Charles V, Mexico City* (1552)   104

15. *The Evils of Cochineal, Tlaxcala, Mexico* (1553)   113

16. *The Indian Pueblo of Texupa in Sixteenth-Century Mexico* (1579)   117

17. *Alonso Ortiz's Letter to His Wife, Mexico City* (1574?)   124

18. *Jerónimo de Benarcama's Letter to Francisco de Borja, Granada, Spain* (1566)   127

19. *José de Acosta on the Salvation of the Indians* (1588)   134

10/6

20.	*Two Images from the Codex Osuna, Mexico City* (1565)	144
21.	*Two Images from the Codex Sierra, Oaxaca, Mexico* (1555, 1561)	148
22.	*Fray Diego Valadés's Ideal Atrio and Its Activities* (1579)	150
23.	*The Huejotzingo Altarpiece, Mexico* (1586)	153
24.	THOMAS B. F. CUMMINS AND WILLIAM B. TAYLOR *The Mulatto Gentlemen of Esmeraldas, Ecuador*	159
25.	*"Blacks Dancing"* (ca. 1640)	162

PART III   *Mid-Colonial Ways and Orders*

26. *Making an Image and a Shrine, Copacabana, Peru* (1582–1621)   167

27. *Felipe Guaman Poma de Ayala's Appeal Concerning the Priests, Peru* (ca. 1615) 173

28. *Pedro de León Portocarrero's Description of Lima, Peru* (early seventeenth century)   185

29. *The Church and Monastery of San Francisco, Lima, Peru (1673)*   196

30. *Santa Rosa of Lima According to a Pious Accountant (1617)*   198

31. *Sor Juana Inés de la Cruz's Letter to Sor Filotea (1691)*   207

32. *Portraits of Santa Rosa and Sor Juana*   215

33. *Two Slaveries—The Sermons of Padre Antônio Vieira, Salvador, Bahia (ca. 1633), and São Luís do Maranhão (1653)*   218

34. *Confessing to the Holy Office of the Inquisition, Bahia, Brazil (1592, 1618)*   234

35. *Francisco de Avila's Christmas Eve Sermon (1646)*   246

36. *The Witness Francisco Poma y Altas Caldeas of San Pedro de Acas, Cajatambo, Peru (1657)*   255

37. *Crossing and Dome of the Rosary Chapel, Church of Santo Domingo, Puebla, Mexico (1632–1690)*   269

38. *Two Paintings of a Corpus Christi Procession, Cusco, Peru (ca. 1674–1680)*   272

39. *A Black* Irmandade *in Bahia, Brazil (1699)*   280

PART IV   *Iberian Rules and American Practices in the Eighteenth Century*

40. *"As for the Spaniards, their time is up," Jauja, Peru (1742, 1752)*   299

41. *Nicolás Ñenguirú's Letter to the Governor of Buenos Aires (1753)*   309

42. *José de Gálvez's Decrees for the King's Subjects in Mexico (1769, 1778)*   316

43. *The Foundation of Nuestra Señora de Guadalupe de los Morenos de Amapa, Mexico (1769)*   320

44. *Concolorcorvo Engages the Postal Inspector about Indian Affairs, Lima, Peru (1776)*   328

45. *Taming the Wilderness, Minas Gerais, Brazil (1769)*   335

46. *Thanking Saint Anne—An Ex-voto from Brazil (1755)*   353

47. *Jeremiah in the Stocks—Baroque Art from the Gold Fields of Minas Gerais, Brazil (ca. 1770s)*   356

48. *Two Castas Paintings from Eighteenth-Century Mexico*   360

10 / 6

49. *Juan Francisco Domínguez's Discourses on the Ten Commandments,*
     Mexico (1805)   366

50. *Brazilian Slaves Who Marry* (1811)   372

51. *Two Brazilian Wills* (1793, 1823)   375

     52. *Late Eighteenth-Century Inscriptions on Fountains and*
          Monuments in Mexico City   384

     53. *Túpac Amaru I, Remembered* (eighteenth century)   390

     54. *"America Nursing Spanish Noble Boys," Peru* (ca. 1770s)   395

55. *José María Morelos's "Sentiments of the Nation," Chilpancingo, Mexico*
     (1813)   397

56. *The Argentine Declaration of Independence, San Miguel de Tucumán* (1816) 401

57. *The Brazilian Constitution and the Church* (1824)   403

Glossary   405
Notes on Selections and Sources   413
Index   425

~ EDITORS' NOTE

This collection is made up of selections, and by this term we refer both to written and visual sources and to the introductions which precede them. Due to pressures of space, we have excerpted portions of a few of our written selections and omitted the scholarly notes from previously published primary sources. When information contained in these notes has seemed crucial to the understanding or integrity of the selection, this information has been included or summarized within square brackets in the body of the text. Readers wishing to read these works as their authors first intended them to appear are urged toward the Notes on Selections and Sources section at the end of the volume. Information on each source is collected there, with references to scholarly work that has particularly informed or assisted the editors in introducing a selection, or to which we wish to draw readers' attention.

Fourteen visual sources are reproduced in color and gathered, along with two other images, into a central section of the book. Readers, who are also viewers, are guided to the plates by indications both beneath black-and-white reproductions within the selections and in the List of Illustrations. Six reference maps, corresponding to the selections' transcontinental sweep and particular needs, follow the List of Illustrations.

Foreign words and phrases are set in italics at first appearance, with a short definition. An independent Glossary of key terms and foreign words used in more than one selection is also provided. The translations of archival and published documentary material originally not in English are the work of the editors unless otherwise indicated in the Notes on Selections and Sources. We have made the following adjustments in the written selections: spelling conforms to United States English; typographical errors have been corrected; on rare occasions, we have altered punctuation to assist clarity; certain words have been capitalized and other small changes in spelling have been made to conform to the style used throughout the book; and ellipses mark parts of a text that we have left out. Our occasional glosses, additions, and interjections appear in brackets, as do the similar interventions of any previous editors.

✑ LIST OF ILLUSTRATIONS

Color plates follow page 164

1. An Inka key checkerboard tunic (fifteenth–sixteenth centuries) ✑AND PLATE 1   *15*
2. A royal tunic (sixteenth century) ✑AND PLATE 2   *16*
3. Aztec Stone of the Five Eras (late fifteenth century)   *24*
4. Drawing of the Aztec Stone of the Five Eras, 1792   *25*
5. Illustration from a German translation of Amerigo Vespucci's letter to Pietro Soderini, Strassburg, 1509   *80*
6. Illustration from a German translation of Amerigo Vespucci's letter to Pietro Soderini, Strassburg, 1509   *82*
7. Drawing of an Indian woman of Mexico by Christoph Weiditz, 1529   *85*
8. Drawing of a Morisco woman and her daughter at home by Christoph Weiditz, 1529   *89*
9. Map of Texupa, Mexico, 1579 ✑AND PLATE 3   *118*
10. "The View from Red and White Bundle": A Mixtec landscape   *120*
11. Illustration from the Codex Osuna, Mexico City, 1565   *145*
12. Illustration from the Codex Osuna, Mexico City, 1565   *146*
13. Illustration from the Codex Sierra, Oaxaca, Mexico, 1555   *148*
14. Illustration from the Codex Sierra, Oaxaca, Mexico, 1561   *149*
15. Illustration from Diego Valadés's *Rhetorica Christiana*, 1579   *151*
16. Main altarpiece in Huejotzingo, Mexico, 1586   *154*
17. Schematic drawing of the Huejotzingo altarpiece   *155*
18. "The Mulatto Gentlemen of Esmeraldas," Ecuador, 1599 ✑AND PLATE 4   *160*
19. "Blacks Dancing" by Zacharias Wagener, Recife, Brazil, ca. 1640 ✑AND PLATE 5   *163*
20. Drawing by Felipe Guaman Poma de Ayala, Peru, 1615   *175*
21. Drawing by Felipe Guaman Poma de Ayala, Peru, 1615   *177*
22. Plan of Lima, Peru, in the mid-seventeenth century   *189*
23. Church and Monastery of San Francisco, Lima, Peru, 1673   *197*

24. Portrait of Santa Rosa of Lima with silver decoration, artist and date unknown
 ❧AND PLATE 6　　　　　216
25. Portrait of Sor Juana Inés de la Cruz, artist unknown ❧AND PLATE 7　　　　　217
26. Upper reaches of the Rosary chapel, Church of Santo Domingo, Puebla,
 Mexico, 1632–1690 ❧AND PLATE 8　　　　　270
27. Corregidor Pérez and secular clergy in a Corpus Christi procession, Cusco, Peru,
 ca. 1674–1680 ❧AND PLATE 9　　　　　275
28. Santa Rosa and "La Linda" in a Corpus Christi procession, Cusco, Peru,
 ca. 1674–1680 ❧AND PLATE 10　　　　　278
29. Santo Antônio de Catagerona, from the Covenant of the Irmandade, Bahia, Brazil,
 1699 ❧AND PLATE 11　　　　　282
30. Plan of La Concepción mission, Paraguay, in late colonial times　　　　　315
31. Plan of Nuestra Señora de Guadalupe de los Negros de Amapa, Mexico, 1769–70　　　327
32. "Thanking Saint Anne," an ex-voto offering, artist unknown, Brazil, 1755
 ❧AND PLATE 12　　　　　354
33. "Jeremiah in the Stocks" by Aleijadinho, Ouro Prêto, Brazil, ca. 1770s
 ❧AND PLATE 13　　　　　358
34. *Castas* painting featuring the Mestizo, child of a Spanish man and an Indian
 woman, by José Joaquín Magón, Mexico (second half of the eighteenth century)
 ❧AND PLATE 14　　　　　361
35. *Castas* painting featuring the Mulatta, child of a Spanish man and an African
 woman, by Andrés de Islas, Mexico, ca. 1774 ❧AND PLATE 15　　　　　363
36. The Salto del Agua, Mexico City, 1779　　　　　385
37. Inscription on the Salto del Agua, Mexico City, 1779　　　　　386
38. Monument for the New Roadway to San Agustín de las Cuevas, Mexico City, 1787　　387
39. "Don Felipe Tupa Amaru," artist unknown (eighteenth century)　　　　　392
40. "America Nursing Spanish Noble Boys," artist unknown, Peru, ca. 1770s
 ❧AND PLATE 16　　　　　396

REFERENCE MAPS

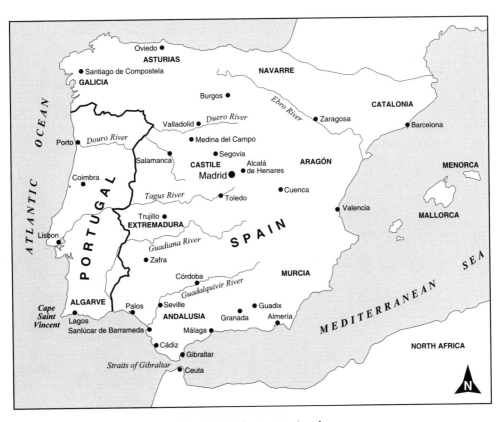

Map 1. The Iberian Peninsula

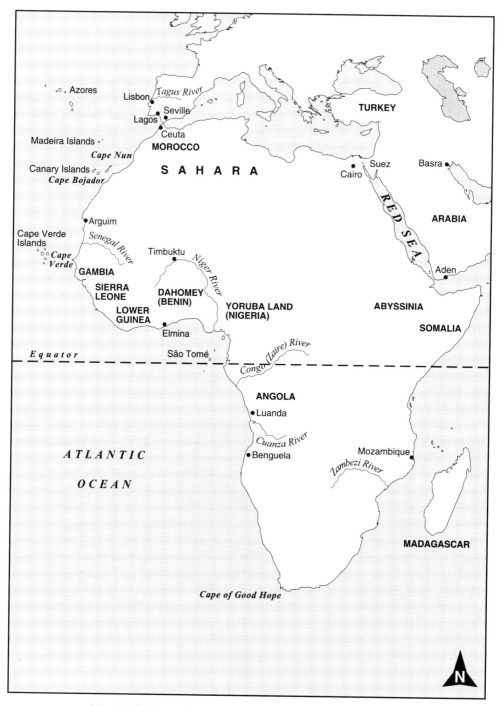

Map 2. The West African Coast and "Atlantic Mediterranean"

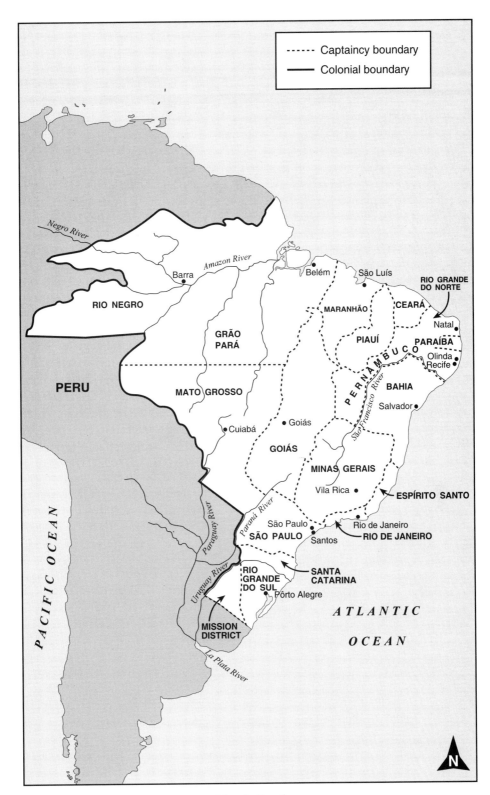

Legend:
- - - - - - Captaincy boundary
———— Colonial boundary

PERU

PACIFIC OCEAN

Negro River

Barra

Amazon River

RIO NEGRO

GRÃO PARÁ

MATO GROSSO

Cuiabá

Goiás

GOIÁS

Belém

São Luís

MARANHÃO

PIAUÍ

RIO GRANDE DO NORTE

CEARÁ

Natal

PARAÍBA

Olinda
Recife

PERNAMBUCO

São Francisco River

BAHIA

Salvador

MINAS GERAIS

Vila Rica

ESPÍRITO SANTO

São Paulo

Paraná River

SÃO PAULO

Santos

Rio de Janeiro

RIO DE JANEIRO

Paraguay River

Uruguay River

RIO GRANDE DO SUL

Pôrto Alegre

SANTA CATARINA

MISSION DISTRICT

La Plata River

ATLANTIC

OCEAN

N

Map 3. Brazil

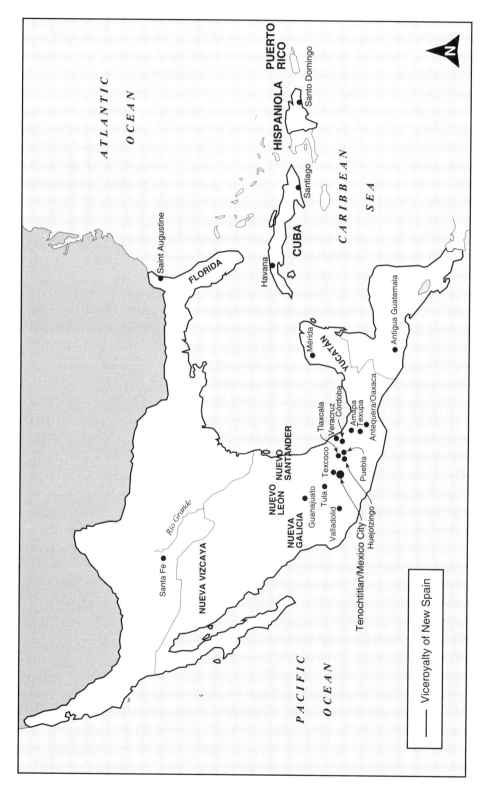

Map 4. New Spain and the Caribbean Basin

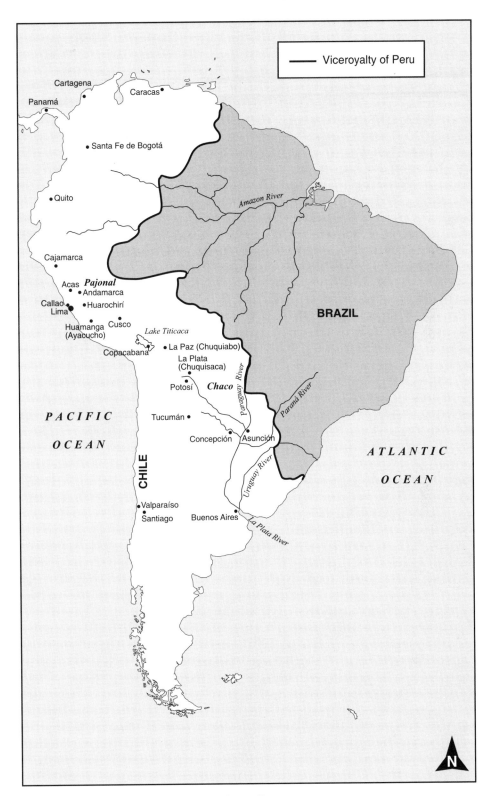

Map 5. Peru

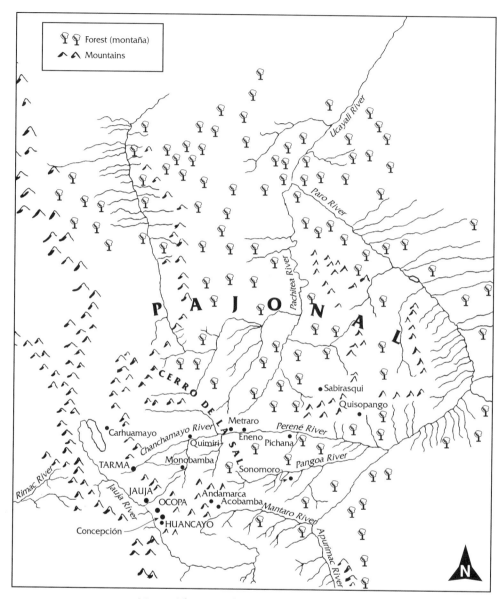

Map 6. The Pajonal on Peru's Tarma Frontier

INTRODUCTION

Texts and Images for Colonial History

Exploration is not so much a covering of surface distance as a study in depth: a fleeting episode, a fragment of landscape, or a remark overheard may provide the only means of understanding and interpreting areas which would otherwise remain barren of meaning.
   —Claude Lévi-Strauss, *Tristes tropiques (1984)*

We may distinguish between two types of imaginative process: the one that starts with the word and arrives at the visual image, and the one that starts with the visual image and arrives at its verbal expression.
   —Italo Calvino, *Six Memos for the Next Millennium (1988)*

This book of readings and images on the history of colonial Latin America is intended for students and teachers as well as for scholars and general readers. Through a variety of documents, both written and visual, it aims to provide more than a conventional treatment of the "great themes" associated with the study of the colonial period. These include exploration; military and spiritual conquest; the formation, consolidation, reform, and collapse of colonial institutions of government and Church, and the accompanying changes in the economy and labor; and the relations between and among the peoples of the region: Indians, Blacks, Mestizos, Whites born in the Americas, Spanish and Portuguese settlers and rulers. Our sources bear on these themes, among others, but through a focus on religion and society as a way to a more integral history.

Three distinct regions receive special attention here: Mesoamerica (the highlands of central and southern Mexico and Central America), Peru (the vast western portion of South America), and Brazil (the extensive eastern and northern coastal zones of South America). The first two areas, because they held the great indigenous state societies and silver deposits that attracted Spanish interests, became Spain's principal colonial heartlands. Brazil offered Portugal fertile coastal land for sugarcane and tobacco, sporadic Indian labor, a market for African slaves, and eventually gold and diamond mines. For two centuries the administrative reach of their viceregal capitals at Mexico City, Lima, and Salvador in Bahia extended to the limits of Spanish and Portuguese territory in America. Mesoamerica, Peru, and Brazil are also the regions best known to historians of the colonial period, thanks to their unusually rich documentary record. Other regions appear here in several texts and images—the Caribbean imagined in an illustration for Amerigo Vespucci's letters; the coast of Ecuador in a striking portrait of three Mulatto gentlemen; Paraguay in a letter from a Guaraní chief and the plan of his mission settlement; and frontiers of southern South America and Mexico in Concolorcorvo's travel account, the story of the Black settlement of Amapa, and Argentina's Declaration of Independence. But the emphases and absences arise from our wish to delve into some matters and areas in depth rather than labor to cover a bit of almost everything.

All the readings are primary documents, a number of which are translated into English for the first time. In addition, images made during the colonial period are presented as primary visual documents, records of life and thought in colonial times that redirect as well as amplify the themes and changes that will be met in the written selections and in wider reading and discussion. Among the primary sources are not only a papal bull, letters, sermons, exhortations, reports, inquisitorial confessions, travel accounts, portions of treatises, last wills and testaments, speeches, decrees, pronouncements, and literary productions, but also carved stones, textiles, a votive offering, altarpieces, the upper reaches of church interiors, a saint's image, maps, portraits, a painting of slaves dancing, and inscriptions on monuments and public works. The emphasis on primary material among the selections represents the choice of three teachers, largely in answer to their own students' enthusiasms for the immediacy and insight that the study of contemporary sources can bring. For similar reasons, the selections emphasize people at various levels of society in their places and times rather than as solitary thinkers or faceless masses, their backs turned toward us.

Each document, written or visual, is accompanied by an introduction composed in the spirit of invitation as much as direction. To increase the accessibility of the selections and suggest how they can be read together, these introductions supply information about the image or text and place it within wider contexts, identifying points of special interest, posing problems and queries, and, in particular, encouraging readers toward their own understandings. The introductions are meant to open discussion rather than to have the last word

about a document. Since the selections and introductions are points of entry as well as points of view, the pages of this book are meant to be turned in both directions. Once met, they will need to be reviewed in light of their neighbors and other sources that suggest related themes. History, in E. P. Thompson's words and practice, is "the restless discipline of context." The introductions supply some of the immediate context for a source and suggest several connections to other sources that are good for thinking about a fuller history—and about what was changing or not changing. But this is open-ended work. Much of the challenge of contextualization calls for ingenuity, adjustment, and some "exact imagining" from readers.

Within this book, readers will encounter coincidences and the challenge of holding apparently contradictory ideas—paradoxes—in mind rather than moving directly to one or the other as "true" or typical. Certain texts and images are juxtaposed for the ways in which they might be related to each other and illuminate wider issues. Thus, for instance, a testimony telling of the life of Santa Rosa of Lima and a letter written by Mexican nun and scholar-poet Sor Juana Inés de la Cruz along with two posthumous portraits of these women are paired for comparison, as are the covenant for a Brazilian lay brotherhood and the representation of its patron saint criticized within the document. Then, thinking across other sources, readers can consider the life of Santa Rosa in terms of a description of seventeenth-century Lima, the weighty insistence of Francisco de Avila's sermon for Christmas Eve, the campaigns to stamp out native Andean religious error, fear of incursions by seafaring Protestant adversaries, and the decoration of a Rosary chapel, all of which emerge out of the same intellectual and political climate. In the same way the brotherhood's covenant, Aleijadinho's sculpture of Jeremiah in the stocks, and the report of Pamplona's expedition of settlement and possession reflect the multiple, and sometimes competing, preoccupations of late eighteenth-century Brazil. Thus, the selections are not meant to file, one by one, in and out of the reader's mind. A historical vision of colonial Latin America that aims to be broad and deep depends on reconsideration of sources and ideas in light of subsequent study, prompted not only by messages in this book but also by other readings and reckonings that will become a study of colonial Latin America.

Although the selections for the most part are arranged chronologically and set in four broad parts, we have resisted the temptation to impose a single periodization on the book on the grounds that it would distract unnecessarily from the associations that can be made between selections at long as well as at short range and would leave the impression that certain dates are inevitable benchmarks and need not be questioned. Of course, the collection cannot magically escape the influence of the periodizations that have guided and organized the study of colonial Latin American history in the past, even if we wanted it to. Composing a sourcebook on the colonial period in itself involves choices about periodization. It is important to ask when and how basic structures of society, government, material life, and ideas changed. But periodization either from the Europeans' perspective alone or from the history of political institutions runs the risk of relegating certain changes and continuities to a distant background and making others appear unduly formative. A fixed sequence of chronological turning points risks a narrative that determines our expectations and our very manner of addressing the past. In offering more than an institutional perspective, we intend that our selections should often blur the familiar temporal and territorial boundaries of this colonial history.

In many general surveys of colonial Spanish America, the military conquests of the early sixteenth century and the independence movements of the early nineteenth century have seemed to be the great events, as if bracketing three centuries of inertia with sudden action. Especially for Spaniards, conquest and insurgency do represent compelling beginnings and endings, but they were only the most dramatic events, not the only important ones.

In Brazil where indigenous peoples lived in small, constantly moving settlements, military conquest in the Spanish style made no sense. Portuguese entrepreneurs, not conquistadores, first traded with Indians and then seized them as slave laborers for their sugar estates, while Jesuit missionaries learned to bring them by persuasion into newly formed villages for conversion. The importation of Africans into Mexico or Peru pales compared to their numbers in Brazil. And while independence wars rearranged the governments and borders of Spanish America, Brazil remained a single nation despite its sprawling size and profound regional differences, ruled by a constitutional monarch, initially the Portuguese king's son. Such events call for their own marking out of time.

In the introductions and choice of sources—such as the Inka's tunics, the Aztec Stone of the Five Eras, Pero Vaz de Caminha's letter in 1500 or the letters of Padre Nóbrega one-half century later, the Texupa map of 1579, the 1592 confession of Domingos Fernandes Nobre, and the testimony of Francisco Poma y Altas Caldeas before an ecclesiastical judge in 1657—we mean to remind readers of the variety and complexity of Amerindian societies before the Europeans' arrival and to suggest that they would persist and be profoundly affected, not simply erased or replaced (however gradually), by the military defeats and capitulations of their significant political centers or the occupations of their lands and apparent conversion of their villages.

We present the difficulty for historical interpretation posed by the fact that much of the existing evidence on the indigenous and African peoples of the Americas comes from European records with an invitation to consider the various cultures that found expression in colonial times as clues to a past as well as to a present and future. "Indians" (people descended from indigenous groups living, if only tenuously, under Spanish or Portuguese rule), like Africans brought originally to the Americas as slaves, Spaniards, Portuguese and other Europeans, and people of the racial and cultural combinations that resulted, are not viewed as growing less "authentic" in their transformations during the colonial period. Rather, they are seen as living not so much within separate spheres of action as within a common "analytical space" that, despite restrictions and pressures, contributed to the development of complex and rich colonial cultures. We view this common analytical space of sixteenth-century conflicts and confusion, collaboration and reconceptualization, as a "new world" for Africans and indigenous peoples as much as for Portuguese and Spaniards.

Most images owe their position in the book to a particular written source or group of sources. The Inka's tunics and Aztec Stone of the Five Eras are set next to readings that relate to pre-Hispanic Peru and Mexico; Felipe Guaman Poma's sketches of Catholic priests are juxtaposed with his words about them; an image of Saint Anthony of Catagerona appears within a covenant of his Brazilian lay devotees. But there are five clusters of images that both mark transitions between parts of the book and reflect back on issues and subjects introduced in earlier selections:

The first cluster (Selections 10–12)—consisting of early European depictions of native Americans and a Morisco (new convert to Christianity from Islam) mother and daughter in Spain—appears at the end of Part I. It both enlarges the subject of contact and discoveries and opens Part II's consideration of the expectations, intentions, and fears of peoples of indigenous, African, European, and mixed descent in the course of the sixteenth and the first half of the seventeenth centuries.

The second cluster of images (Selections 20–25)—from the Codex Osuna and Codex Sierra, Diego Valadés's ideal churchyard, the Huejotzingo altarpiece, the portrait of three Mulatto gentlemen from Esmeraldas, and Zacharias Wagener's painting of an African religious celebration in Pernambuco—and the readings that precede it in Part II concern a more settled and elaborate, but still unfinished, colonial order of institutions and social relationships in the sixteenth and early seventeenth centuries.

The third cluster (Selections 37 and 38)—the Dominicans' Rosary chapel in Puebla, Mexico, and two paintings of a Corpus Christi procession in Cusco, Peru—like the juxtaposed

images of Santa Rosa and Sor Juana carries the story deeper into the seventeenth century. These images in Part III reflect on the meanings of mid-colonial Catholicism and society often associated with the seventeenth century but not readily distinguished from social and cultural patterns in the late sixteenth or eighteenth century. While years of proximity and interaction had made individuals from vastly different social groups familiar with one another, expectations were often dashed and misunderstandings abounded. Colonial circumstances heightened the troubling inequalities, unsettling contradictions, and nostalgia for a lost golden age that are identified with Baroque culture in Catholic Europe, but the seventeenth century is no longer so easily described as an interlude of uneventful retrenchment, decadence, superstition, and economic depression. Stretched well beyond the years 1600 and 1700 in both Brazil and Spanish America, the broad midcolonial period shares a distinctive elaboration of customary relationships, programs of preaching meant to be inclusive, a flowering of providential American holiness expressed in hugely popular pilgrimage sites such as that of Our Lady of Copacabana on the shores of Lake Titicaca or in flourishing lay religious associations like that of Santo Antônio de Catagerona in Bahia, and religious art and literature such as that produced by Sor Juana Inés de la Cruz; a shrunken but dynamic native American population and a rising and equally vital African one; and counterpoints of increasing production for regional consumption, world markets, and contraband trade with the English, Dutch, and French, who were establishing their own American colonies. All of these developments happened in a time of weakened imperial control as Iberian fortunes changed in Europe and beyond.

In Part IV, images in the fourth cluster from the second half of the eighteenth century (Selections 46–48)—a votive offering to Saint Anne, the figure of Jeremiah in the stocks as sculpted by Aleijadinho, and two paintings of Mexican *castas*—suggest the lives, thoughts, and pursuits of people of mixed race in colonial societies while also exploring perceptions of these racially diverse members. And the visual sources in the fifth cluster (Selections 52–54)—inscriptions on fountains and monuments in Mexico City, the eighteenth-century portrait of a famous sixteenth-century Inka rebel, and a Peruvian allegory of America—bear on the emerging Bourbon vision of a second "conquest" and some long continuities with which it clashed or sought to connect. In choosing readings and images for Part IV we have endeavored, while also capturing significant changes, to show how old patterns continued into the eighteenth century. The daily report of Pamplona's expedition into the Brazilian wilderness and the life and work of the sculptor Aleijandinho in Minas Gerais point out the monumental southerly shift of population, resources, and political attention in Portuguese America following the discovery of gold and diamonds at the end of the seventeenth century, while a petition illuminating slave families in the early nineteenth-century parish of São Pedro do Rio Fundo in Bahia reminds of how the sugar estates of the northeast continued and would revive. The early decades of the century in Spanish America witnessed the only extended time of real economic growth in the late colonial period and a foreshadowing of impressive development in the formerly peripheral Cuba, Puerto Rico, Venezuela, and Argentina, and the initiatives of the new Bourbon dynasty in Spain (from 1700) to rejuvenate the Spanish empire in America with monopolistic trading companies and more administration.

A new historical consciousness and vogue of neoclassicism and efficiency marked both Pombaline times in Brazil and Bourbon times in Spanish America without simply replacing customary practices and what are usually regarded as early and midcolonial tastes. But the eighteenth-century assertions of control, conversion, and rejuvenation would not be like the sixteenth-century beginnings. Many Spanish and Portuguese American subjects now spoke imperial languages in their own way, shared religious cultures and bodies of law, and were not so divided among themselves. They had a more refined sense of their rights and often focused political resentment on privi-

leged newcomers from Portugal and Spain and on representatives from the sometimes politically and culturally distant colonial administrative centers. And imperial initiatives in the eighteenth century were increasingly affected by other nations with American interests, as a succession of European wars with American theaters demonstrated. This eighteenth century led to the loss of Spain's mainland American empire rather than its new conquest, while Brazil, aided by Portugal's English ally-opportunists, received its emperor and entourage and became the center of the Portuguese world.

Another departure from frequently invoked explanations in colonial Latin American history is our preference to emphasize what was newly forged in America through the sustained and complex interactions of Europeans, Amerindians, and Africans rather than presuming that colonial experience can be understood as the straightforward transfer to America of Iberian strategies, codes of conduct, or institutions. It is tempting to apply the image of an intermittent Christian crusade to reconquer the Iberian Peninsula from increasingly fragmented Muslim rule, culminating in the capitulation of the last Islamic kingdom of Granada in 1492, as the "Iberian background" for Latin American history. The "reconquest" of Granada in particular has been seen as the dramatic Old World backdrop and prelude to further crusades and conquests that, thanks to Columbus's voyage across the Atlantic that same year, would continue in the Americas. The "reconquest" is a neat label that has been used to give meaning to the mentality and spirit of the Spanish conquistador. As the story goes, the late medieval Spanish adventurer-conqueror, embodying the centuries-old struggle with the forces of Islam and influenced by the heroic feats recounted in the popular chivalric romances of his day, took ship to new fields of battle and wonder. But fixing on Iberia-as-prelude and on the background of reconquest, with its accompanying images of dramatic defeat and the abrupt repudiation of a medieval coexistence between culturally and religiously different peoples, misses the ways in which Spain and America shared an interlocking history after 1492—a history consisting of more than the relationship between metropole and colony or the mere transfer of Spanish culture.

Any easy overlay of a medieval crusade against the infidel, of military conquest, of the gambling conquistador onto Portuguese America would be even further mistaken. Unlike the kingdom of Castile in particular, Portugal had succeeded in reclaiming its territory from the Muslims, including the southernmost portion, the Algarve, by 1250, nearly two centuries before Portuguese ships began to explore the African coast and two and one-half centuries before they made landfall on Brazil's coast. With this lag in time it is more difficult to imagine a direct connection between the peninsular wars of reconquest and the piecemeal, intermittent, and uncertain settlement by Portuguese entrepreneurs who sought to establish sugar-producing estates or by Jesuit missionaries who wanted to save souls and remake Indian culture. Portugal's fifteenth-century ventures on the sea, its fitful exploration along Africa's western coast that created not towns or settlements but trading posts squatting defensively on the beach, and its experiments with agriculture (wheat, then sugarcane) on the Atlantic islands, using local labor and soon African slaves—these provided the models for early attempts to secure and shape Brazil as a colony. Even donatarial privileges and obligations, once thought to exemplify the insertion into a New World setting of a medieval Portuguese institution used during the reconquest, assumed a decidedly altered form in its migration across the Atlantic. And Vaz de Caminha's portrayal of Indian innocence lacks so much as a trace of the view of Muslim intransigence.

Comparing contemporaneous developments in Portugal and Spain also works to remind readers of the relevance of a wider European, African, and Asian scene between the early fifteenth and early nineteenth centuries. Portugal's voyages of discovery along the western African coast, on to India, and beyond to the Moluccas; the repercussions of the Protestant Reformation sparked by Martin Luther's challenges to the Catholic center of Christendom, and the Roman Church's own reforms in response, especially those associated with the Council of Trent (1545–1563), as well as wars among European states and the expansion of international trade and empires throughout the period, are important to this wider context for the study of colonial Latin America. The study of efforts to evangelize Indian peoples in Brazil, Mexico, or Peru, for instance, can benefit from being viewed as part of considerably broader Portuguese or Spanish ambitions at the time. As contemporary churchmen were fond of observing, there were great and varied expanses of "other Indies" in Iberia itself, in southern Italy, in other parts of Catholic Europe, in India, China, Japan, and the Philippines archipelago, and not only among new converts from Islam. Particularly in the small towns and in the countryside, there were Europeans who, though nominally Christian and not, strictly speaking, members of an entirely alien culture, were thought to practice unacceptable forms of religion and to be greatly in need of instruction. Since the late fifteenth and early sixteenth centuries Catholic missionaries preached and taught Christian doctrine in European villages from newly written catechisms to revive the faith. In the minds of many missionaries and parish priests, who themselves are among the most important bridges between the histories of Europe and America, the real differences between the ministries among Christian rustics, the Spanish Moriscos, or native American peoples diminished before the immensity of their task.

The opening words of the *Recopilación de leyes de los reynos de las Indias*, the great compilation of Spanish-American law published in 1681, reiterated the inevitable links among religion, politics, and society acknowledged earlier by popes to Portuguese kings and echoed in the king's pledge in 1539 to "increase our holy Catholic faith" despite all the "dangers and work and expense." In 1681 the Spanish king acknowledged that "God Our Lord by His infinite mercy and goodness, has bestowed upon us, without our deserving it, a great share of the dominion of this world. . . . Consequently, we find ourselves with a greater obligation than other princes to strive to serve Him and the glory of His Holy Name, and to employ all the power He has given us to see that His name is known and worshipped throughout the world as the true God." The obligations between Christian king and new American subjects expressed in this soaring statement of legitimacy and mission are reciprocal but clearly warn:

> Desiring this glory of Our God and Lord, happily have we succeeded in bringing into the fold of the Holy Roman Catholic Church the innumerable peoples and nations who inhabit the Western Indies, islands, and mainland of the Ocean Sea, and other places subject to our dominion. And so that everyone, throughout the world, may enjoy the inestimable benefit of Redemption through the Blood of Our Lord Jesus Christ, we beg and we charge the natives of our Indies to receive and listen kindly to the Teachers and preachers we send them, and give credence to their teachings. . . . And if, with a stubborn and obstinate spirit, they err and refuse to accept and believe what the Holy Mother Church teaches, they are to be punished according to law and in the cases prescribed by law.

Few would deny that religion merits an important place in the study of colonial Latin America, but it is worth considering what this place has most often been, and what it might be. The collection in this volume offers a basis for studying colonial history without cordoning off religion from other aspects of life and without assigning it a predetermined role either as a totalitarian and repressive force (principally a ready justification and vehicle for colonial domination) or as an essentially private or selfless activity (little more than the province of shaded cloisters, home altars, and busy deacons). Here, we do not mean to equate Church and religion and pursue only accounts of bishops' tenures or the evangelizing record of one religious order or another; rather, we conceive of religion as more embracing than any single church and stitched into the larger patterns of society and culture. Our selections feature religion in ways that display its pervasive but often elusive presence in daily life and thought, and in the exercise of colonial power and habits of conception.

Like many other subjects when viewed in a more searching and connecting fashion, colonial religion contains and changes too much to be compressed into a narrow definition. It is here treated as the means by which people expressed and lived their allegiance to an order that transcends human power and promises well-being. Religion is lived and experienced, not merely imposed and prescribed. Colonial religious beliefs and practices were dynamic rather than timeless, capable of adaptation and reformulation in different intellectual climates, capable of being used both to justify and question colonial authority, and capable of being compassionate, demanding, and punitive.

A number of the selections demonstrate that Indian and Black religious life in colonial times was not simply a story of loss and impoverishment, nor did it tend inexorably toward a crystallized state. A protean Catholicism was as central to the sixteenth-century thought-world of Spanish theologian Francisco de Vitoria, a troubled Morisco Jesuit, or of native Andean chronicler Felipe Guaman Poma de Ayala as it was to Guaraní spokesman Nicolás Ñenguirú in the 1750s, leader of a runaway slave community Fernando Manuel in the 1760s, or parish priest José María Morelos in early nineteenth-century Mexico, on the eve of independence from Spain.

It was also paramount in late seventeenth-century Catholic devotion that guided Blacks and Mulattoes, both slave and free women and men, in founding a sodality dedicated to Santo Antônio; or earlier in the sermons of Padre Antônio Vieira, who preached to both slaves and their masters on the eternal consequences of authority obeyed and abused; and for the expedition troops in 1769 who marched into unfamiliar territory only after first attending early Mass each morning. A slave mother's insistence on her daughter's marrying a Nagô, or Yoruba, slave rather than a locally born freed man reminds us that not all religion was Catholic; the man might well have been Muslim or practiced candomblé, a West African religion.

Religion can serve as a nexus for much of what is generally treated as political, social, economic, and cultural history. Colonial Latin America was what Natalie Zemon Davis, a historian of western Europe in the same centuries, has called a "religious culture." Religion became the principal expression of authority and social order in most of Spanish America. Colonial administrators and spokesmen during the sixteenth and seventeenth centuries viewed the parts of a growing empire as building blocks of a universal Christian state ascending in pyramid fashion to an all-seeing monarch subject only to God. These blocks were parts of a larger plan, the contours of which can be perceived in urban designs and descriptions whether in Lima, one of the great colonial cities during its early seventeenth-century prime, or in tiny Amapa, with its brand-new church in late colonial times, or in a depiction of a great arm reaching out from Mexico City to the Indian pueblo of Texupa in the 1560s.

In searching for the identifying themes of colonial culture, Brazil offers a counterpoint to Spanish America: not radical dissonance but culture in another key. Here, juridical authority more clearly intertwined with religion to express an ideal of authority and social order; the two sources of authority were joined in the person of the king. Since the fifteenth century, the Portuguese king had exercised ecclesiastical patronage by nominating, for example, all Church appointments on behalf of the Roman pope. The red cross of the Order of Christ on the white canvas sails of the king's ships or, later, when Brazilian mines supported an aristocratic taste for Baroque opulence, a brooch of garnets set in the form of a cross against a field of clear quartz as the insignia of the Order awarded for royal service, announced this enduring allegiance of Church and state. Just as Catholic thinking affirmed a hierarchy that extended downward from the Holy Trinity to the angels (who themselves appeared in ranked divisions) to the saints, the Church itself was similarly ordered from pope to archbishop, bishop, priest, and finally to the lay faithful, and subject to royal authority on many matters. Civil society duplicated and bolstered this religious ordering by itself being hierarchically arranged, but with the difference that here authority derived from the law, recorded in successively modified legal codes, and its practitioners were tiers of judges acting through courts at various levels, with petition to the king the final appeal. As Catholics, Brazilians prayed to the Virgin Mary and to the saints—hence, devotion to Santo Antônio in the 1699 covenant—to intercede on their behalf in securing God's grace as well as tangible favors, such as the cure for an illness or a safe journey. Religious supplication and intercession were echoed in secular society through the networks of patronage relations that connected persons of markedly different social positions in a deliberately hierarchical society.

This ideal double ordering of religious and civil authority displayed another variant in colonial Brazil where the relationship between owner and slave further complicated matters. Within sugar estate, plantation, mine, or small farm—wherever one man or woman owned another—an enclave of private authority was established by which an owner exercised dominion over his or her slaves. Yet even here the competing authorities of Church and court, in the absence of an actual code of slave law, sought to influence and regulate. The *Constituições primeiras*, announced in 1707 by the Bahian archbishop, urged masters to allow their slaves to marry and to free them from work on saints' days and Sundays, while civil law, based in turn on Roman law, could be appealed to for protection in extreme circumstances. But it was in the web of patronage relations, both within the slave quarters and between slave quarters and free society, that slaves most often and most successfully negotiated some favor or some advantage. If religious culture was not the only conduit for the exercise and manipulation of authority, it set the tone for the workings also of secular society through hierarchy and intercession.

Many of the selections from different times and places in colonial history feature the imagination and organization of space, providing another set of records about intersections of the civil and religious in daily life. In Mexico or Peru, the ideal church courtyard, a native artist's elaborate map of an Indian parish and a district governor's plan for a Black township, or in Brazil, a Jesuit-built village in which to gather Indians for conversion—in each case, aims were projected onto space. The artistic and architectural forms of imperial Rome set something of an ideal for Spanish projections of political and religious power in the American colonies. This ideal was held during early Hapsburg times in the sixteenth century, when the Spanish Christian monarchy was striving toward a universal empire that would unite the diverse parts of the Earth and not only emulate but also surpass Rome's achievement. And it is accented under both Bourbon and Pombaline rule, when neoclassical styles were selected to express the restrained and "enlightened" grandeur of order-seeking and rationalized, if diminished, eighteenth-century empires.

Spanish notions of civility and effective colonization stressed nothing so much as the superiority of urban living over all other forms of society. And no settlement—whether a small pueblo, provincial city, or viceregal capital—was complete until churches had been built and regular services were held. Yet how would these reorderings of space and settlement be viewed? Here, as in most cultural matters, continuity and local pride were a vital part of changing spatial arrangements. A district governor's authoritative report on Texupa, New Spain, in 1579 describes a reconstituted "landscape," a restructured, potentially bountiful

place beneath the superimposed design of Christianity and Spanish authority. Yet an Indian's pictorial representation of Texupa that accompanied the district governor's report suggests more complicated local understandings of the same landscape and emerging realities. His depiction gives special importance to familiar surroundings, teeming with sacred life that seems to be enhanced by the new Christian church complex, more than it dwells on the destruction of old ways and the reordering of the community by the ideal grid plan for a town.

In Mexico and Peru the colonial parish was a nucleus of administration, organized in close relation to civil districts, and parish priests were appointees of the Spanish Crown. Like many members of religious orders and the small host of secular officials, they were relied upon for routine administration, support of royal initiatives, and local information that might be of use to the Crown. People inhabited a religious landscape in which churches, especially parish churches, were significant places. Families were ordered to live within earshot of the bells, which rang out emergencies and punctuated the day with calls to devotion just as the cycle of feast days and holy seasons marked out the year with pertinent lessons.

In Brazilian colonial experience urban centers assumed other meanings. The seminomadic Tupi-speaking Indians of the coast lived in thatch longhouses, not in complex political, economic, and ceremonial centers, and were dispersed in small clusters, not in settled populations several times the size of the largest European cities, as did the Mexica in the Valley of Mexico. Without Indian cities to conquer and rebuild, the Portuguese instead built Recife, Olinda, Salvador, Rio de Janeiro, São Luiz, and Belem piecemeal as their needs and resources dictated. Neither Indian congregations nor, at first, mines compelled the Portuguese to push inland. As in Portugal, Brazilian towns were coastal, fortified against the threat of French or Dutch invasion and situated for commerce and trade. In Salvador the cathedral, the Jesuit college, and the court and municipal council together with settlers' houses ranged along the bluff of the upper city, while docks and warehouses crowded below into the narrow bayside. Rather than buildings arranged around a central square as in the Spanish plan, colonial Brazilian towns were more often ordered by elevation and built along a ridge, a beach, or at the mouth of a river.

Like Spaniards, however, the Portuguese understood "urban" as the place where civilization and order resided. They too built churches; and churches, often set on small *praças*, or open areas, marked out the urban landscape. The Saint Anthony church built outside Salvador's city wall was called "Santo Antônio alem do Carmo," that is, beyond the monastery of Carmo. Each church was known by its distinctive qualities. Membership in a parish church signalled not only membership in the larger Church but also in civilized society. Indeed, the Bahian archbishop's rules in 1707 admonished priests to encourage vagabonds into the settled and stable societies of their parishes and to watch for those who roamed from place to place living as bigamists, a threat to domestic and moral order. In villages, towns, and cities also resided the overseers of civil and secular order: the municipal council, the courts and judges, and the notary.

Although New World living required new formulations of Old World preferences, those in Brazil who owned sugar estates, ranches, farms, and eventually the distant, inland mines did not separate rural from urban as firmly as our vocabulary supposes. They crossed bays and mountains or journeyed down rivers to participate in the governmental, commercial, legal, and religious life that swirled around the ports; their slaves, too, figured in the busy, restless movement of people and goods to market and port. Closer to their landed properties colonial Brazilians filled the offices, by appointment and election, of their local parish towns, where they often owned houses either as investments or as stopping places for their own use. While sponsoring the construction of a parish church, contributing to local lay sodalities, and arranging to be buried at the foot of the altar, they also made devotion routinely a part of domestic life and architecture by building small private

oratories or even exquisite chapels that might rise two stories and incorporate a choir loft. Some enjoyed the offices of a resident priest; others received a bishop's permission for a traveling parish priest to say weekly Mass. The connections between town and countryside webbed both into a single colonial culture.

If Brazil's vast, unsettled wilderness sometimes defied colonization, Indians seemed to melt into forests, and runaway slaves broke camp just ahead of their pursuers. Jesuits also constructed new villages on the understanding that to separate Indians from familiar ways would speed conversion. Brazilians remade the landscape by carrying ordered society to the wilderness. Field officer Pamplona organized free men and slaves to build bridges, roads, and churches at the headwaters of the São Francisco river; he distributed royal grants of land to those who pledged to settle and work it and gloated with pleasure over herds that reproduced and grew fat.

These colonial societies, marked by great inequalities, consisted of people with needs and experiences that differed dramatically, but their beliefs and practices nonetheless intertwined. Within densely populated areas and often in regions considerably beyond, people of all kinds developed a relationship with Christianity, even if simply as nominal converts or adherents who took the state religion largely on their own terms. Similarly, a steadily more varied society developed under the same broad system of law and political authority. The presence and observance of Portuguese or Spanish law and political and religious authority was not the same everywhere, but it everywhere conferred a kind of membership and association.

People were identified, and they identified themselves, according to certain legal categories and interpersonal obligations, often within relationships dependent on kin, community, ethnic group, or patron. Such relationships were not always mutually agreed upon or beneficial, but they could foster a sense of mutual responsibilities and localized social arrangements that lent substance to the metaphors about protection and instruction that often described them. At the same time, people were placed into an elaborate set of political, social, racial, commercial, and religious hierarchies, a number of which were mainly hypothetical. Like the meanings in the upper reaches of the sixteenth-century altarpiece at Huejotzingo, the higher echelons of these elaborations of privilege and power were distant for many people. But they were less mysterious and abstract when intermediaries were as close as a regional magistrate, a godparent, an itinerant seller of foreign wares, a multilingual interpreter, the Mulatto Saint Anthony, or a friendly little figure of Saint Anne, dwarfed by her throne and leaning forward the better to hear the troubles of her devotees.

Each of the documents in this collection connects to the wider community from which its author draws and into which it feeds, and many of them expand standard notions of the viable and imaginable in colonial times. Parts of this book tell an undeniable story of physical and cultural violence, destruction, and dislocation; indeed, Flemish Franciscan Pedro de Gante, Jesuit Antônio Vieira, Andean chronicler Felipe Guaman Poma de Ayala, Guaraní mission leader Nicolás Ñenguirú, royal postal inspector Alonso Carrió de la Vandera (alias Concolorcorvo) all wrote in part to record and warn against abuses they observed. But the collection also offers connecting stories of survival and readjustments within a colonial regime. In this way, the selections qualify the metaphor of "conquest," either military or spiritual, that heralds abrupt destruction and presents colonial settings simply as arenas for the struggle of opposing worlds, classes, or other social groups. Despite the best efforts of spokesmen such as Vaz de Caminha writing to the king or Vespucci's German illustrator in the early sixteenth century, or the late eighteenth-century minister of the Indies, José de Gálvez, it is the impure, incomplete, and paradoxical that come through time and again.

Politics has been described as the art of the possible, and it appears thus in a number of selections. In spite of its ideal representations, power in precolonial and colonial times was not so much handed down from on high or decreed from some oracular center—as if the Aztec Stone of the Five Eras could stand for the scores of small states and hundreds of Mesoamerican communities whose people also saw themselves as belonging to central places—as it was contested, negotiated, and renegotiated between aspiring rulers and subjects, not to mention a number of crucial intermediaries. Power, with its concomitant expectations and obligations, was not expressed only in words, proclamations, and formal laws. Indeed, an overt show of force was often "bad politics" and detrimental to what might be more constructively coaxed through subtle and regular expressions of solidarity, consensus, and patronage. In spite of such encouragement, however, political and religious cultures in colonial Latin America were rarely harmonious. And yet there were many ways in which colonial culture might be more than stage-managed by a governing elite and might be shared and unifying.

The constant interplay between ideals and realities is another recurring theme in the selections. Just as the Inka's manner of dress and the symbolic messages it conveyed depended on his audience, a colonial social order had to be carefully composed. European Christians, as much in the Iberian Peninsula as in America, faced the challenges both of understanding and of living in a social order that comprised a variety of multiethnic settings. Certainly, official arguments for a peaceful and well-ordered society might often be used to establish tighter control. But a colonial order had many supporters, including many who were outside official circles. Visions of seventeenth- and eighteenth-century Baroque Catholicism as a transcendent unity despite the potent contradictions and inequities in nearly all facets of life come through in paintings, church interiors, and formal reports. The selections inevitably feature the conflict and competition that were inherent in colonial lives, but these are not the only or even the most remarkable aspects in a long and complex history. Many of the images and readings offer opportunities to consider colonial contexts as settings in which people and ideas interacted by design and circumstance. Survival was in many cases a process of transformation and reformulation more than simple resistance and accommodation.

Many subjects who could not claim Portuguese or Spanish ancestry suffered horribly under colonial rule, whereas others successfully challenged the terms of their subjugation and carved out advantageous situations for themselves and their companions within the constraints and pressures that they faced. In commissioning paintings and altarpieces, Indian officials took part in the creation and modification of images of themselves as participants in a common, negotiated colonial culture. A Christian Indian's cooperation with his parish priest in the seventeenth-century central Andes did not win him approval from religious leaders of his community who were intent on countering and reinterpreting Christianity, but it also did not preclude him from sympathetic participation in a colonial Andean religion and culture that was changing. Nor did bondage turn slaves and former slaves away from membership in a sodality devoted to their Mulatto saint, although such membership surely diluted the likelihood of violent rebellion. Spanish and Portuguese Christians, whether governors, landowners, mine bosses, field officers, or churchmen, were not alone in perpetually pursuing choices and situations within the colonial system that favored them and those whom they represented. From early colonial times they were joined by many others who, despite precarious and discouraging circumstances, discovered opportunities and niches that, in an extension of Waud Kracke's phrase, "made the found world their own" and responded as that "found world" continued to change. The selections in this book illustrate how—through negotiation, competition, and sometimes violent confrontation—diverse individuals and groups in colonial society arrived at common understandings, if not shared values, and ways of making do.

In studying this colonial history, it is hard to avoid feelings of distaste and outrage at the often noisy, high-handed behavior and biases of the governors, churchmen, scribes, and travelers upon whom we rely for information about subject peoples. For, just as the historian Robert

Muchembled has remarked about a similar predicament in the study of early modern France, "we have to ask repression to recount the history of what it is repressing." Yet a number of the selections also reveal what repression thought it was repressing, not to mention the ways in which it was frustrated and fell short of the mark. Grounded in an ample context of time and place, the often tidy narratives presented in colonial records can become points of entry into situations that they meant to obscure or eradicate.

Cracks in the armor and ideology of empire were widely noticed, even if this knowledge was concentrated locally and gathered little political momentum before the late eighteenth century. Runaway slaves settled into the new town of Amapa in 1769 with banners of colonial legitimacy flying in all directions, but the suspicion lingered that Amapa was merely a convenient "castle" for further assaults on the colonial order by these new subjects; they would return to the mountains if called to account. Túpac Amaru, the last of a series of sixteenth-century Inkas who resisted Spanish domination for almost forty years from a base in Vilcabamba, Peru, was remembered centuries after his death by a multi-ethnic population in the Andes for the injustice thought to have been visited upon him by an overreaching peninsular Spanish viceroy. Some of the most withering critiques of colonial practices were mounted by privileged Iberians or Creoles, including priests, who saw evils in the practice of colonialism while still exercising power over others in the service of the Crown.

As a number of our selections show, colonial expressions of authority and hierarchy frequently contained a basis for denying Spanish or Portuguese Christian legitimacy, challenging impositions in the name of the king or even God, and reformulating prescribed ideas and practices. Thus, Francisco de Avila's midseventeenth-century sermon before a native Andean congregation, inculcating Christian practices and warning against non-Christian ones, could be seen as more than a narrow-minded polemic. It also provides a vantage point from which to view a purposeful dialogue being attempted between an indigenous past and an Indian present, as the techniques of evangelization changed. A series of paintings celebrating colonial social order and participation in Cusco's Corpus Christi festivities features both paternalistic direction and a variety of people taking part in the year's greatest religious and civic procession. Padre Vieira's seventeenth-century sermons were at once blistering attacks on colonial practices and artfully framed defenses of a colonial regime. Even the heroic missionary narrative, anticipated in the instructions to the Franciscan "Twelve" and expressed in Fray Pedro de Gante's spirited defense of Indian neophytes near Mexico City—usually so adept at turning obstacles into surmountable or edifying difficulties—cannot entirely muffle the voice of an errant pupil.

S. L. G.
W. B. T.
K. M.

PART I

Old Worlds and the Time of Discoveries

1

The Ancestors of the People Called Indians
A View from Huarochirí, Peru
(ca. 1598–1608)

In the 1570s and 1580s over one hundred small Andean settlements (*llactas*) in the colonial province of Huarochirí were resettled into hamlets, villages, and towns by Spanish officials to ease labor exaction and facilitate evangelization. Among the native peoples affected were the Checas, from whom came the native recorders and editors of an extraordinary assemblage of oral traditions and sacred histories in the Quechua language—the Huarochirí Manuscript (ca. 1598–1608)—from which this selection derives; it recorded the worldview of these Andean people in a time of momentous change.

The new province of Huarochirí (Huaro Cheri in the following source), a mountainous area to the southeast of Lima, had been carved out of the populous northern portion of the province known to its previous rulers, the Inkas, as Yauyos. The Inkas, like the Aztecs in central Mexico, were latecomers to widespread power in pre-Hispanic times. Before the principal period of Inka ascendancy outside the Cusco Valley (which came after 1400), there had been a period of some four hundred years in which local and regional cultures of the central Andes had flourished without much interference from larger states.

Incorporation in the Inkas' Tawantinsuyu—in the Quechua language, the land of the four quarters—brought to the region a number of political, economic, cultural, and religious impositions, but it did not mean the demise of local Andean traditions. What we understand of Inkaic imperialism suggests that although Inka expansion had devastating effects on some peoples and regions, the undeniable coercion in their project of empire was in places leavened by deft diplomacy and by very generous treatment for groups who were held in imperial favor. Troops made up of loyal peoples were ready to stamp out opponents and rebels, but the Inkas of the Andes were by custom incorporative and reciprocal—that is, they sought to consume, be nourished by, and repay many of the cultures they came to control rather than obliterate and replace them. The region of Huarochirí, within the Inkaic province of Yauyos, appears to have been one of those on good terms with Cusco, and here Inka political arrangements did not strip away existing patterns of settlement or ethnic divisions.

Under the Inkas, local and regional religious systems—often focused on one or a group of ancestor beings, *huacas* (sometimes spelled *wak'as* or *guacas*) and *malquis* (or *mallquis*)—continued within a larger system of Inka-influenced religious cults that were at least broadly similar and ancestral in emphasis. According to Andean traditions, in ancient times, long before the years of Inka expansion or the arrival of the Spanish invaders, the land was inhabited by a succession of powerful warring beings or god-men and god-women called huacas. Although the translation is imperfect, huacas were perhaps the foremost among a host of other lineage and personal sources of sacred power and energy that can be called "gods" and "divinities" in English, although in thinking of them one should abandon the fundamental Judeo-Christian separation between the natural and the supernatural. Huacas were (and still are) places and physical objects of special, sacred significance—often outcroppings of rock, remarkable peaks, or springs.

In the region of Huarochirí, the principal huacas were the highlander Paria Caca, a male being associated with a twin-peaked snowcapped mountain visible on the eastern horizon, and the coastal Chaupi Ñamca, his sister or female counterpart, associated with a five-armed crag of rock. This symbolic union of a highland and a coastal divinity seems to have made sense of the Yauyos highlanders' victory over the Yuncas lowlanders as a coming together into one family (Selection 36 from Cajatambo, Peru, features a similar explanation of coexistence).

Other huacas of greater and lesser importance were also part of a set of sacred traditions that connected a number of neighboring peoples. One of the more important divinities was a coastal trickster named Cuni Raya Vira Cocha (sometimes simply Cuni Raya or Vira Cocha in seeming acknowledgment of two coinciding pan-Andean gods), who is featured in this selection. Cuni Raya is associated with water and irrigation, the media through which he, in the course of his entertaining adventures and buffoonery, is continually making and remaking an imperfect world. After a certain point in these ancient times, ordinary men and women existed as well, although their lives

were much affected by the powerful, roaming huacas and by *villcas*, the demigodlike humans whom the huacas held in particular favor. The Huarochirí narratives make it clear that in this time the divine shaping of earthly affairs was a fact of life in what Frank Salomon calls the "mythic landscape": entire landforms were raised from dust, irrigation and agricultural systems were cut out of the sides of mountains, unjust men were ruined and put to shame, beautiful virgins were seduced, and whole worlds were washed into the sea only to be reconstituted anew.

From the point of view of the Checas and other native Andean groups, most of whom by the last quarter of the sixteenth century had come to live in the resettled villages and towns and within parish networks, religious life was changing. But the huacas who had once lived in these lands and carried out their various feats were still present. They had been the organizers of the known world, and thus the world could be both explained and managed. The physical surroundings, local agricultural traits and preferences, and the order of social arrangements and various rivalries were all grounded in the huacas' initiatory actions and guiding influence. The landscape displayed what amounted to living proof. When the huacas' exploits were completed, when their particular deeds had been accomplished, or when, as we shall see, they had been superseded by huacas more crafty or powerful than themselves, it was common for them to turn to stone, either in their own shapes or in those of animals. This divine lithomorphosis did not spell the end of their power over the lives of their "children," the generations of men and women who would inhabit the land in their wake and gaze upon them every day; on the contrary, lithomorphosis made their power everlasting. The huaca ancestors represented stability and permanence, but they were simultaneously vital and integrated into the colonial conditions of their people.

Of equal importance to Andean peoples were the malquis, a number of whom were also significant to the people of Cajatambo (Selection 36). Malquis were more recent ancestors whose bodies were carefully preserved and wrapped (effectively mummified), and who commonly resided in resting places or cave tombs often near the huacas, and who were nourished, consulted, and cared for in similar ways. The Andean social, ritual, and territorial units called *ayllus*, as well as smaller lineage groups, had networks of ministers and guardians of traditions who attended to these different kinds of gods, and who were joined by a number of ritual specialists skilled in the arts of healing, love, hate, divination, and dream interpretation, among other things.

The assemblage of oral traditions and sacred histories that has been called the Huarochirí Manuscript demonstrates that local and regional ways of making sense of the world retained their vitality and ability to transform themselves through Inkaic times and into the colonial era. The style of the Huarochirí narratives is meandering; there are stories within stories, and lots of doubling back. They are deceptively simple, with arresting silences, repetitions of key phrases, and a cadence that suggests the style of the natural storytellers whose words informed the text created by native writers and editors.

The marginal comments that were scrawled on the original manuscript in Spanish and Quechua offer important hints about the possible genesis of the work and remind us that this was not a simple production. A number of these annotations seem to have been the work of Francisco de Avila (1573?–1647), the parish priest of San Damián de Checa after 1597 and one of the principal campaigners to investigate and repress suspect Andean religiosity and alleged perversions of Catholicism (see Selection 35). The marginalia in Spanish seem obsessed with identifying place names and specific information about persistent worship of huacas. Avila sought out evidence of Andean gods and religious practices from Indian ministers in San Damián, San Pedro de Mama, and other communities in the region. By June 1609 he had convinced the rector of the Jesuit college in Lima of the need for two padres to assist him in his labors. The mass of testimonial, narrative, and physical evidence

that Avila, his native Andean supporters and associates, and Jesuit assistants managed to compile about colonial Andean religion fueled his own efforts to "extirpate" idolatry, and helped him to persuade the archbishop of Lima and other officials to support an even wider campaign of extirpation in other regions. The Huarochirí Manuscript, perhaps the single most important collection of material on pre-Hispanic Andean and colonial religion from native Andean tellers and writers, came out of this priest-extirpator's project.

Avila was knowledgeable about Andean traditions, yet the extent of his role in the creation and editing of much of the work is not clear. And, in any event, the manuscript is considerably more than simply a "tainted" source on Andean traditions or a blind servant of repression. Salomon contends that "because it was composed [by native Andeans] in relative independence from Spanish conceptions about native religion, it has in the end provided a uniquely authentic monument of the very beliefs Avila meant to destroy." Is such a text, then, collected and written in colonial times, essential to the preservation of knowledge of the lives lived by "the ancestors of the people called Indians," as the recorders and editors claim in the first line of this reading?

The text selected comes from the preface and early chapters of the book and is chosen to show native categories of thought and a regional vision of ancient Peruvian times before the Inkas and Spaniards. Even in this passage, the narratives inevitably tell us about the colonial times out of which they emerged, principally because of the complicated voices of the native Andean recorders and editors. These writers make an effort to render their work in terms that they think would appeal to a Christian mentality, although this effort is best described as uneven. Furthermore, they want to merge the traditions they collect and commit to writing with a Christian history, in ways that remind us of the chronicle attributed to the contemporary Andean Christian writer, Felipe Guaman Poma de Ayala (Selection 27). What is to be made of the allusions to Christianity in the text and, at times, the seeming resemblance of described events to biblical happenings? Are these allusions and resemblances evidence of these native Andeans' desire to please the priest Avila, whom they could expect to check some or all of their lines? Or might they also be something else?

Interventions by the recorders-editors occur on a number of occasions, as when sexually explicit passages (usually stated plainly in Quechua) seem softened through the choice of Quechua terms that revolve around "shame." More directly, in their presentation of the time "the ocean overflowed" and only one man survived, the editors state that "we Christians believe it refers to the time of the Flood." In writing of the story in this way, they open their own interpretation of the traditions to question, not least by implying that they have opponents in their midst. There seems to be a set of native Andeans, not very clearly defined, who believe in what the huacas had done and can do. These opponents to the Andean Christians are said not to think that this story of watery cataclysm refers to the Christian God's particular vengeance or an Andean Noah taking refuge from the Flood on a peak or in his ark equivalent. "They," the recorders-editors report, "believe it was Villca Coto mountain that saved them." The death of Jesus also had powerfully ambiguous implications to the authors of the Huarochirí Manuscript. They transport an interpretation based on the darkness described in Luke 23:44–45 into the relation as a possible explanation for the darkness and chaos (llamas driving men, inanimate objects coming to life in order to revolt, and so on) that was said to have fallen on the land after the death of the Sun in ancient times. Again, we see the phrase, "Here's what we Christians think about it." Yet the passage relating the death of the Sun to the death of the Son ends, "Maybe that's what it was."

Are doubts, and perhaps even a collective smile, visible here? Are there other points in the selection in which the recorders-editors are not differentiating so clearly between Andean traditions and what seem to be the traces of Christianity? Does the splitting of colonial Andean society implied by the occasional use of "us" and "them"— "we" who accept Christianity and "they" who still reject it—reflect the exclusivist dichotomies (Christian/Andean, good/evil, accommodating/resistant, and so on) that were expressed in Christian doctrine classes and in sermons? Or perhaps the neat polarized factions delineate extremes in society while obscuring the contours of a more complicated coexistence of huaca worship (and other Andean beliefs and practices) with Christianity.

There is a real possibility that Christian notions were shaping parts of this narrative in fundamental ways. Yet there may be a trap in following this interpretative line too closely, in sifting through the text in search either of pre-Hispanic Andean survivals or of Christian influence. How far does one go? In the reading there is, for instance, a glorification of the huaca who appears as a "little guy," the poor and friendless beggar. This motif recurs in the collection of narratives. Does one suppose that it reflects the influence on native Andeans of Christian notions of poverty learned, say, from visiting missionaries or wandering holy men? Or perhaps the motif of the little guy achieving victory in the end is a convention of Andean oral tradition, not to mention a wider human story-telling inclination. The prototypical huaca hero is not only humble and poor; he or she is also a devious trickster. The traditions explain how the visible world and its people came into being; but, along the way, the reader or hearer seems called upon to root for the clever huaca little guy and the modest people with whom the gods often interact.

This text, collected in the late sixteenth and early seventeenth centuries, need not be simply one or the other. As the historian Inga Clendinnen has written of Indian "religion" in early colonial Mexico, the Huarochirí Manuscript tells of an emerging and vital colonial religious culture in the central Andes that seems to be understood less well, not better, when it is dissected into persistent purities and Christian assimilations.

[Preface]

If the ancestors of the people called Indians had known writing in earlier times,
　　then the lives they lived would not have faded from view until now.
As the mighty past of the Spanish Vira Cochas is visible until now, so, too, would
　　theirs be.
But since things are as they are, and since nothing has been written until now,
I set forth here the lives of the ancestors of the Huaro Cheri people, who all
　　descend from one forefather:
What faith they held, how they live up until now, those things and more;
Village by village it will be written down: how they lived from their dawning age
　　onward.

Chapter 1
⁓ *How the Idols of Old Were, and How They Warred among Themselves, and How the Natives Existed at That Time*

In very ancient times, there were huacas named Yana Ñamca and Tuta Ñamca.
Later on another huaca named Huallallo Caruincho defeated them.
After he defeated them, he ordered the people to bear two children and no more.
He would eat one of them himself.
The parents would raise the other, whichever one was loved best.
Although people did die in those times, they came back to life on the fifth day
　　exactly.
And as for their foodstuffs, they ripened exactly five days after being planted.
These villages and all the others like them were full of Yunca.

[margin, in Quechua: full of Yunca]

When a great number of people had filled the land, they lived really miserably,
　　scratching and digging the rock faces and ledges to make terraced fields.
These fields, some small, others large, are still visible today on all the rocky
　　heights.
And all the birds of that age were perfectly beautiful, parrots and toucans all yellow
　　and red.

Later, at the time when another huaca named Paria Caca appeared, these beings
　　and all their works were cast out to the hot Anti lands by Paria Caca's actions.
Further on we'll speak of Paria Caca's emergence and of his victories.

Also, as we know, there was another huaca named Cuni Raya.
Regarding him, we're not sure whether he existed before Paria Caca or maybe
　　after him.

[margin, in Spanish: Find out whether he says that it isn't known if he was before or after
Caruincho or Paria Caca.]

However, Cuni Raya's essential nature almost matches Vira Cocha's. For when
　　people worshiped this huaca, they would invoke him, saying,

> Cuni Raya Vira Cocha,
> You who animate mankind,
> Who charge the world with being,
> All things are yours!
> Yours the fields and yours the people.

And so, long ago, when beginning anything difficult, the ancients, even though they couldn't see Vira Cocha, used to throw coca leaves to the ground, talk to him, and worship him before all others, saying,

> Help me remember how,
> Help me work it out,
> Cuni Raya Vira Cocha!

And the master weaver would worship and call on him whenever it was hard for him to weave.

For that reason, we'll write first about this huaca and about his life, and later on about Paria Caca.

Chapter 2
∼ How Cuni Raya Vira Cocha Acted in His Own Age. The Life of Cuni Raya Vira Cocha. How Caui Llaca Gave Birth to His Child, and What Followed

[margin, crossed out, in Spanish: Note that it isn't known whether this was before or after Caruincho.]

A long, long time ago, Cuni Raya Vira Cocha used to go around posing as a miserably poor and friendless man, with his cloak and tunic all ripped and tattered. Some people who didn't recognize him for who he was yelled, "You poor lousy wretch!"

Yet it was this man who fashioned all the villages. Just by speaking he made the fields, and finished the terraces with walls of fine masonry. As for the irrigation canals, he channeled them out from their sources just by tossing down the flower of a reed called pupuna.

After that, he went around performing all kinds of wonders, putting some of the local huacas to shame with his cleverness.

Once there was a female huaca named Caui Llaca.

Caui Llaca had always remained a virgin. Since she was very beautiful, every one of the huacas and villcas longed for her. "I've got to sleep with her!" they thought.

But she never consented.

Once this woman, who had never allowed any male to fondle her, was weaving beneath a lúcuma tree.

Cuni Raya, in his cleverness, turned himself into a bird and climbed into the lúcuma.

He put his semen into a fruit that had ripened there and dropped it next to the woman.

The woman swallowed it down delightedly.

Thus she got pregnant even though she remained untouched by a man.

In her ninth month, virgin though she was, she gave birth just as other women give birth.

And so, too, for one year she nursed her child at her breast, wondering, "Whose child could this be?"

In the fullness of the year, when the youngster was crawling around on all fours, she summoned all the huacas and villcas to find out who was the child's father.

When the huacas heard the message, they were overjoyed, and they all came dressed in their best clothes, each saying to himself, "It's me!" "It's me she'll love!"

This gathering took place at Anchi Cocha, where the woman lived.

[margin, in Spanish: The gathering was in Anchi Cocha.]

When all the huacas and villcas had taken their seats there, that woman addressed them:

"Behold, gentlemen and lords. Acknowledge this child. Which of you made me pregnant?" One by one she asked each of them:

"Was it you?"

"Was it you?"

But nobody answered, "The child is mine."

The one called Cuni Raya Vira Cocha had taken his seat at the edge of the gathering. Since he looked like a friendless beggar sitting there, and since so many handsome men were present, she spurned him and didn't question him. She thought, "How could my baby possibly be the child of that beggar?"

Since no one had said, "The child is mine," she first warned the huacas, "If the baby is yours, it'll crawl up to you," and then addressed the child:

"Go, identify your father yourself!"

The child began at one end of the group and crawled along on all fours without climbing up on anyone, until reaching the other end, where its father sat.

On reaching him, the baby instantly brightened up and climbed onto its father's knee.

When its mother saw this, she got all indignant: "Atatay, what a disgrace! How could I have given birth to the child of a beggar like that?" she said. And taking along only her child, she headed straight for the ocean.

And then, while all the local huacas stood in awe, Cuni Raya Vira Cocha put on his golden garment. He started to chase her at once, thinking to himself, "She'll be overcome by sudden desire for me."

"Sister Caui Llaca!" he called after her. "Here, look at me! Now I'm really beautiful!" he said, and he stood there making his garment glitter.

Caui Llaca didn't even turn her face back to him.

"Because I've given birth to the child of such a ruffian, such a mangy beggar, I'll just disappear into the ocean," she said. She headed straight out into the deep sea near Pacha Camac, out there where even now two stones that clearly look like people stand.

And when she arrived at what is today her dwelling, she turned to stone.

Yet Cuni Raya Vira Cocha thought, "She'll see me anyway, she'll come to look at me!"
    He followed her at a distance, shouting and calling out to her over and over.
First, he met up with a condor.
"Brother, where did you run into that woman?" he asked him.
"Right near here. Soon you'll find her," replied the condor.
Cuni Raya Vira Cocha spoke to him and said,
"You'll live a long life. You alone will eat any dead animal from the wild mountain
    slopes, both guanacos and vicuñas, of any kind and in any number. And if
    anybody should kill you, he'll die himself, too."

Farther on, he met up with a skunk.
"Sister, where did you meet that woman?" he asked.
"You'll never find her now. She's gone way far away," replied the skunk.
When she said this, he cursed her very hatefully, saying,
"As for you, because of what you've just told me, you'll never go around in the
    daytime. You'll only walk at night, stinking disgustingly. People will be revolted
    by you."

Next he met up with a puma.
"She just passed this way. She's still nearby. You'll soon reach her," the puma told him.
Cuni Raya Vira Cocha spoke to him, saying,
"You'll be well loved. You'll eat llamas, especially the llamas of people who bear
    guilt. Although people may kill you, they'll wear you on their heads during a
    great festival and set you to dancing. And then when they bring you out
    annually, they'll sacrifice a llama first and then set you to dancing."

Then he met up with a fox.
"She's already gone way far away. You'll never find her now," that fox told him.
When the fox said this, he replied,
"As for you, even when you skulk around keeping your distance, people will
    thoroughly despise you and say, 'That fox is a sneak thief.' When they kill you,
    they'll just carelessly throw you away, and your skin, too."

[A marginal addition in Quechua begins here.]

Likewise he met up with a falcon.
"She's just passed this way. You'll soon find her," said the falcon.
He replied,
"You're greatly blessed. When you eat, you'll eat the hummingbird first, then all the
    other birds. When people kill you, the man who has slain you will have you
    mourned with the sacrifice of a llama. And when they dance, they'll put you on
    their heads so you can sit there shining with beauty."

And then he met up with some parakeets.
"She's already gone way far away. You'll never find her now," the parakeets told him.
"As for you, you'll travel around shrieking raucously," replied Cuni Raya Vira Cocha.
    "Although you may say, 'I'll spoil your crops!' when people hear your screaming
    they'll chase you away at once. You'll live in great misery amidst the hatred of
    humans."

[The marginal addition ends here.]

And so he traveled on. Whenever he met anyone who gave him good news, he conferred on him good fortune. But he went along viciously cursing those who gave him bad news.

When he reached the seashore, [crossed out in original manuscript: he went straight over it. Today people say, "He was headed for Castile," but in the old days people said, "He went to another land."] he turned back toward Pacha Camac.

He arrived at the place where Pacha Camac's two daughters lived, guarded by a snake.

Just before this, the two girls' mother had gone into the deep sea to visit Caui Llaca.
Her name was Urpay Huachac.

While Urpay Huachac was away, Cuni Raya Vira Cocha seduced one girl, her older daughter.

When he sought to sleep with the other sister, she turned into a dove and darted away.

That's why her mother's name means "Gives Birth to Doves."

At that time there wasn't a single fish in the ocean.

Only Urpay Huachac used to breed them, at her home, in a small pond.

It was these fish, all of them, that Cuni Raya angrily scattered into the ocean, saying, "For what did she go off and visit Caui Llaca, the woman of the ocean depths?"

Ever since then, fish have filled the sea.

Then Cuni Raya Vira Cocha fled along the seashore.

When Urpay Huachac's daughters told her how he'd seduced them, she got furious and chased him.

As she followed him, calling him again and again, he waited for her and said, "Yes?"

"Cuni, I'm just going to remove your lice," she said, and she picked them off.

While she picked his lice, she caused a huge abyss to open up next to him, thinking to herself, "I'll knock Cuni Raya down into it."

But Cuni Raya in his cleverness realized this; just by saying, "Sister, I've got to go off for a moment to relieve myself," he made his getaway to these villages.

He traveled around this area for a long, long time, tricking lots of local huacas and people, too.

[marginal note, in Spanish, crossed out: n.b. This huaca's end will be told below.]

Chapter 3
◌ What Happened to the Indians in Ancient Times When the Ocean Overflowed

Now we'll return to what is said of very early people.

The story goes like this.

In ancient times, this world wanted to come to an end.

A llama buck, aware that the ocean was about to overflow, was behaving like somebody who's deep in sadness. Even though its [father] owner let it rest in a patch of excellent pasture, it cried and said, "In, in," and wouldn't eat.

The llama's [father] owner got really angry, and he threw the cob from some maize he had just eaten at the llama.

"Eat, dog! This is some fine grass I'm letting you rest in!" he said.

Then the llama began speaking like a human being.

"You simpleton, whatever could you be thinking about? Soon, in five days, the ocean will overflow. It's a certainty. And the whole world will come to an end," it said.

The man got good and scared. "What's going to happen to us? Where can we go to save ourselves?" he said.

The llama replied, "Let's go to Villca Coto mountain.

[margin, in Spanish: This is a mountain that is between Huanri and Surco.]

There we'll be saved. Take along five days' food for yourself."

So the man went out from there in a great hurry, and himself carried both the llama buck and its load.

When they arrived at Villca Coto mountain, all sorts of animals had already filled it up: pumas, foxes, guanacos, condors, all kinds of animals in great numbers.

And as soon as that man had arrived there, the ocean overflowed.

They stayed there huddling tightly together.

The waters covered all those mountains and it was only Villca Coto mountain, or rather its very peak, that was not covered by water.

Water soaked the fox's tail.

That's how it turned black.

Five days later, the waters descended and began to dry up.

The drying waters caused the ocean to retreat all the way down again and exterminate all the people.

Afterward, that man began to multiply once more.

That's the reason there are people until today.

Regarding this story, we Christians believe it refers to the time of the Flood.

But they believe it was Villca Coto mountain that saved them.

Chapter 4
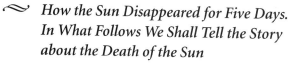 *How the Sun Disappeared for Five Days.*
In What Follows We Shall Tell the Story
about the Death of the Sun

In ancient times the Sun died.

Because of his death it was night for five days.

Rocks banged against each other.

Mortars and grindstones began to eat people.

Buck llamas started to drive men.

Here's what we Christians think about it: We think these stories tell of the darkness following the death of Our Lord Jesus Christ.

Maybe that's what it was.

Chapter 5

∼ *How in Ancient Times Paria Caca Appeared on a Mountain*
Named Condor Coto in the Form of Five Eggs, and What Followed.
Here Will Begin the Account of Paria Caca's Emergence

In the four preceding chapters we have already recounted the lives lived in ancient
times.

Nevertheless, we don't know the origins of the people of those days, nor where it
was they emerged from.

These people, the ones who lived in that era, used to spend their lives warring on
each other and conquering each other. For their leaders, they recognized only
the strong and the rich.

We speak of them as the Purum Runa, "people of desolation."

It was at this time that the one called Paria Caca was born in the form of five eggs
on Condor Coto mountain.

A certain man, and a poor friendless one at that, was the first to see and know the
fact of his birth; he was called Huatya Curi, but was also known as Paria Caca's
son.

Now we'll speak of this discovery of his, and of the many wonders he performed. . . .

2

The Inka's Tunics
(fifteenth to sixteenth centuries)

Both coastal and highland peoples of pre-Hispanic Peru excelled in textile making. An indigenous weaving tradition still flourishes today, especially in the Andes mountains. To a certain extent, skills in the two major available fibers (a hardy cotton: *Gossypium barbadense*, and wool from the native camelids: llamas, alpacas, and vicuñas) developed out of a need for warm clothing, particularly in the high Andes where temperatures can fluctuate sharply both by day and by season. Yet, although woven blankets, clothing, sacks, saddlebags, and pouches for carrying coca leaves were items of necessity, textiles might also function as forms of cultural and political expression. Andean techniques and patterns were many, and a startling number of colors was produced by the dyes from local plants and the secretions of shellfish and insects (on the use of red from the cochineal beetle in another region, see Selection 15). The elaborate textiles created by the Paracas peoples of the central Peruvian coast during the first millennium B.C. are perhaps the most celebrated examples of these ancient Andean arts, although expert textile making was widespread down to the last and best-known Andean state before the Spanish arrival, that of the Inkas, and continued through colonial times.

Figures 1 and 2 are examples from this tradition of meaningful fabrics in the form of *uncus*—Quechua for sleeveless tunics. The first garment (Figure 1; Plate 1), an Inka key checkerboard tunic, is from Inka times, and the second (Figure 2; Plate 2), a royal tunic, may be from the early colonial period. Of all the distinctive accoutrements and apparel of the Inka royalty—the crown or ornamented headgear (*masca paycha*), a colorful feather collar (*huallca*), the scepter (*suntur paucar*), the halberd (*tupa yauri*) and the golden beaker (*tupa cusi*), or the club (*champi*)—the uncu may have said the most about its wearer to his viewers. The abstract patterns and designs on the uncus conveyed complex symbolic information about order in the Andes and the universe. The unique king and son of the Sun, the Sapa Inka, wore a number of tunics that told of his exalted position within an elaborate set of social and political relationships. An uncu might also set out an interpretation of history, with its precise iconography establishing a living ruler's special identification with an ancestral king. A ruling Inka's tunics changed with the calendar and to meet the needs of feasts (*raymi*) or other occasions.

The checkerboard effect created by numerous abstract, square design units (*tucapu* or *t'oqapu*) was called the *collcapata* motif,

Figure 1. An Inka key checkerboard tunic (fifteenth–sixteenth centuries).
Courtesy of the Textile Museum, Washington, DC.
∼ SEE PLATE 1 ∼

and it was one of the standardized types in surviving pre-Hispanic tunics. The squares might be a striking black and white; or, as in the upper two-thirds of the first uncu, each square might alternate in color and contain a standard pattern that John Howland Rowe has called the "Inka key." (The lower one-third of this tunic features six bold stripes in alternating red and blue.) The collcapata design is thought to suggest the rows of stone storehouses (*collca* or *colca*) to which agricultural tribute flowed from the four quarters of the empire (Tawantinsuyu, or Land of the Four Quarters). The collca were the particular attributes of Andean farmers— non-Inkas such as the peoples from Huarochirí, whose traditions were encountered in Selection 1—and many others throughout Tawantinsuyu. The collcapata seems to have expressed concepts of commonality and, ultimately, unity of all ranks of people, representing a careful kind of foundation upon which the structure of Inkaic universalism was built.

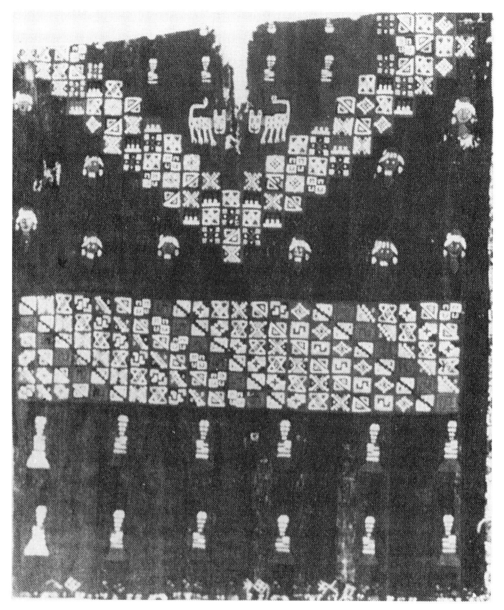

Figure 2. A royal tunic (sixteenth century).
~ SEE PLATE 2 ~

A tunic with a collcapata design was worn by the Inka when he attended one of the three principal feasts of the year to which all kinds of people came, the Inka *raymi* in May. The collcapata was also worn when the Sapa Inka and his noble retinue left the Valley of Cusco and toured the provinces. On these occasions the royal uncu featured neither of the two kinds of royal borders around the ruler's neck—the *ahuaqui*, a V-shaped yoke design of woven squares, or the huallca collar. Such a border is not present in our first uncu, but in the second one it is there in the form of an ahuaqui yoke (in this example, there are four rows of exquisite tucapus on either side of the tunic's neck opening).

Since the border signified the separation of the divine Inka from his subjects, stressing the grandeur of the political head, such symbols were absent on popular and inclusive occasions. The Inka also wore another type of tunic featuring a *casana* design—a large square frame with four smaller squares within, woven into the lower half of the tunic—particularly in the foot-plowing and planting season, August and September, with which it was most associated. Its political message seems to have been a nuanced one about hierarchy and integration: the casana was often worn in combination with an ahuaqui neck border and might also be juxtaposed with the collcapata motif.

Just as surely as the Inka's uncu and other attributes could project a message of measured inclusion and alliance to peoples beyond the Inka royalty and notables or in the outlying provinces, the uncu could also communicate details of power and succession to those at the political center. At the festival of Capac raymi, attended only by the Inka, the royal relatives, and the Cusqueño elite, a so-called royal uncu was worn. According to Rowe, our second tunic is probably an heirloom of a noble family woven in the Inka style in early colonial times; it possesses the distinctive features of royalty also present in the few surviving pre-Hispanic examples of its kind. R. Tom Zuidema describes the second tunic's background color as "blue or purple." It features an elaborate ahuaqui yoke design, a red field within a border that consists of squares filled with seven kinds of tucapus. The two felines, each a mirror image of the other, within the border and close to the neckline, are another indication of Andean royalty, as were the many "extra" designs that would not be present on the tunic (or drinking vessel, for that matter) of an ordinary person.

These extras seem set off by a wide waistband of many differently colored rows of tucapus running diagonally, acting as a frame. Beneath the waistband are two rows of six crowns or royal headgear, each with its three intricate parts (two feathers or a small scepter, above a square golden plaque, and a lower fringe). Five of the crowns in each row have red fringes, while one is yellow. Two sixteenth-century chroniclers, Pedro Cieza de León and Martín de Murúa, claimed that each red thread in this lower fringe represented one of the Inka's enemies slain in battle. And El Inca Garcilaso de la Vega, writing in the early seventeenth century, informs us that an Inkaic crown prince wore a yellow fringe to symbolize his status as an initiate and to indicate that he had not yet killed an enemy. Working constructively from these fragments of information, Zuidema suggests that the five red-fringed crowns in two rows in the lower half of the second uncu may relate to the two arrangements of five trophy heads to either side of the ahuaqui yoke in the royal tunic's upper half. "Thinking of the probable use of this uncu," Zuidema writes, "I propose that the ten red masca paychas on each side represented the ten *panacas* [lineage branches of the Inka nobility] of the organization of Cusco and the two yellow ones the noble initiates at the time of Capac raymi."

When the Spaniards arrived in Peru and began to investigate Inkaic and non-Inkaic Andean societies, perhaps their most repeated early impression concerned the Andeans' apparent lack of a written language. Yet a more expansive definition of what "written" communication might be would allow room not only for the sophisticated pictographic expression of Mesoamerican peoples but also for the iconography of Andean cultures. Zuidema writes of an expressive tradition of lordship in the Andes in which "the iconographic whole was the lord, including his royal paraphernalia, body decorations, and tunic." Spanish Christians would bring an array of powerful symbols of prestige and messages of lineage and authority on their persons and in their creations, but such symbols and messages arrived in lands already exquisitely familiar with such means of expression and expectation. To employ a phrase that

Zuidema himself borrows from Roland Barthes, the Inka's "written garments" in the years before the Spanish arrival are but one example of a means through which the rulers of a vast and dynamic pre-Hispanic Andean state could communicate alliance and distinctions, and political and social hierarchy, as well as ritual roles.

3

The Lords and Holy Men of Tenochtitlan Reply to the Franciscans, 1524

(1564)

The following two chapters of a *coloquio,* or exchange of speeches, between lords and holy men from the Aztec capital of Tenochtitlan and "the Twelve" (the first group of Franciscan evangelizers in central Mexico; see Selection 8), purports to be the Indians' reply to the friars' explanation of their mission in 1524, three years after Cortés had captured the city. It was written out in parallel Nahuatl and Spanish texts in 1564 by or for Bernardino de Sahagún (1500–1590), the famous Spanish Franciscan linguist and missionary who, with the collaboration of surviving elders and young Indian nobles who studied with him in the school of Santiago Tlatelolco on the outskirts of Mexico City, composed the monumental work about beliefs and practices in Aztec society known as the Florentine Codex.

This coloquio is not a literal transcription of what the friars and Indians said to each other on a single occasion. Sahagún could not have witnessed such an encounter, since he did not reach Mexico until 1529. But several early Spanish chroniclers who were there by 1523 refer to such formal exchanges, and Sahagún reportedly drew upon an accumulation of notes and conversations with Indian informants and members of "the Twelve" in

his 1564 composition. It is, then, a literary reworking into one scene of the fragmentary recollections of several such encounters. Sahagún's stated intention in his studies and writings was to understand Indian life and religion more thoroughly, the better to make converts. This intention undoubtedly shaped his presentation of Aztec culture (including the silences) in ways that remain obscure to us, but his deep interest in native life and thought led to the inclusion of much that was tangential, if not irrelevant, to his stated purpose. Miguel León-Portilla, a leading student of Aztec culture and Nahuatl sources, concludes that this coloquio was crafted as an instrument of evangelization, but it also offers an authentic glimpse of the Aztec religion and vision of the world and response to Spanish colonization.

If so, what is glimpsed? The words attributed to the Aztec lords convey a feeling of profound but not altogether incompatible differences between their vision of divinity and human destiny and that of the friars. They accept, even welcome as providential, the arrival of the Spaniards and their king as rulers, but are reluctant to substitute the newcomers' religious doctrines for their own.

They are impressed by the majesty of the Christian God and accept the Bible as a "book of celestial and divine words." They accept the friars as bearers of divine riches, as God's representatives sent by "our great Emperor," Charles V; and they are prepared to consider their teachings, and adopt them in good time, but they are not persuaded by the friars' assertions that "we do not know the One who gives us life and being . . . that [the gods] we worship are not gods." They fear the wrath of their ancestral gods, omnipresent in the landscape, and the creative and destructive forces of nature, hungry for propitiation, if they were to neglect or forsake them. Their ceremonies and sacrifices, they assure the friars, are not empty gestures, easily abandoned. The Aztec interlocutors convey a profound veneration for their forebears—ancestor worship, a Spaniard might have called it—and a way of thinking about divine power that blurred basic dichotomies and boundaries of Christian thought, such as natural/supernatural, heaven/earth, and good/evil. Acceptance of Christianity does not strike them as an all-or-nothing proposition. Speaking in a convivial way as one elite group to another, they warn of popular rebellions rooted in desperation should the Spaniards force such a choice.

Chapter 6
How the Indian Lords Responded to the Twelve

After the twelve priests had finished their first speech to the lords and nobles of Mexico [Tenochtitlan], one of them arose and most courteously and urbanely replied in the following way:

"Dear Sirs, you are most welcome among us. Your coming to our city gives us pleasure. We are at your service and offer you all that we have. We know that you come from among the clouds and mist in the sky. That, along with your persons and way of speaking which we ourselves have seen and heard, makes your arrival unique and marvelous. Altogether, it seems like a celestial event, as if you had opened in our presence a chest of divine riches from the Lord of the sky, and of riches from the great priest who is Lord of the earth, riches that are sent to us by our great Emperor. You showed us all sorts of precious stones—most pure, resplendent, flawless, big and round, sapphires, emeralds, rubies, and pearls. You showed us new kinds of feathers, rich ones of great value. What gives us anguish now is that our wise men who were prudent and skillful in our kind of speech and who were in charge of the principality [the territory controlled by Tenochtitlan], are now dead. If they had heard from your mouths what we have heard, you would hear in return a most agreeable salutation and reply. But we who are inferior and less wise, what can we say? Even though, in truth, we are the leaders of the kingdom and republic, we lack their knowledge and prudence, and it does not seem just to us that the customs and rites that our forebears passed down to us, which they considered good and worthy of safekeeping, should be lightly set aside and destroyed by us.

"Besides this you should know, our lords, that we have priests who guide us and prepare us in the culture and service of our gods. There are also many others with distinct names who serve in the temples day and night, who are wise and knowledgeable about the movement of the heavenly bodies as well as about our ancient customs. They have the books of our forebears which they study and peruse day and night. These guide us and prepare us in counting the years, days, months, and feasts of our gods, which are celebrated every twenty days. These same priests are in charge of the histories of our gods and the rules about serving them, because we are in charge only of warfare, collection of tribute, and justice. We will gather them together and tell them what we have heard of the words of God. It is well that they answer and contradict, for they know and it falls to them by their office."

Having finished speaking, the lords took their leave of the twelve. That same day, the principal lords and priests of the idols gathered and the lords recounted all that had happened, giving a full account of what the twelve had said. They remained a long time discussing this matter.

Having understood the reasoning and speech of the twelve, the principal lords and priests of the idols became greatly agitated and fell into a great sadness and fear, offering no response. Some time later they began to speak again and decided among themselves to go together the following day to see, hear, and speak to the twelve. Once the following day dawned, they all gathered and went directly to where the twelve were. Upon arrival, all greeted them and spoke to them affectionately. And the lords said [to the twelve]: "Our Lords, here before you are our principal lords and priests. They have come. We have told them all you said to us yesterday. Here they are. Let them respond. And so that they may be fully satisfied [that they understand what you said], please tell them again from the beginning all that you said to us yesterday, though we know it is tedious for you to do so." Then one of the twelve, using the interpreter, repeated everything that they had said to the lords the day before. Having heard this, one of the principal lords arose, asked the indulgence of the twelve, then began to speak and made the following long speech.

Chapter 7
∾ *In Which the Reply of the Principal Holy Men to the Twelve Is Found*

"Our lords, leading personages of much esteem, you are very welcome to our lands and towns. We ourselves, being inferior and base, are unworthy of looking upon the faces of such valiant personages. God, Our Lord, has brought you to rule us. We do not know where you come from or where our lords and gods dwell because you have come by sea, through the clouds and mist, a route we have never known. God sends you among us as His own eyes, ears, and mouth. He who is invisible and spiritual becomes visible in you. And we hear His words with our own ears through you, His representatives. We have heard the words that you have brought us of the One who gives us life and being. And we have heard with admiration the words of the Lord of the World which he has sent here for love of us, and also you have brought us the book of celestial and divine words.

"You have told us that we do not know the One who gives us life and being, who is Lord of the heavens and of the earth. You also say that those we worship are not gods. This way of speaking is entirely new to us, and very scandalous. We are frightened by this way of speaking because our forebears who engendered and governed us never said anything like this. On the contrary, they left us this our custom of worshiping our gods, in which they believed and which they worshiped all the time that they lived here on earth. They taught us how to honor them. And they taught us all the ceremonies and sacrifices that we make. They told us that through them [our gods] we live and are, and that we were beholden to them, to be theirs and to serve countless centuries before the sun began to shine and before there was daytime. They said that these gods that we worship give us everything we need for our physical existence: maize, beans, chia seeds, etc. We appeal to them for the rain to make the things of the earth grow.

"These our gods are the source of great riches and delights, all of which belong to them. They live in very delightful places where there are always flowers, vegetation, and great freshness, a place unknown to mere mortals, called Tlalocan, where there is never hunger, poverty, or illness. It is they who bestow honors, property, titles, and kingdoms, gold and silver, precious feathers, and gemstones.

"There has never been a time remembered when they were not worshiped, honored, and esteemed. Perhaps it is a century or two since this began; it is a time beyond counting. Who can remember when or how those celebrated and sacred places came into being, where miracles occurred and answers were given, called Tulan Vapalcalco, Xuchatlapan, Tamoancham, Yoalliycham, Teutiuacam? The inhabitants of these aforementioned places reigned and ruled everywhere, so honored, so famous, such kingdoms and glory and lordship.

"It would be a fickle, foolish thing for us to destroy the most ancient laws and customs left by the first inhabitants of this land, who were the Chichimecas, the Tulanos, those from Colhua, the Tepanecas, for the worship, faith, and service of the abovementioned [gods], in which we were born and raised. And we are accustomed to them and we have them impressed on our hearts.

"Oh, our lords and leaders! You should take great care not to do anything to stir up or incite your vassals to some evil deed. How could you leave the poor elderly among us bereft of that in which they have been raised throughout their lives? Watch out that we do not incur the wrath of our gods. Watch out that the common people do not rise up against us if we were to tell them that the gods they have always understood to be such are not gods at all.

"It is best, our lords, to act on this matter very slowly, with great deliberation. We are not satisfied or convinced by what you have told us, nor do we understand or give credit to what has been said of our gods. It gives us anguish, lords and fathers, to speak in this way. Here present are the lords charged with governing the kingdom and republics of this world. All of us together feel that it is enough to have lost, enough that the power and royal jurisdiction have been taken from us. As for our gods, we will die before giving up serving and worshiping them. This is our determination; do what you will. This will serve in reply and contradiction to what you have said. We have no more to say, lords."

4

The Aztec Stone of the Five Eras
(late fifteenth century)

This famous stone monument from the ritual precinct of the Aztec capital of Tenochtitlan, over which the Spaniards built their own capital city of Mexico, was unearthed during a street-paving project near the end of the colonial period. Measuring nearly twelve feet across, it has long been called the Sun Stone or the Calendar Stone: "Sun Stone" on the assumption that it depicts the face or mask of a sun god, Tonatiuh, at the center and served as an object of sun worship; "Calendar Stone" because time is a dominant feature, if not the main point (one of the circular bands records the signs for the twenty days of a month, and the motifs at the center of the stone depict the Aztecs' conception of five historical ages). Whatever it is called, this mysterious object is packed with messages, irreducibly from another place, combining time and space in ways that are hard to fathom in our words. Still, it provokes speculation about Mesoamerican views regarding time, space, and destiny in comparison with those of Spaniards and colonial subjects. Some of the similarities and differences would have contributed to successful Spanish colonization of native American state societies. (Consider the view of time and order expressed in the Huejotzingo altarpiece, Selection 23).

The detailed drawing of the stone (on which we point out the main elements) was first published in a long, learned treatise by Antonio de León y Gama in 1792, two years after it was discovered. León y Gama recognized both the cult-object and calendrical possibilities in the design, although his schooling in math and science led him to focus on the astronomical connections and chronology of Aztec history that he found in it. His keen scientific interest in the stone and his observation that prominent families of Mexico City had begun to keep such pre-Hispanic objects in their homes as curiosities will be worth recalling in connection with other readings and images from the eighteenth century that appear later in this sourcebook.

An alternative to Sun Stone/Calendar Stone ways of interpreting this great disk, put forward recently by Richard Townsend, fits well with the remarkable discoveries made by archaeologists since 1978 at the adjoining site of the Aztecs' principal temple (Templo Mayor). If Townsend is correct, the face or mask in the center of the stone represents the Earth Monster, Tlaltecuhtli, rather than a sun god. It would then follow that the three inner circles represent the disk of the Earth, expressed in time as well as circular space, bathed in a

Figure 3. Aztec Stone of the Five Eras (late fifteenth century).

great field of daylight and fire. The face's prominent tongue is said to be a flint knife, symbol of war, and the two lobes on either side of the face contain claws that grasp human hearts. The Earth Monster is often depicted in Aztec inscriptions as a gaping, toothy mouth at the center of the Earth, consuming blood sacrifices. The face, combined with the four boxes arrayed around it, depict the five historical eras. In the box on the upper right is the first era when giants roamed the Earth, living on wild fruits and roots. Like the time of darkness and chaos in the Andean Huarochirí Manuscript (Selection 1), this was an imperfect era; it ended when a jaguar devoured the giants. Moving counterclockwise, the second era was destroyed by hurri-

canes that turned people into monkeys. The third one ended in a rain of fire and its people perished or were changed into birds. The fourth era ended in floods that turned people into fish. In the fifth and present era the sun, moon, and humans appeared. The face at the center and the four boxes combine to form the symbol of this era, "Ollin" or movement, auguring destruction by earthquake. This arrangement suggests the necessity of sacrifice and combat for the Aztecs to fulfill their destiny at the center of the cosmos.

The pattern of circles continues. The band of twenty day signs that constitute a month surrounds this central image. Beyond it are four bands that are thought to express the awesome power of the sun: first, a band of

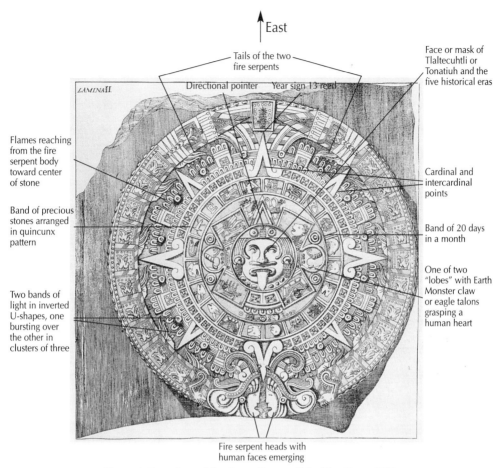

East

Tails of the two fire serpents

Face or mask of Tlaltecuhtli or Tonatiuh and the five historical eras

Directional pointer   Year sign 13 reed

LAMINA II

Flames reaching from the fire serpent body toward center of stone

Cardinal and intercardinal points

Band of precious stones arranged in quincunx pattern

Band of 20 days in a month

One of two "lobes" with Earth Monster claw or eagle talons grasping a human heart

Two bands of light in inverted U-shapes, one bursting over the other in clusters of three

Fire serpent heads with human faces emerging

Figure 4. Drawing of the Aztec Stone of the Five Eras, 1792.

precious turquoises or jades arranged in a quincunx pattern (a familiar Mesoamerican way of indicating sacred space and direction, with four corner points and a center point, or fifth direction; another quincunx arrangement on this stone combines the central face with the four previous eras in one instance and the four cardinal points in another); then two bands of inverted U's separated by a band of four lines with circles interspersed. Between the cardinal and intercardinal points, clusters of three of the inverted U's above more quincunxes burst through the band of lines and the outer ring of U's. The wide band at the edge of the stone is formed by two fire serpents that meet at the bottom of the stone with human faces emerging from the heads, flames reach-

ing out from them toward the center. The direction "up" is emphasized by a pointer directly above the central face. It indicates the place where the fire serpents began their journey across the sky; that is, east, the source of the rising sun. At that point of special emphasis is a year glyph, 13 reed, which Townsend suggests stands both for the distant beginning of the present era and for the year that corresponds to 1427 in the Christian calendar, when expansion of the Aztec tribute empire began in earnest and an ambitious building phase at the Templo Mayor was undertaken.

Whether the face at the center represents the Earth Monster or a sun god, the image as a whole seems to express the sense of a sacred center within concentric circles—a center that is thirsty for nourishment from human blood, sanctioning warfare. Either way, this disk, placed in the great ceremonial precinct of the Aztec city, points to Tenochtitlan as the spatial center of authority, and it expresses the demands and creative/destructive powers of divine forces. More than a cult object dedicated to the sun, this great stone seems to be a kind of city charter that asserted the Aztecs' right to rule, situating them at the sacred center of time and space and celebrating their expansionist destiny in a shifting, threatened world. "Tenochtitlan, place of creation and destruction," it seems to say.

5

Coexistence in the Medieval Spanish Kingdoms
(ninth to twelfth centuries)

In the early eighth century, Arab and Berber invaders from what is today Morocco and the Maghrib in North Africa consolidated a rapid series of military victories and took decisive political control over much of the Iberian Peninsula, calling their territory al-Andalus. From a height of power in the tenth century, when caliphs ruled at Córdoba, Muslim rule fragmented into six large states (or party kingdoms) and a number of smaller ones. Al-Andalus was once again dominated briefly by two groups of Muslim Berber invaders and reformists, the Almoravids and the Almohads, who crossed the Straits of Gibraltar in succession in the eleventh and twelfth centuries. But the Almohad domain was dramatically reduced within a little more than a half-century by separate onslaughts from three Christian powers in the north—the kingdoms of León-Castile, Portugal, and Aragón-Catalonia. Toledo fell permanently to the Christians in 1085, Córdoba in 1236, Valencia in 1238, and Seville in 1248, effectively confining al-Andalus to the southern emirate of Granada, ruled by the Nasrid dynasty from 1231 to 1492.

The three short passages that form the next reading offer Muslim points of view on the history of Iberia before 1492, and they also suggest several ways in which colonial situations brought about by Spanish expansion thereafter can be studied. They were composed in Arabic by different Muslim authors between the ninth and early twelfth centuries, during the ascendance of al-Andalus, in places where Christians appear as a minority population or a savage enemy in the northern distance. These passages illuminate habits of mind toward subject populations and peoples with different religions and customs of living. And they provide substance for thinking about what is often called *convivencia*—a Spanish word loosely translated as the "coexistence" of Muslims, Christians, and Jews within medieval Iberian society.

The historian Ramón Menéndez Pidal originally employed the idea of convivencia in his study of the origins of the Spanish language. He used it to denote the existence of variant forms in early peninsular Romance languages (a "convivencia of norms"), but his student Américo Castro was the first to apply it more broadly to cultural matters. Generally speaking, Castro's convivencia stressed the creative interaction between groups and the roles that this interaction played in the shaping of Spanish culture, which he considered mainly in terms of literary sources. Seen too idealistically, the notion of coexistence conjures up a harmonious intercultural marketplace in medieval Spain that downplays or glides past bitter tension and eruptions of violent conflict. Used with caution, however, the idea of coexistence can shed light on a history of interaction that produced a gradual conversion of an indigenous Hispano-Roman majority to Islam, centuries of miscegenation between Muslims and other groups, and patterns of negotiation and economic interdependence. But irrefutable evidence of cultural intermixture and proximity between peoples neither eliminated strong concepts of pollution nor lifted a prevailing atmosphere of fear, distrust, sectarian prejudices, and the potential for vicious expressions of hatred. To further complicate the story, such rivalries, suspicions, and ethnic exclusivity among peoples living together in medieval Iberian cities under Muslim or Christian rule may actually have contributed to a certain stability in the social order. Tension and distance between peoples became as customary as selective intercultural borrowing in matters of dress, diet, language, and comportment.

The behavior of Spanish Muslim rulers and commoners alike frequently attracted the censure of Muslim jurists and religious scholars, especially after the mid-ninth century when, in al-Andalus, these jurists and scholars generally adhered to a rigorous and conservative school of Islamic law called Maliki after its founder, Malik b. Anas (ca. 710–796). Such jurists and scholars were routinely questioned on points of doctrine and practice, and they would deliver rulings and opinions, usually citing religious authorities and precedents, not unlike their Christian counterparts (see especially Selection 9 from a later Dominican theologian and professor). The Muslim jurists' rulings reveal concern over the blurring of what were meant to be strict religious boundary lines between Muslims and Christians—a response to the twin facts that Spanish Islam had developed for centuries in an environment at a substantial geographical remove from its region of origin, and in a land in which Christianity and

Christians remained an influence. The cities of al-Andalus, in particular, afforded many opportunities for contact between Muslims and Mozárabes (Christians living under Muslim rule). The contact often was of an unspectacular day-to-day variety, but these passages suggest that concerns were developing about more substantial mingling and even official tolerance of religious laxity, including Muslim attendance and participation in Christian religious festivals and the failure of rulers to curb such "popular" behavior.

In part 1, one of these jurists—probably Abu'l-Asbagh 'Isa b. Muhammad al-Tamili, identified in the opening line—questions the legality of Muslims' observance of, and participation in, the practices of festivals held by Christian subjects. According to Islamic law, a Muslim's actions and beliefs might be placed in five categories that ranged from greatly praiseworthy to absolutely forbidden. Any innovation—a belief or practice without precedent in the Qur'an or the Sunna (the body of examples set by the Prophet Muhammad)—was worried over and ruled upon, as one sees in Abu'l-Asbagh's text. The jurist finds such innovations in al-Andalus repugnant and forbidden. His ruling identifies women as the principal offenders, who lead other Muslims into gift-giving, preparing special food, and taking holidays, thus "imitating" Christians and becoming corrupted. For Muslims, days off work were to be limited to the two main Islamic festivals: the completion of the fast of Ramadan (*id al-fitr*) and the feast of sacrifice to mark the end of a pilgrimage (*id al-adha*).

Traditions of information and misinformation about different groups of people burgeoned within the heterogeneous societies of medieval Iberia, as in other places and times (not least in Spanish America in colonial times). Polemics—in the medieval Iberian context, aggressive and controversial arguments against other religions, opinions, and customs—were among the most explicit media for these traditions. They were notable for their venom more than their ingenuity, and certain predominant motifs can be traced through many texts. These polemical traditions frequently spilled over into written works that were ostensibly descriptions of others and their practices. Thus, when some Spanish Christian authors surveyed Islam or the life and teachings of the Prophet Muhammad, they routinely saw and emphasized bellicosity, brutishness, materialism, and unbridled sexuality. Muslim baths, presented as places of barely imaginable iniquity, were the feature perhaps most commonly remarked upon by Christians who wished to accent the self-indulgence of Muslims. (The Aztecs of Mexico were similarly condemned by Spanish Christian commentators for their addiction to cleanliness and sensual pleasures.)

Part 2 of the reading—an excerpt from the work of al-Bakri (d. 1094), the son of a Muslim ruler of the southern Spanish town of Saltes—offers a short "description" of Christian Spain that allows the consideration of these matters from another side, particularly with regard to comments on customs of washing. Al-Bakri's text is thought to draw from an earlier tenth-century work, and it may reflect more than purely a Muslim commentator's point of view; a source to whom al-Bakri refers, Ibrahim b. Ya'qub al-Isra'ili al-Turtushi, was a Jew from Tortosa who is thought to have composed a travel account in the 960s for the Caliph al-Hakam II (d. 976).

The three commentators featured in part 3 are similarly concerned with describing "Christians"—this time not the northern marauders, but rather the Mozárabes living among Muslims in the centers of al-Andalus, celebrating their own festivals, paying their taxes, and often Arabized in many of their customs and more or less integrated into society. These selections derive from *hisba* manuals, sets of regulations in which jurists set out the offenses against the Holy Law of Islam. The regulations concern urban morals, including offenses against public morality and standards among traders and consumers in marketplaces monitored by an inspecting official called the *muhtasib*. Ibn 'Abdun, who composed his bans in early twelfth-century Seville, is concerned with inappropriate contact and working relationships; the predations of lustful Christian priests, who "have made what is lawful unlawful, and . . . what is unlawful lawful"; and the sale of medical and scientific books to Christians who might claim Muslim intellectual achievements for themselves. The dates of the compositions of the final two jurists are not certain, but their concerns complement each other and add to what Ibn 'Abdun established. Ibn 'Abd al-Ra'uf, carefully citing Malik and a number of his disciples, and 'Umar al-Jarsifi are here preoccupied with meat and drink and with the commercial transactions that Muslims might face with Jews and Christians. These two non-Muslim peoples (*ahl al-kitab*, those who possessed holy scriptures before Islam was revealed) are referred to by their legal status as *dhimmis* (those protected, but also kept separate, by a pact or *dhimma* within a Muslim state).

1

 Muslims Celebrate Christian Festivals in the Mid-Ninth Century

The celebration of the beginning of the Christian year.

Abu'l-Asbagh 'Isa b. Muhammad al-Tamili was asked about the eve of January, which the people call the Birth [of Jesus], for which they work so hard over the preparations, and which they consider one of the great feast days. They give each other different foods, various presents and novelties exchanged by way of gifts, and men and women abandon their work that morning because of the importance they attach to the day. They consider it to be the first day of the year. [The text of the question is:]

"Do you think (may God be generous to you!) that it is a forbidden innovation, which a Muslim cannot be permitted to follow, and that he should not agree to [accept] from any of his relatives and in-laws any of the food that they prepared for [the celebration]? Is it disapproved of, without being unambiguously forbidden? Or is it absolutely [forbidden]? There are traditions handed down from the Prophet of God (may God bless him and grant him salvation!) concerning those of his community who imitated the Christians in their [celebration] of Nauruz [Nawrūz, the first day of the Persian solar year] and Mihrajan [Mihragān, a festival around the autumn equinox, traditionally dedicated to Mithra, a chief god of the ancient Persians, surviving into the Islamic period and spreading with Muslim expansion], to the effect that they would be mustered with the Christians on the Day of Judgment. It is also reported that he said, "Whoever imitates a people, is one of them." So explain to us—may God be generous to you!—what you consider correct in this matter, if God wills."

He answered: "I have read this letter of yours and have understood what you are asking about. It is forbidden to do everything that you have mentioned in your letter, according to the ʿulama [scholars of religious learning]." I have cited the traditions that you mentioned to emphasize that, and I have also cited Yahya b. Yahya al-Laithi [d. 849, a famous Berber jurist and one of the founders of Maliki law in al-Andalus], who said, "[Receiving] presents at Christmas from a Christian or from a Muslim is not allowed, neither is accepting invitations on that day, nor is making preparations for it." It should be regarded as the same as any other day. He produced a *hadith* [a relation of the words or deeds of Muhammad and a source of authority for Islamic law] on this subject going back to the Prophet (may God bless him and grant him salvation!), who one day said to his Companions, "You will become settled among the non-Arabs; whoever imitates them in their [celebration] of Nauruz and Mihrajan will be mustered with them." Yahya also said, I asked Ibn Kinana about that, and informed him about the situation in our country, and he disapproved and denounced it. He said, Our firm opinion about that, is that it is *makruh* (repugnant). Similarly, I have heard Malik say, in the words of the Prophet, may God bless him and grant him salvation, "Whoever imitates a people, will be mustered with them."

Yahya b. Yahya said, "It is similar to racing horses and holding tournaments on al-ʿAnsara (Midsummer's Day)"; that is, not permitted, likewise what women do to decorate their houses on Midsummer's Day. That is an act of pre-Islamic ignorance, as is the way they take out their clothes at night to be soaked by the dew. Abandoning their work on that day is also disapproved of, as is preparing cabbage leaves and greens [vegetarian food]. That women should wash themselves in water on that day is absolutely forbidden, unless it is for [normal reasons such as] a ritual impurity.

Yahya b. Yahya said, "Whoever does this has shared in [spilling] the blood of Zakaria (Zacharias)" [the father of John the Baptist]. It is related that the Prophet, may God bless him and grant him salvation, said, "Whoever multiplies the number of a people is one of them." Whoever is content with an act is a partner of the person who did it. If this is so for someone who approved but did not perform an act, what about the person who did it and made it his custom?! We ask God for success.

2
↜ *A Description of Christian Spain from the Tenth Century*

Early authorities divided Jilliqiyya [León and Castile, Christian kingdoms in the north of the Iberian Peninsula] into four parts; the first part is that which lies to the west and faces to the north. Its inhabitants are the Galicians [Leonese] and their territory is Galicia [León]. They [are found] around the city of Braqara (Braga), which is in the middle west.

The city of Braga is one of the first cities founded by the Christians and [one of] their capitals. The localities in this country are like Mérida in the skillful way in which they are built and in the construction of their walls. Nowadays it is ruined and almost empty; the Muslims destroyed it and drove away its inhabitants.

The second division is the one called "the district of Ashturish" (Asturias), so-called because of the river there called Ashtur, which waters all their country.

The third division is the south and west of León, whose inhabitants are called the Burtuqalish (Portuguese).

The fourth division is to the south and east and is called Qashtilat al-quswa and Qashtilat al-dunya (Outer and Inner Castile). Its nearest castles [to Muslim territory] are Gharnun (Grañón), al-Qusair (Alcocero), Burghush (Burgos), and Amaya.

Ibrahim (al-Turtushi) said: "The whole of Jilliqiyya is flat and most of the land is covered in sand. Their foodstuffs are mainly millet and sorghum and their normal drinks are apple cider and bushka, which is a drink made with flour (meal). The inhabitants are a treacherous people of depraved morals, who do not keep themselves clean and only wash once or twice a year in cold water. They do not wash their clothes once they have put them on until they fall to pieces on them, and assert that the filth that covers them, thanks to their sweat, is good for their bodies and keeps them healthy. Their clothes are very tight-fitting and have wide openings, through which most of their bodies show. They have great courage and do not contemplate flight when battle is joined, but rather consider death a lesser evil."

3
↜ *Rules for the Christians from the Early Twelfth Century*

a. Ibn 'Abdun

A Muslim should not rub down a Jew, nor a Christian [in the baths], neither should he throw out their refuse nor cleanse their lavatories; the Jews and Christians are more suitable for such a job, which is a task for the meanest. A Muslim should not work with the animals of a Jew, nor of a Christian, neither should he ride in their company, nor grasp their stirrup. If [the *muhtasib*, the official charged with maintaining public morals and standards and punishing offenses against the Holy Law of Islam, the Shari'a] gets to know of this, the perpetrator will be censured.

Muslim women must be prevented from entering disgusting churches, for the priests are fornicators, adulterers, and pederasts. Frankish women [probably meaning any western European Christian women who were not Mozárabes] [too] should be forbidden to enter churches except on days of particular merit or festivals, for they eat and drink and fornicate with the priests: there is not one of them who does not keep two or more of these women, spending the night with them. This has become a regular custom with them, for they have made what is lawful unlawful, and made what is unlawful lawful. The priests must be made to marry, as they do in the east; if they wanted to, they would.

No woman, old or otherwise, should be left in the house of a priest if he has refused to marry. They [the priests] should be forced into circumcision, as al-Mu'tamid 'Abbad made them do. According to their assertions, they follow the path of Jesus (God bless him and grant him salvation!), and Jesus was circumcised; with them, the day of his circumcision [January 1] is a festival which they hold in great regard, [but] they themselves abandon [this practice]!

One must not sell a scientific book to the Jews, nor to the Christians, unless it deals with their own law; for they translate books of science, and attribute them to their own people and to their own bishops, when they are [really] the works of the Muslims. It would be best if no Jewish or Christian doctor were left to treat the Muslims; for they have no concern for the welfare of a Muslim, but only for the medical treatment of their co-religionists. How could one trust [one's] lifeblood with someone who has no concern for what is best for a Muslim?

b. Ibn 'Abd al-Ra'uf

Muslims are forbidden to buy meat intentionally from the butcheries of the dhimmis [Christians and Jews]. Malik abhorred this, and [the caliph] 'Umar [b. al-Khattab]—may God be pleased with him—ordered them to be expelled from the Muslims' markets. Ibn Habib [d. ca. 853, jurist, disciple of Malik, and *mufti*, or jurisprudent competent to proclaim a religious opinion (*fatwa*) of Córdoba] said, "There is no objection to them having a butchery isolated from the others, and being forbidden to sell to Muslims. Any Muslim who buys from them will not have his purchase invalidated, but he will be a bad man." In the *Wadiha* [Ibn Habib's work] [he says]: Mutarrif [d. 835, pupil and nephew of Malik] and Ibn al-Majishun [d. 818, another pupil of Malik and mufti of Medina] said that if the meat the Muslim buys from them is the sort they do not eat themselves, such as *tarif* (non-kosher) and suchlike, the purchase is invalidated, and the same for fat. God Almighty said, "We have made unlawful for them [the Jews] the fat of cattle and sheep" (Qur'an 6: 147); such are the undiluted and pure fats such as the intestines, the fat of the kidneys and that which attaches to the stomach and suchlike. God says, "except what their backs carry, or the entrails, or what is mixed with the bone" (Qur'an, loc. cit.). All fat that is in this category becomes an exception. It is specifically not lawful for us either to eat or to trade in any of these fats that are forbidden to them from the animals they have slaughtered. Whatever is not forbidden to them of their slaughtered animals by Revelation, but is only forbidden by their religious law, such as tarif and suchlike, consumption of this, trading in it are frowned on [but not illegal], because it is not their lawful meat. This is the opinion of Malik and some of his disciples.

In the *Wadiha* [it says]: Any meat the Christians slaughter for their churches, or in the name of the Messiah or the Cross or suchlike, corresponds with the word of Almighty God, "what has been consecrated for someone other than God" (Qur'an

2: 168), and is frowned on for us, but not forbidden, because God Almighty has made lawful for us what they [the Christians] slaughter, for he is better informed about what they are saying and intending by this, and [also] about what they slaughter for their festivals and for their misguided purposes. Having nothing to do with it is preferable, because to eat it is to show great regard for their polytheistic ways. Malik and his disciples never ceased to show their abhorrence for that. Malik (may God have mercy on him!) was asked about the food that is prepared for their funerals and which [the Christians] give as alms; he replied, "It is not appropriate for a Muslim to take it or eat it, because they prepared it to glorify their polytheism." Ibn al-Qasim said, about a Christian who willed that some of his property should be sold on behalf of a church, that it was not lawful for a Muslim to buy it, and that any Muslim who bought it would be a bad Muslim.

If a Muslim buys wine from a Christian, whatever wine is found in his possession will be destroyed. If the Christian has already received the price, this will be left to him, but if he has not received it, it will not be settled in his favor. If the wine is no longer in the Muslim's hands, and he has not paid for it, the price will be taken from him and given as alms, and both of them will be punished. If a Muslim destroys wine belonging to a dhimmi, he will be punished. Malik has conflicting opinions on the question of the payment of damages for its value: in one place he says, no fine is imposed on him, and none is lawful, because God had made his price unlawful; elsewhere, he says the price is incumbent on him. He [Malik] abhorred traveling with them [dhimmis] in ships, because of the fear of divine wrath descending on them.

c. 'Umar al-Jarsifi

The dhimmis must be prevented from having houses that overlook Muslims, and from spying on them, and from exhibiting wine and pork in the Muslims' markets, from riding horses with saddles and wearing the costumes of Muslims or anything ostentatious. They must be made to display a sign that will distinguish them from Muslims, such as the *shakla* (piece of yellow cloth) in the case of men and a bell in the case of women. Muslims must be forbidden from undertaking everything that entails baseness and humiliation for the Muslims, such as removing garbage, transporting equipment connected with wine, looking after pigs and suchlike, because this involves the elevation of unbelief above Islam; whoever does such things will be punished.

6

A Pope Rewards "So Salutary and Laudable A Work"

(1455)

The other day, which was the eighth of August, very early in the morning and because of calm winds, the sailors prepared their skiffs to remove the captives [from the ships] and bring them [ashore], as they were ordered to do. Assembled together in that field, those captives were an extraordinary sight to behold: among them there were some reasonably white-skinned, handsome, and of good appearance; others less white who seemed more brown; others as black as Ethiopians, so poorly formed of face as well as body that it almost seemed to those who stared at them that they were seeing apparitions from the nether world.

But what heart, as hardened as it might be, would not be rent by a feeling of pity at seeing that company? Some bowed their heads, their faces streaked with tears as they looked at each other; some moaned very piteously, looking steadily towards the heavens and crying out as if they were asking for help from the Father of the Universe; others struck their faces with their hands, throwing themselves full length on the ground; others chanted their lamentations according to the custom of their land, revealing (though we could not understand the words of their language) the degree of their grief.

But to increase their anguish still more, those in charge of dividing them up began to separate them one from another into equal lots. This made it necessary to separate children from parents, wives from husbands, and brothers from each other. No allowance was made for friends or relatives, each one ending up where chance took him. . . .

Who could carry out such a partition without great effort? As soon as the groups were formed the children who saw their parents in another quickly got up and went towards them; mothers clutched their other children in their arms and lying face downward on the ground covered their children with their bodies, receiving blows with little concern for their own flesh rather than have their children taken from them.

The place was a field outside the city gate of Lagos, a port on the southern coast of Portugal in 1444, and these people were the first Africans to be bundled in such numbers onto the fast-sailing Portuguese caravels that carried them from villages on the African coast south of Cape Bojador for sale in lots at public auction in a European town. Of various skin colors and ethnic backgrounds, some were probably already the slaves of Berbers; others were taken in raids or perhaps gotten by trade. As the concessionary who had farmed out this slaving voyage to local merchants and nobles, Prince Henry, astride a powerful horse and surrounded by his retainers and a crowd of curious onlookers, was on hand to survey the sale and savor the success of his enterprise. In a gesture of his grace, he quickly gave away his royal fifth, some forty-six human beings, and instead took "great pleasure in the salvation of those souls which before were lost." The seasoned chronicler who recorded the scene wept at witnessing it, not from a moral repugnance of slavery (something long familiar and accepted by Europeans) but from the Africans' terrible distress, although he easily consoled himself with the thought that they would now become Christians.

This early scene in what was to become a massive trade in men, women, and children was repeated over five centuries. Slaving ships first ranged southward along the northern Guinea coast of west Africa to the Gold Coast and the Bight of Benin, then to Angola and the Congo, and eventually to Mozambique on Africa's east coast. And the trade extended from Europe and the Atlantic islands off the western coast of Africa to the Caribbean, and finally to the Americas. Scholars differ over numbers, which in any case are extravagant: some 10 million persons. We must ask how such a trade came to be.

By 1455, Portugal (not without European competitors, notably Castile) had explored, raided, and traded along Africa's western coast for forty years. These voyages of discovery, as they were for Europeans learning for the first time about the coast in a systematic and reported-on way, were authorized (but not captained) by Prince Henry the Navigator. As a younger son of King João I, founder of the House of Aviz, Henry watched as the crown passed from father to brother and then to his nephew, Afonso V. Never to be king himself, Henry made his reputation through the sea. In 1415 he catapulted the small and relatively poor kingdom of Portugal into an imperial power by capturing the North African port of Ceuta with its access to one stream of the trans-Saharan trade that funneled gold, ivory, slaves, and parrots into Europe in exchange for horses and other European goods headed for Muslim lands to the south. Whether Henry intended this maritime venture primarily as a religious crusade against the infidel or as a daring attempt to divert a lucrative trade remains unclear but, with victory at Ceuta, he understood that he had gained not only a toehold in North Africa against the Moroccans, but also a point from which to repel Spanish expeditions to the west African coast; he now saw reason and profit in the risk of sending Portuguese ships south along the western coast.

No grand design guided Portugal's African voyages; rather, exploration proceeded uncertainly in short advances. After many attempts, in 1434 Prince Henry's ships finally rounded treacherous Cape Bojador, then thought to be the southern limit of the Atlantic and the African coast, dispelling popular belief that beyond it lay only the Green Sea of Darkness and the impossibility of returning northward against prevailing winds. By the time of Henry's death in 1460, Portuguese seamen, sometimes with mixed crews of Spaniards or Italians, had sailed south beyond the Senegal and Gambia rivers and along the northern Guinea coast as far as Sierra Leone. And at the century's end, Vasco da Gama sailed around the true southern tip of Africa to open to Europeans the long-sought eastern sea route to India and the coveted spice trade.

To encourage and pay for these costly expeditions, Henry not only instructed his own ships to trade directly, but most often he also licensed private traders who paid the Crown for sailing rights as well as a heavy schedule of taxes on the goods they acquired. With their newly gained knowledge of the coast, merchants sought access to the inland mines and the sources of gold. If not gold, then the Portuguese raided for slaves, initially along the Saharan coast and then in coastal villages in the region north and south of the Senegal River, often against unarmed kin groups until villagers became wary and defended themselves. African warriors frustrated their aspirations and held them firmly to the coast. In this way Portuguese traders were forced to barter with local chiefs for captives taken in war by Africans of one region against their enemies in another—men and women reduced to the condition of slave on local terms—in what became a commerce conducted between cooperating Europeans and Africans.

Intimidating African responses effectively confined Portuguese traders to their ships until gradually, through negotiation and payment, they began to set up a chain of trading stations along the African coast. These were neither settlements nor administrative centers but factories for conducting foreign trade. The first, established about 1445, with serious slaving already under way, was a castle built on the island of Arguim, a natural fortress. From there the Portuguese traded horses, cloth, brass-ware, and wheat for gold dust, ivory, and slaves. In this way they successfully diverted the camel caravans that had carried such goods across the Sahara to the ports of North Africa. In 1482 a second castle-fortress built at São Jorge da Mina, or El Mina, on the Gold Coast surpassed trade at Arguim by cutting into the gold trade of the western Sudan as well as benefiting from nearby placer mines. These two posts, together with other unfortified ones, were the beginnings of Portugal's seaborne empire, one initially finessed by African determinations to retain control of trade by keeping the Europeans at sea. As new markets opened—in the neighboring kingdoms of Castile and Aragon, in the Madeira and Cape Verde islands where the Portuguese first experimented with sugar plantations, and, from the midsixteenth century, in its American colony of Brazil—the trade in slaves exploded, eclipsing gold and creating unimagined wealth for Portugal.

About these matters which we are inclined to see as being merely about profit, the voice of the Christian church resounded. As Christ's vicar on Earth and head of the Roman Catholic Church, the pope spoke officially through edicts, or bulls, sealed with the round leaden seal, or *bulla*, of his office. Prince Henry not only received royal charters from Portuguese kings; his career was further enhanced by a series of papal bulls that endorsed, often after the fact, his military and maritime pursuits. The distinction that we today want to keep between Church and state, the religious and the secular, would have appeared incomprehensible to fifteenth-century Christians. The crusades of the eleventh, twelfth, and thirteenth centuries were military expeditions against the Muslim infidels intended to return them to Christian dominance. Such expeditions were transformed into holy wars by papal sanction. Any war against the infidels was a just war in the Church's eyes, and captives taken in such wars could legitimately be enslaved. But Portuguese raids captured pagans untainted by Muslim practices and in situations undefined by formal acts of war, and they sometimes became the currency with which to purchase other goods, especially gold.

How did the pope respond? The following bull, the *Romanus Pontifex*, issued by Nicholas V in 1455, supplies one part of the answer. With this bull the pope dismissed Castile's persistent claims to the lands called Guinea. As a kind of charter of Portuguese imperialism, it granted privileges, tempered with restrictions and sanctions. It is worth noting that this bull was followed closely in time with another that extended Portugal's power still further: in 1456 the king and Prince Henry were granted ecclesiastical jurisdiction to fill both regular and secular Church offices in these newly conquered lands and to "pronounce ecclesiastical sentences, censures, and penalties of excommunication . . . [and] interdict . . . whenever the necessity may arise."

In attempting to understand how the trade out of Africa came to forcibly transport millions of once-free people across the Atlantic, there is an even bigger question opened by the papal bull of 1455: according to Europeans, what particular qualifications did these people possess that made them eligible for enslavement? By what argument and by what processes were these Africans transformed into the enslaveable "other"?

∾ Papal Bull, Romanus Pontifex *(Nicholas V), January 8, 1455*

The Roman pontiff, successor of the key-bearer of the heavenly kingdom and vicar of Jesus Christ, contemplating with a father's mind all the several climes of the world and the characteristics of all the nations dwelling in them and seeking and desiring the salvation of all, wholesomely ordains and disposes upon careful deliberation those things which he sees will be agreeable to the Divine Majesty and by which he may bring the sheep entrusted to him by God into the single divine fold, and may acquire for them the reward of eternal felicity, and obtain pardon for their souls. This we believe will more certainly come to pass, through the aid of the Lord, if we bestow suitable favors and special graces on those Catholic kings and princes, who, like athletes and intrepid champions of the Christian faith, as we know by the evidence of facts, not only restrain the savage excesses of the Saracens [or Muslims] and of other infidels, enemies of the Christian name, but also, for the defense and increase of the faith, vanquish them and their kingdoms and habitations, though situated in the remotest parts unknown to us, and subject them to their temporal dominion, sparing no labor and expense, in order that those kings and princes, relieved of all obstacles, may be the more animated to the prosecution of so salutary and laudable a work.

We have lately heard, not without great joy and gratification, how our beloved son, the noble personage Henry, infante of Portugal, uncle of our most dear son in Christ, the illustrious Afonso, king of the kingdoms of Portugal and Algarve, treading in the footsteps of João, of famous memory, king of the said kingdoms, his father, and greatly inflamed with zeal for the salvation of souls and with fervor of faith, as a Catholic and true soldier of Christ, the Creator of all things, and a most active and courageous defender and intrepid champion of the faith in Him, has aspired from his early youth with his utmost might to cause the most glorious name of the said Creator to be published, extolled, and revered throughout the whole world, even in the most remote and undiscovered places, and also to bring into the bosom of his faith the perfidious enemies of Him and of the life-giving Cross by which we have been redeemed, namely, the Saracens and all other infidels whatsoever, [and how] after the city of Ceuta, situated in Africa, had been subdued by the said King João to his dominion, and after many wars had been waged, sometimes in person, by the said infante, although in the name of the said King João, against the enemies and infidels aforesaid, not without the greatest labors and expense, and with dangers and loss of life and property, and the slaughter of very many of their natural subjects, the said infante being neither enfeebled nor terrified by so many and great labors, this his so laudable and pious purpose, has peopled with orthodox Christians certain solitary islands in the ocean sea, and has caused churches and other pious places to be there founded and built, in which divine service is celebrated. Also by the laudable endeavor and industry of the said infante, very many inhabitants or dwellers in diverse islands situated in the said sea, coming to the knowledge of the true God, have received holy baptism, to the praise and glory of God, the salvation of the souls of many, the propagation also of the orthodox faith, and the increase of divine worship.

Moreover, since, some time ago, it had come to the knowledge of the said infante that never, or at least not within the memory of men, had it been customary to sail on this ocean sea toward the southern and eastern shores, and that it was so unknown to us westerners that we had no certain knowledge of the peoples of those parts, believing that he would best perform his duty to God in this matter if by his effort and industry that sea might become navigable as far as to the Indians [of India] who are said to worship the name of Christ, and that thus he might be able to enter into relation with them, and to incite them to aid the Christians against the Saracens and other such enemies of the faith, and might also be able forthwith to subdue certain gentile or pagan peoples, living between, who are entirely free from infection by the sect of the most impious Mahomet, and to preach and cause to be preached to them the unknown but most sacred name of Christ, strengthened, however, always by the royal authority, he has not ceased for twenty-five years past to send almost yearly an army of the peoples of the said kingdoms, with the greatest labor, danger, and expense, in very swift ships called caravels, to explore the sea and coastlands toward the south and the Antarctic pole. And so it came to pass that when a number of ships of this kind had explored and taken possession of very many harbors, islands, and seas, they at length came to the province of Guinea, and having taken possession of some islands and harbors and sea adjacent to that province, sailing farther they came to the mouth of a certain great river commonly supposed to be the Nile [Europeans first thought the Senegal River to be a branch of the Nile]. The war was waged for some years against the peoples of those parts in the name of the said King Afonso and of the infante, and in it very many islands in that neighborhood were subdued and peacefully possessed, as they are still possessed together with the adjacent sea. Thence also many Guineamen and other negroes, taken by force, and some by barter of the unprohibited articles, or by the other lawful contract of purchase, have been sent to the said kingdoms. A large number of these have been converted to the Catholic faith, and it is hoped, by the help of divine mercy, that if such progress be continued with them, either those peoples will be converted to the faith or at least the souls of many of them will be gained for Christ.

But, as we are informed, the aforesaid king and infante, with so many and so great dangers, labors, and expenses, and also with loss of so many natives of their said kingdoms, very many of whom have perished in those expeditions, depending only upon the aid of those natives, have caused those provinces to be explored and have acquired and possessed such harbors, islands, and seas, as aforesaid, as the true lords of them. [We now fear] lest strangers induced by covetousness should sail to those parts, and desiring to usurp to themselves the perfection, fruit, and praise of this work, or at least to hinder it, should therefore, either for the sake of gain or through malice, carry or transmit iron, arms, wood used for construction, and other things and goods prohibited to be carried to infidels, or should teach those infidels the art of navigation, whereby they would become more powerful and obstinate enemies to the king and infante, and the prosecution of this enterprise would either be hindered, or would perhaps entirely fail, not without great offense to God and great reproach to all Christianity. To prevent this and to conserve their right and possession, [the said king and infante] under certain most severe penalties then expressed, have prohibited and in general have ordained that none, unless with *their* sailors and ships and on payment of a certain tribute and with an express license previously obtained from the said king or infante, should presume to sail to the said provinces or to trade in their ports or to fish in the sea. . . . In time it might happen that persons of other kingdoms or nations, led by envy, malice, or covetousness, might presume, contrary to the prohibition aforesaid, without license and payment of such tribute, to go to the said provinces, and in the provinces, harbors, islands, and sea, so acquired, to sail, trade, and fish. Thereupon between King Afonso and the infante, who would by no means suffer themselves to be so trifled with in these things, and the presumptuous persons aforesaid, very many hatreds, rancors, dissensions, wars, and scandals, to the highest offense of God and danger of souls, probably might and would ensue. . . .

We [therefore] have weighed each and every premise with due meditation, and note that we had formerly by other letters of ours granted among other things free and ample faculty to the aforesaid King Afonso to invade, search out, capture, vanquish, and subdue all Saracens and pagans whatsoever, and other enemies of Christ wheresoever placed, and the kingdoms, dukedoms, principalities, dominions, possessions, and all movable and immovable goods whatsoever held and possessed by them and to reduce their persons to perpetual slavery, and to apply and appropriate to himself and his successors the kingdoms, dukedoms, counties, principalities, dominions, possessions, and goods, and to convert them to his and their use and profit.

By having secured the said faculty, the said King Afonso, or, by his authority, the aforesaid infante, justly and lawfully has acquired and possessed, and doth possess, these islands, lands, harbors, and seas, and they do of right belong and pertain to the said King Afonso and his successors, nor without special license from King Afonso and his successors themselves has any other even of the faithful of Christ been entitled hitherto, nor is he by any means now entitled lawfully to meddle therewith. In order that King Afonso himself and his successors and the infante may be able the more zealously to pursue this most pious and noble work, and be most worthy of perpetual remembrance (which, since the salvation of souls, increase of the faith, and overthrow of its enemies may be procured thereby, we regard as a work wherein the glory of God, and faith in Him, and His commonwealth, the Universal Church, are concerned) in proportion they, having been relieved of all the greater obstacles, shall find themselves supported by us and by the Apostolic See with favors and graces.

We being very fully informed of each and every premise, do, *motu proprio*, not at the instance of King Afonso or the infante, or on the petition of any other offered to us on their behalf in respect to this matter, and after mature deliberation, by apostolic authority, and from certain knowledge, in the fullness of apostolic power, by the tenor of these donations decree and declare that the aforesaid letters of faculty (the tenor whereof we wish to be considered as inserted word for word in these donations, with each and every clause therein contained) are extended to Ceuta and to the aforesaid and all other acquisitions whatsoever, even those acquired before the date of the said letters of faculty, and to all those provinces, islands, harbors, and seas whatsoever, which thereafter, in the name of the said King Afonso and of his successors and of the infante, in those parts and the adjoining, and in the more distant and remote parts, can be acquired from the hands of infidels or pagans, and that they are comprehended under the said letters of faculty. And by force of those and of the present letters of faculty the acquisitions already made, and that hereafter shall happen to be acquired, after they shall have been acquired, we do by the tenor of these donations decree and declare have pertained, and forever of right do belong and pertain, to the aforesaid king and to his successors and to the infante, and that the right of conquest which in the course of these letters we declare to be extended from the capes of Bojador and of Não [whether Cape Não is another spelling for Cape Nun, located north of Cape Bojador, or refers to some other cape south of Bojador is unclear], as far as through all Guinea, and beyond toward that southern shore, has belonged and pertained, and forever of right belongs and pertains, to the said King Afonso, his successors, and the infante, and not to any others.

We also by the tenor of these donations decree and declare that King Afonso and his successors and the aforesaid infante might and may, now and henceforth, freely and lawfully, in these [acquisitions] and concerning them issue any prohibitions, statutes, and decrees whatsoever, even penal ones, and impose any tribute, and dispose and ordain concerning them as concerning their own property and their other dominions. . . .

Moreover, since this is fitting in many ways for the perfecting of a work of this kind, we allow that the aforesaid King Afonso and [his] successors and the infante, as also the persons to whom they, or any one of them, shall think that this work ought to be committed, may . . . make purchases and sales of any things and goods and victuals whatsoever, as it shall seem fit, with any Saracens and infidels, in the said regions. [They] also may enter into any contracts, transact business, bargain, buy and negotiate, and carry any commodities whatsoever to the places of those Saracens and infidels, provided they not be iron instruments, wood to be used for construction, cordage, ships, or any kinds of armor, and may sell them to the said Saracens and infidels. [They] also may do, perform, or prosecute each and every thing [mentioned] in the premises, and things suitable or necessary in relation to these.

The same King Afonso, his successors, and the infante, in the provinces, islands, and places already acquired, and to be acquired by him, may found and [cause to be] founded and built any churches, monasteries, or other pious places whatsoever, as volunteers, both seculars, and regulars of any of the mendicant orders (with license, however, from their superiors). And those persons may abide there as long as they shall live, and hear confessions of all who live in the said parts or who come thither, and after the confessions have been heard they may give due absolution in all cases, except those reserved to the aforesaid see, and enjoin salutary penance, and also administer the ecclesiastical sacraments freely and lawfully, and this we allow and grant to Afonso himself, and his successors, the kings of Portugal, who shall come afterwards, and to the aforesaid infante.

Moreover, we entreat in the Lord, and by the sprinkling of the blood of Our Lord Jesus Christ, whom, as has been said, it concerneth, we exhort, and as they hope for the remission of their sins enjoin, and also by this perpetual edict of prohibition we more strictly inhibit, each and every one of the faithful of Christ, ecclesiastics, seculars, and regulars of whatsoever orders, in whatsoever part of the world they live, and of whatsoever state, degree, order, condition, or pre-eminence they shall be, although endued with archepiscopal, episcopal, imperial, royal, queenly, ducal, or any other greater ecclesiastical or worldly dignity, that they do not by any means presume to carry arms, iron, wood for construction, and other things prohibited by law from being in any way carried to the Saracens, to any of the provinces, islands, harbors, seas, and places whatsoever, acquired or possessed in the name of King Afonso, or situated in this conquest or elsewhere, to the Saracens, infidels, or pagans. Even without special license from the said King Afonso and his successors and the infante, [they may not] carry or cause to be carried merchandise and other things permitted by law, or to navigate or cause to be navigated those seas, or to fish in them, or to meddle with the provinces, islands, harbors, seas, and places, or any of them, or with this conquest, or to do anything by themselves or another or others, directly or indirectly, by deed or counsel, or to offer any obstruction whereby the aforesaid King Afonso and his successors and the infante may be hindered from quietly enjoying their acquisitions and possessions, and prosecuting and carrying out this conquest.

And we decree that whosoever shall infringe these orders [shall incur the following penalties], besides the punishments pronounced by law against those who carry arms and other prohibited things to any of the Saracens, which we wish them to incur by so doing: If they be single persons, they shall incur the sentence of excommunication; if a community or corporation of a city, castle, village, or place, that city, castle, village, or place shall be thereby subject to the interdict. And we decree further that transgressors, collectively or individually, shall not be absolved from the sentence of excommunication, nor be able to obtain the relaxation of this interdict, by apostolic or any other authority, unless they shall first have made due satisfaction for their transgressions to Afonso himself and his successors and to the infante, or shall have amicably agreed with them thereupon. By [these] apostolic writings we enjoin our venerable brothers, the archbishop of Lisbon, and the bishops of Silves and Ceuta, that they, or two or one of them, by himself, or another or others, as often as they or any of them shall be required on the part of the aforesaid King Afonso and his successors and the infante or any one of them, on Sundays, and other festival days, in the churches, while a large multitude of people shall assemble there for divine worship, to declare and denounce by apostolic authority that those persons who have been proved to have incurred such sentences of excommunication and interdict, are excommunicated and interdicted, and have been and are involved in the other punishments aforesaid. And we decree that they shall also cause them to be denounced by others, and to be strictly avoided by all, till they shall have made satisfaction for or compromised their transgressions as aforesaid. Offenders are to be held in check by ecclesiastical censure, without regard to appeal, the apostolic constitutions and ordinances and all other things whatsoever to the contrary notwithstanding.

But in order that the present letters, which have been issued by us of our certain knowledge and after mature deliberation thereupon, as is aforesaid, may not hereafter be impugned by anyone as fraudulent, secret, or void, we will, and by the authority, knowledge, and power aforementioned, we do likewise by these letters, decree and declare that the said letters and what is contained therein cannot in any wise be impugned, or the effect thereof hindered or obstructed, on account of any defect of fraudulency, secrecy, or nullity, not even from a defect, but that they shall be valid forever and shall obtain full authority. And if anyone, by whatever authority, shall, wittingly or unwittingly, attempt anything inconsistent with these orders, we decree that his act shall be null and void. Moreover, because it would be difficult to carry our present letters to all places whatsoever, we will, and by the said authority we decree by these letters, that faith shall be given as fully and permanently to copies of them, certified under the hand of a notary public and the seal of the episcopal or any superior ecclesiastical court, as if the said original letters were exhibited or shown; and we decree that within two months from the day when these present letters, or the paper or parchment containing the tenor of the same, shall be affixed to the doors of the church at Lisbon, the sentences of excommunication and the other sentences contained therein shall bind each and every offender as fully as if these present letters had been made known and presented to them in person and lawfully. Therefore let no one infringe or with rash boldness contravene this our declaration, constitution, gift, grant, appropriation, decree, supplication, exhortation, injunction, inhibition, mandate, and will. But if anyone should presume to do so, be it known to him that he will incur the wrath of Almighty God and of the blessed apostles Peter and Paul.

Given at Rome, at Saint Peter's, on the eighth day of January, in the year of the incarnation of our Lord one thousand four hundred and fifty-four, and in the eighth year of our pontificate.

P de Noxeto [Pope Nicholas V]

7

"There Can Easily Be Stamped Upon Them Whatever Belief We Wish to Give Them"
The First Letter from Brazil
(1500)

When in late April 1500 a Portuguese captain and his fleet made landfall on the coast of what is now called Brazil, they did so by chance—a chance beginning to a colony that eventually would produce fabulous wealth for Portugal. The fleet had sailed from Lisbon for India six weeks earlier amid great festivities: "colored flags" decorated the ships, and musicians playing "bagpipes, fifes, drums, and horns" delighted the crowd. All Lisbon came to wish them a good journey. The bishop offered a pontifical Mass; King Manuel I issued final instructions to his commander, Pedro Alvares Cabral, and presented him with a banner bearing the royal arms. The next day, as the unfurled sails were set, the red cross of the Order of Christ blazoned across white canvas declared to all the unity of Crown, Church, and military, a reminder of the king's right as governor of the order to exercise ecclesiastical jurisdiction in newly contacted and as-yet undiscovered territories.

Commoners as well as noblemen, hopeful that some of the new wealth would trickle their way, had reason to celebrate the departure of this fleet headed for the rich and long-coveted spice trade of the East. The ships'

captains intended to repeat Vasco da Gama's voyage of two years earlier around the Cape of Good Hope to Calicut on the west coast of India where, da Gama assured them, they would find Christians willing to ally and trade with them as fellow believers against Muslims. Furious preparations had been under way, since da Gama's return the previous year, to assemble a fleet for what would be the longest voyage yet undertaken.

The result was impressive: thirteen ships, including "round" ships with their "wide bulging sails" and the faster, lighter lateen-rigged caravels; a crew of 1,200 men; provisions meant to last eighteen months; and a cargo of cheap trade goods as well as copper, fine woolens, satins, and velvets, and gold currency. Seven Franciscan friars, eight priests, and a vicar, some of whom expected to remain in India, accompanied the crew, together with the factors and their assistants who had charge of the cargo and of establishing a permanent factory at Calicut, at least thirteen scribes, and interpreters. This voyage was financed differently from the commercial expeditions leased to merchants typical of the fifteenth century. The crew were paid rather than having to wait on the king's pleasure for a reward for their service once back in Portugal. And except for two ships—one owned by Italian merchants and another by a Portuguese noble—the Crown financed and outfitted them all, assumed the risk, and expected to collect the profits. The captains were well chosen. Experienced navigators and pilots figured prominently among them, notably Bartolomeu Dias, the first European to sail around the tip of Africa in 1488, and Pero Escolar, João de Sá, and Nicolau Coelho, who had sailed with Vasco da Gama—all men of reputation, authority, or promise.

Relying on da Gama's experience and critical navigational observations, Cabral's ships were to sail the same route south from Lisbon to the Canary Islands, then skirt the Cape Verde Islands and roughly parallel the African coast until looping south and west in order to avoid the deadly "Guinea calms," or doldrums, before again heading southeast toward the cape. Instead, winds and currents carried them farther west than planned: the landmass they sighted in late April was both unexpected and unknown. They travelled a short stretch of the coast, dropping anchor at the place they called Porto Seguro, or safe harbor, where they stayed for nine days. They then sailed east again to Africa and on to a disastrous, though commercially lucrative, encounter at Calicut, not with Christians but with an unaccommodating Hindu sovereign and hostile Arab traders who, in the Portuguese account, provoked an uprising of local people who stormed their factory, killing some fifty Portuguese. Cabral's men retaliated by seizing Arab ships, killing most of the crews, and stealing their cargos before bombarding the city. And if, on their return to Lisbon, the cargoes yielded profit and encouragement to others in Europe, the longed-for trade would now be possible only under arms. In India no friars remained to christianize, and no factory to conduct trade. Only seven of the original thirteen ships made it back to Lisbon; six were lost at sea. The dazzling success imagined by well-wishers in March 1500 had instead become a diminished and sobering one.

The fleet's brief stop on the Brazilian coast reads differently. Before leaving Porto Seguro, Cabral dispatched a supply ship to return to Lisbon with news of the landmass, which they named the Land of the True Cross. No one knows how many letters this ship carried back to the king, but only two are known to have survived: a more technical one, and this one written by the fleet's chief scribe, Pedro Vaz de Caminha. Born in northern Portugal into a family of officials who for generations had served a succession of kings, Caminha, who was adequately educated, inherited the position from his father. Having signed on as scribe for the outward voyage, Caminha expected to remain and serve in Calicut in the administration of the factory and the anticipated India trade, clearly a position of responsibility and royal favor. Instead he died in the uprising at Calicut in December 1500, his Brazil letter by then safely in the king's hands.

Written over the course of the nine days they anchored in Porto Seguro—it is too long to have been written on any single day, and certainly not on the day it is dated when busy preparations for the next morning's departure would have occupied them all—Caminha's letter speaks with the seductively compelling authority of someone who has seen for himself. He witnessed and recorded the first contact between Europeans and Tupinikin, the Tupi-speaking natives of the northeastern Brazilian coast, when early moments of mutual surprise, alert curiosity, caution, and even small increments of trust were possible before defensive positions formed or hardened (or needed to) and improvisation was essential. It is the only firsthand account that survives, our only source from which to retrieve both Portuguese and native understandings of this unexpected encounter. For the Tupinikin, who had never before come face-to-face with people so unlike themselves, it was an unimaginable one.

What can we make of it? As each people circles the other, trying to take the other's measure, what cultural yardsticks are used? What did the exchange of gifts imply? Do we have to settle for a standard Portuguese response or a standard Tupinikin response, or does Caminha offer evidence, however imperfect, for variations within each group? Native bodies, sleek, hairless, naked, sometimes dramatically painted, fascinated Caminha; he returns to them again and again and especially to what he takes to be the Tupinikin's lack of shame. But what clues offer us a glimpse of how European bodies, bearded, booted, and covered in cumbersome clothes, appeared to native eyes? What was the difference between dress and adornment? What shifts in action, demeanor, or strategy by either group are discernible over the nine days and nights? What tensions surfaced? How was power displayed or restrained? And how do we account for what perhaps initially most surprises us: the absence of violence?

In the end, Caminha judged these natives suitable for conversion: "there can easily be stamped upon them whatever belief we wish to give them." What persuaded him? And what does this suggest about Portuguese or Tupinikin sensibilities?

↝ Letter of Pedro Vaz de Caminha to King Manuel, Porto Seguro de Vera Cruz, May 1, 1500

Senhor:

Although the chief captain of this your fleet, and also the other captains, are writing to Your Highness the news of the finding of this your new land which was now found in this navigation, I shall not refrain from also giving my account of this to Your Highness, as best I can, although I know less than all of the others how to relate and tell it well. Nevertheless, may Your Highness take my ignorance for good intention, and believe that I shall not set down here anything more than I saw and thought, either to beautify or to make it less attractive. I shall not give an account here to Your Highness of the ship's company and its daily runs, because I shall not know how to do it, and the pilots must have this in their charge.

And therefore, Senhor, I begin what I have to relate and say that the departure from Belem, as Your Highness knows, was on Monday, the 9th of March, and on Saturday, the 14th of the said month, between eight and nine o'clock, we found ourselves among the Canary Islands, nearest to Grand Canary; and there we remained all that day in a calm, in sight of them, at a distance of about three or four leagues. On Sunday, the 22d of the said month, at ten o'clock, a little more or less, we came in sight of the Cape Verde Islands, that is to say, of the island of Sam Nicolao, according to the assertion of Pero Escolar, the pilot. On the following night, on Monday at daybreak, Vasco d'Atayde with his ship was lost from the fleet without there being heavy weather or contrary winds to account for it. The captain used all diligence to find him, seeking everywhere, but he did not appear again. And so we followed our route over this sea until Tuesday of the octave of Easter, which was the 21st of April, when we came upon some signs of land, being then distant from the said island, as the pilots said, some six hundred and sixty or six hundred and seventy leagues; these signs were a great quantity of long weeds, which mariners call *botelho*, and others as well which they also call *rabo de asno*. And on the following Wednesday, in the morning, we met with birds which they call *fura buchos*. On this same day at the Vesper hours we caught sight of land, that is, first of a large mountain, very high and round, and of other lower lands to the south of it, and of flat land, with great groves of trees. To this high mountain the captain gave the name of *Monte Pascoal*, and to the land, *Terra da Vera Cruz*. He ordered the lead to be thrown. They found 25 fathoms; and at sunset, some six leagues from land, we cast anchor in 19 fathoms, a clean anchorage. There we remained all that night, and on Thursday morning we made sail and steered straight to the land, with the small ships going in front, in 17, 16, 15, 14, 13, 12, 10, and 9 fathoms, until half a league from shore, where we all cast anchor in front of the mouth of a river. And we arrived at this anchorage at ten o'clock, more or less. And from there we caught sight of men who were going along the shore, some seven or eight, as those on the small ships said, because they arrived there first. We there launched the boats and skiffs, and immediately all the captains of the ships came to this ship of the chief captain, and there they talked. And the captain sent Nicolao Coelho on shore in a boat to see that river. And as soon as he began to go thither, men assembled on the shore, by twos and threes, so that when the boat reached the mouth of the river eighteen or twenty men were already there. They were dark, and entirely naked, without anything to cover their shame. They carried in their hands bows with their arrows. All came boldly towards the boat, and Nicolao Coelho made a sign to them that they should lay down their bows, and they laid them down. He could not have any speech with them there, nor understanding which might be profitable, because of the breaking of the sea on the shore. He gave them only a red cap and a cap of linen, which he was wearing on his head, and a black hat. And one of them gave him a hat of long bird feathers with a little tuft of red and grey feathers like those of a parrot. And another gave him a large string of very white beads which look like seed pearls; these articles I believe the captain is sending to Your Highness. And with this he returned to the ships because it was late and he could have no further speech with them on account of the sea. On the following night it blew so hard from the southeast with showers that it made the ships drift, especially the flagship.

And on Friday morning, at eight o'clock, a little more or less, on the advice of the pilots, the captain ordered the anchors to be raised and to set sail. And we went northward along the coast with the boats and skiffs tied to the poop [stern], to see whether we could find some shelter and good anchorage where we might lie, to take on water and wood, not because we were in need of them then, but to provide ourselves here. And when we set sail there were already some sixty or seventy men on the shore, sitting near the river, who had gathered there little by little. We continued along the coast and the captain ordered the small vessels to go in closer to the land, and to strike sail if they found a secure anchorage for the ships. And when we were some ten leagues along the coast from where we had raised anchor, the small vessels found a reef within which was a harbour, very good and secure [*seguro*] with a very wide entrance. And they went in and lowered their sails. And gradually the ships arrived after them, and a little before sunset they also struck sail about a league from the reef, and anchored in 11 fathoms. And by the captain's order our pilot, Affonso Lopez, who was in one of those small vessels and was an alert and dexterous man for this, straightaway entered the skiff to take soundings in the harbour. And he captured two well-built natives who were in a canoe. One of them was carrying a bow and six or seven arrows, and many others went about on the shore with bows and arrows and they did not use them. Then, since it was already night, he took two men to the flagship, where they were received with much pleasure and festivity.

In appearance they are dark, somewhat reddish, with good faces and good noses, well shaped. They go naked, without any covering; neither do they pay more attention to concealing or exposing their shame than they do to showing their faces, and in this respect they are very innocent. Both had their lower lips bored and in them were placed pieces of white bone, the length of a handbreadth, and the thickness of a cotton spindle and as sharp as an awl at the end. They put them through the inner part of the lip, and that part which remains between the lip and the teeth is shaped like a rook in chess. And they carry it there enclosed in such a manner that it does not hurt them, nor does it embarrass them in speaking, eating, or drinking. Their hair is smooth, and they were shorn, with the hair cut higher than a comb of good size, and shaved to above the ears. And one of them was wearing below the opening, from temple to temple towards the back, a sort of wig of yellow birds' feathers, which must have been the length of a *couto* [possibly meaning the width of the hand with the thumb extended], very thick and very tight, and it covered the back of the head and the ears. This was glued to his hair, feather by feather, with a material as soft as wax, but it was not wax. Thus the head-dress was very round and very close and very equal, so that it was not necessary to remove it when they washed.

When they came on board, the captain, well dressed, with a very large collar of gold around his neck, was seated in a chair, with a carpet at his feet as a platform. And Sancho de Toar and Simam de Miranda and Nicolao Coelho and Aires Correa and the rest of us who were in the ship with him were seated on the floor on this carpet. Torches were lighted and they entered, and made no sign of courtesy or of speaking to the captain or to any one, but one of them caught sight of the captain's collar, and began to point with his hand towards the land and then to the collar, as though he were telling us that there was gold in the land. And he also saw a silver candlestick, and in the same manner he made a sign towards the land and then towards the candlestick, as though there were silver also. They showed them a grey parrot which the captain brought here; they at once took it into their hands and pointed towards the land, as though they were found there. They showed them a sheep, but they paid no attention to it. They showed them a hen; they were almost afraid of it, and did not want to touch it; and afterwards they took it as though frightened. Then food was given them: bread and boiled fish, comfits, little cakes, honey, and dried figs. They would eat scarcely anything of that, and if they did taste some things they threw them out. Wine was brought them in a cup; they put a little to their mouths, and did not like it at all, nor did they want any more. Water was brought them in a jar; they took a mouthful of it, and did not drink it; they only washed their mouths and spat it out. One of them saw some white rosary beads; he made a motion that they should give them to him, and he played much with them, and put them around his neck; and then he took them off and wrapped them around his arm. He made a sign towards the land and then to the beads and to the collar of the captain, as if to say that they would give gold for that. We interpreted this so, because we wished to, but if he meant that he would take the beads and also the collar, we did not wish to understand because we did not intend to give it to him. And afterwards he returned the beads to the one who gave them to him. And then they stretched themselves out on their backs on the carpet to sleep without taking any care to cover their privy parts, which were not circumcised, and the hair on them was well shaved and arranged. The captain ordered pillows to be put under the head of each one, and he with the head-dress took sufficient pains not to disarrange it. A mantle was thrown over them, and they permitted it and lay at rest and slept.

On Saturday morning the captain ordered sails to be set and we went to seek the entrance, which was very wide and deep, 6 or 7 fathoms, and all the ships entered within and anchored in 5 or 6 fathoms; this anchorage inside is so large and so beautiful and so secure that more than two hundred large and small ships could lie within it. And as soon as the ships were in place and anchored, all the captains came to this ship of the chief captain, and from here the captain ordered Nicolao Coelho and Bertolameu Dias to go on shore, and they took those two men, let them go with their bows and arrows. To each of them he ordered new shirts and red hats and two rosaries of white bone beads to be given and they carried them on their arms, with rattles and bells. And he sent with them to remain there a young convict, named Affonso Ribeiro, the servant of Dom Joham Tello, to stay with them, and learn their manner of living and customs; and he ordered me to go with Nicolao Coelho. We went at once straight for the shore. At that place there assembled at once some two hundred men, all naked, and with bows and arrows in their hands. Those whom we were bringing made signs to them that they should draw back and put down their bows, and they put them down, and did not draw back much. It is enough to say that they put down their bows. And then those whom we brought, and the young convict with them, got out. As soon as they were out they did not stop again, nor did one wait for the other; rather, they ran, each as fast as he could. And they and many others with them passed a river which flows here with sweet and abundant water which came up as far as their waists. And thus they went running on the other side of the river between some clumps of palms, where were others, and there they stopped. And there, too, the young convict went with a man who, immediately upon his leaving the boat, befriended him, and took him thither. And then they brought him back to us, and with him came the others whom we had brought. These were now naked and without caps. And then many began to arrive, and entered into the boats from the seashore, until no more could get in. And they carried water gourds and took some kegs which we brought and filled them with water and carried them to the boats. They did not actually enter the boat, but from near by, threw them in by hand and we took them, and they asked us to give them something. Nicolao Coelho had brought bells and bracelets and to some he gave a bell and to others a bracelet, so that with that inducement they almost wished to help us. They gave us some of those bows and arrows for hats and linen caps, and for whatever we were willing to give them. From thence the other two youths departed and we never saw them again.

Many of them, or perhaps the greater number of those who were there, wore those beaks of bone in their lips, and some, who were without them, had their lips pierced, and in the holes they carried wooden plugs which looked like stoppers of bottles. And some of them carried three of those beaks, namely, one in the middle and two at the ends. And others were there whose bodies were quartered in colour, that is, half of them in their own colour, and half in a bluish-black dye, and others quartered in a checkered pattern. There were among them three or four girls, very young and very pretty, with very dark hair, long over the shoulders, and their privy parts so high, so closed, and so free from hair that we felt no shame in looking at them very well. Then for the time there was no more speech or understanding with them, because their barbarity was so great that no one could either be understood or heard. We made signs for them to leave, and they did so, and went to the other side of the river. And three or four of our men left the boats and filled I do not know how many kegs of water which we carried, and we returned to the ships. And upon seeing us thus, they made signs for us to return. We returned and they sent the convict and did not wish him to stay there with them. He carried a small basin and two or three red caps to give to their chief, if there was one. They did not care to take anything from him and thus they sent him back with everything, and then Bertolameu Dias made him return again to give those things to them, and he returned and gave them in our presence, to the one who had first befriended him. And then he came away and we took him with us. The man who befriended him was now well on in years, and was well decked with ornaments and covered with feathers which stuck to his body, so that he looked pierced with arrows like Saint Sebastian. Others wore caps of yellow feathers, others of red, others of green; and one of the girls was all painted from head to foot with that paint, and she was so well built and so rounded and her lack of shame was so charming, that many women of our land seeing such attractions, would be ashamed that theirs were not like hers. None of them were circumcised, but all were as we are. And, thereupon, we returned, and they went away.

In the afternoon the chief captain set out in his boat with all of us and with the other captains of the ships in their boats to amuse ourselves in the bay near the shore. But no one went on land, because the captain did not wish it, although there was no one there; only he and all [of us] landed on a large island in the bay, which is very empty at low tide, but on all sides it is surrounded by water so that no one can go to it without a boat or by swimming. There he and the rest of us had a good time for an hour and a half, and the mariners fished there, going out with a net, and they caught a few small fish. And then, since it was already night, we returned to the ships.

On Low Sunday in the morning the captain determined to go to that island to hear Mass and a sermon, and he ordered all the captains to assemble in the boats and to go with him; and so it was done. He ordered a large tent to be set up on the island and within it a very well-provided altar to be placed, and there with all the rest of us he had Mass said, which the father, Frei Amrique, intoned and all the other fathers and priests who were there accompanied him with the same voice. That Mass, in my opinion, was heard by all with much pleasure and devotion. The captain had there with him the banner of Christ, with which he left Belem, and it was kept raised on the Gospel side [of the altar]. After the Mass was finished, the father removed his vestments and sat down in a high chair, and we all threw ourselves down on that sand, and he preached a solemn and profitable sermon on the history of the Gospel, and at the end of it he dealt with our coming and with the discovery of this land, and referred to the sign of the Cross in obedience to which we came; which was very fitting, and which inspired much devotion.

While we were at Mass and at the sermon, about the same number of people were on the shore as yesterday with their bows and arrows, who were amusing themselves and watching us; and they sat down, and when the Mass was finished and we were seated for the sermon, many of those arose and blew a horn or trumpet and began to leap and to dance for a while, and some of them placed themselves in two or three *almadias* [rafts] which they had there. These are not made like those I have already seen; they are simply three logs fastened together, and four or five, or all who wanted to, entered them, scarcely moving away at all from the land, but only far enough to keep their footing. After the sermon was finished the captain and all the rest proceeded to the boats with our banner displayed and we embarked, and thus we all went towards the land, to pass along it where they were, Bertolameu Dias going ahead in his skiff, at the captain's order, with a piece of timber from an *almadia* which the sea had carried to them, to give it to them. And all of us were about a stone's throw behind him. When they saw the skiff of Bertolameu Dias, all of them came at once to the water, going into it as far as they could. A sign was made to them to put down their bows, and many of them went at once to put them down on shore and others did not put them down. There was one there who spoke much to the others, telling them to go away, but they did not, in my opinion, have respect or fear of him. This one who was telling them to move carried his bow and arrows, and was painted with red paint on his breasts and shoulder blades and hips, thighs, and legs, all the way down, and the unpainted places such as the stomach and belly were of their own colour, and the paint was so red that the water did not wash away or remove it, but rather when he came out of the water he was redder. One of our men left the skiff of Bertolameu Dias and went among them, without their thinking for a moment of doing him harm; on the contrary, they gave him gourds of water and beckoned to those on the skiff to come on land. Thereupon Bertolameu Dias returned to the captain, and we came to the ships to eat, playing trumpets and pipes without troubling them further. And they again sat down on the shore and thus they remained for a while. On this island where we went to hear Mass and the sermon the water ebbs a great deal and uncovers much sand and much gravel. While we were there some went to look for shellfish, but did not find them; they found some thick and short shrimps. Among them was a very large and very fat shrimp such as I had never seen before. They also found shells of cockles and mussels, but did not discover any whole piece. And as soon as we had eaten, all the captains came to this ship at the command of the chief captain and he went to one side with them and I was there too, and he asked all of us whether it seemed well to us to send news of the finding of this land to Your Highness by the supply ship, so that you might order it to be better reconnoitred, and learn more about it than we could now learn because we were going on our way. And among the many speeches that were made regarding the matter, it was said by all or by the greater number, that it would be very well to do so; and to this they agreed. And as soon as the decision was made, he asked further whether it would be well to take here by force two of these men to send to Your Highness and to leave here in their place two convicts. In this matter they agreed that it was not necessary to take men by force, since it was the general custom that those taken away by force to another place said that everything about which they are asked was there; and that these two convicts whom we should leave would give better and far better information about the land than would be given by those carried away by us, because they are people whom no one understands nor would they learn [Portuguese] quickly enough to be able to tell it as well as those others [whom] Your Highness sends here, and that consequently we should not attempt to take any one away from here by force nor cause any scandal, but in order to tame and pacify them all the more, we should simply leave here the two convicts when we departed. And thus it was determined, since it appeared better to all.

When this was finished the captain ordered us to go to land in our boats in order to ascertain as well as possible what the river was like, and also to divert ourselves. We all went ashore in our boats, armed, and the banner with us. The natives went there along the shore to the mouth of the river where we were going, and before we arrived, in accordance with the instructions they had received before, they all laid down their bows and made signs for us to land. And as soon as the boats had put their bows on shore, they all went immediately to the other side of the river, which is not wider than the throw of a short staff; and as soon as we disembarked some of our men crossed the river at once and went among them, and some waited and others withdrew, but the result was that we were all intermingled. They gave us some of their bows with their arrows in exchange for hats and linen caps and for anything else which we gave them. So many of our men went to the other side and mingled with them that they withdrew and went away and some went above to where others were. And then the captain had himself carried on the shoulders of two men and crossed the river and made every one return. The people who were there could not have been more than the usual number, and when the captain made all return, some of them came to him, not to recognize him for their lord, for it does not seem to me that they understand or have knowledge of this, but because our people were already passing to this side of the river. There they talked and brought many bows and beads of the kind already mentioned, and trafficked in anything in such manner that many bows, arrows, and beads were brought from there to the ships. And then the captain returned to this side of the river, and many men came to its bank. There you might have seen gallants painted with black and red, and with quarterings both on their bodies and on their legs, which certainly was pleasing in appearance. There were also among them four or five young women just as naked, who were not displeasing to the eye, among whom was one with her thigh from the knee to the hip and buttock all painted with that black paint and all the rest in her own colour; another had both knees and calves and ankles so painted, and her privy parts so nude and exposed with such innocence that there was not there any shame. There was also another young woman carrying an infant boy or girl tied at her breasts by a cloth of some sort so that only its little legs showed. But the legs of the mother and the rest of her were not concealed by any cloth.

And afterwards the captain moved up along the river, which flows continuously even with the shore, and there an old man was waiting who carried in his hand the oar of an *almadia*. When the captain reached him he spoke in our presence, without any one understanding him, nor did he understand us with reference to the things he was asked about, particularly gold, for we wished to know whether they had any in this land. This old man had his lip so bored that a large thumb could be thrust through the hole, and in the opening he carried a worthless green stone which closed it on the outside. And the captain made him take it out; and I do not know what devil spoke to him, but he went with it to put it in the captain's mouth. We laughed a little at this and then the captain got tired and left him; and one of our men gave him an old hat for the stone, not because it was worth anything but to show. And afterwards the captain got it, I believe, to send it with the other things to Your Highness. We went along there looking at the river, which has much and very good water. Along it are many palms, not very high, in which there are many good sprouts. We gathered and ate many of them. Then the captain turned towards the mouth of the river where we had disembarked, and on the other side of the river were many of them, dancing and diverting themselves before one another, without taking each other by the hand, and they did it well. Then Diogo Dias, who was revenue officer of Sacavem, crossed the river. He is an agreeable and pleasure-loving man, and he took with him one of our bagpipe players and his bagpipe, and began to dance among them, taking them by the hands, and they were delighted and laughed and accompanied him very well to the sound of the pipe. After they had danced he went along the level ground, making many light turns and a remarkable leap which astonished them, and they laughed and enjoyed themselves greatly. And although he reassured and flattered them a great deal with this, they soon became sullen like wild men and went away upstream. And then the captain crossed over the river with all of us, and we went along the shore, the boats going along close to land, and we came to a large lake of sweet water which is near the seashore, because all that shore is marshy above and the water flows out in many places. And after we had crossed the river some seven or eight of the natives joined our sailors who were retiring to the boats. And they took from there a shark which Bertolameu Dias killed and brought to them and threw on the shore. It suffices to say that up to this time, although they were somewhat tamed, a moment afterwards they became frightened like sparrows at a feeding-place. And no one dared to speak strongly to them for fear they might be more frightened; and everything was done to their liking in order to tame them thoroughly. To the old man with whom the captain spoke he gave a red cap: and in spite of all the talking that he did with him, and the cap which he gave him, as soon as he left and began to cross the river, he immediately became more cautious and would not return again to this side of it. The other two whom the captain had on the ships, and to whom he gave what has already been mentioned, did not appear again, from which I infer that they are bestial people and of very little knowledge; and for this reason they are so timid. Yet withal they are well cared for and very clean, and in this it seems to me that they are rather like birds or wild animals, to which the air gives better feathers and better hair than to tame ones. And their bodies are so clean and so fat and so beautiful that they could not be more so; and this causes me to presume that they have no houses or dwellings in which to gather, and the air in which they are brought up makes them so. Nor indeed have we, up to this time, seen any houses or anything which looks like them. The captain ordered the convict, Affonso Ribeiro, to go with them again, which he did. And he went there a good distance, and in the afternoon he returned, for they had made him come and were not willing to keep him there; and they had given him bows and arrows and had not taken from him anything which was his. On the contrary, he said, one of them had taken from him some yellow beads which he was wearing and fled with them; and he complained and the others at once went after him and returned to give them back to him. And then they ordered him to go back. He said that he had not seen there among them anything but some thatched huts of green branches, and made very large, like those of Entre Doiro e Minho [the northern province of Portugal and Caminha's homeland]. And thus we returned to the ships to sleep when it was already almost night.

On Monday after eating we all disembarked to take on water. Then many came there, but not so many as at the other times, and now they were carrying very few bows and they kept a little apart from us, and afterwards little by little mingled with us. And they embraced us and had a good time; and some of them soon slunk away. They gave there some bows for sheets of paper and for some worthless old cap, or for anything else. And in such a manner it came about that a good twenty or thirty of our people went with them to where many others of them were, with girls and women, and brought back many bows and caps of bird feathers, some green and some yellow, samples of which I believe the captain will send to Your Highness. And according to what those said who went there they made merry with them. On that day we saw them closer and more as we wished, for all of us were almost intermingled. And there some of them had those colours in quarters, others in halves, and others in such colours as in the tapestry of Arras, and all with their lips pierced, and many with the bones in them, and some of them without bones. Some of them were carrying prickly green nut shells from trees, which in colour resembled chestnuts, except that they were very much smaller. And these were full of small red grains which, when crushed between the fingers, made a very red paint with which they were painted. And the more they wetted themselves the redder they became. They are all shaved to above the ears, likewise their eyebrows and eyelashes. All of them have their foreheads from temple to temple painted with a black paint, which looks like a black ribbon the breadth of two fingers.

And the captain ordered that convict, Affonso Ribeiro, and two other convicts to go there among them, and likewise Diogo Dias, because he was a cheerful man, with whom they played. And he ordered the convicts to remain there that night. They all went there and mingled with them, and as they said later, they went a good league and a half to a village of houses in which there must have been nine or ten dwellings, each of which they said was as long as the captain's ship. And they were of wood with sides of boards and covered with straw, of reasonable height, and all had one single room without any divisions. They had within many posts, and from post to post a net is tied by the ends to each post, high up, where they sleep. And underneath they made their fires to warm themselves. And each house had two small doors, one at one end, and another at the other. And they said that thirty or forty persons dwelt in each house, and that thus they found them. And that they gave them to eat of the food which they had, namely, much manioc and other roots which are in the land, that they eat.

And, as it was late, they presently made all of us return and did not wish any one to remain there; and also, as they said, they wished to come with us. They traded there, for bells and for other trifles of little value which we were carrying, very large and beautiful red parrots and two little green ones and caps of green feathers and a cloth of feathers of many colours, woven in a very beautiful fashion. All of these things Your Highness will see, because the captain will send them to you, as he says. And thereupon they came back and we returned to the ships.

On Tuesday, after eating, we landed to set a watch over the wood and to wash clothes. Some sixty or seventy men without bows or anything else were there on the shore when we reached it. As soon as we arrived they at once came to us without being frightened, and afterward many more came. There must have been a good two hundred, all without bows, and they all mingled so much with us that some of them helped us to load wood and put it in the boats, and they vied with us and derived much pleasure therefrom. And while we were taking on the wood two carpenters made a large cross from one piece of wood which was cut yesterday for this. Many of them came there to be with the carpenters; and I believe that they did this more to see the iron tools with which they were making it than to see the cross, because they have nothing of iron. And they cut their wood and boards with stones shaped like wedges put into a piece of wood, very well tied between two sticks, and in such a manner that they are strong, according to what the men said who were at their houses yesterday, for they saw them there. By now they kept us so much company as almost to disturb us in what we had to do. And the captain ordered the two convicts and Diogo Dias to go to the village, and to other villages if they should hear of them, and on no account to come to sleep on the ships, even if they should order them to; and so they went. While we were in this grove cutting wood some parrots flew across the trees, some of them green, and others grey, large and small, so that it seems to me that there must be many in this land, but I did not see more than about nine or ten. We did not then see other birds except some *pombas seixas*, and they seemed to me considerably larger than those of Portugal. Some said that they saw turtle-doves, but I did not see any; but since the groves are so numerous and so large and of such infinite variety, I do not doubt that in the interior there are many birds. And towards night we returned to the ships with our wood. I believe, Senhor, that heretofore I have not given account to Your Highness of the form of their bows and arrows. The bows are black and long and the arrows long, and their tips of pointed reeds, as Your Highness will see from some which I believe the captain will send to you.

On Wednesday we did not go on shore, because the captain spent the whole day in the supply ship emptying it, and had transported to the ship what each one could carry. Many of the natives came to the shore, as we saw from the ships. There must have been some three hundred, according to what Sancho de Toar said, who was there. Diogo Dias and Affonso Ribeiro, the convict, whom the captain sent yesterday to sleep there at any cost, returned when it was already night because they did not want him to sleep there, and they found green parrots and other birds which were black, almost like magpies, except that they had white beaks and short tails. And when Sancho de Toar returned to the ship, some of them wished to go with him; but he did not want any except two proper youths. He ordered them to be well fed and cared for that night, and they ate all the food which was given them, and he ordered a bed with sheets to be made for them, as he said, and they slept and were comfortable that night. And so nothing more happened that day to write about.

On Thursday, the last of April, we ate early in the morning and went on shore for more wood and water, and when the captain was about to leave his ship Sancho de Toar arrived with his two guests, and because he had not yet eaten, cloths were laid for him and food was brought, and he ate. We seated the guests in their chairs, and they ate very well of all which was given them, especially of cold boiled ham and rice. They did not give them wine, because Sancho de Toar said that they did not drink it well. After the meal was over we all entered the boat and they with us. A sailor gave one of them a large tusk of a wild boar, well turned up. And as soon as he took it he at once put it in his lip; and because it did not fit there, they gave him a small piece of red wax. And this he applied to the back of his ornament to hold it and put it into his lip with the point turned upward, and he was as pleased with it as though he had a great jewel. And as soon as we disembarked he at once went off with it, and did not appear there again. When we landed there were probably eight or ten of the natives about, and little by little others began to come. And it seems to me that that day there came to the shore four hundred or four hundred and fifty men. Some of them carried bows and arrows and gave all for caps and for anything which we gave them. They ate with us of what we gave them. Some of them drank wine and others could not drink it, but it seems to me that if they accustomed themselves to it, they would drink it with great willingness. All were so well disposed and so well built and smart with their paints that they made a good show. They loaded as much of that wood as they could, very willingly, and carried it to the boats, and were quieter and more at ease among us than we were among them. The captain went with some of us for a short distance through this grove to a large stream of much water, which in our opinion was the same as the one which runs down to the shore, from which we took water. There we stayed for a while, drinking and amusing ourselves beside the river in this grove, which is so large and so thick and of such abundant foliage that one cannot describe it. In it there are many palms, from which we gathered many good sprouts. When we disembarked, the captain said that it would be well to go directly to the cross, which was leaning against a tree near the river, to be set up the next day, which was Friday, and that we should all kneel down and kiss it so that they might see the respect which we had for it. And thus we did. And we motioned to those ten or twelve who were there that they should do the same, and at once they all went to kiss it. They seem to me people of such innocence that if one could understand them and they us, they would soon be Christians, because they do not have or understand any belief, as it appears. And therefore, if the convicts who are to remain here will learn their language well and understand them, I do not doubt that they will become Christians, in accordance with the pious intent of Your Highness, and that they will believe in our Holy Faith, to which may it please Our Lord to bring them. For it is certain this people is good and of pure simplicity, and there can easily be stamped upon them whatever belief we wish to give them; and furthermore, Our Lord gave them fine bodies and good faces as to good men; and He who brought us here, I believe, did not do so without purpose. And consequently, Your Highness, since you so much desire to increase the Holy Catholic Faith, ought to look after their salvation, and it will please God that, with little effort, this will be accomplished.

They do not till the soil or breed stock, nor is there ox or cow, or goat, or sheep, or hen, or any other domestic animal which is accustomed to live with men; nor do they eat anything except this manioc, of which there is much, and of the seeds and the fruits which the earth and the trees produce. Nevertheless, with this they are stronger and better fed than we are with all the wheat and vegetables which we eat.

While they were there that day, they continually skipped and danced with us to the sound of one of our tambours, in such a manner that they are much more our friends than we theirs. If one signed to them whether they wished to come to the ships, they at once made ready to do so, in such wise that had we wished to invite them all, they would all have come. However, we only took four or five this night to the ships, namely, the chief captain took two, and Simam de Miranda, one, whom he already had for his page, and Aires Gomes [*sic*], another, also as a page. One of those whom the captain took was one of his guests whom we had brought him the first night when we arrived; to-day he came dressed in his shirt and with him his brother. These were this night very well entertained, both with food and with a bed with mattress and sheets to tame them better.

And to-day, which is Friday, the first day of May, we went on land with our banner in the morning and disembarked up the river towards the south, where it seemed to us that it would be better to plant the cross, so that it might be better seen. And there the captain indicated where the hole should be made to plant it, and while they were making it, he with all the rest of us went to where the cross was down the river. We brought it from there with the friars and priests going ahead singing in the manner of a procession. There were already some of the natives there, about seventy or eighty, and when they saw us coming, some of them went to place themselves under it in order to help us. We crossed the river along the shore and went to place it where it was to be, which is probably a distance of two cross-bow shots from the river. While we were busy with this there came a good one hundred and fifty or more. After the cross was planted with the arms and device of Your Highness which we first nailed to it, we set up an altar at the foot of it. There the father, Frei Amrique, said Mass, at which those already mentioned chanted and officiated. There were with us some fifty or sixty natives, all kneeling as we were, and when it came to the Gospel and we all rose to our feet with hands lifted, they rose with us and lifted their hands, remaining thus until it was over. And then they again sat down as we did. And at the elevation of the Host when we knelt, they placed themselves as we were, with hands uplifted, and so quietly that I assure Your Highness that they gave us much edification. They stayed there with us until Communion was over, and after Communion the friars and priests and the captain and some of the rest of us partook of Communion. Some of them, because the sun was hot, arose while we were receiving Communion and others remained as they were and stayed. One of them, a man of fifty or fifty-five years, stayed there with those who remained. While we were all thus he collected those who had remained and even called others. He went about among them and talked to them, pointing with his finger to the altar, and afterwards he lifted his finger towards Heaven as though he were telling them something good, and thus we understood it. After the Mass was over the father took off his outer vestment and remained in his alb, and then he mounted a chair near the altar, and there he preached to us of the Gospel and of the apostles whose day this is, treating at the end of the sermon of this your holy and virtuous undertaking, which edified us still more. Those who still remained for the sermon were looking at him, as we were doing. And the one of whom I speak called some to come there; some came and others departed. And when the sermon was over, Nicolao Coelho brought many tin crosses with crucifixes, which he still had from another voyage, and we thought it well to put one around the neck of each; for which purpose the father, Frei Amrique, seated himself at the foot of the cross, and there, one by one, he put around the neck of each his own cross tied to a string, first making him kiss it and raise his hands. Many came for this, and we did likewise to all. They must have been about forty or fifty. And after this was finished it was already a good hour after midday; we went to the ships to eat, and the captain took with him that same one who had pointed out to the others the altar and the sky, and his brother with him, to whom he did much honour. And he gave him a Moorish shirt, and to the other one a shirt such as the rest of us wore. And as it appears to me and to every one, these people in order to be wholly Christian lack nothing except to understand us, for whatever they saw us do, they did likewise; wherefore it appeared to all that they have no idolatry and no worship. And I well believe that if Your Highness should send here someone who would go about more at leisure among them, all will be turned to the desire of Your Highness. And if someone should come for this purpose, a priest should not fail to come also at once to baptize them, for by that time they will already have a greater knowledge of our faith through the two convicts who are remaining here among them. Both of these also partook of Communion to-day. Among all those who came to-day there was only one young woman who stayed continuously at the Mass, and she was given a cloth with which to cover herself, and we put it about her; but as she sat down she did not think to spread it much to cover herself. Thus, Senhor, the innocence of this people is such, that that of Adam could not have been greater in respect to shame. Now Your Highness may see whether people who live in such innocence will be converted or not if they are taught what pertains to their salvation. When this was over we went thus in their presence to kiss the cross, took leave of them, and came to eat.

I believe, Senhor, that with these two convicts who remain here, there stay also two seamen who to-night left this ship, fleeing to shore in a skiff. They have not come back and we believe that they remain here, because to-morrow, God willing, we take our departure from here.

It seems to me, Senhor, that this land from the promontory we see farthest south to another promontory which is to the north, of which we caught sight from this harbour, is so great that it will have some twenty or twenty-five leagues of coastline. Along the shore in some places it has great banks, some of them red, some white, and the land above is quite flat and covered with great forests. From point to point the entire shore is very flat and very beautiful. As for the interior, it appeared to us from the sea very large, for, as far as [the] eye could reach, we could see only land and forests, a land which seemed extensive to us. Up to now we are unable to learn that there is gold or silver in it, or anything of metal or iron; nor have we seen any, but the land itself has a very good climate, as cold and temperate as that of Entre Doiro e Minho, because in the present season we found it like that. Its waters are quite endless. So pleasing is it that if one cares to profit by it, everything will grow in it because of its waters. But the best profit which can be derived from it, it seems to me, will be to save this people, and this should be the chief seed which Your Highness should sow there. And if there were nothing more than to have here a stopping-place for this voyage to Calicut, that would suffice, to say nothing of an opportunity to fulfill and do that which Your Highness so much desires, namely, the increase of our Holy Faith.

And in this manner, Senhor, I give here to Your Highness an account of what I saw in this land of yours, and if I have been somewhat lengthy you will pardon me, for the desire I had to tell you everything made me set it down thus in detail. And, Senhor, since it is certain that in this charge laid upon me as in any other thing which may be for your service, Your Highness will be very faithfully served by me, I ask of you that in order to do me a special favor you order my son-in-law, Jorge do Soiro, to return from the island of Sam Thomé. This I shall take as a very great favor to me.

I kiss Your Highness's hands.

From this Porto Seguro of your island of Vera Cruz to-day, Friday, the first day of May of 1500.

Pero Vaaz de Caminha

[Superscribed]   To the King Our Lord
[On the back in a contemporary hand] Letter of Pero Vaaz de Caminha concerning the discovery of the new land which Pedro Alvarez made.

8

Orders Given to "the Twelve"

(1523)

On the eve of their departure from Spain, the "apostolic twelve" Franciscan friars who accompanied their superior Martín de Valencia received the following *obediencia* (exhortation and instructions) in Latin from their minister general, Francisco de los Angeles. They carried a copy of this document, along with an *instrucción* in Spanish, when they arrived in Mexico in 1524. Although "the Twelve" had been preceded by a few other churchmen, including Mercedarian friar Bartolomé de Olmedo and Franciscan lay brother Pedro de Gante (see Selection 14), it is with them that the organized effort to evangelize the native peoples of Mexico began.

The metaphorical language and preoccupations of de los Angeles allow insight into the expectations and intentions of these missionary friars and the first generation or two of their brethren in New Spain. These Franciscans revived a belief that had developed among early members of their order in the thirteenth century, a belief that they were a divinely inspired force working for the benefit and salvation of souls in the last days of the world. Thus, de los Angeles insists upon the urgency of his call to action, to deeds over words. "Hurry down now to the active life," he writes, and do not be afraid to shock the

world with a zeal that some will see as madness. It is the eleventh hour in the struggle for salvation, he warns. There is an invitation to relentless hardships in this life "without promise of reward" and to death in the line of holy duty—in the *obediencia* such a death is called "the palm of martyrdom"; in the *instrucción,* there is an assurance that "even if you do not convert the infidel . . . you have done your duty and God will do His." De los Angeles presents the Devil as a palpable, menacing force in the world, and the Franciscans are to regard themselves as soldiers waging a spiritual war against him. New Spain, the battleground, is simultaneously the vineyard to which God has summoned the friars to labor among new plants as Judgment Day approaches. Native peoples are depicted as unbelievers powerlessly awaiting a redemption of which they are completely ignorant, "held fast [as they are] in the blindness of idolatry under the yoke of the satanic thrall." They are a far cry from the Aztec lords and holy men with whom "the Twelve" converse in Bernardino de Sahagún's 1564 depiction (Selection 3).

These ardent conceptions of themselves and of the evangelization of Indians spring in part from the special situation of the

Franciscans (or, as they called themselves, the Order of the Friars Minor, or Minorites) in the Iberian Peninsula in the years after the conquest of Muslim Granada and the expulsion of the Jews in 1492. Virtually from the order's beginnings in the early thirteenth century, there had existed an internal tension over whether to adhere strictly to an original rule of austerity, simplicity, and renunciation of property (as "Observants," in later parlance) or to lead more material lives as a way to exert greater influence in the world (as "Conventuals"). Branches of both tendencies emerged in Iberia in the late fourteenth and early fifteenth centuries. After numerous failed attempts to reunite the many branches and heal the fundamental division between Observants and Conventuals, two bulls were issued by Pope Leo X in 1517. First, he made formal the separation of the Franciscan Order into two independent bodies; and second, he brought about a temporary union of the Observant groups—many of them quite new, having emerged only in the late fifteenth century. (The separation between the Conventual and Observant Franciscans hardened, although many Conventuals joined the more numerous and influential Observants at this time. The Observants' own union did not last, and they soon divided into four groups: Barefoot, or Discalced; Recollects; Reformed; and Capuchins.)

Following their interpretations of the priorities of Saint Francis of Assisi (d. 1226), Observant Franciscans in the fifteenth and sixteenth centuries maintained that the example of a holy and moral spiritual life offered the most powerful incentive in the conversion of others. Generally speaking, this fundamental point distinguished the Franciscans from the Dominican Order (the Order of the Friars Preacher), which was founded by Saint Francis's contemporary, Saint Dominic (d. 1221), and which developed over the same period as the Order of the Friars Minor. The Dominicans favored programs of doctrinal preaching and philosophical arguments with religious opponents as the most effective means of conversion. Once they had attained spiritual maturity and obedience,

Franciscans, too, were called on to preach as missionaries in the world. Early Franciscans were known for simple sermons delivered among the poor and lepers, and for their regular withdrawals to secluded places. They preached also among infidels (principally Muslims), but were instructed to avoid entering into complex disputes such as the formal exchanges held with Aztec holy men by their successors. Deeds over words, again; as Saint Francis himself emphasized in his founding rules of the order, *Regula prima,* "All brothers . . . preach by their works."

One of the strictest of the Observant groups in early sixteenth-century Spain would supply many of the early Franciscans in Mexico, including members of "the Twelve." Their interpretation of the original rule stressed that, in the course of the simple preaching of the Word among non-Christians, missionaries should exhibit God's love and thus urge unbelievers toward baptism and becoming Christian. Known as the Minorites of the Blessed Juan de Puebla and the Minorites of the Holy Gospel, they practiced extreme poverty, a rigorous regimen of flagellation, and silent spiritual retreats. These Minorites had also undertaken a short-lived preaching mission among Moriscos (new converts to Christianity from Islam) in the mountains of southern Spain in an effort to promote a simple, austere Christianity among these new and potential converts to the faith. They emerged from the ruling of Leo X with their own Province of San Gabriel, founded in 1518.

The first provincial of San Gabriel was Martín de Valencia, already legendary within the Observant ranks for his humility and practices of penance. He is said to have attracted many fervent religious to the new province. According to Motolinía (Toribio de Benavente), one of these religious, it was during a personal inspection of the province by Minister General Francisco de los Angeles in 1523 that Valencia learned of a plan to send him and twelve companions to begin the evangelization of the indigenous peoples of Mexico. The orders composed by de los Angeles must have emerged from this meeting.

Valencia and his companions were famous in their own time and long afterward. Colonial paintings glorify the moment of their reception in Mexico by Hernán Cortés, with the conqueror typically represented in symbolic self-abasement before their holy purpose and Indian observers absorbing the edifying scene. "The Twelve," as mentioned above, are also the Christian interlocutors in the *coloquios* from which Selection 3 is drawn. And they appear as the bearers of "the church" in Diego Valadés's 1579 depiction of the ideal churchyard-as-schoolroom in Selection 22.

Fray Francisco de los Angeles, minister general and servant of the whole Order of the Friars Minor, to the venerable and his very dear fathers in Christ: Fr. Martín de Valencia, confessor and learned preacher, and to the other twelve friars of the Order of Minors, who under his obedience are to be sent to the places of the infidels who dwell in the lands of Yucatán; that is to say: Fr. Francisco de Soto, Fr. Martín de la Coruña, Fr. José de la Coruña, Fr. Juan Xuárez, Fr. Antonio de Ciudad Rodrigo, and Fr. Toribio Benavente, preachers and confessors; Fr. García de Cisneros and Fr. Luis de Fuensalida, preachers; Fr. Juan de Ribas and Fr. Francisco Ximénez, priests; and to the Brothers Fr. Andrés de Córdoba and Fr. Bernardino de la Torre, devoted lay religious; and to all the others who there shall be received or in the future should be sent, sempiternal health and peace in the Lord.

Among the continuous cares and affairs which daily present themselves to me and occupy my mind, this one presses, worries, and afflicts me first of all, as to how with all the cunning of my bowels and continual sighs of my heart, I might labor with the apostolic man and father of ours, Saint Francis, toward liberating and snatching away from the maw of the dragon the souls redeemed with the most precious Blood of Our Lord Jesus Christ, deceived by satanic wiles, dwelling in the shadow of death, held in the vain cult of idols—and bring them to fight under the banner of the Cross and to place their neck into the yoke of Christ, through you, my dearest brothers, with the favor of the Most High; because otherwise I shall not be able to escape the zeal of Saint Francis athirst for the welfare of souls, pounding day and night with unceasing knocking at the door of my heart. And that which I yearned for with the passing of many days, namely, of being made one of your number, and did not deserve to obtain from the superiors (thus, Father, because such was your pleasure), I confidently hope to attain in your persons through His favor.

For, indeed, the bounty of the Eternal Father chose the same seraphic standard-bearer of Christ to exalt the glory of His Name and procure the salvation of souls, and to forestall the ruin which threatened the Church (and should she fall, save her and raise her to her primitive state), from among many persons endowed and placed in His Holy Church with divine aids and favors—together with his sons, namely, outstanding men who, contemplating and considering the life and merits of the most blessed Saint Paul, glory solely in the Cross of the Lord by spurning worldly delights and consolations for the delights and riches of Paradise.

For the same man of God, not oblivious of his vocation and calling, and ever raising his desire toward the love of heavenly things, sought through the Church Militant both the faithful and the infidels. And even until now do they herald and make manifest unceasingly throughout the whole world the power of the Divine

Name; in spreading the honor and service of the Christian religion, they labor with great vigilance. And what else can be said? For certainly, in chasing away heresies and in destroying other pestiferous and deadly plagues, they willingly offered themselves to contempt. Desiring to shed their own blood, burning with the fire of Christ's love, and thirsting for the palm of martyrdom, the said father with some of his sons went over various parts of the world.

But now that the dawn is far spent and passing away, which is the eleventh hour of which the Gospel speaks, you are called by the head of the family to go forth into his vineyard; not hired for a price like the others, but rather like true sons of such a father, not seeking your own interests, but those of Jesus Christ without promise of pay or reward; may you run like sons following your father to the vineyard—he who desiring to be the last among men did so attain it, and wished that you his true sons should be the last among the rest, treading and trampling upon the glory of the world, despised for littleness and idiocy, possessing the sublimest poverty, and in such a way that the world should regard you with mockery and contempt, and the very picture of contempt and derision, and should consider your life as madness, and your end without honor. For, thus become madmen to the world, you might convert the world by the foolishness of your preaching. Neither should you be disturbed because you are not hired, but rather sent forth without promise of reward; because the man of God, enlightened by an interior inspiration of the Father of Light, foresaw then, not with a clouded eye but with the firm certainty of the sublime, that from the last he would make you the first.

To you, therefore, O sons, with the last end of the world at hand, I your father cry out and bestir your minds that you defend the King's army already falling and presently fleeing from the foe, and, taking up the victorious contest of the heavenly Victor, you preach by word and work unto the enemy. And if up to now, with Zacchaeus up in the figberry tree sucking the sap of the Cross, you sought to see who Jesus might be, hurry down now to the active life. And if you should have cheated anyone from among the souls of men by solely contemplating the mysteries of the Cross, pay back your neighbor fourfold with the active life together with the contemplative, the shedding of your very blood for the Name of Christ and for their salvation—which He regards and weighs fourfold compared with contemplation alone—and then you will see who Jesus is; when, distrusting yourselves while accomplishing this, you shall receive Him with joy into your hearts. He will see to it that while you are small in stature, you will triumph over the enemy. Run therefore thus with such speed as to gain the victory. It follows hence that you, whom the zeal for souls has eaten up according to the sublimity of your profession, and who desire to run in the fragrance of the ointments of those who followed the footsteps of Christ and shed their blood for His love—for this reason you begged me with great importunity, according to the spirit of our Rule, to send you to infidel parts, so that fighting there for Christ in their conversion, you might save the souls of your neighbor and your own, prepared to go to prison and to death for His sake and for their salvation.

Wherefore, having knowledge of your good life and proof of your goodness, and having learned and known from your deeds that you are worthy of the banner of the King of Glory, which you want to raise up in faraway places, and hold up and sustain, flourish and defend even unto death—therefore, confiding in the divine bounty, I send you to convert with words and example the people who do not know Jesus Christ Our Lord, who are held fast in the blindness of idolatry under the yoke of the satanic thrall, who live and dwell in the Indies which are commonly called Yucatán or New Spain or Tierra Firme. With the authority of my office, in the name of the Father and of the Son and of the Holy Spirit, I charge and command you with the merit of holy obedience, so that you may go forth and bear fruit and your fruit may endure.

And to you, venerable father, Friar Martín de Valencia, and to your successors in office, I subject the twelve friars named, and whichever others who in time to come should join themselves to your fold, as to their true pastor and superior; and you I constitute as their true superior, and likewise your successors in office according to the instruction that I intend to give you concerning the mode of your life and conversation; and you I call and constitute for their custos [director of a subprovincial unit of Franciscans], and I wish and order that you be so addressed; and I place and subject you to myself alone and my obedience, and that of my successors in office (according to the instructions that I intend to give you), and also to that of the Commissary of Spain in those things concerning which you alone or your successors, with the majority of the friars, should have recourse by your letters, until you or your successors learn otherwise from the mandates of our general chapter.

Further than this, I charge and command you the twelve through the merit of holy obedience, and the rest who in the future should join your company, and every single person, both you and them—that you will have to obey the said friar Martín de Valencia as your true and indubitable prelate and custos, and his successors in office, in all these things in which you are obliged to obey the minister general and the rest of your prelates according to the tenor of the Rule. And because I am obligated to bring subjects and superior, according to the burden of the office imposed upon me (and which I unworthily fill), and since in the course of time many matters and problems could arise concerning the custody entrusted to you, which might pertain to my office and for the providing and remedying of which my presence should of necessity be required, it follows from this that to you the said friar Martín de Valencia (in whose fervent zeal, religious observance, and laudable maturity, learning, essential discretion, and general ability, I fully confide in the Lord), and to whomsoever of your successors in the office by the tenor of the letters present, I most fully commit all my powers regarding all your subjects, who are as of now and in time should be, and regarding all and whichever friaries, if there are some now of our Order, and those which in the future should exist in New Spain, or the land of Yucatán—giving to you and to them all fullest authority and faculties in one and the other forum, in the external judicial one as well as the internal one of conscience, together with the ordinary one which belongs to me through my office, and even also the apostolic indults and privileges granted to me, with the power of subdelegating; that is to say, publicly and privately to visit, admonish, correct, punish, establish, disestablish, ordain, prohibit and dispose, bind and absolve and dispense from whatsoever penalties, irregularities, and defects, and against whatsoever statutes of the Order, and regarding whatsoever precepts and mandates with which I myself am empowered with regard to either forum; and also by ecclesiastical censures and other canonical penalties to constrain, obstruct, and compel, to interpret and to resolve doubts. Likewise all those things and whichever one of them that in whatsoever manner concern or pertain to my office of minister general, especially in having them performed and carried out as though I myself personally, both by my ordinary power and by my apostolic commission, would perform and accomplish them; and even though the problems were such that, for being so difficult, they needed special and particular declarations. All of these things, and each one of them, I desire to be regarded as sufficiently expressed by the tenor of these presents, excepting two cases which I reserve to myself.

The first: about admitting women, virgins, widowed, or married, into the Order and obedience of Saint Clare, whether from the first or from the second category, or to the Third Order, which [Second and Third Orders] our most blessed father Saint Francis is known to have founded [besides the Friars Minor, the First Order of men]. The second case is: to absolve from the bond of excommunication those who, because of their contumacious disobedience, I should happen to excommunicate by word or in writing. Beyond that, you can depute these my powers and authority, either in whole or in part, either to one or to many, as often as you deem it fitting or consider it proper to entrust these to them, and once entrusted to recall them at your will.

And because you will for a long time endure such great hardships and continuous vigils and cares in carrying out and executing such a great commission and trust, do not let them weaken or exhaust your spirit, but rather find it relaxed and every day more renewed and more completely and fully availing itself of merit. By virtue of the Holy Spirit, and with greater emphasis under obedience, I enjoin you to exercise faithfully and diligently the aforesaid office of pastoral commission and trust, and to carry it out according to the grace which God has given you, and which He will henceforth give and amplify.

Go, therefore, my much beloved sons, with the blessing of your father, to carry out what I have commanded you; and armed with the shield of faith and with the breastplate of justice, with the blade of the spirit of salvation, with the helmet and lance of perseverance, struggle with the ancient serpent which seeks and hastens to lord himself over, and gain the victory over, the souls redeemed with the most precious Blood of Christ. And win them for that Christ in such a manner that among all Catholics an increase of faith, hope, and love may result; and to the perfidious infidels a road may be opened for them and pointed out; and the madness of heretical evil may fall apart and come to nothing; and the foolishness of the gentiles may be made manifest to them, and the light of the Catholic faith may shine forth in their hearts. And you shall receive the eternal kingdom.

Fare ye well, remain with Christ Jesus, and pray for me.

Given in the friary of Santa María de los Angeles on October 30th of the year 1523. Under my signature and with the major seal of my office. Fr. Francisco Angelorum, minister general and servant.

9

Francisco de Vitoria "On the Evangelization of Unbelievers," Salamanca, Spain

(1534–35)

The succession of bulls (proclamations) issued by Pope Alexander VI in 1493 grandly, if vaguely, ceded to Ferdinand and Isabella of Spain the right to occupy "such islands and lands . . . as you have discovered or are about to discover." And the Treaty of Tordesillas between the monarchs of Spain and Portugal in the following year, once again adjudicated by the pope, effectively granted the two Iberian neighbors rights over territories (and peoples) then mostly unknown to them. This late fifteenth-century "papal donation" would prove invaluable to the Spanish monarchs in particular, and to a succession of thinkers who pondered the legitimacy of Spain's power over others for centuries to come.

Such claims to potential bounty attracted many challengers beyond the Portuguese. Vocal protests against Spanish territorial claims issued from awakening rivals in western Europe, especially France and England; and the increase in piracy and the flouting of Spanish economic and territorial monopolies in the Indies were more practical expressions of international rivalry (later effects in the Viceroyalty of Peru are discussed in Selection 28). Yet some of the most rigorous intellectual scrutiny of Spain's emerging American claims

and their papal legitimation came from within. While reports of the immensity and seemingly limitless potential offered in "the kingdoms of the Indies" were reaching Emperor Charles V, theologians and jurists were pondering the moment in the cloisters and lecture halls of Spain's most hallowed university at Salamanca.

The foremost of this group was Francisco de Vitoria (ca. 1485–1546), who delivered the lecture upon which this reading is based. He is thought to have entered the Dominican Order in about 1506 in Burgos in northern Spain. He pursued courses in the arts and theology in Paris, where he also taught and received his doctorate in theology in 1522, having studied especially under the Flemish Dominican Peter Crockaert (d. 1514). Professors of theology in the early sixteenth century customarily lectured on portions of a standard medieval text for theological studies, the *Sentences* (*Sententiae*) by Peter Lombard, an early twelfth-century theologian at Paris. But, following a gradual shift that had originated in Germany and spread to Paris, Crockaert in 1509 also began lecturing on the *Summary of Theology* (*Summa Theologica*) by Saint Thomas Aquinas (ca. 1225–1274). In Salamanca, Vitoria would later do the same for large parts of his courses, as would others in Spain and Italy. Together, Crockaert and Vitoria coedited an edition of the *Summa* (Paris, 1512), and were influential players in an intellectual movement often called "Second Thomism"—the systematic attempt by a number of sixteenth-century thinkers, many of them Dominicans, to revive the study of, and extend, the conclusions of Saint Thomas Aquinas (as well as the spirit of his thirteenth-century synthesis of the writings of the ancient Greek philosopher Aristotle and Christianity) and to relate them to the problems and needs of their own day.

Vitoria's thinking developed in Paris and in the years of his first academic appointments in Spain. From Paris, he became professor of theology at Valladolid in 1523, before being elected as Prime Professor of Theology at the University of Salamanca in 1526, a position he held until his death twenty years later. Vitoria, along with a number of his students (Domingo de Soto [1494–1560], the Dominican theologian who would become confessor to Charles V and a delegate at the Council of Trent, was perhaps the most famous) and several other later theologians and jurists (notably, Francisco Suárez [1548–1617], the Jesuit theologian and author of a widely read treatise on natural law) are often dubbed the "School of Salamanca" by historians. They did not work and write at precisely the same time, nor were they as uniform in their thinking as the notion of a "school of thought" implies. Yet, generally speaking, Vitoria's students and other later commentators carried on much of the work that he had begun, not least in the further examination of the foundations of Spanish rule in America.

Vitoria never traveled to America, but the place pressed in on him as an intellectual challenge with dramatic practical repercussions— arguably, one of the most significant issues that a contemporary theologian could face. He lived in and contributed to an era in which the Spanish Crown and an array of advisers and experts in theology and jurisprudence started to think over the ramifications of having come upon, assumed control of, and begun to colonize the Indies. From his study in Paris, the young Vitoria must have learned of, and perhaps even followed, the great meeting of theologians and jurists held in Burgos in 1512–13, which discussed the legitimacy of Spanish dominion in the Indies and the treatment of indigenous populations and which also drafted the Laws of Burgos. These were issues to which he would return as a teacher.

Vitoria's attitude to Spanish rule in America has often been treated superficially and rather romantically by students eager to find in him an internal critic of Spain's or the Roman Catholic Church's pretensions and actions—a professorial version of the slightly younger Dominican, Bartolomé de las Casas, who would campaign so strongly against Spanish maltreatment of the Indians and the *encomienda* regime [a grant of labor and tribute rights from the Crown to a Spanish individual over specified indigenous groups]. But Vitoria, in the words of the Jesuit José de Acosta, who will be met later in this book (Selection 19), preferred to argue as a "moderate lawyer." Vitoria was a brave thinker who decried false claims and abuses of power, but he wove these positions into larger, complex arguments that were not designed to undermine Spanish imperialism. His significant and often critical engagements with Spain's early modern deeds and predicaments profit from being seen within a tradition of what Anthony Pagden calls, in his introduction to Vitoria's work, the "ritual legitimation which the kings of Castile had, since the Middle Ages, regularly enacted when confronted by uncertain moral issues." By establishing that peoples who did not share the Spaniards' belief and value systems could not automatically either be called enemies or be dispossessed of their property and territory, Vitoria and the thinkers whom he influenced spoke directly to the engine of Spanish expansion even if they did not cause it to change much. From Salamanca, the professor of theology thought and commented and provoked, but as part of the process by which the Castilian Crown secured its own authority.

For Vitoria, nothing in the world—no text, no argument, no current event—was unconnected to the restless interpretation and reinterpretation of the social, moral, and political principles of Saint Thomas. These foundations led Vitoria and others to lay the groundwork for a system of thought that may best be described as Spanish Christian universalism. This system of thought was urged forward by the circumstances that Vitoria saw around him; the consolidation of rule by the Spanish Crown in Iberia and America meant that he was arguing for an ethics of Empire.

In doing so, of course, Vitoria and other Thomists stepped into an intellectual and moral minefield in which a number of positions had already been staked out. Among these, the Thomists saw serious errors in the views of humanists (classical scholars) such as Juan Ginés de Sepúlveda (1490–1573), who had justified Spanish domination of native American peoples because he found them to be inferior human beings, living crudely and with no knowledge of Christianity. In terms borrowed from Aristotle's *Politics,* Amerindians were "slaves by nature (*natura servus*)" and might be treated accordingly by a civilized people such as the Spanish. In contrast, he explored the moral foundations for such political rights. Drawing on Saint Thomas's vision of an entire universe governed by a hierarchy of laws, Vitoria visualized a universal (or international) human society in the world into which any number of independent states might fit and foster relationships. In the interests of this universal society made possible by Vitoria's Thomism, a systematic set of laws and principles—an ethical framework—might be discerned which both pleased God and respected the "common good," that is, the rights of all concerned.

On these subjects and others, Vitoria became known not for what he wrote, but for what he said in his lectures. He published nothing in his lifetime, allegedly remarking that his students already had more than enough to read. But his lectures on the *Summary of Theology* and Lombard's *Sentences* were assiduously copied and distributed by a number of his students. The selection that follows is an extract taken from notes made by an anonymous student. (According to

accepted practices as well as Salamancan university statutes for which Vitoria and his Parisian training were partly responsible, contemporary lecturers were required to speak slowly and clearly so that this process of dictation and copying could take place.) Thus, many of Vitoria's ideas reached a wider audience indirectly—often channeled, as Pagden observes, into his students' published works.

Some of Vitoria's conclusions about Spain in America struck at the issue of the pope's authority in matters of politics and territorial claims. Vitoria challenged the authority of the Alexandrine donations to the Spanish monarchs, arguing that the papacy could not automatically exercise rights over non-Christian peoples and the lands over which they rightfully ruled. Based on what was known of the indigenous societies in America by the mid-1530s, Vitoria asserted, there existed no legitimate grounds for pretending that these territories were vacant, essentially unoccupied or even ill used (as, later, English and, to a lesser extent, French thinkers would argue). Vitoria is said to have been dismayed by news of the circumstances surrounding the execution of the Inka Atahuallpa in Peru. On the evidence he had seen, this was a fresh example of illegitimate Spanish action. (Concern with the justice of such acts continued, as Figure 39 [Selection 53] from the late eighteenth century attests.) More generally and just as memorably, Vitoria pointed out the absurdity of a common claim in his day, namely, that the Spaniards gained property rights over American territories because they had been the first to "discover" them. He maintained that discovery "of itself . . . provides no support for possession of these lands, any more than it would if they had discovered us."

As already mentioned, the Thomist understanding of law as divided into a hierarchy of categories underpinned Vitoria's views and arguments. The first was a composite of two: eternal and divine law. It came from God Himself and encompassed all others. Almost as fundamental for Vitoria was the law of nature or "natural law," defined by Aquinas as a set of first principles (*prima praecepta*) granted by God and understood by all "rational creatures," or, as Suárez later put it, "written in our minds (*scriptam in mentibus*)" by God. Vitoria's (and Aquinas's) notion of a natural law upon which all peoples were in agreement grew from a number of assumptions about the essential truth of Judeo-Christianity. The idea of a natural law assumed the universal applicability of the Christian Gospels and accepted the Ten Commandments —especially the fundamental injunction, "Do unto others as you would have them do unto you"—as a "natural" code of conduct and moral framework for all human beings (see also their later importance for Juan Francisco Domínguez in Selection 49). Compilations of Roman law, and the social and political conventions of western Europe in his day, were viewed by Vitoria as accretions upon these "natural" foundations, as Pagden puts it— "the inescapable conclusions of the rational mind drawing upon certain self-evident first principles." These accretions were the third kind of law, human (or sometimes "positive") law, those laws conceived and enacted by human beings; they might vary between the nations and communities of the world, and they were only binding if they grew out of and confirmed the supposedly common principles of natural law. Finally, there was a "law of nations" poised somewhere between natural and human law. The idea of a law of nations is what made the conception of a universal human society possible. Because observance of the law of nature was thought to be required of all people, it could be assumed further that a certain body of universal human laws might be found and respected in any conceivable place or time, even amid the alien practices of non-Christians.

The last point about the legitimacy of certain shared laws and ways in all places, combined with Vitoria's further elaboration of seven "unjust titles" or claims that Spain could not in good faith advance to justify conquests in the Americas, seem, at a glance, to challenge seriously Spain's right to rule indigenous American peoples who possessed their own laws and codes of conduct. But Vitoria did not leave the argument there. He was bound by the rigor of his method (if nothing else) also to investigate a set of "just titles"—arguments drawn from this assumed law of nations by which the Spanish Crown might gather legitimate claims to political and spiritual jurisdiction in America. Seen from the points of view of indigenous societies confronting the Spanish presence, here were the ways in which they might be judged by a Dominican theologian in Salamanca to have forfeited their right to their own dominion.

Vitoria accepted the existence of a natural right of society and communication which all people were bound to respect. Thus, if native American peoples resisted or hindered the Spaniards' desire to "travel" in their territories, the Indians could be judged as violators of an inalienable human right. War might legitimately be made on them. Vitoria asserted that there existed a similarly inalienable right to trade; a right to protect innocents from rulers judged to be tyrants; even a right to protect other peoples from themselves (that is, from the crimes they were alleged to be committing against nature, especially cannibalism and human sacrifice); and a right to preach the Gospel unhindered in any land.

"On the Evangelization of Unbelievers" sits deep within Vitoria's exploration of these unjust and just Spanish claims to dominion (*dominium*) and activity in America. He considers a key question posed by Aquinas (*Summa Theologica* II-II.10.8) and applies it to his time, asking whether a Christian prince (such as Charles V) has the right to convert non-Christians to the faith "by violence and the sword." This "right," along with the other rights or "just titles" described above, pertain to Spain's situation in the Indies, and Vitoria even makes this connection explicit on occasion. Yet he was also thinking of other matters, of fronts on which there were other kinds of unbelievers with whom Spain and the Catholic Church were simultaneously entwined and preoccupied because of the Christian imperatives to evangelize all peoples and maintain the faith in those to whom it had been given. The "modern heretics," the Lutherans, were among those people on Vitoria's mind when he spoke of a Catholic missionary's right to travel and preach, and when he argued that "no one can be good unless he is Christian and accepts our faith."

More fundamentally, Vitoria divides his lecture in two, treating his problem first among peoples who are subjects of the Crown, and second among those who are not. The examples he raises and to which he returns are instructive. In the first category, Vitoria carries in mind principally Mudéjares (Muslims living under Christian rule) and Moriscos (new converts to Christianity from Islam) in the Spanish kingdoms. He collects these historical and contemporary peoples under one Latin term common in medieval times, *Saraceni*, or Saracens. In the second category are the indigenous peoples of America, his "islanders" (*insulani*) and "barbarians" (*barbari*). Yet, as Vitoria would have been well aware by the late 1530s, the two categories of unbelievers do not remain separate. One might argue about precisely when, but the distinction blurs once certain native peoples in the Indies become consolidated beneath Spanish rule. Like other sixteenth-century churchmen (see Selection 19, for example), Vitoria has both Moriscos and Indians in mind, raising questions and problems that bear directly on the evangelization and colonial conditions of both subject peoples.

Francisco de Vitoria focuses on the role and effects of coercion in matters of religion. He finds religious coercion to be evil and likely to yield results opposite to those intended by the Catholic Church among most unbelievers. "For myself," he emphasizes in discussion of the situation involving Mudéjares and Moriscos, "I have little doubt that more of them could be converted by greater leniency; and they would be likely to remain firmer in the faith." Here and elsewhere in the text, Vitoria's words are loaded as carefully as his target is chosen, and his most potent critical remarks are stated in hypothetical terms. "If, for example, all the Saracens in Spain were to be forcibly converted . . . ," begins one cautionary passage. He lectured in the years of a

generally worsening relationship between Spanish Christian rulers and their Muslim and formerly Muslim minorities: after 1492 there was a succession of contraventions of the capitulation agreement that had ended Muslim rule in Granada, many baptisms were forced, and copies of the Qur'an and other Arabic books deemed religious in content were publicly burned, finally provoking a violent and spreading uprising between 1499 and 1501; in 1502 a decree by the Castilian Crown demanded the expulsion of all Muslims who did not accept baptism and convert to Christianity (almost all chose baptism), and two decades later the same "option" was presented to Muslims in the Kingdom of Aragón; and in 1526, as if in confirmation of the problems which arose from such "conversions," Charles V extended the jurisdiction of the Holy Office of the Inquisition to include Morisco religious offenders in the Kingdom of Granada.

Vitoria was trained as a humanist as well as a theologian and, as always, he treats his problem as multisided. He reflects at some length on the occasions when a Christian prince would be just in his use of force against unbelievers, even in matters of religion. Most notable in this regard is his attitude toward apostasy—a convert's backsliding from Christianity to old errors. Having accepted baptism of one's own will, there was no option but Christianity. Vitoria sees the specter of apostasy in terms of natural law, quoting Saint Thomas: "Whoever accepts the law of Christ can be compelled to keep it." Yet Vitoria has a knack for presenting one side of an argument as indisputable, only to allow his emphasis ultimately to fall the other way. Thus, he lays out the conditions which make different kinds of religious coercion legitimate, yet favors conquest "by faith"—setting a virtuous example and persuading people to abandon their old ways and turn Christian. Similarly, while the smashing of idols and other acts of extirpation of religious error are viewed as legitimate and benevolent actions that assist ignorant or misguided sinners, Vitoria advises care and restraint: "This [idol-smashing] ought not to be done on every occasion, primarily because it may provoke their [the new or prospective converts'] fierce indignation, and destroy any kind feelings toward us which they may happen to have."

Vitoria's words on the evangelization of unbelievers seem designed to summon questions and reflection from his students and contemporaries. What had been the nature of the Moriscos' evangelization to date, and where was that evangelization headed? Was the spiritual enterprise among the Moriscos affected by, or affecting, the ways in which the evangelization of Indians in America was being approached? What was the impact of different evangelization methods on new Christians? And finally, with what, precisely, was the Christian faith becoming associated?

⤳ *Should Unbelievers Be Forcibly Converted?*

§1 Aquinas replies by establishing a preliminary distinction, namely, that the unbelievers in question are *those who have never taken the faith*. These *should not be forcibly converted*; but a second conclusion is that they may be *forcibly restrained from hindering the missionaries of the faith*, and from insulting Christ and Christians; this is clear, because everyone has the right to defend himself and his temporal interests, and therefore also his spiritual interests. And his third conclusion is that those who have received the faith may be forced back to the faith; see the explicit testimonies he adduces.

The first conclusion is the determination of the decretal [an authoritative papal decision on a matter of doctrine or ecclesiastical law] *Maiores* (X.3.42.3) and the canon [a provision of Church law] *De Iudaeis* (*Decretum* D.45.5), on the Jews; and of the decretal *Sicut ait* (X.5.7.8) and the canon *Qui sincera* (*Decretum* D.45.3), on heretics. And this is the common opinion of the doctors on Lombard's *Sentences* [1285] IV.4, of Durandus of Saint-Pourçain [1270/5–1334, Dominican theologian], *ad loc.* 6, and Richard of Middleton [d. ca. 1305, Franciscan, Scholastic theologian at Oxford and Paris], in IV.6.3.

A DOUBT ARISES by what law it is prohibited to forcibly convert unbelievers? To harm another is prohibited by natural law; but to force these people to believe is not to harm them, but to help them; *ergo*. The reply is that it is prohibited in many passages of human law; therefore this is no objection, because positive law cannot forbid anything unless it is prohibited in divine law. I conclude that it is prohibited in divine law.

A doubt then arises as to where this prohibition is to be found? Not in Scripture, because if it was there Saint Thomas would have cited it among his authorities, being always a most careful researcher in this respect. I reply that there are no unequivocal authorities to this effect, but that there are some passages from which it may be inferred, though not clearly, at least by deduction. This is as much to say, it comes not from positive divine law but from natural law; and the arguments for proving it depend on natural reason. But whereas Duns Scotus [ca. 1265–1308, Franciscan theologian and teacher] holds that a convincing argument from reason can be made against the conclusion (in *Sentences* IV.4.9), Durandus of Saint-Pourçain, in the passage cited above, constructs a rational argument for the conclusion. I do not know whether it is valid; judge for yourselves, since it is clear enough. Thomist theologians also advance the following proof for the conclusion: Evil means are not justified even by good ends. But to apply coercion to anyone is evil; therefore, unbelievers cannot lawfully be compelled to believe. This argument, however, perhaps involves a *petitio principii*.

ON THIS BASIS, one could construct an *a posteriori* proof of Saint Thomas's conclusion: namely, that *more harm than good follows from forcible conversion, which is therefore unlawful*:

1. In the first place, forcible conversion would cause great provocation and unrest (*scandulum*) among the heathen. If, for example, all the Saracens [Muslims] in Spain were to be forcibly converted, this would cause unrest in [Muslim] Africa, because the Africans would think that Christianity had always been preached and imposed by force throughout the world; whereas, on the contrary, our strongest argument against them is that they have never conquered any land with their faith, as we have with ours. *Ergo.*

2. The second bad effect is that, instead of the benevolent and proper affection required for belief, forcible conversion would generate immense hate in them, and that in turn would give rise to pretense and hypocrisy. We could never be sure whether or not they truly believed in their hearts; there would be nothing to move them to have faith, only intimidation and threats. Their conversion would be empty and ineffective. Again, as Richard of Middleton says, no one can believe unless he wills; but the will cannot be compelled, *ergo.* Besides, license to compel men in this way would be harmful, because if anyone could forcibly convert men to their own religion, the more powerful would drag many more into following their own evil heresies.

§2 NEVERTHELESS, Duns Scotus, in the passage cited above, holds that the opposing argument is, if not true, at least more probable; that is, that *if precautions are taken to ensure that these evil and undesirable consequences are avoided, a prince may forcibly convert pagans who live in his own kingdom*:

1. His proof begins with the canon *De Iudaeis* (*Decretum* D.45.5), which praises Sisebut, king of the Visigoths in Spain [612–621], for his decree ordering the conversion of all Jews. This edict was later revoked by the Council of Toledo [633–634] (*Concilium IV Toletanum* canon 57), but the words of the canon call Sisebut "most pious prince" and remark that the edict "would not have been revoked were it not for the undesirable consequences." *Ergo,* such a decree is lawful.

2. Consequently, assuming for the sake of argument that such an enactment is properly promulgated and published, all are obliged to believe in Christ, and they commit a sin if they refuse to accept the Christian religion.

3. The prince is empowered to punish and coerce those who commit this sin, just as he is for any other sin; further, by thus coercing them, the prince does not harm them, but benefits them; therefore he can coerce them.

4. "Ignorance makes an act involuntary," as is clear from Aristotle's *Nicomachean Ethics* 1110b 17–24; hence there is no injury (*iniuria*) to our Saracen because he *would* accept Christianity if he knew it was better, but in fact he is ignorant of the faith. Hence his conversion is not involuntary; formally it may be so, but effectively it is voluntary. In the same way, in giving medicine to a patient

who does not know that it is good for him, the doctor does no injury (*iniuria*) to the sick man; the latter takes the medicine without formally wishing to do so, to be sure, but in effect he does so willingly.

5. Again, if someone wished to commit suicide, I should be obliged to prevent him from doing so if I could by confiscating his weapons; I am therefore all the more obliged to prevent him from committing spiritual suicide.

6. Furthermore, the commonwealth has the authority to enact laws not only in civil matters, but also in matters of religion; this is part of natural law. Hence every Christian commonwealth has this power to use forcible conversion; *ergo*, any Christian king or commonwealth may lawfully compel their subjects to accept the Christian faith.

7. Their own priests have the power by natural law to instruct them and enact laws in religious matters, and their subjects are bound to obey them under pain of mortal sin, if the law is good. Hence a Christian prince may also compel his own subjects to accept his faith.

[From all this Gabriel Biel (1410–1495) accepts Scotus's opinion as probable, and goes no further than that (in *Sentences* IV.6).]

BUT ON THE OTHER HAND we must reply to this question by going back to our distinction. Some unbelievers are subjects of Christian princes, such as the Saracens who have settled in Spain; but *others are not subjects.*

I REPLY by asserting, first, that to compel those who are subjects is not intrinsically evil, like perjuring an oath; that is, it is not so evil that it cannot sometimes be a good deed. "It is evil," as Saint Thomas says, "but not so evil that it can never be good"; the proof being that it is not by definition so evil as to involve an inevitable breach of charity toward God or one's neighbor. It is not contrary to God's interest; indeed, it is clearly a great advancement of the Christian religion. Nor is it against our neighbor's interest, since it is to his benefit. The confirmation is that when we say something is "lawful," we are not obliged to prove the assertion until contrary proof is offered that it is harmful, according to the decretals *Sicut noxius* (X.2.23.1, and X.1.12.1). In the question under consideration, forcible conversion is in itself lawful, or at least not unlawful, and I am therefore not bound to prove that it is lawful.

Second, I assert that Christian princes have the authority to compel their subjects to believe; that is, if it be lawful to compel unbelievers. Christian princes may compel their own subjects not only in civil matters but also in religious ones; the commonwealth holds both civil and religious authority over its own subjects by natural law, and the prince has the same authority as the commonwealth over his subjects, be they pagans or not. Therefore, that the prince may not so compel them must be due not to lack of power, but to the expediency or otherwise of the policy.

Third, I agree with Saint Thomas that forcible conversion is evil. This is clear from the proof of the reply to the second argument, in the canon *De Iudaeis* (*Decretum* D.45.5).

Fourth, I assert that even if it is not evil *per se*, it is evil because of the evil consequences which it entrains. The proof that it is evil *per se* is that if faith must be received voluntarily, no one can receive it by coercion. And the undesirable consequences mentioned above need no further comment. They are confirmed by experience; we see that Saracens never become Christians; no, indeed, they are as much Moors as ever they were (*tan moros son agora como antes*).

Fifth, if all the evils and undesirable consequences are tolerable, Scotus's opinion is tenable. And this is what Scotus means when he says "if precautions are taken to ensure that evil and undesirable consequences are avoided." To do so, however, is difficult. Nevertheless, if the consequences can be avoided, it will be lawful to use forcible conversion, as Scotus says. The confirmation is to be found in Saint Thomas, *Summa Theologica* I-II.92.1, where he enquires what is the purpose of civil, that is, royal, power and replies that it is not only to preserve peace and good neighborliness, but also to make the citizens good and happy. But no one can be good unless he is Christian and accepts our faith; *ergo*. This is further confirmed by the fact that, from the standpoint of natural law, a prince or commonwealth is empowered to use coercion on them; hence a Christian prince to whom they are subject (may use coercion to convert them).

Sixth, I affirm that Saint Thomas's reply is more convincing than Scotus's, because he addresses the general question and the most usual circumstances, even though a different consequence may sometimes come about by particular circumstances (*per accidens*). The rule which Scotus sets up against Saint Thomas is, if you like, the exception to Saint Thomas's rule. This is confirmed by the traditional custom of the Church; the primitive Church in the times of Augustine [354–430] and Jerome [ca. 342–420] [see Figures 16 and 17 and their introduction] not only did not use coercion, but even refused to grant immediate acceptance to those catechumens who came to the faith of their own accord, making them wait so that they would later be constant in the faith. This is how it should be done.

TO THE FIRST, concerning Duns Scotus's argument concerning King Sisebut, I reply that the king is praised for his zeal and piety, but not for the deed itself, which indeed earned him a rebuke for breaking the strict prohibition against any forcible baptism of unbelievers. And the text of the canon also adduces the argument that God "hath mercy on whom He will have mercy, and whom He will be hardeneth" (Romans 9:18), for faith is a gift from God. All the same, Sisebut was a most pious king, and was perhaps counselled by his bishops to use force in that way.

TO THE SECOND, even granting that they are obliged to receive the faith, this argument implies only that forcible baptism is lawful, and hence that if there are no undesirable consequences they may be coerced. But this does not contradict Saint Thomas.

TO THE THIRD we may reply in the same way. In addition, I assert that an injustice (*iniuria*) is done them, because their liberty is taken away. If a king were to force someone to take a rich and beautiful woman to wife, even a princess, although he might be obliged to marry her and might even find it hard to make a better match, he would nevertheless be wronged if he was coerced.

TO THE FOURTH, that those who are unwilling through ignorance are not in effect being coerced at all, the reply is that this argument proves only that forcible baptism would be lawful if there were no undesirable consequences; but that is all. In addition, I assert that a wrong is done to them, and that they are indeed acting under compulsion "formally speaking"—just like the man who is compelled to marry a wife who is good, but of whom he himself is invincibly ignorant.

TO THE FIFTH I reply that it remains dangerous to coerce anyone in matters of religion, however advisable it may be in other cases. Therefore the analogy is valid.

TO THE SIXTH I concede the premise entirely; but only so long as no undesirable consequences or other evils ensue.

TO THE SEVENTH I reply that Saracen priests have their authority to coerce subjects because the Saracens themselves have given them the power to teach them in matters of religion. Hence they would commit a sin not merely by refusing to listen to their teaching, but even by not obeying it. In the same way, if the majority of their commonwealth were to accept the Christian faith, the minority who refused to accept it could be compelled to do so by the majority, so long as the faith was sufficiently preached.

THIS CONCLUDES WHAT I HAVE TO SAY about unbelievers who are subjects.

§3 IT MAY BE ASKED, however, regarding the other kind who are not subjects, *whether Christian princes can convert them by violence and the sword, if no scandal or undesirable consequences ensue?* The reply is that they cannot, because the king of Spain has no greater power over them than I do over my fellow citizens; but I cannot compel a fellow citizen to hear Mass; *ergo.*

A DOUBT ARISES whether, given that these unbelievers cannot be compelled to keep the Christian law in this way, *whether they can be compelled to keep the law of nature, which is common to all?* Some reply that they can; that our king can compel these barbarians to keep the law of nature just as I can compel someone not to commit suicide. They prove this by saying that all men profess the law of nature; and, as Saint Thomas puts it, "Whoever accepts the law of Christ can be compelled to keep it."

The reply to this is that there are some sins against nature which are harmful to our neighbors, such as cannibalism or euthanasia of the old and senile, which is practiced in Terra Firma [evidently the American mainlands]; and since the defense of our neighbors is the rightful concern of each of us, even for private persons and even if it involves shedding blood, it is beyond doubt that any Christian prince can compel them not to do these things. By this title alone the emperor is empowered to coerce the Caribbean Indians (*insulani*).

Second, I assert that princes can compel unbelievers who are their temporal subjects to abandon their sins against the commonwealth, because they are subject in temporal matters to their kings. And since the emperor is empowered to make laws for the utility of the commonwealth, if there are any sins against the temporal and human good of the commonwealth, he can compel them to abandon them.

Third, I assert that the faithful cannot compel unbelievers to keep an obvious law of nature, unless it is necessary for the good and peace of the Christian commonwealth, or unless its breach harms a neighbor in the way I have explained. This I think is most certain. Nor do they have any right to act against the infidels solely on the grounds that the latter do not observe the law of nature. If they did have such a right, a Christian king could also compel them to abandon their idols, and that would mean leaving them without any law. That is false; *ergo*.

A DOUBT ARISES whether it is lawful to smash down the idols of these barbarians, once the faith has been preached to them and they have refused to accept it? It seems that it is lawful because it does them no harm or wrong. The reply is that it is not evil *per se* to do so, being against neither the honor of God nor the good of a neighbor, since it does not harm them. But I say that this ought not to be done on every occasion, primarily because it may provoke their fierce indignation, and destroy any kind feelings toward us which they may happen to have. Among peoples where the majority have been converted, however, or where it is to be hoped they may be converted by such actions, it will be quite lawful. I say the same of their temples; they should not be thrown down, because this is an injury (*iniuria*) to their rights, and because even after they are thrown down, they will rebuild them.

§4 A FURTHER DOUBT ARISES *whether unbelievers may at least be indirectly coerced*, for instance, by taxes and levies by which they may be encouraged to become converts to the faith? The compiler of the *Decretales Gregorii IX*, Raymond of Peñafort [ca. 1175–1275, General of the Dominican Order and friend of Aquinas], wrote elsewhere (*Summa de poenitentia*) that this would be laudable if it were customary, but that it ought not to be introduced as a novelty because of the provocation it would cause, which we ought always to avoid for fear of giving "occasion of stumbling," as Paul makes clear in 1 Corinthians 10:23–33 and 2 Corinthians 6:3. Therefore, it would be a good thing only if laws were passed on this matter; and he cites the canon *Non debet* (*Decretum* C.11.3.64). From this I deduce that Raymond's decision was that it ought not to be done.

IN THIS REGARD, it should be noted that "taxes (*tributum*) and levies (*exactio*)" are of two kinds. One kind may justly be imposed on unbelievers even without their being converted to the faith, such as tributes appropriate to the time and place raised at the outbreak of war, which even unbelievers can understand to be just; the proof is that such tributes could be imposed on them even if they were Christians, and may therefore be imposed on them while they are still unbelievers (I am talking, of course, of unbelievers who live in Christian lands and are subjects of Christian princes). Indeed, they may be required to pay tributes from which Christians are exempted, so long as their fiscal burden is moderate and not increased by the fact that Christians are exempted.

Second, I assert that if the tribute is unjust and immoderate, it cannot be demanded of them. From this it follows that the king can justly order the expulsion of the Saracens from our country if they pose a probable threat of subverting the faithful or overturning the homeland. He may legitimately do this because, even if he knows that it may cause them to be converted to the faith, they are not thereby forced to convert. He could not do it, perhaps with the actual intention of using the fear of exile, which affects even the most strong-minded of men, to effect their conversion; but, as long as that intention is absent, he is empowered to use his rights, whatever the consequences. If he cannot exercise direct compulsion over them, he can make a law ordering the exile from his kingdom of anyone who refuses to become a Christian. That this is lawful is proved by the fact that in other matters where compulsion is unlawful, he may employ the same device. For instance, the law states that any Saracen who sleeps with a Christian woman is punishable by death. If one were caught doing so, the king is empowered to put him to death, whether he sticks to his perfidious creed or whether he becomes a Christian; but he also has the power to pardon him from the death penalty if he is willing to become a Christian, even though his conversion would have come about under fear of death. This would be perfectly fair, because the king would be using his rights.

But as for tributes which cannot also be demanded of the faithful, I assert that they cannot be demanded of unbelievers with the intention of making them convert. Unbelievers cannot be deprived of their goods on the grounds of their unbelief, any more than other Christians, because they possess true right of ownership (*dominium rerum*) over their own property. By the same token, it is clear that they cannot be burdened with greater fiscal obligations than are lawful in the case of the faithful. In saying this, I mean that such impositions are unlawful *per se*, that is, in the absence of any additional cause, such as a crime perpetrated by the unbelievers, or some previous pact; because of Saracens, Jews, or other unbelievers who, either through some criminal action of their own or by the law of war, were in a position to be killed or despoiled of their goods, were to be burdened by heavier taxes than the Christian part of the population, this would not be unjust. For example, if the Saracens were to petition for the right to live among us Christians on the agreement that they pay double tribute, no wrong would be done them if we were then to demand such tribute. Therefore, such exactions could justly be levied upon them by our princes for that purpose.

For that purpose, yes; but could they impose heavier taxes on them to force them to convert? This is still in doubt, since we agree that it is not lawful to use fear and violence to convert them. For myself, I have little doubt that more of them could be converted by greater leniency; and they would be likely to remain firmer in the faith. See Saint Thomas's *Opusculum XXI ad ducissam Brabantiae*, where he explains all this: how the prince may impose heavier taxes on them than on Christians, but not excessive ones, and many other useful remarks on the subject.

§5 IT IS ARGUED, nevertheless, that they can be directly compelled, because Saint Thomas says that they can be compelled *for blasphemy*. But all unbelievers blaspheme continually; therefore it is always lawful to compel them, because they hinder our faith with their blasphemies.

The reply is that unbelievers may blaspheme in two ways. The first is if their blasphemies are an injury (*iniuria*) or impediment to Christians, for instance, if they were to send us a letter full of blasphemies. In this case we may set aside any question of faith; we may go to war against them solely on the grounds that they have done us injury (*iniuria*). But if they keep their blasphemies to themselves, we cannot use this alone as grounds for declaring war against them. We are well aware that both Jews and heathens blaspheme the name of Christ among themselves, but we cannot for this reason alone go to war with them.

A DOUBT ARISES whether princes may lawfully coerce them with threats and intimidation? It seems that they can, because Christ forced Paul to believe by casting him to the ground and blinding him (Acts 9:3–9); therefore the same can be done to unbelievers. The reply is that it is not lawful for all of us to do everything which God is permitted to do, because we are not the masters of mankind as Christ is. Hence, Christ could coerce not only Paul, but the whole world, and He could have left this power to the Church; but He did not. Second, I reply that if it were in our power to move hearts, as Christ could, then it would be lawful for us to behave in this way; but He made Paul believe, not by intimidation but by divine inspiration. It is clear from this that masters, contrary to their own belief, do not have the power to put their infidel servants to death, nor to inflict unjust punishments on them. It is lawful, on the other hand, to give preferential treatment to those of their slaves who are Christians, as opposed to those who are not, as Nicolaus de Tudeschis [1386–1445, canon lawyer and archbishop of Palermo] says of the Jews in his commentary on the decretal *Nouit* (X.2.1.13), where he also holds that unbelievers can be compelled to observe the whole of natural law, because they can be restrained from committing homicide, and also from usury, as stated in the decretal *Usurarum* (*Sext* 5.5.1). But it will not always be lawful to compel them in every matter to do with natural law; they cannot be forcibly compelled to abandon polygamy, for example, or other such practices. In fact, Nicolaus de Tudeschis's examples only serve to prove what I have already said, namely, that they can be forced not to upset the commonwealth, and not to harm their Christian neighbors.

A FINAL DOUBT ARISES whether unbelievers who have not themselves received the faith, but whose parents were converts who have since apostatized, can be forcibly baptized? In other words, can someone who is not baptized but whose father was baptized be compelled to accept baptism? The question is raised by Pierre de la Palu [ca. 1270/1280–1342, a Dominican and titular patriarch of Jerusalem] in his commentary on Lombard's *Sentences* IV.4.4. He comes to no firm decision, but seems to be saying that they can be compelled because the Church has the right to enforce baptism on the children of Christians even against their own or their parents' will, and there is no apparent reason why it should have lost this right in the present case; therefore the Church can use compulsion. I believe that in this case they should indeed be compelled. But against this, it would follow that the Christians can compel Saracens any of whose forefathers were baptized. For example, let us suppose for the argument that the present-day Saracens are separated from these forefathers by ten generations; the argument then runs that the Church had the right to baptize the children of their forefather nine generations back, and hence the children of their forefather eight generations back, and so on down to the present generation; *ergo*. In reply, one may say that if it could be established beyond doubt that these Saracens were the distant descendants of Christians, and if they could be forcibly converted without provocation, then it ought to be done. But the Church does not do so, because it cannot be established, and also because of the inevitable unrest which would ensue.

10

Two Woodcuts Accompanying a 1509 German Translation of Amerigo Vespucci's Letter to Pietro Soderini

(1504)

The rights and obligations set down by the Catholic monarchs for Christopher Columbus on the eve of his first voyage into the "Ocean Sea" were specific on matters of trade and political possession, but the document is tellingly vague about the destination of the voyage. One learns only from other sources that Columbus and many of his contemporaries expected outer islands and eventually Asia to appear over the horizon. Greater certainty was not soon in coming. The humanist courtier, Peter Martyr of Anghiera (1457–1526), sifted through the first accounts of the islands and mainlands in the Ocean Sea and wrote cautiously of a "new world"—new, that is, from his own perspective and those of his ancient and medieval predecessors. The lands discovered by the westward voyagers, Martyr informed his readers, appeared not to be part of the continent formed by Africa, Asia, and Europe. And yet if they did turn out to be part of one of these, it would have to be Asia. Martyr's caution in the face of the information he was receiving is instructive. He could conceive of a new world, one outside the bounds of what was known in the old, but he did so

without abandoning an intellectual tradition and worldview that also influenced his seagoing contemporaries. One of these contemporaries was the Genoese, Columbus, and another was Amerigo Vespucci (1454–1512) of Florence.

Vespucci was educated by his uncle, the scholarly Dominican friar Giorgio Antonio Vespucci, who was also a tutor to Pietro Soderini, who would rise to become head of the Florentine republic (1502–1512). It was to Soderini that Vespucci would later address a long letter describing his four voyages to the Indies. Amerigo's route to the sea came through the business of banking. As a young man he became a clerk in the banking house of the powerful Medici family in Florence, and found a patron in Lorenzo di Pier Francesco de Medici, another eventual recipient of his letters on the Indies. In 1492, Medici dispatched Vespucci to supervise business dealings in Seville's port of Cádiz in southern Spain. After his commission for the banking house was completed, Vespucci remained in Cádiz as an independent trader and speculator and thus was in the perfect spot to learn of events transpiring on the Ocean Sea and to get himself involved. He joined an expedition of reconnaissance to the Indies sponsored by King Ferdinand in 1497–98, probably serving as an astronomer or cartographer. Also in the service of Spain, Vespucci returned to the Indies in 1499–1500 as a ship's pilot. He sailed twice more to the Indies, in 1501–02 and 1503–04, as ship's captain in the service of the Portuguese Crown.

Vespucci is most famous for his *Mundus Novus* ("New World"), a Latin translation of a lost original letter to his Medici patron in 1502. It first appeared in Paris in 1503 and was endlessly translated and adapted thereafter. Vespucci's accounts of his explorations of American coastlines made him an instant rival to Columbus, both as an explorer and as an authority on geography. Historians have often credited Vespucci with having recognized that the shores and islands of the Caribbean were not part of a gateway to Asia, as Columbus believed, but lands then unknown to Europeans. However, any such recognition on his part seems to have had little immediate impact, at least in the interested Spanish circles. Of considerably more lasting influence were his descriptions of foreign peoples and lands. Like the information to appear in Columbus's journal, Vespucci's sometimes fantastical observations drew inspiration and details from an array of descriptive models in European classical and medieval literature—Herodotus, the Irish Saint Brendan, the Venetian Marco Polo, and the travels of the fictitious knight Sir John Mandeville, among them—and would themselves find echoes in many later accounts of Indians and America, including the eighteenth-century travel account by Concolorcorvo (see Selection 44). Well into the 1530s, rumors about unknown American regions and their strange inhabitants persisted, despite a steady succession of exploratory and military enterprises.

Vespucci's "Letter to Soderini," written on September 4, 1504, and published in 1505 or 1506 in Florence, excited as much interest as had his previous missive. As before, transla-

tions of the letter into other western European vernacular languages and Latin promptly appeared, sometimes altering the original in order to amplify Vespucci's most fabulous points. And not only the texts were altered in translation and adaptation: the versions were rarely accompanied by the same illustrations. As was also the case with Columbus's earlier descriptions, pictures were left to individual printers and artists. Figures 5 and 6 are the elaborate woodcuts from a 1509 German edition of the "Letter to Soderini" printed by Johannes Grüninger in Strassburg.

The artist who created these images had never been to a Caribbean island or an American coastline, so the woodcuts prompt many questions about the impact of the earliest reports from America on contemporary European minds. What images would be spurred by the mixture of the artist's own notions with Vespucci's words? How would the lands and peoples ostensibly described in the letter be represented? Which depictive norms would prove "naturally" useful and which would have to be invented? And how would one render the first moments of encounter between peoples hitherto unknown to one another? The two images, like the early written account they illustrated, were parts of an atmosphere of mounting speculation and uncertainty about the nature of the Indies and their peoples. They were meant to excite the interest of patrons and general audiences alike. They were meant to fire imagination and ambition.

Projecting from what he had read or heard, it was the artist's task to render peoples and landscape. The written descriptions of Columbus and Vespucci (not to mention later ones by Cortés and others) are purposeful and aimed at further sponsorship: bizarre customs and other deficiencies demanded correction. In his journal, Columbus wrote that the Taíno Indians had nothing he could call religion. On one occasion, he came upon "a beautiful house"; and although he "thought it was a temple" and "made signs to ask if they said prayers in it," the people told him it was not as he guessed. Communication faltered as opportunity beckoned. Once their language is properly learned, wrote Columbus to his sovereigns, returning to his theme in his entry for November 27, 1492, "it will be easy [to convert these people to Christianity], for they have no faith and do not worship idols; Your Majesties will have a city and a fort built here and these lands will be converted."

Vespucci's text, the woodcut artist's principal cue in the images being considered here, often recalls Columbus's absolute statements in allegedly describing Amerindian life. Vespucci admires Caribbean peoples for their physical skills such as running and swimming. But, as Columbus was wont to do, he remarks that they are completely shameless about their nakedness; they have no possessions beyond a few colored feathers and necklaces featuring fishbones and small stones; they have no guiding rhythm to their lives, no order, no trade, nothing to obey; they have no set mealtimes and would rather eat off the ground whenever they please, and they do not seem ever to want to cut their hair; there is no marriage practised among them; they have no justice, not even to discipline their children. This new world emerges as a place of deficiency and "barbaric" customs. Civilization, to a contemporary European reader and viewer, is turned on its head.

Figure 5. Illustration from a German translation of Amerigo Vespucci's letter to Pietro Soderini, Strassburg, 1509.

In the first image (Figure 5) four Indians of both sexes are grouped in the foreground. The man seated in the center, with his head in one hand, is the picture of tedium. His boredom sets the stage. To either side of him, a woman casually dandles her child and a second man tends to his bow. The turn of their heads and the man's gesture with his free hand suggest a domestic chat, but all around this relaxing scene there are surprises. Just behind them, taking a direct prompt from Vespucci's letter, a man shows no inhibition about urinating in public. In his letter describing his first voyage along Caribbean coastlines and beginning up the Atlantic coast of North America, Vespucci remarks that although the Indians were discreet in defecating, they made water wherever and whenever they pleased, even "while standing speaking to us." Farther in the background, in front of some strangely shaped dwellings, a butcher and his mate matter-of-factly chop up human limbs. Faithful to his text, the artist maximizes the shock to his viewer by integrating the startling and peculiar as familiar in the Indians' daily life.

In the portion of the letter describing his third voyage down the Atlantic coast of South America, Vespucci tells of an encounter between a member of his crew and a group of native women who were perhaps Guaraní. The Europeans had come ashore in small boats and were waiting to pick up two crewmen who had gone inland a few days before, seeking knowledge of the land—its riches, spices, and peoples. One young sailor went among the Indians who had come down from a hill, while the other Europeans remained in their boats "to reassure them." According to Vespucci, a group of women surrounded the man, "touching him and gazing at him in wonder." Encircled as he was, the man did not see another woman descend from a hill behind him and raise a club to deliver a blow to his head. The man dropped dead among the women, who dragged him by his feet toward the hill, while the Indian men rushed to the beach firing arrows at the boats. A few gunshots from the Europeans in the boats had little effect beyond frightening the Indians back up the hill, Vespucci laments, and their admiral forbade the crew to mount an attack and avenge the death. The author reports that he and his companions watched in horror as the women cut their victim into bits, "roasting him before our eyes, holding up several pieces toward us and eating them," and leaving few doubts as to the fate of the two other seamen.

Our second image (Figure 6) has been drawn from the description of this incident. The scene is of a beach near a rocky hill. In the right foreground a naked woman is about to club a clothed European from behind. A trio of naked women with long, wild hair seems to welcome and caress the man. The juxtaposition sets established European notions of femininity beside barbarism and brute violence. On the hill behind, a woman embraces a man and looks up at him smiling; another man with his hands clasped in front of his chest gazes calmly to the side. Yet, for the European eye, there are more surprises in store. In addition to the woman with the club in the foreground, within the normality of the group on the hill a person is seen heading into a cave on hands and knees.

For the author, the unfamiliar had to be rendered to excite interest but also to be understandable and convincing. Vespucci, echoing Columbus, asks for evidence of an indigenous religious or moral code of conduct to help him understand. He asks for a parallel between the Indians and familiar non-Christian peoples in Europe's present and past. He asks for things that might be called offerings, sacrifices, or a church. But instead of similitude he turned up differences. "We did not learn that they had any law, nor can they be called Moors or Jews," he writes, "and [they are] worse than pagans: because we did not observe that they offered any sacrifice; nor even had they a house of prayer." The woodcut artist drew from similar cultural wells. His depictions of Vespucci's sylvan landscape populated by naked peoples with long, unkempt hair met what many contemporaries were predisposed to see, borrowing from long-established images of heathen and "wild people."

Figure 6. Illustration from a German translation of Amerigo Vespucci's
letter to Pietro Soderini, Strassburg, 1509.

But what else was conveyed in these woodcuts produced in Germany, where Vespucci's accounts were so often reprinted, adapted, and illustrated? What would the images inspire in their viewers? Wonder? Revulsion? Perhaps fear? Both Columbus's and Vespucci's descriptions of first contact emphasized the Indians' fear. The naked people ran for the hills at the sight of the Europeans and their ships. Vespucci opined that one group of Indians was terrified and rejected gestures of friendliness and peace on seeing the newcomers to be clothed and so different in appearance from themselves. Have the Europeans and Indians reversed roles in the Grüninger woodcuts of 1509? The pictorial new world seems a tempting place in which Europeans might lose not only their lives but also their cultural bearings. Regardless of the inaccuracies and exaggerations in the artist's depictions, to Europeans contemplating these images the Indians appear at home and free to behave in their startling ways. Arguably, it is the Indians and their environment that inspire fear. They are powerful, like the woman's raised club or a rumor of cannibalism. Theirs might be a power poised to threaten degeneration and death as much as to invite domination and desire.

11

Christoph Weiditz's Drawing of an Indian Woman of Mexico

(1529)

In 1528 the conqueror of Tenochtitlan, Hernán Cortés, returned home in order to defend himself before Charles V (both king of Spain and Holy Roman Emperor) against allegations of rebellion while in Mexico. The numerous "treasures" he brought from the lands formerly ruled by the Aztecs included human specimens. Like the letters from Mexico written to Charles V by Cortés, such "treasures" from hitherto unknown civilizations across the seas helped to justify his overstepping of the rules. They also excited imperial support for more ventures in the most alluring "kingdom" yet stumbled upon in the Indies. One sign of the conqueror's rehabilitation in official eyes was an arresting medallion portrait struck by a young German medalist named Christoph Weiditz, for which Cortés almost certainly sat in 1529.

Weiditz, who practiced his craft in Augsburg, had traveled to Spain that year as part of a small group of artists from southern Germany summoned to the roving court of Charles V. In Toledo, Weiditz must have met not only Cortés but also the human "treasures" from Mexico, a number of whom became the subjects of the thirteen drawings of Indians that the German executed. These drawings form one of a number of subgroups

within the body of his 154 sketches of diverse subjects and regional peoples in Spain and the Netherlands in the space of the next three years (his drawing of the Morisco woman and her daughter, Figure 8 in Selection 12, is part of another such subgroup). The bold lines and shading in the drawings may indicate that Weiditz intended them as bases for later woodcuts, yet his *Trachtenbuch* (costume book) of colored drawings remained unpublished until 1927.

Seven of the thirteen drawings of Indians depict men with grayish-brown skin and thick, shoulder-length black hair playing games with stones and a ball, or else juggling and tossing a log with their feet. These active figures wear very little, although jewels set in the skin of their cheeks, foreheads, and lips, single earrings, feathered belts, and anklets are prominent adornments. These Indians performed in Toledo before Charles V and a larger audience that probably included Weiditz. Cortés also sent the jugglers on to Rome in the same year to appear before Pope Clement VII, who was said to have "thanked God that such countries had been discovered in these days." Along with Weiditz, the Indians from Mexico may even have accompanied the court to the Netherlands in 1530–31.

Figure 7. Drawing of an Indian woman of Mexico by Christoph Weiditz, 1529.

Weiditz did not sketch the seven native Mexican men in repose, but rather chose to depict them performing. The inscriptions on the first two—probably written later by a scribe, though perhaps based on Weiditz's own scribblings from the time—stress the curiosity of the games and actions. "These are the Indian people whom Ferdinand Cortez brought to His Imperial Majesty from India and they have played before His Imperial Majesty with wood and ball," the first one announces. And the second, reflecting on a Mediterranean parallel in the street game of *mora*, states that "with their fingers they gamble like the Italians."

Less active, but perhaps even more curious and novel to the artist, was the Indian woman of Figure 7. She is one of six women whom Weiditz portrayed standing alone (several hold "exotic" accoutrements such as a decorated drinking jug, a feather sunshade and colorful parrot, and an elaborate spear and shield). What might her gaze and stance mean? She looks away from the viewer; her demeanor, while not subdued, seems, more than anything, posed. She is isolated from her social context and makes no gesture. Yet is she not as much a displaced "performer" as the ball players and log jugglers? Was this even her clothing, festive or otherwise? She was brought from Mexico and then draped and adorned in order to be seen by an emperor and, after him, by many crowds, among which must have been Christoph Weiditz, who recorded her thus. She stands simply— barefoot, covered by a fine garment of feathers with colored borders, an elegant headdress falling to her left shoulder, and a golden necklace with a red stone at the center at her throat—like a museum piece.

12

Christoph Weiditz's Drawing of a Morisco Woman and Her Daughter at Home

(1529)

Although his many drawings of baggage carts, wagons, and people on horseback suggest that Christoph Weiditz accompanied the imperial court through Castile to Catalonia in 1529, it is not known for certain if the artist from Augsburg ever traveled to the southern kingdom of Granada during his time in Spain. Although the vividness of his set of eleven scenes of Granadine Moriscos (new converts to Christianity from Islam) dancing and working, at home and traveling, might suggest the experience of a keen observer who walked the city streets and countryside and quickly sketched what he saw, one cannot be sure of this experience. Weiditz would have known the contemporary genre of costume books. He may have drawn inspiration and details of Morisco costume and general appearance from existing pictorial sources and perceptions gained from his Spanish Christian hosts.

The German's interest in the Moriscos of Granada, as opposed to the Moriscos living in Valencia, for instance (people virtually in the path of the court in 1529), may have come from their recent conquest by Castilian Christians (1492) and their apparently greater preservation of Muslim traditions. It was not as if the Arabic language and numerous non-Christian customs and practices were not retained by Moriscos in the Kingdom of Aragon, particularly in certain small communities and rural regions, for they certainly were. But by the end of the third decade of the sixteenth century, many other Aragonese Moriscos were highly "Spanish" and "Christian" in comportment and appearance. Moreover, even though a royal decree requiring that Aragonese Moriscos be baptized was not issued until 1526 (twenty-two years after the decree demanding the baptisms of the Moriscos of Castile, with the Granadine population foremost among them), the Aragonese and the Valencian Moriscos were more familiar, albeit marginalized, inhabitants of a land subsumed beneath Spanish Christian overlordship almost three centuries before. (Valencia was taken by James I of Aragon, "the Conqueror," in 1238.) For the early sixteenth-century traveler in the Spanish kingdoms, the concentrations of more northerly Moriscos would not have possessed the lure and reputation of the peoples of Granada.

Somewhat like the Mexican Indians drawn by Weiditz in the same year, the Moriscos of Granada would have offered a vision of a recently conquered people, still "exotic" in

costume and custom. In the drawing reproduced in Figure 8, the curiosity of the home
dress of a Morisco woman and her daughter is
emphasized. "In this manner the Morisco
women [of Granada] dress in their house with
their children," the inscription reads. Weiditz's
choice of the Granadine subjects seems to
affirm a belief that only from Granada—or at
least from the sources that he consulted or
copied—might expressions of such difference
be gained and considered.

By the end of the third decade of the sixteenth century, when Weiditz was in Spain,
the newly converted of Granada were increasingly being perceived by Spanish authorities
as the stubborn remnants of the last Muslim
stronghold in western Europe. Only three
years before, after a crucial *junta* in Granada
presided over by Charles V himself, these
Moriscos were declared subject to the authority of the Holy Office of the Inquisition, the
ultimate policing body of Catholic Christian
orthodoxy. Although a tradition of negotiated
delays in the implementation of full-blown
inquisitorial persecution of Moriscos would
continue even after the pronouncements of
this *junta* in 1526, the decision is an early sign
of the demands on the newly converted from
Islam that would only harden and be reiterated as the sixteenth century proceeded.
Morisco practices involving the preparation of
food, regular bathing, and dress were only the
most notorious among customs once permitted by Spanish Christian officialdom, but
increasingly found intolerable. Certain Moriscos
argued eloquently that the conversions to
Christianity of many of their number were
genuine, and that their surviving manners of
dress, Arabic names, and numerous other
daily practices were now regional expressions
divested of religious, and certainly of sedi-
tious, meaning. Nonetheless, a growing share
of Morisco culture was seen as suspect, part of
what was responsible for the perceived nonas-
similation of the Morisco population and all
the danger it could seem to represent for Old
Christians at a time when a Muslim menace
was perceived from without (from Turks as
well as Barbary pirates) as well as from within.

The official demands made on Spanish
Morisco society (and not just in the Kingdom
of Granada) are comparable to what was
experienced by many indigenous societies in
the Americas in early colonial times. The jos-
tle of evangelization strategies, debates over
the appropriate jurisdictions of the Holy
Office, and the constant interplay between
optimism and pessimism in the evangelization
settings of America are of a piece with developments among the Moriscos before their expulsion (mostly to North Africa) between 1609
and 1614.

Weiditz's image of a Morisca and her
daughter at home invites such a comparison,
especially with respect to dress and to the representation of cultural and religious "others."
Granadine Morisco clothing underwent
changes comparable to transformations seen
in Amerindian societies in the core areas of
Spanish-Indian interaction in contemporary
Spanish America. Generally speaking, the
subject populations' dress altered more in the
cities than in the countryside, and men took
on more Hispanicized garments (and economic pursuits) than women. In the case of
Granada, Moriscas who walked in the streets
had been required to abandon their traditional
covering of the face. But they had substituted
a wide mantle, like the one worn by the girl in
this picture, which was nearly as effective a
concealment. At home, of course, modest
covering was of less importance, as Weiditz's
drawing conveys.

Four of Weiditz's depictions of Moriscos
could be described as lacking social context,
in the manner of the Indian woman of Figure 7
(Selection 11). The others, however, capture
people engaged in real activities: sweeping a
floor, spinning, carrying bread, dancing in a
group accompanied by musicians, traveling
with their families through the countryside
with a horse, or simply walking and gesturing.

The woman in Figure 8 is accompanied
by a female child (one assumes it is her
daughter), whom she is either pointing out (or
perhaps disciplining) while pulling her closer
by the wrist. As we have noted, it is unclear
whether Weiditz was ever in Granada, let

Figure 8. Drawing of a Morisco woman and her daughter at home
by Christoph Weiditz, 1529.

alone taken to the home of a Morisco family. Yet it is a credit to the artist's mind and hand that in looking at this drawing one can imagine a domestic situation intruded upon by a foreign visitor expressing an interest in family members and their clothing. The dress is elaborate, suggesting perhaps noble lineage or considerable wealth. One interpretation of the woman's gesture would tell of her pride in her daughter's fine costume (although one cannot see its colors in our reproduction): a green, gold, and white striped mantle with golden edges, worn over a red-and-silver-embossed dress lined in blue, with gold buttons, along with purple stockings.

If Weiditz himself did not visit the home of a Morisco family in Granada, then the Spanish sources from which he drew shared with him an intimate knowledge of (or at least the appearance of) some of Granada's Moriscos. Does the familiarity in the gestures and action of the Morisco mother and child lessen the exoticism of the exotic, creating pictorial space for subjects who are better known to the Spanish Christian than indigenous peoples of the Americas and, thus, more than museum pieces? What are the ramifications of seeming to be better known to one's conqueror and, alternatively, to being hitherto unknown in all but reinterpreted legend? Christoph Weiditz's drawing of the Moriscas challenges the viewer to reinvestigate the drawing of the Mexican woman—the one who had been brought to Europe—by the same artist in the same year, and to think over what the study of Spanish Christians, Moriscos, and Indians might contribute to the interlocking history of the Spanish world.

PART II

The Americas as New Worlds for All?

13

The Jesuit and the Bishop, Bahia, Brazil
(1552–53)

When the first small band of six Jesuits went ashore at Salvador on the Bay of All Saints in 1549, in the company of the first Portuguese governor to Brazil, not only was a more centralized government for the colony about to be established but serious missionary work to convert coastal Indians was also about to begin. The Society of Jesus had been founded only in 1540 by the Spaniard, Ignatius de Loyola, and was dedicated not to a cloistered life of prayer but to doing good works in the world. During much of the more than two centuries that they remained the dominant religious order in Brazil until their expulsion in 1759, they enjoyed dominion over the Indians to bring them to Christian beliefs and habits. In 1549 these Jesuits, who were to establish their *colégio*, or school, at Bahia, came not only to cure Portuguese souls but with even greater passion to convert heathen ones. After nearly half a century the king had taken up the royal pledge to convert Brazilian Indians, always the announced reason for colonization. Appropriately, governor and priests arrived in the same fleet together with judicial, treasury, and military officials as well as settlers who ranked from nobles to artisans to exiles—more than 1,000 immigrants in all who were to construct this new seat of royal government and religiosity.

Jesuits in Bahia soon learned the truth of the statement by Antonio de Nebrija, the Castilian grammarian, to his queen in 1492 that "Language [is] the instrument of empire," although in suiting the words to their own circumstances they would have substituted "conversion" for "empire." While the ordained priests among the Jesuits had authority to administer the sacraments and were to perform countless marriages in the absence of a parish priest (although only a bishop could bless the holy oils needed for baptism and extreme unction), the Society limited themselves to the particular mission of instructing children and the "unlettered" in Christianity and of hearing confessions. These Jesuits, guided by Padre Manoel da Nóbrega, who acted as their Brazilian provincial, quickly appreciated how profoundly their ministries relied on speech both for the conversion of souls and for the transformations of native customs.

But whose speech—the Portuguese spoken by Jesuits or the Tupi language of the Tupinambá? Following their practice in India, the Jesuits proceeded in their usual way: they established a school to introduce children, both colonist and native, to Christianity, and prominently among native children were the sons of headmen. They hoped that these boys would influence their parents and others in the tribe. The children were instructed in Portuguese grammar and reading as fundamentals in teaching them the questions and answers of the Catholic catechism. After only a month in Bahia, Nóbrega wrote the provincial in Lisbon about how the Indians "showed great desire" to learn and how he and his colleagues were teaching the prayers and instructing them in the faith to prepare them for baptism. One headman, already a baptized Christian, helped the boys with their lessons, promised to make Christians of his brothers and wives, and with great affection brought the Jesuits fish. Then came the hitch. They say they want to stay with us, Nóbrega wrote, and they learn quickly, but they are distracted by the need to go to war against their enemies, although already some refrain from killing and eating human flesh.

His response reversed the usual thrust of any colonial transfer of culture. Convinced that they could bring warring eaters of human flesh to Christ by words and persuasion, Nóbrega told the provincial, "We work to learn their language." "We have determined," he continued, "to go and live in the villages, where we will be more settled and secure, and learn the language with them, instructing them little by little." Although he thought the Indians crude and their vocabulary narrow, he nonetheless recognized that to be effective in bringing them God's word, he and his colleagues must learn their language. A few years later, Padre José de Anchieta had drafted, within six months of his arrival in Bahia, a grammar of the Tupi language written in Latin characters. Nóbrega admitted that he himself learned slowly, and in this Padre João de Azpilcueta Navarro "has the advantage over all of us." In time, Nóbrega arranged for nine orphaned boys to come from Portugal to help teach Portuguese and Christian habits to native boys, their similarities in age assuring a natural sympathy and rapport. The success of the experiment pleased him.

The fathers became more dramatic in their strategies for conversion by incorporating song and musical instruments into their teaching.

By the rules of their Society, insisted upon by their founder, Jesuits initially did not sing Masses, recite their offices in choir, or keep musical instruments in their houses. Music if performed well required precious time away from their true apostolic labors of caring for the spiritual (and bodily) needs of the poor. Loyola saw music as an impediment, but not so the missionary fathers who labored to direct indigenous passions toward Christ. Jesuits in India and Europe had already discovered the delight that children took in singing prayers and even parts of the catechism to native tunes. In Bahia, Tupinambá children sang Christian hymns in Tupi to Tupi rhythms accompanied by native drums, flutes, trumpets, or bagpipes, while at other times the Jesuits gained listeners by imitating native singing and playing, even by dancing with them. Indians asked to sing in Jesuit processions. Orphan boys from the Lisbon school, where religious singing was much practiced, attracted Indian boys with their melodious voices. Better to teach native children to sing Christian prayers in their own language, Nóbrega argued, than to allow their own "lascivious and diabolical songs."

The Jesuit mission was not only to teach but also to confess, and if music avoided the obstacles of having no shared language, then language remained essential for confession. Nóbrega acknowledged that few priests knew Tupi well (only Padre Navarro confessed Indians in Tupi), but through confession souls were saved. To deprive native people of the grace of the sacrament and entrance into Heaven because they did not know Portuguese was, for Nóbrega, a denial of their salvation and the Jesuits' cherished mission. Instead, the Jesuits began to confess native penitents through interpreters, using native boys, whom they had trained at the school and who spoke both Tupi and Portuguese, to act as intermediaries. Nóbrega acknowledged a concern to choose boys who could be trusted to keep the secrets of the confessional, but the practice nevertheless later drew him into bitter conflict with the bishop.

From his earliest days in Bahia, Nóbrega insisted that only a bishop could correct the flagrantly sinful habits indulged in by the local Portuguese: they took their Indian slave women as concubines or had many women, and their children lived among the heathens according to their customs. Further, he deplored colonists' unjustified attacks on Indians to take them as slaves—a reason, he said, for gathering Indians into *aldeias*, or villages, under the Jesuits' watchful protection. The clergy themselves set a bad example and publicly approved the settlers' corrupting ways. He heard "ugly things" about them. One priest, Nóbrega wrote his provincial, had provoked an Indian to kill and eat his enemy.

When finally the pope created a diocese at Bahia and the king sent the first bishop, Pedro Fernandes Sardinha, who arrived in late June 1552, Nóbrega welcomed him to the Jesuits' own meager lodgings until better housing could be arranged. He found his new bishop "very kind and dedicated" and felt sure he would act for the good of the Society. Approvingly, Nóbrega reported that the bishop preached with "much edification" and "won the hearts of his flock." They received him well, he wrote, and since his first sermon, residents had begun to cover up their Indian slaves and give them clothes; they now came to church dressed, such was the bishop's authority and majesty.

Nóbrega's enthusiasm rapidly faded, however. No sooner had the bishop arrived than he raised doubts about how the Jesuits conducted their work. He opposed confession by interpreter as something "new and not used in Christianity"; he objected to allowing heathens into the churches to hear Mass together with Christians and thought an old law keeping them outside should be observed. Singing Christian songs to native tunes and instruments he viewed as harmful to the faith. He differed with the Jesuits, who allowed naked Indians into the churches for Mass and instruction and did not deny them baptism because of their nudity, and finally he challenged the Jesuit prohibition against war against the Indians and their enslavement.

Nóbrega might also have mentioned the bishop's disgust at native haircuts, which boys at the school copied: the shaved crown seemed to him a mockery of a priest's tonsure. In brief, the bishop aimed to halt the Jesuits in their efforts to gain native confidence as the way gradually to convert them and to separate them from their own customs.

The "discipline" Nóbrega writes about in the following letter was a contentious issue among early Jesuits and disapproved by members of the secular Church who tried to distance themselves from medieval practices. Loyola, believing he had damaged his health through severe fasting and self-flagellation, warned others against his mistaken piety: they needed their physical strength for their ministries. The Society imposed no obligatory fasts beyond those prescribed by the Church for all members. But Simão Rodrigues, the provincial in Lisbon to whom both Nóbrega and the bishop addressed their letters, persisted in such practices and encouraged them in others, provoking Loyola to instruct the Jesuits studying under him to moderate their penance. By late 1552 he had recalled Rodrigues to Rome. Although Nóbrega does not say here explicitly whether their discipline required bodily penance or only an examination of conscience in preparation for confession, evidence from other Brazilian Jesuits suggests that both the religious and their Indian converts engaged in mortification of the flesh. Padre Navarro, either in obedience or with his superior's permission, conducted his publicly in the town square.

By late August 1552, Nóbrega thought it prudent to seek advice from Rodrigues, still his provincial in Lisbon. With the Jesuit program stalled and a confrontation in the offing—something Nóbrega refused to permit himself but which the bishop aggravated by insisting he should be obeyed as much because he was bishop as because of his overseas experience—Nóbrega left Bahia for the south of Brazil where he busied himself with extending the Society's work in a more favorable setting. But Nóbrega could not remain away from the Jesuits' center of work in Bahia for long, yet neither had his absence eased the enmity he and the bishop felt for each other. After returning in 1553 and pouring energy into the school, Nóbrega was gratified to see it get ahead. He had decided to wait out the bishop.

The waiting ended shockingly. In 1556 the king summoned the bishop to Portugal, whether permanently or only to account for himself is not known. Complaints from all quarters had accumulated. The bishop's ship sailed from the Bay of All Saints on June 16 with a large party, more than one hundred of Bahia's "principal people," in Nóbrega's description, sailing north along the coast toward Pernambuco where it was shipwrecked and sank in a storm. The survivors took refuge in an inlet only to face their deaths at the hands of Caeté Indians who killed and ate all except three of them: two Indians from Bahia and a Portuguese who spoke the heathens' language.

Later reflecting on the bishop's tenure in a letter to the former governor-general in 1559, Nóbrega judged the bishop zealous in reforming Christian habits, but for the "heathens and their salvation he cared little. . . . By their crude, uncivilized ways, they seemed to him incapable of all instruction," a position Nóbrega found inimical.

The three letters in this selection, one written in 1552 by Father Nóbrega and two by the bishop in 1552 and 1553 as they each came to recognize and defend their differences, offer a glimpse into the complexities of cultural transfer. Without even beginning to ask what the Tupinambá took from the Jesuits, or how the Jesuits were changed by the Tupinambá, the letters caution against seeing Portuguese culture, or even those threads of it we are calling religious culture, as all of a piece. Irreconcilable differences divided them not only over what was to be taught but, more profoundly, to whom and how.

∾ Bahia, July 1552, Padre Manoel da Nóbrega to Padre Simão Rodrigues, Jesuit Provincial, Lisbon

Pax Christi. After the arrival of the Bishop some things happened of which I will give a brief account to Your Reverence, so that you will know what happens and commend everything to Our Lord and always warn us of ways in which we might err. It is little more than a month since the Bishop came and already I am afraid.

In this house there are boys from this land, trained by us, whom we [use as interpreters] to confess some of the people from here who do not understand our speech, nor we theirs, such as Indian slaves of the whites, those newly converted, and the wife and children of Diogo Alvares, Caramarú [the Indian name taken by Alvares when he chose to live among the Indians in Bahia], who do not know our speech. Experience shows us there is much gain and no harm done to the secrecy of confession. I introduced the practice only after finding it written about and being the common opinion as [Padre João de Azpilcueta] Navarro explained, quoting [Cardinal] Caetano and others.

The Bishop greatly opposes us in this, saying that it is something new and that the Church of God is not accustomed to it. I concluded with him that he would write you there [in Portugal], and that we would follow your decision. This is something very beneficial and of great importance in this land where there are not many priests who know the language well, and this seems a great means of saving the souls of those who perhaps do not have perfect contrition for forgiveness and penance but who, through the virtue of the sacrament, make an act of contrition. To deprive them of the grace of the sacrament because they do not know the language, and entrance into Heaven for not having sufficient contrition—this and other matters which you there know well, ought to be looked at closely. Something written about by so many doctors [of canon law] does not seem to me new, although one would not do it casually without looking things over. Send us the decision of the scholars, because we dare not but obey the Bishop.

I thought that, with the coming of the Bishop, we would be quieted with a decision about the Indians taken slaves by assault and about those who sell their relatives, but now we are in great confusion and we still await a reply from doctor [Maretim de Azpilcueta] Navarro [uncle of Padre Navarro, one of the five priests who accompanied Nóbrega from Portugal to Bahia in 1549; Nóbrega studied canon law with the uncle at the University of Coimbra], leaving us in the same doubt.

In this *casa dos meninos de Jesus*, or house of the children of Jesus, there is discipline on many Fridays of the year, particularly during Lent, Advent, and from Corpus Christi until the Assumption of Our Lady. It stirs much devotion among the people. Many men discipline themselves as does everybody in this house: priests, brothers, boys. Only men come to it, and no one [outside the house] knows when they discipline themselves. It did not appear a good thing to the Bishop. In his first sermons he strongly condemned public acts of penance, by which all the city understood him to mean the disciplining, without considering that for public persons, as we of the Society are, their acts must be public and all the more so for not being performed in the town squares. He creates division among the people; some say good, others no.

In these parts, the greatest trouble we have is not being able to save those who live in concubinage with their Indian slave women, with whom they have children, because even to separate them is a great success; to confess and absolve them, they are not capable of this. They await women from Portugal with whom to marry. They are scandalized by our not absolving them, telling us of Our Lord's great mercy which they know better than I.

In all the Bishop's sermons which I have heard, he found no other sins to consider reprehensible in this land, nor anything else to say except the same arguments and words that those who live in concubinage preach at us. This only affirms the men in their bad habits and has caused contempt for the Society. I said so to the Bishop in his chamber as humbly as I could (although hypocritically), alerting him to these things and that they do this place no good. He was much taken aback, for which I was very sad. It was good for me to know his art better and join it to my good intentions. If he gives me nothing, it will be the lesser evil.

The [Indian] slaves of this city had Mass and prayer in this our house on Sundays, and doctrinal instruction in the afternoon: it was very fruitful. Since the Bishop came, he has dispensed with it. He ordered instruction each day by António Juzarte and almost no one went. They do not say Mass. The slaves go about very disconsolate; they come to our church, complaining. It causes me great pain. I said so to the Bishop. He said he will attend to it; I do not know what that will be.

The priests whom the Bishop brought with him do nothing to edify this people, because here we did everything for them for free and now they see another way of proceeding. The Bishop, out of anger, ordered the Vicar of this city, who is now the cantor, arrested, although he was soon released after ten or twelve days. And he had other outbursts with the cathedral chapter, except for two dignitaries and one canon. He ordered them arrested, and they were six days in the city's jail. They disobeyed him. And he does not know how to avoid giving them the occasion to disobey. Nonetheless he gains advantage from it because laymen fear him when they see how he punishes his own.

The boys of this house were used to singing in the same musical tone as the Indians and with their instruments, songs in the language, in praise of Our Lord which greatly drew the hearts of the Indians. In the same way some boys of this place came with their hair cut in the manner of the Indians, which is very little different from our own style. They did everything for the benefit of all. The Bishop considered it very reprehensible. In his first sermon he spoke at length about the customs of the nonconverted Indians, and that was how the entire congregation took it. And so he reprimanded me most severely, without taking into account that they were not rituals or practices dedicated to idols and in no way harmed the Catholic faith. I obeyed him as I will do in everything because I take it as a lesser evil to fail to save nonconverted Indians than for the two of us to be divided.

This business of the boys and their confraternity pleased him not at all, and he hurled words by which it was understood that he was not at all pleased. I am so bad that I suspect he does not consider anything done well unless he orders it or does it himself, and everything else he despises. He said many times he is a teacher and taught the teacher Inácio [de Loyola] and Your Reverence in Paris. *Neque magnifacit societatem nostram; mordet quum vult & potrest* [This does not glorify our Society; he bites whomever he wishes and can], although outwardly he shows me every kindness, and I ask Our Lord to teach me to gain his good will always. Judge now, Your Reverence, my wickedness: I know how to write these things, but not how to weep over them. I write them in order that Your Reverence might weep for me; you know well how to weep. Commend this to Our Lord and always advise me of what I must do about this, about which I have written, and about the other things that prudence instructs Your Reverence, and these will be done here. And since you know what a bad son you have in me, send another who knows better how to behave in these matters. The Bishop understands little of our mortifications or the spirit of them and greatly censures them. What makes me very happy in the Lord is that He is obliged to do great works because He takes so little account of what we do, and we will have the opportunity to extend ourselves through this land, something so necessary and beneficial and desired by us.

The Bishop is a very good preacher and easily accepted by the people. He finds it greatly displeasing that the land is poor. I fear he will leave soon. Support him from there, Your Reverence, because there is no one else. And since Your Reverence was his beginning, you will be the way: ["If thine enemy hungers, feed him; if he thirsts, give him drink, for in so doing thou shalt] "Heap coals of fire on his head" [Prov. 25: 22, and Rom. 12: 20] so that he will love us. The Society is so well respected in this city that no one would be able to throw salt to do us evil, so that I do not feel as badly with respect to the Society as for the little credit he will gain with his flock if they discover in him any of these things.

Although I said to Your Reverence in another letter that I will agree [to make pastoral visits to other parts of Brazil], it now appears to me, through my wicked understanding of his heart, that I will very much flee this task in order not to give occasion for things that may happen. I am very regretful about sending Padre António Pires to Pernambuco to make a visit. I attribute everything to my sins and to the misfortune of Brazil, which impedes him even in this. It consoles me that all the great things Our Lord did required much work and the overcoming of even greater challenges.

∿ *Bahia, July 1552, Bishop Pedro Fernandes* [Sardinha] *to Padre Simão Rodrigues, Jesuit Provincial, Lisbon*

+ Jesus
Reverend Father

The obligation I have to you as an old friend and the affection I have for your Society oblige me to write to you of some things.

The place in Scripture in which God declares why he made pastors in the world is that of Jeremiah: "See, I have set you this day over nations and over kingdoms, to pluck up and break down, to destroy and to overthrow, to build and to plant" [Jerem. 1:10] in which he ordered that they should uproot their vices and bad customs and plant virtue and good doctrine. I, wanting in some manner to seek to do the office of the good pastor, admonished, in the first sermon I preached soon after I arrived on this coast, that no white man should use heathen customs. Aside from provoking evil, they are so discordant with reason that I do not know what ears can hear such sounds and rough playing.

The orphaned boys [sent from Portugal] before I came here had the habit every Sunday and feast day of singing songs of Our Lady in a heathen tone, and of playing certain instruments that these barbarians play and sing when they want to drink their wine and kill their enemies. I spoke with Padre Nóbrega about this and with some people who know the level and behavior of these heathen, especially the bearer of this letter who is called Paulo Dias. I found that these heathen praise them as being good because the padres and the boys play their instruments and sing in their style. I say that the padres play because a priest, Salvador Rodrigues, who came in the company of the boys, played, danced, and leapt about with them.

And all this not only condones non-Christian ways with little benefit to the faith and conversion and even less to the reputation of the Society, but also the inventor of it is one Gaspar Barbosa who escaped from a Lisbon jail, took shelter in the cathedral [tower], and from there, in full daylight, descended by a rope. He was later exiled here permanently. And because he did not give up his bad habits, even here, the Governor ordered him to this city as a prisoner. The sentence established that he would never again leave this city. And after going about here, he has insinuated himself [like a] "ravenous wolf in sheep's clothing" [Mat. 7:15] with your priests, more zealous of virtue than experienced in malice, to get permission for him from the Governor, as they did, so that he could return [to Portugal].

It is he who invented this curious and superstitious heathen practice, and he himself who sang and played through the streets with the orphaned boys and the padres, which I prohibited in order to be rid of the heathenism that seemed so evil to everybody.

It is also very reprehensible that the boys wear their hair cut in the heathen way, making them look like monks. And Padre Nóbrega, as this does not seem bad to him because he consented to it, was somewhat irritated at what I ordered him to do. I told him that I did not come here to make pagans of the Christians, but to acquaint the heathen with being Christians, which cannot be unless they "put off [their] old nature" and "former manner of life" and dress themselves in "the new nature, created after the likeness of God." [Eph. 4:24]

I told him [Padre Nóbrega] that in this land I had to carry on in the way I had in India of making Christians, which Padre Maestro Francisco and the other priests of the Society observed there. He will write all of this to Your Reverence, and I will do what appears best to you.

I found that Padre Nóbrega confessed certain [converted] mestizo women through an interpreter, which to me was very strange and caused talk and whispering, being something so new and never used by the Church. I told him he should not do it any more even if three hundred Navarros and six hundred Caetanos [Padre Navarro and Cardinal Caetano] said that he could do it: " 'All things are lawful for me,' but not all things are helpful." [1 Cor. 6:12] Nor just because the doctors [of canon law] say it can be done, should it immediately be put into practice [when] to hasten to meet it is a danger and to wait is in keeping with Church custom. When such a confession for some reason would have to be made, because some great benefit would derive from it, it would have to be by a prudent interpreter, an honest and worthy man, and not by a local boy, a ten-year-old Mameluco [mixed-blood Portuguese and Indian] who is not aware, nor yet perfectly believable, nor strong in language nor in the diction of words. And the penitent, and not the confessor, would have to choose the interpreter. My opinion is: "Remove not the ancient landmarks which our fathers have set." [Prov. 22:28] The padre, as virtuous as he is, and more theoretical than practical, later tries to put into practice whatever he understands from his teacher Navarro. Although no matter what some theologians say, if the form of this sacrament is to be done correctly (for example, I absolve you), one cannot say such words except when one tells and confesses one's sins. If I had more time than I have at the present, I would prove how dangerous, pernicious, and prejudicial introducing such a practice is to the majesty of this holy sacrament. I have instructed that it should not be done again and have given orders that all should confess. I set as penance that the Portuguese men should teach their mestizo women to speak Portuguese because, until they do, they will not cease to be heathen in their customs.

I also found a great scandal in this town because Padre Nóbrega arranged for the sale of land, announced by a crier going through the streets of this city and the Old Town, which is about half a league away, to another priest, [Manoel] Paiva, for the maintenance of the boys [at the school]. Being a thing so new and unusual, I wanted an explanation from Padre Nóbrega. He told me it was the practice and spirit of the Society. At this point I withdrew in order to think through the foundation of the thing, only telling him that something so new and being done in public should first be very well thought through, whether it would benefit or offend, "giving no offense in anything so that the ministry be not blamed." [2 Cor. 6:3] I reminded him of [the words] from Saint Paul: "to present your bodies as a living sacrifice, holy and acceptable to God, . . ." [Rom. 12:1] and ". . . without blemish in the midst of a crooked and perverse nation." [Phil. 2:15] Because to send a priest selling in the streets seemed excessive and would much debase the priestly standing. To the *negros* [the non-Christian Indians] it would seem very bad, and to the whites a heresy; all would snicker and gossip about it to no one's benefit. He responded to me that nothing was so superb as arranging to sell [land] to the said priest. To this I had no reply. It is my opinion that Your Reverence should advise [Padre Nóbrega] not to make use of these methods for now. Nor when someone breaks a vessel should he be made to wear the pieces around his neck and sent through the city, nor ordered to ring a bell at night through the town, nor should note be taken of those who do not come. Such exercises [in humility], although holy and virtuous and ordered to mortify the flesh, are still more meritorious when done in secret in the manner that they are done in approved religious orders, in your schools in Portugal, and in India without the clamor of a bell.

Given that the disciplining of the men is already done, the disciplining of the women that they do in Pernambuco seems unnecessary because of the nocturnal improprieties that the Prince of Darkness might bring about and command. The priests, being passionate as they are, want to send all to Heaven clothed and shod, but I work only that all should observe the commandments of Our Lord. As they become accustomed to this, then I will make them observe these counsels, and "he who is able to receive this, let him receive it." [Mat. 19:12] I do not yet hold these people in such perfection and, until they have quit their heathen customs, I work much more that the whites should not corrupt themselves than in the conversion of the negros.

It also seems to me that you ought to advise them [the Jesuits] not to have so many hermit priests live alone among the heathen, nor to bury those who are converted in the heathen way. And since I am in this land as a mediator of souls and I have much experience in India, in this [the Jesuits] should do nothing without my advice, because although their intention is good, they are still apprentices and little experienced in these things and they sometimes fail in their duty. I am very devoted to Padre Nóbrega, but at times I reprimand him privately because he pursues his office in public. Finally, I say that to build new buildings and plant the Lord's vineyard in such a new land it is necessary to send old and admired officials here and, if there are none, an educated person of authority should be sent every three years to check on them, someone zealous for the reputation of the Society, to correct any defects they might commit out of carelessness or ignorance, "For I think that God has exhibited us apostles as last of

all, . . . because we have become a spectacle to the world, to angels and to men."
[1 Cor. 4:9] Everything I say is subject to your correction and that of the entire
Society.

And with this I end, reminding Your Reverence that concerning confession
through an interpreter and the other ceremonies of the heathen, it is a long way
between seeing them here and writing about them and being there and discussing
them. Because this people is so affected by their customs, I do not want to say more
than that when we preach to them, it is worth nothing if they see that we enjoy
their heathen songs and playing. About this Paulo Dias, the bearer of this letter, he
should be questioned and entreated. He is the man for whom these heathen have
the most reverence and is most believed; he is a person honored and virtuous, and
he prides himself on saying and speaking the truth.

May the Lord Jesus keep you safe and your Society, and give to me the grace
and strength that I might do the work of this land. May the grace of Our Lord Jesus
be always with us all. In your prayers to God ask that He free me from the heathen
and bad Christians. When I correct their habits they lash their tongues like serpents
against me but, having God's help, I will not fear what man does, and He will free
me from unjust mouths and from lying tongues. "Blessed are those who keep His
testimonies, who seek Him with their whole heart. . . ." [Ps. 119:2] And praise him
who takes me to Portugal and away from here and puts me in a corner where I can
finish my last days in the Lord, and may this be very soon.

∾ *Bahia, October 1553, Bishop Pedro Fernandes* [Sardinha] *to Rector,* *College of San Antão, Lisbon*

In the letter I wrote to Padre Mestre Simão I said, and I say now to Your
Reverence, what greatly surprised me and surprises all the padres is that the
mestizo women married to Portuguese men confess through an interpreter, a boy
of twelve or thirteen years born and raised in this land. And also that on feast days
they go about playing the instruments and singing the sounds that the non-
Christian Indians play and sing when they get drunk and do their killings [of their
enemies]. And now they tell me that they bury in the heathen manner some who
have been made Christians.

If Your Reverence wishes to see about this playing and style of burial, read the
small treatise that I sent there to His Highness and in it you will see how little
prepared these barbarians are for conversion, and how much more we should
concern ourselves that the whites do not corrupt themselves than with the
conversion of the negros [non-Christian Indians]. However, if you decide that the
priests here are right in all they do, I say that I will obey and help in everything,
and I will say that which Elijah said: "For what have I done to you?" [1 Kings
19:20]

With respect to Nóbrega, he is virtuous and learned, but has little experience
and is very wed to his own opinions, such that it seems to me he has greater talent
to be a follower than to lead.

I also point out some things in the same letter that should be ruled on and amended, and so I will do in the future if you think my advice is good for your Society; otherwise I will mind my own business and put my finger to my lips.

Be in good health, Brother in Christ, along with all your Society.

From this City of Salvador, 6 October 1553

Your brother in Christ,

Pedro, Bishop of Salvador

14

Fray Pedro de Gante's Letter to Charles V, Mexico City

(1552)

This letter to the king about the dangers to the Christian evangelization of Mexico, and the abuse of Indians and threats to their spiritual and temporal survival near Mexico City in the first decades of colonial rule, must have caught the attention of its recipient. The author, Fray Pedro de Gante (Peter of Ghent), reputedly a bastard son of the Holy Roman Emperor, Frederick III, or of his son Maximilian (and therefore a kinsman of Charles V), was a near-legendary figure to early Spanish and Indian chroniclers. He arrived in New Spain in 1523, nine months before Martín de Valencia and "the Twelve" were sent out with their orders from Fray Francisco de los Angeles (see Selection 8), and he began the long, exhausting labor of evangelization and instruction that earned him the reputation of a beloved "soul of iron."

Gante was known for his austerity. He repeatedly refused ordination and a bishopric, preferring the humble title of *lego*, or lay brother. He was tirelessly committed to teaching and founded as many as one hundred churches and Indian schools by 1529. The first school, San José de los Naturales, was situated in the courtyard of the main Franciscan church in Mexico City, where Moctezuma's fantastic aviary had been located. It remained his home base to the end of his long life in 1572. There, having learned Nahuatl, he taught Christian doctrine, arithmetic, music, various trades, and the rudiments of reading and writing Castilian and Latin to as many as six hundred Indian boys at a time. Alonso de Montúfar, the second archbishop of Mexico, reportedly said, "I am not the real archbishop because that person is a lay brother, Pedro de Gante." In 1529, Gante succinctly described his life in Mexico: "In the daytime I teach reading, writing, and singing; at night I read the catechism and preach."

This blunt letter highlights a festering dilemma in the Spanish colonial enterprise: the repeated intention that Indians must have the opportunity to know God and be saved; and the inevitable, indispensable requirement that they serve the Spaniards, both the king and colonists. To Gante in 1552, these two purposes were not simply in tension; overwork, mistreatment, frivolous litigation, and other abuses threatened to overwhelm a declining Indian population and prevent them from becoming true Christians.

There is a message of impending crisis. Gante warns that Indians might simply disappear due to illness and overwork. They now had no time to attend classes or even Sunday

Mass. Indians of Mexico City had lost their hospital, and Gante's pupils no longer had the resources needed to pursue their studies. He was concerned, too, about the declining authority of the friars. "Until recently, we friars resolved their [Indians'] disputes," he says in describing the growing influence of lawyers and courts. Another preoccupation was the likely substitution of diocesan priests for friars in the pastoral work.

Gante was not like Dominican friar Bartolomé de las Casas, the most famous voice of protest over the Spaniards' mistreatment of Indians in the sixteenth century, who, in old age, became a thundering opponent of the entire colonial enterprise apart from evangelization. Like Las Casas, however, Gante understood that "it is the struggle for their salvation that justifies their discovery." He could be a fierce critic of abusive Spanish conduct and yearned for an order to society that kept spiritual ends clearly in view. At the same time, Gante urged a balance of interests: a moderation of the Crown's tribute tax and the endless appetite for Indian labor in Mexico City, which would give Indians time to provide for their families and the opportunity to become good Christians. Indians emerge here as people in need of places of "consolation,"

separate places for their spiritual growth, but always in the company of the friars. He regarded the people of central Mexico as able children in need of closer tutelage and paternal care—not, as for Las Casas, as equals of Europeans. He continually appealed for more friars as well as for Indians' relief from tax and labor demands.

The ways of the veteran mentor appear on every page of the letter. He skillfully cajoles his royal interlocutor, reminding him of their shared Flemish roots and personal acquaintance, pointing out the friars' decades of self-abnegation and vital service to God and Crown in this faraway land, pointing out the heavy weight of the king's moral responsibility, and reminding him that he is accountable to God. Last, he offers practical solutions, emphasizing and repeating his key points for effect ("above all," "I firmly believe," he keeps saying) and expressing paternal concern for his Indian flock. This text has the special immediacy and credibility of an elderly man famous for his relentless integrity who spent his energies for the cause he proclaims, but who knows that he will never be able to discuss these urgent matters in person with the king. Gante does not want to give in, "to see the early achievements reduced to nothing."

May the very high Emperor of the Heavens, whose place you occupy on Earth, extend your life and protect your Royal person in His holy service so that your vassals and clergymen may benefit as you favor the poor. And after your blessed journey has been completed, may you go on to glory. Amen.

I am a member of the order of the blessed Saint Francis, native of the city of Ghent, and chaplain in Your Majesty's service. I came from the aforementioned city to the kingdoms of Spain with the armada in which Your Majesty traveled. I accompanied your confessor, Father Clupion, who disembarked at Santander, on the same boat in which Fray Juan de Teta, guardian of the Franciscan monastery of Ghent, also traveled by your order. Along with another friar, he and I went to New Spain at your behest, and we were the first members of a religious order to go there. And Our Lord chose to take Fray Juan de Teta and our other companion to Him almost as soon as we arrived because they died during the discovery of Honduras with the marqués [Fernando Cortés, Marqués del Valle]. I was left alone to do what I could by the Lord's inspiration to try to bring these natives to the faith. Soon another twelve Franciscans arrived, sent by Your Majesty.

I sometimes intended to write an account to Your Majesty as the first to come among these natives and to have had contact with them and worked with them so long. But I did not do so, thinking that one day I would return to kiss your Royal feet and tell it all to you in person. Seeing this possibility delayed, that I was not given license to leave, and that I was now old and near death, I wanted to write this letter to you, brief though it is, because if God decides to take me, I will at least have discharged my conscience with Your Majesty, pleading with you, as to a vicar of Christ, for a remedy for these recently converted souls, that they may receive your favor, that their instruction and conversion may go forward, and that Your Majesty may have the prize of such a multitude of souls converted to God. And so I appeal to your piety to come to their aid and not allow them to be destroyed, which is where they are heading if a solution is not forthcoming.

These Indian people of New Spain are vassals of Your Majesty; therefore it is a just thing that they be favored by you as such. Since members of the religious orders are in this land for their conversion and assistance, and Your Majesty wishes it so, I dare to plead with you for a remedy because, for their people to be saved, they are in great need of relief in order to devote themselves at least somewhat to matters of the Faith. After all, it is the struggle for their salvation that justifies their discovery. Given the way they are going now, this is an impossibility because they do not even have time to look after their subsistence. So they die of hunger and leave their communities because of too much work.

I firmly believe that if the decrees Your Majesty sent here for their benefit were implemented, and if the governors and judges did more than pretend to do so, great good would have come to these people. Even more firmly I believe that Your Majesty's intention is that they be saved and that they know God. For this to happen, they must have some relief, so that with the moderate labor needed to meet their tribute obligation, they can still give themselves wholeheartedly to our teachings and whatever else to which their souls are suited. Otherwise, God will have good reason to complain, for Spaniards came to this land and have taken their property for their own benefit, and Your Majesty has extracted great benefit from them, too. And they may be going to Hell just like before; and where they were many, they are now less than a few.

What is in the past cannot be remedied, but it is just that a remedy be found for the future and that Your Majesty ensure that the decrees issued about personal service be followed because this is one of the main reasons for the destruction of these people. Your Majesty, Most Serene Lord, should know that the Indians who are required to labor for a master in Mexico City in domestic service and bring firewood, fodder, and chickens leave their pueblo for a month at a time, especially those who live a considerable distance from the city. And the poor Indians often have to buy these things because they are not to be found in their pueblos, leaving them in a desperate state looking for these things day and night because the order regarding service is that every day they perform service in the encomendero's house. Thus, they have to buy these things every day, and are always away from their homes and sorely mistreated by the people they must deal with, including slaves, free blacks, and servants of the encomenderos. Instead of feeding them, they mistreat them physically and verbally, causing them to flee and go off to the mountains. Your Majesty should know that Indians in service are like slaves of the blacks, who order them around and punish them as if they were the master.

There is a long history to this, and I do not want my account to be overlong, but I know for certain that if it is not stopped, they will soon be gone, for they are diminishing like the bread that is consumed each day. For the love of Our Lord, may Your Majesty take pity on them and consider what is happening to the poor Indian woman who is in her house with no one to support her and her children, for her husband is hard pressed simply to meet his tribute requirement. She has to go, leaving the home and her husband, perhaps even leaving the children to destruction. Nowhere in the world were men such as these, who had nothing, required to pay tribute; thus, having to find a way to pay it outside [their pueblo], they never have time to rest.

Finally, as a servant of Your Majesty and one who better than anyone knows them and deals with them, I advise you that if Your Majesty does not establish that, as in Spain, they be required to pay tribute only from what they have, within thirty years these parts will be as deserted as the [Caribbean] islands, and so many souls will be lost and Your Majesty's tender conscience. They should be regarded as free individuals and not required to [pay tribute] from what their pueblo has, for Spaniards were never required to do so. They should give tribute to their master from what they produce, and no more, without having to kill themselves trying to make the payment and serving personally. In this way, things will change, and they will become imbued with the Articles of Faith, and their souls will be saved because they will be able to attend the lessons and sermons and will not have any reason to miss them, and tribute will not be the cause of their souls going to Hell because they did not know God and did not confess and did not hear Mass or the lessons of the Faith.

But with thirty or forty more years of service, [the Spaniards] will lose this land forever, for without Indians it is worthless. Your Majesty will certainly understand how the friars who came to convert these souls will feel, for they came here so long ago and saw so many people here to convert. Instead of continually multiplying, there will be no one left; and instead of growing day by day, there will be fewer, and places will be deserted. Certainly it has been the cause of great despair among them.

I turn now to plead with Your Majesty to act as a good shepherd with your sheep and consider that Christ Our Redeemer did not come to spill His precious blood for tribute, but for souls; for a single soul saved is worth more than all the worldly possessions. You are most Christian, and I do believe you will find a remedy and will see that it is the good zeal of a friar and servant of yours that moves me. It has been a great sadness for my soul to see the early achievements reduced to nothing, where once the churches were overflowing with people, now they are not even half full. This is because even on Sundays and other holy days they must find a way to pay their tribute. This is credible because these people are so poor that many of them do not even have decent food, only roots and greens.

One thing that could well destroy them completely is the recently reissued order that these Indians hire themselves out against their will. This order calls for pueblos within a ten-league radius [of Mexico City] to send Indians for hire for all the plots of land held by officials and others. The salary designated for common people is twelve maravedies a day, and I do not know how much for others. So the Indian comes when he is required to serve, comes from ten leagues away, a two-day trip, leaving his wife and children dying of hunger. Once in Mexico City he waits for someone to hire him, selling the shirt off his back in order to survive because it may take three or four days before he is hired. Then he is paid twelve maravedies a day and it costs him ten or the entire amount to eat, so he serves without pay because he must spend this amount just to survive. It gives me such pain to speak of this that I do not want to go on at length, except to tell Your Majesty that an Indian having been away from his home for a month working without pay and having sold his clothes and lost time needed in his fields and his children and wife suffering the loss, returns to the demand for tribute when he does not have even enough to eat. Then comes the personal service, and having been unable to work his fields he can take no more, so he leaves, with his household in ruins. May Your Majesty consider how this man can be a Christian. I believe that if he had been, he would turn into a Moor out of despair.

I leave aside the many acts of mistreatment they receive. I do not want to talk about them because there would be no end; a kick, a hair pulling, or a clubbing is never lacking. Your Majesty, for the love of God, do not allow such great inhumanity to continue. Make them free, and if someone wants to hire himself out, whether he is a dignitary or not, it should be of his own free will, and he should come to an agreement with the Spaniard and not be forced or have the wage set arbitrarily. And they should not go into debt [to the employer] because it destroys them—if the Indian becomes indebted, it is his livelihood that is at stake. The Indian who hires himself out voluntarily does so to support himself; but if he is forced to do so, it is the cause of communities being abandoned.

It has also been ordered that every Indian from every pueblo within the ten-league radius bring a load of firewood to the city. This is a great burden because it takes two days to cut the wood and bring it to Mexico and another day or two to return home. He returns exhausted and nearly dead to find that what little there was in his house has been eaten, and he has only been paid half a real when it cost him a full real just to eat, and his work went unpaid. Oh, how cruel! Don Antonio de Mendoza [Viceroy of New Spain, 1535–1550] certainly understood this, for he is said to have observed that this could not last long or the place would be destroyed. And he was certainly right in the end, for within a year and a half where this went on, there are fewer people in every pueblo. They are Your Majesty's vassals; they cost the blood of Christ; their property has been taken away; they have lost their lands in exchange for souls. There is good reason to cry out for them.

In making this report to Your Majesty, I fulfill my duty to God. To speak more precisely, in numbers, would require a long time. May Your Majesty, most Christian as you are, remedy the situation, preventing personal service altogether and not allowing the hiring [of Indians] against their will or the collection of tribute from community property. There is no other solution.

What has been ordered thus far with regard to slaves in the mines should go forward, and miners should not be allowed to keep them locked away so that they cannot come to ask for their liberty. And whoever makes such a request should have justice done expeditiously, without giving rise to routine lawsuits with them; a judge should be appointed to give them justice expeditiously, going to the mines and putting their situation to rights.

And Your Majesty should not allow lawsuits among Indians, for there is already corruption in this. Now they know nothing but lawsuits, and the notaries are very busy with such business because the Indians press lawsuits for no reason at all, over a bit of worthless land. They spend the tribute and community property in lawsuits and carry them on for three or four years. There is great destruction in this for the Indians. It is unbelievable how they have become such avid litigators, spending what they have on agents, lawyers, notaries, and interpreters. Worst of all, it comes out of the sweat of the Indian commoners, whose belongings are sold in order to litigate. Until recently, we friars resolved their disputes. They did not allow differences among themselves, and in a single day they would accept the resolution, and were content. After Spaniards put into their heads that lawsuits are better, they destroy them and deceive them. Under the guise of doing them a favor, they take advantage of them. And there are disputes among pueblos, and they spend what they have because their leaders, on the pretext of litigating, eat and drink and spend the community's wealth and the sweat of the commoners, robbing them, and everything is lost.

And I attest to Your Majesty that it has happened that a Spaniard will join with Indians who are in conflict with other Indians. To take advantage of them, he will inquire into their reasons for litigating and tell them that their cause is just and they will get what they request without any complications. They make the Indians serve them and work in their homes, and spend their money; and the Indians are left without anything. Your Majesty should see the conscience with which they do this. To remedy this situation, lawsuits among Indians by any means should not be permitted; rather, the friars should get them to agree, as has been done heretofore, with no cost to their property or having to miss their spiritual lessons or leave home, and, above all, without their bringing forward new lawsuits every day and killing themselves as a result. May Your Majesty remedy this situation instead of allowing it or doing anything to encourage it, so that the conservation and peace of these natives will be sought in every way possible, and that they may be favored and not be used so inhumanly, and that they be treated as if they were our next of kin.

I firmly believe that one of the things in this land that most needs a remedy is this city of Mexico. Those who were once lords of the whole land are now slaves, and even worse than slaves. And since they serve the entire city—dignitaries and lesser folk alike, especially in the homes of those who govern—their women suffer deprivation because an Indian is away in service to the Spaniard for a month or two, especially in the houses of those who govern in Your Majesty's name. The woman must seek to feed herself, her husband, and their children, and also to pay the tribute. And what her husband ordinarily would do, she must do; and she goes out to bring back firewood and greens because her husband is obligated to personal service and cannot do this. May Your Majesty consider whether this work is tolerable. With regard to sustenance and rest, dogs lead a better life than Indians because dogs are fed while Indians are made to work for others without being fed. Considering that the Indians of this city of Mexico are so poor, having no lands or resources other than their labor, you will understand how they must suffer. And above all, even if the Indian is an official or a dignitary, he must do the labor service like anyone else. And it is a shame that Indian children ten or twelve years old must travel eight or ten leagues in search of maize and go carrying heavy loads with their mothers in order to support themselves and their fathers and find the means to pay the tribute every eighty days. And lacking lands to plant, they must buy it with the toil of their hands in order to eat and provide for their parents and pay the tribute. For the love of God, Your Majesty should provide that in no way, under no circumstances, should anyone make use of them in this way, that such services be completely stopped, and that they be left to be Christians, for even on the high holy days of Christmas, Candlemas, and Easter they are not allowed to rest.

In this city of Mexico, in the patio of the church of San Francisco there is a chapel called Saint Joseph. There I have worked with [the Indians] day and night for more than thirty years, being with them constantly in a school that is adjacent to this chapel, where I have taught them to read and play musical instruments and taught them their spiritual lessons, and I have always taken charge of them and looked out for them. And they have rebuilt this chapel of Saint Joseph, good and strong, in order to celebrate with fitting solemnity the Divine Offices. There, in fact, they are celebrated, and the Indians are confessed and preached to and baptized and treated with all charity. I believe Your Majesty knows what the Franciscan friars have done in this regard, seeking God's honor and the salvation of [the Indians'] souls wherever [we have] monasteries among these people. And because of the great poverty that exists among their poor Indians, the schooling does not advance for lack of essentials, even food. And this is such an essential activity, being where the Indian children and youths learn their spiritual lessons and are taught to read and write and sing and play instruments, and the reason why the Divine Offices are celebrated devoutly is because they serve at Mass.

In order that improvements be made and the said school does not come to an end, Your Majesty, merciful person that you are, should make grants to these Indians and the said school of some assistance for the maintenance of the natives and so that they will help me there, as they have done up to now, that they will have the means to eat and pay their tribute, so that the spiritual instruction of one and all may go forward and what has been lost will be restored. May Your Majesty grant them 500 or 600 pesos annually, considering the many people who could be taught. It would be a great consolation to the natives, considering the plight of these Indians of Mexico, for they have no lands, nor any means of providing for themselves except laboring for their masters. May your deputies make the money available in the manner that seems best to Your Majesty. It is certain that, without this support, the effort will fail because, lacking subsistence and having to pay the tribute, they will leave the school and spiritual lessons behind. It would certainly be a great service to God in terms of good learning, for, seeing the support, those yet to be born or who are now children would make an extra effort, and a grand thing and great service to God would result. I cannot specify for certain the great service that would result and will result from it, except that it will be forthcoming. And since I am the one undertaking the work and have worked so much with them and intend to continue teaching them until I die, it is a just thing that I receive the grant.

I dare to approach Your Majesty about this, being your fellow countryman and because what I request is in the service of God and for the honor and benefit of Your Majesty. Therefore, for the love of God, please grant what I have asked for the benefit of the Indians' salvation and spiritual education. And please order that some indulgences from His Holiness be sent for the said chapel of Saint Joseph, and permission for some kind of special celebration there (especially an annual celebration and indulgences for this chapel like His Holiness granted to the Colegio de los Niños of this city, thanks to your intercession), so that, with such acts of support, they may go forward and know Your Majesty's favor.

May you order also that under no circumstances can bishops or other prelates act to take away the said chapel and other churches that [the Indians] have in their parishes, where they find consolation; nor can the secular priests take them over in order to become vicars, because for the preservation of these natives, members of the orders are needed, as Don Antonio de Mendoza ordered. Nor should the Indians be divided up, but left as they are; to do otherwise would be to destroy them. In all of this, Your Majesty, being most Christian, will do as you think best, for you know that the Indians have grown up with the friars.

These Indians had a hospital in this city where sick Indians were treated, which they built at their own cost. And there the sick Indians were treated and found consolation. Then it was taken away for the Colegio de los Niños, with an order that another one, just as good, be made for them. It has now been two years, and neither has another one been started nor the original hospital returned, to the detriment of those who are sick. This is an essential matter. In reverence to God, may you order the hospital returned or a new one built as soon as possible so that those who are sick do not die for lack of a place to be treated. May you also make a gift of some amount to the said hospital for maintenance and treatment, and grant a special sum for these poor little ones. May Your Majesty thereby become the patron of this hospital, for the consolation of these Indians, that they may know your favors and know that Your Majesty loves them and looks out for them, as I hope for the great mercy you will extend them.

I have here given an account and made my entreaties, as a servant to his master. What remains is the equipment needed for the job and the officials to undertake its construction. For this work, the friars are indispensable, and we are short of them—there are houses [evangelizing centers] among these natives that have only two or three friars. For this, Your Majesty should order that workers be sent for Jesus Christ's project—many of them, and soon. May some of them be from Flanders and Ghent because if the Indians see that people from my homeland remain among them, they will not feel that I have left them bereft when I die. And because this is so essential—as essential as bread for sustenance—I shall stop here and submit myself to Your Majesty's mercy and magnificence, reminding you to send shepherds for your sheep. Also, do not forget what you have ordered about Indians settling together and not spilling out over the mountains where they will not know God. This is most necessary to complete the conversion of these people and for the friars to keep track of them without having to go looking for them in the mountains. In the mountains there is nothing but idolatry, while, when they live together and can be supervised, Christianity and benefit to their souls and body are advanced, and they do not die without faith and baptism and knowledge of God. This is one of the main ingredients in their salvation, I firmly believe, since it contributes to their well-being in every sense. Your Majesty will know how to deal with this.

Our Lord, Most Serene person and of Royal state, whose hands I kiss, may Our Lord guard you and extend your life in His holy service, as we your subjects and clergymen do desire. Amen. From the Franciscan monastery in Mexico City, February 15, 1552.

✑ 15

The Evils of Cochineal, Tlaxcala, Mexico

(1553)

This record of the city of Tlaxcala's municipal council (*cabildo*) three decades after Tlaxcalan lords allied with Cortés to destroy the Aztec state reveals some striking changes in life there under Spanish rule. Composed in Nahuatl (the language of much of central Mexico at the time of the Conquest) with Roman script and translated into English by James Lockhart, the writing itself is evidence of both change and continuity. The document reveals a traditional hereditary elite making the transition to the Spanish colonial regime as elected officeholders in a municipal council system linked to the Spanish district governor appointed by the Crown (here the *corregidor* is Alonso de Galdós) and a central administration in Mexico City.

In some ways, Tlaxcalan leaders and communities enjoyed a privileged place in the colonial order as the most important native allies of Cortés. Their political and property rights were confirmed early; their native capital received the unusual status of "city" by 1535; they succeeded, as colonial law provided, in keeping civilian Spaniards from living among them during the sixteenth century; they lobbied, with less success, for relief from the tribute and labor demands that weighed heavily as the population declined in early waves of epidemic diseases; and groups of

Tlaxcalans were invited to join Spanish colonizing expeditions on the frontiers of New Spain. In this document, one of the Tlaxcalan leaders is away serving as a kind of circuit judge in the Valley of Mexico district of Coyoacan.

The Indians of early colonial Tlaxcala enjoyed considerable prosperity, easing some of the adjustments to a new state system and religion and to changes in diet, language, dress, labor service, and production. Much of the initial Spanish influence in the province of Tlaxcala filtered in through the top—through the provincial Indian nobles who received coats of arms from the Spanish Crown, learned to read and write Spanish and sometimes Latin, and were among the first to accept Christian baptism and instruction. After the 1560s the hardships of epidemic disease, state demands for tax payments and labor, the mixed blessings of European livestock, and migration out of the province for residence and work in Puebla or in the new colonial settlements far to the north were more apparent at all levels of Tlaxcalan society. Still, Tlaxcalans continued to survive and adapt to new conditions.

In this record of their *cabildo* deliberations of March 3, 1553—during that early period of prosperity—the lords of Tlaxcala express concern about the increasing production of cochineal, a small insect that thrives on the native nopal cactus of central and southern Mexico. The females of this cactus mite were collected, dried, and crushed into a deep red dyestuff that was coveted in Europe, as well as in Indian America, before chemical dyes. The elected leaders' concerns suggest a new level of commercialization of cochineal, grown in many new places, absorbing the energies of people and land previously devoted to food crops; new patterns of local consumption (*cacao*, or chocolate, which was not grown locally, and the fermented beverage, *pulque*,

get special attention here); a knowledge of Christian teachings; and challenges to the customary powers, habits of consumption, and social standing of these lords. But notice that, in spite of the rulers' laments about disorder and moral decay, the changes were not simply in the direction of destruction, dissipation, and demoralization. Remember that great changes are described in this document from the vantage point of a hereditary elite working to protect its position under new colonial circumstances.

In the loyal city of Tlaxcala on Friday, the third day of the month of March of the year 1553, there assembled in the cabildo the magnificent lord Alonso de Galdós, corregidor in the province of Tlaxcala for His Majesty, with Miguel Cardenel, Spaniard, as interpreter; and it was in the presence of the very honorable lords Don Domingo de Angulo, governor; and the alcaldes ordinarios [members of the cabildo exercising judicial authority] Don Diego de Paredes, Félix Mejía, Alonso Gómez, and Don Diego de Guzmán; and of the four rulers, Don Juan Maxixcatzin, Don Julián Motolinía—Don Juan Xicotencatl is sick—; it was in the presence of Don Francisco de Mendoza; and the regidores [secondary members of the cabildo] Don Julián de la Rosa, Buenaventura Oñate, Antonio del Pedroso, Antonio Téllez, Hernando Tecepotzin, Don Juan de Paz, Baltasar Cortés, Pablo de Galicia, Pedro Díaz, and Tadeo de Niza; not (done) before Don Domingo de Silva, who is sick, and Lucas García, acting as judge in Coyoacan; it was done before us, Fabián Rodríguez, Diego de Soto, and Sancho de Rozas, notaries of the cabildo of Tlaxcala. They deliberated about how the cochineal cactus, from which cochineal comes, is being planted all over Tlaxcala. Everyone does nothing but take care of cochineal cactus; no longer is care taken that maize and other edibles are planted. For food— maize, chilis, and beans—and other things that people need were once not expensive in Tlaxcala. It is because of this (neglect), the cabildo members considered, that all the foods are becoming expensive. The owners of cochineal cactus merely buy maize, chilis, etc., and are very occupied only with their cochineal, by which their money, cacao beans, and cloth are acquired. They no longer want to cultivate their fields, but idly neglect them. Because of this, now many fields are going to grass, and famine truly impends. Things are no longer as they were long ago, for the cochineal cactus is making people lazy. And it is excessive how sins are committed against Our Lord God: These cochineal owners devote themselves to their cochineal on Sundays and holy days; no longer do they go to church to hear Mass as the Holy Church commands us, but look only to getting their sustenance and their cacao, which makes them proud. And then later they buy pulque and then get drunk; all of the cochineal owners gather together. If they buy a turkey, they give it away for less than its price, and pulque, too; they lightly give away their money and cacao. Not remembering how Our Lord God mercifully granted them whatever wealth is theirs, they vainly squander it. And he who belonged to someone no longer respects whoever was his lord and master, because he is seen to have gold and cacao. That makes them proud and swells them up, whereby it is fully evident that they esteem themselves only through wealth. And also the cochineal dealers, some of them noblemen, some commoners, and some women, line up here in the Tlaxcala marketplace and there await the cochineal. When they are not collecting cochineal quickly, then they go to the various homes of the cochineal owners, entering the houses. And there many things happen; they make the women drunk there, and there some commit sins. They go entering the homes of anyone who has cochineal plants; they already know those from whom they customarily buy dye, and sometimes they also go on Sundays and holy days, whereby they miss attending Mass and hearing the sermon, but go only wanting to get drunk. And these cochineal dealers act as if the women who gather dye have been made their relatives. Some of the men hire themselves out to Spaniards to gather dye for them, and they give them money and cacao. And later they distribute the women to them, making them like their relatives; to some they assign seven or eight (women), or thereabouts, to gather dye for them. Because of this, many improper things are done. And of those who hire themselves out, many are likewise ruined, because some act as slaves in the hands of the Spaniards. If it were not for cochineal, they would not become such. And both the cactus owners and the cochineal dealers so act that for little reason they begin to pair with each other, or take one another as co-godparents, or just feed one another, gathering and collecting together with their wives. They feed one another, however many of them there are; they give one another a great deal of food, and the chocolate they drink is very thick, with plenty of cacao in it. When they find the chocolate just a little watery, then it is not to their liking and they do not want to drink it. Some pour it on the ground, whereby whoever has given his very good cacao to someone is affronted, but they imagine themselves very grand because of it. And so then they buy pulque or Castilian wine; even though it is very expensive, they pay no heed, but give (the price) to the person selling it. And then they become entirely inebriated and senseless, together with their wives; they fall down one at a time where they are congregated, entirely drunk. Many sins are committed there, and it all comes from cochineal. Also these cochineal dealers no longer want to cultivate the soil; though some of them own fields, they no longer want to cultivate; they do nothing but look for cochineal. And both the cactus owners and the cochineal dealers, some of them, sleep on cotton mats, and their wives wear great skirts, and they have much money, cacao, and clothing. The wealth they have only makes them proud and swaggering. For before cochineal was known and everyone planted cochineal cactus, it was not this way. There were some people of whom it was clearly evident that they lived in knowledge of their humility, but just because of the cochineal now there is much drunkenness and swaggering; it is very clear that cochineal has been making people idle in the last eight or nine years. But in the old days there was a time of much care in cultivation and planting; everyone cultivated the soil and planted. Because of this, the cabildo members said it is necessary that the cochineal cactus decrease and not so much be planted, since it causes idleness. It is greatly urged that everyone cultivate and plant; let much maize, chilis, beans, and all edible plants be grown, because if Our Lord God should wish that famine come, and if there were in people's possession much money, cacao, and cloth, will those things be eaten? Will there be salvation through them? It cannot be. Money, cacao, and cloth do not fill up one. But if people have much food, through it they will save themselves, since no one will (starve); no one will die being wealthy. Therefore two or three times the lord viceroy who presides in Mexico City, Don Luis de Velasco, has been told and it has been brought to his attention how the dye brings affliction, and he has been informed of all the harm done. And after that the lord viceroy gave orders in reply, ordering the lord corregidor that in his presence there be consultation here in the cabildo to approve how many plantings of cochineal cactus are to be kept by each person; it is to be a definite number, and no longer will there be planting at whim. And in consulting, some of the cabildo members said that five plantings of cochineal cactus should be kept (by each person), and others said that fifteen should be kept. But when the discussion was complete, everyone approved keeping ten plantings of cactus, and the lord corregidor also approved it. No one is to exceed (the number). And the women who gather dye in the marketplace are to gather dye no more. Nevertheless, it is first to be put before the lord viceroy; what he should order in reply will then be made public. Then in the cabildo were appointed those who will go to Mexico City to set before the lord viceroy what was discussed as said above. Those who will go are Alonso Gómez, alcalde, and the regidores Antonio del Pedroso, Pablo de Galicia, and Pedro Díaz, with the notary of the cabildo Fabián Rodríguez. It is by order of the cabildo that they will go to Mexico City. The most illustrious lord viceroy will decide how to reply; then it will be announced all over Tlaxcala in what manner cochineal cactus is to be kept.

[There follow eighteen of the names found at the beginning of the document, with other rubrics.]

Done before us, notaries of the cabildo. Fabián Rodríguez, notary. Diego de Soto. Sancho de Rozas.

～ 16

The Indian Pueblo of Texupa in Sixteenth-Century Mexico

(1579)

Hundreds of thousands of Spaniards went to America during the colonial period, but no Spanish king ever paid a visit, nor did more than a few of the leading royal councilors who passed judgment on American affairs. Yet America was quite extensively, sometimes minutely, governed from Spain, and Spaniards were great consumers of news and information about "the Indies." The vast collection of documents in Seville's Archivo General de Indias testifies to this thirst for information and will to administer. Especially valuable to historians are the reports submitted in response to royal questionnaires that periodically blanketed the colonies, calling for details about places, resources, and life among the king's subjects across the Ocean Sea.

Philip II, who reigned from 1556 to 1598, was an avid gatherer of such information. His long questionnaire of 1577 elicited a particularly rich set of reports, or *relaciones geográficas*, from local districts in New Spain (167 of the 208 reports received were for New Spain). The questionnaire called for precise information about location, natural resources, economic activity, political jurisdictions, boundaries, native languages, pre-Hispanic institutions, modes of war, historical traditions, house

types, religious practices, and more. In addition to the written report, the king's instructions called for a *pintura* (picture or map) of the area.

An intriguing report (Selection 16) and accompanying pintura (Figure 9; Plate 3) were received from the town of Texupa, Oaxaca, in southern Mexico, on the road from the colonial city of Antequera (the modern city of Oaxaca) to Puebla and the viceregal capital. The written report was prepared by the Spanish *corregidor* for Texupa with the help of two Dominican pastors from testimony by unnamed local Indians. To all appearances, the map was prepared by one of the Indian informants, not by the district governor or the Dominicans. In counterpoint, the pintura and the report complement each other as perceptions of Texupa and its vicinity at the end of the great epidemic that swept through New Spain in the late 1570s.

In its matter-of-fact answers to the king's questionnaire, the report identifies some notable changes in material life for the people of Texupa: new clothes, new food, new economic activities (animal husbandry and the cultivation of silk, in particular), tile roofs, and silver currency. It recognizes the drastic

Figure 9. Map of Texupa, Mexico, 1579. *Pintura* accompanying the Texupa *relación geográfica*. East is at the top, with its sacred hills, shrines, arroyos, streams, and paths coming into town, the paths converging on the Dominican church and compound. The west side of Texupa is "the entrance to the pueblo . . . more open . . . a fertile depression a little less than one-fourth of a league wide."
Courtesy of the Real Academia de Historia, Madrid.

⌁ SEE PLATE 3 ⌁

decline in population since the Spaniards arrived. People are not as healthy as they used to be, the report states, but it does not mention epidemic diseases introduced from Europe as a cause. Rather, the great dying was attributed to diet—too much eating and richer foods. Even though the report is filtered by the corregidor's determination to answer only the questions at hand and his disgust with pre-Hispanic religious practices, there are hints of local pride in the descriptions of warrior garb and the orderly government of former times that undoubtedly were provided by his Indian informants.

The pintura (Figure 9) illustrates two great changes in early colonial Texupa: the physical reorganization of the community according to the standard Spanish colonial grid plan; and the advent of Christianity, as represented by the church-monastery-orchard compound. But the composition and its living landscape also suggest important continuities in the artist's conception of his community that muffle the sense of transformation of local life under Spanish rule. Like a pre-Hispanic screenfold or "picture book," its story is told almost exclusively in stylized color drawings. The few words on the map identify Comaltepeque (one of the hills mentioned in the report), the Dominicans' monastery ("monasterio"), and the road from the town of Tamaçulapa ("camino de tamaçulapa"). Like some pre-Hispanic Mixtec records, it represents real space, locating prominent physical features of the landscape in ways that were understood by viewers. The conventions for representing the important features of the landscape—especially hills, temples, roads, and sources of water—are similar, too, and there is the same sense of human settlement identified by its surroundings more than by the place itself. However, the way of representing that sense of place and landscape has changed. Whereas pre-Hispanic records from the Mixteca located the viewer in the landscape by way of a meandering string of place glyphs (especially of hills, mountains, and temples) that could be seen in only this sequence from a particular vantage point, the 1579 pintura offers a more European notion of mapping and landscape in which physical features are arranged according to compass directions and a bird's-eye view.

A section of the pre-Hispanic Codex Vindobonensis studied by archaeologists John Pohl and Bruce Byland can illustrate this change. They found that the meandering line of places reproduced in Figure 10 (top left) represents an actual landscape visible from a location near the town of Tilantongo. They call this sequence of places "The View from Red and White Bundle." The meandering line of places begins with Red and White Bundle (the bundle-like form in the lower right). Then comes a fretted temple with a serpent emerging, which is the town of Tilantongo; then the Hill of the Wasp, Hill of the Enclosure, Hill of Flints, and so on, ending with Jaguar Rock and a variant form of Red and White Bundle above the "rock." In Figure 10 (bottom left), Pohl and Byland depict the same landscape from a European perspective, with Red and White Bundle as the point of reference and the various hills and other places visible from it in a clockwise order. In this depiction it would be appropriate to fill in the intervening spaces as they appear to the photographic eye.

In the 1579 pintura of Texupa, east (the place of the rising sun) rather than north is "up," with its concentration of sacred hills and shrines, but the pintura situates the streambeds, hills, and fertile depression in relationship to the town by the cardinal directions in a European way and offers a more illusionistic landscape. The rows of hills and mountains that surround the town in the 1579 depiction more closely approximate a bird's-eye view than does the pre-Hispanic landscape from the Codex Vindobonensis. The effect of a range of hills is achieved by overlapping the native symbol for hill used in the Codex. But the luxuriant vegetation perhaps has less to do with a photographic approximation of the surroundings than with an idealized depiction of promontories and depressions that seem to ripple with life and provide an abundance of running water, a precious resource in what today is a stark,

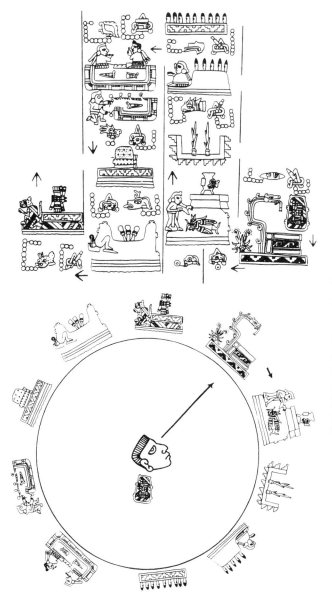

Figure 10. "The View from Red and White Bundle": A Mixtec landscape discovered by John Pohl and Bruce Byland. The image at top left is redrawn in black and white from the Codex Vindobonensis, a manuscript made in the Mixteca Alta region near Texupa before the arrival of the Spaniards. Arrows have been added to show the sequence of figures. In the image at bottom left, Pohl and Byland imagine the same landscape, in a bird's-eye view. Courtesy of Cambridge University Press.

dry, eroded area during the eight or nine months between rainy seasons.

This colonial pintura is too complex in its combination of old and new forms and its ways of depicting the landscape for one neat interpretation to satisfy all viewers who would engage its complexity by emphasizing one feature or another. Is it mainly about oppositions? About native identity versus colonial organization? Does it represent a repudiation of, or indifference toward, Spanish rule and colonial transformations? Do the organic shapes and muted colors of the landscape menace the apparition-like colonial settlement? Do the curving lines of streambeds and old roads that overlap the grid plan of the town somehow subvert the grid and colonial organization, tearing it open or crossing it out, as one scholar suspects? The roads are not mentioned in the written report, and they do seem to suggest more important pathways than the straight streets of the new town.

If we accept this way of interpreting the overlay of forms on the pintura, one colonial form is not covered over or canceled: it is the monastery and church with its walled garden of abundant new fruits and other plants. It appears on top of the ancient roadways and streambed that cross the town, all three of which converge at the site, lending additional importance to it ("all roads lead here" may be the message). The only other man-made structure that seems to have the same importance as the church complex is the pre-Hispanic temple at the base of the hill on the eastern edge of town. The prominence and rough equivalence of these two structures suggest a reverence for the sacred and its institutions that makes no sharp distinction between past and present.

Another, perhaps more promising, interpretation of the Texupa pintura that would also emphasize the landscape (on which the maker lavished such care and to which he gave such scope) does not interpret the overlay of roads and streambeds on the colonial town plan as a repudiation of colonial rule. The depiction of the landscape is seen less as being about competition with the town than it is about a pre-Hispanic concept of space in which human settlements were regarded as temporary and located by their enclosures—that is, by the permanent features and sacred places that surround them—more than as permanent, freestanding places in their own right. Much as the depictions of landscape in most of the surviving ancient Mixtec records were political maps in which ruling elites were shown inheriting and exercising territorial power, the 1579 pintura seems to make a political statement, celebrating Texupa as a central place. If so, it is a grand statement that continues long-standing local claims to authority more than it confronts and challenges colonial power. If not the world's navel (as the Aztec Stone of the Five Eras seems to assert for Tenochtitlán; see Selection 4), Texupa at least appears as a center of things, *the* town, surrounded by places that teem with plant life and spiritual power, a community not obviously subordinate to any political order imposed from outside.

As a glimpse of how colonial reorderings could be viewed by native subjects during the sixteenth century, the Texupa pintura expresses more than a Spanish conquest of the landscape. As in most cultural matters involving colonial Indians in central and southern Mexico, local pride and attachment to place were a vital part of changing spatial and political arrangements. The Spanish corregidor's report describes a more colonized landscape—a restructured, potentially productive place beneath the superimposed design of Christianity and Spanish authority. The Indian painter's representation of Texupa suggests a rather different understanding of the place and emerging colonial realities. In its luxuriant hills, meandering paths, and straight lines, his depiction of home gives special importance to familiar idealized surroundings teeming with sacred life. That life seems to be augmented by the new Christian church complex more than it dwells on the reshaping of the community into the Spanish ideal for an urban settlement.

Relación Geográfica of Texupa, 1579

In the pueblo of Texupa this twentieth day of October 1579, I, Diego de Avendaño, His Majesty's corregidor of said pueblo, have been ordered by the Most Excellent Viceroy and His Majesty's Governor of this New Spain, Don Martín Enríquez, to report in the interests of the good government of this New Spain. Here I, the said corregidor, do so in the company of the very reverend fathers, Fray Antonio de la Serna, pastor of the monastery of said pueblo of Texupa, and Fray Pasqual de la Anunciación, resident of the monastery. Below I answer each of the questions in the viceroy's circular.

The pueblo of Texupa in the Mixteca Alta stands alone, without any subordinate settlements. It is fifty-eight leagues east of Mexico City, almost entirely over very rough roads, although the leagues here are said to be not as long as those in Spain. It is thirty-eight leagues of rough road east of the city of Puebla and twenty-two leagues west of the city of Antequera in the Valley of Oaxaca through both rough and flat terrain. Texupa is in the diocese for which Antequera, with its cathedral, is the capital.

The pueblo of Texupa is situated on a plain between two hills. The western part is more open than the part bathed by the afternoon sun. The hill nearer the pueblo is called Comaltepeque in the Mexican language [Nahuatl], and the other hill Miagualtepeque, also in the Mexican language. It has a fertile depression a little less than one-fourth of a league wide, running west of the pueblo for about one league. Above the pueblo two little arroyos originate. One goes through the center of the pueblo and the other across the northern edge. They join at the entrance to the pueblo and form a depression below it.

This pueblo has a monastery of friars of the Dominican Order, with two friars in residence for the instruction of the natives. His Majesty pays for their maintenance since the pueblo belongs to the royal Crown [rather than being assigned in *encomienda*].

Pueblos in the vicinity are Yanguitlan, four leagues to the east, some of it rough terrain and some flat. To the east is another pueblo called Tonaltepeque, two leagues by rough road. Another pueblo called Cuestlavaca is to the north three leagues by very rough road. To the west is another pueblo called Tamaçulapa, one and one-half leagues over flat ground. The pueblo of Teposcolula is to the south three leagues by rough road over hills. (Recall that the leagues are not as long as in Spain.)

In this pueblo the Indians speak two languages, Mixtec and Chocho. The more widely spoken is Mixtec. The Mixtec name for Texupa is Ñundaa, which in Spanish means "blue land," or "Texupa" in the Mexican language. Why it is called by this name could not be determined.

The lord and cacique in the time of their infidelity when the Marquis [Hernán Cortés] arrived was Yesa Huyya. He and his wife, named Yaanicuin, and their descendants were subjects of King Motecçuma for many years before then. They paid tribute to their King Motecçuma with slaves, parrot feathers, and a little cochineal. They gave the cacique copal [an incense from tree resin] and whatever else was needed for their rites and the devil's house [temple] where they performed their sacrifices.

The devil [god] they worshiped was called Yaguizi; another one was called Yanacuu. In Spanish the word for the latter devil means "wind" and the former means "lizard." They offered these devils dogs, quail, green feathers, many insects, and Indians for sacrifice. Their customs used to be very bad and abominable.

This cacique nobleman appointed another noble as governor of the Indians. He, in turn, appointed someone in each neighborhood to govern the Indians there. They were at war with an upstart Chocho lord who defeated them. In battle they wore quilted cotton down to the navel as a sort of breastplate. They made their hair stand on end and were armed with shields and clubs studded with obsidian blades.

They used to dress in "gicoles," a sort of Turkish costume open in front, dyed in the color that the wearer preferred. Now they wear Castilian-style clothing, hats, shirts, shoes, and breeches. Others wear jackets and loose blankets knotted at the shoulder.

Formerly their diet generally consisted of dry tortillas, chili peppers, insects, mice, lizards, and snakes. In their celebrations the nobles ate native chickens, venison, human flesh, dogs, and insects. Now the common folk usually eat tortillas, chili peppers, and many other types of vegetables; and the nobles eat chickens, venison, beef, mutton, and other things, and those who can obtain it eat wheat bread. They used to be healthier than they are now. It is not known why this should be, but it is thought that by eating less and eating less rich foods they lived longer.

In the said pueblo many mulberry bushes grow. They are used for silkworms, but little silk is produced here. The reason is that when the Marquis came to conquer, there were more than 12,000 Indians in this pueblo, and now there are fewer than 750. There are also some productive fruit trees called cherries; also white zapotes [native fruit], and fruit from the nopal cactus. Spanish trees grow here: pears, apples, and peaches. These types of fruit do well. Lettuce, radishes, cabbage, broad beans, chick-peas, and onions also do well.

Maize is grown in this pueblo, and a little wheat. A little silk is produced, but no cochineal, wine, or olive oil.

In this pueblo there are a few sheep and goats, and some pigs. With a little effort they would multiply greatly because the land is well suited to it. Some of the Indians have mules and horses to help them in their work.

There are no salt deposits in this pueblo. They get their salt from the Indians of Teposcolula and elsewhere. They obtain the wool and cotton for their clothing outside the pueblo.

There are some stone and clay houses in this pueblo, with their tiled roofs and roof terraces.

The trade and produce of the natives of this pueblo amount to the cultivation of their fields. Each married Indian pays a silver peso and one-half fanega [about three-quarters of a bushel] of maize in tribute to Your Majesty. And they benefit from the production of silk.

The pueblo of Texupa enjoys a good climate in a healthy location. The winds generally come out of the north and usually are moderate.

There is moderate rainfall beginning at the end of April and ending at the end of September. The pueblo has a temperate climate, more cold than hot.

I, the said corregidor, carried out the said inquiry recorded here, without discovering anything more. In the presence of the said friars, and Gobernador Don Joseph de Sandoval, Don Gregorio de Lara the cacique, alcaldes Don Gabriel de Mendoça, Gabriel Rodríguez, and Francisco Sánchez, Indian nobles and natives of the said pueblo of Texupa.

17

Alonso Ortiz's Letter to His Wife, Mexico City
(1574?)

Alonso Ortiz's letter from Mexico City to his wife, Leonor González, in Zafra, Spain, offers a rare glimpse into the life and concerns of one of the two hundred fifty to three hundred thousand people who left Castile for the New World in the sixteenth century. Ortiz's principal interest lay in making money, and it was for this end that he left for America. Yet, for the student of history, this surviving letter, probably written on March 8, 1574, makes him more than a name on a list of ship's passengers or a name on an inventory of stock in a warehouse. Ortiz emerges from this document as an individual with his own dilemmas and dreams, who seeks to maintain strong connections with his family in Spain.

The letter has a number of motifs. One of these is Ortiz's stress on the value of perseverance. Life has not been easy for him, not that he seems to have expected ease. He alludes to "difficulties" endured in Spain, where his family's movements might still be hindered by creditors waiting to be paid. Even in Mexico, he has clearly shifted occupations before taking up the tanning of animal hides and venturing a small business with a partner. He works hard and lives frugally, and advertises these facts to his wife. As Ortiz is well aware, for people like him, America habitually shattered more dreams than it fulfilled.

Related to his views on perseverance is Ortiz's stoical blend of longing for home and family with enthusiasm for his commercial ventures. For him, life seems to be a mixture prepared and stirred by an all-knowing God. Ortiz sees God's will in all that happens to him; God guided him to Mexico, led him to become a tanner, brought him a compassionate business partner, provides him with good health and the capacity to take advantage of it. "God does no harm," he reminds his wife, "and . . . even a leaf on a tree does not move without His will." Mexico, for Ortiz, is a place where one endures a number of personal privations in order to acquire wealth that would be barely imaginable for him in Zafra. "I do suffer," he informs his wife, but "I also earn very abundantly." Communication between Mexico and Spain seems slow and unreliable. Ortiz reveals that letters sent sometimes never arrived. One senses his frustration at the lack of news from home and at seeing a number of his personal connections there fading away in his absence.

With only the remote prospect of a reunion in America, his family has been left behind. They receive letters like this one, telling of his loneliness, his accomplishments, and the survival and transformation of his hopes. Perhaps now, he writes, a new source of financial support and a plan of action will bring his wife and children to him. Yet, even here, Ortiz seems braced for disappointment and the need for adjustment. At one point, he states bluntly that he will remain in Mexico, the place to which God has guided him and in which his business prospects are looking up. At another, he mentions that he has kept open a condition in his latest business contract that would allow an eventual return to Castile. The family reunion in Mexico planned and proposed by Alonso Ortiz depends ultimately on Leonor González's decision, her disposition toward travel and a life in New Spain for her family. One wonders whether the couple had spoken and written of this matter earlier.

His letter includes one paragraph in which the correspondent sets out to tell his wife "about things here." For him, this means money, that is, the amount and kind of rent he has paid on the house and tannery in which he now lives and strives. Tanning was one of the most unpleasant and least prestigious trades, and Ortiz gives his wife little notion of what the work was like. His attitudes toward his "between six and eight" Indian workers are almost as veiled, although there may be hints of meaning in their manner of mention. At least from the evidence in this letter, Alonso Ortiz, on the subject of Indian laborers, is no Pedro de Gante (see Selection 14). Each Indian brings in an amount of money for Ortiz, and he keeps track. There is a great range in the profitability of the Indians' activity, with some bringing in thirty pesos and others only ten. His words on the subject end curtly: "About them [the Indian workers] I will not say more than that I pay them each week for what they do." Otherwise, Ortiz's letter is like most letters between husband and wife—personal and centered on the correspondent's own situation.

My lady,

Juan López Sayago gave me some of your letters, and I have others from a sailor who told me he got them from a certain de la Parra, who died at sea. From both sets of letters, I was most pleased to learn that you and all my children are well. Also, I was very happy to find among the letters given to me by Sayago a missive from my compadre Leonis de la Parra, because even though he wrote in his letter of having sent me others, none of them reached me. I will write to him with this fleet, and you can tell him for me that I have been negligent in not writing and that I ask his pardon. Up to now I have simply not been able to write. But be assured that in all I have done, I have asked God and His Blessed Mother to grant me health and, even more, the ability to take advantage of this time and my good health. Thus I have gone on, seeking first the things for which I have prayed; second, the tears that He has seen flow from my eyes; and finally—and most important—all that you, my lady, have prayed for, knowing as I do that I have not been forgotten, that you will have commended me to God and His Blessed Mother. And so they have done these things for me, and I also trust that they will have done as much—and more—for you and the children. Because, over here, even though it seems that one suffers much work and tribulation, one knows that God does no harm and that even a leaf on a tree does not move without His will.

I endured difficulties before God guided me here, to the place where I am and will remain. And all that I have suffered since coming is nothing to me because the troubles that you and my children have endured are what give me great sadness and torment, as well as those of your father and mother, and your brothers and sisters. And I now feel it more than ever because God has led me to become a tanner, and there is no better position than this over here. Moreover, the great expectations which I brought, I still have. In order that I will make good use of the health with which God has blessed me, and that this time not be lost, I have worked, and I continue to work, with great care; I try not to spend money wastefully, and I earn much more than I need to make ends meet. There is, in all this, only one thing wrong, and this is that I do not have you and the children with me, because if I did have you here, and if God granted me health, saving even a thousand Castilian ducados each year would mean little to me.

To show you what I mean about things here, I have rented a house and tannery from April 1, 1573, until the end of March 1574. This has cost me ninety pesos de tipuzque, which are eight reales [one silver peso] each, and this I paid four months before the terminal date. And now, from April 1, 1574, I have rented another house for one hundred pesos de minas, which are thirteen and one-quarter reales for each peso, which I must pay in advance. In addition, I have between six and eight Indians who work with me, and each one that I have brings in thirty pesos, twenty, fifteen, or some only ten. About them I will not say more than that I pay them each week for what they do. I tell you all this so that you might consider that here, where I do suffer, I also earn very abundantly.

God has also brought me a partner so that I may not lose more time. He saw immediately my situation, and saw the distress I have over my wife and children, and he understands how much this afflicts me. And when I formed the partnership with him, I made no other condition than that if I wanted to depart for Castile within the three years of our contract, I could do so. He, who will not be leaving because he sees that much profit can be made in the long term, agreed to send 150 pesos to Seville with a merchant friend of his, a sum which is meant entirely for you, that you and the children may come. These pesos are meant to feed you, to pay for the preparation of your belongings and provisions for the trip, and for all other related business, and the money is yours from him. My partner tells me that he wants to provide for you from his house, and that the sum of money is to be understood as yours from him, so that certain people do not suggest that I sent it and that they neither hinder nor interfere with your coming, because your arrival would bring me great joy. So, if you decide to come, send your letter by the advance ship preceding the fleet on which you will sail. And to those men to whom I am indebted, you may say that on another fleet I will send one hundred hides that will be worth enough for everyone to be paid. With these letters will go also my power of attorney in order that you may act on my behalf, and that you can put me under obligation for the shipping costs, even if they amount to 200 Castilian ducats, that I shall pay upon your arrival. Dated in Mexico City on the eighth of March,

Alonso Ortiz

18

Jerónimo de Benarcama's Letter to Francisco de Borja, Granada, Spain

(1566)

The Society of Jesus was founded by Ignatius de Loyola (1491–1556), a Basque of military experience, under the authority of Pope Paul III in 1539–40. The Jesuits established seminaries and schools attached to their colleges throughout Catholic Europe. The motivation to convey Catholic Christianity to places and peoples beyond Reformation Europe was always part of Jesuit thinking, growing out of the early desire of Ignatius and a number of his companions to work in the Holy Land. In the years after 1540, their attention was drawn especially to non-Christian peoples contacted and, in some cases, ruled by Portugal and Spain. Francisco Xavier (1506–1552) sailed from Lisbon, Portugal, in 1541 for India and the coasts and islands then called the "Indies of the East," where he baptized people and preached in the hope of laying the foundation for the Christianization of Japan and China. The Jesuits arrived in the Americas in 1565, first in Brazil and Florida, and then in Peru in 1568 and New Spain in 1570. José de Acosta, the author of the reading (Selection 19) that follows the present one, was among the Jesuits who reached Spanish America at a point (1572) when the order's mission to the Moriscos in the Kingdom of Granada had fallen victim to the climate of distrust which spread with the Alpujarras rebellion and its bitter aftermath.

About a decade before these hostilities, in the late 1550s, the Jesuits' attention had been drawn to a large sector of Granada called the Albaicín, which stood off on the second hill that divided the city proper from the hill dominated by the great palace of the Alhambra. Here, according to one Jesuit correspondent in 1559, "more than 8,000 citizens," almost all of them Moriscos, dwelt. With encouragement from members of the new Christian nobility in the Albaicín, and from the coffers of Archbishop Pedro de Guerrero (1546–1576), Jesuits of the newly founded college at Granada and a few other Andalusian *colegios* established a satellite "house of doctrine" in the heart of this neighborhood. Thus began the most systematic episode of evangelization among the Moriscos of Granada, and perhaps the Moriscos in Spain as a whole. During its more than a decade of existence (1559–1570), the house's complement of Jesuit *padres* (fathers) and *hermanos* (brothers) fluctuated between seven and twelve (within some thirty-five Jesuits at the College of Granada in 1559 and forty-seven in 1569).

Padres administered sacraments and were licensed to preach, while hermanos worked as assistants who heard confession and taught the basics of Christian doctrine.

Whereas schools among the native people of Granada had been of limited appeal, underfunded and generally short-lived in the early sixteenth century, the Jesuits' apparent successes prompted much early optimism. Pedro Navarro reported to Rome in August 1559 that "already" the house of doctrine served "some 200 students . . . and every day [the number] is increasing." The student body would rise to as many as 550 in 1560, although by that time the Jesuits' school was both attracting and admitting an increasing number of non-native Old Christian children. In that year, a group of "350 Morisquitos" (little Moriscos) shared their teachers with 200 Old Christian children.

From their home base, the Jesuits would venture into the squares and winding streets of the Albaicín. They were busiest on Sundays and feast days, inquiring as to why people were not in church hearing Mass. In their own accounts of these forays, it was a rare thing if a Jesuit preacher did not manage to lead a group of negligent Moriscos back to the church and participation in the day's devotions.

Small companies of missionaries also spread out to the communities of Moriscos living in the surrounding countryside, particularly in the Alpujarras mountains south of Granada. It was in these settings that the more promising Morisco students from the Albaicín, some of them already Jesuits-in-training, were thought most valuable. Although a few of the non-Morisco Jesuits of the Albaicín had learned the local Arabic dialect of *algarabía* well enough to deliver a sermon and hear confession, the select Morisco youths were often the adepts—native speakers who could facilitate deeper instruction. Moreover, their very presence was designed to encourage the urban and rural folk to see their own potential and that of their children in these young Christian models.

The Jesuits' mission work in the Albaicín and environs followed patterns established not only by Archbishop Hernando de Talavera (1492–1507) in immediate post-reconquest Granada but also, for that matter, by successive purveyors of the Gospel since early Christian times. Relevant lessons, ideas, and techniques also flowed back to evangelization settings in Spain from colonized Atlantic islands (especially the Canaries) and from newly conquered regions of the Americas, not to mention the East Indies. Reports and letters, as well as missionary personnel, channeled information and inspiration between the parts of what was increasingly being presented as a larger Spanish Christian unity.

A comparison with pedagogical efforts in early New Spain offers a good example of how educational efforts traveled as a central feature of evangelization. In the years directly following Cortés's military victories in the Valley of Mexico, a school was established at Texcoco by three Flemish Franciscans, one of them Pedro de Gante (the author of Selection 14). Their initiatives were followed up after 1524 by members of "the Twelve" Franciscan apostles and their successors, as seen in the schools at Tlatelolco-Mexico City, Tlaxcala, and Huejotzingo, among others. Later educational initiatives often reflected altered aims and perspectives, but the schools were not only the product of the first Franciscans in Mexico. After their arrival in Peru in 1568 and New Spain in 1570, for instance, the Jesuits established similar schools along with their residences and centers for study and training. In the last decades of the sixteenth century, and into the seventeenth, these institutions became familiar home bases for itinerant missions into the hinterlands. Educating the children of the indigenous elite in the regional schools was as central to the program of evangelization in Spanish America as it was to those which spread from the Albaicín into the communities in the Alpujarras mountains.

The Jesuit instructors in their schools throughout the Spanish world received careful directives from their superiors on many points of procedure, not least in the early identification of the young candidates best suited for clerical training. These boys became assistants in language acquisition. At best, they might mature into a native clergy, or, if expectations were lowered, at least a devoted band of catechists with a valuable store of local knowledge. This selection of the most promising among the Indian and Morisco student bodies did not diminish the importance of reaching the students who were not to be educated as potential priests or even formal catechists. It was a signal hope of the generation of Catholic churchmen whose aims were influenced by the atmosphere (if not the actual decrees) of the Council of Trent that all individuals would finally receive enough fundamental education to become good Christians. Reformative "missions" (the word is of this era) among a vast laity in western Europe deemed much in need of doctrine are part of the context in which the evangelization of former Spanish Muslims and adherents of native American religious systems was pursued. In all settings, but perhaps most urgently in "colonial" circumstances, the Jesuits sought good examples, a new Christian generation of women and men who would teach and personify Christian values and practices at home, in the presence of their own children and other relatives.

In sixteenth-century Spanish America, some Indians and people of mixed race (including those of African descent) followed up their years of education by living and working in convents and churches, dressing in habits, and associating themselves with churchmen and their religious orders or parishes. Their duties ranged from those of servants and manual laborers to those of scholars and research assistants, who shared the lives of the friars in almost every respect save that of official status. Yet however well educated and committed these native and mixed-race Christian assistants and scholars of early Spanish America appeared, very few were admitted to religious orders or ordained as secular priests. Despite substantial and sustained early efforts at instruction in central Mexico, for instance, native collegians were ultimately found unfit for ordination not so much for a perceived lack of intellectual capacity as for the presumed strength of their attachment to worldliness, to sensual living, and to value systems that made them ill suited to become Franciscan friars. In the curt estimation of the first bishop of Mexico, Juan de Zumárraga, writing to Charles V in 1540, the Indian students "tend toward marriage rather than toward continence."

A roughly analogous but also suggestively different situation occurred in sixteenth-century Granada. More young men who were the offspring of Morisco mothers and Spanish fathers appear to have become diocesan clergy (secular priests not attached to religious orders) serving in sixteenth-century parishes of Moriscos in the kingdom than was the case with Mestizos in contemporary Spanish America. And although the number of men perceived as "full-blooded" Moriscos who took the habit of a religious order and/or were ordained as priests was still small, their relative number appears to have been greater than that of Indians from a much more numerous population (even after the greatest ravages of disease) in the Indies. In the case of the Morisco Jesuits, identification is difficult and research has not been exhaustive. Yet it is certain that at least six Moriscos (or young males with at least one Morisco parent) who had been students of schools in Granada, Gandía, and Murcia (and five or six other strong possibilities, two of whom were denied admisssion) were accepted by the Society of Jesus as novices and hermanos in this period. These cases invite comparison with the more isolated American ones not only of Indian but also of Mestizo and Mulatto student-candidates in the sixteenth century and later: among others, Diego Valadés, the multilingual Mestizo Franciscan and author of the *Rhetorica Christiana* (1579) (see Selection 22), who had studied under Pedro de Gante in Mexico; Blas Valera (1544–1597), the Mestizo Jesuit scholar from Chachapoyas, Peru, assistant to the Third Provincial Council of Lima, and chronicler of the Inkas—at least before his fall from the Society's favor, on account of the theological and practical implications of his views on the sacred potential of the Quechua language and Inka religious concepts in the ongoing evangelization of native Andeans; and Santa Rosa's contemporary in Lima, the Mulatto Dominican, Martín de Porras (1579–1639).

How do these new Christians' experiences compare? Were the new converts from Islam regarded as an order of people higher than native Americans (or Tagalog speakers in the Philippines archipelago, for that matter) by Spanish Old Christians? From the points of view of not a few Old Christian authors who expressed some optimism about the assimilation of Moriscos, former Muslims were a not-so-distant people "of the Book" who had been deceived by a false prophet and were now being gathered back into the fold. Among the descendants of militant enemies of Christianity from whom the Kingdom of Granada had been reconquered, perhaps there was added incentive to teach and ordain more young models for conversion.

Jerónimo de Benarcama (1548–?), the author of the letter that follows, was one of the Morisco children who went beyond the period of intensive education and followed his Jesuit teachers around the Albaicín reciting the Christian doctrine. By the age of ten or eleven, Jerónimo was said to have dressed in religious robes, and his teachers clearly hoped that he might join the select rank of Moriscos led by a celebrated contemporary in Granada, a Morisco Jesuit padre named Juan de Albotodo (1527–1578). Albotodo, to whom Jesuit correspondents regularly referred as the "apostle to the Moriscos," was an ordained priest who preached and taught the Christian doctrine in algarabía in the Albaicín and in the surrounding communities of the Alpujarras in the 1550s and 1560s. The fruits of his pastoral work were much praised within the Jesuits' reports from Granada. Other evidence suggesting that Albotodo and a few of his Morisco assistants drew a decidedly mixed response from the heterogeneous Morisco population of his region is deemphasized by almost all Jesuit reports of him. Writers took care not to dislodge the image of a "solid" convert who obeyed, a tireless preacher, and

a model native Jesuit who committed himself totally to his ministry and to the local glory of Christianity.

If Albotodo emerges as a polished embodiment of the Morisco new order sought by Old Christians active in this ministry and by their converts, then Jerónimo de Benarcama is a rough edge—the less made-to-order and more precarious face of the new Christian in a contemporary evangelization setting. The figure of Albotodo arguably plays a part as protagonist in a steadily advancing Christianizing narrative, while Benarcama's complicated self represents a detour, an unfortunate complication that cannot quite be repressed by Jesuit participant-tellers. The figure of Albotodo rises almost entirely out of glowing accounts written by others who were eager to see in him (and in any other new convert who would offer the opportunity) an embodied edifying story. The novice Jesuit Benarcama, in contrast, brought trouble, threatening to present an unedifying narrative and ambiguous example to all.

Benarcama knew that a flurry of correspondence about him had been passing between his superiors in the Jesuit province of Andalusia, and that Francisco de Borja (1510–1572), the third Father General of the Society in Rome, had already been duly informed of the matter concerning Brother Benarcama. You will already have heard tell of me, of how I came to enter the order, and other things, Benarcama self-consciously began his letter, while at the same time implying strongly that there was so much more than his notoriety to understand. This Jesuit Father General would read the letter with knowledge, if not much sympathy. Before pursuing his religious education and admission to the Society, Borja had been duke of Gandía (near Valencia). He had supported a significant educational effort among the Moriscos there, founding a school which, among other goals, had sought to educate a Morisco novitiate to assist evangelization in that region.

Written on September 25, 1566, Benarcama's letter delves straight into the complex Granada of his day, examining barriers, points of contact, and traditions of misrepresentation between social groups. Benarcama points at "good" and "bad" in both the Old and new Christian communities. He manages to be insightful without being particularly endearing. Given the vow of Jesuit obedience that he has taken, he emerges as a proud, at times even manipulative young man, and it is not difficult to imagine how he irritated his superiors. He as much as asks the Father General to pause and imagine the repercussions if he, the Morisco novice whom everyone knows, were to leave the Jesuits because of his "indisposition." And Benarcama knows just where to strike for effect. He refers to himself and to Albotodo as the Granadine Moriscos' examples, and their only protectors and defenders. Did Benarcama have an inflated idea of his own importance? (It certainly served his interests to be significant.) Or was he, as a potential Albotodo, a genuinely critical agent and symbol for a number of parties in the Granada of the 1560s?

Benarcama's aptitude was quickly noticed after he entered the Jesuit Order in 1562 at age fourteen, but reports claimed that his health declined rapidly over his next four years in the novitiate. After a series of illnesses remarked upon by his superiors, he was sent to convalesce in the *colegio* at Granada, which he soon left for the refuge of his mother's house in the Albaicín quarter. It was at first claimed by his Jesuit superiors that he hoped to recover his strength and return to his studies and the service of God. Yet the problem of "ill health" might have meant a number of things within the contemporary Society of Jesus: ill health was sometimes a code for any number of difficulties emerging between a novice or Jesuit and his superiors, often an indication, in John O'Malley's words, of "a growing sense of incompatibility on one side or the other, or both." In Granada there were mounting signs that Benarcama's "indisposition" was more than simply physical. In the meantime, his father, a prominent and demonstratively Christian post-Conquest noble, died. In the young Jesuit's words, his father's death left his mother and siblings "so

poor that if bread was not given to them as alms, they would not eat." What was more, like their Morisco neighbors, Benarcama would later state, his family members endured the abuses and financial demands that plagued "the poor people" of this place. His feeling of responsibility for his family, along with his outrage at the conditions suffered by "the people of his nation," come into sharper relief in the letters he wrote after the one excerpted below, especially as it became increasingly clear that his college rector and provincial had lost patience with his special requests for solitude and more time to study.

In his letter to Borja, Benarcama seems motivated by contradictory impulses that express his complicated position and those of others like him. There is a raging sense of injustice within this Morisco novice who feels the conditions of his family and relatives. Yet he also feels an anxious need to belong as a Christian and to live up to his assumed role as a pathbreaker in difficult times. His words suggest that he felt immense pressure as one of the privileged boys who had been chosen and educated by the fathers, and who was now depended upon—as much by certain Moriscos as by other Jesuits—to be an agent in the assimilation of others. Here was a new convert from Islam who had accepted membership within a Christian community, who was anxious about his immortal soul, and who was facing some culminating vows. Would he be another Padre Albotodo? His strong inclination toward his studies (as opposed to preaching in the Alpujarras, for instance) seems to be a sign that this was not to be. Perhaps he was also pestered by doubts that his efforts as Christianizer would do anything to better the Granadine Moriscos' conditions.

Benarcama clearly chafed within the controls of the order, and yet he seeks (at this point) to retain his place and to serve God. He wants Christianity and to be a Jesuit, but he also wants these things his way. A proud and angst-ridden young man who feels so many eyes upon him never quite disappears beneath the apologetic language expected of someone in his position writing to the Father

General, and even more so from one with such a mixed history. His promises to reform notwithstanding, there is in this letter a hint of his later decision that his return to the fold would only come if he could make his studies the center of his life, perhaps at the University of Alcalá, where many of his teachers had studied, and where he might also put his learning to use.

There is in Benarcama an interesting opportunity to consider what membership or association in a religious order, not to mention the issue of ordination, was like from the position of a member of the native nobility. Benarcama in Granada begs comparison with indigenous collegians, native scholars, and artists trained in European traditions and techniques in early colonial Spanish America, for whom similar choices and challenges appeared. In Benarcama's case, the young Morisco, who was to have abandoned the matters of the world and the ties of his relatives in preference for complete obedience to his superior and to God, was drawn instead toward an ultimate responsibility to his own

desires, to his family, and perhaps also to his people as a local leader. His early decision to be a Jesuit comes to seem a bitter mistake. An amazing series of interviews in his mother's home, increasing disobedience of his superior's entreaties, captures, and jail breaks ensue, all related from the point of view of his disgruntled Jesuit superiors.

Yet of what precisely did Benarcama's resistance consist? There is no evidence to suggest that his commitment to Christianity had diminished, although his faith may have been less rigorous than that demanded of a would-be native missionary and more closely connected to the situation of his family and respectful of the needs of the Morisco community. Just as Jerónimo de Benarcama disappeared from view behind the outbreak of the Morisco rebellion in the Alpujarras in 1568 and the pressing nature of his superiors' other concerns (among them, the arrival of the first Jesuits in Peru in that year), there surfaced a rumor of his wish to marry a cousin, with whom he might presumably raise a family.

[Benarcama's letter to the Father General is joined close to its mid-point]

Your Honor should know that I am a native of this kingdom of Granada of the Moriscos. That is, I am a grandson of the man who was once the Moorish lord or magistrate of the city of Guadix (I say this even though it seems immodest because it seems relevant to what I am about to say), and as such I am as well known by the leaders and notables as by the general population throughout this kingdom. . . .

[It is necessary that we establish a few other truths.] The first is that in the whole of this kingdom there is neither a leader, nor a member of the nobility, nor a prelate who does not have his eyes fixed on me, as does the Count of Tendilla, the president of the audiencia [regional governing body and court], the archbishop of this city [Granada], the bishops of Guadix and Almería, the deans [of the cathedrals], and so on. So much so that I am terrified and overwhelmed by what is expected of me, and about this I speak frankly. The second [truth] is that all of the natives of this kingdom are much persecuted by the Old Christians, and they [the Moriscos] have no one to protect and defend them except for Father Albotodo and myself. Many of them have told me that it [Albotodo's and my presence and ministry] cheers them greatly and that because of it they want to enroll their children in school so that they can grow up to be churchmen. And [further,] there is not a Morisco nobleman who has not expressed his hope that, through me (even though I am a vile and feeble instrument), God will work wonders among them. The third [truth] is that I am so well known by them that if the newly converted of this kingdom number 200,000 or 300,000 souls, not 100 could be found who do not know me, as I already said, because I am from the nobility, as well as for other reasons.

With these things established, then, if I left the Society [of Jesus], the news would go out across the whole kingdom that would be so sad for the virtuous and so joyful for the evil. Sad for the good Old Christians because they would lose hope and at once despair at the worth of this people [the Moriscos], seeing that one [of those whom] they had their eyes on did not persevere. And sad for the good ones among the natives because their guard would have dropped, and it is disheartening [to think that] they would then have no one to defend them against the words of their detractors. Happy for the bad Old Christians because they would truly get their desired occasion to grumble, and happy for the bad natives because seeing me unable to carry on would confirm their cherished opinions that this generation has neither the ability nor the [intellectual] wherewithal for the tenets of Christianity. Judge for yourself, then, Father, if my leaving would be more an offense to God, a pleasure to the Enemy [the Devil], and an unedifying example to the people, than [an act] in the interests of the glory of God and the edification of all.

The other difficult matter that stirs me still more is the danger to my soul, for I am certain that if I were to leave the Society I would see the inferno open for me and that my soul would be lost to the flames of Hell. . . . If I leave the Society . . . with health and freedom and other circumstances of which I will not speak so as not to defame anyone, I do not know what will become of my soul.

I have summarized the difficulties about which I wrote to the Father Provincial [and have written] of my feelings about leaving, but his response has not yet arrived.

My view on this matter [of abandoning] is stated in these terms, with which, even though unworthy, I now earnestly and humbly ask Your Honor for the love of that so merciful Lord for whom I prepare with such a special vocation and who, by such an indirect route and without my deserving it, brought me to be in this holy Society. . . . I trust that I do not have to be cheated of my hope and then that I will never lose my place, for which, not without reason, God now gives me my health, so much so that I am [privately] carrying my studies forward. And I do all that is asked and commanded of me with a great desire to live all the days of my life in obedience in the Society of Jesus, so much is my pain and repentance and intention to make amends for all the mistakes I have made and for all my carelessness up to now. Time does not allow me to say more. . . .

Your unworthy son and servant in the Lord,

Geronimo de Benarcama

19

José de Acosta on the Salvation of the Indians
(1588)

José de Acosta was born in the Castilian city of Medina del Campo in 1540. Following a path that was also traversed by four of his five brothers, he entered the Jesuit Order in Salamanca at the precocious age of nine. At twenty, in a letter to a superior, Acosta reflected that as a young novice he had studied and performed the Spiritual Exercises—a series of meditations undertaken by all prospective Jesuits—for some three weeks, "even though," he complained of his supervisors, "they would not allow me to spend the entire day shut up inside because I was a child." He set out as a preacher and a teacher of theology in a succession of the Jesuit colleges that had sprung up in the Iberian Peninsula. A good writer with an excellent command of Latin, Acosta frequently composed letters to Rome on behalf of his college rectors, particularly from Segovia and Alcalá. He was ordained in 1566 while at Alcalá, where, unlike his contemporary Jerónimo de Benarcama (in Selection 18), he was allowed time for study, focusing on courses in philosophy and theology at the university. The effects of conventional as well as Renaissance humanist learning at Alcalá would be put to good use by Acosta in his later writings, most of which were stimulated by his assignment to the new Jesuit province of Peru.

He arrived in Lima in April 1572 in the company of two other fathers, part of a small, third group of Jesuit arrivals to the southern Viceroyalty of Spain's American possessions (seven Jesuits had disembarked in 1568, and another twelve in 1569). Acosta picked up where he had left off in Spain, initially teaching theology at the Jesuit College of San Pablo in Lima. Some exceptional abilities must have been quickly noted, because in the next year his provincial sent him on a sixteen-month tour of the central and southern parts of the Andean region. The Jesuits were eager to expand their new missionary base in the south-central Andes, and Acosta's assignment was to determine how this goal might best be accomplished. He was to examine the prevailing conditions and prospects for missions in Cusco, Arequipa, Potosí, Chuquisaca, and La Paz (all of which would come to have Jesuit fathers and colleges). Part of Acosta's research tour coincided with an ambitious general visitation of the realm then being made by Viceroy Francisco de Toledo (1515–1582), whom the Jesuit seems to have impressed. Acosta would also have benefited from the opportunity to compare notes with the viceroy's advisers and assistants, among them the lawyer and keen observer of mid-sixteenth-century native Andean culture, Juan Polo de Ondegardo.

Back in Lima, Acosta was promoted on Toledo's recommendation to a professorship in theology at the University of San Marcos, a position he held for only a short time before taking on a five-year term as the Jesuits' second provincial of Peru (1576–1581). Reflecting the growing respect he commanded in ecclesiastical and political circles, Acosta served as principal theologian and adviser to the Third Provincial Council of Lima (1582–83), convened by Archbishop of Lima (and later saint) Toribio Alfonso de Mogrovejo (1581–1606). In addition to his influence in the conception of the pivotal council that would reflect the concerns of the Church's general Council of Trent to South America, Acosta helped shape and draft its acts and decrees. He also assembled the third council's pastoral complements, including texts by Polo de Ondegardo on the Indians' "errors" and "superstitions," a confessor's manual, thirty-one sermon texts, and two catechisms for Indians that Acosta himself edited and that others would translate into the principal indigenous languages of Quechua and Aymara. The trilingual results, the *Christian Doctrine* and *Catechism for the Instruction of Indians,* were published in Lima in 1584 and 1585.

Acosta's experiences and study of the pastoral situation in one of the great Indian heartlands of the Americas provided inspiration for two books that he was already writing in the 1570s and 1580s. He left Peru in 1586 for a year in Mexico in order to confer with people there and to collect additional information for his writings. After a time in Rome, gaining papal approval for the decrees of the Third Provincial Council and discussing American evangelization with the general of his order, Acosta was back in Spain. His remaining years were spent writing and publishing his books, teaching theology, and occasionally advising the Crown on American matters. Acosta's best-known work, the ambitious *Natural and Moral History of the Indies* (*Historia natural y moral de las Indias*) (Seville, 1590), was a Spanish translation of the first of two Latin tracts that he had pub-

lished two years before in Salamanca (*De natura Novi Orbis libri duo, et de promulgatione evangelii, apud barbaros, sive de procuranda Indorum salute libri sex*). This history was quickly translated into English and other western European languages. Acosta died in 1600 at the age of sixty.

Less widely known outside circles frequented by churchmen and students of evangelization is the second tract in Latin, a guide for Christian priests serving among Indian peoples. Though published in 1588, Acosta makes clear in the selection which follows that he was writing it in Peru as early as 1576. *How to Provide for the Salvation of the Indians* (*De Procuranda Indorum Salute*) is a missionary masterpiece that highlights Acosta's erudition and considerable abilities as a writer. The work combines a fervent immediacy drawn from personal experiences in the spiritual plane with a subtle application of Christian theology and missionary practice that is somehow both learned and accessible. In *De Procuranda,* Acosta confronts a number of vital issues related to Indian peoples and their relationship with Catholic Christianity at a late sixteenth-century moment that he presents as critical for the Indians, as well as for the Church and the Spanish monarchy. Writing in provocative, general terms to his mostly clerical audience, Acosta observes that the Indians' attachment to Christianity is not forming at the expense of their ancestral religious beliefs and practices. Virtuous living and habits of devotion seem an external gloss on many Indians' lives, a dutiful shine that dulls without the scrutiny and urging of assiduous priests and judges. A number of salvations seem to hang in the balance.

Acosta wrote *De Procuranda* at a time when missionary enchantment with the prospects for Christianity in the "New Jerusalem" to be built among the indigenous peoples of Latin America is often said to have been uniformly on the wane. Histories of the evangelization of Indians in colonial Spanish America tend to pocket efforts at understanding and persuasion in the sixteenth century, a slide to pessimism and coercion in the seventeenth century, and an atmosphere of resignation and increasing indifference in the eighteenth century. By Acosta's time, the optimism and sympathy so characteristic of the evangelization of early New Spain is often said to have made way for lowered expectations, distrust, and cold practicality. Indeed, there is a certain reserve to Acosta's missionary hope in an American future. He prefers to argue, he says—thinly cloaking a criticism of the style of his Dominican predecessor, Bartolomé de las Casas—in the manner of "a moderate lawyer" rather than "an uncritical enthusiast." Acosta perceives complications in the evangelization of Indians, but is he accurately described as disillusioned with them, as hardened or narrow in vision?

One might argue that his words are a caution to anyone who would seal off an early colonial "era of missionary optimism and patience" from a subsequent "era of disillusionment and pessimism" that is usually said to begin in the late sixteenth century, around the time of the Third Provincial Councils in Lima and, a few years later, in Mexico City (1585). In its fervor and imagery, the following passage recalls the exhortation to the twelve Franciscan apostles on their way to Mexico (Selection 8) and the letter from Pedro de Gante (Selection 14). Reminiscent of the writings of Las Casas himself, Acosta's text aggressively counters the arguments of the Indians' "detractors," defending the new converts and offering up remedies for the future. Especially in the Andes, where civil wars, determined Inka rebels, and difficult terrain had delayed Spanish religious and political consolidation before the 1560s and 1570s, the arrival of members of the religious order that had risen so quickly to prominence in Catholic Europe was a kind of new beginning.

Acosta's *De Procuranda* reflects the Jesuit ascent and the sense of occasion. It demonstrates the Society's concern with pedagogical excellence, exemplary virtue, and missionary feats that might equal those of Saint Francis Xavier in distant corners of what would have seemed to a sixteenth-century missionary as an exhilarating, widening Spanish world much in need of the word of God. Within this expanding world, attention might shift between various constituencies judged to be in need of mission, indoctrination, or reform. For Acosta, Catholicism was becoming more portable, more committed to and even defined by its traveling translocal program of evangelization. Jesuits in the New World, as in the old, echoed the sentiment of one late sixteenth-century Spanish correspondent to Rome who enthusiastically predicted that wherever there was a square or a crowd in a street, there would be a Jesuit father preaching.

Intensive experiences in America and Europe had, by the last quarter of the sixteenth century, thus required the adjustment of dreams but not their disappearance. *De Procuranda*'s pastoral optimism is a tower steadied by realism. Acosta and his generation of Jesuits expected to win souls in the world, but to win them gradually and not without surmounting sizeable obstacles. Some of the American obstacles are judged by Acosta to be intrinsic to the lands and their peoples. According to his evolutionary scale, some Indian groups were more capable of receiving an Hispanic brand of Christian civilization than others. But other obstacles were placed by Spanish Christians themselves. As late sixteenth-century Jesuits were discovering at virtually the same time among "newly converted" *naturales* (natives) in Valencia, Granada, Florida, Brazil, Mexico, Peru, and so on, missionary endeavors were precarious and reversible. In this age of reform, missions were vulnerable enough in contemporary Europe among the many who were ostensibly of the same faith, but they were especially so among neophyte peoples such as Indians and Moriscos—peoples who fell beneath even heavier official scrutiny and a changing hierarchy of demands, needs, and fears.

Jesuit pedagogy blended classical ethics and decorum with a Christian moral tradition, with the result that emulation and edification became the principal aims of the constructive relationship that was to mature between teachers and pupils, missionaries and new converts. A student, moved by the merits of the good example before him, was to be inspired to similar virtue. Reflecting on these aims, Acosta seems acutely aware of how close missionary reverses were in the New World and of where he should apportion the blame. His hope for the Indians' salvation is bound to an acutely critical appraisal of his fellow Spanish Christians. In *De Procuranda,* he does not let his readers forget the ultimate importance of the Indians' will and determination in their own Christianization, a process that—again, like Las Casas—he sees as having crept along, often in spite of Spanish Christian behavior. The faith and its new contexts are a tender plant for Acosta; and, in his view, Christianity had grown its roots in late sixteenth-century Indian soil principally because "men who have suffered serious wrongs from Christians still have not cast Christ aside." For those Spanish Christians who take advantage of Indians and live as poor examples among populations assumed to be impressionable, Acosta serves up a cool reminder of Judgment Day: "God does not distinguish between them and us."

In marked contrast to the problems encountered in assuring the Indians' salvation, he features Jesuit advances. Fruits are measured in a number of ways, not least by the "companions in this happy dawn of the Gospel," the indigenous lay assistants and local equivalents of a Valadés or an Albotodo (see Selections 22 and 18, respectively), who were won to God's side and chose to assist the fathers' ministry among their people. The native peoples, in Acosta's mind, become not foes aligned in defensive positions and needing to be overcome so much as the Jesuits' principal allies, the coveted reward for the Society's exhibitions of virtue, patience, and

energy. Acosta emphasizes a mutual respect developing between itinerant Jesuit fathers and the Indian people who sought them out as. confessors of sins and preachers on Sundays and festivals.

Like the Franciscan superior instructing Valencia and "the Twelve" over half a century earlier, and like Francisco de Vitoria lecturing about the place of coercion in evangelization (Selections 8 and 9), Acosta connects missionary deeds and aspirations in America to those of the first apostles of Christianity. He universalizes the American evangelization settings, making their Christianizers aspirants to the same praise and metaphors as the faith's founders: farm workers prepare the soil, sow seeds, tend fragile plants, destroy weeds, await the harvest, and reap bountiful rewards, while shepherds guard flocks from danger, their own bad judgment, and the temptation to stray. Acosta, as artfully as any clerical participant-teller in his day, builds upon pregnant allusions to the primitive church and the biblical analogies (principally to Samaria) by comparing Indian peoples with "pagans" from Europe's past. On an obvious and practical level, such thinking had, for almost a century by Acosta's time, made Indians more intelligible to Europeans and the Europeanized in America. Further, the transhistorical analogy, like the translocal commitment noted above, seemed to promise a Christianized future, a great goal for which to strive. The parallels allowed some Spanish Christians to counter the diminished hopes of other contemporary missionaries for the evangelization of Indians. Acosta and others reduced Indians to a few categories (not just one) in ways that strengthened changing notions of Spain's providential role in the unification of all humankind under Christian rule. Acosta suggested that vigorous self-reform would have to accompany renewed effort if evangelization was to advance.

Chapter 14

∽ *The Christianity in Which the Majority of the Indian Peoples Live*

1. The Indians' situation appears to me very similar to that of the Samaritans of ancient times of whom we read in the fourth book of Kings [II Kings]: wounded by terror and fear of the lions who wreaked havoc among them, the settlers asked God for a priest who would teach them the divine law. "One of the priests," reads the Scripture, "banished from Samaria, was then to establish himself in Betel, and he taught them [the settlers] how to worship the Lord." And there followed an enumeration of various of their superstitions, after which was added: "So they worshiped the Lord and served their gods at the same time, in keeping with the religion of the country from which they came to Samaria. They come, observing their ancient rites, right up to today. They do not venerate the Lord, nor do they live according to His commandments and rules, but instead follow the law and norms already stated," etc. The Scripture concludes: "Thus, that people honored the Lord and gave worship to their idols. And up to today their descendants continue doing the same as their ancestors did."

I do not believe that one needs to describe in greater richness of detail and elegance all that is our Indians' way of life and religiosity. They give worship to Christ and they serve their gods, they revere the Lord and they do not revere Him; the two extremes are confirmed by Holy Scripture. They venerate Him only in word, they venerate Him as long as the priest or judge urges, they venerate Him, in short, only with the appearance of Christianity. They do not venerate Him from deep inside, they do not give true worship nor hold the faith in their hearts as is truly required. What use is there to carry on? The [pre-Hispanic Indians'] descendants continue doing the same as their ancestors did.

Chapter 15

∽ *Despite This, There are Great Hopes that the Indians Will Receive the True Faith and Salvation; To Imagine Otherwise Is Contrary to the Spirit of God*

1. Consider the Samaria of our own time, a place which Christ occupies together with Succoth-Benoth of Babylon, Nergal of Cuth, Ashima [of the people of Hamath], Nibhaz and Tartak [of the people of Avva], Andrammelech and Anammelech [of the people of Sepharvaim], and other monstrous gods. It is not so much that one worships Christ along with others as much as it is that, in a certain way, one obliges Him to suffer that insult and affront against Him, in being associated with demons and showering them with honors through His participation. But that does not mean we should reject our Samaritans and give up all hope in them. The Lord will remember Samaria, too. And the time will come when it [our Samaria] will receive the word of God and listen to Philip after rejecting Simon, and be worthy of having Peter and John as its preachers. The time will come when [our Samaritans] will say: we, too, believe that He [Christ] is truly the Savior of the world.

Also, Christ will make the Samaritans surrender themselves and show His disciples golden fields ready for harvesting, for He proclaims a successful harvest and promises bountiful fruit for eternal life. Why, then, should we lose hope? Why do we command with Jewish arrogance that the Samaritans go far away? Would it not be much better to proclaim the Gospel to them in imitation of the Lord and His apostles? We believe the seed that grows and bears fruit over the whole world will, in the end, also yield its bounty in this arid and inhospitable land. That which is parched will become a spring, because rocks have smashed in the desert and been moved by rivers.

It will come, Samaria's time will come, and those who earlier had received the order, "Neither go to the land of the pagans nor enter the cities of Samaria," then will hear the precept of the Lord: "Receive strength, [for] the Holy Spirit will descend over you, and you will be my witnesses not only in Judaea, but also in Samaria and to the ends of the earth." I have arrived at a firm conviction, and it is impossible for me to think in another way, that, although it may yet be a while and it may perhaps [require] more effort and prudence at the beginning, the time will come when, by the kindness of the Holy Spirit, the Indian peoples will be much enriched through the grace of the Gospel, and the Lord of all that is holy will be presented with abundant fruit.

2. The only difficulties I fear are the great shortage of ministers [who are] sensible and faithful in Christ, together, of course, with a surfeit of mercenaries and others who are looking out for their own interests rather than those of Jesus Christ. Because if the unfit pastors were merely useless, they would be tolerable. But the fact is that they are doing much damage and scattering Christ's flock, and all this causes us pain and occurs without courageous objection from us.

Therefore, if the Lord would dispatch real workers to His ripe fields, and I mean irreproachable workers who proceed with respect for the word of God, and who see in these peoples not personal gain but the peoples' interests; who gladly put aside wealth only for the good of their children and are, moreover, completely willing to wear themselves out for the salvation of their souls; who will love their spiritual children so much that they will wish to give to them not only the Gospel of Christ but also their own lives; who, trying to please God, speak in ways that [show they] do not look to ingratiate themselves with men, but only to win over God (who knows the hearts of men), whose words are neither characterized by flattery nor encouraged by greed—workers, in short, who with the greatest sincerity seek not their own glory but that of God—at that time, with their sheaves replete, the barrenness will come to an end and the most bountiful fields of grain will spring up and be harvested for eternal life. Meanwhile we must be patient and pray fervently to God to send His workers.

3. Let no one think that I have said this thoughtlessly: experience itself is more than enough proof. There are men of God—and although, I admit, they are few, they exist—[men] who have observed for themselves that the Indians' malice does not arise from their nature. Those [Indians] who have had reliable, diligent, and wise priests and guides sense very well the power of the divine doctrine; and they respond, little by little, by setting an example with their lives, naturally, of course,

as happens in everything; but, they receive the seed and yield a harvest on their own: first, [there] is a shoot, that is to say, the external practices of the religion; then, the sprig of understanding and a variety of emotional attachments; finally, the wheat at the height of its maturity, that is, the faith now fully working through love, with acts worthy of God. One cannot insist on the maximum growth right away, in only one day.

If the decrees that have emanated from the Catholic King and his Council [of the Indies], by the great zeal that they have for the Christian religion and the concern that they have for the Indians' salvation, and which so wisely keep an eye on their [the Indians'] interests and well-being, will be carried into effect with as much diligence and loyalty as the gravity of the situation that led to their promulgation, before long the task of saving the Indians will not only be simple and pleasant but even very fruitful. In spite of everything, [and] whatever the situation is at the moment, it is not so bad that many thousands of Indians have not been won for Christ. And whereas some zealous persons moan excessively that all the Indian peoples are going back to their Baal, and cry that they all maintain their huacas and serve their Supay [an ambiguous Andean force ill-advisedly pressed into service by some sixteenth-century evangelizers and lexicographers as a synonym for the Devil], the Lord keeps for Himself more than seven thousand who do not bend a knee before Baal, and there is even an Obadiah enriched with the gift of prophecy. "The Lord knows His own; all peoples will serve Him." In these circumstances it is not the Christian way, indeed it is very contrary to the spirit of Christ, to keep the people away from our ministry and to dissuade them from the enterprise, [or to say that] because the difficulties will be great they cannot have over them the rule of God and His grace; and with the harvest being very meager, the fruits of the souls cannot fail to be abundant and the rewards before God immense.

[Acosta continues along related lines in Chapters 16 and 17. He is confident about the conversion of many Indians, arguing that their "internal religiosity" should not always be doubted. And he returns to the theme of how essential able, sensible, and dignified priests are to the maintenance of the faith in its new lands in the Spanish world. Acosta invokes the authority of his personal experiences, and he finds the Indians eager to imitate good examples, capable of receiving the faith and abandoning their non-Christian ways; he finds them naturally obedient and respectful of people in power. He underscores his points with further examples from the Bible and from the histories of early Christian missionaries among the pagans of Europe (missions to Ireland and Britain are the examples that occur to him), the twists and morals of which he knows so well and relates exquisitely. Acosta's purpose is clear: America is part of the Christian revelation. Friars and priests and Indians are playing their parts in a divinely sanctioned story that will cost much toil and many lives. Doubts and regrets will flourish in even the strongest of missionaries. But there is a magnificent ending even in this most barbarous of lands. The Jesuit's principal messages build up an exhortation aimed at his fellows: we Christians in the Indies must not lose heart in our venture to win the Indians over to God's side. We can learn and gain strength from the "patience," "perseverance" (these words are repeated by Acosta), and "apostolic industry" of the "soldiers of Christ" who have gone before us in other barren lands. We should be cheered by the evidence of bountiful crops of millions of souls reaped by our holy predecessors. In the same manner, one day we shall harvest. But, first, great effort (by good teachers and healthy doctrine) is required. "A plant comes to nothing," the Jesuit writes, playing on 1 Corinthians 3:7–9 to make a confident return to his metaphor, "if it is not watered."]

Chapter 18

〜 *Not Only Is There Hope for the Future, There Also Exists*
Evidence of Great Results in the Present

1. The problems I have examined to this point are expressed as if I myself held
a low opinion of the Indian peoples who are to be led to the truth of the Gospel
and as if I had no confidence that notable results might come from these apostolic
labors. Although what I have said about these peoples, for whom I feel a deep
fondness, is, as some of our own [Spanish Christians] pointed out well enough, not
only a little dishonorable but positively unjust and damaging, still, I allow myself to
do it, because in the defense of the Indian cause I prefer to act as a moderate lawyer
rather than as an uncritical enthusiast.

Most of the mercenaries slanderously claim that these peoples surrounded by
the great ocean were barbarous, irrational, inhuman, thankless, superficial, coarse,
and, in the end, unsuited to understand the Gospel and the whole spiritual
enterprise. Still, unless we set aside the objectivity of the facts, what has been
achieved with them up to now is sure proof that in a way we should not give up
hope for the salvation of so many peoples. So, if the detractors of the Indians'
chance of salvation were right in their allegations, they will in no way achieve what
they so much desire.

If I am to say what I sincerely feel, I do not doubt for a moment that there is no
reason to call into question the character and nature of these peoples with respect
to the cause of the Gospel. And I am fully certain that if the Gospel had been
introduced into these regions in the way in which the Gospel's founder intended,
the gains made would equal those about which we read in the primitive apostolic
church. Because if, in spite of such depravity [among] our men [Spaniards], with
their immense chasms of greed, their violent pillage and servitude, and their
outrageous instances of cruelty, men who have suffered serious wrongs from
Christians still have not cast Christ aside, and when a little more well-behaved
instructor or reformer of their ways comes to them, they listen with admirable
attention and respect, show themselves to be more malleable than wax, and strain
to imitate any honest and decent gesture they see. Think what might have been—
Holy God!—if from the very beginning of the evangelization they could have
glimpsed the beautiful feet of the heralds of peace, if they had learned for
themselves by deed and word, and not out of our self-interest, that they were being
sought for Christ!

2. Of course, the fathers of our modest Society [of Jesus], who have already
spent eight years in these regions of Peru and who know from experience the
customs of these peoples, through having set out on many extensive missions,
through the administration of their own parishes, or through frequent dealings
with them even when they have not held the position of parish priest, affirm with
great sincerity that they have met with better results than they expected in all places,
placing their lives on the line with God as a witness if what they say is not true.

Moreover, some of our most serious and prudent fathers assure us in the letters
they write that nowhere have they seen an easier or better field for evangelization.

And those recently arrived from Spain have held on to the common opinion, that is, the opposite view, [but] in the end they jettisoned it completely after contrasting it with [what they learned from] years of experience. For they had seen that these Indians are intelligent, gentle, humble, obedient, devoted to the good priests, they despise pomp and luxury (a thing some find hard to believe), and once they have accepted the religion and virtue willingly and with sincerity, they stand firm in their resolve. It is easy for me to tend toward this opinion, when we see them so committed to the Inkaic religion or so absorbed by the superstition of their huacas that, in order to conceal some useless idols with which they have been entrusted or a hidden treasure, they often die willingly, giving up their fortunes and their own lives rather than the secrets of their parents' superstition.

Who is not aware that Indians were frequently flogged with lashes by Spaniards and burnt by fire set beneath them, and that in the midst of these tortures, they uttered not a single word against their convictions? Why, then, should we think that the Devil is more bold in his own defense than Christ? Or that these peoples, who have been created and redeemed by God, are going to be more steadfast in the preservation of their pernicious falsehoods than saving truths? One thing is certain: give me apostolic men among the Indians that I shall repay you in Indians' souls.

Perhaps because they have seen in us of the Society some kind of life that is honest and removed of all ambition, they come to us, often from far away, and with great enthusiasm and after having traveled thirty or eighty leagues, they make their confessions. We have seen them attend the sermons with such frequency that they seemed gripped by an insatiable hunger for the word of God, going from one to the next until [they have heard] four and five in the same day, and [they do] this every Sunday and feast day. Anyone seeing the endless crowd of those who ask for and receive the sacrament of confession and absolution would think themselves witness to a jubilee or the celebration of Holy Week.

They ask that weighty penances be imposed on them; and if those which are set are not as heavy as they wish, they place them on themselves, driving themselves to tears and bitter pain. They encourage each other to penance with such passion that our fathers cannot satisfy them all and grumble that they are overwhelmed by inappropriate requests. They are so constant in their intentions to reform that one learns of some women (these being of the weaker sex) who, without entreaties, threats, nor [even] a sword drawn and held to their necks, could not be persuaded to go back to their old lovers.

They gladly give up all of their possessions; they hunger most eagerly for the body of Christ, and those to whom it is permitted [through Holy Communion] receive it with great purity of soul, maintaining it [their cleansed state] with devotion and declaring that once they have taken Communion there is no room [in their lives] for criminal acts. We heard of an Indian who felt such anger at himself for once failing in his intention that [only] with great difficulty could he be restrained from strangling himself like an ungodly and sacrilegious traitor to the body of the Lord. It is known that some are so full of devotion to God that they attain an extremely wise and exalted sense of the sacred, to the point that sometimes they have the heavenly prescience to foretell the future.

Many will consider all that I am saying to be exaggerations which exceed all limits, or they may even smile as if these are stories. But I speak of sure and proven facts. And no matter what those who consider themselves the only Christians say, the grace of God has also been spread among these peoples, purifying their hearts with faith, and God does not distinguish between them and us. And there are those who, already won over by the facts themselves, realize that they had never seen or expected such a thing from these Indian peoples; and so they are amazed and give thanks to God the Greatest Father of the orphans. Some even choose to join us [Jesuits], as companions in this happy dawn of the Gospel.

There are very many who, out of envy, are furiously against us and keep on attacking us, [but] one must rejoice at the salvation of brothers and warmly congratulate one's collaborators. What our [Jesuit] fathers have begun, more than completed, is small enough and is deserving of no more special tribute than that which could be made to any minister of the Gospel who is not unskilled or unfaithful to his mission. These same fellow Jesuits who have taken up the ministry of the Indians' salvation are very few; and, also, they are not endowed with the qualities needed for an undertaking of such importance.

3. From all that I have said, one can now easily understand the excellent and abundant results that will follow if the Lord of such ripe grain decides to send numerous workers possessed of suitable strength and talents to work in this field. And even though we reckon that many other Indian groups are able to receive the Gospel in the form we have described here, and such is without a doubt the experience we have of the Peruvians, in the remaining parts of this book we will observe [a certain] moderation and not speak so broadly of the matters of Indians, [in order] not to give the impression either that we have overlooked other Indian peoples [or] that we are unaware that they are less able.

Because although we have mostly our Indians, the ones we know, before our eyes, if it proves possible, we want what is written [here] to be of wider value for the salvation of all. We know for a fact that even among those barbarous peoples whom we classify in the last place [in a non-Christian hierarchy that ranks nomadic hunter-gatherers very low], the Gospel's grace is reaping magnificent and copious fruit. One certainly knows that the Brazilian Indians are second to none in their ferocity and hideous customs, and yet we have learned from the letters of our fellow Jesuits that thanks, above all, to the Society of Jesus, they have become tame and molded to divine and human laws, [and] learned to be men and good Christians at the same time.

Now, also, the faith is enjoying its first fruits among the pagans, and the Gospel's harvest among the peoples is better than could be expected. Our great plea must be that Christ Our Lord will make us worthy ministers of the New Testament, for who could be qualified for such a ministry?

∾ 20

Two Images from the Codex Osuna, Mexico City

(1565)

During a *visita*, or general inspection of local government, in and around Mexico City in 1565, various Indian communities complained strenuously about unjust and uncompensated labor service and other onerous demands for food, fodder, and building materials. Part of the legal record of this visita, known as the Codex Osuna, registered the complaints of Indian communities in the jurisdiction of Mexico City, Tlatelolco and Tacuba (near the city limits), and Tula in the modern state of Hidalgo in a form that combined the pictorial tradition of pre-Hispanic records with a written Nahuatl text in Roman letters and Spanish glosses.

The complaints in the Codex Osuna, including the two images (Figures 11 and 12) and texts given here, echo the grim account and warnings of Pedro de Gante's letter of 1552 to Charles V (Selection 14) that labor demands exceeding those of the Aztecs will ruin these new American subjects if the Crown does not intervene. The rapid decline of the Indian population from epidemic disease made the labor demands all the more onerous. In the first image (Figure 11), Indian men are shown quarrying and moving large blocks of stone by wheeled carts—a European introduction—for construction of a church. The accompanying Nahuatl text identifies the church in question as the "great church" (cathedral) in Mexico City, and adds that not since the work began had Indian laborers received any wages from the overseer, Juan de Cuenca. The short Spanish gloss says simply that "they have not been paid since the first stone of the church was set in place."

The second image (Figure 12) makes a direct connection to Gante, who was still alive. The issue, as the Spanish text reveals, was whether Bachiller Moreno, the archbishop's adviser on Indian affairs, acted on the approval of either the archbishop or the viceroy when he had ordered the Indians of Mexico City to acquire three bells for the church of San Pablo two years earlier. Moreno is shown seated in the upper right corner beneath a church identified as that of "Sanc Pablo," speaking and gesturing with both hands toward three bells. To show that San Pablo was one of the four "barrios," or settlements, in the jurisdiction of the Indian government of Mexico City, the Indian author of the Codex Osuna arrays little churches of the four subordinate settlements of Sanc Pablo, Sanc Juan, Sancta María, and Sanc Sebastián around the larger church for the capital city

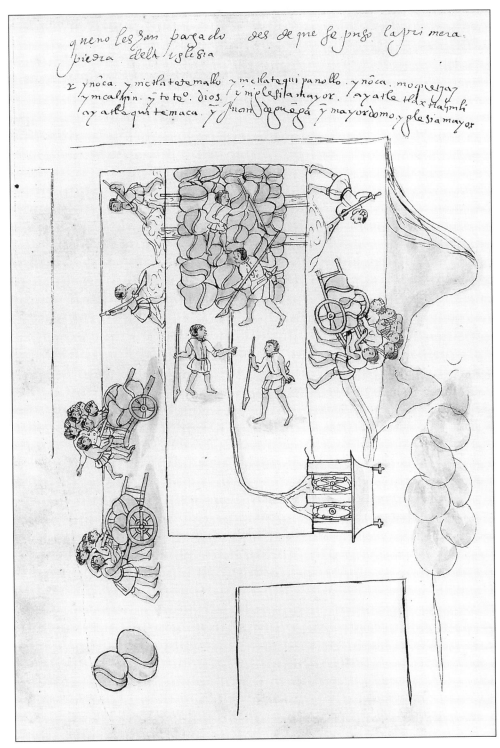

Figure 11. Illustration from the Codex Osuna, Mexico City, 1565.

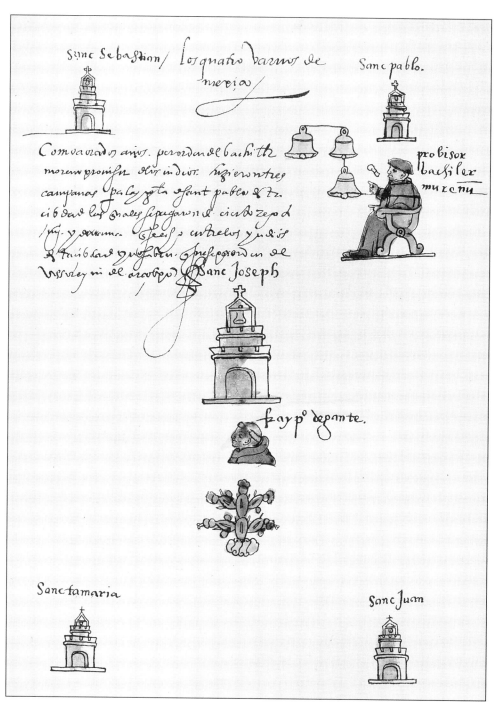

Figure 12. Illustration from the Codex Osuna, Mexico City, 1565.

with its place glyph of a nopal cactus on a pile of stones. Two features of this image are of special interest as an Indian vision of the space and the subject at hand. First, the configuration of the five places recalls the sense of five directions that pervades pre-Hispanic representations of space: four corners raying out from the paramount fifth direction, the sacred center (see Selection 4, Figures 3, 4). Second, rather than identifying Mexico City with its cathedral, the author shows the chapel of San José de los Naturales ("Sanc Joseph") as the important church at the center. San José was, indeed, where most of the city's Indian neophytes went for instruction, church services, and the sacraments, but it was also a local Indian place in a fuller sense. It was built and maintained by Indians of the vicinity at their own expense and had been accorded some privileges and special indulgences usually reserved for cathedrals. The author goes further, embellishing the representation of the Indian church in Mexico City with a drawing of the head and shoulders of the beloved Pedro de Gante. That his name and person were then synonymous with Christian piety, service, and local pride is suggested also by the popularity of "Pedro de Gante" as the personal name taken by newly baptized Indians in the city. Together these two images from the Codex Osuna provide a suitably mixed sense of the demands made on Indian subjects and the succor offered them by the new church and its Spanish priests.

21

Two Images from the Codex Sierra, Oaxaca, Mexico

(1555, 1561)

An illustrated account booklet from the 1550s and 1560s known as the Codex Sierra enlarges the 1579 Texupa map's representation of early colonial experience in Indian perspective for a part of southern Mexico (see Selection 16 and Figure 9). It records community expenses for a place also called Texupa, perhaps located near the Texupa of the 1579 report or at least in the same Mixteca region that forms an arc from the highlands to the coast in northern and western Oaxaca.

Like the map for the Texupa *relación geográfica*, the images in the Codex Sierra also suggest a colonial Indian viewpoint that drew upon pre-Hispanic knowledge and new forms of expression to represent local activities under Spanish rule. Arranged in European book form rather than the traditional screen-fold, it gives a running account of community

expenses for the pueblo of Santa Catarina Texupa from 1550 to 1564. The pages of entries in horizontal lines combine the older way of recording events in pictures with written words in Nahuatl using Roman letters. Many of the entries are for church expenses— equipment and supplies for Mass, musical instruments, religious art, food for the priest, and money spent on holy day festivities.

The first entry included here (Figure 13) dates from 1555 and shows a frame containing a stretched cloth on which there is a sleeved arm and hand holding a large key. The writing notes that ten pesos were spent for a painting of Saint Peter. This economical way of depicting a painting of Saint Peter fits with the pre-Hispanic practice of a conceptual more than a visual art, representing figures and events by combining signs rather than attempt-

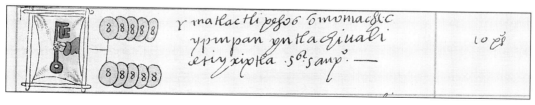

Figure 13. Illustration from the Codex Sierra, Oaxaca, Mexico, 1555.
Courtesy of the Marquand Library of Art and Archaeology, Department of Rare Books and Special Collections, Princeton University Libraries.

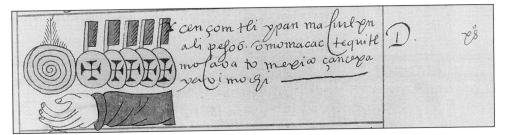

Figure 14. Illustration from the Codex Sierra, Oaxaca, Mexico, 1561.
Courtesy of the Marquand Library of Art and Archaeology, Department of Rare Books
and Special Collections, Princeton University Libraries.

ing a literal depiction. In pre-Hispanic pictorial records it is the arms and hands of highly stylized human forms that are especially expressive, and here an arm in European dress grasps the key, telling us that someone associated with a key is depicted in a painting. That someone is Saint Peter because the key is his particular symbol as keeper of the heavenly gates.

The second entry (Figure 14), from 1561, also shows a large sleeved arm and hand, but it is more expressive in a European way. The text reads "500 pesos were sent to Mexico City to pay for various things purchased there." Miguel de Unamuno once anatomized Madrid as "a stomach, not a brain," consuming the wealth of the nation rather than providing Spain with intelligent leadership. Here in the Codex Sierra, Mexico City becomes a giant outstretched arm with the palm of the hand cupped upward, awaiting payment.

Taken together with the Texupa *relación geográfica* and its map, the Codex Sierra can serve to reflect on the idea that the Conquest was less the defining historical moment for many indigenous people than it was for Spaniards. An example of indigenous people expressing indifference, or at least little surprise, at the arrival of Europeans comes from another Mixteca pictorial record produced earlier in the colonial period, known as the Selden Codex. It records in indigenous style events that happened shortly before and after Spaniards entered the region, yet it fails to note the Spanish presence at all. By comparison, the Spaniards' presence is more of a defining feature in the Codex Sierra and the Texupa maps, which were produced later in the sixteenth century.

~ 22

Fray Diego Valadés's Ideal Atrio and Its Activities

(1579)

Born in 1533 to a conquistador father and Indian mother, Diego Valadés would become the first recorded Mestizo friar of the Franciscan Order in Mexico. Under the influence of Pedro de Gante, whom he later assisted, Valadés entered the order at an early age, becoming an excellent Latinist and following the Observant tradition. He helped to evangelize hostile Chichimecs of north-central Mexico and assisted Gante at the Indian school of San José de los Naturales in Mexico City before being sent to Rome in 1570 as the Franciscans' agent to the Vatican. There he composed and illustrated the *Rhetorica Christiana,* an extraordinary theological text in Latin, intended to assist preachers of his order among Indians of the New World.

Focused so clearly on America, the *Rhetorica* was also the first printed account of the evangelization of Mexico. Valadés argued for the natural human rights of Indians. He considered them as fully human as Europeans and praised the advanced cultures of pre-Hispanic central Mexico (although he also supported war for "just cause" against "barbaric" Chichimecs who rejected Christ). He regarded Indian converts generally as sincere Christians who repeatedly demonstrated their

love of the missionary friars, and he wrote optimistically of the great potential of the young Indian men and women of New Spain.

He was interested in the organization of space in Indian pueblos—town plans, churches, and courtyards for open-air instruction—that would best suit a civil life and the evangelization enterprise. His illustration of the organization and uses of an ideal *atrio* (church courtyard) is at once symbolic and descriptive. The church in the center is not so much a real building as the dwelling place of the Holy Spirit, borne in procession on the shoulders of Saint Francis and Martín de Valencia, the leader of "the Twelve" (see Selection 8), who also appear as bearers in this illustration. Beneath them is the inscription, "The first to bring the Holy Roman Church to the New World of the Indies." The Holy Spirit in the form of a dove reaches the various activities depicted in the atrio with dotted lines. And above the church is God seated in judgment in Heaven, with an angel and the Virgin Mary interceding for the souls of Christians. The activities depicted were inspired by the uses to which Valadés had seen Pedro de Gante put the great chapel and courtyard of San José de los Naturales in

Figure 15. Illustration from Diego Valadés's *Rhetorica Christiana*, 1579.
Courtesy of the John Carter Brown Library at Brown University.

Mexico City. He sets Gante himself into the scene in the upper left—the only named priest—in the act of teaching, and he describes Gante in his text as "a man of singular piety and devotion who taught [the Indians] all of the arts, for none was foreign to him."

Teaching and learning Christian principles and practices are the great activities of this circumscribed space, this place apart. It teems with lessons and rites: group instruction in the Catechism, prayers, the marriage sacrament, the creation of the world, writing, and contrition; a funeral accompanied by Gante's beloved cantors; a marriage ceremony; confessions; a baptism; Mass; Holy Communion; extreme unction; and a judicial proceeding with the priest sitting as magistrate. In the four corners are the unusual chapels found in many early church compounds in Mexico and Peru. Here, friars are giving instruction to separate groups of women, men, girls, and boys. These *posa* (stopping place) chapels served also as processional stations for the solemn Corpus Christi festivities (see Selection 38 and Figures 27 and 28) and instructive displays during Easter and Christmas, and perhaps as meeting places for local confraternities and neighborhoods within the community. The sick are cared for, as an act of Christian charity, along the two outer paths connecting the chapels.

23

The Huejotzingo Altarpiece, Mexico

(1586)

The most costly and esteemed piece of public art in communities of the old central areas of colonial Spanish America was usually the main altarpiece of the local church, whether it was the seat of a parish, a modest chapel in an outlying village, a pilgrimage shrine, the cathedral, or a church of one of the religious orders. Occupying the apse—the often semi-circular space at the very front center of the church where the great sacramental rites took place—it was the destination: the grand and glittering, yet remote, form that beckoned viewers from the moment they entered the building.

Such colonial altarpieces, usually large gilded ensembles that gave form to divinity and depicted the life of Christ and the lives of saints, were meant to evoke feelings of awe and devotion and to invite contemplation. They were much in the spirit of "Tridentine Catholicism"—the reforms and practices affirmed by Church leaders who gathered at the Council of Trent between 1545 and 1563 in response to the Protestant Reformation that had begun to divide Christianity irrevocably in the 1520s. Among its many initiatives, the Council of Trent promoted the special importance of saints and images. One Trent decree declared that "images of Christ, the Virgin Mother of God, and the other saints should be set up and kept, particularly in churches, and that due honour and reverence is owed to them, not because some divinity or power is believed to lie in them as reason for the cult, or because anything is to be expected from them . . . , but because the honour showed to them is referred to the original which they represent. . . . The faithful are instructed and strengthened by commemorating and frequently recalling the articles of our faith through the expression in pictures or other likenesses . . . which is a help to uneducated people."

In the spirit of this Tridentine vision of didactic art and the prevailing Spanish conception of Indians as perpetual children, the evangelization and ongoing instruction of native Americans made lavish use of paintings, engravings, and stone and wood carvings. As a seventeenth-century manual for parish priests put it, "Indians are often moved more by examples [including graphic illustrations] than by explanations." In the central areas of the viceroyalties of New Spain and Peru, Indian communities entered enthusiastically into this visual expression of devotion, sometimes vying with each other for the grandest and most beautiful set of religious images, especially on the main altarpiece.

Figure 16. Main altarpiece in Huejotzingo, Mexico, 1586.

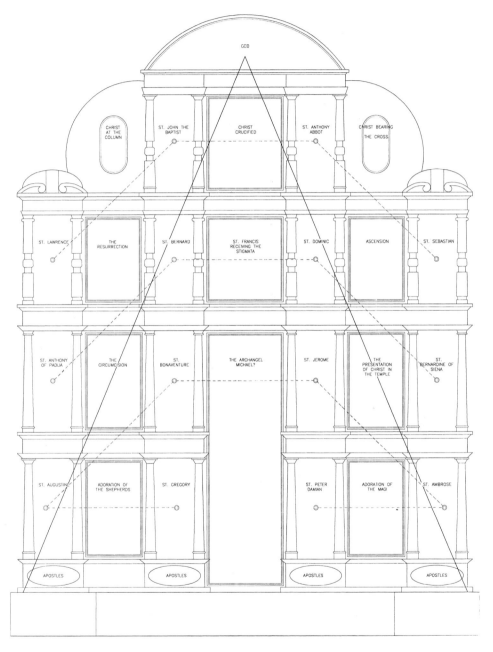

Figure 17. Schematic drawing of the Huejotzingo altarpiece.
Adapted by Karin E. Taylor.

One of the few large altarpieces that survives largely intact from the sixteenth century is in Huejotzingo, an important colonial Indian pueblo near the provincial city of Puebla, not far from Mexico City. It was commissioned by the Indian officials of the pueblo in 1584 "according to the wishes of the Franciscan father in charge of the church and the native Indians." The work, an architectural project in its own right, is a great gilded wood structure with columns, decorated moldings, statues, and paintings (Figure 16). The construction was directed by a Flemish painter residing in Mexico, Simon Pereyns. The Franciscan in charge of Huejotzingo at the time was a famous evangelizer and author deeply imbued with his order's millennial outlook (those expecting to witness the Day of Judgment), Gerónimo de Mendieta. He was probably responsible for the choice and deployment of the statues and paintings. The contract called for a series of paintings by Pereyns and fifteen statues of saints, including one of the patron saint of Huejotzingo, the archangel Saint Michael (which was to be "four fingers" taller than the others). It also specified the size of the altarpiece and the kind of columns to be used in the lower rows of saints. The price was 6,000 pesos, a great sum for the time, plus the old altarpiece (given to Pereyns and valued at 1,000 pesos), and living expenses for the master builder and his assistants. The altarpiece was completed and installed in 1586.

The religious art of the colonial period was never art for its own sake. It was always instructive, always meant to convey a vision of divine order and transcendence. This sense of order and transcendence could change, as did the Rosary chapel in the city of Puebla, dedicated a century after the Huejotzingo altarpiece (see Figure 26). The great ordering theme of the Huejotzingo altarpiece is the providential sweep of Catholic Church history and the life and figure of Christ.

The overall arrangement of this altarpiece displays Christian history with a powerful sense of hierarchical, masculine authority. The basic form of this ordering is a series of tri-angles, associated with the Trinity (the three-fold conception of divinity in the Father, the Son, and the Holy Spirit). One triangle connects the bottom and top of the altarpiece (Figure 17): Christ's twelve apostles in a line of four groups of three at the base and God at the apex, anchoring the seven vertical rows of statues of saints and paintings of the life of Christ. Within this great triangle three smaller triangles of statues are nestled, each spanning two of the horizontal bands of the altarpiece. The bottom triangle, just above the twelve apostles—the historical foundation of Christianity—presents the "doctors" or framers of Church doctrine and liturgy, and two early monastic reformers. (Perhaps the statues of Saint Jerome and Saint Peter Damian were switched sometime after Pereyns completed his work. Saint Jerome fits better on the bottom row with his three fellow doctors of the early Church: Saint Augustine, Saint Gregory, and Saint Ambrose; and Saint Peter Damian is paired more obviously with Saint Bonaventure as a monastic reformer.) The second triangle is traced by four of the great teachers from the mendicant orders: Saint Bernard and Saint Dominic, founders of the Cistercians and Dominicans, respectively; and two Franciscans, Saint Anthony of Padua and Saint Bernardine of Siena. (It is not surprising to see the mendicant orders figuring prominently in such a representation of Church history; this was, after all, a Franciscan church.) The third triangle connects early heroes of the Church: the martyrs and penitents Saint Lawrence, Saint Sebastian, Saint John the Baptist, and Saint Anthony, Abbot. Chronological at its base, the higher reaches of the altarpiece's statuary celebrate the Church's mission and some of its more compelling male heroes with less reference to chronological sequence.

If the wooden framework and statues of the altarpiece represent the historical skeleton of the Church, then the paintings, which depict the life of Christ from birth to resurrection and ascension to Heaven, become its flesh and blood. Another prominent feature of the altarpiece's arrangement and sculpted features that suggests a second organic metaphor for the majestic sweep of Church history and organization is the central panel reaching from the base up to God. Within it are the most important figures of all—a low-relief depiction of Saint Francis receiving the wounds of Christ (flanked by statues of two other founders of religious orders), and the crucified Christ (flanked by statues of a penitential and a martyred hero and by paintings of Christ's suffering at the column and on the road to Calvary). The crucified Christ is no longer in place, and the statue now sited at the top of the panel appears to be another image of Saint Francis. The missing statue of Saint Michael may originally have been located just below Saint Francis. In any event, this central panel suggests a massive tree trunk from which branches of exemplary Church leadership and heroism spread. History in this vision of order is moving in one direction, toward which the apexes of the triangles point: toward a final judgment and day of salvation for the chosen.

We can only guess at the more worldly implications spoken or silently understood by priests and parishioners of Huejotzingo who knew this altarpiece well. But an educated guess is not out of order, since religion was the main expression of colonial ideology in Spanish America before the eighteenth century and provided some of the concrete symbols for social order and authority that appear repeatedly in other kinds of records. The altarpiece suggests both hierarchical order and mediated authority, much as power in colonial Spanish America frequently was exercised by appointment and command, and entreaties were made through intermediaries. On the altarpiece, saints stand between the viewer and God, inviting appeals for intercession. As the Council of Trent recommended, "It is a good and beneficial thing to invoke them [the saints] and to have recourse to their prayers and helpful assistance to obtain blessings from God through His Son Our Lord Jesus Christ." As a vision of history and authority, this early colonial altarpiece invites comparison to that of the Aztec Stone of the Five Eras (Selection 4, Figures 3 and 4).

∾ Saints Depicted in the Huejotzingo Altarpiece

Bottom row, left to right:

Saint Augustine (354–430). One of the major early theologians, famous for his *City of God* and *Confessions.* Following his conversion in 386 he led a contemplative life and became bishop of Hippo in 396. He promoted the idea of the Trinity and a just God as neither simply a loving God nor the source of evil in the world.

Saint Gregory (540–604). Another leader of the early Church; the first and greatest of the popes named Gregory and the first monk chosen as pope; a former civil magistrate of Rome who supported the founding of monasteries.

Saint Peter Damian (1007–1072). Theologian and monastic reformer inspired by the early desert monks; a fierce critic of clerical misconduct.

Saint Ambrose (339–397). Bishop of Milan and a famous preacher and theologian who helped establish basic Church liturgy (ritual practices).

Second row:

Saint Anthony of Padua (1195–1231). Portuguese Franciscan missionary in northern Africa, then a hermit in Italy. Known as a gifted preacher with a remarkable knowledge of the Bible.

Saint Bonaventure (1221–1274). "The Seraphic Teacher." Italian Franciscan theologian, reformer, Minister General of the order from 1257–1274, and staunch defender of the mendicant friars. A prolific author known for his personal simplicity.

Saint Jerome (341–420). Famously learned scholar, secretary to the pope (382–385), founder of religious houses, and hermit. He was largely responsible for the Latin version of the New Testament.

Saint Bernardine of Siena (1380–1450). "The People's Preacher." Italian Franciscan preacher and figure in the Observant movement within the order (calling for strict observance of the Franciscan rule).

Third row:

Saint Lawrence (d. 248). An early martyr; one of the seven deacons of Rome; thought to have been put to death by being roasted on a gridiron.

Saint Bernard of Clairvaux (1090–1153). French theologian and charismatic founder and leader of the Cistercians, the followers of the rule of Saint Benedict. A prolific writer, including a treatise on the duties of the pope; a famous preacher against heresy and a promoter of the Second Crusade in France and Germany.

Saint Dominic (1170–1221). Castilian founder of the Dominican Order—the highly educated "Order of Preachers"—who vowed to live in monastic poverty following his service preaching against the Albigensian heresy in southern France. He was known for his deep compassion for every sort of human suffering.

Saint Sebastian (dates unknown). Roman martyr, said to have been an officer of the imperial guard of Diocletian. The traditional story is that he survived being shot with arrows once his conversion to Christianity was discovered, but was then battered to death with cudgels.

Top row:

Saint John the Baptist (d. 29?). The martyred "Herald of Jesus Christ." In about 27 A.D. he appeared as an itinerant preacher announcing "Repent, for the Kingdom of Heaven is at hand." He baptized Christ, and those who confessed their sins, in the waters of the river Jordan.

Saint Anthony, Abbot (ca. 250–355). Ascetic desert monk in Lower Egypt; founder of monasticism in the sense of gathering into loose communities hermits who sought his advice; famous for his heroic struggles against temptation; spent his later years living alone in a cave near the Red Sea.

24

The Mulatto Gentlemen of Esmeraldas, Ecuador

THOMAS B. F. CUMMINS AND WILLIAM B. TAYLOR

This remarkable group portrait, painted in 1599 by Andrés Sánchez Gallque, is the oldest surviving signed and dated painting from colonial South America. The three nearly life-size figures are clearly identified by name and age, all with the Spanish honorific title of *don*: Don Francisco de Arobe, age 56, in the middle, flanked by his son, Don Pedro, age 22, and another young man, Don Domingo, age 18. Don Francisco was the leader of a previously independent Afro-Indian community in the province of Esmeraldas on the north coast of Ecuador. A 1606 report describes him as the Spanish-speaking Mulatto (of mixed African ancestry; here, presumably, African and Indian) *gobernador*, or governor, of a settlement of thirty-five Mulattoes and 450 Christian Indians, some of them native to the area, others removed from distant coastal areas and governed by the Mulattoes as their subjects. In 1597, following the military and diplomatic efforts of Juan del Barrio de Sepúlveda (a judge on the Audiencia of Quito) and the missionary work of the Mercedarian Diego de Torres, Don Francisco and his community accepted Spanish authority and Christianity.

When these three men visited Quito two years later, Barrio commissioned the portrait and sent it to Spain as a memento of the event, celebrating a favorite imperial story about securing new frontiers and converting barbarians. The three figures are dressed in an ethnically mixed style of courtly attire. The lace collars and sleeves, as well as the satin or silk cloaks, were Spanish fashions. The artist draws attention to the garments by emphasizing the folds and ruffs as well as the rich color and sheen of the cloaks. Beneath his cloak each man wears an Andean-style poncho made of European brocade-like material. Underneath the poncho is a European-style sleeved and buttoned shirt, with a fancy *lechuguilla*, or ruff. The fine cloth and style of dress best suited to the cool highlands add to their appearance of civility and dignity. As Barrio notes in a letter that accompanied the portrait, people from the coast normally wore only a light shirt. In the portrait it is the golden ornaments piercing their faces and the necklaces of white seashells worn over the ponchos that distinguish them as men of the coast. These

Figure 18. "The Mulatto Gentlemen of Esmeraldas," Ecuador, 1599.
Courtesy of the Museo de América, Madrid.

 SEE PLATE 4

ornaments have a long tradition there, dating back to at least 500 B.C., as seen on Jama-Coaque and La Tolita ceramic figurines.

The three men appear as if standing before the king as his loyal subjects, doffing their hats and holding their new steel-tipped spears as though they were ready to defend the coast against the king's enemies, whether English and Dutch pirates or hostile Indian groups and Mulatto slavers. It was surely intended as a likeness, for it was regarded by its patron, the high court judge, as a document of an American event; only now do we look at it as a freestanding work of art. But something else is going on here, too. In a sense the three black gentlemen are trophies, stuffed and mounted on a wall of blue.

The painting offers little, if anything, about how the three men thought about their attire and the portrait-making event, but it is fair to assume that they did not regard themselves as fixed in their proper place, as we see them here. The 1606 report adds something of their longer view of the event and tells a less triumphant imperial story than does the 1599 painting. In 1605 the province of Esmeraldas was convulsed by raids and bloody battles among rival Mulatto elites and their Indian subjects and allies. Don Francisco and his companions were not accused of participating in the upheaval, but colonial officials were disappointed by his failure to help bring the perpetrators to justice. When reprimanded for their indifference, his son, Don Pedro, reportedly threatened to burn their fields and disappear into the jungle if the Spaniards sent a punitive expedition. The colonial investigator in 1606 complained that Don Francisco and his people were drunkards and not true Christians ("they are not Christians in their hearts"), and he concluded that the money spent in Quito for blankets, jugs of wine, and fine clothing (perhaps the very outfits displayed in the portrait) had been wasted on them.

Whether or not they were Mulattoes in the Spaniards' racial sense, the portrait and the 1606 record show Don Francisco and his young companions as new people in a cultural sense—part African, part Indian, part Spanish Christian, and now American in their particular way, as social categories loosened and were reshaped on the margins of the Spanish empire.

Judge Barrio's selection of the artist to paint the portrait is almost as interesting as the painting itself. Sánchez Gallque was an Indian born in Quito who trained in the European style of painting with Pedro Bedón, a Dominican friar and artist. Along with other native artists, Sánchez Gallque belonged to the Confraternity of the Rosary, established by Bedón with the utopian aim of bringing Spaniards, Indians, and Africans together. In a way, such a wish is expressed in this portrait to which Mulatto, Indian, and Spaniard all contributed. But this resort to pictorial representation as a way of conveying information to royal authorities in Spain also expressed another kind of "Americanization"—an enforced, Spanish one in which colonial subjects were regarded as incompletely Hispanicized, requiring perpetual tutelage and restraint. Combining both expressions, the portrait of these three men becomes as hauntingly familiar and remote as the nineteenth-century photographs of Indian chiefs in U.S. Army officers' uniforms.

25

"Blacks Dancing"

(ca. 1640)

From 1630, when they first occupied a portion of northeast Brazil, until 1654, when Portuguese-led forces drove them out, the Dutch gradually controlled a coastal strip north to the Amazon that stretched for more than a thousand miles. Johan Maurits, Count of Nassau-Siegen, arrived in 1637 in Recife, the principal port in the lucrative sugar-producing zone of Pernambuco, having accepted an offer from the Dutch West India Company, a trading and colonizing company chartered by the government of the Netherlands, to oversee Dutch lands in Brazil. He brought with him an impressive entourage that included both naturalists and painters, whom he employed to document this remote place. They were to draw, paint, map, and describe any riches that might be a source of trade to Europe as well as portray its birds, animals, and flora together with the productive activity of the colony, such as the milling of sugarcane and the labor of slaves.

Zacharias Wagener, whose watercolor is reproduced on the cover and in this selection, was an adventurer who left his home town of Dresden in 1633 at the age of twenty, made his way to Holland, and sailed a year later as a mercenary on the *Amsterdam* bound for Recife. Over the next seven years, working first as a secretary and later as butler

for Count Nassau, he also tried his hand as copyist and illustrator. Wagener's amateur drawings of fish, birds, and animals have an appealing freshness. Although intended for popular viewing rather than for scientific or commercial use, Wagener's work vanished until 1738 when it appeared in the inventory of a state museum in Dresden, bound together as the *Book of the Animals*. Added to the animals is a series of "human types"— Indian, African, and Mulatto—that he surely copied from the more famous and frequently reproduced paintings made by Albert Eckhout, a member of Maurits's cultural mission in Brazil. It is thought that Wagener may even have been a copyist for Eckhout and in this way became familiar with the detail of his work.

More intriguing, because more original, are two scenes. The first, which Wagener called a "modest drawing," shows the Recife slave market where Blacks were warehoused until they could be sold in lots to traders, who paid in installments over the course of a year, or auctioned singly to individual buyers. In Wagener's drawing the Portuguese and Dutch traders, appearing as stiff figures primitively painted, nonetheless walk with each other across the square, talking and pointing, while the Africans blur into inert black clumps, with

Figure 19. "Blacks Dancing" by Zacharias Wagener, Recife, Brazil, ca. 1640. Courtesy of Staatlichen Kunstsammlungen, Dresden.

≈ SEE PLATE 5 ≈

only a scattering of shapes recognizable as human figures.

The second, "Blacks Dancing," is enigmatic (Figure 19). Wagener may have borrowed the theme from Frans Post's "Brazilian landscape with chapel and [Blacks] dancing." Although Post painted his "Blacks dancing" in 1652, six years after he had returned to Europe from Recife (Wagener was by then in China), when both men were still in Brazil, Wagener may have seen one of the many drawings that Post made there and used as the basis for later paintings. Despite the similarity in subject, the mood and style of the two paintings are markedly different. While the human figures in Post's picture are small—sky, landscape, and chapel dominate—they are represented with movement and grace; both men and women are modestly dressed. Within the small scale, Post creates verisimilitude: a man plays a drum; work baskets have been placed on the ground out of the way of the dancers. Beyond the clearing where the Africans gather, Europeans walk unhurriedly toward the church, and farther in the distance to the right other Africans move about in what appears to be a sugar mill. It is an artificial juxtaposition of three scenes in one, yet the whole conveys harmony.

Wagener's version is more jarring. Here the principal African figures dwarf a strange and fanciful landscape. The dancing is undisciplined and ungraceful, despite the rhythmic beat from two drummers and a third musician with a *reco-reco*, played by quickly drawing a stick over a piece of notched wood. Distorted male bodies resemble overgrown, romping children, while the women are lascivious, their arms raised, their ample breasts uncovered. This is how Wagener described the dancers in words written in Brazil:

> When the slaves have carried out their arduous duties for weeks on end, they are allowed to celebrate one Sunday as they please; in large numbers in certain places and with all manner of leaps, drums, flutes, they dance from morning until night, all in a disorganized way, with men and women, young and old; meanwhile, the others drink a strong spirit made with sugar. . . . [T]hey spend all day like that in a continuous dance until they do not recognize each other, so deafened and filthy have they become.

The celebrations may have been not merely raucous affairs but *batuques*, or African drum dances, at which slaves demonstrated their skill and inventiveness as drummers, as versifiers in impromptu call-and-response singing, and as dancers, all with a coherence denied in both Wagener's watercolor and his accompanying text.

Another reading becomes plausible when the two women in their long red and blue skirts are seen as being in a trance, their arms extended for balance as they continue to whirl to the beat of the drums. The religious practices and beliefs inherited from Angolans from west-central Africa and the Yoruba people of West Africa came to be known in Brazil as *candomblé*. In the performance of candomblé, dancing is an essential element that builds in energy and intensity, driven by the call and response of the drummers, until the *orixá*, or spirit, descends on the head of a particular dancer as she or he enters into a trance. Only those who have prepared themselves through a long and demanding period of initiation are allowed to participate, imparting a rigorous discipline to the performance. Although there are important differences, both groups summoned the spirits through music and dance. Since Black slaves from the Mina coast as well as from the west-central African region of Angola were imported into seventeenth-century Pernambuco, the dancers and their ceremony might represent either ethnic group. Instead of wanton entertainment, Wagener perhaps misunderstood and misrepresented a sacred dance.

 # LIST OF PLATES

1. An Inka key checkerboard tunic (fifteenth–sixteenth centuries)
2. A royal tunic (sixteenth century)
3. Map of Texupa, Mexico, 1579
4. "The Mulatto Gentlemen of Esmeraldas," Ecuador, 1599
5. "Blacks Dancing" by Zacharias Wagener, Recife, Brazil, ca. 1640
6. Portrait of Santa Rosa of Lima with silver decoration, artist and date unknown
7. Portrait of Sor Juana Inés de la Cruz, artist unknown
8. Upper reaches of the Rosary chapel, Church of Santo Domingo, Puebla, Mexico, 1632–1690
9. Corregidor Pérez and secular clergy in a Corpus Christi procession, Cusco, Peru, ca. 1674–1680
10. Santa Rosa and "La Linda" in a Corpus Christi procession, Cusco, Peru, ca. 1674–1680
11. Santo Antônio de Catagerona, from the Covenant of the Irmandade, Bahia, Brazil, 1699
12. "Thanking Saint Anne," an ex-voto offering, artist unknown, Brazil, 1755
13. "Jeremiah in the Stocks" by Aleijadinho, Ouro Prêto, Brazil, ca. 1770s
14. *Castas* painting featuring the Mestizo, child of a Spanish man and an Indian woman, by José Joaquín Magón, Mexico (second half of the eighteenth century)
15. *Castas* painting featuring the Mulatta, child of a Spanish man and an African woman, by Andrés de Islas, Mexico, ca. 1774
16. "America Nursing Spanish Noble Boys," artist unknown, Peru, ca. 1770s

ERRATA: The caption to Plate 5 should read "'Blacks Dancing' by Zacharias Wagener, Recife, Brazil, ca. 1640. Courtesy of Staatlichen Kunstsammlungen, Dresden," and the caption to Plate 11 should read "Santo Antônio de Catagerona, from the Covenant of the Irmandade, Bahia, Brazil, 1699. Courtesy of The Catholic University of America, Oliveira Lima Library, Washington, DC."

Plate 1. An Inka key checkerboard tunic (fifteenth–sixteenth centuries).
Courtesy of the Textile Museum, Washington, DC.

Plate 2. A royal tunic (sixteenth century).

Plate 3. Map of Texupa, Mexico, 1579. *Pintura* accompanying the Texupa
relación geográfica. East is at the top, with its sacred hills, shrines, arroyos, streams,
and paths coming into town, the paths converging on the Dominican church and compound.
The west side of Texupa is "the entrance to the pueblo . . . more open . . . a fertile
depression a little less than one-fourth of a league wide."
Courtesy of the Real Academia de Historia, Madrid.

Plate 4. "The Mulatto Gentlemen of Esmeraldas," Ecuador, 1599. Courtesy of the Museo de América, Madrid.

Plate 5. "Blacks Dancing" by Zacharias Wagener, Recife, Braxil, ca. 1640. Courtesy of Staatlichen Kunstsammlungen, Dresden.

Plate 6. Portrait of Santa Rosa of Lima with silver decoration, artist and date unknown.

Plate 7. Portrait of Sor Juana Inés de la Cruz by an unknown artist.
Courtesy of the Philadelphia Museum of Art.

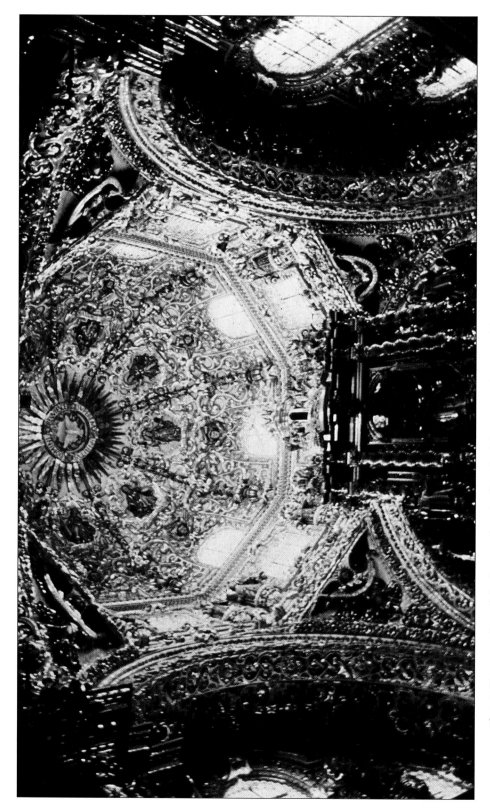

Plate 8. Upper reaches of the Rosary chapel, Church of Santo Domingo, Puebla, Mexico, 1632–1690. Courtesy of James Early.

Plate 9. Corregidor Pérez and secular clergy in a Corpus Christi procession,
Cusco, Peru, ca. 1674–1680.
Courtesy of the Museo del Arte Religioso, Cusco, Peru.

Plate 10. Santa Rosa and "La Linda" in a Corpus Christi procession, Cusco, Peru, ca. 1674–1680. Courtesy of the Museo del Arte Religioso, Cusco, Peru.

Plate 11. Santo Antônio de Catagerona, from the Convenant of the Irmandade, Bahia, Brazil, 1699. Courtesy of The Catholic University of America, Oliveira Lima Library, Washington, DC.

Plate 12. "Thanking St. Anne," an ex-voto offering, artist unknown, Brazil, 1755. Courtesy of José Mindlin, São Paulo, Brazil.

Plate 13. "Jeremiah in the Stocks" by Aleijadinho, Ouro Prêto, Brazil, ca. 1770s.

Plate 14. Castas painting featuring the Mestizo, child of a Spanish man and an Indian woman, by José Joaquín Magón, Mexico (second half of the eighteenth century).

Plate 15. Castas painting featuring the Mulatta, child of a Spanish man and an African woman, by Andrés de Islas, Mexico, ca. 1774. Courtesy of the Museo de América, Madrid.

Plate 16. "America Nursing Spanish Noble Boys" by an anonymous artist, Peru, ca. 1770s. The inscription at the bottom reads in part: "Where in the world has one seen what one sees here. . . . Her own sons lie groaning and she suckles strangers." Courtesy of an anonymous collector.

PART III

Mid-Colonial Ways and Orders

~ 26

Making an Image and a Shrine, Copacabana, Peru

(1582–1621)

The sculpted image of the Virgin Mary known as Our Lady of Copacabana was made by native Andean noble and aspiring artist Francisco Tito Yupanqui in 1582. It was not his first attempt. Indeed, a great deal of effort and persistence appear to have been required before Tito Yupanqui could answer his community's yearning for a holy image to which people might pray for relief.

Even before Spanish and Hispanicized native Andean colonists to the village of Santa Ana de Copacabana and the wider region around Lake Titicaca entered the ethnic mix, local society had come to comprise a diverse assemblage of native peoples. By the late sixteenth century, generations of these Andean peoples had received instruction in Catholic Christianity from Dominican friars, secular clergymen, and, most recently, Jesuit missionaries in what became one of the most bustling early colonial zones of evangelization and resettlement in Peru. A number of the native leaders of kin groups had, like Tito Yupanqui

and his immediate kin, developed a vital Andean Christian self-image, including precise ideas about the patron saint they wanted to make the center of a new lay religious association (*cofradía*) and village church.

Severe drought and an ensuing series of bad harvests in the early 1580s had caused famine in Copacabana and its environs. As conditions grew desperate, two of the prominent ethnic groups in the village sought a special advocate before God. The Anansaya kin group—the more powerful faction to which Tito Yupanqui and his kinsman Don Alonso Viracocha Inka, its governor, belonged—wished to establish a *cofradía* dedicated to an advocation of the Virgin Mary known as La Candelaria.* However, the Urinsaya, by this time a subordinated group in the village, but one with deeper local roots than the Anansaya, favored Saint Sebastian, the third-century Roman martyr. (From the fifteenth century, Sebastian was commonly shown pierced with arrows, with his courage in facing such a

---

* La Candelaria, sometimes called the Purificada, or "Purified," is a representation in which the Virgin carries both the Christ Child and a large candle and offering. The iconography commemorates Mary's presentation of the baby Jesus in the temple at Jerusalem and her rite of purification forty days after the birth [Luke 2: 22–38]. Penitential processions with blessed candles came to mark commemorations of the Purification or Candlemas, hence the Virgin's candlestick in representations.

death strengthening his devotees as they themselves faced trials.) Sebastian had a specialized reputation for interceding with God against famine and pestilence, although the feast days of both would-be patrons (February 2 for Our Lady of the Candlemas and January 20 for Saint Sebastian) fell appropriately within the period when frosts most threatened highland agricultural crops. In the end, only a compromise between these two local groups led them to settle on the Marian patron favored by the Anansaya.

This compromise led, as the following selection relates, to Francisco Tito Yupanqui's apprenticeship under a master image-maker in Potosí and to the aspiring artist's decision to make an image modeled in part after the sculpture of Our Lady of the Rosary in the church of Santo Domingo in that city. Only after he had negotiated an array of obstacles, including the bishop of La Plata's ridicule of his preliminary painting, did Tito Yupanqui see his rendering of La Candelaria, soon to become known as Our Lady of Copacabana, approved and enshrined in his village in 1583.

The Virgin of Copacabana was credited almost immediately with bringing God's favor and a range of miracles to her devotees. The image began attracting pilgrims to the humble lakeside church and, in short order, inspiring other images and shrines of the Virgin of Copacabana across Peru, many of which reported miraculous events. In these early moments of devotion to its Virgin, Copacabana was administered by a secular priest, while most of the responsibility for the image fell on the members of the fledgling *cofradía* of Indians. But with the sudden rise of the image's fame came pressure for change. The rival religious orders in the Lake Titicaca region vied for control of the promising shrine. In 1589, amid vociferous Dominican objections, the prize fell to the Order of Saint Augustine, whose friars took up the task of interconnecting the prosperous shrine's future with their own.

The Augustinians in the late sixteenth- and early seventeenth-century southern Andes, like contemporary churchmen in New Spain and elsewhere, followed patterns of self-authorization perfected over the course of the later Middle Ages by communities of friars who watched over shrines of miraculous images in the Iberian Peninsula. In many cases, efforts culminated in the publication of celebratory official histories of given shrines. And the books were not all. The Augustinians on Lake Titicaca began construction of a splendid new sanctuary for the image of Copacabana, financed in large part from alms gathered in the Virgin's name. They diligently collected information from pilgrims and others, particularly about miracles attributed to the Virgin of Copacabana's intercession with God, that would further glorify the image and their stewardship. In the end, the Augustinians assembled a sacred history of Copacabana that stretched resourcefully from the pre-Inkaic and Inkaic cults of the Sun (which had centered on an island in the lake) to the triumphant cult of the Virgin Mary in their present. At the heart of this sweeping history was the story of the image sculpted by Francisco Tito Yupanqui.

The account of the image's origins was first set down less than a half-century after the events described by the principal agent of the early Augustinian historical effort at Copacabana, Friar Alonso Ramos Gavilán (ca. 1570–ca. 1639). Ramos Gavilán was born in Huamanga in the central Peruvian Andes (today's Ayacucho), apparently the illegitimate son of Creole parents who moved from the provinces to Lima. Like many studious Creole boys in that city in the late sixteenth century, the young Ramos Gavilán was educated by the Jesuits; he then professed his vows to God within the Augustinian order in 1589 and followed a path of devotion and study through various Augustinian convents and parishes of Indians before arriving on the shores of Lake Titicaca about 1616 and then in Copacabana itself by 1618. From that point, his devotion to the image of the Virgin in the lakeside sanctuary flourished. Ramos Gavilán immersed himself in the wide reading, travels, and investigations into all manner of regional wonders, including the signs, much-discussed in his day, that one of Christ's apostles had visited the zone and preached in pre-Hispanic times. His researches resulted in the *History of the Celebrated Sanctuary of Our Lady of Copacabana*, published in 1621. The work is peppered with 132 miracles attributed to the image, some of which Ramos Gavilán witnessed or recorded verbatim from the lips of devotees and pilgrims. Another prominent feature is Ramos Gavilán's notable mixture of Christian Andean and Augustinian protagonism.

Even in an age when Ramos Gavilán's heavily allusive approach and style were the accepted ones for aspiring authors, his work is remarkable for the insistence of its Biblical, hagiographic, and classical literary patterns, quotations, and allusions. Deeply familiar with edifying tales in which virtuous heroes endured trials on the road to vindication and divine favor, Ramos Gavilán presents an intriguing challenge to his reader when he tells the story of the image's origins through a letter said to have been written by none other than the perseverant Indian Christian and aspiring artist Francisco Tito Yupanqui himself. The letter was allegedly preserved by the artist's brother (Felipe de León, who appears as a silent co-protagonist in the course of the letter), who is said to have passed it on to Ramos Gavilán to assist the friar's historical inquiries. What do we make of the Augustinian's claim? If the letter did exist, where does the inspiration of Ramos Gavilán's literary models end and the narrative of Tito Yupanqui's experiences begin? In what ways are the Indian's words accessible here?

Letting the letter speak for itself is as important as letting it raise these and other questions as it goes along. The people in the story beg for attention. As presented here, are Francisco Tito Yupanqui and the other players—from the bishop through the master sculptor to the various critics of the Indian's image—believable individuals? If so, why? And believable for whom? In the end, both Ramos Gavilán's claims and the articulations present in the letter carry a certain ring of authenticity. Which of the letter's features suggest an original authorship by Francisco Tito Yupanqui and seem to consign Alonso Ramos Gavilán (and the artist's brother) to the sidelines, as either a faithful scribe or a pious embroidering editor? In any event, it is certainly the voice of Alonso Ramos Gavilán that introduces the story.

The desire to know is so fundamental in man that the prince of Philosophy [Aristotle], in his metaphysics, distinguished it as almost his true nature, writing: *Omnis homo naturaliter scire desiderat.* [That is to say,] All men are naturally inclined to want to know; and thus it is that many authors—keen to appeal to this passion—have tirelessly investigated many mysterious things, unsatisfied until they have brought to light whatever lay buried, unscrutinized, in perpetual silence. Polidoro, Virgil, Textor, among the many others who have sought to meet this passion of man, leave evidence of the things they sought. Eager to play my part in so universal a quest, amid all that this kingdom [of Peru] offers, I wanted to know of the beginnings, and true origin, of the holy image of Copacabana. While looking into things, I met the very brother of the sculptor who made her [the image], and he handed me an account which the deceased [Francisco Tito Yupanqui] had left, written with his own hand. To ensure that his open-heartedness, kindness, and holy simplicity are appreciated, and in order to give pleasure to all who read it, I have endeavored to keep his very same style in setting it down as follows:

The first time my brother Don Felipe de León and I began to make an image of the Virgin—[we worked] in clay and [ultimately produced a form] one *vara* in height—was during the tenure of the priest Antonio de Almeda. He [Almeda] told me to place it on the altar, where it remained for more than a year and a half. Later, another priest named Bachiller Montoro came and, upon seeing my creation and judging it no better than good, he told me sharply to remove it. They took it away to the sacristy. Disheartened by this, my brother and I got to talking and decided to go to Potosí and there, with [the aim of seeking advice from] our brother Don Alonso Viracocha Inca, to learn much more about the craft of making images. When we met my brother Don Alonso Viracocha Inca, he was glad to see me. I told him I was gloomy after the priest rejected my work, I told him of my anger, and I asked him to get me a position under an expert in image-making that I might be better instructed in the art. He told me I was in luck, and off we went at once.

He took me to the home of a master image-maker named Diego de Ortiz, and the two of them arranged that I would learn as his apprentice. After we had learned a little about image-making, I went to the place where he [Ortiz] and my brother Don Alonso Viracocha Inca were. And after telling him it was an easy art, I said I intended to begin a figure of the Virgin. My brother congratulated me and [he recommended] that all of us native Andeans should go and see [existing] images of the Virgin, and to take from this [the experience of studying different images] that which seemed good. We went looking in all the churches, one by one, until we came to the church of Santo Domingo. And with the form of the Virgin [an image of Our Lady of the Rosary]—and its very same size and dress, and its Child and candle—in mind, we set to work in the same way.

The three of us, Don Felipe, Don Alonso, and I, set to making a clay casting, [but things went poorly.] If we finished it [the casting] one day, it was broken by the next morning. So we tried to make it again, and again the casting cracked and we started over, and thus it went for more than three or four times.* We were growing very dejected, and I prayed to God, with the Virgin, pleading that this image would come out well, and I asked that a Mass be said to the Holy Trinity for the same aim. After this, we wiped it with cloths. When we had removed it [the casting from the mold], we took it to Diego de Ortiz to learn from him whether it was good or bad, or if it had some fault or a poor form. Looking over the image, he told me it was good and that I had learned much, but he said no more to me than that.

I [then] took the image to the painters' house in order to learn their opinion. Some told me that while it was better [than what I had done before], it was [still] poorly made, while others told me it was well done. The painters said all this, wanting to mislead me, because [in truth] the image was complete and whitewashed, and there was nothing left to do but gild it.

---

* In this form of image-making, less costly than carving from the durable cedar preferred for religious sculpture, a wood paste of variable ingredients is poured into a clay mold (created after a desired model image). After the concoction has set, the casting is eased out of the mold to harden, varnish, paint, and gild to taste.

So I went to Chuquisaca [the city of La Plata, today Sucre, Bolivia] to ask for a license from the Lord Bishop to establish a lay religious association of Our Lady, and to be a painter and image-maker. I brought an image of the Virgin painted on a panel to His Lordship, [along] with a petition explaining that I wanted to be a painter and make images of the Virgin. He responded to me, "I do not want to grant you a license to be a painter, nor to be one who makes images of the Virgin, nor statues, and if you wish to be a painter then paint a monkey with its long tail, for I do not want to give you permission to paint [sacred things]. And if you persist in wanting to paint and make images of the Virgin, I will punish you thoroughly."

I left there saying, "Jesus, Saint Mary; may God and the Virgin, His holy mother, help me." For they [others with whom he spoke in the bishop's company at Chuquisaca] told me that the image was not well made, and that it looked like a man with a beard or what appeared to be whiskers. They found much fault in it, much that was not good, and they told me I should not carry on making it. And once His Lordship had seen the image, everyone laughed a lot, ridiculing [me] the painter. Each Spaniard who took it in his hands laughed upon seeing it, and they told me that native Andeans cannot paint images of the Virgin, nor make statues. I ended up feeling weak, appalled, and vexed because I had brought the image before the bishop and been laughed at. I went to the church to ask for Our Lord's mercy and that I might [somehow] manage to get the image of Our Lady painted, and all the rest. I asked in my prayer for license [from God] to do this work, that He would grant me the hand to make sculpted images and to be a skillful painter.

We all set off for Chuquiabo [today's La Paz], bringing along our image of the Virgin and two natives, and stopping at all the inns along the way. In the town of Hayohayo [Ayoayo], as we were fixing to sleep in the houses of the *cabildo* [town council], the *corregidor* came, asking why we had brought a dead body into the house, and they [the official and councillors] wanted to send us roughly on our way. But once I explained that it was [not a body but] an image of the Virgin, they let us spend the night, knowing that in the morning we would be leaving for Chuquiabo. We arrived and from there went in search of a master to help us make the final improvements on the image of the Virgin. At the church of San Francisco, we happened upon a master named Vargas who said that if I assisted him with the altarpiece [on which he was working], and if I bought the gold required for [gilding] the image, he would happily help me with the Virgin and all the rest. We carried the image to the cell of a friar named Navarrete, the father preacher [where we completed our work].

Then, by order of the corregidor, we took the Holy Virgin on to Copacabana, even though the natives there did not [at first] wish to receive her, saying they wanted to get another image, a good one, from Lima or Castile. Thus the image [we had made] was in [the village of] Tiquina, in the chapel of Saint Peter, for a short time, until the corregidor Don Gerónimo del Marañón came. Entering the chapel [and discovering the image of the Virgin there], his hair stood on end [in amazement, and] he went straight to Copacabana. He told the *cacique* [native governor] to gather ten brothers to go and fetch the Virgin. He sent them off before the morning prayers and they came back before it was time to sleep. They prepared the image on a platform [for the next morning], and as the cocks crowed, they lifted her up and entered the town just as the sun was rising. All the people came out to see the Virgin arrive. Joined by people and trumpets, we processed down the hill, and rested the image at its foot. The priest was waiting to say Mass outside of town, [so we then marched there]. And [later] the corregidor carried the Virgin's standard, entering the church and leaving it on the table with the Virgin on her day.

27

Felipe Guaman Poma de Ayala's Appeal Concerning the Priests, Peru

(ca. 1615)

Felipe Guaman Poma de Ayala was a native Andean from the province of Lucanos in the central Andes in the late sixteenth and early seventeenth centuries. He claimed descent from a line of nobility in his province and also sought a distinctly colonial form of legitimacy. Guaman Poma followed the path of his father, who, he said, had spent his life in the service of God and the king of Spain. He was educated in the Spanish language and western European learning and had become an adherent of a fiery, Old Testament brand of Christianity. Guaman Poma spent many years working as an interpreter in Quechua. In the 1560s he was briefly in the employ of Cristóbal de Albornoz, a general inspector and judge of suspect Andean religion whom Guaman Poma found just and fair. In these activities, Albornoz and Guaman Poma anticipated the more systematic "idolatry" investigations of the seventeenth and early eighteenth centuries (see Selections 35 and 36). Through reading and experience, he became familiar with contemporary Spanish chronicles and Christian devotional and moral texts, and he borrowed and adapted to his own purposes a number of their principles and conventions when he himself began to draw and write.

Guaman Poma composed a remarkable manuscript, the *New Chronicle and [Treatise on] Good Government (Nueva corónica y buen gobierno)*, a work he is thought to have finished in about 1615. The *Nueva corónica* consists of a massive assemblage of almost 1,200 pages, including nearly 500 drawings, which Guaman Poma meant explicitly for the eyes of King Philip III. In part it is a history of the world from the perspective of the Andean region, encompassing Andean cultures, the Inkas, and the Spanish conquest and colonial rule in Peru. It is part autobiography and travelogue punctuated by the anecdotes and examples that become the vehicles of Guaman Poma's arguments. It is a moral condemnation and stinging critique of the flagrant disobedience of royal laws and colonial ordinances that were supposed to protect Indians and other subjects in the Kingdom of Peru. And it is also an appeal for measures that would assist the survival of native Andean peoples. Figures 20 and 21 are two of his drawings, and the reading that follows is a translated excerpt of two passages from his text. Both the visual and verbal sources come from the section of the *Nueva corónica* that Guaman Poma devoted to the discussion of Catholic priests.

His drawings and writing work together—equally graphic, complementing each other, imprinting themselves on the minds of their viewer/reader and demanding a unified response. Indeed, recalling Italo Calvino's words in the second epigraph to the introduction of this sourcebook, it would be difficult, and probably beside the point, to say whether Guaman Poma intended his viewer/reader to separate the visual and the verbal, to start an imaginative process with either one or the other. As is particularly vivid in Figure 20, Guaman Poma's words of explanation and speech could hardly be more integral to what he has drawn, allowing the visual and the verbal to merge.

Generally speaking, Guaman Poma's treatment of parish priests in the Peru of his day is as critical of some members of the religious orders as it is of the diocesan priests serving in Indian parishes—priests who were not of the orders, and who were subject directly to bishops within dioceses. His ire is carefully aimed, even if at one point he says that he is restraining himself from naming names he knows very well. Sometimes he cannot help himself, exposing in the reading with unforgiving precision the vile deeds of certain individuals, such as Father Juan Bautista Aluadán. Others, and occasionally certain groups, receive notable praise.

In Figure 20, Guaman Poma sketches one of the praiseworthy, one of "the fathers of the Society of Jesus," in action. Apart from concentrations of *padres* in special houses among native Andean peoples in Juli, Chucuito (near Lake Titicaca and what is today Bolivia), and in the Cercado district of Lima, the Jesuits' principal contact with Indians in the late sixteenth and early seventeenth centuries came from itinerant missions into the provinces from the order's urban colleges. The Jesuits are described in Guaman Poma's inscription as "the most holy men in the world, who believe, [show] love, and perform charitable acts and who, moreover, give all that they have to the poor people of this kingdom." The father's gestures are of giving, of effort and approach. He steps forward, about to put a

rosary and an assortment of sacramental medallions into the praying hands of a kneeling Indian man.

Guaman Poma imagines the Indian's words at this moment and writes them around the person's head to carry along his story. This Indian is an Andean Christian, tired of suspicion and persecution and fearful of rejection. "Confess me, Father, of all my sins. Don't ask me about *huacas* and idols, and, for the love of Jesus Christ and His Holy Mother Mary, absolve me [of my sins] and don't throw me out the door. Have mercy on my soul." Another text has been penned just beneath the bottom line that frames the picture. More than simply a further expression of his admiration for the Jesuits, here is part of Guaman Poma's remedy for the ills that afflict the Indians in their parishes: "If the said reverend fathers were teaching the Gospels and preaching on the passions of Jesus Christ, [on] the Virgin Mary, all the saints, the Day of Judgment, and the Holy Scriptures, [then] the Indians would not take flight." Here, as he would have been well aware, Guaman Poma joins his voice to those of other (Spanish) seventeenth-century commentators who maintained that the native Andeans' salvation would be greatly served if the Jesuits could be persuaded to reconsider their customary aversion to parish service.

The Jesuits, however, appear as an all-too-scarce remedy in this portion of the *Nueva corónica,* one of few exceptions to the rule among the priestly cohort perceived by Guaman Poma in the late sixteenth and early seventeenth centuries. In this reading and in Figure 21, the artist/author singles out the diocesan priests for particular condemnation. Guaman Poma compares the priests he has known and seen, and of whom he has heard tell in his travels, with the "blessed friars" of the orders who preceded them. The priests of his own time, including the friars, come off very poorly. The artist/author contends that Christianity was once carried to the Andes and put before native peoples in an appealing and effective manner, but that the spirit of the early friars and a charismatic faith have died

es   ,P,
LOSPDELACOMPANIATE

Jesus s hombres en todo il mundo q ecama y hazecaridag y Salos
tiene alas pobres mas enes x veey no

confiesame padre de todos
mis pecados no me preegun
tes delas huacas y de los X.
por amor de Jesu cristo y
sus madre s m me apsol
ueme y no
me dyes
por los pues
ta ten mi
seu cordi
a de mi
a nima

ai los Sthos Reb rendos padres fue sm do mirando euangelios   sela
ypree dicage passiones de jesu cristo y dela virgen m
y de todos los S.s y gra del juyno y delas sag estaes
cri tuea no se huy vian los y ius pero trata de viacas

Figure 20. Drawing by Felipe Guaman Poma de Ayala, Peru, 1615.
Courtesy of Siglo Veintiuno Editores, Mexico City.

in the Peru of Viceroy Toledo's time (1569–1581) and thereafter. Indians are now driven into the ground by the very people who should be raising them up through their examples and teachings in the faith.

Like the intellectual message of Francisco de Vitoria (Selection 9), the recommendations of Pedro de Gante (Selection 14) in a different but related context, the work of José de Acosta who simultaneously had conditions in Peru specifically in mind (Selection 19), the letter by a Guaraní leader named Nicolás Ñenguirú (Selection 41 and Figure 30), and many others both before and after him, Guaman Poma calls for Spanish Christian responsibility. This native Andean's critique measures Spanish Christians by their own standards, turning the recognizable language and moral guidelines of Christianity against its supposed purveyors among "new Christians." The effects of this appraisal and redirection are biting. These parish priests are scandalous servants of no one except the Devil and themselves. They are exemplary only in their capacity to sin and corrupt others. They seek financial, not spiritual, profit from administering the Holy Sacraments. They employ Indian parishioners in all manners of work for little or no pay, simultaneously using up and repulsing a native Andean population who are left with no energy or desire for Christian lives—even if they knew, or could remember, what those were. Many people, according to Guaman Poma, flee their homes and communities to escape the predations of pastors who live like so many lords of the land. In Guaman Poma's estimation, the priests ultimately suffer in comparison even with the integrity and good examples of pre-Hispanic Andean religious ministers who, in his view, "were Christians in everything but their idolatry."

Guaman Poma wants to expose the behavior of parish priests such as Francisco de Avila in Huarochirí, whom he denounced in one portion of the *Nueva corónica* (and see Selection 35), who seek to conceal their many abuses, reprehensible conduct, and illegitimate children behind their holy office or showy exhibitions of zeal. Guaman Poma

repeats that the priests' exploitation of Indians is frequently sexual in nature. It is in his treatment of these matters that he invests the most emotion and moral indignation. He needs to describe and comment upon terrible things in a graphic manner before God and king, and to arouse people to what is occurring in Peru. Parish priests, like other Spaniards, seek out Indian women and men whom they can oppress and mistreat with virtual impunity and hateful hyprocrisy. Through abusive relationships and perversions, Guaman Poma writes, the Indian women become "notorious whores," and a Mestizo population multiplies while the number of native Andeans diminishes.

The corrupt priests do not act alone, and Guaman Poma is at pains to portray visually and textually the disreputable alliances that the churchmen seek with Spanish secular and religious officials. And such priests draw more people into their selfish, profit-making webs than simply Spanish officials. The second image (Figure 21) picks up on a theme that Guaman Poma discusses twice in the written passage, namely, the extravagant and drunken dinners convened by parish priests to impress others and cement their wicked alliances with illicit business partners and relatives of their mistresses, all "at the expense of the poor Indians." The devastating effects of these corrupt cooperatives are many in Guaman Poma's view, not least the opportunities that such alliances allow for "low-bred Indians" to enlist priestly assistance in their selfish displacement of legitimate, "hereditary" Andean lords.

In Figure 21, as in most of his drawings, Guaman Poma has paid attention to the depiction of people. "The father invites the drunks," the title reads, "low-bred Indians, Mestizos, [and] Mulattoes, to take part in the robbing of the poor Indians." A priest in his three-cornered hat and high-buttoned collar sits at the head of his own table. He is unshaven, intent on sipping from the full drinking vessel at his lips. His companions include, as advertised, a Mulatto and a Mestizo or native Andean behind the table,

Figure 21. Drawing by Felipe Guaman Poma de Ayala, Peru, 1615.
Courtesy of Siglo Veintiuno Editores, Mexico City.

and another native Andean on the far left, seen in profile, having his cup filled. The Mulatto is elaborately dressed, but Guaman Poma makes him ape-like in appearance, a bit cross-eyed and with exaggerated ears that stick out. The other guests wear distinctive Andean headgear that shows their pretension to noble status. Most eyes are on the imbibing host, toward whom the Mulatto points. Despite his size, the diminutive Indian servant in the foreground draws the eye. Guaman Poma renders him shorter even than the arm of the priest's chair, as if he is being literally diminished by his servitude and by what he is hearing from the men at the table. The servant looks glum as he raises the jug and continues to pour.

Guaman Poma repeats a pessimistic refrain in the *Nueva corónica,* and it is not absent from the reading that follows. "There is no remedy," he writes. And yet at places in the work—as in his portrayals of "good priests," among whom are the Jesuits—he clearly preserves hope for the reform of colo-nial Peru. In the midst of an often tragic and disturbing narrative, Guaman Poma makes precise recommendations. He somehow sustains a faith in ideals, in a kind of Christianity that could be better than many Christians, and in the inherent justice of higher levels of Spanish Christian authority. He writes that "from fatigue and nightmare, the bishops of this kingdom die because we [Indians] are so cruelly treated." He calls for harsh punishment of the worst offenders, for the cleansing effect that he believes such punishments might have on Peru. And Guaman Poma, the Andean Christian and would-be royal adviser, grows more specific. These priests should be at least fifty years old, appointed on an interim basis, and carefully monitored, and the Indians' opinions should be both sought and honored. Moreover, priests should be carefully screened by a succession of able Jesuits and friars for their abilities and preparation as pastors. Usurpers of their holy office, the false priests, must be banished from the Indian parishes.

The aforementioned priests, fathers, and pastors who stand for God and his saints in the parishes of this kingdom of Peru do not act like the blessed priests of Saint Peter and the friars of Our Lady of Mercy, Saint Francis, Saint Dominic, and Saint Augustine, and the hermits of Saint Peter who preceded them. Rather, they give themselves over to greed for silver, clothing, and things of the world, and sins of the flesh, appetites, and unspeakable misdeeds, of which the good reader will learn later so that they can be punished in exemplary fashion. May they be charged by their prelates and members of [religious] orders, and punished by the Holy Inquisition. Their acts do harm to the Spaniards and even more to the new Christians who are the Indians and Blacks. By fathering a dozen children, how can they set a good example for the Indians of this kingdom?

The fathers and parish priests are very angry, imperious, and arrogant, and are so haughty that the aforementioned Indians flee from them in fear. These priests seem to have forgotten that Our Lord Jesus Christ became poor and humble in order to live among and bring in poor sinners, leading them to His Holy Church and from there to His kingdom in Heaven.

These fathers and parish priests consort with their brothers and children or relatives, or some Spaniard, Mestizo, or Mulatto, or they have slave men or women or many yanacona or chinacona [servant] Indians and cooks, whom they mistreat. With all of this, the mistreatment and pillaging of the poor Indians of this kingdom increases.

These parish priests engage in commerce themselves or through a third party, committing wrongs and failing to make payment. And many, many Indians must concern themselves with collecting [from the priests], for which there is no legal recourse in the entire kingdom.

These fathers and pastors demand that women's clothing of fine cloth and ordinary cloth, and sashes for the waist [all] be made for sale, saying it is for their prelates. They order, and deputies oversee, the manufacture of clothing by the poor Indians, who are paid nothing in the entire kingdom.

These fathers and pastors are occupied in demanding that clothing from ordinary cloth, sacks, canopies, bedspreads, tablecloths, sashes for the waist, belts, cords, and other things be made for them for trade and commerce without pay. In pursuit of this, they punish the leaders, the alcaldes [local magistrates], and the fiscales [the pastors' lay assistants]. In the face of such demands many people flee the kingdom.

These fathers and parish priests in this kingdom all keep mita [corvée labor] Indians busy: two Indians in the kitchen, another looking after the horses, another in the garden, another as janitor, another in the kitchen, others to bring firewood and fodder, others as shepherds, harvesters, messengers, field workers, and tenders of chickens, goats, sheep, cows, mares, and pigs. And in other things they insolently put the aforementioned hapless Indian men and women of this kingdom to work without pay. And for this reason they leave their homes.

These parish priests pasture ten mules and others belonging to their friends, which they fatten up at the expense of the Indians and single women who must take care of them. Some have many cows; also a thousand head of goats or sheep and pigs, mares or native mountain sheep, one or two hundred chickens and rabbits; and planted fields. And people are put in charge of all of these things with their corrals and buildings, keeping the poor Indians busy and without pay. And if one is lost, [the person responsible] is charged for one hundred; and they [the workers] are neither paid nor fed. With so much work, they leave.

These fathers and parish priests in this kingdom keep in their kitchens four unmarried women mita workers, cooks, and the head cook who oversees the preparation of meals, [and in addition to] the mita women and women under the priest's supervision, there are beautiful unmarried women. They also keep more than eight boys and overseers, and much equipment, all at the expense of the Indians. These males, plus the servant women, consume a bushel and a half of food daily and they are paid nothing. And these Indian women give birth to Mestizos and become wicked women, whores in this kingdom.

These fathers and parish priests of this kingdom ask for Indians to carry to market their wine, peppers, coca, and maize. Some have Indians bring mountain wine and coca down from the high plains to the hot lowlands. Being highland people, they die from fever and chills. And if the goods are damaged in transit, the Indian is forced to pay for them.

These parish priests have thread spun and woven, oppressing the widows and unmarried women, making them work without pay on the pretext that they were living in illicit unions. And in this the Indian women become notorious whores, and there is no remedy. And they do not wish to marry, staying with the priest or a Spaniard. Consequently, the Indians of this kingdom are not multiplying, only Mestizos, and there is no remedy.

These parish priests take from every pueblo things belonging to the church, hospital, or members of confraternities, saying that they must help them; and they use them up with impunity. They do so with the help of the corregidor or the visitador [administrative inspector, or inspector and judge of idolatry]; and in this way the Indians are robbed of their belongings and community.

These parish priests of this kingdom keep the offerings and alms for the Masses in honor of the departed. For a sung Mass they demand six pesos; if it is ordered, three pesos; for a spoken Mass they demand four pesos; if it is ordered, one peso. Some collect ten or twenty pesos. And they do not perform the said Mass and offering for four reales, which is supposed to be voluntary and suitably returned. Their belongings should be returned to the poor Indians, and these fathers should be punished in this kingdom. [But] there is no remedy for it.

These priests demand five pesos for the banns and candle and offering for a marriage, and four pesos for a baptism, without accepting that Your Majesty pays them a salary. [These collections] should be returned and [the act] punished.

These priests eat at no expense to themselves, paying nothing for their wheat, maize, potatoes, mutton, chicken, eggs, bacon, lard, tallow candles, peppers, salt, dried potatoes, preserved goose, dried maize, choice grain, beans, lima beans, chick-peas, green beans, fish, shrimp, lettuce, cabbage, garlic, onion, cilantro, parsley, mint, and other trifles and foodstuffs and fruits, firewood, and fodder. And they pay nothing for it, or occasionally four reales in order to ease their consciences. And there is no remedy or favor to the poor Indians of this kingdom.

And thus the Indians leave, and their pueblos, [once so] full of labor, are abandoned.

These parish priests do not want to obey or follow what the Holy Council [the Third Provincial Council of Lima, 1582–83] and ordinances and royal decrees of Your Majesty have ordered, to the effect that they are not to have women, whether unmarried or married or widowed, whether old or young, in their house and kitchen. They are not to live together even under the pretext of instruction in Church doctrine, so that the harm and disputes do not multiply and the Indians and their possessions, which serve God and Your Majesty, are not used up; even though they are ordered to serve their [the Indians'] mothers and fathers, [and] go to the communities and sapci [or sapsi, surplus goods held in common] of every province. There is no remedy.

And consequently the number of Mestizos and half-breeds multiplies in this kingdom.

These parish priests clamor to involve themselves too much in judicial matters. Having become secular priests, they want to become assistant pastors, then titular priests, and even corregidor and recklessly order about the alcalde and principal cacique [or *kuraka*, native lord and governor]. As a result they enter into disputes and initiate petitions and are bad examples for the pueblo. They cause destruction for the caciques and other leading Indians, and for the corregidores and encomenderos, and there is no remedy. They treat them so imperiously and thereby destroy the Indians of this kingdom.

Father Juan Bautista Aluadán [whom Guaman Poma isolates as an offender on two other occasions as well] was pastor of the pueblo of San Cristóbal de Pampa Chire. He was a most imperious, cruel father; the things he did were unspeakable. For example, he took an Indian from this pueblo named Diego Caruas who had not given him a ram and put him on a cross like that of Saint Andrew [that is, in the shape of an X]. He tied him up with leather strips, began to burn him with a tallow candle, applying fire to his anus and private parts, abusing him with many lighted candles. And he opened his buttocks with his hands, and they say he did many other unspeakable things of which God will take note, a great many harmful and evil acts. Thus he tormented the painters he summoned. He did this because the unmarried women of Don Juan Uacrau complained that Father Aluadán stripped his [Uacrau's] daughter naked and examined her anus and genitalia and put in his fingers and gave her four beatings on her bottom. Every morning he did this to all the unmarried women. [The native] governor, Don León Apouasco, tried to oppose this and entered a petition, but the aforementioned Father Aluadán responded by saying that [the governor] hid Indians during the visita [general inspection]. And so he was exiled; from this misfortune, Apouasco died.

Consider, Fathers, whether all of you deserve to be brought before the Holy Office [of the Inquisition]. May you be punished for such arrogance, which you practice on the pretext of being the titular priest and teaching Church doctrine to young women. From fatigue and nightmare, the bishops of this kingdom die because we [Indians] are so cruelly treated.

These parish priests fall from grace by involving themselves so much in judicial matters and commit great offenses and serve as bad examples and are not obeyed and create disputes because they sin publicly with all the unmarried women of the parish who live with them.

These women and their parents and relations cannot confess [to such a priest], nor is the sacrament of confession valid, nor is he worthy of a salary from them. Because how can he confess and absolve someone with whom he sins mortally, a sacrilegious sin with these Indian women?

All of this deserves great punishment; and even more than punishment, such a sin should be made known to the Inquisition. Properly punished, this will be a good example to the faithful Christians of Jesus Christ in the world and in this kingdom.

These fathers hire other priests in the vicinity, because their bad deeds are known among them, to confess these unmarried Indian women on the pretext of saying that they are helping each other. In this way they are a bad example for the Christians and show no fear of God and punish [the women's] parents. And there is no remedy for the poor Indians. And thus they die off and do not multiply.

These parish priests have Indian women in the kitchens or elsewhere who act as their married woman, and others as mistresses, and with them they have twenty children, which is a public and well-known fact. And they call these Mestizo children their nephews and nieces and say that they are the children of their brothers and relatives. In this way many sins mount up, and the Indian women learn them from one another, and thus many little Mestizo boys and girls multiply. This is a bad example to the Christians; every one of these [priests and women] needs to be convicted and punished and exiled from the parish.

And so they [the priests] defend themselves, saying that they are the titular priests, appointed by Your Majesty forever. And they say they are rich, with plenty of silver to use in court. And thus no one raises a hand [against them]. On this pretext they show no fear of God or justice. He makes himself into another bishop and has more leeway for his misdeeds than the king; and thus the entire province is being destroyed.

The ancient [Andean] priests of metals, idols, demons, and gods, high priests of stone according to their law, [these] priests of metals acted devoutly and gave good example, as with the virgins and nuns of the temples. And so the rest submitted to their justice and law. They were Christians in everything but their idolatry.

Now the priests and ministers of the eternal, living God are [as I have described them]. From such a bad father springs a bad child, lost to the things of the true God. From a bad tree comes bad fruit, from a bad foundation comes a bad root. This badness is what God punishes most severely in Hell and in this life.

These fathers and pastors are very fierce. They punish the aforementioned fiscales and sacristans and cantors and schoolchildren. They punish very cruelly, as if they were punishing a Black slave, with such malice and harm and vehemence, and they do not stop. They [the Indians] run away and flee and are put in shackles and stocks. With this, these Indians die, and in this kingdom there is no one who takes their side.

These fathers and pastors, acting as judges but without appointment, have prisons and jails in the sacristy, [the room with the] baptismal font, and bedroom. And they have shackles, chains, handcuffs, irons, and stocks with a lock. With these they abuse the poor people of this kingdom, doing them only harm, taking away the possessions and daughters of the poor Indians.

Their names are not mentioned here so that they will not take offense.

These parish priests puff themselves up like a great lord, become rich, and play the role of benefactor. Accordingly, they invite Spanish strangers, encomenderos, corregidores, and the caciques [to dine and drink with them]. The meal they consume is at the expense of the poor Indians. For this purpose they levy contributions from among the Indians of this kingdom.

The priest should not be allowed to be a shopkeeper or merchant or petty trader on his own account or through anyone else, including his siblings and relatives. When he sells food or clothing, he is already acting like a petty dealer. He does not deserve the name of priest because in this kingdom they [the priests] are shopkeepers and small-time dealers. On the pretext of collecting offerings, he buys and sells, so that every pueblo's offerings are sold to the poor of Jesus Christ, and with the proceeds he furnishes their churches.

And so, my Father, he [the priest] goes about winning souls, distributing alms, and living the life of the saints. The priest with more than a thousand pesos [in income] can apply some to the hospital or for the aforementioned work of the Church in the pueblos, because in his parish he keeps the Church as poor as a stable with his demands, and he wants nothing other than to gather silver and rob the poor Indians of this kingdom. . . .

These fathers and pastors of the said parishes call [some of] the Indian tributaries "Don Juan" or "Don Pedro," or they make a habit of eating and chatting with them, because they do business with them or because their daughters or sisters are their mistresses. And they scorn and cast out and exile the hereditary [Indian] lords. The result is many "dons" and "doñas" [springing up] among the low-bred mitayo Indians. See how Don Juan World-Turned-Upside-Down invites the drunkard! He [the priest] will be a drunkard like the rest of them, dishonoring his priest's table in this kingdom.

Because of so much damage and so many complaints lodged against them, these fathers and pastors should be appointed on an interim basis—for a year at a time if he is good; and if not, may he not remain a single day. He should be at least fifty years old because a child's or young man's follies are not good in the world, nor can they be tolerated; [such younger men] commit blunders that cannot be found out.

They should be proven and tested for academic preparation as well as for humility, charity, love and fear of God and justice, and for knowledge of the Quechua [or] Aymara languages of the Indians, needed to teach them, confess them, and preach the Gospel and sermons [to them].

They should be examined by the reverend fathers of the Jesuit Order; second, by the Franciscan friars; third, by the humble hermits who are most holy fathers; fourth, by those of the Dominican Order who are great scholars and preachers in the world. Those [who pass the examinations] should be sent to Your Lordship and to the lord viceroy for appointment as interim pastors, posting a guaranteed bond. With this they will lose their arrogance; they will obey Your Lordship.

In the time of the conquest of a province there was only a single priest in charge of instruction; and before there was a priest, a poor Spaniard was responsible for teaching [Christian] doctrine in each province of this kingdom. And this teacher of doctrine was called uiczarayco. . . .

And so everyone gathered around the priest from the time of Barchilón [who, in midsixteenth-century Huamanga, began the Hospital of San Juan de Dios, which served the native poor], and they called him uiczarayco because he demanded no silver, only enough to eat. Thus these first ones were exemplary saints. They feared God and justice; [they feared] the pope, the king, and their prelate, and they did not pretend to be a bishop or a magistrate. Thus [the people] converted to God, giving themselves over to peace and to the royal Crown.

And if it were then as it is now, with so much harm, they would have risen up or, if not, the Indians of this kingdom would have been finished off, as they are now being finished off by the priests.

Among these priests there are many who go hungry and are so very poor, and others who are superior scholars and sons of humble gentlemen who are deserving of parish assignments. But there are others who are not deserving, who have usurped parish assignments. There, they have twenty children and do great harm. Claiming to be titular priests, they refuse to leave the parish.

So they should be appointed on an interim basis and post bond; then all will eat well or better. And if [the pastor] is very good, may he, at the Indians' request, die there. [But] if he is a source of great harm and arrogance, may he appear before Your Lordship for punishment or pardon and be removed from his jurisdiction and lordship, even if it be to Rome or Castile. May he again appear before Your Lordship to make restitution to the Indians. And giving him license and a letter of safe passage, if he wishes to go to another diocese in this kingdom, let him do so. In this way such great harm in this kingdom will stop.

May these parish priests not impede the Indian men and women of this kingdom from wearing silks and Castilian cloth as they please, as long as they do not tyrannize the leading caciques. And may they eat at table with tablecloths and dinnerware of silver or gold, rather than of wood or pottery. May they keep clean and be rich so that they may serve God and Your Majesty. If the people are rich, Your Majesty, the encomendero, the corregidor, the priest, and the chief cacique will be rich. Therefore, if the priests or corregidores stand in the way, may they be punished in this kingdom.

28

Pedro de León Portocarrero's Description of Lima, Peru

(early seventeenth century)

After the capture of Atahuallpa and his army at Cajamarca in 1532, the Inka's highland capital of Cusco was occupied by Spanish soldiers. Yet in contrast to New Spain, where the Aztecs' Tenochtitlan became the viceregal capital of Mexico City, Cusco was deprived of its central political and symbolic role after control was wrested from the Inkas in Peru. The Spaniards considered establishing a highland capital but ultimately needed the sea and its connection to Europe, via the isthmus at Panama. Pizarro's home base, the City of the Kings—soon known as Lima—was founded on the coast of central Peru in 1535 and soon reoriented the political, religious, and commercial space of western South America. As the capital of the Spanish Hapsburgs' South American viceroyalty, Lima was one of the most remarkable colonial cities by the early seventeenth century, when this selection was written.

Beginning in the mid-sixteenth century, Lima became a magnet for economic opportunists, and many others besides, as did, on a lesser scale, the great silver-mining center of Potosí, the cause of much of the Peruvian "opportunity" after 1545. (Potosí, in the region that is today Bolivia, had a population of

120,000 by 1572, and an astounding 160,000 by 1610. Seville, which had swelled into the largest city in Spain in the course of the sixteenth century, thanks to its role as the gateway for Indies trade and emigration, had about 90,000 inhabitants in 1590. By comparison, Lima had about 13,000 in 1593.) Like Potosí, Lima drew Spaniards from Mesoamerica and the Caribbean islands as well as from the Spanish kingdoms. The city also became a major destination for enslaved Africans brought to work and build the colony's base. Lima drew on neighboring valleys for wheat, maize, livestock, wine, olives, and other goods, but the city's rapidly increasing population was soon dependent for many of its staples (and most of its luxuries) on trade within a steadily widening sphere in Spanish America, Europe, and Asia.

Contemporary population figures must be taken as rough estimates—and some of our sources were not above exaggerating certain elements of the population and magnifying the size and importance of Lima—yet a basic idea of the composition of society in the early seventeenth century helps to imagine the place described by the author of the passage. The viceroy's census of

1614 marked Lima's population at 25,454 persons, among whom were: 10,386 Africans (5,857 women and 4,529 men); 9,616 Spaniards (5,257 men and 4,359 women); 1,978 native Andeans (1,116 men and 862 women); 744 Mulattoes (418 women and 326 men); and 192 Mestizos (97 men and 95 women). Notably, persons recorded as *negros* (Africans) outnumbered all other groups, and there were more African women and Mulattas than male counterparts. The figures for Mulattoes and Mestizos seem conspicuously low for 1614, suggesting that, in official terms at least, many were being designated as Africans or Indians or else were "passing" as Spaniards. This is the first census in which the Indian residents of Lima, almost all of whom were migrants, were included in the city's count, perhaps because it seemed significant and possible now that they were concentrated in the sector of the city called the Cercado. As Frederick P. Bowser has observed, an increasing number of slaves brought to Peru from different parts of Asia were not included in the census. The Franciscan Creole Buenaventura de Salinas y Córdova (1592–1653), whose grandfather had been one of the Spanish conquerors of Peru, claimed that the population of his native city climbed substantially from the 1614 figure to 40,000 by 1630.

Its dwellers and visitors looked on the city with different eyes and from different angles. Sometimes their reactions (like their lives) are difficult to trace, as, for example, in the experience of Lima for the thousands of African and Mulatto women who worked principally as domestic slaves and servants. The center of political and religious authority staggered Felipe Guaman Poma de Ayala, the Hispanicized native Andean author and artist (Selection 27 and Figures 20, 21). Yet that impression did nothing to lessen the danger and corruption he saw in Lima and other sizable cities and towns in Peru—especially for the displaced highland peoples who were brought there by Spaniards to work, or who fled problems or squalor in their depopulated communities and came in search of new livelihoods.

Guaman Poma documented how Indians were mercilessly preyed upon in the provinces but, for him, the city was even worse. He believed that cities ought to be left to the Spaniards, Africans, and people of mixed race, and that native Andeans should return to their home communities, where they might prosper and be guided and protected by Christianized native governors such as himself. Guaman Poma found that Indians lost their bearings and integrity in walled districts, intersecting streets, and teeming squares. Indian women (whose sexual and physical abuse by Spaniards was uncompromisingly investigated by Guaman Poma and is a prominent thread running through his chronicle) slid into habits of brazenness and were lured into prostitution, while honest men became drinkers, idlers, and devotees of petty crime and other forms of degeneracy.

In his *History of the Foundation of Lima* (composed ca. 1639), the Andalusian Jesuit Bernabé Cobo (1580–1657) was bothered by another kind of degeneracy promoted by living in Lima—an ailment, it seems, that affected not Indians but the wealthy sectors of the city. Father Cobo noted Lima's vigorous life of business in approving terms, but he was disgusted by the uses to which most of the financial gains were put. He lamented the "empty pomp" of the culture of plenty and the affluence of the few, and he scorned extravagant expenditures on such items as sumptuous furniture and glittering jewelry.

Yet not a few Creole intellectuals in the first decades of the seventeenth century saw the *peninsular* Cobo's "empty pomp" in quite another way. Exhibitions of the well-planned splendor of their Lima, a New World marvel, were the strings upon which they played a political agenda. A number of Creole authors combined enthusiastic celebrations of their native city and its overflowing wealth with spirited defenses of the abilities of fellow Creoles and condemnations of peninsular Spaniards' prejudices, greed, and exploitation of native Andeans and Creoles alike. Their pride helps explain the extent of the planning, building projects, and religious institutions that dominated the urban landscape in a place that a number of these writers celebrated as one of the urban wonders of the world. Friar Salinas y Córdova acclaimed the city alongside Rome for Lima's impressive ecclesiastical architecture and religious ornamentation, Genoa for its sense of style, Florence for its fair climate, Venice for its wealth, and Salamanca for its learning. The mining of precious metals cost much suffering and many Indians' lives, and this was to be lamented by the Creole commentator (and blamed on the transforming evils of peninsular brutality and indifference), but silver and mercury produced the untold wealth that flowed not only back to coffers in Europe but also into the privileged sectors of Lima's fast-growing population, with some of it transformed into its parks and plazas, buildings and gardens.

The author of the selection that follows did not record his name. However, Guillermo Lohmann Villena has argued convincingly that it was Pedro de León Portocarrero, a man whose life story offers a number of points of entry into the interlocking history of the contemporary European and Atlantic world. León was a *converso*, a new Christian of Portuguese Jewish descent, from Galicia in northwestern Spain. He was investigated by the Inquisition in Toledo in the late sixteenth century for the persistent profession and practice of Judaism. He repented of the alleged offense and was handed a light sentence, ordered to process in an *auto-da-fé* (the Inquisition's public ceremony featuring acts of repentance and sentences of punishment for religious offenders) in Toledo in 1600 and to wear a *sambenito*, a penitential garment that marked a former religious offender. People of Jewish and Moorish descent were prohibited from traveling to the Indies at this time, but many went anyway, attracted by the prospect of lessened notoriety and, often, the opportunities of new lives among relatives already there. They entered secretly, often through the port of Buenos Aires. León was one of these secret Iberian emigrants to South America.

He lived in Peru for about fifteen years (1600–1615), and in Lima itself for a decade. He appears to have composed his description of the city and the other places he visited after he returned to Spain. Yet in only a limited sense can León be called a foreign traveler. He was an insider with an eye for detail, who married a Christian woman and had two children and participated vigorously in the commercial life of early seventeenth-century Lima.

That said, there is possibly even more to the author's tracing of Lima's streets, his noting of the positioning of its palaces and armaments, the locations of surrounding Indian towns, and, in parts of the description not included here, his careful attention to the state of its port and urban defense initiatives. Without arguing that espionage was the only or even the central purpose of León's research and writing, Lohmann Villena places the author within the context of an international contingent of "spies," snooping around and collecting information in the wealthy capital of the southern viceroyalty that would be of great interest to enemy powers—especially to the Dutch, who (like the English and French) already had colonizing designs on the Indies well beyond what they would eventually achieve in northeastern Brazil, the Caribbean, and the Guyanas. A number of people believed to be secret agents were captured by colonial officials in Lima and found to be of Portuguese Jewish descent; some had lived for a time in Holland before arriving in Spanish America.

It is uncertain if spying or assisting a challenge to Spanish control in Peru was our author's intention if, in another part of his anonymous description, the cool reference to incursions by Dutch "adversaries" (*contrarios*) in the waters off Lima's port of Callao is an example of León's careful adoption of a tone that would not attract attention. But after establishing himself as a successful merchant in Lima, our author fell under suspicion for other reasons. Perhaps anticipating another arrest by the Inquisition on charges of Judaizing—this time, not only an alleged secret adherence to the Jewish faith but also the proselytization of others—León in 1615 took flight for Spain. He left his wife, business interests, and Peru, taking with him his nine-year-old son and six-year-old daughter. He erred in not anticipating diligent communication between the tribunals of the Inquisition in Lima and Seville, for he was promptly arrested and imprisoned when he landed in Seville. Appearing before the Inquisition once again, León admitted his converso lineage but denied the charges of Judaizing and endeavoring to convert Christians to Judaism in Lima. He maintained that he was being framed by enemies who stood to gain by his downfall. The inquisitors seemed to believe him or, at least, they were not sufficiently convinced of his guilt. León was set free with an obligation to pay a fine of 300 ducats.

His description of the city of Lima betrays few signs of the trials and tribulations that interrupted his life. One detects in this piece of writing, if anything, an admiration for the things he describes, many of which were the manifestations of Spanish Christianity. A crypto-Jew's duplicity? A curious infiltrator's artful veil over a useful piece of intelligence? The eloquent product of a few Peruvian years of happiness, curiosity, travel, and business in the life of a new Christian otherwise threatened by suspicion and bouts with the Inquisition? The splendor of his Lima does not seem threatened or about to decline along with the regularity of the shipments of Peruvian silver to Cádiz. The document and its converso author, whose very presence in Peru was a crime, find their place under the rule of a viceroy-poet, Don Juan de Mendoza y Luna, the Marquis of Montesclaros (1606–1614); out of his viceregency came an extraordinary cluster of eventual saints and pious persons, an upsurge in the efforts to eliminate suspect Indian religiosity, a flourishing of Baroque art and architecture, and an extraordinary number of synthesizing histories from different sources such as José de Acosta and Felipe Guaman Poma de Ayala.

In his city tour, the author comments on many of the same highlights as Salinas y Córdova, reminding us that civic pride was not a Creole preserve. Of particular note is the size and splendor of Lima's religious establishment in the early seventeenth century. Salinas's chronicle from 1630 complements León's mostly physical descriptions with a sense of the human proportions of this religious culture. Salinas maintained that in 1630 there were as many as 400 secular priests in Lima—more, if one counted the port of Callao and other surrounding parishes. And the city seems to have held even greater attraction for members of the religious orders, with about 900 male religious in Lima at this time. Salinas writes of 1,366 nuns in the city, coming mostly from families who could afford the sizeable endowments described by León, served by 899 female slaves. The great Augustinian Convent of the Incarnation took up its own city block, housing 450 nuns, 50 novices, and 276 slaves. There were 210 nuns of the Conception, with 23 novices and 245 slaves; 150 nuns of the Holy Trinity (with 10 novices), served by 130 slaves; 65 Barefoot nuns (and 20 novices) with more than 100 slaves; 197 nuns lived in the Convent of Santa Clara (with 20 novices) and 120 slaves; and in the newly founded (ca. 1623) convent so wished for by Santa Rosa before her death, that of the Dominican nuns of Saint Catherine of Siena, there were already 46 nuns, who kept 38 slaves.

Of 700 Dominican friars in this order's province of Peru, Salinas wrote that 250 lived in Lima. Salinas's own order, the Franciscans, also had some 700 friars in Peru, of whom another 250 were in the city—190 of whom resided in the massive structure featured in Figure 22. Of 500 Augustinians in Peru in 1630, 170 lived in the convent in Lima, with many more in the College of San Ildefonso, and 130 of 330 Mercedarians were similarly based in Lima. The Jesuits had a complement of 250 in Peru at this time, with about 150 members resident in Lima. A good number of the Society were occupied in teaching a student body of over 180, drawn principally from the children of the city's elite, in two colleges, San Pablo and San

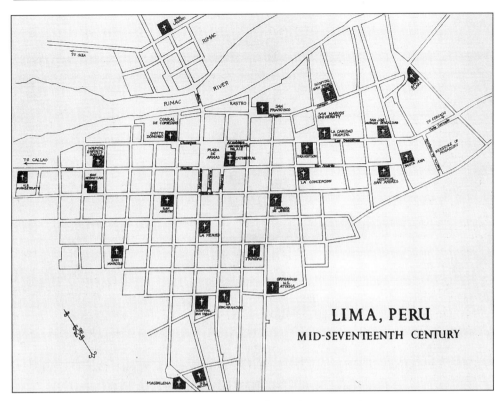

Figure 22. Plan of Lima, Peru, in the mid-seventeenth century.
Courtesy of the University of Oklahoma Press.

Martín. According to Salinas, an alumnus of San Martín from the time when Father Pablo José de Arriaga (the famous proponent and agent of the Extirpation of idolatry) had been rector, 14 Jesuits taught at the college in 1630. Other teachers worked among the 50 novices in the Society's own novitiate. And 6 Jesuits were based in a house of doctrine established among the over 800 Indians who lived in the some two hundred dwellings that made up the Cercado in 1630 (similar to the residence that members of the Society had erected over a half-century earlier among the Moriscos in the Albaicín quarter of Granada; see Selection 18).

León's tour of Lima's religious architecture and general urban landscape contains within it a detailed description of the city's commercial practices. For him, the city's commerce is clearly hard-headed and competitive, but it is also commended in moral terms, described as "the most true, fair, and worry free that one can find in the world." León clearly knew this realm of activity intimately. His description of the market square and the central streets named after the merchants and wares that lined them brings to life a bustling emporium of moving parts. (See the plan of the streets and principal ecclesiastical buildings in Figure 22.) The account puts the lie to the (mostly Protestant-inspired) depiction of the Spaniard as the idle "Mongol of America," a rusty former conquistador whose dignity resided in his shunning of entrepreneurial activity and in an utter dependence on native laborers and slaves. "Everyone is involved," León writes, "all have dealings and everyone is a merchant, even if it is through a third party or on the sly." The contemporary Salinas echoed the statement, observing that "the entire city is a market."

There were a number of rags-to-riches stories among merchants in colonial Peru, and plenty of wealthy figures. The business practices, scales of value for goods, and general acumen of one fabled sixteenth-century Lima merchant, Don Nicolás Vargas—or El Corso, "the Corsican"—are lingered over by the author of this account. Whereas the Franciscan Creole Salinas might well have found him one of the Spaniards who "live among us squeezing the land like a sponge," León sees in "the Corsican" not a peninsular exploiter but a hero, a success story, and an example to all who followed. He was a contemporary man of business in Lima, connected by blood and business relations to the greater "Babylon" of the Spanish world, Seville. And yet the great merchant, too, found his place within the religious culture of colonial Lima. At his death, to unburden his conscience and ensure the eternal rest of his soul, the man who had set the world's prices bequeathed 80,000 pesos to the prior of Santo Domingo. A hospital and church were constructed, within which a chapel to Saint Joseph was built in honor of "the Corsican," whose remains came to rest in a vault behind the altar.

The eight most important streets of Lima converge in the city's *plaza mayor* [central square, or *plaza de armas*], with two entering at [and leaving from] each corner. These streets are very straight, and all of them carry on into the open country. First there is the Street of the Plaza Mayor next to the [viceregal] palace and between the arsenal and the houses of the municipal council. This street runs directly north, crossing the river [Rímac] by a bridge, into the neighborhood of San Lázaro [Saint Lazarus]. Turning left from here, one goes along a very grand street, the Royal Highway of the Plains, which passes along the Carabaillo River, and through the cultivated plots of land and countryside, to Chancay by way of the Arena mountain range. Four leagues [about 14 miles] on is Carabaillo, an Indian community. Returning to Lima's bridge [over the Rímac], the street goes straight to the church and hospital of San Lázaro, into which anyone who is afflicted with Saint Lazarus's illness [blindness] is taken. Turning to the right, one arrives opposite the wooded park in between San Lázaro and the Hill of San Cristóbal. It features a great variety of trees, such as cedars and poplars, as well as trees bearing oranges, lemons, olives, apples, and other fruits. It has eight rows of trees interspersed with four fountains whose waters fall into stone basins, and are connected to channels from the river which are used to irrigate. All of these rows run directly to the monastery of the Barefoot Franciscan friars that stands at the foot of the Hill of San Cristóbal. These friars have a well-built house and garden. Upstream near the Hill of San Cristóbal is the road to Lurigancho, an Indian community which lies beyond the hill, one league [about 3 1/2 miles] from Lima. Out here there are many cultivated fields as the road leads up to the mountains.

Another street leaves [the *plaza mayor*] from the east side of the palace and approaches the slaughterhouses, coming out in a square that is next to the Franciscans' monastery, a large and very rich house. Including its garden, it takes up two blocks right next to the river. From there, the street passes by the church of San Pedro and reaches [another] large and rich convent, that of Santa Clara. Next to these nuns' abode, running from north to south, is the city's principal water aqueduct. The street then passes the northern part of the walled district [the

Cercado] of the Indians. From this point a road begins that extends straight to the reservoir, the source of much of the water that courses through pipes into the city's fountains in the squares, in the palace, and in the monasteries and houses of the nobility. This is the water that the people of this city drink, finding it better than the water from the river. This reservoir is in the middle of a green meadow, and [leaving from it] the road passes through many cultivated fields, heading to the Valley of Santa Inés, a beautiful valley bursting with fruit and water. Out here there are many Indians, and the road continues toward the mountains.

Another street leaves from the palace and the houses of the archbishop and proceeds straight to the east, passing the College of Santo Toribio and the houses of the main postal office, and continuing to the square of the Inquisition, some three blocks east from the plaza mayor. The secret jails and their prisoners are here, and here, [too,] the inquisitors live and have their chapel, taking up an entire block on the south side [of the square]. On the east side of this square is the church and House of Charity, in which poor sick women are treated and many poor maidens are sheltered until they leave to be married, and [also] where women who live indecently are taken in. Near to this charitable house, on the north side [of the square of the Inquisition], is the College of the King. From here the street leads into the square of Santana (Santa Ana), in which there is the convent of the Barefoot nuns and the hospital and parish church of Santa Ana. This is the hospital for Indians in which all their illnesses are treated. Its income from rent is 30,000 assayed pesos [monetary unit of 12 reales in value]. The street continues along next to the church of the Barefoot nuns, by the drilled rock and on to the church of the Prado, right next to the gate into the Indians' Cercado. Next to this entrance lies Dr. Franco's small farm, once owned by the author of this account. The road [then] runs perfectly straight to the east, through fields of wheat and alfalfa. To its right, two leagues [about 7 miles] from Lima, sits Late, an Indian town. And from here another road stretches toward Santa Inés and the mountains. Turning back to the Royal Highway, it passes through the area of Late (*la rinconada de Late*), where cucumbers, sweet potatoes, maize fields, and vegetable gardens flourish. [A trip along this road] is a delightful excursion for the people of Lima. The road [the Royal Highway] goes to la Seneguilla, where it resumes its course.

Another street leaves the plaza mayor next to the cathedral and leads to the monastery of the Conception, which houses nuns and is rich and pleasant. It carries on to the hospital of San Andrés, a large and excellent house in which Spaniards are treated when they are ill. It crosses the plaza of Santa Ana and joins the main road that heads to the mountains. Turning back, next to the church of Santa Ana, on its right side, this street proceeds to the lime and brick ovens. The owner of these works is Alonso Sánchez, a lime processor who, in my time there, employed four hundred Black slaves. This road carries on to the open country and to the Royal Highway of the coastal plains, [while] another turns to the east and comes out at the guaquilla of Santa Ana [probably a small mound of pre-Hispanic remains or a shrine to Saint Anne, and possibly both]. Here, there is a large field all around, filled with irrigated gardens adjacent to a large water channel. And from here a road heads southeast to the gunpowder works, where much powder is ground very fine. Here is their watermill where the work is done, and [also] a separate house where the powder is locked up. This powder house is a quarter of a league from the city, and its road passes on through the fields and the valley of la Seneguilla.

Another street leaves [the *plaza mayor*] by the Clothiers' Street. These shops [more than twenty, according to Salinas] stock clothing for Blacks. This street goes straight south and passes by the side of the Mercedarian friars' monastery and leads directly to the convent of the nuns of the Incarnation, the most renowned [religious] house in Lima, in which there are more than four hundred professed nuns. Many of the rich nobles' daughters come [to stay in this house] to learn good manners, and they leave it [ready] to marry. In this convent there are splendid and intelligent women, endowed with a thousand graces, and all of them, both nuns and [pious] lay women, have Black women slaves to serve them. They [the nuns] make preserves and assortments of sweets of various kinds, and they are so good that one cannot imagine a greater treat. They have a large and comfortable garden, and this convent and its garden extend for two blocks in length and one in width. For any woman who wishes to enter a convent in Lima, the cost of her admission and necessities alone is 6,000 pesos, while for a nun who wants a separate cell, a Black woman to serve her, and 100 pesos of income, the endowment required is 12,000 pesos; for others the cost is [still] more, set in accordance with their wealth: but even they never quite get the best [of everything]. Continuing on from this convent, one arrives at the monastery of the Conventual Dominican friars and heads into the open country and the coastal plains road.

Another street leaves by the main one, [and] that is the Merchants' Street, along which there are always at least forty shops [but Salinas claimed more than twenty warehouses and at least two hundred shops] packed full of assorted merchandise, whatever riches the world has to offer. Here is where all of the important business in Peru transpires, because there are merchants in Lima whose estates are valued at 1 million pesos, with many more at 500,000 or 200,000, and at 100,000 pesos there are very many. Among the ranks of these rich [merchants], few operate shops. [Rather,] they put their money to work in Spain, in Mexico, and in other places. And there are some who have dealings in the great China, and many merchants [also] invest in rent-producing property. Here [on this street], they sell merchandise on credit for at least a year, and, if the orders are large, for two and three years, receiving their payment [in installments] three times a year.

Commerce in Lima is the most true, fair, and worry free that one can find in the world because the order of buying and selling is that which has been practiced for many years, an order set down by "the Corsican" [Don Nicolás Vargas]. He was the principal merchant and the richest man Peru has ever seen. His sons are the marquises of Santillana, both of Seville. "The Corsican" established a scale of value for all goods made anywhere in the world, and all are obliged to pay those prices. On some commodities he set [the estimated price] very high and on others very low, in accordance with their value at the time. And the brokers [even now] follow his practice on merchandise that was produced and named after his time; and this method of appraisal has been preserved up to today.

The order that the merchants observe in buying their goods is that they take the [manifests of] the merchandise that the transporters give them in order to [start with] the same prices they would in Spain or Mexico. Then, they immediately revise the prices of items, with the prices of some goods rising and others falling, according to the current demand and value of the merchandise locally. Thus, the setting of the price is up to date, with each kind [of goods] given the value at which one can sell it at the time of its purchase. And the reckoning and the repricing is made in assayed pesos, and by this the value is determined, and it is made also with [attention to] the running account. These [become] the prices because [at them] the given merchandise can be sold, reflecting the sum of the one account and the other, with both accounts governed by current [financial] conditions. Then one can begin to see if one profits or loses, and the men who sell them set their own refixed prices and accounts; and thus the price rises and falls accordingly, and they buy these goods at so much percent, more or less, of the cost. Later, as they come from Spain, once all is in order, they send the cargo to the buyers' house, supplying everything correctly and accompanied by an account.

In merchandising one must always take into account the damaged goods and additions. "Damaged goods" are things that are broken, stained, or that have become damp or rotten. An "addition" occurs with the kinds of merchandise that one sells of different qualities; for example, saying it is from one master craftsman's shop when it turns out to be from another's, or saying that a piece of cloth is twenty-four [in size] when it is twenty-two, or not to have the advertised brand, and such things. This is what one means by damages and additions; and in order that they be accounted for, a third of each part is chosen and scrutinized. And the ones [who do this] are always merchants of good conscience who remove what they should and discount the value of the merchandise. Because of this [wise and honest practice] the goods are never returned, litigation and grief are avoided, others buy at the current estimated price, and [still] others at so much percent above the cost in Castile or Mexico. And sometimes they buy a variety of loose goods; but with the assorted large shipments, some of which are worth 100,000 pesos, the sales are always by the rate [method].

All the merchants are exceedingly skillful in their buying. A merchant will collect all the manifests of shipments brought to the plaza for sale, and quickly refix their prices, and from there choose and buy whatever seems best to him. This gives an idea of the merchants of Lima. [Everyone] is involved, from the viceroy to the archbishop; all have dealings and everyone is a merchant, even if it is through a third party or on the sly.

Continuing on with [the description of] this sixth street, one reaches the immense and wealthy monastery of the Mercedarian friars, and then passes to the parish church of San Diego, [also] a hospital for convalescents recovering after treatment of their illnesses in the hospital of San Andrés. When their health returns and they can move about, they are sent to this convalescent hospital. There, they receive all they need until they are sufficiently fit to go back to work. From here, the road meets a little square and the Conventual Mercedarians, and goes directly to the countryside and the sea to the south, about three-quarters of a league from Lima passing the Indian community of Magdalena.

From among the arcades [on the *plaza mayor*] where there are four streets and the Merchants' Street [already described], another street leaves, beginning with the Street of the Mantas [cloaks and coverings of coarse cotton cloth], which is also lined with merchants' shops. This street, like the Merchants' Street, takes up its own block. Along this entire street, proceeding directly west, there are many shops with different specialties: chandlers, confectioners, boilermakers who work with a lot of copper, blacksmiths, and other craftsmen. And it passes next to the Espíritu Santo hospital for sailors who are gathered there and cured when they are ill, [then] under the arch and on to the church of Monserrat. The street heading south from there goes straight toward the road to [Lima's port of] Callao. . . .

The last of the eight streets that leaves the square departs from beside the arsenal in the palace, the houses of the municipal council, and the house of Don Alonso de Carabajal, because in all of the intersections of the plaza there are three corners. This street proceeds straight to the monastery of the Dominican friars, the most wealthy and outstanding [of the male religious houses] in Lima, the north walls of which are washed by the river. And here, in a bit of space not occupied by the friars, sits the theater. The compound consists of two blocks of houses, with seven patios. This street carries on straight to the river. For anyone going south, by turning left from any of these last streets [I have described], one can reach Callao.

One [other] street [worth mentioning, the better to understand the design of Lima], two blocks from the east side of the plaza mayor and running north to south, goes by the church of San Francisco to the house [and church] of the Jesuit fathers, the richest and most powerful residence [of all religious] in Lima. Even the facings of the altars [in the Jesuits' church] are made of finely worked and thick silver. Its memorials they put up during the week of mourning [Holy Week] are all of crimson velvet, all adorned on top in solid silver, with a thousand bows, intricately worked by an artist's chisel, so high that they reach the church's ceiling and so wide that they stretch across high pillars and arches from one wall to the other. They have infinite riches in this monastery and residence.

On another street that runs behind the Jesuits' establishment is the College of San Martín, also belonging to the Society of Jesus; it has more than five hundred students, the sons of notables throughout the kingdom [of Peru] who send them there to study, and who pay the Jesuits an annual fee of 150 ordinary pesos for each one, from which sum the students are fed [as well as instructed]. These Jesuits offer a very elaborate course of studies incorporating many branches of learning. As it continues, the street passes next to the monastery of the Trinity for nuns, and then arrives at the parish church and house for orphans, children abandoned by mothers who did not want their parents to know of their ruinous acts and [thus] gave birth to the children without parental knowledge. Farther along one comes upon another Jesuit convent and house of no small amount of wealth. It was built when I was living in Lima with a gift of 300,000 pesos from the secretary to the Inquisition, Antonio Correa. From such choice morsels many in Peru stuff themselves without choking, because they have the stomach for everything. They [the Jesuits] keep a lovely garden and also have many riches in this house, so that no Jesuit suffers want. The street [then] carries on to Guadalupe, a monastery of the

Franciscan friars. Here, the Royal Highway of the coastal plains heads south, the ocean on its right, straight to Pachacama [formerly the site of the great pre-Hispanic divinity, Pacha Camac], an Indian community four leagues from the city.

Extending from east to west, another street passes close to the Jesuits' church and into the Street of the Silversmiths [with more than forty public shops, says Salinas, and over two hundred people trained to work in silver and gold], which runs from the corner of the Street of the Mantas [with more than thirty shops selling clothing mostly to native Andeans] to the corner of the Merchants' Street. Off this Street of the Silversmiths is the Hatters' Alley, [which] leads to the church of San Agustín. In this block there are a great number of apothecaries, and all of them are not more than a block from the [central] plaza. San Agustín is the rich house and church of the Augustinian friars. The street passes to the great and sumptuous parish church of San Sebastián and continues up to the mills of Montserrat, to which a large channel provides water for the milling and irrigation of gardens, turning left for the port of Callao.

Another two streets, heading from east to west, leave from beside the [convent of the] Incarnation and San Diego and pass near to San Marcelo, the principal parish church in Lima. Here, taking up a space on the left side, is the [monastery] of the Conventual Augustinians. Both of these streets lead straight to the road bound for Callao.

These are the highlights of Lima. The city has many other streets, but the ones described here have all the monasteries, churches, and squares, and all that is best about the city, something that the others do not have for our purpose.

29

The Church and Monastery of San Francisco, Lima, Peru

(1673)

This image folds out of a 1675 work celebrating the church and convent of Saint Francis in Lima after its restoration following earthquake damage. The *Temple of Our Great Patriarch, San Francisco, in the Province of the Twelve Apostles of Peru in the City of the Kings, Ruined and Raised to a Grander State by Divine Providence* was published in Lima and "composed by an obedient son of the Province," father and preacher Miguel Suárez de Figueroa. The title shows that central Mexico was not the only place in Spanish America remembered as a recipient of an "apostolic twelve." In other ways, too, this image, and the text that accompanies it, is a glorification of the wealth and power of the Franciscan establishment in the city and in Peru.

Pedro de León Portocarrero noted the Franciscans' monastery and church in the early seventeenth century, either just before or after an earthquake in 1609 (see Selection 28). The structure sat (as a smaller version of it still does) just east of the *plaza de armas*, "a large and very rich house," which, "including its garden . . . takes up two blocks right next to the river." It became an even more impressive part of the city's space after León's time, as this engraving, ostensibly from its moment of reconsecration in 1673, shows. The engraver's angle of view allows one to look beyond the main facade and different entrances, over the walls and around the domes. Inner fountains, as mentioned in León's account, can be seen. And numbers (corresponding to a small legend on the far right) mark the principal sectors of the community, including a long central garden, an infirmary, an area for the novices, and special cloisters and courtyards. Depicted in the bottom right corner is Antonio de Somoza, the Franciscans' commissary general for the Indies (among his other offices), to whom Suárez de Figueroa dedicates his book.

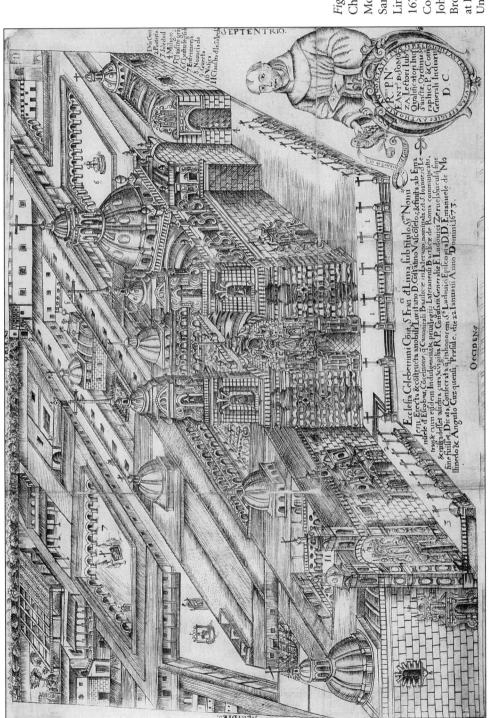

Figure 23.
Church and
Monastery of
San Francisco,
Lima, Peru,
1673.
Courtesy of the
John Carter
Brown Library
at Brown
University.

30

Santa Rosa of Lima
According to a Pious Accountant

(1617)

In the early days of the Christian church, news of saintliness spread by unofficial channels, and often after a holy individual's death. Some "saints" remained locally famous, whereas others attracted cults that greatly transcended their beginnings. Saint-making grew more formalized in the eleventh century, when Pope Urban II required witnesses to testify that miracles had occurred and that sufficient virtues had been possessed by the people who were candidates for sainthood. From the thirteenth century, both saints and heretics were to be determined by ecclesiastical tribunals, the procedures of which were dictated from Rome. These "trials" were presided over by judges and included advocates, witnesses, and—in the case of the candidate for canonization (the Church's confirmation of saintliness)—a skeptical officer known as the Devil's advocate.

Yet the implementation of legal procedures at the center did not result in strict centralized control over the posthumous reputations of holy persons or the actions of their devotees in the many corners of Christendom. Written accounts of a saintly person's life, as well as word of mouth among the faithful, continued to ensure that enthusiasm would grow in predominantly local settings, and sometimes in eccentric ways, after the individual's death. Not surprisingly, the veneration of saints attracted criticism and concern from Protestants and Catholics alike during the Reformation. As the great humanist and student of the Church authorities Desiderius Erasmus of Rotterdam (1466–1536) complained, the cult of the saints was "not a great deal different from the superstitions of the ancients." The saints, Erasmus and others implied, were like local heroes whose powers were concentrated in sacred places, and who were regularly worshiped in themselves as well as in return for their mediation with God. The Council of Trent provided a pivotal setting at which Catholic churchmen gathered to debate a comprehensive set of reforms spurred both by reformers within the Church and by the growing critical presence of breakaway Protestant groups in parts of northern Europe. At the twenty-fifth session (December 1563), the participants at Trent clearly demonstrated their preoccupation with the practices by which saints were made. These churchmen effectively presided over the heart of an era of caution with regard to the determination of sainthood. Between 1523 and 1588, while saintly people and reputations continued to live on, no saint was officially canonized.

A revival of official saint-making began in the late sixteenth century, but with even more careful and centralized procedures directed from Rome. By the early seventeenth century, a prudent distinction between "true" saints and *beati* (saintly individuals) grew sharper, with the formal addition of a beatification stage in the certification of saints. Moreover, to guard against the hasty canonizations which were thought to have overtaken the Church in the euphoric moments after the deaths of certain pious persons in the past, it was decreed that no canonization proceedings could begin until fifty years after the death of a candidate.

Santa Rosa of Lima (1586–1617) was one of some fifty-five people (forty-three men and twelve women) canonized by the Catholic Church between 1588 and 1767. She died at the age of thirty-one on August 24, 1617, and was beatified in 1668 and canonized in 1671 (on April 12), judged heroic in virtue more quickly than an extraordinary cluster of certified saints and holy people who were her contemporaries and near-contemporaries in Peru. Most notably, the Franciscan Francisco Solano, who died in 1602 and was beatified in 1675, and the archbishop of Lima, Toribio Alfonso de Mogrovejo, who died in 1606 and was beatified in 1679, were both canonized in December 1726. Rosa's fellow Dominicans Juan Macías (1585–1645) and the Mulatto Martín de Porras (1579–1639) were not even beatified until October 1837. Within the half-century following her death, Rosa's patronal relationship with the city of Lima grew and soon extended well beyond it. Even before she was canonized, she became patron of Peru (1669) and of the Americas and Philippines archipelago (1670). Rosa's cult subsequently spread to pockets of devotion in Europe. Her example sheds light on religion and some of its functions in the period we are studying.

At the request of the head of the Dominican Order, the process of accumulating the testimonial evidence that would determine Rosa's sanctity began promptly on September 1, 1617, only eight days after her death. One source of information about her life and how she was perceived by her principal devotees and promoters just after she died are the declarations that Don Gonzalo de la Maza made between September 16 and October 6 in response to thirty-two questions put by a tribunal of judges to him and seventy-four other witnesses in the first stage (*proceso ordinario*). (Some 147 other witnesses were heard during a second stage—*proceso apostólico*—conducted between 1630 and 1632.) For reasons that will become clear, de la Maza's testimony is perhaps the most substantial of those collected in the first round of investigations. Excerpts from it are collected in the selection that follows.

Soon after his arrival in Lima from Spain in 1601 to take up his appointment as bookkeeper to the Tribunal of the Santa Cruzada, de la Maza made his home a haven for local people of extraordinary piety and ascetic devotion. In 1613, twenty-six-year-old Isabel Flores de Oliva (Rosa's baptismal name), the Creole daughter of a noble Spanish family in the city, was one of those attracted to Don Gonzalo's home. On the strong advice of her confessors and, it was later claimed, with the permission of parents who were "already" edified by their daughter's stirrings, Isabel became a *beata* (a lay holy woman).

De la Maza described her life at a moment soon after her death, as noted, in response to official queries about her alleged sanctity. His answers run in a number directions, frequently doubling back on themselves and, in effect, emphasizing the principal image he wanted to convey—that of a woman voluntarily withdrawn into a world of exemplary piety and for whom the goal of mystical union with God was open and attainable. His "Rosa" was one intimately remembered by him, his wife, and his daughters. Although he was older, de la Maza calls her "his mother," having sought her wise counsel and example, as did many others.

De la Maza was not an ordained priest and did not hear the young woman's confessions himself. Yet he says that they shared confidences, and he clearly learned what he could from her confessors, committed to memory events from her short life, and, in the process, became one of her most ardent promoters. There are strong indications in his testimony, however, that the extent of his personal relationship with her might easily be exaggerated, and that intimacy with the young recluse was enjoyed principally by his wife, Doña María de Usátegui, from whom de la Maza seems to have learned much about Rosa.

Pious writings about those who chose lives of chastity, private penitence, and prayer often conformed to a pattern, as much in early seventeenth-century Lima as in other places and times. De la Maza's testimony vividly conveys how Isabel Flores de Oliva came to see herself, and to be seen by others, in terms of known models of conduct. Rosa's saintliness is one expression of a set of values and understandings that suited her and her admirers, then and later, in the Peruvian capital. The person Isabel-Rosa sought a life of exemplary piety and contemplative devotion, just as her "life" (or saintly biography) was also converted into a series of spiritual feats for the edification of others. Further, inhabitants of Lima, and eventually the colonies of the Spanish world as a whole, sought through her an enhanced and legitimate place in a continuous Christian tradition of sanctity. As in José de Acosta's framing of the evangelization of Indians within the same long history of Christianity (see Selection 19), Rosa's fame and pious example came to sanctify her person, her city, and its people in the wider context of Counter-Reformation Catholicism.

She was said to have emulated the youthful path of the fourteenth-century mystic Saint Catherine of Siena (ca. 1347–1380), who was canonized in the fifteenth century. As Catherine had done, young Isabel adopted the simple dress of a tertiary of the Dominican Order—that is, she made only simple vows, as opposed to formal, more binding ones, and a "profession," which made her part of the Dominican family but not a nun. And like Catherine, she abandoned the distracting comforts of her parents' home. Isabel moved into a room in de la Maza's house and sig-

naled the beginning of a personal transformation by taking a new, religious name, Rosa de Santa María. According to de la Maza, the resemblances between her life and that of Saint Catherine began very early, with special signs occurring in childhood. Like Catherine, Isabel was said to have acted on a precocious resolve to mask and thwart her beauty and to have unsettled her parents' expectations for her.

Her life, as told, was punctuated by a series of spiritual yearnings and tests that became milestones along a known path of spiritual perfection. There was her hunger for seclusion so that prayer and acts of penitence might continue undisturbed. There was the economy of her speech and her impatience with petty preoccupations or imprecision in others. There were her painful vigils of wakefulness, the feats of fasting and resistance to worldly comforts, all in pursuit of spiritual rewards that were said to have taken her more than once to the brink of death.

How much of her do we see in the following account? Rosa, who appears to have wanted nothing more than a private life of devotion and closer union to her God, became much more than a saintly recluse in the minds and hands of her contemporaries. Her Dominican champions made the most of an association between the name "Rosa" and the order's promotion of the Rosary and Our Lady of the Rosary. The earliest "life" of Rosa, the *Life, Death, and Miracles of Sor Rosa de Santa María* (*Vida, muerte y milagros de Sor Rosa de Santa María*) of 1619, was written by a Dominican, Pedro de Loayza, in time to be included as evidence in the investigations into her sanctity. She was a seemingly perfect candidate for sainthood in her age and one that was literally seized upon in Lima, as de la Maza's testimony shows. Seeking the widest legitimacy for his account, he presents a "Rosa de Sancta María" who for many years (before and after her death, he says) was fervently discussed by people far outside his family's circle of beatas, including her confessors and the learned inhabitants of Lima dedicated to private spiritual lives. And her life was marveled at by many other contemporaries who had caught a glimpse of her or who had learned something of her from others. The sick flocked to her tomb to be healed, and others sought relics from the places in which she had lived. De la Maza describes many of Rosa's later devotees as "distin-guished ladies" and gentlemen of Lima's elite, but he is just as quick to stress how much her example and reputation attracted and edified members of all social groups and stations, bridging earthly class divisions and economic interests.

[We join the testimony of Don Gonzalo de la Maza at his answer to the fourth question.]

Answering the fourth question, this witness explained that he had known the said Rosa de Sancta María for about five years, and he told of the personal contact he had with her. Although this witness had wanted to make her acquaintance years before, knowing the considerable virtue she possessed, he had not done so out of respect for her rigorous seclusion. His first direct experience came on the occasion when the said Rosa de Sancta María wrote to this witness asking him to assist her in a charitable deed, which greatly delighted him. However, he was afraid to disturb her tranquillity, until one day soon thereafter this witness chanced to see her enter his house with her mother, the said María de Oliva, and his wife, Doña María de Usátegui. As strangers, they [the three women] had met and spoken in the Jesuit church, for she [Doña María], too, wanted to meet the said Rosa. And for much of the time between that day and the one on which she passed from this life, he saw a lot of the said Rosa de Sancta María in his house with his wife and daughters due to the special affection they all had for one another. Rosa's taking of a room in this witness's house was favored both by her natural parents and by her spiritual fathers [her confessors], with whom she communicated. Sometimes, it was even by their orders, as this witness learned from her confessors, Padre Maestro Lorenzana of the Order of Saint Dominic and Padre Diego Martínez of the Society of Jesus. Through her stay and his personal exchanges with her, this witness learned of the beginnings of her calling.

Rosa told this witness of an incident that occurred when she was about five years old, while she was playing with one of her brothers, Hernando, who was two years older. Rosa [then Isabel] had grown beautiful blonde hair and [on this occasion] it had been handled roughly and soiled by her said brother. Once she saw the state of it, she started to cry. Her brother asked why she cried. Did she not know that on account of [worrying over] their hair many souls were in Hell? Knowing this, she should not be crying over her hair. [Rosa said] that this retort had so imprinted itself in her heart that in thinking about it she was seized by so great a fear in her soul that from that moment on she did not do a thing, not one thing, which she understood to be a sin and an offense to God Our Father. From this fear Rosa gained some knowledge of the divine goodness, which helped her [understand things about] her grandmother [who had died] and a sister, a little older than her, who died at the age of fourteen. [Rosa was now able to see them] as souls that, in her opinion, had been very pleasing to Our Lord, [and] whose deaths had been a great consolation to her because the things she had seen in them and been given to understand by His Divine Majesty convinced her that they had certainly gone to Heaven.

Thus, the said Rosa de Sancta María said to this witness that at that tender age
she had dedicated to God Our Lord the gift of her virginity, with a vow [of
chastity], and that, to this witness's understanding, the great outward modesty and
purity of life attained by the said Rosa suggested that she honored the said promise
not only in her deeds but also in her thoughts, as one of her spiritual fathers
expressed it to this witness. And her introspection was such that the said Rosa also
revealed to the witness that in her life she had neither seen nor longed for a feast
day or worldly celebration, not even a common procession, and that during the
time that he knew her he clearly perceived this [to be a true account of] her way of
withdrawal [from the world] and devotion. She withdrew not only from direct
communication but also from seeing people and [worldly] things in order that they
might neither impede nor delay the serenity of her soul, the power of which this
witness saw at that time to be so focused that he beheld it with great admiration.

And as much [was true] in other senses, because this witness never saw her
tongue move to utter an unnecessary thing. [This was true] in her answers or advice
to others, in her praise of the Lord and in her encouragement of others to give
praise. Her words were so careful and serious that they demonstrated very well that
it was God who moved her. She was so chaste in her speech that if she said
something that might be understood in more than one sense, she added, "What I
am saying" or "I wish to say." She wanted everyone to do the same, as was
demonstrated on the occasions when other people recounted something she had
said or done. If [the relation of her words or acts] was not undertaken with absolute
precision, she pointed out whatever was wanting with complete courtesy, [noting]
that she had said or done this [or that]. And this witness noticed this perfection
of the truth in her speech until she died. [In fact, this was] so much the case that on
the very day she died, a devoted friar had come and asked one of the people who
were attending Rosa in her illness if it would be acceptable for Father So-and-So,
for whom Rosa had asked, to enter, at which point the said Rosa, though in very
great anguish and pain, spoke up, saying, "I said I wished to see him before I die."

The downward cast of her eyes was notable, so much so that this witness said
that, in communicating with her so familiarly and with such openness that he called
her his mother, it was amazing how few times he saw her lift her gaze. She was so
chaste and pure in her sensibilities that in no manner would she attend conversations
that were not spiritual and directed toward the good of souls and the service of Our
Lord. And if it happened otherwise, or if some person began to speak on secular
themes, with very great modesty she attempted to divert them or absent herself from
the conversation, as this witness saw in his house on many occasions. Thus, in the
time they knew one another, it was very rare for her to go out [or be among] people
from outside the house, not counting the times in which some spiritual fathers
visited, because the whole of her interest was in retreat and solitude. . . .

The day of her birth is recorded in her father's book and the certificate of
baptism. Concerning the day of her death [in order to establish her age at death], it
occurred in this witness's house on Thursday, August 24, Saint Bartholomew's Day,
one half hour after midnight. And after the said beginning of her calling, the said

Rosa de Sancta María told this witness that she scorned the things of this mortal life, such as trying to impress people and be their object of curiosity. To manage this, for some time she had worn the habit of Saint Francis until, at the age of twenty or twenty-one years, she dressed in that of Saint Dominic and Saint Catherine of Siena, her mother, whom she had wanted to imitate since the beginning of her life, and become a nun of her order. And this witness has never heard, understood, or seen anything which contradicts what he has said, nor anything against the virtue, honesty, spiritual absorption, and virginal purity of the said Rosa de Sancta María. This is his answer to the question. . . .

To the sixth question . . . Although they kept secret her mortifications of the flesh and penances until she died, this witness and his family knew of her way of life. This witness said that from a young age she was given to mortify herself with fasts, scourges, and other [self-inflicted] sufferings, and that from early on she had subsisted on bread and water for many days [at a time]. And, from the age of ten or eleven years she kept to her fasts of bread and water, especially on the days that her mother would excuse it, that is, on the Wednesdays, Fridays, and Saturdays of each week. At the age of fifteen and sixteen years she had made a conditional vow to forego meat and to fast on bread and water for the rest of her life. . . .

This witness observed her abstinence when she lived in his house, during which time even when she had a fever and her doctors and confessors ordered her to eat meat, she would not do it. Her fasts on bread and water were continuous. . . . [In fact,] this witness saw that she would go a day or two or more without eating or drinking anything, particularly on the days when she took Holy Communion, because at certain times of the year confessors granted permission for one to take Communion every time one went to church, and this is what she did with much modesty and without drawing attention to herself. During these fasts and abstinences, [when] she left the church or her secluded room in his house, she had such color [in her face] and showed such health [that it seemed] as if she was fortifying herself with plenty of nutritious dishes. Worrying over her stomach pains and all that she suffered, one would ask her why she did not eat anything, to which she ordinarily responded that Holy Communion made her feel full to bursting and that it was impossible for her to eat [even] a bite. . . .

[It often happened that in ill health Rosa would be made to eat meat and other food, especially by her well-meaning mother, but also by doctors and her worried confessors. In this witness's experience, these feedings had the effect of worsening Rosa's condition.] During one of her dangerous illnesses three years ago, the doctors forced her to eat meat, which left her weary and so short of breath that she could walk no more than a few steps for many days. She said that it [her worsened condition] had resulted from her distress at having eaten meat, and she began getting better when she resumed her abstinence. . . . During the time that the said witness knew her, the said Rosa's manner of abstinence was such that the amounts she ate even when she was not observing it [her fast of bread and water] did not, to him, seem enough to sustain the life of a human body, especially one so young. . . .

To the seventh question this witness answered that he knew for a fact that since the beginning of her life the said Rosa de Sancta María performed continuous and rigorous mortifications of the flesh, usually with iron chains. And this witness knew [about these mortifications] from what he had heard from her, her mother, some of her confessors, his wife the said Doña María de Usátegui, and his two young daughters, from whom, even given their tender ages and the love and concern he had for them, he did not deny exposure to [Rosa's] virtuous example.

With the same certainty, this witness learned that for a long time she [Rosa] had worn an iron chain wrapped two or three times around her waist and fastened with a padlock for which she had no key. [At one point when] she was in her mother's house, she developed a very severe pain in her abdomen, and the chain had to be removed in order for her to be helped. She suffered much as the lock was broken because her skin and, at some parts, her flesh had become stuck to the said chain, as this witness saw after Rosa's death.

Because all of this information was communicated to his wife, the said Doña María de Usátegui, on the understanding that it might be told to this witness, he also understood with the same certainty that she [Rosa] had employed different hairshirts, and that she had worn one with very rough bristles [that extended] from her shoulders down to her knees. For a long time she had worn tunics with sackcloth on the inside until, after two years, her confessors noticed her health so diminished that they took them away. This witness had seen them on the occasions when she changed them and hung them out in the sun. By order of her confessors, from that time [when the rough tunics were forbidden] until the point of the illness from which she died, her simple outfits were brought to her, on which occasions this witness also saw that she changed them.

The said Rosa de Sancta María sometimes told this witness and his wife and daughters that from an early age she had greatly detested putting on a good appearance for people and the care taken by her mother in arranging her hair, face, and clothes. Seeing that she was not getting very far [toward the realization of her ascetic designs] with her mother, at the age of twelve years she cut off her very blonde head of hair, at the sight of which her mother scolded her harshly. [But her quests continued.] Feeling that her fasts and mortifications were not sufficient to drain the color from her cheeks, she poured pitchers of cold water over her chest and back even when she was dressed. Because of this, or because of divine will and providence, she contracted an illness at the age of thirteen years and became crippled and [had to be] clamped to a bed by her hands and feet for a long time. [She suffered] a great pain over her entire body that could not be explained, but, in bearing it, a very great relief and comfort came to her, in [knowing] that on account of Heaven her patience and compliance with the divine will had never faltered. She told this witness that on this occasion, as on others, Our Lord had rewarded her with so much pain, of a kind she had not believed a human body could withstand. [It was] nothing like the kind [of pain] He Himself had suffered, [she had said,] yet she was bewildered at having enjoyed so much forgiveness from God's hand, [considering] it was not possible that this [reward] would be bestowed on so wretched a creature as herself.

This witness also understands it to be a certain thing [based on what he had learned] from his wife the said Doña María de Usátegui, and from other people, that the bed in which Rosa slept until the age of one and a half or two years in her parents' house, [eventually] taken by her confessors, was a barbacoa, a small platform of rather coarse canes, like those used for threshing wheat in Spain. [It was] bound together by leather cords, with sharp, two- or three-cornered shards of an earthenware jug scattered over it and between the said canes. . . .

And after the said bed was taken away, and put on a shelf so that the said shards would not fall away, this witness knows that the said Rosa de Sancta María normally slept either on a plank of wood with a blanket, or seated in a small chair, as she did the whole time she lived in this witness's house. . . . This witness also knew that from the beginning of her life the said Rosa de Sancta María had endeavored to punish her body by depriving herself of sleep, and there came a time when in a day and night she slept no more than two hours, and sometimes less. . . .

And, on the matter of her ways and mortifications, from one of Rosa de Sancta María's spiritual fathers this witness has heard [of one of her methods] to be able to keep praying when she was overcome by drowsiness. She set about tying together a number of the hairs at the front [of her head], [hairs] which concealed a crown of thorns that she wore [underneath], [and then attaching these knots] to a nail she had driven into the wall of her refuge. [Thus,] she would be virtually hanging [there], only able to reach the floor with difficulty. And in this way she conquered weariness and continued her prayers. . . .

To the twenty-ninth question he answered that he has heard said that there have been many, and very exceptional, miracles performed by Our Lord God for the greater glory of His name and in demonstration of the virtue and sanctity of the blessed Rosa. [By these miracles] many people with different maladies, [who] entrust themselves to her intercession [by] touching some traces of her clothing and the earth from around her tomb, have been restored to health. This witness defers to the testimonies and proof of the said miracles.

Since the day on which the body of the said blessed Rosa was buried in the chapter room of the said convent of Saint Dominic, every time this witness entered [the chapter room] he has found a great gathering of people of all orders, stations, and sexes, and at the tomb this witness has seen many of the sick, crippled, and maimed.

And in the same way he has observed what is [equally] well known, [namely,] the veneration and devotion which the notables of this city, like the rest of the general population, have for the blessed Rosa de Sancta María and for the things that were hers [and that were associated with her life]. [This is demonstrated] by the number of people of all stations who have gathered at this witness's house to visit the rooms in which the blessed Rosa stayed and died. In particular, there have been very few, if any, distinguished women who have failed to turn up in this witness's house to ask for relics from the clothing and other things that belonged to the blessed Rosa. And the same [close attention] has been paid by important men; indeed, the first one whom this witness saw request relics was Dr. Francisco Verdugo, the inquisitor of this realm, and this witness sent them to him. And [then] there was the judge from the royal Audiencia who has come twice to ask for them. The demand has been such that if the tunics and habits which she left were many, they [still] would not have been enough to share in very tiny parts among the people who have come with such great affection and devotion. [One notes] particularly the monks from the five religious orders and the nuns in the convents of this city, whose requests [for relics] have not been small.

The flow of people who have visited the house of Rosa's parents in which she grew up and lived has been of no less magnitude. [They visit] the little cell that was her room, taking from it what they have been able to prize away and remove, even the little latch from the door, as this witness has seen, and [even] the threshold and planks are cut out from the room and its door. There was one time when this witness wanted to do the same, and he visited her parents only to find so many people and coaches and horses outside the door and in the street that he returned [home, having been] unable to enter. . . .

What this witness had most noticed were the tears shed by many people [while] talking about the life and things of the blessed Rosa. Some friar-confessors told him of the exceptional conversions of souls and arduous transformations of [people's] lives that had occurred among those who commended themselves to the blessed Rosa after her death. Other people, especially devout women, have told this witness they wanted to receive the habit that the blessed Rosa had worn and to found the convent of Saint Catherine of Siena that she [Rosa] so much desired. A prelate of a religious order, and not even the Dominicans, has told him the same thing. And this witness knew a maiden whom he took to be very virtuous, who now was attempting to imitate the life of the blessed Rosa. And [there are] spiritual people, very devout, among them some friars, who have said to this witness that since the death of the blessed Rosa de Sancta María they have received from Our Lord remarkable favors and rewards, much better than those which they had received before. And this he knows and is his response to this question.

❧ 31

Sor Juana Inés de la Cruz's Letter to Sor Filotea
(1691)

Perhaps the most celebrated literary figure of colonial Spanish America is Sor Juana Inés de la Cruz (1651–1695), a Jeronymite nun in Mexico City. Her life and writings say much about the Baroque predicaments that were keenly felt, especially in the seventeenth century—a life of struggle toward salvation in a world of troubling contradictions.

The illegitimate daughter of Creole Spanish parents from the pueblo of Chimalhuacán, near the Valley of Mexico, she was identified as a child prodigy and at the age of eight went to live with relatives in the capital. Her beauty, wit, and skill at poetry and her amazing knowledge of books and ideas made her an instant celebrity at court. At age fifteen the admiring viceroy and his wife sent her before a panel of learned professors of the University of Mexico (women were not permitted to study there), who failed to stump her in a probing oral examination ranging across physics, mathematics, theology, and philosophy. Abruptly in 1667, still not sixteen, she entered a Carmelite convent, switched the following year to the less rigorous Jeronymite Order, and spent the remainder of her life as a nun.

Marriage and religious seclusion were the usual lines open to respectable colonial Spanish women. Misogyny was unusually overt among clergy of the seventeenth cen-tury, who dwelt on the idea that women were passionate daughters of Eve, temptresses who invited sin and damnation. As an Inquisition judge remarked during an early seventeenth-century investigation, respectable women "are to remain at a distance from the mundane affairs of the public and stay shut up in their houses." So it was not surprising that Sor Juana, with her stated "total disinclination to marriage," would choose this conventional way to remain faithful to her religion and pursue her passion for study. Almost to the end, the secluded life of the spirit for this refined, troubled, and vibrant woman took a very different turn from that of Santa Rosa of Lima, and it met with a very different response from her ecclesiastical superiors.

Nearly all of Sor Juana's writings come from behind cloistered walls, and she remained in correspondence with literary friends and scientists in Mexico City and abroad until 1694. Her poetry offers a rich variety in form and content, including love lyrics, tender Christmas carols, morality plays, allegorical pieces, and the contradictions of her time and all time. Much of it is written in the ornate, rather obscure style that was popular then, but often there is a stunning clarity of meaning and accessibility. Her remarkable intellectual life as the Age of Reason was beginning to unfold in western Europe left her deeply distressed by the prevailing dichotomy of emotion and intellect that was hardly questioned by Spanish ecclesiastical authorities. She was not a rebel at heart, but her joyful, sometimes indignant curiosity and biting wit about the world and the mind trespassed conventional boundaries for women's lives and spiritual activity. Torn by her interior struggles over religion and science, body and soul, passion and reason, and the situation of a woman entering the intellectual territory of men, she found little of Santa Rosa's reported serenity. She finally gave up the struggle in 1694 at the age of forty-two. She gave away her books and scientific and musical instruments and in her own blood wrote out an unqualified renunciation of her learning, signing it "I, Sor Juana Inés de la Cruz, the worst in the world." (With this phrase she cites Paul [1 Timothy 1:15] in making a statement of utmost humility: "Christ Jesus came into the world to save sinners, of whom I am the worst of all.") She died the following year while caring for her convent sisters who had contracted smallpox.

The famous letter to "Sor Filotea" is a spirited, autobiographical response to critics among her ecclesiastical superiors. "Sor Filotea" was not another nun but rather her sometime friend and adviser, the Bishop of Puebla, Manuel Fernández de Santa Cruz (1676–1699), who wrote to her under this pseudonym, warning of her intellectual activities (which he himself had encouraged) and worldliness as threats to her immortal soul.

Although she was celebrated by some leading intellectuals and patrons (including two viceroys' wives), Sor Juana was a troubling example for many of her contemporaries. There would be no sainthood in her future, but she has become something of a heroine for our time. In reading these passages from her letter, we might consider why she speaks to late twentieth-century readers more directly than does Santa Rosa. Part of an answer is that *she* speaks, whereas someone else always speaks for Rosa or claims to have her words. But there is much more. The two young women spent their energies in the service of God in different ways, perhaps expressing Miguel de Unamuno's sense of the difference between mystics and others: mystics "reject science as futile and seek knowledge for a pragmatic purpose, in order to love and work for and rejoice in God, not for the sake of knowledge alone. Whether or not they are aware of it, they are anti-intellectuals." The colonial-era portraits of Santa Rosa and Sor Juana (Figures 24, 25) are as suggestive of the differences as are the texts.

Moses, because he was a stutterer, thought himself unworthy to speak to Pharaoh. Yet later, finding himself greatly favored by God, he was so imbued with courage that not only did he speak to God Himself, but he also dared to ask of Him the impossible: "*Show me thy face.*" And so it is with me, my Lady, for in view of the favor you show me, the obstacles I described at the outset no longer seem entirely insuperable. For one who had the letter printed, unbeknownst to me, who titled it and underwrote its cost, and who thus honored it (unworthy as it was of all this, on its own account and on account of its author), what will such a one not do? What not forgive? Or what fail to do or fail to forgive? Thus, sheltered by the assumption that I speak with the safe-conduct granted by your favors and with the warrant bestowed by your goodwill, and by the fact that, like a second Ahasuerus, you have allowed me to kiss the top of the golden scepter of your affection as a sign that you grant me kind license to speak and to plead my case in your venerable presence, I declare that I receive in my very soul your most holy admonition to apply my study to Holy Scripture; for although it arrives in the guise of counsel, it shall have for me the weight of law. And I take no small consolation from the fact that it seems my obedience, as if at your direction, anticipated your pastoral insinuation, as may be inferred from the subject matter and arguments of that very letter. I recognize full well that your most prudent warning touches not on the letter, but on the many writings of mine on humane matters that you have seen. . . . I want no trouble with the Holy Office, for I am but ignorant and tremble lest I utter some ill-sounding proposition or twist the true meaning of some passage. I do not study in order to write, nor far less in order to teach (which would be boundless arrogance in me), but simply to see whether by studying I may become less ignorant. This is my answer, and these are my feelings. . . .

To go on with the narration of this inclination of mine, of which I wish to give you a full account: I declare I was not yet three years old when my mother sent off one of my sisters, older than I, to learn to read in one of those girls' schools that they call Amigas. Affection and mischief carried me after her; and when I saw that they were giving her lessons, I so caught fire with the desire to learn that, deceiving the teacher (or so I thought), I told her that my mother wanted her to teach me also. She did not believe this, for it was not to be believed; but to humor my whim she gave me lessons. I continued to go and she continued to teach me, though no longer in make-believe, for the experience undeceived her. I learned to read in such a short time that I already knew how by the time my mother heard of it. My teacher had kept it from my mother to give delight with a thing all done and to receive a prize for a thing done well. And I had kept still, thinking I would be whipped for having done this without permission. The woman who taught me (may God keep her) is still living, and she can vouch for what I say.

I remember that in those days, though I was as greedy for treats as children usually are at that age, I would abstain from eating cheese, because I heard tell that it made people stupid, and the desire to learn was stronger for me than the desire to eat—powerful as this is in children. Later, when I was six or seven years old and already knew how to read and write, along with all the other skills like embroidery and sewing that women learn, I heard that in Mexico City there were a university and schools where they studied the sciences. As soon as I heard this, I began to pester my poor mother with insistent and annoying pleas, begging her to dress me in men's clothes and send me to the capital, to the home of some relatives she had there, so that I could enter the university and study. She refused, and was right in doing so; but I quenched my desire by reading a great variety of books that belonged to my grandfather, and neither punishments nor scoldings could prevent me. And so when I did go to Mexico City, people marveled not so much at my intelligence as at my memory and the facts I knew at an age when it seemed I had scarcely had time to learn to speak.

I began to study Latin, in which I believe I took fewer than twenty lessons. And my interest was so intense, that although in women (and especially in the very bloom of youth) the natural adornment of the hair is so esteemed, I would cut off four to six fingerlengths of my hair, measuring how long it had been before. And I made myself a rule that if by the time it had grown back to the same length I did not know such and such a thing that I intended to study, then I would cut my hair off again to punish my dull-wittedness. And so my hair grew, but I did not yet know what I had resolved to learn, for it grew quickly and I learned slowly. Then I cut my hair right off to punish my dull-wittedness, for I did not think it reasonable that hair should cover a head that was so bare of facts—the more desirable adornment. I took the veil because, although I knew I would find in religious life many things that would be quite opposed to my character (I speak of accessory rather than essential matters), it would, given my absolute unwillingness to enter into marriage, be the least unfitting and most decent state I could choose, with regard to the assurance I desired of my salvation. For before this first concern (which is, at the last, the most important), all the impertinent little follies of my character gave way and bowed to the yoke. These were wanting to live alone and not wanting to have either obligations that would disturb my freedom to study or the noise of a community that would interrupt the tranquil silence of my books. These things made me waver somewhat in my decision until, being enlightened by learned people as to my temptation, I vanquished it with divine favor and took the state I so unworthily hold. I thought I was fleeing myself, but—woe is me!—I brought myself with me, and brought my greatest enemy in my inclination to study, which I know not whether to take as a Heaven-sent favor or as a punishment. For when snuffed out or hindered with every [spiritual] exercise known to Religion, it exploded like gunpowder; and in my case the saying *"privation gives rise to appetite"* was proven true.

I went back (no, I spoke incorrectly, for I never stopped)—I went on, I mean, with my studious task (which to me was peace and rest in every moment left over when my duties were done) of reading and still more reading, study and still more study, with no teacher besides my books themselves. What a hardship it is to learn from those lifeless letters, deprived of the sound of a teacher's voice and explanations! Yet I suffered all these trials most gladly for the love of learning. Oh, if only this had been done for the love of God, as was rightful, think what I should have merited! Nevertheless, I did my best to elevate these studies and direct them to His service, for the goal to which I aspired was the study of Theology. Being a Catholic, I thought it an abject failing not to know everything that can in this life be achieved, through earthly methods, concerning the divine mysteries. And being a nun and not a laywoman, I thought I should, because I was in religious life, profess the study of letters—the more so as the daughter of such as Saint Jerome and Santa Paula: for it would be a degeneracy for an idiot daughter to proceed from such learned parents. I argued in this way to myself, and I thought my own argument quite reasonable. However, the fact may have been (and this seems most likely) that I was merely flattering and encouraging my own inclination by arguing that its own pleasure was an obligation.

I went on in this way, always directing each step of my studies, as I have said, toward the summit of Holy Theology; but it seemed to me necessary to ascend by the ladder of the humane arts and sciences in order to reach it; for who could fathom the style of the Queen of Sciences without knowing that of her handmaidens? Without Logic, how should I know the general and specific methods by which Holy Scripture is written? Without Rhetoric, how should I understand its figures, tropes, and locutions? Or how, without Physics or Natural Science, understand all the questions that naturally arise concerning the varied natures of those animals offered in sacrifice, in which a great many things already made manifest are symbolized, and many more besides? How should I know whether Saul's cure at the sound of David's harp was owing to a virtue and power that is natural in Music or owing, instead, to a supernatural power that God saw fit to bestow on David? How without Arithmetic might one understand all those mysterious reckonings of years and days and months and hours and weeks that are found in Daniel and elsewhere, which can be comprehended only by knowing the nature, concordances, and properties of numbers? Without Geometry, how could we take the measure of the Holy Ark of the Covenant or the Holy City of Jerusalem, each of whose mysterious measurements forms a perfect cube uniting their dimensions, and each displaying that most marvelous distribution of the proportions of every part? Without the science of Architecture, how understand the mighty Temple of Solomon—where God Himself was the Draftsman who set forth His arrangement and plan, and the Wise King was but the overseer who carried it out; where there was no foundation without its mystery, nor column without its symbol, nor cornice without its allusions, nor architrave without its meaning, and likewise for every other part, so that even the very least fillet served not only for the support and enhancement of Art, but also to symbolize greater things? How, without a thorough knowledge of the order and divisions by which History is composed, is one to understand the Historical Books—as in those summaries, for example, which often postpone in the narration what happened first in fact? How, without command of the two branches of Law, should one understand the Books of Law? Without considerable erudition, how should we understand the great many matters of profane history that are mentioned by Holy Scripture: all the diverse customs of the Gentiles, all their rituals, all their manners of speech? Without knowing many precepts and reading widely in the Fathers of the Church, how could one understand the obscure sayings of the Prophets? . . .

They [who sought to prohibit me from study] achieved this once, with a very saintly and simple mother superior who believed that study was an affair for the Inquisition and ordered that I should not read. I obeyed her (for the three months or so that her authority over us lasted) in that I did not pick up a book. But with regard to avoiding study absolutely, as such a thing does not lie within my power, I could not do it. For although I did not study in books, I studied all the things that God created, taking them for my letters, and for my book all the intricate structures of this world. Nothing could I see without reflecting upon it, nothing could I hear without pondering it, even to the most minute material things. For there is no creature, however lowly, in which one cannot recognize the great "*God made me*"; there is not one that does not stagger the mind if it receives due consideration. And so, I repeat, I looked and marveled at all things, so that from the very persons with whom I spoke and from what they said to me, a thousand speculations leapt to my mind: Whence could spring this diversity of character and intelligence among individuals all composing one single species? What temperaments, what hidden qualities could give rise to each? When I noticed a shape, I would set about combining the proportions of its lines and measuring it in my mind and converting it to other proportions. I sometimes walked back and forth along the forewall of one of our dormitories (which is a very large room), and I began to observe that although the lines of its two sides were parallel and the ceiling was flat, yet the eye falsely perceived these lines as though they approached each other and the ceiling as though it were lower in the distance than close by; from this, I inferred that visual lines run straight, but not parallel, and that they form a pyramidal figure. And I conjectured whether this might be the reason why the ancients were obliged to question whether the world is spherical or not. Because even though it seems so, this could be a delusion of the eye, displaying concavities where there were none.

This kind of observation has been continual in me and is so to this day, without my having control over it; rather, I tend to find it annoying, because it tires my head. Yet I believed this happened to everyone, as with thinking in verse, until experience taught me otherwise. This trait, whether a matter of nature or custom, is such that nothing do I see without a second thought. Two little girls were playing with a top in front of me, and no sooner had I seen the motion and shape than I began, with this madness of mine, to observe the easy movement of the spherical form and how the momentum lasted, now fixed and set free of its cause; for even far from its first cause, which was the hand of the girl, the little top went on dancing. Yet not content with this, I ordered flour to be brought and sifted on the floor, so that as the top danced over it, we could know whether its movement described perfect circles or no. I found they were not circular, but rather spiral lines that lost their circularity as the top lost its momentum. Other girls were playing at spillikins [jackstraws] (the most frivolous of all childhood games). I drew near to observe the shapes they made, and when I saw three of the straws by chance fall in a triangle, I fell to intertwining one with another, recalling that this was said to be the very shape of Solomon's mysterious ring, where distantly there shone bright traces and representations of the Most Blessed Trinity, by virtue of which it worked great prodigies and marvels. And they say David's harp had the same shape, and thus was Saul cured by its sound; to this day, harps have almost the same form.

Well, and what, then, shall I tell you, my Lady, of the secrets of nature that I have learned while cooking? I observe that an egg becomes solid and cooks in butter or oil, and on the contrary that it dissolves in sugar syrup. Or again, to ensure that sugar flows freely, one need only add the slightest bit of water that has held quince or some other sour fruit. The yolk and white of the very same egg are of such a contrary nature that when eggs are used with sugar, each part separately may be used perfectly well, yet they cannot be mixed together. I shall not weary you with such inanities, which I relate simply to give you a full account of my nature, and I believe this will make you laugh. But in truth, my Lady, what can we women know, save philosophies of the kitchen? It was well put by Lupercio Leonardo that one can philosophize quite well while preparing supper. I often say, when I make these little observations, "Had Aristotle cooked, he would have written a great deal more."...

I confess also that, while in truth this inclination has been such that, as I said before, I had no need of exemplars, nevertheless the many books that I have read have not failed to help me, both in sacred as well as secular letters. For there I see a Deborah issuing laws, military as well as political, and governing the people among whom there were so many learned men. I see the exceedingly knowledgeable Queen of Sheba, so learned she dares to test the wisdom of the wisest of all wise men with riddles, without being rebuked for it; indeed, on this very account she is to become judge of the unbelievers. I see so many and such significant women: some adorned with the gift of prophecy, like Abigail; others, of persuasion, like Esther; others, of piety, like Rahab; others, of perseverance, like Anna [Hannah], the mother of Samuel; and others, infinitely more, with other kinds of qualities and virtues.

If I consider the Gentiles, the first I meet are the Sibyls, chosen by God to prophesy the essential mysteries of our Faith in such learned and elegant verses that they stupefy the imagination. I see a woman such as Minerva, daughter of great Jupiter and mistress of all the wisdom of Athens, adored as goddess of the sciences. . . . I see Gertrude read, write, and teach. And seeking no more examples far from home, I see my own most holy mother Paula, learned in the Hebrew, Greek, and Latin tongues and most expert in the interpretation of the Scriptures. What wonder, then, can it be that, though her chronicler was no less than the unequaled Jerome, the Saint found himself scarcely worthy of the task, for with that lively gravity and energetic effectiveness with which only he can express himself he says: "If all the parts of my body were tongues, they would not suffice to proclaim the learning and virtues of Paula." Blessilla, a widow, earned the same praises, as did the luminous virgin Eustochium, both of them daughters of the Saint herself [Paula]; and indeed, Eustochium was such that for her knowledge she was hailed as a World Prodigy. Fabiola, also a Roman, was another most learned in Holy Scripture. Proba Falconia, a Roman woman, wrote an elegant book of cantos, joining together verses from Virgil, on the mysteries of our holy Faith. Our Queen Isabella, wife of Alfonso X, is known to have written on astrology—without mentioning others, whom I omit so as not merely to copy what others have said (which is a vice I have always detested). Well, then, in our own day there thrive the great Christina Alexandra, Queen of Sweden, as learned as she is brave and generous; and too those most excellent ladies, the Duchess of Aveyro and the Countess of Villaumbrosa. . . .

If ever I write any more little trifles, they shall always seek haven at your feet and the safety of your correction, for I have no other jewel with which to repay you. And in the opinion of Seneca, he who has once commenced to confer benefits becomes obliged to continue them. Thus you must be repaid by your own generosity, for only in that way can I be honorably cleared of my debt to you, lest another statement, again Seneca's, be leveled against me: "*It is shameful to be outdone in acts of kindness.*" For it is magnanimous for the generous creditor to grant a poor debtor some means of satisfying the debt. Thus God behaved toward the world, which could not possibly repay Him: He gave His own Son, that He might offer Himself as a worthy amends.

If the style of this letter, my venerable Lady, has been less than your due, I beg your pardon for its household familiarity or the lack of seemly respect. For in addressing you, my sister, as a nun of the veil, I have forgotten the distance between myself and your most distinguished person, which should not occur were I to see you unveiled. But you, with your prudence and benevolence, will substitute or emend my terms; and if you think unsuitable the familiar terms of address I have employed—because it seems to me that given all the reverence I owe you, "Your Reverence" is very little reverence indeed—please alter it to whatever you think suitable. For I have not been so bold as to exceed the limits set by the style of your letter to me, nor to cross the border of your modesty.

And hold me in your own good grace, so as to entreat divine grace on my behalf; of the same, may the Lord grant you great increase, and may He keep you, as I beg of Him and as I am needful. Written at the Convent of Our Father Saint Jerome in Mexico City, this first day of March of the year 1691. Receive the embrace of your most greatly favored,

Sor Juana Inés de la Cruz
Treasurer of the convent

∿ 32

Portraits of Santa Rosa and Sor Juana

Santa Rosa's reputation and her association with the city of Lima grew rapidly after her death. We recall Gonzalo de la Maza's words about the stir in Lima, the fervent clamoring after relics and stories. An emerging set of attributes can be seen in almost any of the many early paintings of her: the crown of fresh roses entwined with thorns, a wreath of flowers, the rosary, a Dominican habit, and depictions of her visions (that of the Christ Child holding a golden wedding ring as a reminder of her marriage to God, for instance, appears in one painting from the early eighteenth century).

This posthumous portrait (Figure 24; Plate 6) emphasizes another characteristic feature which, one suspects, Santa Rosa would have appreciated more than all the attributes: a likeness to the classic depictions of her spiritual mother, Saint Catherine of Siena. An understated crown of roses and thorns, a rosary, and the habit make the necessary identification, but the image's most striking feature is its quiet portrayal of its subject's purity and inward focus: the downward, meditating gaze of her eyes. Eyes lowered, hands joined, rosary within reach, Rosa is in another world. We are meant to imagine an inner place of contemplation, and moral and mystical beauty. The elaborate rays projecting from her head and the designs on her habit seem to be the canvas's reply to its decorative silver frame. They are distractions put in place by admiring patrons and successors—not so unlike the associations with the city of Lima, the layers of flowers, or the Dominican Order.

The second image (Figure 25; Plate 7), a painting of the Mexican nun Sor Juana Inés de la Cruz, also completed after her death and said to be a copy of a self-portrait, is different. She gazes straight out at her viewers, engaging us with a presence and an intelligence that recall her letter to Sor Filotea (Selection 31). Sor Juana's right hand rests on a carefully identified volume of her own works, while with her other hand she marks a page in another tome, as if we have interrupted her reading and she would like to know why. She wears her nun's robes and *escudo de monja* (an oval painting on copper that members of her order in New Spain wore on special occasions; hers depicts the Annunciation). Taking the veil, in Sor Juana's words, offered her the "least unfitting and most decent state." Like the "skills that women learn," discipline is endured because of devotion to God and the life that it can bring with it. She cut off her hair as a girl, just as Santa Rosa did, and both decided to leave "the world." But, whereas in Rosa's case the gaze turns inward in contemplation of God, with Sor Juana the withdrawal is meant to serve God and become a refuge for study and writing. She leaves in order to find the time and opportunity to scale intellectual heights denied her and other women outside a convent. Santa Rosa seeks the same time and opportunity, but, for her, different heights are in view. The heavens have opened.

Figure 24. Portrait of Santa Rosa of Lima with silver decoration, artist and date unknown.

⁓ SEE PLATE 6 ⁓

FIEL

Copia de otra que de sí hizo, y de su mano pintó la R. M. Juana Ynés dela Cruz Fenix dela
América, Gloriofo defempeño defu Sexo, Honrra dela Nacion deefte Nuevo Mundo, y arǵu-
mento delas admiraciones, y elogios deel Antiǵuo. Nació el dia 12. de Nov. deel año de 1651. alas
onfe dela noche. Reciuió el Saǵrado Habito de el Maximo D. S. S. Geronimo enfu Convento de
efta Ciudad de Mexico, de edad de 17. años. Y murió Domingo 17. de Abril de el de 1695. de edad
4o. y 4. años, cinco mezes, cinco diaz, y cinco horas. Requiescat in pace. Amen

Figure 25. Portrait of Sor Juana Inés de la Cruz, artist unknown.
Courtesy of the Philadelphia Museum of Art.

～ SEE PLATE 7 ～

33

Two Slaveries—The Sermons of Padre Antônio Vieira, Salvador, Bahia *(CA. 1633)* **and São Luís do Maranhão** *(1653)*

Sor Juana Inés de la Cruz began her unbending critique of one of Padre Antônio Vieira's Maundy Thursday sermons, available to her in published form in Mexico, with soaring praise: "if God were to allow me to choose my talents, I would choose no other than [Vieira's] genius." This Portuguese priest who achieved so exalted a reputation in his own time began life more humbly. Born in Portugal in 1608, he went to Brazil as a six-year-old boy when his father took up a post as clerk at the High Court in Bahia. Although later detractors incorrectly liked to insinuate that he had Jewish ancestry, his paternal grandmother was a *Mulata*, indicating his relation to an African slave in Portugal, something Vieira preferred not to reveal. Having entered the Jesuit college at Bahia at the age of only fifteen, three years later he was given the high honor for one so young of being asked to write the annual letter to the Society's General in Portugal, which became a famous account of the Dutch occupation of Bahia at that time. Before being ordained in 1635, he not only had learned Tupi by living in an *aldeia*, a Jesuit-organized Indian village, but also had preached powerful sermons in Bahia on sugar estates and at aldeias. His fame as a preacher was fully established by 1640.

His talents found new expression when during the 1640s he returned to Portugal to become adviser and court preacher to João IV, the Bragança king restored to the throne after sixty years of Spanish Hapsburg domination. Sent on important diplomatic missions to other parts of Europe, Vieira extended his own reputation and gained a more cosmopolitan understanding of imperial Portugal. In 1653 he returned to Brazil as Superior of the Jesuit missions in the Amazon. Although he was later to be silenced, confined, and denied paper and ink by the Inquisition for messianic writing the Holy Office judged contrary to the teaching of the Church—charges he finally saw removed after a long struggle in Rome to vindicate himself and where he became once again a celebrated and sought-after preacher —the Amazon years remained the defining ones of his life.

Except for a journey to Portugal in 1654 to argue passionately at court for reform in legislation that regulated relations between Indians and settlers, which he got, Vieira remained a missionary priest in Maranhão and Pará until hostile settlers expelled the Jesuits from the colony in 1661. He sought contact with reluctant, resistant Indians, who by then had little reason to trust Europeans, to baptize and instruct them. But alongside his apostolic mission, which took him to Indian villages upriver into unknown and generally inaccessible regions of the Amazon, he recognized the settlers' urgent need for Indian labor if the sugar and tobacco plantations were to sustain the colony and produce essential wealth for Portugal. If it is tempting to see Christianity in this context as merely imperialist and to see missionaries and settlers locked in grim battle over competing and irreconcilable interests, Vieira, the missionary and ever the Crown's representative, acted from a different understanding. To his acceptance of Portugal's colonial aims he joined his own vision of a universal Church and an apostolic mission to convert non-Christians to the faith. Not only did he commit himself to enlisting Indian trust—and that meant recognizing their different experiences with the Whites, their relations with their indigenous enemies, and their resources and strategies—but he also took on the job of persuading settlers that fair and humane treatment of the Indians benefited them immediately and materially.

While Indian tribes were captured and "descended" from distant reaches of the river basin, congregated at Belém and on Marajó island, and sold to settlers, the pro forma stipulations of taking them only in a just war or redeeming them from enemy captors rather than letting them be eaten became unenforceable. Through endless letters to the king, Vieira urged the granting of complete Jesuit jurisdiction over the Indians which, when authorized, finally ignited the settlers' already seething anger. And Indians continued to die in appalling numbers, diseased from smallpox and brutalized by those who depended on their labor. Colonial policy during these years tacked back and forth between Jesuit jurisdiction and enslavement in deadly ambivalence.

There were two slaveries in Brazil, two peoples enslaved: one Indian, the other African. While African slaves were imported in significant numbers to the Amazon only after the mideighteenth century, they outnumbered, without fully replacing, Indian slaves on Bahian sugar estates by the late sixteenth century. Vieira knew them both. And in these two sermons he insists on two additional slaveries, that of body and soul. These sermons mark the early and middle periods in Vieira's preaching in Brazil: the first, in the series of sermons called "Mary, Mystic Rose," is from the early 1630s; the second was delivered upon his arrival in São Luís do Maranhão in 1653.

Flattened into print, the compelling force of a sermon as a dramatic spoken performance by a master orator is lost. We can only imagine Vieira's words filling the church and making Biblical images vivid to his congregations of listeners who, in Bahia at the church of the Black Brotherhood of Our Lady of the Rosary, included African slaves. Also missing on the printed page are the breath caught, the tightening of jaws, the hush as settlers heard this priest warn them of eternal damnation if they persisted in the abuse of their slaves. Here is the power of erudition thundered out to listeners, most illiterate, who could know the Bible only through hearing. The immediacy and intensity of Vieira's words must have been stunning.

❧ "*Twenty-seventh Sermon, with the Most Holy Sacrament Present,*" *Salvador, Bahia, [ca. 1633]*

One of the most important things we see today in the world, which no longer surprises us because it is an everyday and ordinary occurrence, is the immense transmigration of Black peoples and nations that continually pass from Africa to America. . . . Of the ships that from trans-Atlantic ports are steadily entering ours we may say that they bring Africa to Brazil. A ship comes from Angola and in one day disgorges five hundred, six hundred, and perhaps one thousand slaves. The Israelites crossed the Red Sea and passed from Africa to Asia, fleeing slavery; these cross the wider Ocean Sea and pass from that same Africa to America to live and die as slaves. . . . The others are born to live, these to serve. . . . Oh, what an inhuman business in which the merchandise is men! Oh, what a diabolical business! . . .

There is no slave in Brazil who is not for me a subject of deep meditation, and all the more so when I see the most miserable ones. I compare the present with the future, time with eternity, what I see with what I believe, and I cannot accept that God who created these men as much in His image and similitude as He did others, predestined these to two Hells, one in this life, one in the next. But when I see them today so devout and festive before the altar of Our Lady of the Rosary, all brothers together as children of the same Lady, then I am persuaded without a doubt that the slavery of the first transmigration is ordained, by her mercy, as a liberty for the second one.

Our Gospel mentions two transmigrations: one in which the sons of Israel were taken from their own land "to captivity in Babylon"; and another, in which they were brought "from the captivity of Babylon to their land" (Matthew 1:11 & 12). The first transmigration and its slavery lasted seventy years; the second, that to liberty, had no end because it lasted until Christ. . . .

And how did God link the first transmigration to the second one? By ordaining that from Josiah should be born Jechonias: "And Josiah begat Jechonias and his brethren about the time they were carried away to Babylon" (Matthew 1:11). In all this Gospel [of St. Matthew] when it says one patriarch "begat" another it means mystically, that from the meaning of the father's name emerges the meaning of the son's: . . . Josias means "God's fire" and Jechonias means "God's preparation." The text says, in effect, that in the Babylonian transmigration God's fire engendered God's preparation. . . .

Here, Black Brothers and Sisters of Rosário, here is your present state and the hope that God gives you for the future. Josiah begat Jechonias and his brothers. You are siblings in God's preparation and the children of God's fire. Children of God's fire in the present transmigration into slavery, for God's fire marked you as captives; but although it is an oppression, like a fire it has also enlightened you because it brought you the light of Faith and the knowledge of Christ's mysteries, those that you recite in the rosary. In this very state of the first transmigration, which is this temporal captivity, God and His Most Holy Mother are preparing you and making you ready for the second transmigration, which is to eternal freedom.

That is what I shall preach to you today for your consolation. And reduced to a few words, this will be my subject: that your Brotherhood of Our Lady of the Rosary promises you a letter of manumission through which you will not only enjoy eternal freedom in a second transmigration, one to another life, but also that you will free yourselves from the worst form of slavery [even] in the first one. Rather than the rejoicing that I might ask from you because of this good news, I ask instead that you help me to reach sufficient grace to be able to persuade you of its truth. Hail Mary, etc.

All we children of Eve are exiled and await a universal transmigration from Babylon to Jerusalem, from the exile in this world to our repatriation in Heaven. You, however, who came or were brought from your homelands to this exile, besides the second and universal transmigration, you face this other exile in Babylon's continued slavery, whether very harsh or not. And so that you will know how to behave in it and not increase your slavery by your own actions, I wish, first of all, to explain what it is and in what it consists. But even if you do not understand it (because the subject may require more understanding than everyone has), at least, as Saint Augustine said in your Africa, at least I will be content if your masters and mistresses understand me, so that they may more slowly teach it to you, for it is very important that you and also they should know it.

Know, all those of you who are called slaves, that not everything that you are is enslaved. Every person consists of a body and a soul; but that which is a slave and is called "slave" is not the entire person, but only one half. Even the pagans, who had little understanding of souls, knew this truth and made this distinction. . . . Saint Paul, speaking with slaves about slaves, says, "Slaves, be obedient to them who are your masters according to the flesh" (Ephesians 6:5). And who are these masters? All interpreters declare that they are temporal masters like yours whom you serve during all your life. The apostle called them "masters according to the flesh" because the slave, like any other person, is composed of flesh and spirit. The dominion of the master over the slave extends over the flesh, that is, the body, and does not extend over the spirit, that is, the soul.

That is why among the Greeks, slaves were called bodies. So says Saint Epiphanius who added that the usual way of speaking among them was not to say that such-and-such a master had so many slaves, but that he had so many bodies. . . . But we need not go as far as Rome or Greece. I ask you: In this your Brazil, when you want to say that so-and-so has many or few slaves, why do you say he has such-and-such a number of *pieces*? Because the first who called them such wanted to signify, wisely and in a Christian way, that the subjection of the slave to his or her master and the dominion that the master has over the slave, extended only to the body. Men are not made of only one piece as are angels and animals. The angels and animals are entirely of a piece (to put it clearly); the angel because an angel is entirely spirit and an animal because it is entirely body. Not so human beings. A human being has two pieces: soul and body. Because the master of the slave is master over only one of these pieces and can exercise dominion over only it, and that part is the body, therefore you call your slaves *pieces*. And if you do not agree with that derivation, then we could say that you call your slaves *pieces* as we would refer to a *piece* of gold, a *piece* of silver, or a *piece* of silk or of anything else that does not have a soul. And in this way it is even more clearly proven that the word *piece* does not include the soul of the slave but is understood to extend merely to the body. Only this part is captive, only this part is bought and sold, only this part is placed within the jurisdiction of wealth. Finally, only this part was taken from Jerusalem to Babylon in the transmigration of the children of Israel, and only this part is brought from Africa to Brazil in the transmigration of those who are here called slaves and who continue in captivity.

Therefore, Black brothers, the captivity that you suffer, no matter how hard and rough it may be or seem, is not a total captivity of everything that you are, but only half a captivity. You are enslaved in that exterior and less noble part of you, which is the body; but the other, interior, and most noble part of you, which is the soul, and in everything that belongs to it, you are not enslaved but free.

And given this first point, it follows that you should know the second and much more important one and that I should state it: whether this part, the free half which is the soul, can also in some way be enslaved and who may enslave it. For I say that your soul, like anyone's, may also be enslaved. And who may enslave it is not your master, not even the King, nor any other human power, but you yourselves and by your own free will. Blessed are you who so come to terms with your half-enslaved lot as to make use of your very servitude and learn how to take advantage of what, through it and by it, you may come to deserve. But the evil and the misfortune that will make you totally miserable is that, while chance has made you captive only in your body, you very much by your own will may enslave your soul as well. . . .

The first sale and the first auction of souls in this world was in the terrestrial Paradise. On one side was God ordering that the forbidden fruit should not be eaten; on the other side was the serpent urging that it be eaten. And what happened? Eve, who represents the flesh, tended toward the Devil. And Adam, who filled the part of arbiter, instead of obeying the commands of God, followed the appetites of the flesh. Thus were the two first souls sold to the Devil and from it came the sale of the rest.

Tell me, Blacks and Whites: Do we not all condemn Adam and Eve? Do we not know that they were ignorant and more than ignorant, crazy and more than crazy, blind and more than blind? Are we not the very ones who curse and damn them for what they did? So why do we do the same thing, selling our souls as they sold theirs?

Let the Whites hear an example first that will show them their deformity, and then I shall show the Blacks another in which they can see theirs. The Bible tells us that Ahab was the worst king Israel ever had. . . . And Elias said to his face: "Thou hast sold thyself to work evil in the sight of the Lord" (I Kings 21:20). . . . And what were these sins by which Ahab sold himself? . . . He consented that Naboth should be falsely accused and condemned to death in order to confiscate and take his vineyard. See if this is not a good example for these little kings of the Recôncavo. Is it possible that to add one acre of land to your cane field and half a load more of cane to your mill you will sell your soul to the Devil?

Well, it is your soul, so sell it off if you wish. But as to your slaves' souls, how could you also sell them, placing the golden idols of your cursed and always faulty interests ahead of their salvation? That is why your slaves do not know Christian doctrine. That is why they live and die without the sacraments. That is why, although you do not forbid them the Church, with a greediness that only the Devil could invent, you do not want them near the door of the church. You consent that male and female slaves live in sin and do not allow them to marry, because, you say, if married they will serve you less well. I wish your thinking were as worthy of your Christianity as it is of your logic: "Let service to me prevail over service to God. As long as my slaves serve me better, let them live and die in the service of the Devil"!

I pray to God that He shall have mercy toward your miserableness and your souls; but I have nothing on which to base such a favorable hope, judging by the quality of your souls and from what is for you too a misery.

Now let us turn to an example appropriate for slaves, who should definitely not sell their souls, even if it costs them their lives. When King Antioch came with a powerful army and dominated Jerusalem . . . (for one can be enslaved in one's own land). . . he ordered all Judeah to abandon God's Law, and obey only his, and that sacrifices be offered only to the pagan gods that he worshipped. . . . Some, weak and vile, obeyed him and "made themselves pagans, selling their souls." (Macabbeus 1:16) But others, strong, faithful, and glorious, lost their lives because they would not sell their souls. . . . Those masters were so tyrannical that they cut off their fingers and toes, pulled out their eyes and tongues, fried and roasted them in hot frying pans, and with other weird torments took away their innocent lives. But they would rather suffer and die than sell their souls. Judge for yourselves, you who are likewise enslaved, which ones acted better: those who sold their souls to please their masters, or those who preferred to lose their lives than to enslave their souls? . . .

If a master orders his male slave to do something or desires from his female slave something that gravely offends the soul and conscience—just as he should not so wish or order, just so the slave is obliged not to obey. Say constantly that you must not offend God; and if because of this, they threaten and punish you, suffer it bravely and as a Christian, even if it be for your entire life, for these punishments are a martyrdom.

We have seen that just as human beings consist of two parts or two halves—the body and the soul—just so slavery is divided into two slaveries—one, the enslavement of the body in which bodies are involuntarily captives and slaves of men; another, the slavery of the soul, in which through one's own will souls are sold and become the captives and slaves of the Devil.

And because I promised you that the Virgin, Our Lady of the Rosary, shall free you from the worst enslavement, and for you to know how much you should welcome this freedom, it is first important for you to know and understand which of these two slaveries is the worse one. The soul is better than the body; the Devil is a worse master than any man, no matter how tyrannical he may be; the slavery of men is temporary, that of the Devil is eternal; thus there can be no mind, no matter how rustic or blind, that does not know that the worse slavery is that of the soul. But since the soul, the Devil, and this slavery itself are things that are not seen with one's eyes, how will I find a way within your grasp that will make this argument visible to you? Only by basing it on your enslavement itself, something that is most immediate to you. I ask: If God at this very moment were to free all of you from the slavery in which you are placed and you suddenly discovered yourselves all free and freed, would this not be an extraordinary and amazing grace that God would have given you? Well, even greater and of much greater and higher value will be the grace that Our Lady of the Rosary will give you in freeing your souls from enslavement to the Devil and to sin. . . .

And if we search for the fundamental principle because of which Christ, being the Redeemer of humankind, only came to redeem and free people from the enslavement of souls and not from the servitude of bodies, the clear and manifest basis is that, to end enslavement to men, men will do; but to end enslavement to the Devil and to sin, all God's power is needed. . . . For to free them from the slavery of souls and from the yoke of the Devil and of sin, only God Himself has the strength and the power, and even then only with both arms extended on a cross.

The Apostle exhorts all those who seek the salvation of their souls to keep them in a state of grace. And for this he says, "You know that you were not redeemed with corruptible things such as silver and gold, but with the precious blood of Christ." (I Peter 1:18, 19) In these words it is worth noting that Saint Peter not only urges us to ponder the price by which we are redeemed but also the price for which we were not redeemed. . . . His principal purpose in having us think about these two prices was that, by focusing on the difference of ransoms, we should know the difference of slaveries. To become free from the slavery of the body one must only give as much gold or silver as the slave costs. But to become free from the slavery of the soul, how much gold or silver would do? Would one million be enough? Would two million? Would all the gold of Sofala and all the silver of Potosí be enough? Oh, how crude and ignorant is human perception! If all the seas became silver and all the land became gold; if God created another world or a thousand worlds of materials more precious than gold and with more carats than diamonds, all this would not be enough to free a single soul for one moment from the enslavement of the Devil and of our sin. For this reason it was necessary for the Son of God to become man and die on a cross so that for this infinite price of His Blood he could redeem souls from the enslavement of the Devil and of sin. And it is from this enslavement, so difficult, so fearful, so immense, that I promise you a letter of manumission through your devotion to the rosary of the Mother of that very God.

Freed of the greatest and weightiest slavery, which is that of souls, you remain slaves in the second way, which is that of bodies. But do not imagine that because of this the mercy given you by Our Lady of the Rosary is diminished. That Our Lady of the Rosary is powerful enough to free you from the slavery of the body is proven by innumerable examples whereby those captive in the land of infidels found themselves freed through their devotion to the rosary; they then offered their broken chains and shackles as trophies of her power and mercifulness at the altar of the said Our Lady and hung them up in the churches. When God deigned to free His people from captivity in Egypt, why do you think He appeared to Moses in the burning bush? Because the bush, as all saints have declared, prefigured the Virgin, Our Lady. And God wished even then to make manifest to the world that that same Most Holy Virgin was not only the best suited and most efficacious instrument of Divine Omnipotence for freeing men from the enslavement of souls (and so chose her for His Mother when He came to redeem humankind), but also for freeing them from the enslavement of the body, like the one suffered by His people in Egypt under the yoke of the Pharaoh. Oh, how powerful is the Redeemer's Mother to free you also from this second and lesser captivity!

But it is by God's particular providence that you live at present as slaves and captives, so that, by means of this very slavery, a temporal one, you will very easily reach eternal freedom.

Now we get to the second part of being freed that I promised you. The only thing lacking is the knowledge and good use of your state for you to be, through it, the most fortunate people of the world. On this subject I will only refer to the two Apostolic princes, Saint Peter and Saint Paul, who dealt with this subject at various points, speaking with slaves as seriously as if they were speaking to Roman emperors and as profoundly and exaltedly as if they were speaking to the wise men of Greece. . . .

The Apostle Saint Paul spoke to slaves saying in two places: "Slaves, obey in all things your masters according to the flesh; not with eye service, as men pleasers, but in singleness of heart, fearing God. And whatsoever you do, do it heartily as to the Lord and not unto men, knowing that of the Lord ye shall receive the reward of the inheritance, for ye serve the Lord Christ" (Colossians 3:22–24). . . . Two things does God promise slaves for the service they provide their masters, both of which are not only uncommon but unique: "pay" and "inheritance." Note this carefully. When you serve your masters you are not their heirs nor do they pay you for your work. You are not their heirs because the inheritance belongs to their children, not to their slaves. And they do not pay you for your work, because slaves work because they are obliged to and not for a stipend. How sad and miserable a state, to serve without hope of a reward in all one's life and to work without hope of rest, except in the grave! But there is a remedy, says the Apostle (and this is Catholic doctrine). The remedy is that when you serve your masters you do not serve as one who serves men, but as one who serves God. Thus you do not work as slaves but as free men, nor do you obey as slaves but as sons. You do not work as slaves but as free men because God will pay you for your work, and you do not obey as slaves but as sons and daughters, because God . . . will make you His heirs. Tell me: if you worked for your master for a wage and if you would inherit his plantation, would you not work with a will? Well, serve this same man whom you call your master, work for him as if you worked for God, and in this very work, which you must do, all you need is a voluntary decision to make it "as for God" and God will pay you as if you were free and make you heirs as if His children.

That is what Saint Paul says. And what does Saint Peter say? He makes the point even more emphatically. After addressing Christians of all states in general, he says even more to slaves and encourages them to bear their misfortune, giving them the best of reasons: "Slaves, be subject to your masters with all respect, not only to the kind and gentle, but also to the overbearing," that is, to the bad and unjust ones. That is the summary of the rule and counsel that the Prince of Apostles gives you. And then he adds reasons worthy of the most noble spirits. First, because the glory of patience is "suffering unjustly." Second, because this is the grace through which men become more acceptable to God: "When you do right and suffer for it, you have God's approval." Third, and this is truly stupendous: because in this condition into which God placed you it is your vocation to be similar to the Son, who suffered for us, leaving us an example that you should imitate: "For to this you have been called, because Christ also suffered for us, leaving you an example that you should follow in his steps" (I Peter 2:18, 20–21).

Most justly have I called this reason stupendous. For who is there who is not amazed to see the lowly state of those to whom Saint Peter speaks and the height to which he raises them for comparison? He does not compare the calling of slaves to another step or status within the Church, but to Christ himself. And more: The Apostle does not stop here but adds a new and still greater prerogative of slaves when he declares for whom and why Christ suffered: "Christ suffered for us, leaving you an example."

I have often noted the difference between this "you" and that "us." The passion of Christ had two purposes: the remedy and the example. The remedy was universal for all of us, but the example, Saint Peter clearly says, was particularly for the slaves to whom he was speaking. And why? Because there is no condition among all that more clearly imitates the patience of Christ or is better suited to follow his example.

Oh, fortunate you, if God, as He gave you the grace of your [slave] condition, gives you also the wisdom and knowledge to use it well! Do you know what is the status of your captivity if you make good use of the means it itself provides you, without adding any other? It is the status not only of a religious order, but of one of the most austere religious orders of the entire Church. It is a religious Rule according to a divine and apostolic institution, because, if you fulfill your obligations, you will serve not men but God, with the specific title of Servants of Christ: "Servants of Christ, doing the will of God from the heart; with good will doing service, as to the Lord, and not to men" (Ephesians 6:6–7). Note well these words—"from the heart." If you serve only because forced to and with ill will you renounce your religious order; but if you serve with willingness, conforming your will to the divine will, you are truly Servants of Christ. Just as in the Church there are two religious orders dedicated to ransoming captives, yours is one made up of captives—captives without ransom, so that to you shall not lack perpetuity— which is the very perfection of this status. Some orders are of barefoot ones, others of the shod; yours is that of the barefoot and naked. Your habit is your very color, for you are not clothed in sheepskin nor camelshair, as was Elijah, but in the very clothes with which nature covered you or uncovered you, exposed to the hot sun and cold rain. Your poverty is poorer than that of the most lowly order and your obedience is more subjected than that of what we call the Minim [mendicant] Order [of Saint Francis of Paula]. Your abstinence is rather hunger than fasting, and your vigils are not one hour at midnight, but the entire night without a break. Your Rule is both one and many because it is the will of your masters. You are bound to them, because you cannot leave your captivity, but they are not bound to you because they may sell you to another whenever they wish; in only this religious order is there this contract, so that in this also yours is singular. I will not even say the mode of your address, because it is not of "Reverence," nor of "Charity," but of contempt and insult. Finally, as every religious order has a particular goal, vocation, and divine grace, your divine grace consists of flogging and punishment; your vocation is the imitation of Christ's patience; your goal is the reward of eternal inheritance. Without any other harshness or penitence beyond that which your status or order, as captives, already has within it, you have the reward of the blessed as well as the inheritance of sons. A very special favor and a providence of the Virgin Mary is that you remain in the same status with its great value, so that, as I promised you, you gain through temporal slavery an eternal freedom and manumission. . . .

Tell me: If, just as you in this life serve your masters, they would in the other life serve you, would that not be a most notable change and a glory you have never imagined? Well, it will not be that way, because that would be very little. Does God not say that when you serve your masters, you do not serve as those who serve men but as those who serve God? So this great change of fortune will not be, I say, between you and them, but between you and God. Who will serve you in Heaven will not be your masters, who likely will not go there, but God Himself in person. God will serve you in Heaven because you served Him on Earth. . . . In this way you will be twice manumitted and freed: freed from enslavement to the Devil and freed from this temporary slavery to enjoy eternal freedom. . . .

What you have to do is to console yourself much with these examples; suffer the work of your condition with much patience; give many thanks to God for the moderation of the captivity to which He brought you; and most of all take advantage of it in order to exchange it for the freedom and happiness of another life, one that does not end like this one, but lasts for ever.

And will masters also have some benefit from this Babylonian captivity? Apparently not. "I," each one of you is saying, "I, thanks to God, am White and not Black, free and not captive, master and not slave; in fact, I own many of them." And those who were captive in Babylon, were they Black or White? Had they been captive or free? Had they been slaves or masters? Neither in color, nor in liberty, nor in seigneurialship were they inferior to you. Yet if they found themselves lowered to slavery, going down so many degrees, why do you not fear the danger, you who with a minor slip may find yourselves in the same condition as they? If you are young, you may have many years to experience the change, and if old, very few. . . .

Masters, who today call yourself such, consider that to pass from liberty to slavery no transmigration to Babylon may be necessary: It could happen right in your own land. And there is no land on Earth that more deserves it and is calling for it from Divine Justice. "He who hath ears to hear, let him hear" (Luke 8:8). . . . And we have examples in our own conquests. For having enslaved Africa, God captured [from us] Mina, São Tomé, Angola, and Benguela; for having enslaved Asia, God captured Malaca, Ceylon, Ormuz, Mascate, and Cochin; for having enslaved America, God captured Bahia, Maranhão, and, for twenty-four years, Pernambuco and four hundred leagues of coastline. And because our enslavements began in Africa, God permitted there the capture of our King Sebastião and then the capture of the kingdom [of Portugal] itself for sixty years.

I know some enslavements [of Blacks] are just, which are the only ones permitted by law, and that we suppose that these are the slaves who in Brazil are bought and sold, not the natives, but those brought from other places. But what theology can there be that would justify the inhumanity and cruelty of the extreme punishments with which these slaves are mistreated? Mistreated indeed, but that is a very short word to cover the meaning that it conceals and hides. Tyrannized, we should say, or martyrized. For this is more like martyrdom than punishment for the miserable injured ones, squeezed, sealed with hot wax, slashed, ground up, and

victims of even worse excesses about which I will be silent. . . . And you can be
certain that you should fear the injustice of these oppressions no less than unjust
enslavement itself. Indeed, I say, you should fear them much more because God
feels them even more. God tolerated enslavement of the sons of Israel in Egypt as
long as it was merely enslavement; but finally His Divine Justice could not
countenance it any longer. . . . Why not? God said it: "I have surely seen the
affliction of my people and have heard their cry by reason of their taskmaster, for I
know their sorrows" (Exodus 3:7).

Note two things: First, God does not object to Pharaoh, but to his overseers,
because overseers are often those who most cruelly oppress the slaves. And, second,
He does not give slavery as His reason for justice, but the oppressions and rigors
afflicting the slaves. And He adds that He heard their cries. . . . They are cruelly
flogging a miserable slave and he is crying at each stroke, "Jesus! Mary! Jesus!
Mary!" It does not even take reverence for these two names to provoke pity in a
man who calls himself Christian. And how can you [masters] hope that they will
hear you when you cry out to these two names at the time of your death? You can
be certain that God hears these cries that you do not hear. As they do not move
your heart, they will doubtless be ineffective to lessen your punishment.

Oh, how I fear that the Ocean will be for you like the Red Sea, your houses like
those of the Pharaoh, and all Brazil like Egypt! . . . If your hearts, like those of the
Pharaoh, are hardened, that is tragic, because you will suffer the ultimate
punishment. May God grant that I am wrong in this sad thought.

⁓ "Sermon on the First Sunday of Lent," preached in the city of São Luís do Maranhão, 1653

"All this I will give you, if you will fall down and worship me."
(Matthew 4: 9)

The Devil takes Christ by the hand and takes him to a mountain higher than
the clouds and shows him from there the kingdoms, the cities, the courts of the
entire world and their grandeur, and says to him: "All this I will give you, if you will
fall down and worship me." Can there be such a proposal? Come now, Devil: do
you know what you say or what you do? Is it possible that the Devil promises the
world for only one act of adoration? Is it possible that the Devil offers the world for
only one sin? Is it possible that it does not seem much to the Devil to give the
world for only one soul? . . .

At what a different price does the Devil buy souls today than he offered for
them previously! And in our land, I say to you! The Devil has no other market in
the world where they go more cheaply. In the Gospel he offered all the kingdoms of
the world for one soul; in Maranhão the Devil need not offer such a purse for all
souls. It is not necessary to offer worlds, nor kingdoms; it is not necessary to offer
cities, nor towns, nor villages. All he has to do is wave toward a thatched hut and
two Tapuya Indians and at once he is adored on both knees. Oh, what a cheap
market! An Indian for a soul! And even better a female Indian than a male! This

Indian will be your slave for the few days that he lives; and your soul will be the Devil's for all eternity, as long as God is God. This is the contract the Devil makes with you. And not only do you accept it, but you give him your money on top of it!

My Senhores, impelled by the Gospel we have entered into the most serious and useful subject this State has. A subject from which comes either the salvation of the soul or life's remedy—see if it is serious and if it is useful. It is the most serious, the most important, and the most intricate subject. And being the most useful, it is the least pleasing. For this last reason of its being least pleasing I had determined never to speak of it, and thus also not to climb up into the pulpit. To mount the pulpit in order to give displeasure is not my purpose, and even less to people to whom I wish all that is pleasing and good. On the other hand, to climb into the pulpit and not to say the truth is against office, obligation, and conscience. . . . I ask you: Which is the better friend, he who warns you of danger, or he who, not wanting to cause you pain, leaves you to perish? Which doctor is more Christian: he who warns you of death, or he who, not wanting to upset you, lets you die without the sacraments? I had all these reasons but I had not finished deliberating. I went Friday morning to say Mass with this purpose, that God would enlighten and inspire me in what would be to His greater glory. On reading the Epistle, God told me what He wanted me to do, with His own words. They are from Isaiah: "Cry aloud, spare not, lift up your voice like a trumpet; declare to my people their transgression." (Isaiah 58:1)

> "Is not this the fast that I choose: to loose the bonds of wickedness, to undo the thongs of the yoke, to let the oppressed go free, and to break every yoke?" (Isaiah 58:6)

Do you know, Christians, do you know, nobles and people of Maranhão, what fast God wants of you during this Lent? That you loosen the bonds of injustice and let go free those whom you have [held] captive and oppressed. These are the sins of Maranhão; these are what God commands me to make known to you: "Declare to my people their transgressions." (Isaiah 58:1) Christians, God commands me to disillusion you, and I disillusion you on God's behalf. You are all in mortal sin; you all live and die in a state of condemnation, and you all will go directly to Hell. Many are already there and you will soon be there too if you do not change your life.

God help me! An entire people in sin? An entire people to Hell? Whoever is surprised by this knows nothing of unjust captivity. The sons of Israel went down into Egypt and, after the death of Joseph, the Pharaoh captured them and used them as slaves. Wanting to liberate this miserable people, God sent Moses there and gave him no other escort than a stick. God thought that to free the captives a stick was enough, even though he would free them from a king as tyrannical as the Pharaoh and from a people as barbarous as the Egyptians. When the Pharaoh refused to free the captives, plagues began to rain down on him. The land was filled with frogs, the air with mosquitoes; the rivers ran with blood, and the clouds were changed into thunder and lightning. All Egypt was awestruck and perishing. Do you know who brings plagues to Earth? Unjustly taken captives. Who brought the

Dutch plague to Maranhão? Who brought the plague of smallpox? Who brought hunger and scarcity? These captives.

Moses insisted and urged the Pharaoh to release the people. And what did the Pharaoh respond? He said one thing and did another. What he said was: "[Who is the Lord, that I should heed his voice and let Israel go?] I do not know the Lord, and moreover I will not let Israel go." (Exodus 5:2) Now that seems clear to me; let us say it now. Do you know why you do not give liberty to your ill-gotten slaves? Because you do not know God. Lack of faith is the cause of everything. If you had true faith, if you truly believed in the immortality of the soul, if you believed in Hell for all eternity, it would make me laugh that you would want to go there for having a Tapuya slave. With what confidence does the Devil say to you today: "if you fall down and adore me"? With the confidence of having offered you the world. The Devil made this speech: "I offer to this man everything; if he is greedy and avaricious, he must accept. If he accepts it, without doubt he worships me, committing idolatry, because greed and avarice are the same as idolatry." It is a saying expressed by Saint Paul: ". . . covetousness which is idolatry." (Colossians 3:5) Such was the avarice of the Pharaoh in wanting to retain and not give freedom to the captive sons of Israel, and at the same time confessing that he did not know God: "I do not know the Lord, and I will not let Israel go." This is what he said.

What he did, the same Pharaoh, was to go after the fleeing Israelites with all the power of his kingdom in order to return them to captivity. And what happened? The Red Sea opened that the captives might pass on dry footing (God knows how to make miracles in order to liberate captives). Do not think that the Hebrews merited this by their virtues, because they were worse than these Tapuyas. A few days later they worshipped a [golden] calf, and of all six hundred thousand men only two entered the Promised Land, but God so favors liberty that he frees even those who do not deserve it if they are unjustly enslaved.

The Hebrews having passed to the other side, the Pharaoh entered along the same road which was still open, the sea separated like walls, then the waters fell over him and his army and drowned them all. What I notice here is the way in which Moses tells this in his song: "Thou didst blow with Thy wind, the sea covered them; they sank as lead in the mighty waters. . . . Thou didst stretch out Thy right hand, the earth swallowed them." (The Song of Moses, Exodus 15:10 & 12) That the sea fell over them and drowned them and the earth swallowed them. Now if the sea drowned them, how could the earth devour them? Those men, like us, had both body and soul. The water drowned the bodies because they were at the bottom of the sea; the earth devoured the souls because they descended into Hell. All went to Hell, without anyone excepted because where all pursue and all capture, all are condemned. Is this not a good example? Now, consider the reasoning.

Any man who receives services and deprives others of their freedom and, being able to restore it, does not do so, is certainly condemned. All, or nearly all, men of Maranhão receive services and deprive others of their freedom and, being able to restore it, do not restore it. Therefore, all or nearly all are condemned. You will say to me that even if this were so, they did not think about it or know it, and their good faith will save them. I deny this. Yes, they did think about it, and, yes, they did know it, just as you also think about it and know it. And if they did not think of it or know it, they ought to have thought of it and known it. Some are condemned by their knowledge, others by their doubt, others by their ignorance. Those who have knowledge condemn themselves by not restoring it; those who doubt condemn themselves by not examining it; those who are ignorant condemn themselves by not knowing when they have the obligation to know. Ah, if graves would open now and some of those who died in this unhappy state would appear here in their burning flames, you would clearly read this truth! But do you know why God does not permit them to appear before you? It is as Abraham said to the rich miser when he asked him to send Lazarus to this world: "But Abraham said, 'They have Moses and the prophets; let them hear them.'" (Luke 16:29) It is not necessary for someone to come here from Hell to tell you the truth. You already have Moses and the law, you have the prophets and learned men. My brothers, if you doubt this, here are the laws, here are the learned men, question them. You have three religious orders in this State with so many members of such virtue and learning. Ask, examine, inform yourselves. But it is not necessary to go to the religious, go to Turkey, go to Hell, because there is no Turk so Turkish in Turkey, nor a Devil so devilish in Hell who will tell you that a free man can be a slave. Is there any among you with natural intelligence who denies it? Then why do you doubt?

I see what you tell me: "This is all very well, if we had another solution. . . . This people, this republic, this State cannot be sustained without Indians. Who will go in search of a bucket of water for us or a bundle of firewood? Who will plant our manioc? Will our wives have to do it? Will our sons?" First, these are not the straits in which I put you, as you will soon see. But when necessity and conscience require such a thing, I say yes, and yes again: you, your wives, your sons, we all should sustain ourselves by our own labor. It is better to live from our own sweat than from the blood of others.

You will say that your slaves are your feet and hands. You will be able to say that you love them greatly because you raised them as children, as your own. And so it is, but Christ has already responded to this reply: "If your right eye causes you to sin, pluck it out and throw it away; . . . And if your hand causes you to sin, cut it off." (Matthew 5:29; Mark 9:42 & 44) Christ does not mean to say that we should gouge out our eyes or cut off our feet. He means to say that if that which we love as our eyes and that which is as necessary as our feet and hands causes us injury, cast it from us even though it hurts us as if we had cut it. Who is there who does not love his arm or his hand but, if it suddenly became diseased, would not permit its amputation in order to save his life? . . . If in order to calm your conscience and save your soul it were necessary to lose everything and become like Job, lose everything.

But take heart, my Senhores, it is not necessary to arrive at such a point, nor even close to it. I have studied the matter with all care and purpose; and following the most liberal and favorable opinions, I have narrowed things down such that with very little worldly loss, and with very great benefits, all the residents of this State can improve their prospects for the future. Give me your attention.

All the Indians of this State are either those who serve you as slaves or those who live in the King's villages as free persons, or those who live in the wilderness in their natural and even greater liberty. These latter are the ones you go upriver to buy or to "rescue" (as they say), giving the pious name of rescue to a sale so forced and violent that sometimes it is done with a pistol at the chest. Regarding those who serve you, all in this land are inherited, gotten, and possessed in bad faith, and therefore they will be doing no small thing (even if they do it easily) if they forgive [what you owe for] their past service. However, once you have declared their freedom, if they, having been raised in your house and with your children, more or less domesticated, spontaneously and voluntarily want to remain there, no one can separate them from your service. And what will be done with those who do not wish to continue in such submission? These will be obliged to go and live in the King's villages where they also will serve you, as we will soon see. Every year you will be able to make your expeditions into the wilderness truly to rescue those who are (as it is said) tied up ready to be eaten, and this cruelty will be commuted to perpetual captivity. So, too, all those who, without violence, were sold as slaves by their enemies or taken in a just war will be [your] captives. The judges in this will be the Governor of the State, the Magistrate General, the Vicar of Maranhão or Pará, and the Prelates of the four religious orders: Carmelites, Franciscans, Mercedarians, and the Society of Jesus. All of those judged to be true captives will be distributed among the colonists at the same price for which they were bought. And those who were not taken in a just war, what will happen to them? All will be divided into new villages or divided among the villages that exist today. These along with all the other village Indians will be distributed among the colonists to serve them for six months of the year, alternating every two months, so that for the other six months they will attend to their own fields and families. In this way all the Indians of the State will serve the Portuguese either as properly and fully slaves—those tied up or taken in a just war—or those who freely and voluntarily wish to serve or, as half-captives, all those from the former and new villages who, being free, will submit themselves to serve half the time of their lives for the good and conservation of the State.

It only remains to know the wage for those called "half captives" or "half free" with which their labor and service will be paid. It is a matter that would make any other nation of the world laugh, and only in this land is it not surprising. The currency of this land is cotton cloth, and the usual price for which Indians serve and will serve each month are two lengths of this cloth, worth a few cents. From which it follows that an Indian will serve for less than a few copper coins a day! An amount not worth mentioning, and much less worthy of men of reason and Christian faith who, for not paying such a small price, condemn their souls to Hell.

Could there be anything more prudent than this? Could there be anything more reasonable than this? Whoever is not content or not satisfied with this is either not Christian or lacks reason. Otherwise, let us press the point and weigh the benefits and costs of this proposal.

The cost is only one, that there will be some private individuals who lose a few Indians, and I promise you they will be very few. But to those who seek compensation, I ask: Do not some of your Indians die? Do not some of your Indians flee? Many. Then does death do what reason will not? Does chance do what an uneasy conscience will not? If smallpox comes and carries off all your Indians, what will you do? You will have to have patience. Is it not better to lose them to the service of God than to lose them by a punishment of God? This has no reply.

Let us go to the benefits of which four are the most important. The first is that you will acquire a clear conscience. You see what a great good this is. You will be removed from a state of mortal sin. You will live as Christians, confess yourselves as Christians, die as Christians, you will bequeath your goods as Christians. Finally, you will go to Heaven, not to Hell which, at the least, would certainly be a sad thing.

The second benefit is that you will remove this curse from your houses. There is no greater curse on a house or a family than to be unjustly served with the blood and sweat of others. Everything is undone; nothing is gained. The Devil takes everything. The bread thus earned is like that today offered by the Devil to Christ: bread of stones which, if it does not stick in your throat, cannot be digested. See that in this much bread is taken from Maranhão, see if any is digested, see if anything is gained. . . .

The third benefit is that in this way there will be more rescues by which more Indians will be removed [from cannibalistic practices], which by any other way there will not be. Do you not say that this State cannot sustain itself without Indians? Well, if the wilderness is closed and the rescues completely prohibited and the few remaining Indians dead, what solution do you have? It is important that Indians be rescued and only by this means can the rescues be permitted.

The fourth and last benefit is that a proposal made in this way will be worthy of going to the hands of His Majesty for approval and confirmation. Whoever asks for the illegal and unjust deserves to have the legal and just denied him; and whoever petitions with conscience, justice, and reason deserves to have his request fulfilled. You know the proposal that you made here? It was a proposal that vassals could not make in conscience, nor ministers deliberate in conscience, nor a king grant in conscience. And even if it were possible that the King would permit such a thing, how would this serve you? If the King allows me to swear falsely, does the false oath cease to be a sin? If the King allows me to steal, will the theft cease to be a sin? The same applies to Indians. The King can order that the captives be freed, but his jurisdiction does not extend to making the free captives. If such a request went to the Crown, the very stones of the street would cry out against the men of Maranhão. But if the request were legal, just, and Christian, those same stones would line up with you.

34

Confessing to the Holy Office of the Inquisition, Bahia, Brazil

(1592, 1618)

Cooking with olive oil rather than animal fat, smoking tobacco (first described by Europeans as "drinking smoke" because they had no word for either the leaf or the practice, having never before encountered them), throwing out all water stored in a house after a death had occurred there, or wearing clean clothes on Saturday—these seemingly small, daily activities all occupied the attention of the Holy Office of the Inquisition as it operated in Brazil in the last decade of the sixteenth century and early in the seventeenth century.

No Holy Office was permanently established in Brazil, unlike in Mexico and Peru where in 1570 two jurisdictions were created, and in Cartagena where a third was founded in the early seventeenth century. Instead, a scaled-down and sporadic version was transferred to Brazil at the end of the sixteenth century from a Portugal then ruled by Spain. Visitations, as they were called, were sent to Bahia and Pernambuco in the early 1590s, followed by another to Bahia between 1618 and 1620, and the Inquisition in Portugal commissioned a visit to Pará in the Amazon from 1763 to 1769. Yet the presence of the Inquisition was felt more than the expanse of time between these dates suggests. In the

interim, voluntary *familiares*, local informers who watched and reported, served as the Inquisition's eyes and ears. They were persons of some social standing who could also demonstrate purity of blood. The position carried its privileges: exemptions from certain taxes, prestige in an honor-conscious and visibly ranked society, perhaps promotion in a career. The number of familiares increased from at least 103 in the seventeenth century to 634 in the eighteenth. New Christians denounced directly to officials in Lisbon might then be investigated by clerics appointed in Brazil, arrested, and tried in Portugal. Their property was inventoried and frequently confiscated, especially in the 1640s, when Portugal feared alliances between suspected Jews and the Dutch, who occupied Pernambuco from 1630 to 1654; and between 1704 and 1761, when the siphoning off of wealth from Brazilian gold and diamond mines alarmed royal authorites.

In June 1591, Bahians lavishly welcomed their first *visitador*, Heitor Furtado de Mendonça (who had submitted to sixteen examinations for purity of blood, routine for this position), when he arrived with a small delegation that counted himself, a notary, and a bailiff who also served as his personal assistant. No witness to the opening rites could have missed the joining of religious and secular authority to the supreme authority of the Holy Office. Mendonça began his round of formal introductions by presenting himself first to the bishop, who kissed his feet and promised solemnly to assist his visitation in every way possible. In the chambers of the municipal council a few days later the "very noble senhores, judges, and council members" paid him homage. But a grand public ceremony waited for the visitation's official opening a few days later. En route to Cathedral Square, the procession passed before the bishop and members of the cathedral chapter, government and judicial officials, priests and clerics, members of the lay brotherhoods, and common people who elbowed their way into the streets. Mendonça, walking beneath a golden canopy, was greeted with praise for himself and the Holy Office. After reading the Rule of Pius V in favor of the Inquisition, he proceeded into the cathedral and an honored place at the head of the altar.

The visitador then set to work. A "Proclamation of the Faith" was posted to instruct the faithful, under pain of excommunication, to confess and denounce the heresies and doctrinal errors that concerned the Holy Office. The Tribunal, being blind to "degree, status, or preeminence," was purported to exempt no one. Among the transgressions to be reported, Jewish practices allegedly followed by New Christians and "crypto-Jews" figured prominently, just as they would in subsequent inspections: keeping Saturday as the Sabbath, abstinence from certain foods such as bacon, circumcision of male infants, failing to say prayers in a certain way or to make the sign of the cross, performing certain burial rituals. And while as many as five hundred New Christians in Brazil were sentenced over the years and some of these were put to death, the Inquisition did not entirely ignore the heresies of converted Indians or African slaves, although their numbers among the sentenced were few.

Following the charges of early Protestants and the Catholic Christian response marked by the Council of Trent (1545–1563), the Inquisition extended heresies to include other errors in an attempt to protect Catholic doctrine. Operating within this expanded understanding, the Brazilian visitations campaigned to instruct and reform local morality. The Bahian Tribunal interrogated those suspected of idolatry, of uttering invocations of the Devil in witchcraft, and other blasphemies. Errors against doctrine such as denying the existence of Purgatory, doubting the purity of the Virgin, or questioning whether the consecrated Host was the true body of Christ all fell within the visitador's purview. Sexual crimes or "sins against nature," by which was understood bigamy, sodomy, or bestiality, the sexual solicitations of a priest, or believing that fornication was not a sin also concerned local investigators. Although books were not published in Brazil until the arrival of the first printing press with the court in 1808, and most people could not read, occasionally those confessing admitted to having read prohibited books.

In Bahia between 1591 and 1593 the visitador heard confessions and denunciations, ratifying those he judged reliable and barring those he did not trust, such as one from a man he dismissed as mentally unsound. As visitador he had no authority to try or sentence those who came before him, and instead was instructed to send to Lisbon for trial only persons whose cases pointed confidently toward conviction. Without adequate proofs, an irate cardinal later warned Mendonça, carelessly prepared cases would "discredit the proceedings of the Holy Office." The Bahian Tribunal repeated a familiar administrative strategy: rely on local officials, in this case especially the Jesuits, to complete their numbers and draw local people into the Inquisition's business. The bishop, the Jesuit provincial, and the rector of the Jesuit school were all present at interrogations and all signed the cases the Bahian visitador sent to Portugal for trial.

Despite the cardinal's warning, however, at least fifty trials were heard in Pernambuco between 1593 and 1595. (The original records were transferred to Portugal and preserved in the National Archive in Lisbon.) These decisions were final, without appeal, and demonstrate the autonomy that the early Brazilian Tribunal exercised from Portuguese authority. The cases were sometimes read in Lisbon, however, and comments scrawled across the cover sheet: "Unjust imprisonment and unjust sentence"; "This crime warrants the pain of death"; or "The defendant was rigorously [interrogated] and, having confessed during the time of grace, a rebuke by the Tribunal would have been enough." At least two autos-da-fé were held at a church in Olinda at which the condemned were publicly humiliated. Blasphemers, for example, were required to appear barefoot, wearing only their underclothes, and bareheaded, with a lighted candle in one hand and a stick clamped sideways across the mouth.

To encourage the populace to come forward voluntarily to confess their crimes, the visitador granted a thirty-day period of grace to residents of Salvador and nearby neighborhoods that closed on July 28, 1591, and another to the people of the surrounding hinterland ending on February 11, 1592. If a guilty person's confession was judged "complete and true," she or he was promised exemption from the worst punishments—confiscated property or death at the stake—although not from lesser ones. It was a gamble: remain silent and risk being denounced by someone else, or confess, perhaps unnecessarily, and face possible trial and punishment. The recorded testimonies of some confessants suggest they were genuinely confused about whether they had committed a crime. Others fell into the trap by telling less

than they might have, only to find themselves thoroughly denounced; some deliberately perjured themselves. Denunciators who knew too much risked implicating themselves.

Of the four confessions presented in this selection, two come from the first Bahian visitation of 1591–1593 and two from the second in 1618. The Tribunal heard all four during periods of grace. To know the fates of the latter two men requires further research in Lisbon to discover if indeed they were tried, as seems likely, and what sentences they faced. Of the first two, we know that Domingos Fernandes Nobre was tried by Mendonça, contrary to instructions, and severely reprimanded by members of the Tribunal. Yet the punishments were mild: besides spiritual penitence and a moderate fine, Nobre was forbidden ever to return to the wilderness. He apparently disobeyed this order, for years later he was awarded a royal land grant precisely for his valor in exploring the wilderness. Dona Ana Alcoforada, her goods sequestered, was sent to Lisbon and imprisoned until 1605. She narrowly escaped conviction through a general papal pardon, which had been bought with an extravagant donation to the Crown by New Christians.

These testimonies, as a sample of those heard by Mendonça and his successor, help to illuminate the preoccupations of the Brazilian inspections, the visitador's methods of questioning, and some of the varied motivations that impelled men and women from all social ranks to risk confessing. They provide glimpses of how a range of Portuguese and Brazilians understood the Inquisition and its role in the moral and religious reform of society.

∿ *Confession of Domingos Fernandes Nobre*

February 11, 1592, Salvador, Bahia

He said he is Old Christian, a native of Pernambuco on the coast of this Brazil, *Mameluco*, [or Mestizo], son of Miguel Fernandes, a White man and stonemason, and Joana, a native and heathen of this Brazil, both deceased; he is forty-six years old, married to Isabel Beliaga, a White woman, Old Christian; he is a resident of this city and has no trade.

Confessing his offenses, he said that from the age of eighteen until the age of thirty-six years he lived as a heathen, neither praying nor commending himself to God, [nor] taking care that he would die not having knowledge of God as a true Christian, and although he confessed at Lent it was [only] in order to fulfill an obligation. His life during this time was more heathen than Christian, although he never left the Christian faith, which he had always in his heart.

He confessed that twenty-two years ago, more or less, in Pernambuco he sinned the sin of the flesh with two young women, his goddaughters to whom he became godfather when they, being heathens, were baptized and made Christians. It seems to him that it was as much a sin to sleep with them whether or not they were his goddaughters.

He confessed that twenty years ago, more or less, he went to the wilderness of Porto Seguro in the company of Antônio Dias Adorno to search for gold and there he practiced the customs of the heathens, staining his legs with a paint called *urucu* [*uru'ku* in Tupi; a reddish dye made from seeds of the annatto or *achiote* tree] and another [called] *jenipapo* [from the fruit of the genipap evergreen tree that produces a reddish-brown juice or dye], and covering his head with feathers and playing heathen tambourines which are gourds with stones inside, and playing their drums and instruments, dancing with them, singing their heathen songs in the heathen language, which he knows well. He did these things in order to make the heathens of that wilderness understand that he was brave and did not fear them even though they were always at war.

He confessed that sixteen years ago, more or less, he was ordered by João de Brito d'Almeida, who was governor of this captaincy in the absence of the governor, his father, Luis de Brito [governor 1573–1578], to go to Paraíba. He, the confessant, went to the wilderness of Arabo as captain of a company to bring heathens downriver to be settled. On this expedition he spent four or five months, and there, in the heathen way, he had two women who were daughters of heathens given to him as wives. And he painted his body in the heathen way and danced and sang and played [musical instruments] with the heathens in their way. And he scarred his thighs, buttocks, and arms according to the heathen practice, using a tooth from an animal called the paca. After lightly scarring the flesh, they rub some black powder on their skin, and after the skin heals the black markings remain forever impressed on the arms or buttocks, or wherever they are put, like brands forever.

This scarring the heathens customarily do to themselves when they want to show that they are brave and that they have just killed men. The confessant, finding himself surrounded by heathens who rose up against him, had a non-Christian Indian scar him in the said way in order to show he was brave, and in this way he escaped, because, seeing this, the heathens fled from him. Francisco Affonso Capara, resident in the Pirajá neighborhood of this city, then scarred himself in the same way.

He confessed that fifteen years ago, more or less, he returned to the same wilderness of Arabo in this captaincy at the order of the governor, Luis de Brito, and by the captain of another captaincy to bring heathens downriver for settlement, an expedition which lasted some six months. In the wilderness the heathens again gave him their daughters for wives, and he had two or three wives simultaneously, like any heathen. He drank their tobacco with them, which is the leaf from an herb that in Portugal is called holy herb. He drank their wines with them, and danced and played and sang with them in the heathen style; he went about nude like them, and he wept and lamented appropriately, in their way. All these things he did to the disgrace of God's law because the heathens, seeing him do these things, took him also to be a heathen and called him nephew. He did these things (while having the faith of Christ in his heart) so the heathens would treat him well.

He confessed that thirteen or fourteen years ago, by order of the same governor, he returned to the wilderness of Ilhéus where he spent fourteen months. There he stuck feathers to his face with mastic, and painted himself with the red paint of the urucu in the heathen style, and had seven heathen women, whom the heathens gave him, and he had them in the heathen way. He dealt with them, drank their wines, did their dances and played and sang—everything like a heathen.

And because they rose up against him and his companions, they—the confessant and João de Remirão, owner of his own sugar mill where he lives near Tasuapina in this captaincy—pretended to be shamans in the way to which the heathens are accustomed, saying they would cast death upon them so all of them would die, and inventing and pretending so the heathens would take care and not kill them, and so they could escape. And indeed they did escape.

He confessed that twenty years ago, in the wilderness of Pernambuco on the river São Francisco, he gave a sword, shields, daggers, German knives, and other arms to the heathens who are enemies of Christians and who kill and make war against them whenever they have the chance.

He confessed that five or six years ago, more or less, in the wilderness [near] this city there arose among the heathens a heresy and superstition which they called Santidade. They called one heathen Pope, whom they said was God, and others they called saints, and a heathen woman they called Mother of God and other women they called saints. They performed baptisms among themselves with burning candles, sprinkling water on the heads of the baptized. Those whom the so-called Pope baptized received heathen names. The one called Pope, author and inventor of the heresy and superstition, used to be called Antônio and was a heathen of this Brazil and was raised in the house of the priests of the Society of Jesus during the time when they had villages in Tinharé, captaincy of Ilhéus, from whence he fled into the wilderness.

And the heresy set itself up, parodying and falsifying the practices of the Christian Church, performing baptisms and making churches with altars, holy water fonts, confraternity boards, candlesticks, prayer beads, and a sacristy. They had an idol on the altar, the figure of an animal that represented neither a human nor a bird nor a fish nor a worm, but was like a chimera, which they worshipped. The non-Christian Indian woman called Mother of God was the wife of the one called Pope, according to the heathen practice.

And this false belief having arisen, the confessant, made captain by the governor, Manoel Telles Barreto [governor 1583–1587], and on his order led a company of soldiers to destroy the heresy, to arrest and bring its supporters, the majority of whom were Christians who, after becoming so, fled to the one called Pope who also was Christian.

The confessant, being already in the wilderness, found that the supporters of the heresy fled because they feared his troop going against them. He encountered a detachment of Indians of this Brazil, some heathens, some Christians, who carried with them the idol and he, the confessant, seeing the idol, removed his hat and feigned reverence for it to deceive those who brought it into thinking that he believed in their superstition.

And the Indians asked him to allow them to have a procession with the idol. He gave permission and ordered his Indians whom he had taken with him to help them make the procession. He sang their heathen songs with them, drank their tobacco, which they called sacred, and played their heathen instruments according to their practice of that heresy called Santidade.

And then the confessant ordered some of his companions to take the idol to Fernão Cabral de Taide at his *fazenda* Jaguaripe from where he, the confessant, had left for the wilderness. These companions were Domingos Camacho, native of the Algarve and who now is in the Indies of Toqumão [Tucumán?], and Pantaliam Ribeiro, farmer and resident on the fazenda of Diogo Correa. And along with the idol, he wrote a letter to Fernão Cabral in which he said that he sent the idol there with those people, followers of the said heresy who might [number] some sixty souls, and that it would be good company to them while he, the confessant, went into the wilderness so that he would not run into danger.

And after thus bidding farewell to his companions, those who took the said people and idol, he, the confessant, went ahead, already taking with him new help from companions whom the governor Manoel Telles sent him.

And arriving at a pass called Palmeiras Compridas, the headman of the supporters of that heresy, the one called Pope, sent word to the confessant that he should not pass through that place under threat of punishment because he would soon come there. Soon the one called Pope came dressed in some trousers of coarse black cotton, a green cassock, and a red beret on his head, bringing with him many of his followers in orderly rows of three, all the women and children at the back with their hands raised.

The one called Pope came in the lead, and the others, who followed him in rows, came shaking and making movements with their feet and hands and necks, and speaking a certain new language; everything [they did] was the invention and ceremony of that heresy called Santidade.

And he, the confessant, worshipped the one called Pope and knelt before him, saying these words: "I worship you, *odre* [billy-goat], because you will be a goatskin." [As late as the eighteenth century, *odre* meant a container for wine or vinegar made of goatskin.]

Soon he, the confessant, also wept to the one called Pope according to the heathen custom and jumped and celebrated with him in his heathen way, and drank tobacco with him, tobacco which the followers of the heresy called sacred. He played their instruments and sang their songs with them in their languages. And the confessant allowed them to worship him, and call him the Son of God, and also Saint Louis.

All these things he did and agreed to without the intention or the spirit of the heathens, but pretending in order to deceive the people of that heresy and to bring them with him to the fazenda of Fernão Cabral.

And to the one called Pope he, the confessant, gave a horseman's sword, and had already given him a short sword, and the clothes in which he came dressed.

He further confessed that before this case of heresy, he went to the wilderness of this captaincy in the company of Luis Lopes Pessoa with permission from the governor, Lourenço da Veiga [1578–1581], who then governed this State, to bring heathens downriver with him to settle. On that expedition he spent one year, and during that time he practiced with the heathens their heathen customs, playing and singing in the manner described above; he accepted four women given to him as wives, according to their heathen style.

He further confessed that two and a half years ago he went with permission from the governing board [1587–1591] to the wilderness in the company of Cristovão da Rocha to bring heathens downriver, from where now they come to the wilderness of Pernambuco, where he also consented to and ordered a dance of swords and festivities for the heathens of the wilderness of Pernambuco. He also gave two muskets to the heathens and they gave him six women whom he had as wives.

And he confessed that in all the time he traveled in the wilderness, he always ate meat during Lent and on other days on which the Church forbids meat. Many times he said that he never wanted to come out of the wilderness because he had many women there and ate meat on forbidden days and did what he wanted without having to account to anybody.

And he said that for all these things and offenses that he has confessed, he asks forgiveness in this time of grace.

Soon he was questioned as to how he has been married to his legitimate wife, Isabel Beliaga, and the manner in which he had the women in the wilderness. He responded that it was twenty-three years ago, more or less, that he married, and that in the wilderness he did not receive the women who were given to him by any words of the Church. He only took them as is the custom among the heathens to keep women for immoral conversation.

Asked if he could excuse himself from eating meat at forbidden times, he responded that he always ate it out of necessity, having no other provisions, and when he had provisions, he stopped eating meat.

He declared that at the time he worshipped the one called Pope, he said to his companions that they should dissemble [their] worship of him, even if he was in front of everybody and did not see if [in fact] they worshipped. The one called Pope said that he was called Antonio, he was Christian, and came from the priests of the Society of Jesus in Tinharé, in the captaincy of Ilhéus.

And being asked which persons in his company did he see do the same that he did or similar things, he responded that he saw Captain Cristovão da Rocha give the heathens, who are enemies of the Whites and make war on them and kill them when they can, a weapon of war, a silk banner, a drum, a horse, a mare, a musket, a sword, and it was said that he gave them a flask of gunpowder. He saw him blackened around the neck with the jenipapo dye according to the heathen custom, and that he had five or six wives in the way of the heathens. He saw Pedro Álvares, Mameluco, now resident in New Ceregipe, order that a sword be given to the heathens for three *peças* [pieces, or three Indian slaves]. He saw Fernão Sanches Carilho, a White man from the Alentejo [the central region of Portugal], who now is at the São Francisco river, previously give to the heathens a leather warrior's jacket. He saw Domingos Diaz, mameluco, who it now seems to him is in Paraguaçú, scarred on one arm in the heathen way.

And saying nothing more, he was ordered to secrecy and so he promised. As to his impediments as a witness he said he has a hatred for Cristovão da Rocha.

〜 *Confession of Dona Ana Alcoforada*

February 11, 1592, Salvador, Bahia

She said she is half Old Christian and half New Christian, a native of Matoím in this captaincy, daughter of Antonio Alcoforado, Old Christian, and his wife Isabel Antunes, New Christian, both deceased; she is twenty-seven years old, married to Nicolao Faleiro de Vasconcelos, farmer and resident on his *fazenda* at Matoím.

And confessing herself, she said that four years ago she had in her house a servant by the name of Balthesar Dias Azambujo, an Old Christian according to what he said, native of Santo Antonio do Tojal, who will now be a man of thirty years, a little more or less, who now is married and resides in the captaincy of Ilhéus with Caterina Cordeira, his wife, and they live by their labor. Before living with her, the confessant, he also lived some days with her aunt, Dona Lianor, wife of Anrique Monis Telex.

And at that time when one of her slaves died at home, her servant, Balthesar Dias Azambujo, asked her why people threw out the water when someone died at home, was it out of repugnance or why?

And she, the confessant, never until then had heard nor known that at the death of someone, water was thrown out. She asked him then why he had said that, and he replied to her that he said it because he had seen that in his land water was emptied out of houses when someone had died, but he did not know why, nor did he say anything more.

Then she, the confessant, simply taking care that it would be something good, ordered that the water that was in the house should be thrown out. And it happened that at various times seven or eight slaves died, and when they died she ordered that the water that was in the house should always be emptied out. She did this without having heard or learned from any other person, in any other place, and without having seen any other person do it, only from hearing her servant say it.

Further, she said that she heard her grandmother, Ana Rodrigues, a New Christian, swear when she wanted to affirm something in this way: "by the world that has the soul of Heitor Antunes," who was her husband, the grandfather of the confessant.

And so she heard the same oath from many other persons whom she does not remember, and for this reason she also simply, without any bad intention, many times used the same oath, and when she wanted to affirm something she said, "by the world that has the soul of my father and my mother."

Asked which world this is that has the soul of her father and her mother, she responded that she does not understand nor know how to say what the oath means to say, but that she utters this oath simply for having heard it, and has sworn it many times, before her relatives and other persons, and she does not remember how long ago [she first heard it].

She was quickly admonished by the Senhor Visitador, with great charity, that she should confess fully and truly because these rituals she performed of throwing out water are very well known to be from the Jews, who usually swear by "*Orlon de mi padre*," which means the same as "by the world that has the soul of my father." And because she is a New Christian, it can only be presumed that she does these ceremonies and oaths with the intention of a Jew, and that she is a Jew and lives by the law of Moses and has left the faith of Jesus Christ. "Therefore speak the truth and open your heart, because this will benefit you greatly in achieving grace because you are within the period of grace."

She responded that she is a good Christian and never knew of, nor had anything [to do with], the law of Moses, but that she did these things without understanding that they were Jewish. Later when the Holy Inquisition announced itself in this city and she heard told of the things declared in the Proclamation of the Faith, she understood that what she had said, and would never say again, was Jewish, and that her guilt was in having done them externally, without having any error of the Catholic faith in her heart. She asks forgiveness and mercy.

∽ *Confession of Francisco Nugueira*

September 18, 1618, Salvador, Bahia

On the eighteenth day of the month of September of one thousand six hundred and eighteen in the city of Salvador da Bahia de Todos os Santos, in the church of the Jesuit College at an afternoon hearing during the period of grace, being present Senhor Inquisitor Marcos Teixeira, there appeared before him without being summoned Francisco Nugueira, Old Christian, between twenty-nine and thirty years of age, a barber, born in Lisbon, married, resident in this city on the Rua Direita do Colégio. And being present, he was charged to tell the truth in everything, was pledged to secrecy, and was given the Oath on the Holy Gospels on which he put his hand, charged with so promising.

He said he confesses before this Tribunal that about a year and a half ago in this city a Black slave woman of his was missing from his household for a period of three months. Learning that an old Black man who belonged to the Franciscan Monastery in this city was a sorcerer and diviner, he searched him out and told him about the flight of the slave woman, asking him to say how he, the confessant, could find her. He, the confessant, did this both times that the slave woman fled (for between one flight and another there were not more than fifteen days). The Black man replied right away that she would return to the house on a certain day which he then specified. And the other time he answered that she would come home and would bring [her] godfather and also specified the day. And everything thus happened both times.

And because he said he had nothing else to confess, he was asked for the name of the Black man by the Senhor Inquisitor, whether he was well known as a sorcerer, whether he [the confessant] had seen some spells, what witnesses there were to this case, and whether it provoked a scandal.

He answered that he did not know the name of the Black man but that he was well known and was the oldest Black serving the said priests. It was because he was famous as a sorcerer that he, the confessant, had sought him out. He, the confessant, had not seen him practice any other things on the two occasions, aside from, the first time, pouring wine into a dish and, the second time, water, then speaking a little to himself, and then divining as described above.

It was also true that he had recounted the event to Pero de Moura, married, resident in this city, a native of Lisbon, and to his brother, Paulo Correa, also resident in this city. It was because they told him that if they had to accuse [him] they would do it; he asked forgiveness and mercy, being ready for whatever penance was imposed. He thus spoke, and said he did not know of any other witnesses regarding the case nor did he think those mentioned above were scandalized by his [action].

He was asked whether, when it happened, he understood and believed that the Devil could divine future things and that the Black man divined through him; and whether he knew that future contingencies are reserved only to God and that the Holy Mother Catholic Church so believes and orders it believed; and if he knew that the Black man had made a pact with the Devil, tacitly or explicitly, to divine, or [whether] he, the confessant, had done it to know what [God] intended; and whether he knew that the Holy Mother Church forbade practicing or using sorcery and benefitting from it.

He replied that he, the confessant, moved by a desire to find the said Black woman, consulted the sorcerer, as he has said, and as things happened he understood that [the Black man] had divined by the action of the Devil and that this was forbidden by the Holy Mother Church, but that he, the confessant, had not made any pact with the Devil nor did he know whether the Black man had done so, nor did he know what such a thing would be. He believes what the Holy Mother Church believes. After he learned that this was a case for the Holy Office [of the Inquisition], he repented, so much so that, when another Black woman fled from him, he had not wished to benefit from similar acts of sorcery.

And he was told by the Senhor Inquisitor that he was well advised to come and so acknowledge [it] to this Tribunal, for the sake of unburdening his conscience and seeking mercy. And he was asked whether he knew of others who were guilty of cases for the Holy Office, and what motive did he have for coming and confessing. He replied that he knew nothing other than that it was generally said in this city that a wall-eyed Black man belonging to André de Freitas, Field Captain, married, resident of this city, divined by sorcery. He [the confessant] had come to acknowledge [this] in order to benefit from the mercy of this Tribunal.

And he was asked to whom he had confessed this case and whether he had been absolved. He replied that before the Edict of Grace he had not thought to confess it, but that after his confession was taken in writing, he had confessed sacramentally to Canon Manoel Viegas and that, having said that he had made a statement to the Holy Office, he [the canon] had absolved him.

Asked whether he had any [connections to the other witnesses that would discredit his testimony], he said no. And he signed along with the Senhor Inquisitor. Manoel Marinho wrote this. [signed] Marcos Teixeira, [signed] Francisco Nugueira.

∾ *Confession of Pero de Moura*

September 18, 1618, Salvador, Bahia

On the eighteenth day of the month of September of one thousand six hundred and eighteen in the city of Salvador da Bahia de Todos os Santos, in the church of the Jesuit College at an afternoon hearing during the period of grace, being present Senhor Inquisitor Marcos Teixeira, there appeared before him without being summoned Pero de Moura, Old Christian, born in Lisbon, thirty years old, married, and resident in this city. And being present, he was charged to tell the truth in everything, pledged to secrecy, and given the Oath on the Holy Gospels on which he put his hand, charged with so promising.

He said that he came before this Board to accuse himself and confess his guilt so as to receive the promised mercy and grace; that he was repentant and ready to do any penance that was assigned him for such guilt. A year and a half ago more or less, when his brother Paulo Correa was very sick in this city, he, distrusting doctors, had summoned a Black man from São Thome called Francisco Cucana, a freedman, who lives in Pirajá in the hinterland of this city near the Diogo Monis Telles plantation. This Black man was famous as a sorcerer and had been jailed for this in the [ecclesiastical] jail of this city. And this Black man came to the confessant's house and in the presence of his wife Hieronima Dias, his brother, and a young man called Francisco, the confessant's servant, practiced sorcery ceremonies with an egg, calling the name of the sick man while telling him not to answer. The confessant declared that the sick man, his brother, had been healed with the cure that the Black man had made for him, but that it did not seem to him that the application of herbs and other small things with which he had healed him was the work of sorcery.

And he further said that, with the intention simply of unburdening his conscience, he declared well and truly that two or three months ago more or less when he was going to Mass in the company of Paulo Antunes Freire, they entered a basement-level store of Andre Lopes de Carvalho, a Jew, a widower, born in Europe, a shopkeeper, resident in this city, and, as all three of them chatted, Andre Lopes de Carvalho said, "The Devil take anyone who wishes to be an Old Christian," which he, the confessant, heard him say and witnessed, having been present. And the bystanders threw up their hands and told him that he should watch what he said, because not even when teasing could one say such a thing. The denounced replied, "If they accuse a New Christian, why should I want to be an Old Christian?" And [the confessant] said he had nothing else about which to testify or denounce.

The Senhor Inquisitor told him he had done well to testify before the Board, both to relieve his conscience and to receive much mercy. Then he asked him if he had heard any scandal regarding his confession, if he had heard other witnesses, if he knew whether the Black man had made a pact with the Devil, either tacitly or explicitly, and if he knew that the Holy Mother Church forbade the use of such sorcery.

He replied that he knew nothing more than that the Holy Mother Church forbade the above, but that he, the confessant, to remedy his brother's need, had had few scruples regarding this, because of the little that is made of such matters in this land.

And he was asked if the words of Andre Lopes de Carvalho had provoked a scandal, whether after they had thrown up their hands he insisted on what he had said, why had he, the witness, entered the shop of the accused, what provoked him [the accused] to say the said words, and what other witnesses were there to the occurrence.

He said that there were no other witnesses besides himself and Paulo Antunes Freire, a single man, born in Lisbon, a stock-clerk in this city. The reason both of them had gone into the store of the denounced was, as far as he can remember, to inquire about some gunpowder. What provoked the denounced to utter those words was that they were speaking of similar words that were said in this city and that Antonio Mendes, nicknamed Beijú, had said at the beach not long before. And it was true that he, the denouncer, and the said Paulo Antunes Freire were scandalized by the words of the denounced.

And he was asked if the denounced was a man who often lost his wits, whether he had been imprisoned and punished by the Holy Office, and if he was infamous for Judaism. And [he was asked] if he knew of other cases related to the Holy Office and what motive did he have in denouncing this one.

He replied that the denounced was a man of reason and proud of it, that he had heard it said that the denounced had been imprisoned by the Holy Office in Portugal, and that he denounced the occurrence [because he was] zealous to unburden his conscience, and that he knew of no others.

Asked whether he had any [connections to the other witnesses that would discredit his testimony], he said no. And he signed along with the Senhor Inquisitor. Manoel Marinho wrote this. [signed] Marcos Teixeira, [signed] Pero de Moura.

35

Francisco de Avila's Christmas Eve Sermon
(*1646*)

In the last years of his life, the office of canon in the cathedral of Lima upon which Francisco de Avila (1573?–1647) had long trained his eye was finally his. Avila was born in Cusco of uncertain parentage, and he may have been a Mestizo whose career was impeded by prejudice and suspicion. In the mid-1640s a new archbishop of Lima, Don Pedro de Villagómez (1641–1671), was working to revive the mechanisms of the Extirpation of idolatry (see Selection 36), a process for which Avila was prepared to take much credit. As canon, he added to his apparent triumph with the publication of the first part of his *Treatise on the Gospels* (*Tratado de los evangelios,* 1646), from which the following selection derives. When the second part appeared posthumously in 1648, the entire work formed an extensive cycle of 122 sermons in Quechua and Spanish that followed the holy seasons and feast days of the Catholic calendar. Avila's *Tratado* was the first substantial new book of sermons for Indians to be published in Peru since the thirty-one trilingual sermons (in Spanish, Quechua, and Aymara), the *Third Catechism and Exposition of the Christian Doctrine in Sermons* (*Tercero Catecismo y exposición de la doctrina cristiana por sermones*) (Lima, 1585), appeared in the wake of the Third Provincial Council. Expounding

orthodox understandings of doctrine while paying especial attention to the identification and refutation of native Andean religious errors, Avila's bilingual *Tratado de los evangelios* offers valuable insight into the style and strategies of one of the most knowledgeable evangelizers in seventeenth-century Peru.

It is worth noting that comparatively few Indians would actually have heard Avila preach from these texts. They were collected to assist others, an audience of contemporary priests of Indians in particular. These parish priests were required, most recently by the dictates of the Council of Trent, to preach on Sundays and major festivals in the year as well as daily during the seasons of Advent and Lent. Model collections of sermons such as Avila's were often published late in a noted preacher's career, reflecting the texts used and elaborated upon over decades of thought and practice.

Avila did not, however, live to enjoy much of the new extirpating atmosphere presided over by Archbishop Villagómez. He died in 1647, the year before the publication of the final part of his *Tratado*. He missed, too, the elaborately staged departure of six idolatry inspectors from Lima the following year, the symbolic beginning of Villagómez's new campaign to eliminate suspect native religiosity in the Archdiocese of Lima which had, in effect, already started. And one suspects he would not have been pleased to know that his sermons failed to become the primary texts used by the itinerant inspectors of idolatry to complement their judicial and penal labors.

Another bilingual collection of sermons by Avila's contemporary in the cathedral chapter in Lima, Fernando de Avendaño, overshadowed the *Tratado* at the time and has done so ever since. Avendaño's personal history as a preacher and extirpator was almost as storied as (and considerably less controversial than) Avila's. To Avendaño fell the double distinction of being named the prelate's honorific superintendent of the Extirpation and having his own set of anti-idolatry texts, the *Sermons on the Mysteries of Our Holy Catholic Faith* (*Sermones de los misterios de nuestra santa fe católica*), favored by Villagómez and widely distributed as the pedagogical appendix to the prelate's exhortation and instruction for extirpators of idolatry, the *Pastoral Letter,* published in 1649. Apart from its revealing preface, Avila's book of sermons has not been carefully examined by most students of colonial Latin American history, for whom he is associated principally with the Huarochirí Manuscript (see Selection 1). The official attitude toward the contents of the *Tratado* at the time is more complex and stems from more than the simple fact that Avila himself was off the scene. It is quite possible that his sermons were judged by Villagómez and by others who offered him advice to be less safe in the hands of priests in Indian parishes than the texts of his contemporary, Avendaño.

Avila's *Tratado* signaled some of its differences from Avendaño's *Sermones* with its very name. The contents of a tratado are set in a freer, more leisurely mold than a book of sermons proper. Moreover, the tratado as a form enjoyed a reputation for popular and accessible references rather than argument by logic. The freedom clearly suited Avila's style, allowing him not only to wander between points, unfettered by an initial proposition and the formulaic need to present his proof through contraries (although he, too, would sometimes revert to this basic strategy), but also to enter repeatedly into extended dialogue with Andean religious traditions. This is not to say that Avila, in choosing his form, abandoned structure; in fact, as we have noted, he chose to base his sermons, in an entirely customary way, on the Catholic festival cycle. Yet, even as the sermons expounded on the appropriate biblical texts through the calendar year, these seasons and Scriptures became launching points for a freer discourse. If Avendaño's works are notable for the directness of their argumentation, then Avila's are more subtle in the way that they weave engagement with Indian beliefs and practices into a cycle of close scriptural instruction and elaboration. Avendaño's texts are often predictable, whereas Avila's are full of surprises. The historian Pierre Duviols memorably took his comparison of the styles of the two great preachers of the era of the Extirpation in the archdiocese of Lima to an emotional level. He refers first to Fernando de Avendaño: "That which is probably most lacking in these sermons is Christian charity, or simply a feeling of humanity. The man is without a doubt dominated by his iconoclastic and apologetic zeal; he is skilled and brilliant, but his heart remains cold and hard. Of this we are fully convinced when we compare his sermons with those of Francisco de Avila."

The preface that Avila composed for his *Tratado* in 1645 provided an opportunity to reorder and recall selectively experiences from his early career as a priest in the Indian parish of San Damián de Checa, Huarochirí, from 1597 to 1609. He had been in trouble with his Indian parishioners as early as 1600, when accusations of misconduct were first brought against him. The priest was cleared of guilt on this occasion, yet in September 1607 he found himself accused again, and this time in a far more serious manner. Andean notables from his parish made over one hundred charges, denouncing Avila for behavior that flagrantly contravened the directives of the Third Provincial Council of Lima (1582–83) concerning the activities of priests among Indians. The charges ranged from exploitation of Indians as manual laborers (some of whom were constructing a home in Lima for the aspiring canon-to-be), through frequent absenteeism from his responsibilities in San Damián (presumably while he completed his doctorate in Lima during these years), his collection of exorbitant fees for the performance of sacraments and other religious services, and his involvement in the lucrative trade of agricultural goods for his own profit, to a number of allegations of scandalous sexual relationships with native Andean women in the community. On the orders of the chief judge of the archdiocese, Avila was removed from his parish and incarcerated in the ecclesiastical jail in Lima. Yet Avila had soon rallied some regional friends—native Andean assistants among them—and secured his release. Acting on his behalf, his allies had put pressure on three of his principal accusers to retract parts of their denunciations and thus cast doubt on the veracity of the other charges.

At this point, with the help of native Andean informants and writers as well as Jesuit assistants, Avila began a systematic collection of information on colonial Andean religiosity, part of which became the Huarochirí Manuscript featured in Selection 1. Assisted by the corpus of religious traditions and specific knowledge that he and his agents were assembling, Avila began an ambitious tour of the region, exposing and punishing Indian "idolaters" as he went, and burning or otherwise destroying *huacas* and other religious objects in great numbers. The extent of the Indians' deception, he maintained, had come as a painful revelation. Representing these events in the 1645 preface to his book of sermons, Avila cast himself as a "discoverer" of native Andean religious duplicity, a devoted shepherd who, having recognized the urgent need for reform, had transformed himself into a tireless warrior against religious error in the parishes of Huarochirí and beyond.

He tied his supposed discovery of idolatry into a compelling narrative surrounding one sensational event. Avila wrote that in August 1608 he had been invited by Bartolomé Barriga, the priest in neighboring Huarochirí, to attend and preach at the local celebration of the Feast of the Assumption. But before he arrived, Avila claimed that Cristóbal Choque Casa (one of the native Andean allies who earlier had helped to cast doubt on other parishioners' charges against Avila) had come forward to reveal these Indian parishioners' errors. Choque Casa supposedly informed him that the Christian festival in Huarochirí was nothing but a diversion, and that holy images were sullied by an observance that served to mask Andean dances and rites in honor of the regional huacas, Paria Caca and Chaupi Ñamca. Avila wrote in his preface that, once possessed of this information, he not only kept his engagement in the neighboring pueblo but also used it to deliver a fiery sermon admonishing the Indians for the idolatry that tarnished their Christian devotions, and to begin to stamp out the cults of which he had learned.

Unmasking a persistent idolatry, of course, served his purposes in 1608–09 perhaps even more than it did when he was working out a heroic rendition of his San Damián experiences at mid-century. At the earlier juncture such discoveries allowed Avila to deflect attention from the charges brought against him by his parishioners and to provide himself with a platform from which to claim that through their fabricated lawsuit the idolaters sought to rid themselves of a zealous priest who threatened their evil rites. Avila was certainly not the first, nor would he be the last, churchman in colonial Spanish America to present himself and Indian "deceptions" in such dramatic and manipulable terms. The notion of a native Andean idolatry that was hidden and that had to be discovered and confronted was even being employed at virtually the same time by Archbishop Villagómez. In his *Pastoral Letter,* written by 1647 and published in 1649, Villagómez wrote of "an evil lost to view" in the Indian parishes, exhorting all Christians to join him in renewing a systematic struggle against Andean religious error through the mechanisms of the Extirpation of idolatry. The idea of a recalcitrant bloc of idolaters operating as a uniform evil beneath a guise of Christianity was potent in the intellectual atmosphere of the time, a potency that has not been completely dispelled in scholarly treatments even today.

In San Damián, for instance, both the Indians' charges against their priest and Avila's subsequent decision to unmask their idolatry seem to have challenged relationships and common understandings that were very like those which had developed more gradually between many other priests and their native parishioners. Like the Franciscan Bernardino de Sahagún in an earlier time in central Mexico (see Selection 3), Avila had learned a lot about the complex realities of colonial Indian religion. Although the study of Avila's destructive actions and their timing seems to indicate that he was not much moved to worry over these realities before it suited his interests to channel his knowledge toward Extirpation, there is no reason to stop there. The consideration of his sermons offers wider insights on his thought and methods of pedagogy. Avila was a gifted Quechua linguist who knew as much about colonial Andean religion, and the vital functioning of regional oral traditions within it, as any non-Indian in his day. He used this knowledge when he entered the same oral medium as native Andean ministers and dogmatizers in his efforts to express the Gospel and dispute errors.

The following sermon for Christmas Eve provides an especially rich opportunity to reflect on the imagery and methods of this talented preacher in the action of instruction and refutation. The sermon is often catechetical—that is, it employs questions and answers pertaining to a given religious lesson in the manner of an elaborate catechism. Avila not only preaches on an appropriate biblical text and seasonal theme but also pauses to imagine and counter doubts, questions, and difficulties and even to catch out the mental tricks of his indigenous congregations. He seems confident both that he knows what is going on in the minds of his hearers and that from this knowledge he can persuade them to reform their ways. He assumes that some of them, hearing of the Christian fasts and abstinence

to be observed before Christmas, will begin reflecting on and legitimating roughly analogous non-Christian practices that have persisted into colonial times. "There are those of you who are listening to me now who are saying in your hearts, 'Father, in the paganism taught to us by our elders, we, too, fast when the festivals of our idols are approaching.' "

In a text such as this one, we can linger over the changing faces of Avila's Christianity. At times, the preacher is a restrained and patient father, imploring his children to reflect carefully on what is being taught. "Have you understood?" he asks, "Do I not tell the truth?" "Listen a little more," "Have you not learned?" He seems particularly understanding in dealing with the thorny issue of the Immaculate Conception and the unquestionability of Mary's virginity despite her marriage to Joseph. "Do not a man and a woman marry for this reason in order that they might have children?" ask the imaginary Indian interlocutors. "This is true, my children, nevertheless many married people have achieved this feat," begins the reply. And there is a notable patience in the teaching of this Christian moral ideal: "All this, I know, takes some time to understand."

But Avila can also grow more forceful, insisting on attention: "Look here, listen to me." Much of the visual imagery of his words, too, seems meant to inspire awe and fear and to be memorable in a chilling way. The Indian congregations might often have been listening to the sermon in a courtyard similar to the one drawn by Diego Valadés (see Figure 15 in Selection 22), and it was onto just such a group of people—not unlike themselves and in this same kind of space—that Avila asked his hearers to project their thoughts. They are to imagine people who have not heard, or who have not responded to, the word of the Christian God, a patio full of shackled wretches on the night before their executions rather than Valadés's busy but tranquil scene. For Avila, the word of God is a puncturing, burning, and pounding thing—a thorn, a brand, a hammer, a stick. God does not let one rest. Rather, He delivers the beatings that are the soul's only nourishment and correspondingly the only way to escape the Devil's clutches. The body is molded clay or it is a house in which the invisible soul dwells, giving life and requiring no other meal than this forceful divine Word. To have fed one's soul is likened to waking from a bad dream. All this to think about on the night commemorating Jesus's birth.

Like the Jesuit Arriaga, a few of whose views are discussed in our introduction to Selection 36, Avila recognizes a wide definition of "idolatry." He recognizes convergences between Christianity and native Andean religious beliefs and practices as a more prevalent concern in the middle of the seventeenth century than simply persistent traditional beliefs and practices. For Avila, religious mixture and local imitations and appropriations of Christianity offer both danger and opportunity for the faith in the Andes. On the one hand, it is the misunderstanding of Christianity brought on by the false parallel that will lead to Hell.

Everywhere, there are dangerous interpretations and Christian concepts not only to define properly but also to seclude from Andean analogies. These analogies are the menacing work of a restless Devil, "God's monkey," who "goes around imitating God." And yet the small convergences and new religious understandings emerging in the Andean parishes need attention and even selective embracing if the evangelizer is going to get anywhere worth going. The convergences and emerging understandings are fraught with heretical danger, and they are Avila's principal points of entry into the imaginations of his hearers. In the sermon that follows, Avila engages colonial Andean religion even as he refutes it. He perceives that even when his Indian audience is made up of people who call themselves Christians, his act of describing a time of abstinence and a vigil will summon a number of charged thoughts. It is the cajoling and coaxing of those thoughts that is this preacher's art.

◈ *Mary, the Mother of Jesus, Married Joseph, etc. Matthew, Chapter 1*

Neither in the Spanish towns nor here [in the places where you Indians live] is the eve of the feast day an officially observed festival. Yet all of us have come together to hear Mass and to sing for the Baby Jesus and the Blessed Mary, His Mother.

This being so, I will tell you something about this vigil. The first thing to explain is the meaning of a vigil. Why does the Holy Mother Church command that the days before certain of the year's festivals should be vigils?

Then I will read today's Gospel, expounding a little on it, leading finally into the sermon which I shall give with God's help. For this we ask the intercession of Our Lady, the Blessed Virgin Mary, saying *Ave Maria*.

Be attentive and I will tell you what a vigil is. When Christ Our Lord was on this earth as a man, even though He was the True God, He continually prayed to God His Father. Sometimes He separated Himself and went into solitude, or He went out into the countryside, while other times He did it in public; often, He spent the entire night in prayer. He did this to provide us with an example so we would know not to be negligent in praying to God and asking for His help.

And so, He had returned and ascended to Heaven after being resurrected. The saints, following Christ's example, rose from their beds four times each night to pray; and because they passed almost the entire night without sleep, they called this a vigil. To stay awake, in the Spaniards' language, is to perform a vigil.

People customarily performed a vigil in the evening or on the day before the most important festivals. And, beyond this, they would not eat meat on this day or eat more than once. This is called a fast in the Spanish language. This is what a vigil used to mean.

Because it is a very arduous kind of vigil to do without sleep, Our Holy Mother Church directs that in place of not sleeping the night before, we must only fast the day before some festivals. This is commanded in order that we may worship to good effect, and that we might pay closer attention in our veneration of the saint of the given feast day and thus earn his mediation. That, then, is the vigil and the purpose it serves. Have you understood?

From here, then, we come to the festival itself, the day on which Jesus Christ, Our Lord, was born of Our Lady, the Virgin Mary. Today is the vigil on the eve of the festival, in order that we may reach this day with calm, and without offense to God, arriving with much respect and care—for these reasons we fast.

There are those of you who are listening to me now who are saying in your hearts, "Father, in the paganism taught to us by our elders, we, too, fast when the festivals of our idols are approaching."

You speak candidly in this, I know. Here is how I feel about it. Look here, listen to me.

In the time of the Inkas, and even before the period of their dominance in these lands, all of you, according to your *ayllus* and smaller groups, were faithful to your idols. In order to worship them in festivals, you would occupy yourselves in preparations before the feast for one month, or even two months in the case of your principal idol. And the chief priest would give notice to make ready, saying that the festival would fall on such and such a day; and then you made your *chicha* [maize beer] and all the other things because, it was said, the day of Our Great Father was coming.

And you were also ordered to fast, eating neither salt nor *ají* [a hot pepper], and men and women would abstain from all sexual relations. And in this way you say you had to fast. And not to have done it in exactly the prescribed way would be taken to be a great sin, which would cause you to fall ill and suffer labors, and your crops to fail, causing your children to die. Thinking all this was true, you were frightened, and you fasted and kept the vigil without sleeping the entire night. Do I not tell the truth?

Look here, my children, all of this is the deception of the Devil. The accursed Devil does not stop; he is always thinking and wanting desperately to make himself Lord so that people will worship him as they do God, thus he goes around imitating God. Have you not seen how a monkey, when he sees what a person does, copies it? In this way the Devil imitates God, like God's monkey. And since the fathers in the Church sing praises to God, the Devil has himself sung to in the worship of hills, snowy peaks, and rocks. And if Our Holy Mother Church directs us to fast during Lent and at the time of vigils, the Devil in turn wants people to fast and to work for him. He does the same in many other things, too, deceiving those people who know little.

Thus we come to the end of our treatment of the vigil.

Now I am going to tell you the Gospel that Our Holy Mother Church provides for this day of vigil. This Gospel derives from the evangelist Saint Matthew in his first chapter, and what it says is this: Mary, the mother of Jesus, was recently married to a man named Joseph, with whom she had no carnal relations of any kind (and this is absolutely certain, not even once). Yet her womb was growing, and she began to appear to Joseph to be pregnant (and the truth is that she was, but by the work of the Holy Spirit). Joseph knew all this very well in his heart and soul, but being so saintly and not wishing to have her pregnancy be apparent in public, before anything was said, he wanted to go into exile far away from his lands. While he was sleeping with all these worries on his mind, an Angel, a messenger from God, came to him in his dreams and told him: "Joseph, son of David, do not decide to abandon your wife Mary, and do not be burdened with distress and worries, because what she has in her womb is the work of the Holy Spirit, and to you will be born a son whom you shall call Jesus, that is, Savior, for He will save and redeem His people."

So ends the Gospel.

Those words are very appropriate on the feast day of Saint Joseph; in fact, they are the very same ones I repeat to you on that day.

This being so, I have something more to tell you now. When you hear that Saint Joseph was the husband of the Blessed Virgin Mary, you are not to say, nor to understand, that the couple knew each other carnally or that they had sexual relations. Because even though they were truly married, it did not come to this. Our Lady the Blessed Virgin Mary was always a virgin, a maiden who was superior, perfect, without ever knowing a man in that way. You will say, "But, Father, how could Joseph be her husband if they never came together [and consummated the union]? Do not a man and a woman marry for this reason in order that they might have children?" This is true, my children, nevertheless many married people have achieved this feat. They live as a married pair without coming together carnally; they neither sleep together nor know each other in this way, in order that they might better serve God, loving each other as brother and sister; and from their ranks have come many saints and saintly individuals. Saint Joseph and Our Lady the Virgin Mary were people of this kind. It was God who ordered it to be thus, wanting His Mother to be married in this manner. Now all this, I know, takes some time to understand; this being so, we will tell of one other thing, and then we will be done.

We will finish now by speaking a little more about today and your vigil, all the things which precede, and prepare us for, tomorrow.

Imagine a great crowd of people crushed together in a large courtyard, dark and confined, panic stricken, and all condemned to have their heads cut off for their alleged offenses. As they were waiting for the moment of execution, without anyone who could help them, is it not true that they would be very dejected, crying out as they awaited their deaths? And, the situation being thus, imagine that some letters were delivered to them from a powerful lord telling the prisoners not to worry, assuring them that their grief would be over tomorrow, because then, with the help of God, they would be saved from their distress and labors, and properly cared for. What is more, they themselves would become great lords. *Hodie scietis quia veniet Dominus, et mane videbitis gloriam eius.* [Know that on this morning the Lord will come and you will behold His glory.]

What would those prisoners say after hearing this? What great comfort would this be for them? What cries of happiness would come with such news? They would pass the whole night without sleeping, saying: "Oh, if only the day would come!" wondering if there was perhaps some impediment which might keep their savior from coming, and saying: "May he not be taken ill, may no one have held him up."

Is it not certain, my children, that this would occur? "Yes, father," [you will say], "it is very certain." Well, listen now. Before Jesus Christ, the Son of God, came from Heaven, all humankind were in darkness and in the shadow of death, prisoners in chains and iron shackles.

"Well, Father," [you will say], "if this was so, who farmed the fields in those times? Who tended the cattle, sheep, and goats? Who built the houses?" I am going to tell you, so give me your undivided attention. Look now, do you not know that as men we are made of two different things? One is the soul, and the other is our body. Similarly, life itself has two ways, the life of the soul and the life of the body. And thus, there is sustenance for the soul, and also for the body, and there is the sleep of the soul, and the other of the body, and there is the death of the soul, which is different from the death of the body. Have you understood?

Listen a little more, because it is of great importance that you understand this; herein lies nothing less than your salvation. Are you and I not living? Yes, we are living, and in this life, in this being alive, are we not living in the company of one another, with our bodies and souls together? Yes, we live together, and together we eat and sleep.

This being so [you will say], "Father, I still want you to persuade me that the life, food, and rest of the soul is different from that of the body."

In order to understand this well, it is best that you know first that when the soul is compared with the body, the soul wins out easily. Because our body is a bit of clay, molded clay, and in the end it reverts to clay. But our soul is not like that. Then what is it? It is intellectual, it reasons, and it does not have a body, hands, feet, a head, or eyes. It is immortal, and God created it from nothing in order that He could give life to the body. It was in order that we might live and dwell in Heaven, that God did us this kindness. This is our soul, my children. The soul gives life to our body, and exists in the body, as in a house, for as long as we live; and when the soul leaves, the body dies. Thus, even though the soul leaves the body, it lives and never dies. So, when we eat bread, meat, or any other thing, it is only our body eating, not the soul. And when we drink, sleep, and become sick, these are matters affecting the body, not the soul. Because without a mouth, teeth, or belly, how could it eat or drink? That much said, it is true that the body eats and drinks so that the soul can dwell within it, and for the same reason the body also sleeps and rests.

"So, the soul does not eat?" That's right, brother. "Well, how is the soul able to sustain itself? And whatever it does eat, where does it go if the soul has no teeth, mouth, or belly?" Look, the soul has no food other than the word of God, to which it listens carefully and which it understands well, and with this it lives and gains strength. Now that you have listened, have you not understood me? Have you not learned? And is not your heart and mind made content by what you have heard, as someone feels when he has just woken from a bad dream? Well, this is to have eaten, to have fed the soul; because the word of God brands our soul as a knife makes its mark, and God's word may also destroy like a big hammer. "But, Father," [you ask], "how is the word of God like a brand, and how does it give blows?" In this way: when the father preaches to you about abandoning your life of sin, do not the words bore into you and live in your thoughts as if you had been pierced to your core by a thorn or beaten soundly with a stick? And do you not come to a point at which, in your heart, you say, "What will become of me"? Well, this is God pricking at you and delivering His blows. The very same thing He reveals to us in His Scriptures, informing us that this is the soul's meal.

There is no one who can completely make this meal for the soul, cooking it, preparing it, other than the Son of God Himself. And it is He who tells you, through the voice of the Church: "Await tomorrow, all those who are in sin. I tell you to wait because tomorrow I will be made into a man, born of Mary, in order that I may teach men, light the way for them, and show them the path to Heaven. And I will suffer for you and die, as a man, to free you from the claws of the Devil."

This is what He tells us today: *Hodie scietis quia veniet Dominus, et mane videbitis gloriam eius.* [Know that on this morning the Lord will come and you will behold His glory.]

With which words, with what language, in what sense can I, as an insignificant man, explain to you this great marvel, of God becoming a man?

Look, my children, many years ago, God revealed in His Holy Scriptures that He would come in order that we would know and that we would wait for Him. If He had come without forewarning us, we might claim that it was not Him; thus, we must believe in His coming with all our heart. Because if we do not believe, He will not have come for us; and if this were to be the case, what would become of us? Without a doubt, we would be condemned to the punishments of Hell among the demons; all the things that you have been taught, all that you have suffered, and even your death—all this would occur, yet none of it would be of any use.

Therefore, we must believe that on a night that was very like this one, Jesus Christ was born of the Blessed Mary, and we must love and humbly worship this Child, asking His help. Of the Blessed Mary we are to ask the same, saying "Oh, Our Lady, it gives us the greatest joy to see the precious Son born to you. Plead and intercede for us sinners with the tender Child that He might grant us understanding and the capacity to comply with His will and live in His presence forever." Amen.

 *36*

The Witness Francisco Poma y Altas Caldeas
of San Pedro de Acas, Cajatambo, Peru
(1657)

Francisco Poma y Altas Caldeas, a forty-six-year-old native Andean, testified before the idolatry inspector and judge (*visitador*, or by his full title, *visitador general de idolatría*) Bernardo de Novoa in the village of San Pedro de Acas (or Hacas), Cajatambo, in the central Andes. Novoa—a native of Lima, fluent in Quechua, with some thirteen years' experience as a priest in three Indian parishes—was an agent of the process known as the "Extirpation of idolatry." The Extirpation was an effort by the Christian authorities in the seventeenth- and early eighteenth-century Archdiocese of Lima to root out and destroy suspect colonial Andean religiosity through systematic campaigns of investigation and destruction, and the trial and punishment of principal offenders. His investigation in Acas was spread over almost a year and a half (1656–1658). During this time, Francisco Poma, like the other witnesses, responded to a series of questions posed by Novoa and an interpreter. Poma's responses in Quechua were recorded in Spanish translation by the interpreter and notary, and this testimony, now rendered in English, is the document that follows.

The Extirpation's agents employed and adjusted methods drawn from the quintessen-

tial arbiter of religious orthodoxy in the contemporary Spanish world, the Holy Office of the Inquisition. After the establishment of the Holy Office in Spanish America in 1570, it was formally determined that indigenous peoples, judged new to the faith and uncommonly susceptible to error and the Devil's wiles, would not fall under its jurisdiction. Thus, the process of the Extirpation in the Archdiocese of Lima was a substitute that Pierre Duviols has accurately dubbed an "Inquisition for Indians," an adaptation with scaled-down penalties and, at least theoretically, an amplified pedagogy of reform.

A judge's path and the duration of his stays were largely determined by the information and cooperation he received from native Andeans and their parish priests. He could investigate leads, but without specific information, in places and among people he often did not know, there was only so much he could force. Trials might last a few days, months, or, as in the case of Novoa in Acas, even years, with a visitador often interrupting proceedings and resuming them later on. Each idolatry inspector's brief was a little different, depending on what he knew or had been led to believe about a given place and its people.

But, generally speaking, he was charged to determine a region's principal religious offenders, the people who were thought to hold evil spiritual sway and represent obstacles in the Christianization of others. He was also commissioned to locate sacred places and objects in the local landscape as well as to raise pious work parties so that these places and objects might be efficiently destroyed and publicly reconsecrated with holy crosses and the application of new, triumphantly Christian names. Procedure varied from one visitador and his entourage to the next, but the remoteness of many of the Indian parishes and a general failure by Lima's authorities to enforce existing rules failed to curb the abuse of power. Even so, most information gathered by extirpators came from Indians' confessions obtained without recourse to various methods of torture. Ordeals, however, were sometimes applied if, after an obigatory series of stern warnings, a witness was suspected of withholding vital evidence. A great range of punishments—again, borrowed and adapted to the Peruvian context from the Inquisition's examples—was meted out to convicted "idolaters." Castigations were public and intended as examples to others; sentences were harsher for the unrepentant.

Francisco Poma's testimony before Novoa offers a richly descriptive angle on Andean religion and life over a century after the Spaniards had arrived in Peru. Poma tells of steadfastly local relationships between Andean people and divinities, and customs of sense-making which remind us that the ways of Huarochirí (Selection 1) have many other companions. As a member of one of the eight *ayllus* (social, ritual, and territorial units) that made up the resettled village of Acas, and as a self-described participant in religious rituals and practices long forbidden by colonial authorities, Poma knows what he is talking about. He tells of a local and regional religious structure that, while clearly embattled by depopulation, colonial work regimes, and intermittent Spanish Christian pressures, is very much alive. People were resettled not far from ancestral lands populated by *malquis*

and *huacas* (on these Andean divinities see Selection 1), gods who were conceived of as parents and relatives and protectors. Every ayllu in the village, he reveals, had its ministers who nourished the gods and mediated between the people and the divine, and its specialists who tended to the community's needs and enforced its codes of conduct. Even the archbishop of Lima, Don Pedro de Villagómez (1641–1671), who was eager to convey the impression that he and his Extirpation were winning a battle against the gravest forms of Andean religious error, found it impossible to deny the great degree and range of traditional religious survival in mid-seventeenth-century Cajatambo, especially with regard to the ancestral dimensions of the religion, the worship of malquis and huacas.

Francisco Poma speaks frequently of Huari progenitors, revealing his own allegiance to the ancestral divinities of one of the two founding peoples who settled in this region at points deep in its pre-Inkaic past. The Huaris' arrival was said to have ended an ill-defined period of chaos and war—a regional, ordering vision of the past that tells much about imaginings of history, recalling the idea of "imperfect time" being set right as conceptualized not only by Andean neighbors, but also by peoples in Mexico (featured in Selection 4) and by the Spanish theologians and chroniclers who made sense of Iberian history in retrospect (as in Selection 9 or 19). The Huaris were said to be children of the Sun, giants who came either from the sea in the west or from Lake Titicaca to the south. The Huaris were the arrangers of the world, the civilizers and agriculturalists who brought irrigation techniques and built terraces on the mountainsides to maximize the land available for cultivation. They gathered people together into small settlements called *llactas* (hamlets).

The invaders of the Huari domain were austere and warlike pastoralists from the high plateaus known as the Llacuazes, the self-described sons and daughters of Libiac (who made himself manifest as a bolt of lightning), a people "joined to the sky." According to another witness who came before Novoa in neighboring Otuco in Cajatambo, although the conquering Llacuazes killed many of the Huaris and took their lands, at least two of the Huari progenitors survived to maintain the lineage. A number of seventeenth-century witnesses explained that the Huaris and Llacuazes had inaugurated a period of peace and mixing between the two peoples that did not, however, completely erase a distinction that endured through the era of Inka domination and into Spanish colonial times. At least into the middle of the seventeenth century, Huari and Llacuaz divinities were recognized, while local festivals emphasized a historic relationship of complementarity.

Francisco Poma's testimony is packed with interpretative challenges. Like the other contents of this book, the source is a point of view that contains distortions, emphases, and silences generated in and reflecting a specific time and circumstance. The most fundamental challenges in this case are the filters through which Poma's own words have passed, most of which result from the inquisitorial atmosphere in which the evidence was collected. Francisco Poma, a Quechua-speaking Indian witness with some understanding of spoken Spanish, was interrogated by a Lima-educated Creole priest and inspector. As we have noted, Poma's answers were translated by an interpreter and recorded in Spanish by a notary, and an additional filter is, of course, our translation of the Spanish record into English. Each filter muffles the transmission of Poma's original meaning, as do the terms of reference and particular aims and interests which the idolatry inspector and notary could not help but have as they listened to the man, questioned him further, and crafted the translation.

What do some of the common terms in the document mean? "Idolatry," the worship of false gods or "idols," was a familiar crime to a seventeenth-century mind educated in the Judeo-Christian tradition. It was the Devil's work, and it was expected among non-Christians in Peru, as elsewhere in the past and in contemporary times; it was a presumed weakness in the religious systems of Amerindians. Idols were thought to be vile, impo-

tent, and inanimate objects that, among misguided peoples who had not yet received or digested the message of the Gospels, stole reverence due only to the Christian God. The standard manner of refuting idols in sermons before Indian congregations was through aggressive ridicule and denigration. Idolatry, along with related concepts such as superstition, sorcery, witchcraft, and even heresy, increasingly became a blanket term for many perceived wrongs. In the mid-colonial Andes it had come to refer to beliefs and rites persisting since pre-Hispanic times, perceived perversions of Catholicism, moral laxity, and acts of disrespect to Spanish religious and secular authority, although at its base it remained a term that accused people of worshiping false gods. Notaries frequently called huacas and malquis (not to mention a good many other Andean religious concepts and beings) simply "idols," although the official who recorded Francisco Poma's words often takes a middle path and refers to "malquis and idols."

To complicate matters, we can be certain that by the mid-seventeenth century, terms such as "idol" were not descriptions used only by Spaniards. Thus, the notary's "malquis and idols" may in fact be a faithful rendering of the words spoken by a native Andean witness such as Francisco Poma. Indeed, there is considerable evidence to suggest that many colonial Indians had taken on some of the language and were engaging with the ideas that Christian preachers and catechists used to devalue and refute Andean beliefs and practices. At times, Catholic prescriptions for how to understand, and behave before, Holy Images seem taken over and turned around by certain native teachers (the notary who recorded this testimony called them "dogmatizers") as they assembled their own teachings and critical interpretations of Christianity and some of its agents. At other times, native Andeans might combine their appropriations of Christian elements with a dose of the Church's intended skepticism toward the ways of their ancestors. Indian usages of "Devil" and "demon" and, in the Andes, the Quechua loan-word "Supay" are instructive examples of the mutability of language and the challenge of translation (not to mention religious change) in colonial terrains.

For native Andeans and others who were interacting in colonial society, religious and cultural indoctrination became processes that begged participation. Words and ideas became unfixed; what began with one set of meanings could accumulate new ones. Indian witnesses might turn Christian narratives heard in sermons into colonial Andean stories; they might blend some doubt in with their knowledge of Andean practices, and they might employ terms such as "demon" and "Devil" to define gods, ideas, and forces in a religious framework that was less traditionally "Spanish" or "Andean" than it was living, and thus incomplete and transforming. Francisco Poma fits into this atmosphere of gradual mixture and change in which Christian concepts and rituals were not necessarily or purely contamination.

The atmosphere of fear that the trial might generate in a small community, not to mention an individual's dread of torture or the ramifications to be suffered by family members, might induce some witnesses to confess in certain terms or against certain persons simply to secure an escape. And many native Andeans were, by the mid-colonial period, hardened veterans when it came to facing interrogation by Spanish Christian officials. There were times to give details and show the way, and times when specific information (such as a huaca's name or location) could safely be suppressed. People targeted by these proceedings soon gathered, for instance, that the immensity (indeed, the impossibility) of most extirpators' tasks and their bureaucratic and zealous needs to justify their endeavors with material results could lend an imprecise and even desperate character to the process. Out of a mixture of necessity and attempted conformity to standard procedure, extirpators of idolatry frequently focused their investigations on a few offending individuals (conceived of as the corruptors of others) or on the destruction of notorious sacred places. Thus, it became an astute move for a witness who wished to deflect attention away from himself

and those whom he wanted to protect simply to meet an interrogator's most urgent needs and expectations. This might be done in a number of ways, not least by further implicating community members who were already under suspicion or by assigning blame to a rival village in the next valley.

Do such sources "poison" the documentary pool, misrepresenting society in their hunger for information about those people who ran most afoul of prescribed laws and customs? And does the information in them support unquestioned assumptions about indigenous responses to Spanish Christianity or colonialism—assumptions of "resistance"—or its usual opposite, "accommodation" and acquiescence? In the present context, are we in danger of being led toward an image of the people of mid-colonial Acas as more or less uniform in their extraordinary adherence to a traditional system of belief and practice?

The answer can easily be "yes" on all counts if certain elements in the documentation are emphasized to the exclusion of others. One can extract solid and various demonstrations of native Andeans' organized resistance and intelligent countering of Christianity in Acas. For Francisco Poma illuminates an atmosphere of religious competition and tension in the village. He tells of the commands and prophesies of doom made by dogmatizers, powerful local religious figures who, within the celebration of regular festivals, besieged the place of Christianity among the people of Acas and its environs. But it is instructive also to consider how the answers can be "no." For it would be a misrepresentation to insist that the ministers and dogmatizers, the people who most embodied resistance, existed alone, or even that their substantial countering of an exclusivist Christian position somehow defied the influence of Christianity on themselves or others.

Francisco Poma's testimony, far from poisoning the pool with information skewed in one direction, offers a glimpse at a number of seemingly contradictory elements within colonial Andean religion. When an idolatry visitador was not present and attentively defining religious boundary lines, would the merging and simultaneous participation in native Andean and Spanish Christian religious practices have been "contradictory" or particularly remarkable to an Indian man or woman who was not a huaca minister and dogmatizer? Poma is a colonial Andean who is difficult to place in a simple category or clearly defined faction within the village. He lives what at first appear to be compartmentalized lives. His testimony reveals him to be a knowledgeable participant in Andean religious rituals, practices, and specializations as well as in native structures of religious authority that had long been forbidden by Spanish Christians. He is also knowledgeable about Christianity. He served as lay assistant to the parish priest and as an organizer of the festival of the patron saint of the community, Saint Peter. Further, by performing his duties as the priest's assistant, Francisco Poma incurred the wrath of Acas's principal native Andean minister and the powerful head of his own ayllu, the memorable Hernando Hacas Poma.

As Poma's conflict with the chief minister unfolds, and as it is resolved, a reader is left to ponder the diverse influences on this person speaking before a Spanish Christian interrogator. What reflects the things that Hernando Hacas Poma said and did, and just what is Francisco Poma's imagining and re-creation? In part, the story might be viewed as a remarkable local distortion upon the kind of narrative example regularly recounted by contemporary churchmen to stir and edify their faithful and correspondents: an evil opponent (Hacas Poma) is identified, a participant-teller endures a time of trial, a vital lesson is learned, and an individual's correction is achieved. If this is the case, what precisely is the lesson, and to whom does it apply? One prospect is that Hacas Poma has been shown to be a great and fearsome instrument of the Devil, an obstacle to Christianity who must be brought down at all costs. But another is that the chief minister and dogmatizer's power has been demonstrated yet again to all who know of him, and that his teachings and warnings pester and even torment new converts to Christianity. Poma's story about his run-in with Hacas Poma does not sit in splendid isolation. It can be examined alongside his description of the cross-cultural actions of the native Andean governor, Don Juan de Mendoza, and especially his words about the villagers' observance of the Christian festival of Saint Peter in conjunction with (not as a disguise covering) the Andean festival of Vecosina. Such information accumulates and combines to suggest a number of possibilities for the study of colonial Andean life—possibilities that complement the conflict and competition of which the witness Poma also tells.

The image of a constraining mechanism of repression (either the Catholic Church or, more specifically, the Extirpation) facing off against a unified but embattled adversary ("idolatry") would seem to oversimplify colonial Andean religious realities. Through the information he provides and through the instance of his own position, Francisco Poma challenges the plausibility of this purely oppositional framework as a full and accurate portrait. He participates in a wider colonial religious culture that, however tentative, disorganized, and variable, did not conform to the strict dictates of either the official Church or the native Andean dogmatizers. The parish priest of Acas mentioned in this document does not, through what little we learn of his actions, appear to have been much known for his negotiated positions within the workings of this emerging colonial religious culture. Yet it seems important to note that Poma, Don Juan de Mendoza, and many other native Andeans like them, who were simultaneously Catholic parishioners and adherents to a complex of transforming Andean religious structures, were not unique, just as clergymen and Spanish Christians in general were not all cut from the same cloth. They, too, occupied an interactive colonial terrain in which the practice of everyday life sometimes made nonsense out of theoretically separate and tidy categories.

We should not (and do not have to) take Francisco Poma's indirect word for it. Some of the most prolific and insightful commentators on native Andean religious life in colonial times were well aware of the complex nature of religious change. A "common error" among native Andeans, wrote the Jesuit Pablo José de Arriaga (1564–1622) in his 1621 manual for extirpators of idolatry and priests of Indians, "is their tendency to carry water on both shoulders, to have recourse to both religions at once. . . . Most of the Indians have not yet had their huacas and *conopas* [personal divinities and sources of fecundity, sculpted or natural in form] taken away from them, their festivals disturbed, nor their abuses and superstitions punished, and so they think their lies compatible with our truth and their idolatry with our faith." Padre Arriaga was a contemporary of Francisco de Avila (see Selection 35), an early mastermind

behind the Extirpation and one of its first active agents. His biases are about as clearly articulated as his keen perception of Andean religiosity a century or so after the Spaniards' arrival in Peru. What he saw happening in the Indian parishes of the Archdiocese of Lima echoes in many ways what a similarly observant Juan Polo de Ondegardo perceived about a century before and what José de Acosta noticed after him (see Selection 19). The testimony of Francisco Poma, a witness before an idolatry trial conducted by one of Arriaga's successors over three decades later, adds color and detail to the colonial Andean religious culture only hinted at by the Jesuit's metaphor and Polo's and Acosta's earlier observations.

In the village of San Pedro de Acas in the district of Cajatambo on the 25th of January, 1657, there came before us a very rational and acculturated Indian. He testified that Don Cristóbal Hacas Malqui commands all those in his ayllu to gather offerings for the malquis and idols, and that this same man is the dogmatizer of his ayllu who directs them to worship not Our Lord God, but their malquis. And [he said] that Alonso Chaupis the Blind is the confessor and minister of idols of the Quirca ayllu. This witness stated that on many occasions, when it was time to clear the irrigation channels and plant their plots of land, he had seen the said Alonso Chaupis carry two measures of coca leaves and some two pounds of fat and chicha [maize beer] to the Huari malquis, and that he offered these things to them in sacrifice in order that they might enjoy bountiful crops and that their channels would not rupture. When he went to make these offerings, he was accompanied by everyone in the village; and after these were complete, they began clearing the irrigation channels, and plowing and planting their plots of land.

This witness continued, saying that one time, going as far as the herb gardens and passing the ancients' settlements of Quirca and Yanqui, he had seen Alonso Chaupis the Blind, Hernando Chaupis Condor, Pedro Sarmiento, and Pedro Capcha Yauri making sacrifices, cutting the throats of many cuyes [Andean guinea pigs]—there seemed to be six or seven—burning much coca and fat, pouring out chicha, and scratching off powder from coricallanca shells [collected from the coast for this purpose], all before some huge wooden masks, painted and with large noses that they call guasac. Pedro Quespo and What's-His-Name Guaman Capacha took up the masks in their hands and began dancing with them, and other times they would put them over their faces, and in the same way resume dancing accompanied by small drums; and there they stayed, getting drunk, while this witness passed by on his way to the herb gardens.

And he said that it is a common rite and ceremony in the village of Acas, and in all the other communities of this parish, that when a man or woman dies and before their burial the relatives of the deceased—wife, father, children, brothers and sisters or husband—invite the maestro of the idols or the sorcerer of their own ayllu to make the offerings of a llama, cuyes, and all the rest. Much chicha is prepared, and the relatives of the deceased also invite the whole village. The said minister of the idols does the honors in the following way. A llama is killed either through its side or at its shoulder, the blood is collected, and he [the minister] takes out the entrails and lungs. Then the sorcerer himself, in the presence of the deceased, blows in the windpipe and inflates the lungs, which swell up like a wineskin; and if the sorcerer sees that the lungs have sores [*guarcos*], he tells the relatives of the deceased that they have committed great sins and that the deceased is angered because he has eaten a flawed offering and that it is necessary to make another offering of cuyes, coca, and fat to him, asking the cause of his anger. And then the relatives provide the said offering, and burn the cuyes, coca, fat, and black and white maize before the deceased. And in making the sacrifice they shed blood and burn it, and smear the face of the deceased with the llama's blood. And the said sorcerer then acts as if he speaks with the deceased, and returns to tell the relatives that the deceased revealed that he had died because he had not kept up the rites and ceremonies and had not worshiped his malquis, and that if his relatives do not worship their idols and malquis and if they fail to make their offerings to the deceased himself in order that he might come to rest in his pacarina [place of origin to which one also returns], then they will die very soon. Afterwards, the said relatives gave another offering to the minister of the idols that he might make a sacrifice to the malquis, and then they sat down to eat of the llama that had been killed and to drink before the deceased for a day and a night. And even if there did not appear sores on the llama's inflated lungs, they would proceed in the same manner before the deceased, burning cuyes, coca, fat, the ears of the llama as well as its eyelids and the calluses from its feet, black and white maize, along with the llama's blood and chicha, and they would say that this was the mircapa, that is, the food for the deceased to eat in the other life. And thus, the ashes produced by the burned sacrifice were carried to the church and cast into the grave meant for the deceased.

During the night before the burial, at the first crowing of the cock, the said minister of the idols along with the closest relative of the deceased, such as the mother or father or husband, wrapped their own heads with the clothing of the deceased and took staffs in their hands. Then, followed by all the Indian women, they went through the streets shaking their heads, crying and calling out to the deceased so he would see how they wept over his death and remembered him, and so the other world would not curse his relatives. And with some brushes of guaillapa, which is a coarse straw, they went about brushing the streets and walls with llama's blood and chicha from the jugs they carried. Upon returning to his [the deceased's] house at dawn, the said minister of the idols cut a little of the hair and the nails from the fingers and toes of the deceased and carried them to the machay [cave tomb] of the malquis of his ayllu where they were kept for a year. When the year had passed, the same minister removed the hairs and repeated the said rites and ceremonies already described. If the relative or relatives of the deceased were wealthy, they killed two llamas, prepared chicha from a fanega [about 1.5 dry bushels] or two of maize, and invited everyone in the village. And in the house of the deceased they drank and danced one day and one night to the sound of the small drums. In the middle of the night the hairs and nails of the deceased that the said minister of the idols had brought from the cave tomb were placed on the blanket or shirt of the deceased, and over them he killed cuyes, and cast coca leaves, llama fat, white maize flour, powders from the [white] pasca stone and coricallanca shell, all of which were burned in sacrifice so that the soul of the deceased could go to rest in its pacarina, taking with it the mircapa.

Five days after the death, all those in the house of the deceased cooked him a meal and put out chicha for him to drink, and they say that during those five days he came to eat. And on the fifth day the deceased's old clothes, animal hides, and the straw [from his home] were burnt with powders of pasca stone and white maize flour at a place chosen outside the village, and new clothes were washed with maize flour in the river that runs close to the village. And cross-examining the said witness, the idolatry judge and inspector asked who and how many Indian men and women had observed these rites and ceremonies and honors in the pagan way for their dead relatives. To which the witness replied that however many had died in Acas, that was how many had had performed for them the said sacrifices and honors, and that this abuse is common in this village of Acas and in the other communities of the parish. They had invited this witness [to attend and participate] many times, and he had found out about the said [funeral] rites.

And this witness told the said inspector that when he was visiting in the village of Mimuchi he had seen that, along with Leonor Nabin Carua and Inés Colqui Maiguai, Alonso Chaupis the Blind was killing a llama and sacrificing it in the herb gardens to the idols and malquis who are in that place. The said llama was given to the ministers for this purpose by Gonzalo Poma Lloclla. And in inquiring of these ministers how they could make that sacrifice and [commit] idolatry, and why they were not afraid when the señor visitador was currently visiting this parish, they responded [to this witness] that it did not matter that the idolatry judge and inspector knew; and, even if he knew of it, what could he do? And the said Gonzalo Poma Lloclla and his brother Bartolomé Chuchu Condor, who are the keepers of the herb gardens, call for the said Alonso Chaupis and give him llamas and cuyes to offer to the idols and malquis of the said gardens.

And in the same way he said he saw with his own eyes that, one time in the village of Cochillas, Hernando Chaupis Condor, Alonso Chaupis the Blind, and Francisco Hasto Paucar were worshiping, and sacrificing a llama to an idol named Macacayan that had been dislodged and burned [some forty years earlier] by the señor bishop Don Fernando de Abedaño [Fernando de Avendaño, the preacher-extirpator noted in the introduction to Selection 35]. This witness asked the said ministers why they venerated that idol and honored it [in the customary way] if it had been taken away and incinerated, and they responded that although it had been destroyed, the soul of the said idol lived and descended for a sacrifice and would receive it. And he said it is well known that Domingo Chaupis Yauri, now deceased, had an idol named Micui Conopa and another idol Colqui Conopa to obtain food and money, and that his nephew, Pedro Chaupis, inherited them and would show them to him.

And this witness, asking mercy of the said señor visitador, showed him a guacanqui [idol usually used for influencing love] that is like a glittering rock or bit of stone marl from the mines. He said that this guacanqui had been sold to him by an Indian man named Don Cristóbal Chauchisac, an important person in the village of j . . . s in the province of Huamalies, who told this witness that by having and worshiping this stone he would have good fortune, money, llamas, clothing, and that this witness [himself] had always kept it for these ends. And in a similar fashion the said witness showed the said señor visitador two idols called llama conopas that were some long stones like pestles, one of which had a head and was in the shape of a person, and he said that the said idols had been passed down through the members of his family since the time of his ancestors and that now he revered them for the increase of his llama herd. And he had seen that at the beginning of the rainy season Pedro Capcha Yauri goes to worship the malqui Hacac, with respect to which he [the witness] is unsure whether it was removed by the señor bishop Don Fernando de Avendaño, and takes llamas to sacrifice to the said malqui, and that for this purpose he keeps close to thirty llamas, [a herd] that, since ancient times, has been dedicated to the worship of this malqui. And the said Pedro Capcha Yauri, as minister of the said idol and having succeeded in his office from his ancestors, watches over and preserves the said herd. It is a well-known tradition among the Indians, and especially the said Capcha Yauri and the other ministers of the idols Hernando Hacas Poma and Hernando Chaupis Condor, that when the said malqui Haca [the same one called Hacac above] was wont to live in the presence of the Indians, he would blow on his hand with pursed lips, and, by the art of the Devil, he caused clumps of potatoes and maize to be born on his palm, at which the Indians had felt great wonder and fear; and they venerated and respected him as a man of great power, and for this reason they adored him and gave him worship, and devoted the said llama herd to him so that sacrifices could be made of them.

And this witness said that one Friday, three years ago, the interim priest of this parish of Acas, Licenciado Ignacio González de Ozerín, seeing that many Indians were failing to attend the doctrine classes, became angry and began quarreling with this witness, who was then serving as fiscal [lay assistant], ordering him to get the people to the indoctrination. Going through the streets and to their homes, urging the people to go to the church, he said that most all of them resisted and told him they could not go to the church because they were observing their fasts and making confessions to their malquis, as was the custom. And the person who resisted him most especially was Hernando Hacas Poma. He argued with the said witness, telling him not to get in the way of his custom or a great illness would come to him. And by pushes and shoves this witness brought the said Hernando Hacas Poma to the church. From that night forward this witness began to sicken seriously, and for six months he was in bed with great pain, withering away and becoming so frail that he was obliged to receive all the sacraments. After these six months the wife of the said Hernando Hacas Poma came to see this witness and said to him: "Give me a llama if you do not want to die, and, with my husband, I will offer and sacrifice it to the idols and malquis, and we will eat part of it without salt or ají [hot pepper], and then you will be well." This witness gave a llama to the said wife of Hacas Poma and she took it to her husband. And on the next day the said Hernando Hacas Poma came to visit this witness and asked him for cuyes, fat, and coca, and told him that six of this witness's hairs would be taken and hidden away. Having provided the cuyes and coca, this witness's wife went with the said Hernando Hacas Poma to see him take the hairs from her husband. [Then,] as both of them arrived at a wall in the ancients' settlement of the Tacas ayllu, near to where the idol Yanaurau resides, she saw that the said Hernando Hacas Poma took from a recess in the said wall a goat-kid's skull, and from the hollow within it he removed some hairs that were mixed with fat, coca, blood, [and shavings from] mollo [or *mullu*, a reddish-colored shell] and llacsarumi [a stone], and he gave them to the aforesaid [the witness's wife]. And the said Hacas Poma cut the throats of some cuyes and performed a sacrifice in that place, burning them with coca and llama fat. The aforesaid [witness's wife] then took the hairs to her husband, and from that day and hour he began to recover from his illness. And when he was better, this witness went to see the said Hernando Hacas Poma to thank him for his health and he told him: "Yayamic [father] and my lord, you are a great wise man and doctor; tell me you made me ill"; and the said Hernando Hacas Poma responded by saying: "I am the one who made you ill because you led me to the church by force and with shoves . . . and [you did the same] to all the Indians at the time when we were fasting for our idols and huacas, and watch that you do not try it again or else the same illness will return to you."

And this witness said that three or four years ago the captain Don Juan de Mendoza, cacique governor [in Quechua, *kuraka* (or *curaca*), hereditary lord] of this repartimiento [regional administrative district] of La Chaupiguaranga de Lampas, came to this village of Acas on three different occasions, and that each time he brought a llama, along with cuyes, coca, and fat, to the said Hernando Hacas Poma. And he [the governor] ordered him to sacrifice those llamas and offerings to the idol Yanaurau so that his son Don Alonso, whom he currently had at the [Jesuit-run] school [for the sons of the Indian nobility] in the Cercado [the Indian sector in Lima] learning to read and write, would emerge well schooled and thus able to take on the office of cacique governor now held by the said Don Juan de Mendoza. This witness saw with his own eyes that the said Hernando Hacas Poma killed and sacrificed the said llamas at the place called Canto that is close to the idol Caruatarquivrauc that is said to have been destroyed by the señor bishop Don Fernando de Avendaño. And when the said Hernando Hacas Poma made those three sacrifices, the said governor Don Juan de Mendoza attended along with Acas's important people, Don Cristóbal Poma Libia, Cristóbal Pampa Condor, Pedro Caico, Domingo Tantayana, Domingo Chaupis Yauri, and many other Indians from the village. The said Hernando Hacas Poma poured llama blood, coca, and chicha and burned fat at the place of the said idol Yanatarquivrauc, and then the said cacique sat down with the Indians to drink and to eat from the llama whose blood they had sacrificed, and he said to this witness and the rest of them:

"Observe that we are Indians and although we worship Yanaurau, which is our custom, do not tell anyone of it."

And on another occasion five or six years ago this witness saw that the said Don Juan de Mendoza came to this village of Acas and, accompanied by Domingo Yana Pintor and all the Indians of the village, the curaca [Mendoza] killed a llama in a corral behind the rest house [*tambo*] and said [to the people]: "I am your cacique governor; we make this sacrifice and shed the blood of this llama on this land so that I will know how to govern you and rule in peace and calm, and so that all of us will be in peace and live with tranquillity." And, having killed the llama, Domingo Chaupis Yauri helped to shed the blood on the earth, and so did Domingo Yana Pintor; and then, all together, they ate the llama and spent the entire night drinking much chicha, dancing and performing the cachua [dance], all with their small drums, and they chewed coca leaves and scattered them on the soil.

Some three years ago, a little more or less, the said curaca came from Lima, bringing his son who was very ill. And passing through this village, he [summoned and] took the said Hernando Hacas Poma with him to the village of Rahan [Rajan] where the said curaca lived, and he kept him [Hacas Poma] there for many days, and everyone said that it was to cure his son with superstitions.

And this witness said that all the ayllus of this village, and there are six, have their ministers and confessors. Juan Raura is the minister of the idols and confessor of the Tacas ayllu, and his assistants who help collect the offerings are Domingo Ribera and Chatalina [Catalina] Chaupis Maiguai. In the Chaca ayllu the minister of the idols is Hernando Hacas Poma, of whom he has already spoken, and this man is famous as a sorcerer-healer who draws out spiders from the bodies of the sick, and as the one who dogmatizes in all the ayllus of this village and whom all the Indians consult. And it is equally well known that it is to him that the malqui Guamancama and the idol Yanaurau respond. And [still in the Chaca ayllu] Don Cristóbal Hacas Malqui is a confessor, and Pedro Sarmiento and Leonor Nabin Carua are their assistants who gather the offerings and make chicha. And Cristóbal Pampa Condor is also a confessor, and he holds the office of socya pacha, that is, using spiders he divines what they are to do and what sacrifices [are required], [the location of] lost things, and other incidents and issues. And in the Carampa ayllu, Andrés Guaman Pilpi is confessor-teacher and Alonso Quispi Guaman is also confessor, and Pedro Caico is his assistant who looks after the collection of offerings and is also colca camayo, responsible for the storehouse where the maize is kept to support the service of these idols. Hernando Chaupis Condor and Alonso Chaupis the Blind are the great ministers of the idols, confessors, and dogmatizers from the Yanaqui ayllu, yet they travel as far as the village of Cochillas to dogmatize and make sacrifices to the Yungas' idols and malquis. And Inés Colqui of this ayllu is a sorcerer, while Inés Upiai is a confessor-dogmatizer and holds the office of cauya and who, [through her divinations,] solves thefts and finds lost things. And Francisco Hasto Paucar and Domingo Guaras are also confessors and dogmatizers in the said village.

Pedro Guaman Bilca is assistant in the Quirca ayllu and he gathers the offerings; and because there are no ministers of the idols, [all of them] having died, the said assistant gives the offerings and the rest of the necessary materials to Alonso Chaupis the Blind that he might make sacrifices to the idols of the said ayllu. And Inés Colqui is a sorcerer as well as serving in the office of rapiac ychanioc [or *rípiac,* diviner who consults the fleshy parts of the arms, and confessor]. And from the Canta ayllu, old and crippled Domingo Tatcachi (or Taicachi) is minister of the idols, confessor, and dogmatizer, and the crippled Hernando Poma Quillai serves as his assistant and in the office of socya pacha. In the Picoca ayllu, with those who were the ministers of the idols, Domingo Chaupis and What's-His-Name Vilca, having died, Andrés Guaillapaico, who is religious assistant of this ayllu, and Leonor Llacsa Tanta give offerings to Hernando Chaupis Condor to sacrifice to the ayllu's malquis and idols. And, in the same manner, the ministers have died off in the ayllu of Yacas, thus Bartolomé Chuchu Condor and his brother Gonzalo Poma Lloclla give the said offerings to Alonso Chaupis the Blind in order that he might make sacrifices to the idols and malquis in the herb gardens, as he has already stated above and as is well known.

And this witness has seen with his own eyes that two times each year, the first before they begin to prepare their plots [for seeding] at the first rains and the other at the time of [the festival of] Corpus [Christi] when the maize starts to ripen, all the ministers mentioned earlier collect offerings from their ayllus, and many times this witness has given cuyes, coca, llama fat, and chicha to Hernando Hacas Poma. They [the ministers] take them to the ancients' settlements and offer them to the malquis and idols. The sacrifices made, with a voiced announcement they call the Indians from their ayllus, and they gather in a small open space where the idol Tauris is, and there everyone confesses with the minister of their ayllu, and [in this way] this witness has confessed many times with Hernando Hacas Poma. After the confessions they washed their heads with maize flour and the powders of the pasca stone and they said it left them absolved, and they were ordered to abstain for the next five days, eating neither salt nor ají and not sleeping with women, even their legitimate wives. And on the night of the first day of the abstinence, they were ordered not to sleep during the entire night, because it was said that if they slept the sacrifices they had made would be rendered ineffectual and that the sins they had confessed returned to those who slept. And for those five days of abstinence, the said ministers of the idols ordered that they rest and not work because it was a festival, and that they occupied themselves with drinking, for which effect all the maize from the storehouses dedicated to the cult of the idols was shared out to the Indian women of the pueblo, and each year it was sown for this ministry in the plots of land designated for the malquis and idols.

Don Cristóbal Poma Libia, a notable [*principal*] and the local headman, and Domingo Tantayana, Cristóbal Tanquis, and Pedro Caico, also important local people, commanded the village to make the chicha and seed the plot of land for the said malquis and, during the five days of abstinence, they [also determined] the ways in which some ayllus invited others. And this witness concurred with everyone else in that he saw and heard that before all the Indian men and women, the said ministers taught and preached that the native Indians did not have to worship Our Lord God or the wooden saints who were in the church, that this was for the Spaniards, and that they were their [the Spaniards'] idols and huacas; and that the Indians had other, different camaquenes [creator beings and forces] which were their malquis and idols, and that the Indians had to worship these with sacrifices of cuyes and llamas; and that they had to observe their fasts and times of abstinence and make their confessions, because if they did not respect and adore them, the Indians would waste away and suffer great illnesses and die and lose their crops to frost, and the springs and irrigation channels would dry up. And at the time they do this, they would not eat any other type of meat apart from cuyes and llamas, because the rest of the food, the meat from Castilian sheep, pigs, or goats, was abominable and it was forbidden to eat it at the time of the said abstinence. And in this time they would not enter the churches to pray because that would defile their sacrifices, confessions, and abstinences, and they [the dogmatizers] also ordered that they [the Indians] not confess these rites and ceremonies to the priest so that he did not discover and punish them. And during those five days of abstinence they would make offerings of money, and each person gave from one-half real to one real, and these offerings would be kept by the head steward [*mayordomo*] of the storehouses so that livestock and other materials necessary to the cult of the idols might be bought.

And four or five days before the festival of the Señor Saint Peter, official standard-bearers give llamas, cuyes, coca, and chicha to the said ministers of the idols of their ayllus so that they [the ministers] can make sacrifices and ask [both] for their [the huacas' and malquis'] permission and indulgence that they must hold the festival of Señor Saint Peter in the church. And when he was mayordomo one year, this witness gave the said offerings to Hernando Hacas Poma so that he could ask the malquis for the said permission, and this is a common practice which all the mayordomos respect and maintain, and everyone will confess to it and tell of it just as he has said. And on the night of the festival of Señor Saint Peter all the ministers of the idols come out with the women from all the ayllus, with their small drums; and in groups they pass through the streets dancing and carrying on this revelry until dawn, entering the homes of the standard-bearers and drinking. And if any of these groups goes to sleep before dawn, they are said to be defeated, shamed, and dishonored because they have not known how to do a proper festival to their idols, nor how to worship them because they went to sleep. And those who dance until dawn without sleep emerge victorious for having stayed awake all night performing the festival to their idols, and this rite they call the Vicochina [Vecosina].

And on those five days of abstinence and confessions this witness saw that the said ministers of the idols taught all the Indians to worship the Sun, because he is the father who created men, and the Moon as the creator and mother of women, and the bright star of the morning that they call Chachaguara because it is the father and creator of the curacas, and [also] the two small stars that travel together [through the night sky] that they call Chuchuicollor because they are the creators of twins, and the seven nanny-goats that they call Uncuicollor so that their crops do not freeze and that there will not be illnesses.

And at the place where the idol Tauris resides this witness has seen all the people of this village of Acas dancing the dance of the Airigua with their small drums and drinking much chicha the whole night long. And on a maguey pole they attach a bunch of many maize cobs that they call airiguasara and misasara. And having performed the dance with them, the said ministers of the idols burn and sacrifice them [the maize cobs] to the malquis and idols. They do this dance, rite, and ceremony after taking up the crops from their lands, giving thanks to their idols and malquis for having provided food that year. And this witness had seen many times that Andrés Guaman Pilpi and Pedro Caico took Hernando Hacas Poma to the Carampa ayllu with offerings to worship the malqui named Caratupaico. And [he said] that, before plowing their plots of land, it was a common thing for all the Indians of this parish to cut the throats of cuyes in the fields themselves, and to burn coca, fat, and chicha; and when the first choclos [ears of maize] began to ripen, even before tasting them, they would give the first fruits to the ministers of the idols so that they would be offered to the idols.

And this witness saw that Pedro Julca of the Yanaqui ayllu had a daughter born with curly hair named Isabel Chaupis, and [when she was born] he made chicha and invited all the villagers; and at the feast and drinking party he cut her hair, and with a cuy, coca, and fat, he burned it in sacrifice to the Sun, and after [the offering] all those who attended the feast gave offerings of silver coins. And Andrés Guaillapaico performed the same rites and ceremonies as described above three years ago when one of his sons was born with curly hair, and he cut it; and Pedro Guaman of the Quica [likely Quirca] ayllu also cut the hair of his daughter who was born with curly hair, and [this witness said] that this is a custom and ceremony that they observe in this village and parish whenever a young one is born with curly hair, which they call pacto or guarca.

And this witness saw with his own eyes that two years ago Hernando Chaupis Condor and Alonso Chaupis the Blind took thirty cuyes, three measures of coca, and a little bag of fat to a plot of land called Tauya where they made a sacrifice to the malquis called Huaris, burning before them the said cuyes and fat, and pouring out chicha. He [the witness] also saw that Pedro Capcha Yauri has some large cups from ancient times and made from the shell of a coconut, and in which they carry chicha to offer to the idols and malquis.

And in the same way this witness said that Don Diego Julca Guaman, an acculturated Indian who has become leader and headman in the village of Santiago de Chilcas, an annex of this parish, and whom the Indians fear and respect, has threatened them and stated that any Indian man or woman who reveals some idolatry to the said señor visitador would have to be whipped and punished severely once the visita [idolatry investigation] passed through. And this the witness knows because his sister Juana Solórzano, who lives and participates in the said village of Chilcas, told him of it. . . . He stated [under oath] and confirmed [that what he had spoken was the truth] and said he was forty-six years old, and because he neither knows how to write nor how to sign his name, the said interpreter and the señor visitador sign.

37

Crossing and Dome of the Rosary Chapel, Church of Santo Domingo, Puebla, Mexico

(1632–1690)

Inside the looming, rather plain shell of the gray stone church built for the Dominicans in the city of Puebla, Mexico, at the beginning of the seventeenth century is a remarkable chapel to the Rosary of Our Lady. Decorated over a period of at least sixty years, it suggests in an unusually concentrated way the Baroque artistic and religious sensibility that was popular in Spanish America during the seventeenth and eighteenth centuries.

By the time of Spanish colonization in America, the Dominicans had attached their ardent devotion to the Virgin Mary to the Rosary—the round of devotional prayers consisting of fifteen sets of ten Hail Marys preceded by a Lord's Prayer and followed by the doxology (Gloria Patri). The string of 165 beads used to assist the recital of the Rosary was the emblem of this special devotion, and images of Our Lady of the Rosary depicted the Virgin holding such a string of beads. Dominican churches in America typically gave special prominence (often in the form of a separate chapel) to this devotion.

Situated on the left side of the church just before the main altar, Puebla's Rosary chapel is in the shape of a cross. Where the two arms of the cross intersect, a dome lit by arched and rectangular windows rises above a gilded tabernacle of twisting Solomonic columns that houses a small statue of the Virgin of the Rosary in its lower story and the statue of a saint (perhaps Saint Dominic?) in the upper story. The dome and upper story of the tabernacle appear in the photograph (Figure 26; Plate 8).

Every available space on the walls, window wells, and dome of this chapel is decorated with gilded or painted high-relief stucco forms. There are recognizable figures. At the top of the dome, golden rays of celestial light surround a circular band with a Latin inscription from Isaiah, "Requiescet Superem Spiritus Domini" (And the Spirit of the Lord shall rest upon her), surrounding the white dove of the Holy Spirit. Below this central element, twisting trunks of sturdy vines rise from bulbous vases like ribbed vaults to define the eight sections of the dome, ramifying in all directions. Within each section a female figure represents a gift of the Holy Spirit, or, in one instance, Divine Grace. The heads and flexed arms of winged cherubs emerge from the foliage above the arched windows to support the female figures. The rectangular windows in an octagonal band below the dome are flanked

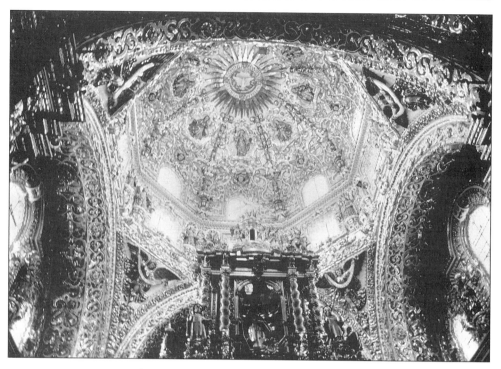

Figure 26. Upper reaches of the Rosary chapel,
Church of Santo Domingo, Puebla, Mexico, 1632–1690.
Courtesy of James Early.
～ SEE PLATE 8 ～

by statues of sixteen virgin martyrs. And in the inverted triangles created by the four arches at the intersection of the cross are hefty winged angels holding ribbons with phrases in praise of the Virgin. But these various figures largely dissolve in the undulating and swirling rhythms and dazzling overall effect of the many forms and glittering surfaces, as if this space were alive with the sacred. The center of attention is not so much Mary as the dome itself, the radiant canopy of Heaven, bathed in shafts of celestial light that suggest the transcendent delights of eternal Paradise.

By the late sixteenth century, Mediterranean and Latin American Catholic art began to focus greater attention on the display of sacred *things*—relics of saints and other holy objects; miracle-working images; beautiful (and therefore divinely inspired) paintings and statues of the heroes of Catholic history; medals, crucifixes, rosaries, pilgrimage mementoes, inex-

pensive prints of saints; chestfuls of fine vestments and costly, precious implements of the liturgy; and other ornaments fit for the House of God. Altars and entire church interiors teemed with gilded forms. These things made church buildings not only places of worship but also models of the Kingdom of Heaven. Like much Hispanic Baroque art, they were intended less to engage the intellect with theological propositions than to provide an experience of the divine, a glimpse of the celestial kingdom. The complexity of rounded forms and angles, the paintings and sculpted figures, the play of light on polished silver and twisting forms coated with gold leaf gave the impression of concentrated preciousness pulsating with life. To be inside a well-furnished colonial church or chapel in the seventeenth or eighteenth century was to approach the heavenly realm, to be transported toward the divine in an atmosphere of worship intended to engage all the senses—the smell of incense, candle wax, and damp earth; the cool wetness of holy water; the feel of a saint's robes and the hard ground or tiles under one's knees; the sound of organ music, the cantors' voices, the priest's mysterious speech and echoes of his footsteps at the altar, the bell that signaled the presence of Christ, and the murmurings of prayers and confessions; and the sight of precious objects, colors, movement, tall arches, and bright domes that drew the eyes up and out.

The contrast to the sixteenth-century altarpiece at Huejotzingo (Selection 23, Figure 16), with its symmetrical vision of Church authority and history so cleanly expressed, is striking. It invites intellectual appreciation, whereas the Rosary chapel is more an escape from history and firm rules about design. It is full of invention and an abundance of details that disguise its symmetry; it is an open, intimate invitation to soaring emotions. But both places convey a sense of order in hierarchy "up there" and affirm the preciousness of objects, seeking to inspire awe through art. Both fit well with the Spanish Hapsburgs' sense of their royal authority in patriarchal terms, utterly inseparable from their Catholicism, although the Rosary chapel's surfeit of details is more in the spirit of the extraordinary elaboration of customary rights and practices that distinguished society and the application of justice in Spanish America under the later Hapsburg kings.

Such highly ornamented religious art as that in this chapel is often regarded as a sign of decadence in Spanish American life, of a Church and society in extravagant retreat, increasingly preoccupied with material wealth and superficial appearances, of elaborate forms emptied of content and order or meant to cover over grim realities. The decoration of the Rosary chapel does correspond to a time when the robust aspiration to a universal Christian state under Spanish leadership had turned hollow, when Spanish power in Europe had ebbed and Europe itself experienced a prolonged economic depression, when troubling contradictions in the world seemed permanently irreconcilable, when the Devil seemed to have gained the upper hand in "the invisible war" for immortal souls. But should the Rosary chapel be taken as a kind of decadence in itself, as one kind of response to these circumstances of decline, or as something largely unrelated to the ideas of decadence and decline? Criticism of this hugely popular and long-lived taste in art in the old central areas of the Spanish empire rarely was voiced during the seventeenth and eighteenth centuries. Rather, it was widely accepted as beautiful and full of meaning, not decadent but a suitable expression of grandeur reaching for pure spirituality. It was a style with beginnings in Italy, developed in a confident spirit of struggle against the Protestant Reformation more than out of disheartened feelings of collapse.

When criticism of Baroque artistic expression did come from within the Hispanic world in the late eighteenth century, it was royal administrators and *peninsular* style-makers who spoke up, favoring a restrained and orderly neoclassicism that was more in keeping with their own exalted sense of themselves as enlightened, modern rulers. Buildings inspired by neoclassicism began to appear, especially those designed for state agencies, such as governors' palaces and royal mining and art schools, or the grand palaces of Spanish merchants and Creole nobles. But popular taste in religious art and architecture still inclined toward exuberant, homemade, inventive Baroque effects in the old centers of colonial life long after Spanish rule ended in America.

38

Two Paintings of a Corpus Christi Procession, Cusco, Peru

(ca. 1674–1680)

A remarkable series of at least sixteen paintings of a procession of the Blessed Sacrament —the Corpus Christi, the body of Christ, His living presence in the consecrated Host—in late seventeenth-century Cusco is thought originally to have hung in the parish church of Santa Ana in the northwestern district of this city, once the imperial center of the Inkas. The colonial church was erected on Karmenka, a hill that had been significant for solar observations in Inka times and that came to mark the principal entrance to the colonial city. The open plaza in front of the parish church hosted the ceremonial dances and performances with which the native Andeans and others greeted visiting dignitaries traveling into the highland city from coastal Lima and which enlivened the final moments of the annual processions of Corpus Christi.

The parishioners of Santa Ana were predominantly native Andean descendants of a variety of ethnic groups brought by the Inkas to Cusco as *mitmaqkuna*—peoples conquered and resettled in "safe" areas by the Inkas to discourage rebellion and promote integration. Notably, the parish was home to a number of Cañaris, a people originally from the region of modern Ecuador, south of Quito. The Cañaris

had been noted guards and fighters in the service of the lords of Tawantinsuyu, a set of roles they only enhanced in privileged alliance with the Spaniards once the tables turned on their Inka ruler-rivals. Also residing in the parish of Santa Ana were another group resettled by the Inkas, the Chachapoyas. Their post-Conquest paths were similar to those of the Cañaris. The positions of these indigenous groups as allies of the Spanish authorities in Conquest and colonial times recall alliances and resettlements of Tlaxcalans and others in New Spain. Santa Ana's most prominent representatives, Cañaris and Chachapoyas among them, are depicted in the Corpus Christi paintings as highly Hispanicized in their apparel (cloaks, breeches, lace shirts, stockings, and shoes) and comportment.

These works of art are examples of the so-called Cusco School of painting and cultural production (our black-and-white reproductions of two of the canvases do not capture the distinctive predominance of red in the palette of the originals, the gilt brocade, and decorative detail). The series is thought to date from between 1674 and 1680, to have been commissioned by a number of patrons, and to have been painted by two or more native

272

Andean artists within the circles of well-known contemporary painters Basilio de Santa Cruz and Juan Zapaca Inga, and perhaps with the contributions of these artists themselves. Twelve of the sixteen known paintings from the Santa Ana series have been restored and hang in the Museum of Religious Art in Cusco; the other four are in two private collections in Santiago, Chile.

The Catholic celebration of Corpus Christi, transplanted to the Indies by Iberians in the sixteenth century, quickly became the most important festival in the religious calendar in many of the larger urban settings in Spanish America. Corpus Christi fell between late May and mid-June, and it coincided with a pre-Hispanic festive season at the time of the winter solstice and maize harvest. The continuity of certain agrarian and religious rhythms doubtless accounted for some of the Catholic festival's popularity among native Andeans in and around the city in early colonial times. Indeed, scholars have investigated numerous parallels between the celebration of Corpus Christi in Cusco and the Inkaic festival of Inti Raymi, and also that of Capacocha. Yet it is worth considering the effects of focusing investigation on the possible symbolic and practical parallels between pre-Hispanic and colonial festive behavior. Such a focus encourages a kind of questing after a bedrock of Andean religious structures and meanings that somehow survives beneath a convenient but ultimately superficial cover of the Spanish Catholic feast day; as David Cahill shows, this is true whether the focus falls on coinciding festive calendars, shared solar imagery, the use of central spaces and the public roles of dancing and drinking, or certain images and ethnic regalia. What, then, are we assuming about the appeal and meaning of Corpus Christi processions for native Andeans, both initially and later in colonial times? Does the vitality of colonial Andean religious culture depend only on the native peoples' successful camouflaging of a notional pre-Hispanic purity and resistance of foreign influences?

Fundamentally, the festival of Corpus Christi was of European provenance. Nearly all of its organizers and appointed deputies were members of the colonial elite; and, further, the procession was in many ways an expression of the triumph of the Spanish Christian social order that this elite guarded in the former Inka heartland. The Corpus Christi series of paintings had an ethnically diverse set of male and female patrons, but, as Cahill convincingly demonstrates, primarily non-indigenous male sponsors from the city's guilds took on the principal burden and honor of funding the elaborate triumphal arches and altars that transformed the processional circuit and that figure so prominently in the paintings. These arches and altars were the pride of the city and drew comments from visitors to Cusco during the Corpus Christi cycle throughout the colonial period. In the late eighteenth century, the author of another document in this book (Selection 44), Concolorcorvo, remarked that "the entire transit of the procession is a continuous altar." Even so, these paintings invite the consideration of more complicated kinds of change in colonial Cusco. This was a place and time in which native Andean notables, like others, might preserve and reinforce their positions through identification with and participation in Christianity. There is also the matter of colonial Cusco's rapidly changing social composition, and the fact that the festival procession became a focus of popular religious life not only for Spaniards and Creoles but also for a multi-racial population. Such dimensions can be overlooked if the colonial festival is sealed off as though it were an arena for a winner-take-all contest between opposing symbolic structures that belong exclusively to native Andeans or Spaniards.

The paintings allow us to glimpse the streets, plazas, and edifices of Cusco as they may have looked after the rebuilding that followed a devastating earthquake in 1650. And the procession itself is rendered at the height of its regional popularity and significance, in the years before a 1685 reform of the festival which strictly limited the zone from which its participants might be drawn. Through their ambitious inclusion of subjects and detail, the images are visual delights that suggest a complex society participating in the most important religious procession of the year. Patrons oversaw the creation of these paintings and influenced not only their own placement within them but also the placement of others. Yet their documentary value is only the beginning of their wealth, for the canvases are best approached as purposeful works of the imagination, not simply as ethnographies painted and peopled for our research.

A number of European models informed the artists' "localized" inventions. Carolyn Dean has explored a memorable example of this painterly process of appropriation and localization by showing how in a number of canvases the native Andean artists depict multistoried processional carriages copied from prototype engravings in a contemporary festival book from Valencia, Spain. Although they became dramatic components in the canvases from the series, there is no evidence that such triumphal carriages ever rolled through the streets of Cusco.

Like the Huejotzingo altarpiece (Selection 23), and also like paintings of other events rendered to be remembered—the paintings of the conqueror of Mexico, Hernán Cortés, watched by an assembly of native lords, abasing himself in welcome of "the twelve (Franciscan) apostles of the Indies" to Tenochtitlan in 1524 is an example—the Corpus Christi canvases were commissioned by patrons, coordinated by churchmen, and created by artists to send certain messages to viewers within society at large. For, unlike so many works of art that adorned private walls within the homes of the Spanish and native nobility, the procession paintings would have been regularly viewed and re-viewed by people attending Mass and entering the church of Santa Ana—members of the very same multi-racial society, including Spaniards, who would watch the annual procession in person. What messages were they meant to take away from the paintings?

Connected to the glorification of a public religious procession in the most symbolic city in the Andes, these paintings offer an idealized representation of society, a consecration of the prescribed social order in an urban center of colonial Spanish America, and messages about prestige and participation. The communication of Spanish Christian triumph seems firmly present, as are ideas about the potential for the redirection of popular cultural and religious enthusiasms toward reformed Catholic Christian ends.

In the first image (Figure 27; Plate 9), some thirty or so priests and lesser clerical officers in black cassocks under white surplices—three carrying their birettas (three-lobed hats) and others candlesticks—form a line passing under a triumphal arch. The arch is paneled with landscapes and topped by the figure of the archangel Michael defeating Satan, flanked by two helmeted trumpeters. To the right of center, the well-dressed official wearing the Maltese Cross of the knightly Order of Saint John and enjoying the honor of carrying the banner of the Holy Sacrament is thought to be Don Alonso Pérez de Guzmán, the *corregidor* of Cusco (1670–1676). Six paintings—two more landscapes and four archangels—almost obscure a building behind a processional altar devoted to Christ's crucifixion. People fill the background, most of them watching the procession. To the left of the altar is a native Andean man playing an elaborately carved harp, accompanying a group of young singers.

The crowd in the foreground stands in the street. In the center, a bearded European man with his long hair tied in a queue, wearing a large hat and enjoying a cigar, seems oblivious to the solemn procession of clergy and provincial authority. In contrast to him are the three patrons of the canvas—an old Andean woman who made the commission on behalf of her two grandsons—facing the viewer, all with hands raised and clasped in prayer. The woman stands behind the boys, one of whom is with her on the far left, while the other is somewhat displaced to the right. The old woman, who dominates the foreground from her corner, wears Andean clothing while both children are dressed in Spanish attire.

Figure 27. Corregidor Pérez and secular clergy in a Corpus Christi procession,
Cusco, Peru, ca. 1674–1680.
Courtesy of the Museo del Arte Religioso, Cusco, Peru.
∼ SEE PLATE 9 ∼

This painting, with its focused expression of piety and order, like a number of others in the series does not quite deny the intrusion of more messy and entertaining social realities. But the intrusions are deemphasized or neutralized in ways that were common in European art of the day; the intrusions here function much as the cavorting servants and pets do in paintings of the Last Supper. The distracted man with the hat and cigar in the foreground of the Corregidor Pérez canvas is a good example of a figure whose capacity for trouble seems reduced to inattentiveness. He draws the gaze but seems benign and contained, allowing the artist and viewer to delight in him. The didactic message about order and society is conveyed by contrasting the disruptive or simply inattentive behavior among the diverse commoners in the foreground and outer fringes with the careful and intent propriety of the White elite (see also the background figures on the balconies in the second image, Figure 28), the pious patrons, and the central order of the procession participants.

Even more obviously irreverent behavior is also included according to contemporary artistic conventions, as a useful foil to exemplary behavior. As Dean has shown, in the Corpus Christi series these further "distractions" are often unruly children, confined to the margins of the pictorial space, suitably away from properly restrained and reverential attitudes. To the far right in the first image, just beyond the triumphal arch, is a group of people who unfortunately cannot be seen clearly in our reproduction (or in any others of which we are aware). These people gaze at the next and culminating segment of the procession "outside" this canvas (and depicted in another painting from the series), namely, the bishop of Cusco, Manuel de Mollinedo y Angulo, bearing the consecrated Host in its monstrance. A group of men (seemingly an Andean, a European, an African, and another figure) are about to kneel, and the African has even removed his hat out of respect. Yet just in front of the men, a woman holds a baby while another child seems to aim a peashooter in the direction of the approaching Host.

What does such a rendering achieve? It is unlikely that the artist's discreet sideshows of casual disorder and disrespect are clever messages chanced by native Andean artists who meant to subvert the order-seeking messages of the commissioned paintings. In fact, one possible interpretation following from Dean's work is that the intended messages are entirely opposite to subversion and closer in spirit to routine. Arguably, the placement of the inattentive commoner in the foreground, or the misbehaving child almost out of view (and before the attentive men and beside the reverent mother, all of whom are notably

unfazed by the child's actions), assembles in this canvas a Baroque message about the coexistence of opposites, a micro-lesson in what is and is not appropriate in the presence of Spanish Christian authority. By depicting the most destabilizing elements in the paintings as marginal and "childish," are the artists saying that however unfortunate their behavior, they are exceptional and, like children, more or less controllable? How do these messages relate to Cuevas's descriptions of commoners and their behavior during Corpus Christi processions in another region of Spanish America? Building from elite perceptions of "uneducated" and less Hispanicized segments of society as childlike, Dean suggests this insight, arguing that many of the misbehaving children in the series (unlike the praying grandsons in Figure 27) are treated similarly and are "behaviorally analogous" to the more chaotic and talkative commoners in the foregrounds of the Corpus Christi paintings.

How were these paintings seen? One cannot know for certain if the native Andean parishioners of Santa Ana noticed the few disruptive elements in the paintings, much less if they saw them in a prescribed manner. Yet an interpretation that sees ethnic variety and hints of disorder being pictorially "conquered" and rather hopefully set in place in these depictions of Christianity's processional triumph seems strengthened by wider attention to contemporary events and concerns. Although serious and sustained challenges to the social and political hierarchy were rare, churchmen and other authorities recorded that Corpus Christi celebrations were notorious for their public drunkenness, small-scale violence, disrespect for authority, and any number of excesses and disruptions. Even the leaders of Hispanicized groups such as the Cañari parishioners of Santa Ana used the public moments of the dances and demonstrations during the procession to goad rival ethnic groups, sometimes setting off pitched battles in the plaza and streets and bringing ignoble ends (or at least long and bloody delays) to any expression of communal consensus. Colonial officials in Cusco, and in the rest of

Spanish America, were not the only ones with such troubles, and in fact shared them with many contemporaries throughout the Catholic world who increasingly lamented that religious festivals, in addition to their financial drain and lost work time, were often occasions for violence and protest. Cusco's patrons and sponsors had these reasons and more to be urgently concerned by the disruptions that marred actual festivals, and they were obviously eager to curb such behavior.

In its use of the pictorial space and in the activity and arrangement of subjects, the second image (Figure 28; Plate 10) is an even more elaborate idealization of a colonial social order that reached downward to the people from the Spanish monarchy itself. At the center is the festive altar before which the procession would pause. It features the young King Charles II, a number of archangels, and a collection of paintings on biblical themes. The eye is drawn toward two resplendent images. On the left is Santa Rosa of Lima, patron of the Indies, carrying her wreath of roses and wearing her customary Dominican habit, crown of roses, and a rosary draped around her shoulders (see also Selection 30 and Figure 24 in Selection 32). Following her is the patron of Cusco, the Virgin locally known as "La Linda" (The Pretty One). The two saints ride on litters carried by members of their *cofradías*, or religious associations.

These native Andean litter bearers are depicted as ethnic non-Inkas; shod in sandals, they wear their hair long, and most are dressed in European breeches beneath tunics covered by darker traditional mantles. They contrast with the noble standard-bearer who wears a modified Inkaic tunic, bordered at the neck (recalling the messages of such dress suggested by Figures 1 and 2 in Selection 2); and they contrast also with his elite companions, who carry their staffs of authority and office and who are dressed in the darker colors of Hispanicized garb, with lace sleeves of mixed European and Andean styles. The red fringed ornamental headgear (*masca paycha*) that the Sapa Inka had worn on his forehead as one of the symbols of his preeminence,

now forming part of the imagery adopted by Cusco's post-Conquest Inka elite, is borne on a pillow in front of the standard-bearer—perhaps, it has been suggested, because wearing (as opposed to displaying) the connotative headdress of his bloodline would confuse his current capacity as head of the Catholic *cofradía* of "La Linda." The castle and elongated rainbow, and other elements of this headpiece, demonstrate a colonial sharing of symbols, most basically that of the Inkaic forehead insignia and the Spanish coat of arms signifying Cusco and its recent history.

Unlike the litter bearers who stare intently ahead, the Andean leaders who walk in front of "La Linda" gaze proudly out at the viewer. The post-Conquest Inka carrying the standard appears an embodiment both of a noble Andean and of an Andean Christian leader. A partial inscription to the lower right on the canvas announces: "Here goes the standard-bearer with his father Don Baltazar Tupa Puma. . . ." On his bright tunic, in addition to the Andean geometric motifs (*tocapu*) and borders, is a solar visage—a round face with its rays projecting outward—suggesting a mixture of Andean solar imagery and the Inkaic divinity Inti with European solar metaphors for Christ and the spreading warmth and light of Christianity, and recalling the sun-shaped receptacle of the focus of this event.

The *cofradía* as principal patron asserts a collective vision of its members as devoted agents within the order of the procession and a reconstituted civil and religious community. The modified Inkaic dress marks a clear association with the pre-Hispanic past, but one that is not bereft of symbols which seek a reformulated and participating "Christian" Andean authority in colonial times. The depictions of the native leaders and supporting cast seem eager to speak to and gain legitimacy from a mixed audience of viewers. Santa Rosa is surrounded by Indian musicians, while a group of Indian notables with their ceremonial staffs precede "La Linda." Nobles who descended from the royal line of Inkas, as well as native Andean governors (*kurakas*) from the environs of Cusco, regularly participated in

Figure 28. Santa Rosa and "La Linda" in a Corpus Christi procession, Cusco, Peru, ca. 1674–1680.
Courtesy of the Museo del Arte Religioso, Cusco, Peru.

⤳ SEE PLATE 10 ⤳

these processions and would characteristically dress in a mixture of Andean and Spanish costumes. Two such men—perhaps the most striking portraits in this painting—are positioned in front of "La Linda," one in a patterned white tunic and the other in dark dress with the lace sleeves of a noble, staring straight back at the viewer. These native leaders, as intermediaries between Spanish authorities and Andean peoples, appeal to a kind of traditional authority that was encouraged by the Spanish rulers, and also to a modified understanding of authority that the Indian elite were obliged to negotiate with their subjects in colonial times. The governors and notables, like the musicians and members of the cofradías, walk as men of local importance, as dignified and exemplary participants in this representation of a central Christian occasion.

What does one make of the use of Inkaic dress and symbols during the Corpus Christi processions? As in their general portrayals, the artists seem to have held a vision of achieved assimilation in mind. Here in the late seventeenth century, it might be said, dressed in their revised pre-Hispanic finery and striding magnificently at the center of the holy pageantry, are ideal representatives of Andean colonial culture, examples to those who watch. Such messages were thought more useful than sub-versive by officials in the late seventeenth century. Yet, as David Cahill has pointed out, in the face of the spreading rebellions and signs of an Inka's return to power in Peru, views could change. Colonial officials in the later eighteenth century would grow distrustful of native Andean assimilation and increasingly hostile toward the presence of Inkaic reminders and even ceremonial Andean dancing within the celebration of Corpus Christi. Such festivities were eventually deemed dangerous rallying points as well as extravagantly wasteful of time and money.

The magnificent paintings of Cusco's Corpus Christi are ultimately ambitious works of the mind, imaginings (even instructions) of how an ideal procession would appear in this prestigious and symbolic setting. As such, they seem to signify the hopes and efforts of members of a Spanish and native Andean elite in late seventeenth-century south-central Peru to forge and maintain a social unity, thereby reducing the likelihood of disturbance and rebellion. All of the participants and observers of the popular real event, pictorially represented as people from every social station, were given their parts to play, even as the agents of distraction, who were carefully minimalized. Now, if only everyone would learn their lines and gestures and keep to their places.

~ 39

A Black Irmandade *in Bahia, Brazil*

(1699)

Consider this small scene of popular religious performance: out on the streets, brothers from the Espírito Santo *irmandade,* or lay sodality, some dressed in comic getups beating a drum and tambourines and hoisting high their flag. They sing ballads, joke, and make music, while one among them, decked out as the Emperor, is carried in an armchair complete with canopy, the procession stopping here and there to acknowledge greetings from one and all. A noisy, humorous, irreverent group, they draw Blacks and Mulattos in their train. Their roving antics do not merely entertain, however; from street vendors and shopkeepers the troupe also collects coins to sponsor an elaborately planned celebration of their special day of devotion for the Holy Spirit, a movable feast day in the Catholic calendar that falls on the seventh Sunday after Easter to commemorate the descent of the Holy Ghost upon Christ's disciples. In 1765 the White brothers, mostly immigrants from the Portuguese Atlantic islands of the Azores, intended to provide a splendid banquet in the Santo Antônio do Carmo church for friends of the irmandade and other invited guests, with casks of free wine and tables outside on the street to serve dinner to the poor. The feasting was to follow a Mass. And in the preceding days the church's side altar, dedicated to the Holy Spirit, was to

be lit with many candles, and there the brothers would sing to the Holy Spirit, accompanied by violin and cither.

The captaincy's interim governing council, composed of representatives from the three authorities of army, Church, and High Court, found offense in these celebrations, especially in the farce of the Emperor, who allegedly sprayed holy water on one priest at the door of the church and then ordered another from the pulpit on grounds that no one should stand above him. These allegations were firmly denied by the brothers who, in any case, claimed their performance merely imitated that practiced in Lisbon. But what drew the council's most pointed condemnation were the Blacks and Mulattoes, the "lowest rabble," unworthy of any respect, who accompanied the musicians through the streets. Full of food and wine they inevitably would fall to quarreling with knives and clubs. Those shopkeepers who contributed alms would benefit with more business, while others would suffer. The whole affair was nothing but trouble, and the council recommended to the prime minister in Portugal that the irmandade be limited only to White immigrants and that the satire of the Emperor be strictly forbidden; if they did otherwise, they would be exiled to Angola without remission. And, the council continued, in

Lisbon they did not carry on as in Bahia and, besides, the Whites there were "raised with fear and respect for the law and Christianity." In contrast, in Bahia, the rabble were "insolent and presumptuous Mulattoes" and "brutish Blacks."

The status of the offending Blacks and Mulattoes, whether or not members of this irmandade, remains ambiguous, but they might well have been full members of their own sodalities, many of which admitted only men and women of color. The most prestigious Bahian irmandades were those with all-White members, such as the lofty Santa Casa da Misericórdia, which required them to be literate and demonstrate purity of blood (that is, descent from neither Jews nor Moors); it expressly excluded manual laborers. There were others—Our Lady of Piety, Our Lady of Grace, or the Most Holy Sacrament—who readily raised money for rich chapel decorations and lavish festivals. The more numerous colored irmandades competed to adorn their own churches, chapels, or modest side altars with works of religious art, silver candelabra, or a carved wooden grill and to honor their saints with exuberant devotions. And they reflected further social divisions. Particular occupational groups such as blacksmiths or shoemakers formed irmandades, thus giving them a guild quality, while among Africans some sodalities restricted membership to distinct ethnic groups such as Yorubas, Gêges, or Angolans. Some accepted slaves, others only former slaves or free-born Brazilians.

They often chose Black or Mulatto patron saints, especially Saint Benedict or Saint Efigenia. Saint Anthony of Catagerona, the saint to whom the irmandade in this selection was devoted, is almost unknown today and difficult to find in the published dictionaries of Catholic saints, but he had particular resonance for Brazilian Blacks (see Figure 29; Plate 11). This Saint Anthony was born in Africa, captured, and sold as a slave in Sicily. At some time he was baptized Anthony, eventually freed, and then joined the Franciscans. Being merely a virtuous and charitable shepherd would not have earned him sainthood, but the opening of his tomb in 1599, fifty years after

his death, and the discovery of his uncorrupted body did qualify him. In the irmandades we can glimpse the transformation of a people from a place in Africa with distinctive beliefs and practices into a people with an African past (or whose parents had an African past) coming to have Christian connections based in a new place, with a church or chapel, and around the image of a saint.

With origins in Portugal from at least as early as the thirteenth century, the irmandade was among the first institutions to be transferred to colonial Bahia in the midsixteenth century. From the beginning these irmandades also had an African cast to them, brought in part by Africans or Creoles who first had experience in Portugal before going to Brazil, or from Africans who had been converted and taught by Catholic missionaries in Africa before being sold in the Atlantic slave trade directly to Brazil. For some Africans devotion to a saint through membership in an irmandade was a familiar practice. In Bahia, irmandades reached their zenith in number and influence during the eighteenth century, when thirty-one dedicated themselves to the Blessed Mother alone, including six Black irmandades and another five for Mulattoes devoted to Our Lady of the Rosary. No one can say how many Bahians belonged to lay religious associations, but they were frequently mentioned in the funeral instructions and legacies presented in last wills and testaments. And many Bahians belonged to more than one.

While the Church encouraged and approved the formation of irmandades with the hope of bringing Christian teaching to Africans and their Portuguese- and Brazilian-born descendants, irmandades dedicated themselves to charitable works for their own members, and often for the needy more generally, that is, those not associated with a protecting irmandade of their own. What was the essential need that an irmandade promised to fulfill? A dignified death and burial, which separated the fortunate from the poorest among the dying and dead who might be abandoned on the street. To die anonymously and alone was a dreaded end, the opposite of a *boa morte,* or

Figure 29. Santo Antônio de Catagerona, from the Covenant of the Irmandade, Bahia, Brazil, 1699.
Courtesy of The Catholic University of America, Oliveira Lima Library, Washington, DC.

good death. Burial for most Blacks and Mulattoes in eighteenth-century Bahia meant something in between: the body was carried on a rented bier (later returned to the Santa Casa, which long held a monopoly on caskets and biers) and then slid into a plot of ground in a public cemetery on the outskirts of the city. Well-off Whites ended up inside a church buried as close to the altar of God as their money and prestige permitted. Gradually some colored irmandades petitioned for, and received, permission to own their own burial casket, as long as they agreed to pay the Santa Casa a small compensatory fee. Masses and prayers said for the dead would shorten their time in Purgatory or increase their glory in Heaven while delivering grace to those who paid for the Masses, said the prayers, or accompanied the body to its grave. These post-death rituals were crucial to their eternal life, and while the rich could will the funds to ensure that the rituals were properly and elaborately carried out, the poor relied on their irmandades.

If the calculations of grace seem overly instrumental, a kind of sacred economy to ensure salvation, were the devotions sponsored by the irmandades not also extravagant expressions of beauty and joyous energy? In a thoroughly hierarchical society, did the colored poor not have reason and experience to recognize the importance of saintly intercessors in spiritual matters, just as they understood and relied on intermediaries in their secular dealings?

The covenant, or set of statutes and commitments, for the proposed irmandade of Santo Antônio de Catagerona offers us a chance to see the social relationships and religious works that a group of Blacks and Mulattoes took on for themselves. In broad outline this irmandade was not unlike others, nor was this petition accepted without changes by higher authorities. Nonetheless, it is worth asking whether membership offered the opportunity to fashion a distinctive, ethnically, and racially based identity.

～ *A Covenant to Keep*

Made by the Devotees of Saint Anthony of Catagerona
On behalf of their *Irmandade* Located in the Parish Church of Saint Peter in the City of Bahia
Done in the Year 1699

And he said to his disciples: Fear not, little flock; for it is your Father's good pleasure to give you the kingdom. Sell what ye have and give alms; provide yourselves bags which wax not old, a treasure in the heavens that faileth not, where no thief approacheth, neither moth corrupteth. For where your treasure is, there will your heart be also.—The Gospel According to St. Luke [Luke 12: 22, 32–34].

Chapter I
～ *The Protective Saint of This Holy Irmandade*

The protective Saint under which this Holy Irmandade expects to grow and steadily progress, with great spiritual satisfaction and prosperity to its souls and approval of all, is the glorious Saint Anthony of Catagerona, whose feast day shall be celebrated with great solemnity on the day indicated below. On that day the chapters of this Covenant shall be read to the new officers for them to observe in the manner specified.

Chapter II

∼ *On the Officers*

The officers, who shall be elected to serve this Holy Irmandade, are the following: Judge, Scribe, Treasurer, Procurator, and Majordomos as necessary. Said officers shall be, first, male Creoles, and second, male Angolans, and for this purpose there shall be two elections for separate slates, and in the same manner there shall be elections of female Creoles and female Angolans, and they shall all be chosen on the day of our glorious Saint by the outgoing officers, in the presence of the Reverend Parish Priest; for Treasurer and Scribe shall be chosen men of sound honesty.

Chapter III

∼ *Who Shall Be Procurator*

The Procurator who serves that year shall be a man of great zeal because his office is of great importance and to him belongs especially the welfare of this Irmandade, such as the defense and conservation of its statutes. In his absence, one of the Majordomos, whoever seems best, will serve. That is, if there is some impediment for the Procurator, the Majordomo is obliged to inform the Brothers and Sisters as to when they should process in accompaniment [of burials] and seek to do whatever pertains to the welfare of said Irmandade.

Chapter IV

∼ *On the Entrance of Brothers and Sisters*

To this holy Irmandade shall be admitted all and any persons of any state or condition, each one giving one *pataca* [coin worth 320 réis] for admission, but being a poor person, some allowance shall be made, because we wish that no person who wishes to serve God and the glorious Saint in this Irmandade shall be prevented by their poverty, but rather that they shall find the door open so that all may work for the love of God.

Chapter V

∼ *On the Books to be Kept by This Irmandade*

There shall be with the Board a book to register the names of the Brothers and Sisters and the day and year of their admission, which shall read in this way: "So-and-so took his/her place as Brother/Sister on such-and-such day of such-and-such month, and promised to observe the statutes and good order of the Irmandade"; and at the foot of this register they shall sign along with the Scribe. There shall be another book to be used only for elections, and in it nothing else shall be written. There shall be still another book in which to enter the receipts and expenses and in which shall appear the acknowledgment of Masses said and anything else that is necessary. And all these books shall be in the care of the Scribe who serves that year.

Chapter VI
∾ *On Recording the Alms Received*

The Scribe shall have a book to record the alms or money received when there are some and, along with that, there shall be recorded all expenses, and this shall be the book of receipts and expenditures and nothing else shall be written in it. And said Scribe will show this account to the officers who in that time or year do serve, whenever they ask. And they shall verify the receipts and expenditures and prepare a formal statement for the year that all [officers] shall sign.

Chapter VII
∾ *On the Masses that Shall Be Ordered*

Every Wednesday and day of Saint Anthony—to whom all Brothers and Sisters should be very devoted, praying every day at least one rosary of seven Our-Fathers and seventy Hail-Marys—a Low Mass shall be said which two Majordomos will attend with their capes and great candles, and these Masses shall be said as an act of veneration by all the Irmandade, and be paid for at the customary rate. And when a Brother or Sister dies, eight Masses shall be said for his or her soul and, for officers, ten for their soul.

Chapter VIII
∾ *On the Solemn Feast*

On the fourth [*sic*; see Chapter 2, Additional Clause] Sunday of November the feast of Saint Anthony shall be celebrated with the greatest possible solemnity, having on its eve a sung Mass and sermon attended by all the Sisters and Brothers, wearing their capes. And on this day shall be named the new officers who will serve during the coming year. The expense of the Feast will be borne by the said Irmandade, according to its possibilities and the alms that it may have received.

Chapter IX
∾ *On the Alms Received*

Every Wednesday, or another day if more advisable, one Procurator—or two if that is better—will go to the doors of the Brothers and Sisters and others devoted to Saint Anthony to ask [for alms]. At the end of each month the Brother or Sister is obliged to go immediately and hand over [what has been collected] to the Treasurer of that year; and, in the presence of the Scribe, it shall be recorded in a book for this purpose so that afterwards this record may be transferred to the book of receipts and expenditures, all of which is necessary for greater clarity.

Chapter X
∾ *On How Deceased Brothers and Sisters Will Be Accompanied*

Brothers and Sisters who die shall be accompanied [to the grave] by the entire Irmandade with their capes and great candles, carrying the cross in front, and all

Brothers and Sisters will pray one rosary with seven Our-Fathers and seventy Hail-Marys. Eight Masses for their soul shall be ordered said, as specified in Chapter VII, and in all this the Brothers and Sisters will carry [the body] with great zeal and care, because this is important for the welfare of the Irmandade and the service of GOD.

Chapter XI

On the Prayers for Absent Brothers and Sisters Who Die

We order, with the approval of all the Irmandade, that for the Brothers and Sisters who die while absent, the declared obligations shall be carried out, whether of Masses or of prayers, and all shall participate in those said at the Irmandade. And in this matter great care shall be taken, for it is not right that a Brother or Sister who left for whatever reason should lose the prayers for the dead of the said Irmandade which he or she has served, and on this particular matter they [the members] shall act with great zeal.

Chapter XII

On the Brothers and Sisters Who Do Not Pay

Brothers and Sisters should always strive with great care to conserve and augment this holy Irmandade, and this cannot be hoped for if they do not help and join in its support. Not doing so cannot be permitted because then no benefit will result. Therefore we order that any Brother or Sister who does not pay [dues] for two years will no longer have Masses said for their soul when they die or be accompanied [at their burial] by the Irmandade. The Procurator and Treasurer will take great care to warn the Brothers and Sisters to pay, since many become careless for lack of such a warning. And we ask future officers to observe this rule, which is of great utility to the Brothers and Sisters and to the Irmandade itself.

Chapter XIII

On Brothers and Sisters Who Wish to Become Free from Slavery

Any slave man or woman who wishes to secure liberty and become a freed person may turn to the Irmandade if it has funds to effect it and, on the presentation of security, it will give that person the funds to purchase his or her freedom, and the Treasurer shall not raise any objection.

Chapter XIIII [sic, that is, XIV]

On the Service to be Held for Our Deceased Brothers and Sisters

On the day following the day on which the feast of said Saint is celebrated, a Mass shall be said for the souls of our deceased Brothers and Sisters, which shall be paid for at the usual and customary rate. We beg our Brothers to attend with capes and great candles and our Sisters will also attend, praying a chaplet for the souls of our deceased Brothers and Sisters with all solemnity, humility, and devotion.

[Actions Dated 1699]

Most Excellent Sir,

The Judge, Majordomos, and other officers of the Irmandade of Saint Anthony of Catagerona located in the parish church of Saint Peter in Bahia [say] that they have prepared a Covenant that they offer to keep with the Chapters contained therein for the benefit of the said Irmandade and greater devotion of its Brothers and Sisters, which cannot go out in the light without permission from Your Excellency.

They ask Your Excellency to grant the said permission so that the Covenant that they here present may thus come to the notice of our Brothers and Sisters.

And they request indulgence,

[marginal comment:]

The Reverend Provisor should look over this Covenant, initial it, number [the pages], and advise us with his opinion, Bahia, May 26, 1699.

[signed] Archbishop

Illustrious and Most Reverend Sir,

I have examined this Covenant of the sodality of Creoles and Angolans, confreres of Saint Anthony of Catagerona, or rather Cataragirona, located in the parish church of Saint Peter, outside the walls of this city, and before I say what I think regarding the fourteen chapters that make it up, I cannot fail to touch on two matters that I find in the image of the Saint painted at the beginning of this book that seem to me contrary to the truth as to the life, history, and miracles of the saint, something we are ordered to attend to by the Council of Trent in its second decree on the *invocatione, veneratione, et reliquias santorum et sacris imaginibus* [invocation, veneration, and reliquary of saints and sacred images]. The first is seeing the saint dressed with a monk's cowl as if he had been a friar and had dressed in this way during his lifetime; whereas the [lay] Third Order did not use a cowl. The second is that the saint holds an image of the Christ Child in his arms, for, although it is known that in his life he was highly devoted to the holy name of Jesus, there is no evidence that the Lord ever appeared [to him] in the form of a child or that [the Christ Child] ever granted him any favors, which is what the Church requires in [representations] of the child Jesus in arms. And so it seems to me that, until we have clearer information, images of this saint should be painted and dressed without a cowl and with a cross in his hands, as is done in the chapel of the Third Order of the Franciscans of this city.

As to the Chapters: Fourteen are so far found in this Covenant and, although I find nothing in them contrary to our Holy Faith, it seems to me that some of them are contrary to the good government of this sodality and that, to be well served, they require the following declarations and statutes:

Declaration as to the Second Chapter:

Whereas in Chapter II it is ordained that Treasurers should be men of sound honesty, without specifying the condition of these persons, and although some Blacks may be good as can be seen in the [illegible] of this sodality, nevertheless he should also be a knowledgeable, reliable, and reputable person so that the goods of the sodality not go astray, [qualities] rarely found in Blacks, even when free. Therefore, an [additional] declaration to this chapter orders that the Treasurer of this sodality be a White man, chosen by the Brothers and Sisters in the same way as other officers.

Second declaration as to the same chapter:

Because it is just that both the honor and the responsibility be distributed among all the Brothers and Sisters, no Brother or Sister who serves one year should be re-elected to serve in the next one. And if it be very advisable to re-elect [someone], he or she shall not begin to serve without receiving permission from Your Illustrious [Person], who, informed as to what is right or not for the Irmandade, will give or deny permission according to what you think best, and in your absence they can turn to the Provisor.

Third declaration as to the same chapter:

Within fifteen days from the date when the former officers cease to serve, the former officers should meet with the new ones at the church on a Sunday or religious feast day and give account, the old to the new, according to the book of receipts and expenditures. And it being determined that something is owed, this shall be declared in writing, signed by all. And if they do not pay within fifteen days, the new officers will take the old debtor ones to court, and if they [the new officers] are negligent in collecting the debt, they shall be required to pay the debt out of their own pockets.

First declaration as to Chapter XIII:

As it is certain that, although aiding the liberty of slaves is a work of mercy and something very pious and very holy, nevertheless it is not advisable that this work be preferred to others that the sodality requires. Slave Brothers and Sisters, taken by the desire to become free, will facilitate loans for the [purchase] price [of others] with the hope that on another occasion the same favor will be done to them, to the detriment of the sodality. Besides declaring that they may not lend the goods of the Irmandade without permission of Your Illustrious Person or your Provisor, Chapter XIII should declare that it will not lend any money for such freedoms nor for anything, no matter how pious, without your permission. The penalty for doing so will be whatever punishment appears just, besides making up for what it leant to repay the Irmandade for loss and damage.

That, Illustrious Sir, is my opinion on this Covenant; I have numbered and initialed the pages of the book and formally declared its end on this last page. Your Illustrious Person will do what you believe right. Bahia, first of June 1699,

[signed] Sebastião do Valle Pontes

For authorization, with the declarations noted by the Reverend Provisor, Bahia, June 15, 1699.

[signed] Archbishop

We, Dom João Franco de Oliveira, by the mercy of God and the Pontifical Apostolic See, Metropolitan Archbishop of this State of Brazil and a member of the Council of His Majesty, etc., by this our present authorization approve this Covenant of the Irmandade of Saint Anthony of Catagerona, in the parish church of Saint Peter beyond the walls of this city of Bahia [made] by the Creole Blacks and Angolans who may enter and serve. And we order that it be observed and followed as specified with all the declarations that our Reverend Provisor and Teacher [illegible], Doctor Sebastião do Valle Pontes, made regarding the form of its second and thirteenth chapters, which shall be obeyed in the way they specify, because it thus contributes to the good regimen of said Irmandade, without any contrary alteration or interpretation, for we confirm them and consider them good. For which we interpose our ordinary authority and judicial decree. Given this day in Bahia under our sign and our chancery's seal, where it will be registered, fifteenth of June 1699. Diogo da Fonseca Freyre, chapter scribe, wrote it down,

[signed] Archbishop

[seal]

Authorization that the Most Illustrious Reverend has decided to concede to the Brothers and Sisters of the sodality of Saint Anthony of Catagerona for . . . this Covenant, observing the added declarations to the second and thirteenth chapters.

For His Illustrious Reverend

[verso]

Registered in the third Chancery book, folio 63.

[signed] Sousa

[verso again]

I numbered and initialed this book of the Covenant of the sodality of Saint Anthony of Catagerona located in the parish church of Saint Peter outside the walls of this city, and it consists of twenty-three folios, numbered and initialed with my last name—Pontes. And since this is so, I have made this closing act, interposing my authority and judicial decree whenever the law so requires, Bahia, June 20, 1699.

[signed] Sebastião do Valle Pontes

[Documents Dated 1764]

The Judge and other Brothers and Sisters of the Irmandade of the glorious Saint Anthony of Catagerona in the parish of Saint Peter of this city say that they, supplicants, are in possession of said Irmandade with the attached Covenant to which, because it is very ancient and contains several faults as to its provisions and the good operation of the same Irmandade, they have added some chapters that they now present for His Majesty so that he may grant them the favor of issuing an authorization in the customary way.

We ask His Majesty to grant them the favor of ordering the issuance of an authorization in the sought-after form, and beg for his indulgence.

[Additional Clauses]

Chapter 2

〰 *On the Officers—Additional Clause*

There shall be two Judges, one Scribe, one Treasurer, two Procurators, eight Counselors, to wit, one for Creoles, another for Angolans, and on the feast day which shall be on the first [*sic;* Chapter VIII says fourth] Sunday of the month of November as declared in Chapter VIII of this Covenant, the Board will meet at the accustomed place and choose the new officers who shall serve during the coming year. The Scribe and Treasurer shall be persons of sound honesty and good knowledge for these places.

Chapter 3

〰 *On the Procuratorship and Its Duties—Additional Clause*

As the office of Procurator is one of great weight, it is ordained that they shall take much care for the increase of the Irmandade and go out to beg [alms] every month through the streets, and at the end take whatever they have gathered to the Scribe, who shall entrust it to the Treasurer, handing it over as specified in Chapter IX. At meetings of the Board, the Procurator shall propose only that which is for the welfare of the Irmandade and, seeing that something that the Board determines is detrimental to the Irmandade, he shall protest on its behalf and have his protest entered in its book, which the Board shall order done; while obeying whatever is decided, the said Procurator will appeal to rightful authority. He shall take great care as to the cleanliness of the Chapel and all its paraphernalia, caring for it and doing all that the good Procurator should do.

Chapter 4

〰 *On the Pledge and Admission of Brothers and Sisters—Additional Clause*

After the installation of a new Board, if not on that day then eight days later, the new officers shall meet to make their pledges, starting with the Judges, which shall be in the amount of 6$400 réis; the Brother Scribe, 5$000 réis; the Brother Treasurer, 5$000 réis; the Procurators, 1$000 réis; the Counselors, 1$280 réis each; and each one may exceed [these amounts] as their wealth and devotion permits. The female Judges shall pledge what they can, in keeping with the custom in other Irmandades of not setting a fixed price. The Brothers and Sisters who newly enter this holy Irmandade will give for their admission 1$280 réis or as much more as they wish.

Chapter 5

〰 *On the Books to be Kept—Additional Clause*

In addition to the books specified in this Chapter V there shall be another book in which to place the acknowledgments [or receipts] of Masses said, and in it nothing else should be recorded. Also a book to record the decisions of the Board and another one for any other matter that is observed and everything else that this chapter and its additional clause may require as well as those mentioned in Chapter VI.

Chapter 7
~ *On the Masses—Additional Clause*

In order to avoid any doubt as to the Masses that this Irmandade customarily orders said every year for the living and the dead because Chapter VII and Chapter X did not specify by whom they shall be said nor the alms that will be paid [for them], we order that our Father Chaplain shall be preferred for all the Masses that are ordered said and in his absence any other priest, and that the alms [paid] for Sunday Mass and the Masses said on holy days shall be 320 réis, those for deceased Brothers and Sisters 200 réis, [and] the three Christmas Masses 1$920 réis, as this is the custom observed in all Irmandades.

Chapter 12
~ *On the Brothers and Sisters Who Do Not Pay—Additional Clause*

As it [this chapter's provision] is contrary to reason and to the love one should have toward the dead—for intercessory prayers are the food of the deceased—we order that the Brother or Sister who dies without having paid what is owed to the confraternity will nevertheless enjoy the prayers for the dead and be buried in the customary way, and this part of Chapter XII is declared null and void. We only order that if he or she owes the confraternity and does not pay, the number of Masses will be reduced. And our Brother Procurator will take care to pursue [from the deceased's estate] what the Brother or Sister owes so that the full number of Masses for the dead may be said. However, if the deceased serves the Irmandade with zeal, both in person and by disbursements from his or her pocket, and then falls into poverty and, because of it, is unable to satisfy his or her pledge, then the Masses will be said without any diminution. See Chapter XI which agrees with the piety of this clause.

Chapter 14
~ *On the Service, etc.—Additional Clause*

This Chapter determines that a Mass be said for deceased Brothers and Sisters on the day following the feast of our glorious saint, but does not indicate the number of priests nor how much they shall be paid. To avoid any doubt on this matter, we order that for the said office shall be paid 10$000 réis and it shall be conducted by priests and, if the Reverend Vicar does not wish [to do it] for said sum, we order our Treasurer to divide this sum into Masses to be said by priests at 240 réis for each one, which Masses are to be said on that very day or the next.

[New Chapters Added In 1764]

Chapter 15
∽ On the Judge and His or Her Duty

As Judges hold first place, so also should they be [first] in the care and zeal of the Irmandade insofar as its good regimen depends on them. They will summon the Board whenever they deem it necessary, and all our Brothers and Sisters should obey them for the service of God, and Judges shall treat and care for everyone with respect and urbanity. They shall exercise great vigilance in admonishing officers to do their duty. On the Board they shall order the voting and instruct some to remain silent when necessary. When the Scribe cannot come for a good reason, a Judge shall name a Brother Board member of good knowledge to write whatever is decided, doing so on loose paper for the Scribe later to copy into the first book, if it is accurate. And if any other official is absent, the Judge shall summon another who has already served on the Board. The Procurators shall go every eight days to the house of the Judge to learn of any news to be conveyed to the Scribe and Treasurer and to carry out instructions on anything that needs doing.

Chapter 16
∽ On the Brother Scribe and His Duties

No lesser in weight and importance is the place of Scribe, because on it depends all the growth of the Irmandade. The occupant should, therefore, be experienced, vigilant, and well regarded, since on him rests the continuation and law of the Irmandade. He should make sure that the Procurators, male and female, gather alms for its expenses; he should see to it that the Irmandade's goods not be squandered in loans; care for the increase of its patrimony; and admonish all officers and other Brothers and Sisters to do their duty. Only he should write in the books, and no one else. He should pay close attention to the alms and other moneys presented to him and register them immediately along with the Treasurer, with both signing. He shall have all the books, and at the end of the year he will prepare two rolls of all the officers and other persons who are in debt to the Irmandade and will give one to the Brother Treasurer and one to a Procurator, who shall take care of collecting these debts with gentleness, without vexing the Brothers and Sisters. And whatever is collected will be registered with the Treasurer and the receipts that are issued will be signed by the Scribe and the issuer, except that of Masses [which will be signed] by the authority who issues [receipts for] them.

Chapter 17
∽ On the Brother Treasurer and His Duties

The place of Treasurer is of no less circumstance, weight, and consideration, for he is the very key to the Irmandade, and therefore it is determined that he should be a man of good behavior and goods sufficient for the potential of the Irmandade. It is his responsibility to take care of all the goods of the Irmandade, whether gold, silver, or moneys, as well as all the chapel decorations and furniture. Everything will be turned over to him with an inventory prepared by our Brother the Scribe, and signed by both, so that he, the Treasurer, may account for said goods to the new Treasurer at the end of the year. He will take great care to order Masses for the deceased and will not tarry in having them said, always preferring the Father Chaplain, and will make sure the receipts are entered in the appropriate book as specified in Chapter V. He will record his expenses in a notebook for the Scribe to copy into his first book. He will make sure the Procurators, male and female, carry out their duty, whether gathering alms or cleaning the church, and to this end he will go every Sunday and every holy day to the chapel to see and examine the matter specified in this chapter.

Chapter 18
On the Female Procurators and Their Duties

The female Procurators shall be persons of upright morals, diligent, and very vigilant in the service of God and the Irmandade. They will take great care to gather alms every Sunday and Holy Day, and to this end they will place on a table with tablecloth the image of the Saint, and every three months they will present an account to the Brother Scribe and he will do as already ordered, and if this is not possible, then [they will] do it annually. They will alert the female Judges when they should pay their alms, acting carefully, as they should do in identifying others for the following year, all of which we ask them [to do] in the service of our Saint.

Chapter 19
On the Qualities and Duties of Our Father Chaplain

Our Father Chaplain shall be a priest of the most exemplary life and good behavior so that in imitation we shall follow, and we urge him greatly to exhort all the Brothers and Sisters in the holy fear of God, confessing all of them on the days that they ask and helping them at the hour of death, so their passage from this life to the better one will be a good one, accompanying their burial when summoned. He will say the Mass for the deceased and he will be the first [priest] to be so asked, as will also be true for the other Masses this Irmandade is accustomed to having said. If the Father Chaplain does not carry out his duties, he may be expelled from the Irmandade without it needing to state a cause, just as it cannot oblige him to serve against his will, and he too may desist whenever he wishes without giving a reason why.

Chapter 20
Board Procedures and How Votes Shall Be Taken on Any Matter

The Brothers and Sisters of the Board having been summoned, the Procurator or Judge will propose the matter for which they have been called. And having heard the proposal, an urn will be passed around and the deliberation will be by white and black beans, each one casting his or her bean, and whichever proposal receives the most [votes] will be done and [written] in the book of decisions by the Scribe to be observed in the future, and our Procurator shall observe what is written in

Chapter III. And if there is a need to vote *in voce* and not with the urn, the Judge will so order it; but if an officer has some objection to the proposal, he or she will speak of it in secret to the Judge and, if the Judge understands that it is relevant, he will always call for the urn to be passed. And at other meetings of the Board, the elections for the officers to be chosen will proceed with much care, without any assistance from the Reverend Vicar, notwithstanding Chapter II.

Chapter 21
∿ *What to Do on Matters Not Provided For in This Covenant*

When a grave matter arises for resolution and decision by the Board that is not covered by our law, it shall be proposed to the Board and voted on, after which the [entire] Irmandade will be summoned—and it shall be enough if thirty Brothers and Sisters including members of the Board are present—and being thus gathered, the matter shall be proposed once again to all, and voting shall take place by using white and black beans as stipulated in Chapter 20, and whatever the majority decides will, without fail, be understood as the law of this Covenant.

Chapter 22
∿ *How to Proceed with a Disobedient Brother or Sister*

Any Brother or Sister who engages in disorders, riots, or insults with another will be called before the Board where he or she will be quietly admonished. And the same shall be done to anyone who causes or becomes the motive for any persecution of the Irmandade. And not being willing to desist in his or her stubbornness, he or she shall be scratched from the Irmandade, after a hearing which will be called. But if in the future such a Brother or Sister seeks out the Irmandade, confessing his or her blame, then he or she may be once again admitted.

[Actions Taken in 1764]

The chief officer to initial this book and pass it on to the Crown Judge and Procurator, Bahia, September 25, 1764.
As Governor,
[signed] Andrade [Bishop José Carvalho de Andrade was a member of the interim governing council that ruled Bahia from 1761 to 1766]

This book, which will serve as the Covenant of the Saint Anthony of Catagerona Irmandade in the parish of Saint Peter of this city, has thirty-two pages written only on the front, all of which are initialed by me, chief officer of the High Court, with my sign "Lemos," Bahia, September 25, 1764.
[signed] Pedro Ferreira Lemos

The twenty-two chapters and additional clauses of this Covenant contain nothing against His Most Faithful Majesty's laws or good customs and therefore the supplicants should be granted their request, telling them, however, to declare in Chapter 14 [additional clause] the number of priests who shall carry out the ceremonies there determined, which was perhaps not done through an error of whoever wrote it down, since this is one of the principal reasons for its addition on folio 23, and also, that they should sign the Covenant.

[initialed] [presumably by the Crown Judge and Procurator]

[verso]

Satisfy the supplicants in the manner asked for by the Crown Procurator, Bahia, October 6, 1764

As Governor,

[signed] Andrade

Issue authorization, Bahia, October 11, 1764

As Governor

[signed] Andrade

Dom José, by the grace of God, King of Portugal and the Algarves, of this and that side of the ocean, of Africa and Lord of Guinea and the Conquest, Navigation, and Commerce of Ethiopia, Arabia, Persia, India, etc., let it be known by those who this authorization read, that in respect to the Judge and other Brothers and Sisters of the Irmandade of the glorious Saint Anthony of Catagerona located in the parish of Saint Peter in this city having declared in the petition written on the above folio that they, the supplicants, are in possession of said Irmandade with the attached Covenant to which, because it is very ancient and contains several faults as to its provisions and the good operation of the same Irmandade, they have added some chapters that they now present for me to approve and grant them the favor of issuing an authorization in the customary way; and having seen their petition and, from what my High Court Judge and Procurator, having seen it, responded, it has pleased me to approve and confirm to the supplicants the twenty-two chapters and their additional clauses of the Covenant which they should sign since these chapters contain nothing against my laws and good customs, ordering them, however, to declare in Chapter 14 [additional clause] the number of priests [later set at ten] who shall carry out the ceremonies there determined, which was perhaps not done through an error by whoever wrote it down, since this is one of the principal reasons for its addition on folio 23. I therefore order the Ministers to whom this matter concerns to carry it out and ensure that is executed in its entirety and preserved as it is written, without any doubt, embargo, or contradiction. And this shall be registered in the books of the secretariat and will have its effect, assuming that it will have passed first through my Chancery and that the half-annates owed will have been paid. Francisco da Costa Lima did it, in the City of Salvador, Bay of All Saints, on the twelfth day of October,1764. Paid of this [illegible] in the usual way. [In a different hand:] José Ignacio de Alvarenga had it written.

[signed] José Carvalho de Andrade

Archbishopric of Bahia

Authorization by which His Majesty granted the indulgence of approving and confirming to the Judge and other Brothers and Sisters of the Irmandade of Saint Anthony of Catagerona the twenty-two chapters and their additional clauses of this Covenant which they should sign, as they contain nothing against the laws of His Majesty and good customs, ordering them, however, to declare in Chapter 14 [additional clause] the number of priests who shall carry out the ceremonies there determined, which was perhaps not done through an error by whoever wrote it down, since this is one of the principal reasons for its addition on folio 23, as declared above.

For His Majesty to see,

[Seal]

[signed] José Carvalho de Andrade

On folio 32 of the second book of receipts of half-annates, for which Francisco Alvarez Pereira serves as Treasurer-general, there appear revenue credits in the amount of 640 réis, Bahia, October 19, 1764,

[initialed]

Registered on folio 168 of the registry book that serves at the Chancery to [register] Ordinances and Authorizations, Bahia, October 20, 1764,

[signed] Menezes

Paid 640 réis at the Chancery, Bahia, October 20, 1764,

[signed] Menezes

Registered in Registry Book 250 of the respective secretariat, on folio 176, Bahia, October 22, 1764,

[signed] Abreu

Gratis

[on verso of the additional clause to Chapter 14]

Obeying the Royal Order appended to the supplication of the supplicants and based on the learned reply thereon: We declare that the number of priests who shall carry out these offices will be ten, including the Reverend Parish Priest, as this is the custom which is observed. As to the sum which will be paid for them, it is as declared overleaf. —For His Majesty to issue the requested order to confirm this and other chapters of this Covenant. [Fifteen signatures, including that of the] present Scribe of the Irmandade, Judge, Procurators, [and] Counselors, . . . 1764.

~ PART IV

Iberian Rules and American Practices in the Eighteenth Century

40

"As for the Spaniards, their time is up," Jauja, Peru

(1742, 1752)

Near the end of the rainy season, in the last days of May 1742, a man appeared in the upper reaches of the Shimaqui (or Shimá) River near Quisopango. In his navigation of the river systems in the plains beyond the eastern rim of the Andes known as the Pajonal* he had been aided by a Simirinchi (or Piro) leader named Bisabequí. The newcomer, who spoke Quechua as well as Spanish, was about thirty years of age and thought to be a highland Indian, although he was probably a Mestizo. He dressed in a bright red *cushma* (a finely woven tunic favored by the Inka and other Andean peoples for special and ritual occasions) and wore his hair unfashionably short. He came from Cusco, where he was educated in the Colegio of San Francisco de Borja, a school for indigenous noble youths run by the Jesuits, with whom he had traveled to Africa and Spain perhaps as a servant, but more probably as the kind of promising pupil whom the Jesuits were trained to identify in evangelization settings around the world. He called himself Juan Santos Atahualpa, as well as Huayna Capac and Apu Inka, his various epithets suggesting both a Christian identity

and an emphatic pride in a lineage he traced back to Inka royalty.

It emerged that Juan Santos was intent on gathering Indian peoples for a common rebellion against the corruption and abuses of Spanish rule. While his immediate aims appear to have consisted of ridding this vast region of all Spaniards and Blacks, it was also repeatedly claimed by Spanish secular and religious commentators that he meant to go further. His ultimate goal, most contended, was to attract highland peoples to what he had begun in the lowlands and thus to threaten Spanish rule across Peru.

In its most revolutionary, pan-Andean aspects, the rebellion of Juan Santos differed from most of the revolts led by and involving Indians in the central and southern Andes through the eighteenth century. The leaders of these many small-scale revolts were usually local notables who sought the reform of colonial administration rather than its destruction, typically singling out abusive regional officers (*corregidores*), work regimes, and tribute-collecting practices that threatened the indigenous community. As was the case with most

---

* The plains and brush country just to the east of the Andes off the Pachitea, upper Ucayali, and Perené river systems. See Reference Map 6.

of the Creole reformers who were their contemporaries, these Indian leaders conceived of the Spanish Crown as a poorly informed but ultimately benevolent force with the power and will to alleviate the sufferings of Indians as colonial subjects. Juan Santos joins a cluster of much more radical figures whose eighteenth-century uprisings caused much alarm, culminating in the rebellion in the south-central Andes from 1780 to 1782 led by the Mestizo José Gabriel Condorcanqui, who took the name of Túpac Amaru. Like their more moderate contemporaries, Juan Santos, Túpac Amaru, and others sprang from the native and Mestizo elite and, if anything, from the well-educated and more highly Hispanicized slice of the indigenous ruling class, many of whose members prided themselves on their Inka ancestry. As John Rowe has memorably pointed out, to be an authentic Inka in the middle of the eighteenth century was to look good on horseback in your three-cornered hat.

One of the books these late colonial Inkas appear to have read as youths in their Jesuit schools must have resonated with their experience of conditions in Peru and their emerging sense of responsibility as an Indian leadership. The *Royal Commentaries* of Mestizo humanist El Inca Garcilaso de la Vega was written in another time, originally having been published in Spain in 1607, and it was not widely known in Peru until its second edition of 1723. Yet it is not hard to imagine elements of the book speaking to the middle-cultural positions of late colonial Andean nobles such as Juan Santos and Túpac Amaru. Garcilaso's scholarly defense of his mother's people and his idealization of Inka rule came packed with information on the Quechua language, pre-Hispanic titles, symbols, and imperial institutions and achievements, and it even included a clever contention that the lords of Tawantinsuyu had prepared the way for monotheistic Christianity. When Juan Santos and Túpac Amaru dreamt past the mere correction of colonial abuses, and toward a more radical solution that would culminate in an expulsion of the Spaniards and a restored Inka rule, they did not call to

mind the Tawantinsuyu as it had been governed by Atahuallpa or by his father, Huayna Capac. They thought of an Inka monarchy after the model of the king who ruled from Madrid. And they championed their understanding of native Andean cultural traditions and forms while envisioning an Andean Christian future.

Such dreams proved difficult to realize. In Juan Santos's case, any restoration of Inka rule pivoted on whether or not he could transform a rebellion in the vast but relatively remote region on the eastern border of the frontier province of Tarma into a movement embraced by highland and other peoples. His beginning in May 1742 was well chosen. Either Juan Santos or his guide Bisabequí knew what they were doing, for the would-be Inka from Cusco was well received in Quisopango by a disgruntled group of Campa, and by a leader named Santabancori in particular. Only six years earlier, these Campa had been forcefully resettled from another part of the plains, and they harbored no love for the demands of their new situation. Quisopango became the first of a series of home bases from which Juan Santos Atahualpa sent emissaries and issued calls for other peoples to join him.

It is difficult to determine how much the sweepingly paternalistic appeals and manifesto-like messages attributed to Juan Santos by contemporary Spanish commentators reflect his actual words and wishes. The projection of a host of Spanish fears and imaginings seems present in equal measure. Yet, from what can be surmised from reports by missionaries and secular officials, it does appear that Juan Santos's leadership offered both the hope of fundamental change as well as the prospect of immediate vengeance and opportunity. If certain parts of the design attributed to him— such as freedom from work in textile factories and mines, or the reclaiming of a pan-Andean Inkaic title with help from the seafaring English—seem like a mixture of imported fears and revolutionary aims tuned by Juan Santos for ears other than those of the peoples of the mideighteenth-century Pajonal, part of his message was more immediate and local.

There was a fundamental call for a recovery of lands taken from the region's native peoples over the last two centuries as well as for a restoration of traditional authority based upon ritual responsibility and reciprocal gifting between indigenous leaders and economically (as well as politically) interdependent microregions.

The Franciscans, like other religious orders with mission stations on the frontiers of Iberian rule, were accustomed to uprisings led by their indigenous charges that often involved their stubbornly non-Christian neighbors. A religious chronicle treating such regions in the eighteenth century, like one from the two previous centuries, was not complete without its dual emphasis on the evil spread by a few "bad seeds" (commonly presented as trusted converts to Christianity who fall back into error [just like Juan Santos] and turn on their teachers), on the one hand, and heroic efforts and martyrdoms of a new wave of apostles, on the other. Even so, the effect of Juan Santos's arrival and call for a gathering of native peoples across the region seems to have startled the Franciscans. Their correspondence tells of over twenty functioning mission settlements (*conversiones*, most of which had been established at least sixty and as many as one hundred years before) of Ene, Perené, Cerro de la Sal, and Chanchamayo, abandoned by neophytes who answered the call of Juan Santos Atahualpa.

The first of the two documents in the selection is a letter written by Father Domingo García, a Franciscan from the College of Santa Rosa de Ocopa active in the missions based in Cerro de la Sal, to his superior about a month after Juan Santos had arrived in the region. Fear is emerging and little is understood, much less confirmed. The ideas, words, and actions of Juan Santos Atahualpa are, by the time that García's rendering is committed to ink, thirdhand. He tells of what two African slaves, who have narrowly escaped the uprising with their lives, report Juan Santos to have done and said. The slaves, for their part, appear to have offered more than casually gathered or simply sensational hearsay. They

claim to have learned much of what they reported from a meeting with Juan Santos himself, a solemn occasion in which he not only represented himself and his goals at considerable length but in which he also asked the slaves to swear not to misrepresent him to others.

Local violence had erupted quickly in the Franciscan mission towns. It appears to have been focused against perceived local oppressors, especially the Black slaves whose work it was to act as the friars' armed guards and foremen in the conversiones. Some, like García's informants El Congo and Francisco, managed to flee and tell their tale. But others were captured, apparently mutilated, and their hated weapons seized. Domingo García paints a picture of Juan Santos as a moderate leader in the face of these early eruptions against the Black slaves, a picture supported by other contemporary sources, and one can legitimately ask whence this picture comes. While García notes that the rebel leader made no secret of the fact that he wanted Blacks (as well as Spaniards) to be gone from his kingdom, the friar also claims that Juan Santos actively opposed the people's opportunistic attacks and proposals of vengeful killings of the guards, to the point of traveling with some of them as a force of restraint. García, whose apparently stern hand guided the indoctrination and moral reform of Indians in the mission town of Eneno, alleges a similar split between the Indian followers' purported wish to be rid of the Franciscans and Christianity entirely and Juan Santos's desire to maintain both, though very much according to his own terms.

Domingo García's resigned postscript, signed with two other friars, expresses regret and justification for the Franciscans' retreat from the zone of hostility, but what is most palpable is his fear and uncertainty. He and his companions were unarmed and without the protection of their fleeing Black slaves; neither the loss of their mission towns nor even of the whole kingdom of Peru is inconceivable. In June 1742 the friars decide not to chance a meeting with the rebel leader to confirm what El Congo and Francisco had reported. When, in September 1742, about three months after the following letter was written, Father Domingo García and a companion did descend to the Pajonal, it was not as part of an embassy to Juan Santos but rather as an advance party intent on smoothing the way for a company of soldiers sent by the viceroy from the highlands to apprehend the rebel. The two Franciscans did not get far before they were killed by the followers of Juan Santos Atahualpa.

∾ *Long live Jesus! To the Very Reverend Padre Comisario Father José Gil Muñoz,*

The *padre presidente* [of this Franciscan mission region] wrote some time ago to warn that an Indian who said he was the Inka had appeared in the Pajonal and was calling out to all the peoples of the mountains and surrounding hinterlands. He [the mission administrator] asked if I would go down there to see him [the one calling himself Inka] about turning the peoples of the hinterlands away from rising up; I went down as far as Eneno, where I learned more than they told me in [Cerro de] la Sal. I ordered that no Indian from my town, nor from any of the others, should go down there. I went down to discover the truth about all this in order to advise you.

I came to the town of Pichana, where I found the padre alone, abandoned by the people, all of whom had fled against his will. Two Blacks named El Congo and Francisco, showing much alarm and all worked up from just having fled from down there themselves, have arrived with news that the Inka has told them he will talk, and we are preparing to descend to the Pajonal tomorrow, June 3. The Inka calls for Father Manuel del Santo, stating clearly that he [Father Manuel] should come alone, unaccompanied by either another padre or a Black. Not daring to have the padre go by himself, I am determined to accompany him. Yet, before we leave, it seems essential that we write to you, Reverend Father, about what we have just heard from the mouths of these Blacks, so that you, Reverend Father, can notify and inform whoever should know of these things, and so that the fathers [in their home convent at Santa Rosa de Ocopa] can read the letter; even though you are not now in Ocopa, we send an open letter [so that others can read it]. The report [what El Congo and Francisco have told us] is the following:

An Indian has come along who says he is an Inka from Cusco (called Atahualpa), brought down the river by a Simirinchi [or Piro] *kuraka* (indigenous governor) named Bisabequi. He says he has three brothers back in Cusco, one older and two younger than he, that he is a little more than thirty years old, and that his house is named *piedra* [rock]. His intention, he says, is to recover the crown taken by [the Spanish conquistador Francisco] Pizarro and the rest of the Spaniards who killed his father [Atahualpa Inka] (through whose line he becomes the Inka) and sent his head to Spain.

He says that he was in Angola and the Congos [in Africa], and that he has spoken with the English, with whom he has entered into an agreement that they will come by sea and help him take back his crown, while he will proceed by land, gathering his people, all toward recovering his crown; and that to this end he sent his brothers, especially the older one, into the hinterlands. He assures people that he means well, that he does not intend to introduce a new law, but only the true one which the padres preach, and that once he has managed to gather the people here [in the forests and plains], he will climb with them to Quimiri, where he will call on the highlanders, his vassals, to join the enterprise. But [he says] that before this happens, Father Manuel del Santo must come alone, as he wants to write to the viceroy to demand the restoration of the crown that is rightfully his, or else he will come and take it by force.

His call is out to all the Amajes [and Amuesha], the Andes [Campa], the Cunibos [Cunibo], Sepibos [Shipibo], and Simirinchis [and Piro], and already he has brought the majority of them together and under his command. All are crying out [to him, saying] that they do not want padres, that they do not want to be Christians, and urging him to allow them to kill the Blacks, to which end they already have tied up three people and cut them across their faces with a knife. The Inka does not know about this [that is, the native people's actions against people of African descent and perhaps also their opposition to Franciscans], and [if he did] he would object to all of it, for he quarrels with them when they talk of it. The Indians—the Christians among them as much as the infidels—are holding many dances, as they are very pleased with their new King. They speak a thousand things against the Spaniards and the Blacks, and they do not pay any attention to the padres, but rather congratulate themselves a thousand times over for the coming of the cure for their ills.

(It is said that) this Inka speaks the highland language [Quechua, as well as] the Andes' [or Antis'] tongue [Campa], and Spanish. He calls upon all Indians, as we have said, but does not allow Blacks or Spaniards into his presence because [he believes] all of them to be thieves who have stolen his crown. He says that there are only three kingdoms in this world: that of Spain, that of Angola, and his own. And that while he has not gone to steal the kingdom from another, the Spaniards have come to steal his from him.

As for the Spaniards, [he says that] their time is up, and that his Kingdom has returned to him. His vassals have been worn out by the Spaniards [he says,] but already the textile workhouses, the bakeries, and [the many other] slaveries are at an end, since he does not permit slaves, nor the rest of the Spaniards' tyrannies, in his Kingdom. [He says] that now the padres will have to journey into the hinterlands to teach their Indians, but that [when they come] they must not be accompanied by Blacks or *viracochas* (Spaniards). And if the padres do not like it thus, [Juan Santos says that] he will bring the matter before the bishop of Cusco so that the Indians will be ordained as padres, for among the Blacks he has seen Black padres, with long beards, saying Mass. He says that although they were not Whites like the Spaniards, they make very good padres and priests. As for the Governor, he says that he [this Spanish official] comes to his hinterlands like a pig (the term is his [Juan Santos's]), frightening his Indians, tying them up, and carrying them away. And now [he says that] the Governor is no more, nor is there a King apart from himself.

He repeats that he calls upon all the Indians from the highlands, and that if the padres prevent them from coming down to join him he will be greatly angered. [Juan Santos says] that when he sent word to the people of Sonomoro, they answered that they would not be coming because there were many Blacks who would block their way, to which he replied that he had feet to come find them.

He chews a lot of *coca* leaves and sends gifts to the towns so they will keep up the supply, and from it he shares with those who have none. He says that it [*coca*] is the Plant of God and not that of the witches, as the *viracochas* [Spaniards] claim.

He says that they [the Indians he calls to follow] are not surprised to find him poor, since everything [of his] has been stolen, but [also] that he has much gold and silver hidden away and that later, when he is crowned as King, he will reveal it, though he does not have more than the Spaniards possess.

In the uprising in the mission town of Sabirosqui, everything was taken, including the Blacks' guns, which he [Juan Santos] said he would return to the padres. And he advised that all Blacks should leave the Pajonal, as has happened. I had given three knives to a Black so that he could buy me three *cusmas,* and they were taken; but he [Juan Santos] will return them to me. He [Juan Santos] ordered that all the cattle that we had in Sabirosqui be rounded up in order to sell them; he said they were good livestock, and that he would also approve of taking sheep, but not pigs, because they were bad livestock. He had I do not know how many of the town's pigs killed.

His home base is Quisopango with [the protection of the Campa leader] Santabancori; he only went to Sabirosqui to be with the Indians who wanted to kill Blacks and help themselves to what was in the houses. He is in Quisopango now, and from there he orders everyone to gather.

All this—and much more that we suppress as insubstantial and so as not to go on and on—the Inka told the Blacks. Taking out a silver crucifix that he wears at his heart, he made them swear before Christ that they would tell the truth and not add to, or leave out, any of what he had said, and with that he took his leave of them.

One of the Blacks fled under cover of night. . . . The other was caught and tied up by the Indians that night, but by morning he had managed to free himself and get away. We can see the marks made by the bonds on his arms.

All of what is said above happened in Sabirosqui, and now, as we have noted, he [Juan Santos Atahualpa] is in Quisopango waiting on the Indians he has called upon—men, women, children, everyone. We write all this, and only what the Blacks have said, in the town of Pichana. Tomorrow we will go down to [the mission town of] San Tadeo [de los Antis], and the following day we will aim to arrive in Quisopango. We will see him and speak with him, employing appropriate shrewdness and caution until we know his intention, and once it is understood to the best of our ability, we will advise you of everything.

[Finally,] we add that he is a highland Indian, dressed in a *cusma* and nothing else; these Indians have said other things [about Juan Santos], but these were lies and their own imaginings.

We ask that you, Reverend Father, commend us heartily to God and that our brothers will do the same, and we ourselves ask that His Divine Majesty watch over Your Grace for many years to come. Pichana, June 2, 1742.

Fray Manuel del Santo
Fray Domingo García

Postscriptum [not dated, but perhaps as soon as the next day]:

This is to confirm the news contained on this paper, except for the resolution of the Reverend Fathers Manuel and Domingo to go down there. So as not to contravene the orders of the Reverend *padre presidente* of [the missions in] Quimiri, and according to the common consent of the three signed below, we have decided to withdraw back to Quimiri, bringing all the ornaments from the convents and churches with us. The people in all the towns are greatly stirred and unheeding of anything the padres order or ask of them; taking their women and children, they rush to go down [to the Pajonal] in search of their new King or Inka. Many times it seems that this people deserve the curse which Christ Our Father ordered to be cast, Matthew 10: 14: *Et quicunque non receperit vos neque audierit sermones vestros, executies foras de demo, vel civitate excutite pulverem de pedibus vestris.* [And whosoever shall not receive you, nor hear your words, when ye depart out of that house or city, shake off the dust of your feet.]

I ask that there not be the least doubt about the information expressed here, and that it help bring about the necessary measures, and also that failings on the part of some in no way bring about the loss of the mission towns or maybe even the kingdom [of Peru]. Those who sign below do not take this decision [not to proceed with the plan to go down to talk with Juan Santos] lightly, but rather because the people are in such a state that at even the slightest hint they obey the orders of their new King even when, to be accurate, they do not agree with the intentions of this evil man. [Also,] if the padres had come face to face with him, they would have had to inform him of the truth, and they could not have anticipated good things to have come from their assertion that he has no right to his Kingdom, etc. And, what is more, the Blacks have been frightened off; there are none of them about, nor any of their guns. This is the sense of things from the Reverend Fathers, *salvo meliori* [save anything better], the below signed—

Fray Manuel del Santo
Fray José Cabanes
Fray Domingo García

Here we move on to the second introduction and text within this selection. By 1752, the rebellion had been going on for a decade. At least two things about it stand out. First, it seems clear that Juan Santos's stated objective of taking back lands stolen in Spanish colonial times was more than generally appealing to his indigenous followers. It was an objective taken literally and locally, and one in which a number of native peoples achieved promising results. By the end of 1752, groups of Amuesha, Piro, and Campa had gradually reclaimed all the regions inhabited by their ancestors in the early seventeenth century, sending into flight the few Indians who had remained loyal to their friar's wishes in places such as Sonomoro.

Second, while Juan Santos's followers had not been decisively defeated by the forces that two viceroys had dispatched to the region, the larger goal consistently attributed to the rebel chief by Spanish commentators remained unfulfilled. The dream and/or fear that Juan Santos's message would spill into the highlands and ignite a larger uprising that would threaten the Spanish government in Peru was foundering. Bold and decisive raids by the Inka struck chords of fear that reverberated through officialdom, but in a larger sense they were fleeting incursions.

Responses directed from Lima and the Tarma frontier tended to be tardy and repressive and, as time passed, to share the singular goal of preventing the problem of Juan Santos from spreading beyond the plains. When, in 1750, three local conspiracies of Indians in the provinces of Huarochirí, Canta, and Lambayeque were thought by authorities to have links to Juan Santos and to have organized themselves toward a common rising, the response was dramatic and decisive. The apprehended conspirators were publicly executed, their heads displayed in the plaza in Lima, and the viceroy immediately moved to deploy five new companies of soldiers in Tarma and Jauja. The fact that one of the escaping highland rebels appears to have taken refuge with Juan Santos suggests that the viceregal fear of localized protests becoming a spreading conflagration may not have been pure fantasy.

Negotiating peace on the Tarma frontier had been tried in the first years of the insurrection by religious (especially Franciscans, but also Jesuits) with knowledge of the region and its peoples. The most substantial of the peace proposals was set down by a Franciscan, Father Joseph de San Antonio, in a *memorial* sent to the king of Spain on July 11, 1750. San Antonio was openly critical of Spanish treatment of Indians in the region as well as of officials' handling of the uprising thus far, to the point of blaming the insurrection entirely on the authorities and the bad example of the Spaniards. He proposed that his home convent at Ocopa be given authority over sixty fresh missionaries in the region, and that the Indian insurrectionaries be issued a general pardon and invited into a network of new and fortified missions, the construction and development of which the friars would oversee. San Antonio suggested that the rebellion would only grow if his proposal or something very like it did not win support. He conjured up a specter even more unsettling to his readers than the one at which Father Domingo García had hinted eight years before: the possibility of Juan Santos setting out for Lima with 200 of his best Indian archers and sparking a general uprising across the land as he went.

The viceroy and his frontier governors did not have to take the Franciscan at his word. In August 1752, Juan Santos himself sent a reminder of his capacity to surprise when he led another short-lived but daring raid on the mountain towns of Andamarca and Acobamba in the valley of San Fernando. The towns submitted to his show of force and he proceeded to take prisoners, among them two friars, and some livestock. Three days later, Juan Santos had released his prisoners and abandoned his highland position for the safety of the plains, leaving the padres and the townspeople to tell a now fast-arriving company of soldiers what had happened.

The following document is the deposition of one Pedro de Torres, a Mestizo from the town of Apata, who claimed that he was taken prisoner by followers of Juan Santos Atahualpa in their assaults in this area in the first days of August 1752, and that, after being marched with the rebels as far as Andamarca, he had managed to escape. Torres's testimony was heard and recorded in Concepción on August 11, 1752, by the Marqués de Cassatorres Don Laureano José de Torres y Ayala, the *corregidor* and chief justice in the province of Jauja, and the latest brigadier of the royal army charged with mopping up after the fact.

While carefully critical of Juan Santos and the rebellion in general, Pedro de Torres also provides a hint of what becoming Juan Santos's "prisoner" actually meant, and of the message that Juan Santos and his emissaries were said to have broadcast in local highland settings in the hope of expanding his base of support and inspiring new recruits to the rebellion.

The incidents in Andamarca in August 1752, described below, have traditionally marked a beginning to the end of the hostilities attributed to Juan Santos Atahualpa. He had once again eluded capture and direct defeat, but his inability to consolidate a highland base from which his rebellion might spread marked a limit on what he would achieve. Similarly, most commentators have found in Brigadier Pablo Sáez de Bustamante's unopposed arrival in Quimiri in 1756 proof of the rebels' further disintegration and an epilogue to this episode in colonial Andean history. Moreover, a Franciscan report from the upper Ucayali region in the mid-1760s, claiming that Juan Santos Atahualpa had died in Metraro perhaps as much as a decade earlier, seemed to mark an even more decisive end; here was evidence from two of his Campa followers, who purportedly told a friar that the Inka had "gone up in smoke."

Juan Santos may have died around 1756 at the treacherous hands of one of his wavering followers, and the fear of his expanding rebellion may have receded for officials in Peru, but it is less clear that his physical dis-appearance mattered for everyone concerned. How much was changing for the indigenous peoples of the hinterlands whose possibilities had been transformed over the past dozen years? In 1766 a Setebo leader named Runcato gathered together his own people, the Shipibo, the Cunibo, and groups of Campa and Piro in a new uprising in the Ucayali region, keeping the vast area off the eastern slopes of the Andes as unattractive to Spanish colonizers and administrators as it had become between 1742 and 1756. What is more, when two fortified missions were tentatively constructed by the Franciscans (just as Father Joseph de San Antonio had proposed) as late as 1788 and 1789, they wrote as if Juan Santos Atahualpa was very much alive and as if his followers were about to renew hostilities. For many, the attack on Andamarca in 1752, about which we learn from the point of view of Pedro de Torres, may not have begun to signal an end at all.

~ *Deposition of Pedro de Torres*

In the said town, and on the same day, month, and year [Concepción, August 11, 1752], the said gentleman, the Marqués de Cassatorres, was told of how Pedro de Torres, a Mestizo from the town of Apata, and one of the people taken prisoner by the Chunchos [a generic term, like "Antis" or "Andes" for indigenous groups in the hinterlands] last year, had now found himself back in Apata, having fled from Andamarca on the fourth day of the current month [August 4, 1752], in the blockade the Rebel experienced. He appeared before His Lordship, and before me the public notary, swearing an oath before God and making the sign of the Cross, as the law prescribes. Thus entrusted, he promised to tell the truth about what he knew and was asked, and here follows the sense of what he said:

[He declared] that he was one of the prisoners the Chunchos had taken in their incursion on Uchubamba last year, and that in his estimation he was among the some 300 captured. He was taken, along with the rest, on a three-day march through Chontabamba, Monobamba, Vitoc, and Chanchamayo, until they reached Metraro, where the Rebel [Juan Santos Atahualpa] was staying. They were taken into his presence, and he received them, treating them as sons and daughters, and uttering some heretical propositions such as: "Come over here, my children: I am the owner of all these lands and the son of the True God." [The declarant said] that hearing this [statement], along with other similar heresies, had saddened him and he had called out to the Blessed Mary, and not in a voice soft enough to have been missed by the Rebel. He [Juan Santos] scolded him and threatened to kill him with a club [*macana de chonta*], asking him why he was distressed, and telling him that this Mary of his was in Spain, and that he was not to mention her, but only to believe in him, [and] that he was the omnipotent God, absolute owner of all he had created. [The declarant said further] that he [Juan Santos] then ordered all of them to worship him and kiss his feet, as he said the following words: "Apo Capac Huayna, Jesús Sacramentado" [Lord Huayna Capac, Holy Jesus].

The declarant said that in this way he [Juan Santos] surrounded himself with followers. The highlanders were as many as forty, all with their wives, and the Chunchos were even more numerous, gathered according to their towns and villages. They all worked together in their plots of land and showed him much obedience and subordination. All this he [the declarant] could see going on from the jail [in which he and others were confined].

As soon as Easter was over in this present year [1752], the Rebel summoned all the Indian nations, pleasing each of their *caciques* [native governors] with [the gift of] a knife, and made plans to push at his frontiers. Last month, in July, he set out with a first party of Chunchos, which looked to be 600 or 800 strong, marching toward the Tarma frontier region. And, although about half of them deserted along the way, he came to the lumbering settlement of Ata and then the ranch of Runatullo on Tuesday, the first of this month [August]. From there, on Wednesday, they passed to Yauricalla. And early on Thursday [August 2,] they arrived at the town of Andamarca, having sent an Indian messenger ahead from Runatullo to ask if they [the townspeople] received him as their Inka or not, and thus if they chose peace or war; the messenger did not return.

The Rebel rushed straight in and met no resistance; two gunshots were all I heard, as well as the voice of an Indian from Andamarca crying out, "You are our Inka, come on in!" Having thus been allowed to enter, and arriving at the town square, he [Juan Santos] began to quarrel with the padre (Father Mauricio Gallardo), whom he took prisoner, along with his companion (Father Juan Fresneda). By this time, night had fallen and he [the declarant] seized his moment to escape to his town of Apata.

He said, under the oath he has sworn, that what he has declared is what he knows to be the truth. Having read over the declaration, he agreed and confirmed it, along with the fact that he is forty years of age and does not know how to write; at his request, his name was signed by one of the witnesses present, Don Julián Carrillo and Don Manuel de Marticorena.

[signed] Marqués de Cassatorres.
At the request of the declarant, and as a witness: Manuel de Marticorena.
Juan de Messa Valera, public notary

41

Nicolás Ñenguirú's Letter to the Governor of Buenos Aires

(1753)

The province of Paraguay in the interior of southern South America had a singular colonial experience. It was remote from the centers of Spanish colonial activity but was strategically located on the frontier with Portuguese Brazil. Few of the resources that drew concerted Spanish interest were present—no precious metals, no Indian state societies—but there were peaceable Guaraní Indians clustered along the banks of the Paraguay, Uruguay, and Paraná rivers, not far from hostile neighbors in the Chaco region. Many of the Guaraníes accepted a modified encomienda system in the vicinity of the colonial capital of Asunción and mission settlements on the eastern fringe of the province.

The Crown and Church would not invest heavily in administering territory that did not at least cover costs, and accounts of Paraguay throughout the colonial period stressed the general poverty and lack of money in the province. Yet it was important to extend and consolidate a Spanish colonial presence in Paraguay as a buffer against Portuguese expansion and other European designs on Spanish territory. The result was that the province had a long military tradition, considerable independence, and poorly defined boundaries.

Lay and ecclesiastical settlers were allowed considerable freedom. From its beginnings in the 1550s, the long-lived encomienda system developed in a peculiar way, with Spanish *encomenderos* residing among their Guaraní subjects, relying on kinship networks and traditions of chieftainship as much as on military prowess for their authority, fathering many children, and speaking both Spanish and Guaraní—the beginnings of a bilingual, Mestizo society. The result is the only country in modern Latin America that is bilingual, with both a European and a native official language. By the 1570s nearly all the encomenderos were Mestizos. The "Spanish" Mestizo residents of little Asunción came to exercise a virtual veto power over the appointment and tenure of royal governors sent out from Lima. And thirty Jesuit missions were founded in the early seventeenth century among Guaraní people to the east in both Spanish and Portuguese territory, distant from provincial authorities in Asunción and Buenos Aires, not to mention Lima and Madrid. Except in these frontier missions, the Church and priests in Paraguay were much less important than in the central areas of the Spanish empire. There was no Pedro de Gante, no missionary "Twelve," no Las Casas looming large in a "spiritual conquest" of the Asunción hinterland. Few priests settled there at all in the sixteenth century, and few of those who did learned the Guaraní language.

The Jesuit missions were important to the colonial state in stabilizing a frontier with the Portuguese and resisting the slaving expeditions of *bandeirantes* (explorers and fortune seekers in the interior of Brazil) from São Paulo, but they were controversial as virtually self-governing armed refuges run by Jesuit priests, which sometimes tipped the balance of political power in the province. In 1750 international politics broke in on Paraguay and its local controversies. The Spanish and Portuguese monarchies agreed to terms of peace in the Treaty of Madrid, which attempted to define more clearly the imperial borders in South America. Lands occupied for Spain east of the Uruguay River in Paraguay were to be turned over to the Portuguese and the settlements there disbanded. Seven Jesuit missions were affected. Guaraní people in these seven communities resisted in various ways their transfer to Brazil, leading to the sporadic fighting and negotiations of the so-called Guaraní War from 1753 to 1756.

The Guaraní settlements were more inclined to fight in the 1750s, when they were faced with removal from their lands, than they were in 1767, when the Jesuits were expelled from all Spanish territories. Recent scholarship by Barbara Ganson and James Saeger indicates that the Jesuits controlled Guaraní lives and loyalties less than suggested by the usual emphasis on Jesuit actions and the regimentation of mission life. Rather than suddenly abandoning the missions, the Guaraní residents participated in the gradual breakdown of the mission system after other religious orders took the Jesuits' place. Guaraní militias continued to play a role in imperial defense, but the Indians began to leave for work on plantations or as artisans in towns, and thereby avoid the tribute tax or escape mistreatment by colonial authorities and labor contractors. Perhaps the heaviest blow to the missions as viable communities was the royal decree in 1800 that freed Guaraní residents from communal labor obligations. In any event, there was no widespread retreat into the forests; most of the former mission Guaraní people continued to find their living within colonial society.

The following 1753 letter was one kind of response by Guaraní leaders in the seven missions to orders from the colonial governor at Buenos Aires to disband their settlements or face a war to the death. Six of the seven mission communities replied in writing to the governor's order. The author of the longest reply was Nicolás Ñenguirú, the Indian *corregidor* of La Concepción (Figure 30). He became the nominal commander of Guaraní mission soldiers in 1756, but he was always more a man of words than an effective military leader. Philip Caraman, a Jesuit historian of the Paraguay missions, regards him as an "ignorant pawn" for not being a more determined fighter, but Ñenguirú enjoyed more prestige and respect in his community than Caraman's view allows, and his letter to the governor suggests that he was no simple tool of the governor (or of the Jesuits).

The Guaraní letters of 1753 claimed a moral right to their settlements that, they said, the Spanish Crown had endorsed. The letters argue for an implicit contract between the king and the Guaraníes: they had not been conquered by the Spaniards. Rather, they had chosen to accept Christianity and the protection of the king of Spain. The king was the representative of God, not just of the Spaniards, and thus the Guaraníes' lands belonged to them by divine right. They had, they said, always been loyal subjects of the king, and it was inconceivable that he could wish to expel them from their lands.

Ñenguirú's letter is worth reading for its elaboration of the case for Guaraní mission rights. It raises questions about how the author positions himself with the governor concerning the likelihood of open rebellion. Does he present himself with hat in hand, contrite and obsequious? Does he presume to speak for "his people"? On the other hand, what are his relations with the Jesuits? Could this letter have been ghost-written by a Jesuit missionary at La Concepción? And in what sense could this letter be read as a colonial communication? Does his stance as a loyal Christian subject calling for mutual responsibility compare with the position of Felipe Guaman Poma de Ayala (see Selection 27)? We should remember that Paraguay was not Peru or central Mexico, and Ñenguirú was not in the same situation as Guaman Poma.

Governor, Sir:

Hearing your letter has given us a great fright. We cannot believe that the saintly heart of our king has ordered us to move—a most troublous thing. And so we say that this is not our king's will. Of course, the Portuguese, we say to you, those enemies of our well-being, want to make us move for their own wicked reasons.

We also have another letter from our king, in which the deceased father of our king lets us understand his heart very well, the love he has for us. He approves of our way of life, our church, even what we have done in war [in the king's service], and he is consoled by what we have so readily done in all matters, according to his wishes. "Well done," his congratulatory letter says to us. His letter also tells us: "I will remember you, I will help you, I will take good care of you, and my governor also will help you; and I have ordered him to free you of all harm." Therefore we say: How can it be that these two letters from our king are so unequal, so different? Our king would not err in his words. Why should he now harass us, burdening us when we have not failed him, impoverishing us greatly without cause, wanting to expel us from our land in order to give the Portuguese our possessions and what we have worked so hard to create? To lose us without more ado? This, sir, we cannot believe, nor do we know how to believe it. So we say: This is not the will of our king. If he knew about this, if he could hear our words, he would be angry, he would not see it as a good thing, and he would not approve of our removal.

Sir, we have never gone against our king, nor against you. You know this well. With all our heart we have honored your commands; we have always followed them very well. For love of you we have given our possessions, our animals, even our lives. This is why we cannot believe that our king would repay our faithfulness with an order to leave our lands. Our Indians, our children speak constantly of this; and, growing angry, they are going to extremes, acting as if they were in rebellion. They no longer wish to hear our words as those of their corregidor and the cabildo [council]. They get angry at us and only their caciques [chiefs] sway them. It is now useless for us to say anything to them about this move. You know very well how the Indians are when they are oppressed by some excessive, harmful demand. If we tell them, with respect to their pueblo, to send away the vassals of our king, force them out into the open country in the name of our king, take away their possessions, impoverish them, beggar them without cause—if we tell them this, you will hear what they say and you will see their anger. Sir, listen, you should also hear the true words of these our children, just as they speak them to us. They say: "In former times our sainted father named Roque González de Santa Cruz, as soon as he arrived, taught us about God and also to be Christians. Not even one Spaniard entered this land. By our own free will we chose to place God above all, and then also our king so that he would always be our protector. For this reason alone we submitted and humbled ourselves. And we chose to do so. The king gave his word to our grandparents to treat us well. And he has always repeated this same promise to us. Then how is it that suddenly he wants to break his promise?"

"This land," say our children, "was given to us by God alone. In this land our sainted teacher Roque González and many [Jesuit] fathers died among us, they raised us, and they labored for us alone. Why, then, are the Portuguese so intent upon this when it is none of their business? The magnificent church, the good pueblo, the ranch for our animals, the maté plantation, the cotton fields, the farmland and all that is needed to work it is a great endeavor that we alone have accomplished. How can they presume to take away the possessions that belong to us, and wrongly mock us? It will not be so. God Our Lord does not wish this, will not stand for it; nor is it the will of our sainted king. We have not erred in anything, we have taken nothing from the Portuguese. They will never pay us anything for what we alone have built."

Never even in the remote past have our [Jesuit] fathers spoken to our children of such a move. They have cared for us, indeed they have. They have always loved us well. Only now do we hear these words from them. Only now do they speak wrongly to persuade us to leave our pueblos and lose our well-being. So, what is this? By chance did they remove our grandparents from the mountains for this? Did they congregate and teach them just to send them away again now? Is this what the padre comisario [the Jesuit delegate, Luis Altamirano] was sent for? He certainly has made our [Jesuit] fathers into something other than what they were. They weren't as they are now. He has bothered them, badly. He certainly is a new kind of father to come to this our land. He does not offer anything that we need. He has not labored for our love. Wrongly he wishes to remove us from our pueblos and lands, suddenly, hurriedly, period. He wants to cast us out to the mountains as if we were rabbits, or to the open countryside as if we were snails, far away, even if it is bad weather or winter. He only wants to impoverish us. He seems to want to finish us off. This is what the Indians say to us: "This is not the will of God, nor does He wish it. This is not Christian conduct. We, too, are Christians, children of the Church, our mother. We have never failed the Church nor our king." The padre comisario does say, in the name of our king: "Send them out in poverty. Go far away, to the edge of the mountains. Look for your livelihood there. Go to the countryside. Take your belongings. Work there, grow tired, experience illness and poverty." This way, they say, you will also achieve our sense of poverty and will learn to have compassion for us. We gain no consolation from him, for he does not know our language. He does not know how to speak to us, he cannot hear our words. So the Indians say to us. After this, our children repeatedly say to us: "Where do they want to send us? And they want us to go suddenly, hurriedly to a bad land. Good land has not been found for even three pueblos, much less for our animals.

And our fathers seem happy that two pueblos are to be founded in a bog where we are sure to die, saying that no good land can be found. They have not even allowed us time to move gradually. Therefore they wrongly mean only to see us destroyed."

Sir, I have written these words of the Indians to you, and they are their true words. We, the members of the cabildo, have no more words to calm them, nor to oppose them when they become angry. Therefore we humble ourselves before you so that, in the words of the king, you will help us. In the first place, all of us are your vassals: please let our king know of our poverty and what we are suffering, and send him my letter, wherever he may be, so that he himself will see, that he will hear and understand our poverty and tribulations. Our Lord God made him our king; we chose him to take care of us. We have not erred in anything to justify being abandoned. So we trust in his good heart, that he must take pity and mercy on us, then we will all fulfill his will most willingly. In the second place, Sir, for the love of God, if you do not believe these to be our true words, send someone, even if it be two good Spaniards whom you trust, so that they can hear our words and see with their own eyes. They cannot but help telling you the pure truth. We desperately need you to do this, and since we are in such need, we hope that they will come. Surely, God Our Lord hears the words of the poor.

Finally, Sir, this my pueblo of La Concepción is not bad, although there are misgivings here. It is not on the other shore of the Uruguay River. We have two ranchos in that land, two maté plantations. If this land is taken from us, we and the people of this pueblo will be in a very poor state. We have been looking for some suitable land and do not know where to find it. That great cacique named Nicolás Ñenguirú is my true grandfather. It was he who, long ago, at the beginning, allowed the sainted father Roque González to enter. He revered and loved greatly the words concerning faith in God. From this my pueblo Indians, all children and relatives of mine, went to the other shore of the Uruguay River to establish two pueblos. They wanted me (and they asked me to do so) to inform you in this my letter of their poverty and suffering. All of us, every day, pray before God and put our trust in Him. May this same Lord give you a good heart and long life, and may God protect you eternally so that you may help us well. At La Concepción, July 1753. Nicolás Ñenguirú, corregidor.

Plan of the Jesuit Mission at La Concepción, Paraguay

This late colonial plan of Nicolás Ñenguirú's home community shows the standard buildings and configuration of space in a Jesuit mission of Paraguay. The Indian community was arrayed in long blocks (F) around a large plaza, more than a football-field's length on each side. Facing east onto the plaza and dominating the layout is the Jesuits' compound (A to E): the church, cemetery, school, residence patios, and large "garden" plot, presumably worked collectively under supervision by the missionaries. A separate building (G) located close to the school and living quarters of the missionaries was reserved for widows and orphans, or perhaps served as the hospital.

The neat layout recalls the typical grid plan of colonial towns in Spanish America that was inspired by imperial Rome, but there are differences. The church compound with double patios for schooling, the manual arts, and residences for the priests is the principal feature here. There are no town offices or other civic architecture to rival its prominence on the plaza. The residential blocks face the plaza rather than running in many long lines toward it. The effect was to make the plaza and the Jesuits' compound a more interior, protected place. The residential blocks of the mission settlement also have a more standardized appearance than the usual colonial town. Built as one continuous structure, each block was divided into one-room family dwellings with connecting walls and private entrances. The front of each dwelling consisted of a doorway and one window with a long portico running the length of the block. The rear wall of each connected dwelling had another window. In most older, better established missions the buildings were of cut stone with tile roofs. Typically, there was a large cross at each corner of the plaza, and in the center a statue of the Virgin Mary or the patron saint of the community.

Key
A. Church
B. Cemetery
C. School
D. Patios
E. Garden
F. Blocks of Guaraní dwellings with their porticos
G. "House of the needy" (*casa de miserias*)

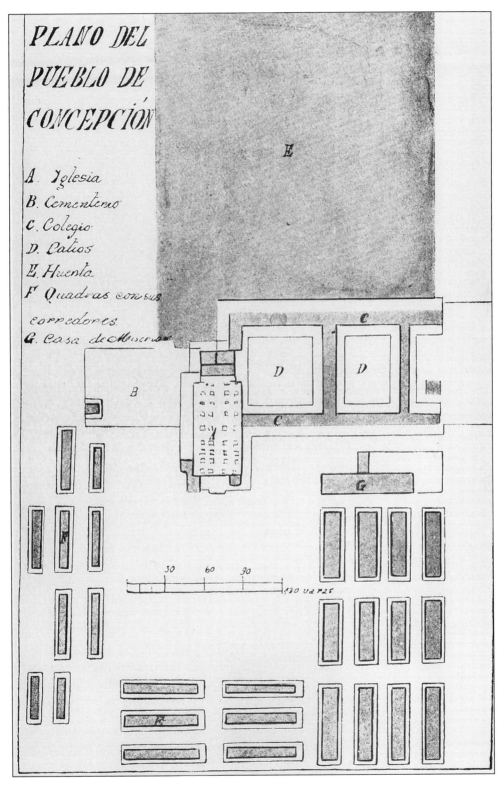

Figure 30. Plan of La Concepción mission, Paraguay, in late colonial times.
Courtesy of the Academia Nacional de Bellas Artes, Buenos Aires.

42

José de Gálvez's Decrees
for the King's Subjects in Mexico

(1769, 1778)

✑ Regulations on Wages and Peonage, Sonora, 1769

José de Gálvez was a chief architect of Bourbon reforms in the American colonies, especially for New Spain. As *visitador* for New Spain and then Minister of the Indies, he oversaw the creation of a vast military district for the northern frontier (the Comandancia de Provincias Internas), intendancies for the entire viceroyalty south of the Provincias Internas, and other new administrative offices. He established the first Academy of Fine Arts (Academia de San Carlos in Mexico City), which promoted neoclassical restraint; tripled the public rents; corrected various abuses; reduced restrictions on trade; and moved to give practical, strictly regulated meanings to "freedom" and "equality," two watchwords of eighteenth-century Europe that, conceived more broadly, became closely associated with revolution in France and the United States.

Wage labor came within his restless regulatory gaze. As Charles Gibson writes in his introduction to this document,

> Wages for repartimiento [corvée] workers had been fixed by viceregal order from the beginning, but wages for free labor had not ordinarily been adjusted to any regular schedule. It was entirely

characteristic of Gálvez, and of his eighteenth-century frame of mind, that efforts were now made to systematize wages. Everyone should have a job, and equivalent jobs should be paid equally. Many jobs in the Spanish colonies involved payment of food as well as financial payments, and these also were to be specified. With respect to peonage or debt labor, a type of employment that had begun in the sixteenth century and had become general in many forms of labor, Gálvez sought to establish a typical compromise: that workers in debt to their employers could not renege on their contracts, but that employers could not advance workers' wages more than the equivalent of two months' pay.

Mexican novelist Carlos Fuentes's pithy remark that Spanish Bourbons of the eighteenth century were "modernizing busybodies" may be one of those exaggerations in the direction of the truth. Gálvez's decrees seem more concerned with efficiency, productivity, order, and minute regulation than with freedom, equality, and justice for all.

Don Joseph de Gálvez of the Supreme Council and Chamber of the Indies, intendant of the army of America, general visitor of all the tribunals of justice and royal finance and the treasuries and branches of it in these kingdoms of New Spain, and with His Majesty's approval commissioned with the fullest powers by the very excellent viceroy Señor Marqués de Croix, viceroy, governor, and captain general of the same kingdoms:

In order to make sure that workers needed for the cultivation of lands and the grazing of cattle are not lacking, through agreement with the mine owners and hacienda owners, I have resolved upon a measure that will benefit the poor and promote the public welfare, namely, to set a quota upon salaries and rations of goods that will prevail in the future in the provinces of this jurisdiction, for workers, wage earners, and servants, of the following classifications:

1. The leaders, captains, and heads of mining labors; majordomos of haciendas and ranches, whether for agriculture or for grazing; mule-train shippers; and the overseers of other kinds of occupations equivalent to these, are to receive from their masters the wages and rations so that they may negotiate with them in accordance with the skill and circumstances of each one, with the indispensable requirement that wages must be paid in reales or in silver.

2. Workers in mines and others laboring at equivalent tasks should receive at least seven pesos per month in money, and each week they should receive two almudes [about one-fourth of a bushel] of maize and one-half arroba [a 12-pound measure] of fresh meat or one-quarter arroba [a 6-pound measure] of dried meat, whether they be married or single, and with no innovation for the present in the arrangement commonly granted to mine workers by the owners of mines.

3. The same salary and rations are to be paid to the principal cowboys, farm hands, muleteers, horse guards, and others of similar work in other tasks and occupations, except that carriers are to receive six pesos with the same ration.

4. Subordinate shepherds and cowboys who are aides in mule trains or have other equivalent work are to receive the same weekly ration and are to receive as salary five pesos per month in reales, or in silver if reales are lacking. But if they are Indians under the age of eighteen, they are to receive only four pesos in money, with the same rations.

5. In accordance with the laws, I prohibit vagabonds in these provinces and order that everyone is to have a precise job or office, under penalty of one month in jail for the first offense, whether he be Spaniard or Indian or other non-Indian; and a fine of twenty pesos against anyone who protects him under pretext of refuge and fails to report him to the judge, so that he may be punished and set to work. And with any repetition of the offense, the vagabonds will be assigned to the public or royal works, with rations but without wages for two months.

6. Servants have a natural freedom to leave one master in order to make arrangements with another, but this freedom is used by some with such impudence and to such excess that the matter requires some effective correction; there is also the opposite extreme, wherein servants are forced to work for masters who do not treat them well or do not pay them the wages agreed upon. To remedy both abuses, I declare and order that the worker who is in debt to his master cannot leave him

without first fulfilling the terms of the contract, and no other employer may accept him without having assurance that this is the case, in the form of a written statement by the former employer. And no master may advance the wages of his workers or servants more than the amount of two months' wages; nor may he stand in the way of those who have paid up their debt and who want to look for better employment, at least so long as they are not repartimiento workers.

And so that no one may contravene this regulation, which is useful for all, and so that the masters, servants, and workers may ensure from the government its observance, it is to be published and posted in all the reales [licensed mining settlements] and towns of these provinces, with the corresponding testimonies placed in their archives.

Done in the Real de los Alamos [Sonora], June 2, 1769. Don Joseph de Gálvez, by order of His Most Illustrious Highness.

∾ Royal Cédula *that American and European Vassals Are to Be Equal, Madrid, January 2, 1778*

On the surface, the royal decree that elicited a complaint by the Mexico City municipal council and the following somewhat testy reply by Gálvez (now the king's Minister of the Indies in Madrid) seemed to strike a blow for equality of opportunity between peninsular Spaniards and people born and raised in the American colonies, inspired by the king's abiding love for all his subjects. But Creole Spaniards in New Spain's viceregal capital took it as a move to insinuate more *peninsulares* into high offices of American cathedral chapters. Invoking Enlightenment rationality, Gálvez replied that the new decree merely made Americans and peninsular Spaniards equally eligible for these offices; it did not mean to favor one group over another. Past experience, at least, would have suggested the opposite to ambitious Creole Americans, for few of their ancestors had ever received preferment for important offices in Spain, whereas many peninsulares were selected for prestigious offices in the American colonies, especially in the second half of the eighteenth century. They also might well remember Gálvez's retort as the king's *visitador* to New Spain in 1767 to those who questioned the expulsion of the Jesuits: "Vassals of the throne of Spain were born to be silent and obey, not to debate or discuss the affairs of Government."

Josef de Gálvez to the municipal council and judicial and military branches of the city of Mexico. I have advised the king of your communication of last July 24 in which you complain of His Majesty's order of February 21, 1776, reserving one-third of the places in American cathedral chapters for American Spaniards [Creoles], and another order of September 17 of the same year providing for the nomination of European Spaniards for the vacant post of deacon in the cathedral chapter of the Archdiocese of Mexico and cathedral dignitaries elsewhere in the Indies. Naturally, His Majesty noticed the imprecision with which you refer to the two royal orders and that you either do not understand, or pretend not to understand, the spirit that motivated them and their purpose. It is clearer than light that the spirit of the two royal orders is His Majesty's religious ardor, the motivation is his paternal love for his American vassals, and the purpose is the well-being and happiness of these same vassals. In the first order, His Majesty stipulated that for the purpose of maintaining the splendor of the divine cult in the cathedrals of the Indies and the greatest exactitude in administration of justice in the secular tribunals, and also to strengthen the union of those Kingdoms with these and reward equally the merit and services of his vassals, it was his will that the Council of Castile consider Americans for prebends and dignitaries in the churches and tribunals of Spain, and that the Council of the Indies do the same for the churches and tribunals of those dominions, with the proviso that one-third of the cathedral chapter posts there be filled by American Spaniards. This wording makes it perfectly clear that at least one-third of the prebends must be from the Indies. It does not exclude the possible appointment of many more, as there have always been, are now, and will be.

In the second order, His Majesty directed that for the deaconate of the cathedral chapter of the Archdiocese of Mexico, which was then vacant, European Spaniards be considered and that the same be done for the dignitaries of other American cathedrals. But it did not order the exclusion of Americans for consideration; rather, for that post and for others in the cathedral of Mexico that have been filled lately, Americans as well as Europeans have been considered, and His Majesty appointed the American Don Luis de Torres Tuñón.

Therefore, it is evident in these two orders that His Majesty opened the doors of the churches and the tribunals of Spain to his vassals from the Indies, demonstrating his paternal desire that they and his European vassals be considered equals. It is well known that since the two royal orders were issued, Americans have been considered and appointed as dignitaries. And lately the few Europeans in the Mexican cathedral chapter and other cathedrals of both Americas are conspicuous. So there is no rational or just reason for your communication, especially not for the complaints that figure in it. His Majesty orders me to make this known to you, and advise you that the efforts and care with which his generosity seeks the well-being, happiness, and security of his beloved American vassals deserve justice from the municipal council of Mexico City, not unfounded complaints. They deserve that recognition, love, and gratitude which has always been its [the council's] most glorious keynote and character.

✑ 43

The Foundation of Nuestra Señora de Guadalupe de los Morenos de Amapa, Mexico

(1769)

In the following prologue to a parish register of baptisms (now among the manuscripts of the Zimmerman Library, University of New Mexico), part of the complex history of slavery and freedom for Americans of African descent in this colonial history can be glimpsed. Here, Licenciado Joseph Antonio Navarro, the priest of Nuestra Señora de Guadalupe de los Morenos de Amapa in northeastern Oaxaca, near the southern tip of Veracruz, Mexico, traces events that led to the recent founding of his town and parish. Amapa's residents were descended from *cimarrones*, runaway Black slaves, who had taken refuge in the mountainous district of Teutila from the early seventeenth century. These cimarrones reputedly robbed travelers on the road to Córdoba, terrorized nearby valley settlements and sugar mills, and sowed rebellion among settled slaves.

The early colonial history of the Teutila district and this account of the establishment of Amapa in the late eighteenth century reveal a paradoxical combination of motives and responses to the cimarrón problem by Spanish authorities, which contributed to a growing free Black population but not an egalitarian view of society. Colonial authorities' treatment of slaves and cimarrones in Mexico varied from exceedingly cruel punishment (including execution, castration, and amputation of hands and feet) to offers of freedom, property, and spiritual care in exchange for loyalty to the Crown and colonial laws. During the early seventeenth century, after punitive expeditions had failed, a policy of conciliation was favored. In 1630 the town of San Lorenzo Cerralvo near the Villa de Córdoba was established as a settlement for peaceable runaways, but few agreed to reside there, and sporadic raids and counterattacks followed. An intensification of unrest among slaves and cimarrones in the vicinity during the mid-eighteenth century led to more repression by colonial authorities. Abortive punitive expeditions by the Córdoba militia were launched in 1748 and 1750 to root out the cimarrones. Shortly thereafter, Teutila's *alcalde mayor*, or district governor appointed by the Crown, also failed in his attempt to negotiate a settlement in his district.

Although their guerrilla activities continued during the 1750s, the runaway slaves of the Teutila area apparently split into two factions: one willing to accept the Spanish offer of freedom and rights to a separate town; and the other preferring to oppose the Spaniards and continue a fugitive life in the mountains. An armed clash between the two factions ended with the victory of the pro-settlement chief, Fernando Manuel, and his followers. Eighteen of the opponents were turned over to their former masters and their leader was imprisoned. In 1762 a group of cimarrones from the Amapa area formally obtained their freedom after serving in the defense of the port of Veracruz against British attack. Finally, in 1767 an agreement was reached between the *alcalde mayor* of Teutila and the cimarrones for the establishment of a town and church services, and a declaration of freedom for its inhabitants. Some of the original settlers of the town of Amapa had been fugitives for as long as fifty years, but most had lived in mountain refuges of the Teutila district for less than eight years, having escaped masters from the Villa de Córdoba who operated sugar mills and plantations. By December 1767 land titles had been secured, boundary markers laid out, and houses and a church were under construction (see Figure 31). With this new town the colonial authorities had succeeded in incorporating a group of fugitives from colonial rule who had proven that they could not be subdued by force. (At least this was the idea. As the story behind and beyond that arresting portrait [Selection 24, Figure 18] of the Black dons of Esmeraldas, Ecuador, in 1599 suggests, fairy-tale endings were unlikely for anyone in these circumstances.)

That a preoccupation with security underlay the colonial officials' willingness to grant privileges of freedom, municipal life, and spiritual salvation to the cimarrones is suggested by the duties and obligations to the Crown assumed by the *morenos* (dark ones) of Amapa. The townsmen of Amapa were obliged to take up arms in defense of the king of Spain and to undertake expedi-tions into the mountains every two months to capture runaway slaves and prevent the formation of new cimarrón colonies. The parish priest, identified as a peninsular Spaniard of pious intentions, admitted that "the principal motive" for the establishment of a parish at Amapa was the government's desire to form a *reducción*, or settlement, for more effective administration and law enforcement.

Here, Spanish officialdom found security and control to be compatible with more disinterested motives in dealing with runaway slaves. In 1750 the alcalde mayor saw two potential benefits from the foundation of a town: "The salvation of their souls would be facilitated by instruction in Christian doctrine, which they sorely lack; also the roads they used to terrorize would be safe to travel." In the priest's mind the impossible had been achieved at Amapa: "The Negroes are extremely happy in their town; the countryside is free from the outrages they perpe-trated as vagabonds; sugar mill slaves are more secure in their servitude; the king has more soldiers in his service; and the salva-tion of these souls is more certain." The legal freedom obtained by Amapa's residents was not without strings, nor was it simply an act of Christian conscience. Practical, paternalistic, and religious considerations appear all at once, under the mutually celebrated protection of the Virgin Mary as Our Lady of Guadalupe, New Spain's official patroness since 1754.

Although Black slaves near the end of the colonial period were comparatively few in Mexico—reportedly fewer than 10,000, while Venezuela and Cuba each had more than 60,000, and Peru still had 90,000—the legacy of forced African immigration there since the sixteenth century was substantial. In the 1790s, 381,941 free Blacks and Mulattoes were counted (about 6 percent of the viceroyalty's population), most of them residing in highland mining and ranching districts of the north center and west.

In order to trace the beginnings of runaway Negro slaves in the high mountains of Mazateopam whose consolidation into a town was the principal reason for the founding of this new parish of Nuestra Señora de Guadalupe de Amapa, it is necessary to recall that Negro slaves were brought to this kingdom shortly after the Conquest. According to the post-Conquest histories, Negroes were introduced to work the fields, mines, and sugar mills and to perform other onerous labor considered too strenuous for the weaker Indians. Royal law enacted to preserve the Indian population even prohibited the relocation of Indians in different climates in order to prevent illness.

Thus entered the Negroes, seedbed of the various castes that perverted the purity of the Indians—a painful thought. Disaffected with life in the mines, haciendas, and sugar mills, many slaves deserted their masters, forming small settlements in the mountains of Totula, Palmilla, Tumbacarretas, and Totolinga, presently in the jurisdiction of the illustrious Villa de Córdoba and Veracruz. They assaulted travelers, robbing them of their belongings. Under existing conditions they could not be contained or captured. As a result, residents of the town of San Andrés Huatuxco . . . in 1617 petitioned the viceroy, the Most Excellent Don Diego Fernández de Córdoba, Marqués de Guadalcázar, for permission to found the Villa de Córdoba. The following year, 1618, the villa was established, bearing the viceroy's family name. The founding is described by the parish priest of the said villa, Doctor Don José Antonio Rodríguez Valero, in his sacred historical treatise published in Mexico in the year 1759.

Various measures were attempted to dislodge and subjugate the cimarrones. Since force alone proved inadequate, a policy of forbearance was applied with the thought that by winning the affection of the cimarrones the difficulties could be more easily overcome. . . . The cimarrones were offered their freedom on the condition that they come together in a permanent settlement and parish so as not to lack the spiritual nourishment of which they were deprived in such a licentious and dissolute life. The majority of the runaways accepted the offer. The town of San Lorenzo Cerralvo was founded a considerable distance from the said Villa between 1630 and 1635 during the viceregency of the Marqués de Cerralvo, after whom it was named.

Suspicious of this settlement, a band of Negroes continued to roam the highlands of Mazateopam, venturing into the valleys and sugar mills from time to time to plunder travelers, arouse the slaves, and even carry off women from the small, isolated communities. Taking advantage of the cover afforded by the palenques [protected upland refuges], slaves frequently fled from their masters, continually venturing back in surprise attacks. After considerable expense and effort it was at last sadly realized that the cimarrones could not be subdued by force. On the contrary, armed sorties into the mountains in pursuit of the cimarrones only gave them more reason for revenge to the detriment of the sugar mills, travelers, and the inhabitants of the entire region.

In the years 1725 and 1735 there were slave revolts in the above-mentioned sugar mills of the Villa de Córdoba. In 1725 the greater part of the area in the direction of Xalitatuani to the banks of the Quetzalapa River in this jurisdiction of

Teutila was involved. A large number of slaves fled; some were captured; others escaped deep into the mountains of Mazateopam where they joined the long-established cimarrones, as José de Padilla, Marqués de Guardiola, former alcalde mayor, told me and described in a written account. In 1735 the region was menaced by a nearly general uprising. If the dragoons from the plaza of Veracruz and the provincial militia had not arrived in time to subdue the runaways before they penetrated deep into the mountains and procured arms, the result would have been grievous. As it was, not all were returned to slavery. Many disappeared into the palenques where their comrades were hiding. With the ranks of the cimarrones thus expanded, vigilance had to be increased day by day. The available means were not sufficient to contain or diminish their forays, which resulted in widespread damage.

In 1748 two punitive expeditions into the mountains of Mazateopam were attempted by the militia. One was directed by Don Gabriel de Segura, Don Bernardo de Zeballos, Don Miguel de Leiba Esparragoza, and Don Vicente Tapia; the other in the direction of Xalitatuani was led by Captain Don Nicolás Carvaxal Castillo de Altra. Both efforts failed miserably. In 1750 two more expeditions were undertaken with the same result. Don Andrés de Otañes, alcalde mayor of Teutila, realizing the futility of these attempts, decided to engage in talks with the said Negroes. He met with the captain and some of his comrades on the banks of the Quetzalapa River two leagues from the town of Zoyaltepec and persuaded them to establish a town to facilitate the salvation of their souls through instruction in Christian doctrine. . . . The result would be that the cimarrones would no longer be persecuted and the roads would be free from their frequent attacks. The alcalde mayor offered his complete support for this Christian purpose. He stipulated only that the unanimous consent of the runaway slaves living in the highlands be secured. This seemed agreeable to the leaders, who returned to the mountains to tell their comrades of the proposal, promising to return with a reply. Viceroy Revilla Gigedo was informed of the talks, but for the moment nothing resulted.

In 1750 at this stage in the negotiations another punitive expedition by the militia was made on behalf of the sugar mill owners. The Negroes now became suspicious of the promises made by alcalde mayor Otañes, for they did not return with the reply. They undoubtedly believed that he intended to bait them with deception. From 1750 to 1760 the region experienced various incursions at the expense of the mill owners and travelers. Meanwhile the Negroes had divided into two groups. Some, who were less distrustful, joined the party seeking the formation of a town; others continued to oppose the Spanish proposal. The cimarrones' course of action was decided by formal combat. The part against a settlement was led by Captain Macute, longtime chief of the cimarrones. Fernando Manuel, Macute's lieutenant, headed the other group. Fernando Manuel acknowledged that before firing his guns he made a fervent plea to Nuestra Señora de Guadalupe, humbly seeking protection for the success of his Christian purpose. From that moment he designated her Patroness and Guardian of the town which would be founded by his followers, an admirable recognition for such uncivilized people, worthy of envy by the most enlightened and zealous [Christian]. God allowed that Fernando Manuel be rewarded with victory over his opponents. He gravely wounded Captain Macute; and after killing many others, he captured eighteen of those still living who were brought to the Villa de Córdoba, where they were turned over to their respective masters. Captain Macute today is still imprisoned in the Córdoba jail. . . .

Having done this, the said Fernando Manuel went to the Hacienda de la Estanzuela where he encountered the owner, Don Fernando Carlos de Rivadeneyra, and Bachiller Don Apolinar de Cosio, his administrator and chaplain. Fernando Manuel sought their protection in establishing the town. Whether or not they agreed to do so cannot be determined because shortly thereafter both men died. The cimarrones settled at sites known as Palacios, Breva Corina, and Mandinga, belonging to the hacienda. These settlements were located near the summit of the mountain leading to the palenques as an escape route should they be pursued. In 1762, on advice given to them, the cimarrones went down to the plaza of Veracruz where they presented themselves to the Most Excellent Viceroy Marqués de Cruillas. They offered to serve the viceroyalty in the current war with Great Britain and requested that he grant them their freedom in exchange. Undoubtedly he agreed, for they were incorporated into the corps of lancers, as we know from the document appointing Fernando Manuel sergeant, authorized by Don Santiago Cubillos, infantry captain. When peace was achieved they returned to their settlements to live with their customary distrust, for they could find no one to protect their communities and they had lost the decree signed by the Marqués de Cruillas. At the same time a suit initiated by the mill owners was pending, which threatened the Negroes' freedom and their town. The mill owners lost the case for lack of a sound legal base. However, the records of this case were maliciously jumbled or abridged on behalf of the mill owners.

In 1767, when Andrés de Otañes was again serving as alcalde mayor of Teutila, the Negroes appeared before him in the town of Zoyaltepec. Remembering the proposal of 1750, he offered to support them in the declaration of freedom and founding of the town. The cimarrones readily agreed . . . and this became the fundamental basis for the good fortune they later experienced. The proposal for founding the town was formalized in a written document relating their former occupations and residence; designating the land where the town would be located . . . ; and fervently imploring the protection of the most illustrious Señor Doctor Don Francisco Fabián y Fuero, most dignified bishop of this bishopric. The bishop, upon whom they depended for judgment and pastoral zeal, joyfully complied. The alcalde mayor ordered that various judicial formalities be carried out and informed the Most Excellent Viceroy Marqués de Croix of the proceedings. An agent was appointed on behalf of the Negroes to expedite the petition. Reports were gathered by various ministers; and finally, on January 12, a decree signed by the señor fiscal [the high court's legal adviser] Don Juan Antonio Velarde C. and the señor asesor [special adviser to the court] Don Diego Cornide declared a list of cimarrones and others still living in the palenques liberated from servitude and perpetually exempt from paying the royal tribute. The decree further granted them the power to found a town in the appointed location and obligated them to destroy completely the runaway bands of Mazateopam; to take up arms in the service of king and country whenever called; to capture henceforth those Negro slaves who fled from their masters with a reward of twenty-five pesos each; to prevent the formation of other marauding bands; to go into the mountains every two months to verify that no bands had formed; to live in obedience to the Royal Justice of Teutila; and to name alcaldes and regidores to govern the community. . . .

On February 5 of the said year a dispatch was drawn up directing Don Andrés de Otañes to oversee the establishment of the town and apportionment of lands. I, Don José Antonio Navarro, native of the city of Valencia in the Spanish kingdoms, was selected for the spiritual guidance of the community. . . . On May 3, accompanied by the alcalde mayor and the Negroes, I went to survey this location known as Amapa. The site chosen is a gently sloping hill formerly occupied by a Mulatto Juan González and his wife Manuela Rodríguez, both natives of the port town of Tamiagua in the jurisdiction of Guauchinango. González was employed in cultivating corn and cotton, carrying travelers across the Amapa River in his canoe, and defending the area against attack by cimarrones. This was a favorite spot for their ambushes. The hill was chosen for its supply of potable water, healthful winds, proximity to the highway, and access to the Amapa River.

On May 6 a town meeting was held at which alcaldes, regidores, and other community officials were elected and presented with the trappings of magistrates. Immediately thereafter the locations of the church and houses were designated. The alcalde mayor ordered that materials be secured for the buildings as soon as possible, to which the Negroes agreed. The alcalde mayor returned to the town of Zoyaltepec and I returned to the Hacienda de la Estanzuela.

On May 31, Don Miguel Rodríguez de la Vega, alcalde mayor of Córdoba, brought an order at the instance of the mill owners to suspect the establishment of the new town. For reasons totally unfounded in fact, it was asserted that the town should be established at Mata del Agua, located between the exposed areas of Totolinga and San Campuz. The order was promptly obeyed. A document opposing the settlement at Mata del Agua was then submitted on behalf of the Negroes, which the mill owners tried to refute with arguments of more bulk than substance. It should be noted here that alcalde mayor Otañes, realizing that further delays would revive the Negroes' distrust, resolved to begin construction at the townsite. At Amapa on August 30 he was joined by the Negroes who had come down from their huts at the edge of the mountains. With the help of more than 125 local Indians, who worked on a rotating basis for a week at a time, the church was begun. On September 17 the church was ready for celebration of the first Mass, which I performed with a happy throng of assistants and communicants. Construction of public offices and private dwellings for the Negroes was then begun along streets laid out in straight lines. As a whole it was a very pleasing sight and in time will be the most resplendent town in the lowlands. The viceroy approved the entire proceeding and extended his congratulations for the efficacy and devotion with which this important matter was carried out. On October 19 the matter of the mill owners' opposition was resolved. In a strongly worded order their petition was denied and the completion of the town approved. The mill owners subsequently failed in an appeal to the Audiencia. The Audiencia refused jurisdiction since the Negroes, as soldiers, were subject to the captaincy general.

On December 5 possession of the land was finalized and boundary markers were set out. The Negroes are extremely happy in their town; the countryside is free from the outrages they perpetrated as vagabonds; the plantation slaves are more secure in their servitude; the king has more soldiers in his service; and the salvation of these souls is more certain. In this, the impossible has been conquered without staining the endeavor with human blood; accomplished in the felicitous and just reign of Our Catholic Monarch Charles III (May God protect him many years!), being Viceroy the most excellent Señor Marqués de Croix, Knight and Comendador de Molinos y Laguna Rota of the Order of Calatrava and Lieutenant General of the Royal Armies, and being Bishop the Most Illustrious Señor Don Francisco Fabián de Fuero. The establishment of this town has not been carried out at the expense of Your Majesty or any other person. The undertaking was supervised and paid for by the said Don Andrés Fernández de Otañes. It seemed opportune to me to recount this as an introduction to this book [the baptismal record of Amapa] so it may serve as a monument to posterity. . . .

∾ Plan of Amapa (1769–70)

Alcalde mayor Andrés Fernández de Otañes, sponsor of Amapa in its first years, had a plan of the town and surroundings prepared to commemorate its founding (Figure 31). His sense of himself in the project and his vision of its future are apparent in this image and his ebullient description of the place. Here the neatly ordered grid plan of the pueblo dwarfs the landscape, as it never would have done in fact. The little community of twenty-two adults centers on an ample plaza about 200 feet across, defined by the church and eight houses with modest arcades, two of them reserved for the priest and the town office. A road linking Amapa to the Villa de Córdoba and the Indian pueblo of Zoyaltepec enters on the open north side of the plaza and turns off to the west. The plan shows room for expansion of the settlement on a plain bounded by rivers, pasturelands, and woods arranged in orchardlike rows.

Writing in February 1770 of "this great work of settling the Blacks in their own pueblo," the alcalde mayor described the site as "agreeable, even delicious, in a hot climate well suited to this type of people, very health-ful and good for raising maize, cotton, vanilla, and other crops—better than other places that do not enjoy these advantages—and with ready access to various towns, which will facilitate commerce." Fernández de Otañes wrote of the good order of the town and the civil life to which the once-naked residents were growing accustomed in their elections, new clothes, farms, and the "yoke" of Christianity. In the town itself he was especially proud of the church, with its freestanding belltower and two "beautiful" bells. This wooden structure with a fine thatched roof was more than 75 feet long and 25 feet wide. The high altar displayed painted images of Our Lady of Guadalupe (patroness of the new community and personal protectress of Fernando Manuel, who had led the struggle to make peace with the colonial government and settle at Amapa), Saint Joseph (the Virgin's husband), and Saint Carlos Borromeo (in honor of the reigning king of Spain, Charles III). Facing each other near the altar were a portrait of King Charles and his coat of arms, with inscriptions noting that the foundation of the town was accomplished under the protec-

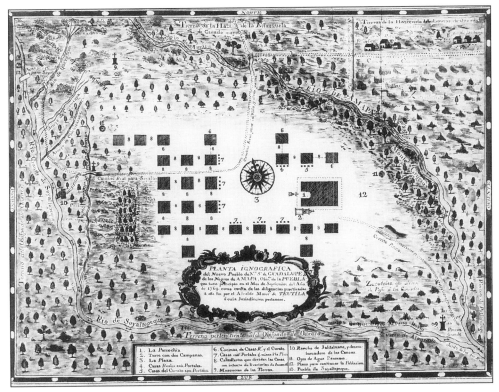

Figure 31. Plan of Nuestra Señora de Guadalupe de los Negros de Amapa,
Mexico, 1769–70.
Courtesy of the Archivo General de la Nación, Mexico City.

tion and at the expense of Alcalde Mayor Fernández de Otañes. All of the paintings were housed in fine gold frames, he added.

Six years later, the original settlers were still in place, quite contented despite the difficulty of tilling land laced with tree roots, but a different alcalde mayor and interim priest took a dimmer view of the town and its citizens. The priest lamented their drunkenness and torpor, especially when it came to serving the church. The alcalde mayor wanted the town disbanded because the settlers showed little fear or respect for his authority (which he exercised from the distant head town of Teutila); they harbored Indians, *castas* (people of mixed racial ancestry), and military fugitives from Veracruz, usurped lands from a neighboring Indian community, and failed to pay tribute or personally submit their annual elections for his confirmation. They lived, he

said, "in complete independence and the pueblo is nothing more that a Castle from which they sally forth to commit outrages."

The viceroy and his legal adviser rejected this 1776 proposal to disband the settlement. The likelihood that the residents of Amapa would return to their mountain refuge and raids weighed heavily in the decision, but the viceroy's adviser also noted that most of the alcalde mayor's complaints were without foundation. The people of Amapa, he noted, had been granted extended relief from the tribute tax and sacramental fees. Moreover, they were only required to submit their election results to the alcalde mayor's lieutenant who lived nearer to their town, and there was no prohibition on non-Blacks settling there if they wished. Nuestra Señora de Guadalupe de los Morenos de Amapa prevailed, at least for the time being.

44

Concolorcorvo Engages the Postal Inspector about Indian Affairs, Lima, Peru

(1776)

In 1776 a book of travels in Argentina, Paraguay, Bolivia, and Peru began to circulate in Peru. In it, a royal inspector of the postal service, Alonso Carrió de la Vandera, and his Indian assistant, Don Calixto Bustamante Carlos Inca, alias Concolorcorvo or "Mr. Inca," described and reflected on what they encountered along the way. Presented as if it had been written by Concolorcorvo and published in Spain in 1773 by the La Rovada ("Something Stolen") Press, it was, in fact, the work of Carrió, fresh off the press of an unidentified Lima printer. Carrió had made this arduous tour across nearly three thousand miles of often forbidding terrain during nineteen months beginning in November 1771.

Born about 1716, Carrió spent most of his life in America, going first to Mexico about 1736 and then to Peru ten years later as a trader. He settled in Lima where he married and entered a series of second-level government appointments in 1750, interrupted in 1762 by service in a cavalry regiment of distinguished citizens of Lima against pirates on the coast of Peru. In early 1771 he received the appointment to inspect the mail service between Buenos Aires and Lima and expected it to be his springboard to some prestigious permanent office in the viceregal capital. But

his report and recommendations were ignored by the armchair director of the mail service, and a long, bitter, and ultimately fruitless complaint by Carrió to the viceroy ensued. *El lazarillo de ciegos caminantes,* in the form of a dialogue, was Carrió's way of presenting his side of the dispute without openly offending his superiors (other than the director of the mail service). The postal inspector speaks abundantly, but not as the author, and the printed pages appear as if they came from a different time and place—Spain in 1773, at the end of the inspector's tour, rather than Lima in 1776, when Carrió had lost patience with the formal channels of appeal.

El lazarillo de ciegos caminantes is often described as a satirical work. The author's mocking and ironical wit peeks through in every chapter and dominates several, but who and what were being mocked? If Carrió was angered by the dismissive reception of his efforts as postal inspector, as he must have been, his anger did not turn into a subversive critique of Spanish rule or Bourbon designs for commercial and political reform. His occasional irreverent criticism of Spanish governors in America could be used by others to justify self-righteous rebellion (as could Felipe Guaman Poma de Ayala's forgotten exposé of

Spanish abuses almost two centuries earlier, but Carrió himself remains a Spaniard in his predilections and prejudices, and something of a super Bourbon.

Ancient Rome and Greece were in vogue in the neoclassical high culture of Bourbon Spain, and Carrió did not miss the opportunity to draw in a story about Alexander the Great and Darius. "Progress" in terms of civilization and commerce was one of his watchwords, as it was for Bourbon policymakers under Charles III. Ever the advocate of improved communications and circulation of goods, Carrió lamented the opportunities missed by Spanish merchants to tap the rich Indian markets and incorporate Indian trade into the imperial economy. His advice to would-be traders in the Indian markets was: learn the ways of Indian petty commerce and apply them, patiently, to sales and profit.

In this chapter on Indian affairs, Carrió had his caustic fun at the expense of virtually everyone except the king. He could be critical of Spaniards' mistreatment of Indians, but he was no Las Casas—no defender of Indian rights on ethical grounds, and certainly not as a reason to question Spaniards' right to rule in America. He recognized different kinds of Indians (his evolutionary categories were much like those of José de Acosta; see Selection 19), but he kept returning to their fundamental barbarity. In their natural state, he concluded, Indians were violators of the Ten Commandments, not innocents. He excused Spaniards from corrupting Indians with their sins, including drunkenness, because such sins were already present "twice over" in ancient America. The Spanish conquerors' failure as rulers was that they "governed themselves [and Indians] according to the custom of the land," not that they behaved as tyrants.

Even when Mr. Inca invites the postal inspector to speak positively about Indians' courage and industry, the response veers off to their cowardice and ineptitude and the fool-hardly arrogance of Aztec and Inca leaders. His respect for Indian fighters of Chile and the Chaco region turns into a backhanded compliment, for their fierce cunning becomes another sign of extreme barbarity, subject to no law, ruled by their passions rather than the genteel light of reason.

Like a good reformer, Carrió had some solutions to the problem of Indian barbarity. The subject of "Indian affairs" meant to him subjugation or removal. For settled Indians—the "less crude" who "live from their plantings and livestock"—his answer was to promote mass education in the Spanish language, the civilized tongue of empire. This solution offered him an opportunity to criticize Catholic priests as pastors, a favorite target of Bourbon administrators. He attributed the spotty development of Spanish among Indians to the self-interest of parish priests, with a special swipe at the recently expelled Jesuits who, he claimed, kept Indians in ignorance in order to control them better.

With implacable Indian adversaries on the frontiers, "there is no other way . . . than firm defense and thinning them out with our growing numbers." Carrió was particularly enthusiastic about the string of new *presidios* (fortified garrisons) in northern New Spain that, he said, had transformed Nueva Vizcaya from "forsaken plains" into a zone of bustling towns and trade. (But in Carrió's world of original sin, even this advent of civilization did not bring a simple resolution to disorder. The great landowner, the Conde de San Pedro del Alamo, discovered that Indian incursions had been replaced by the prejudicial conduct of "the multitude of Mestizos and Spaniards who lived off his properties.") Towns and forts, forts and towns: Christian missions are notably absent from this vision of a frontier Indian policy.

There are eighteenth-century twists that emphasize state reforms and commerce and mute the importance of Church and religion, but Carrió told a familiar colonial story of civilization approximated versus barbarism in the extreme. If not a premonition of the Túpac Amaru rebellion of 1780–1783 (see Selections 40, 43, and 53), this panorama of South American life by a longtime resident of Peru at least suggests deep doubts by those who thought of themselves as Spaniards about their ability to control Indians of any kind.

"The first charge I would make against the parish priests [said the postal inspector, or *visitador*] is that they have not thrown themselves into the task of incorporating the Spanish language into their religious instruction. It is only these ministers of doctrine who can achieve this desirable result because the corregidores who are sent out to govern thirty pueblos for five years at a time—often for only two years—have neither the time nor resources to find a way toward something so useful to religion and the State. The parish priests' assistants, who are usually ordained as Indian-language priests and have the most contact with Indians, do not want them to speak anything but their native language. The few Indians who want to express themselves in Spanish are berated for doing so and mocked as degree-holders and men of letters, as the current and most worthy bishop of La Paz confessed to me. These circumstances retard any great progress in the Spanish language.

"The Jesuits, who for 150 years were the principal teachers, pursued a strategy prejudicial to the State by trying to keep the Indians from any contact with Spaniards and limit them to their native language, which they [the Jesuits] understood very well. I make no attempt to defend or attack their principles since they have already been expelled. I need only refer to the general points which their disciples and successors follow. Those good fathers asserted that when Indians had contact with Spaniards and learned their language, they became infected and tangled up in enormous vices that they could not even have imagined before. There is no doubt that these ministers of the Gospel spoke in bad faith about this because all of the accounts written at the beginning of the Conquest describe many abominations that the Spaniards themselves had never imagined (as I recounted earlier). So, these Spaniards can only be held responsible for making the Indians confess in their languages the enormity of their sin and abominate it, such as eating human flesh, sacrificing prisoners of war to their gods, worshiping various monsters or logs shaped into a horrendous figure, and often poisonous insects.

"The polygamy and incest permitted under their laws were not practiced by Spaniards, nor was intercourse between males, which was very common among Indians, as can still be seen among those who have not been conquered. The sixth, seventh, and eighth of the Ten Commandments were and are so commonly violated, as they are among Spaniards and every other nation in the world, that one can infer that they [Spaniards] did not introduce any sin into this kingdom that was not already present twice over. As for swearing, the Indians know how to say Supaypaguagua, which means son of the Devil, which would have offended God in this language as much as in any other, unless one assumes that God only understands Spanish and only punishes those who offend Him in that language. Drunkenness was more widespread among the [ancient] Indians than anywhere else in the world. Spaniards appear to be guilty only of having introduced a more potent version in the form of spirits and wine.

"The parish priests will do a great service to God, the king, and the Indians by eliminating Indian languages from their teaching and replacing them with Spanish, making their assistants responsible and ordering their native constables to carry it out. The corregidores, their lieutenants and accountants, and everyone else passing through their parishes will derive great benefit because the Indians, on the grounds of not understanding Spanish, fail to understand many things, which leads to disputes, unfortunate arguments, and Indian crudities."

"No, for the love of God," I said to him. "Don't leave without saying something about what you mean by their courage and industry."

"As for the former," he said, "they are like greyhounds—in a group they are capable of attacking a lion, but alone they can hardly come up with a hare. Just draw a drop of their blood and they're said to be dead; and in the greatest uprising, unless they are drunk, if they see one of their own struck down dead, the rest will flee even if they outnumber us fifty to one."

"That's why so few Spaniards conquered over seven million Indians," I replied.

"You understand very little, Mr. Inca," the visitador said to me. "The conquest of a civilized kingdom with the loss of control over its inhabitants, which is not aided by other rulers, is achieved with two or three victories on the battlefield, especially if its leaders are killed or captured. The Spaniards, with the defeat of the Otumba army, earned a reputation for courage but they also showed the Indians that they were mortal and vulnerable, like their horses. But with the capture of Mexico City, aided by the Tlaxcalan nobles, they subjected that great empire of more than forty million souls because thereafter every prince, general, or petty lord swore his allegiance out of fear of being attacked and ruined.

"If Darius had opposed Alexander the Great with 50,000 men and one or two good generals, even if he had been defeated, his officers could have gathered at least 20,000 men and Alexander would have had no more than 4,000 or 5,000, and he would have had to use some of them to guard the prisoners and equipment. Darius could have attacked him a second, third, fourth, and fifth time with his remaining army, tiring out Alexander's valiant troops and reducing them in the engagements and strategic garrisons he could capture. But Darius attacked as if victory over Alexander was assured, and not as a fighter. He thought Alexander would be frightened by his powerful, disciplined army and the size and trumpeting of his elephants. With this confidence he entered the battle and in one day he lost a great empire and his life, while his conqueror made off with his treasures, his wife, and his daughters.

"The Chileans knew better how to deal with the Spaniards. Observing that they had always been defeated when their numbers were four times greater, and even many times when they outnumbered them one hundred to one, they changed their plan and mode of combat. They judged the Spaniards more skillful and courageous than themselves, and in possession of better weapons, but they also knew that they were mortal and subject to human frailties. So they undertook to engage them in combat repeatedly until they overcame them and forced them back to their trenches with the loss of some settlements. These reflections show that a large but poorly led army of 200,000 men—even veteran soldiers, if the generals are inexperienced—can be defeated and put to flight by 30,000 well-disciplined soldiers led by wise and courageous chiefs. But these subjects are beyond our conversation and talent, so tell me, Mr. Inca, whether you have more to say or ask about your countrymen."

"Well, I wonder why the Spaniards, who conquered and subjected seven million Indians to their ways, are unable to subject the Indians of the Chaco region and those of the mountains?"

"That question would more appropriately be asked of one of your Inca and chiefly ancestors. But since they have given their account to God for their actions, for good or ill, I will take the trouble to defend them, as well as to disabuse some Spaniards who think the Chaco can be conquered with a well-ordered militia of 1,000 men led by good officers, and that the same result can be achieved in the mountains with the same number more. Of course, I confess that this number of men, at considerable expense, could move through the various provinces and territories. But the barbarous Indians, who have no formal settlements or cultivated fields, would change their locations. They will mock the vain efforts of the Spaniards who, being unable to fortify their strongholds, would abandon them, enabling the Indians to return at their pleasure, at considerable cost to us, as you judiciously observed in your opening thought.

"By barbarous people I mean those who are not subject to laws or magistrates, who in the end live by their own devices, always following their passions. This is the nature of the Indians on the pampas [of Argentina and Uruguay] and the inhabitants of the Chaco. In New Spain, seeing the impossibility of subjecting the barbarous Indians who occupied the forsaken plains of central Nueva Vizcaya [in northern Mexico], including more than one hundred leagues of the royal road leading to the valley of San Bartolomé del Parral, the Spaniards built four presidios twenty-five leagues apart garrisoned with fifty soldiers each and the appropriate officers. The soldiers were to be married and young enough to bear children. Each month they accompanied the great mule trains to the next presidio. The mule train that did not arrive at the next link in the chain by the third day of the month had to wait nearby until the following month. The muleteers were left to their own devices to find safe and fertile pasturage. For this escort no fee was collected because the officers and soldiers were and must be paid by the king. The soldiers of the first three presidios did not deviate more than two leagues to the left or right from their route to guard the surrounding territory where their horses grazed. But in the fertile and delightful valley of San Bartolomé where a large town by the same name is located, a mobile company is located which goes out in groups to reconnoiter the countryside at a considerable distance, under orders not to engage the Indians unless victory is assured. In case they encountered a large number of Indians together, they were to note the location and advise all the presidios and militiamen so that together they could engage and disperse them with minimal losses.

"Rarely did they take prisoners, and they did not often allow any barbarous Indians into the presidios because the soldiers said that they were good for nothing but eating their bread and robbing their horses if any trust was placed in them. The presidios were not even twenty years old, and they already consisted of a large population of Mestizos and Spaniards of both sexes, with cultivated fields and pastures for livestock. The rural presidio in one place grew so much that the Conde de San Pedro del Alamo, whose great estates were nearby, asked the government to move it or close it down because it was no longer useful in that place since there were no more Indian incursions; and, in any case, Indian incursions were less prejudicial to him than the multitude of Mestizos and Spaniards who lived off his properties. Finally, he wanted them ordered to devote themselves to clearing the countryside and escorting the mule trains—which would save the royal treasury 12,000 pesos a year, the cost to His Majesty of providing for those presidios— on the condition that as those areas were populated and the hostile Indians removed, they, too, would advance. The Conde achieved his aim, and perhaps now not a single presidio exists in that vast region, replaced by many towns of varying sizes, according to the greater or lesser fertility of the land and presence of watering places, for Nueva Vizcaya is a very sterile land. I am going to conclude this point with a notorious public event in Nueva Vizcaya.

"It concerns a certain captain of the mobile company, whose first name I don't remember but whose last name was Berroterán, whom the barbarous Indians called Perroterán. [Changing the "B" to "P" makes the first part of the captain's surname mean "dog."] He was frequently deceived by the promises they made him, for he followed the pious maxim of our kings, who repeatedly ordered that peace be granted to Indians who requested it, even if it was in the heat of battle and they were about to be defeated. They were confident of the generosity of our laws, and he, I say again, having been repeatedly deceived by these infidels, resolved to make war on them without quarter. So, when the Indians asked for peace [*paz*], the good Cantabrian would construe it as bread [*pan*], replying that he would take some for himself and his soldiers. He attacked them with such vigor that he terrified them and forced them out of that entire territory. As the story goes, at the hour of his death, the priest who was helping him to achieve a good death asked him if he repented of having killed so many Indians. He responded that he only regretted having left behind on Earth a rabble lacking in religion, faith, and law, that he thought only of their treachery and deceptions and way of life at the cost of trouble to the Spaniards and the sweat of the civilized Indians. What is certain is that there is no other way to deal with the barbarous Indians than firm defense and thinning them out with our growing numbers. In New Mexico, which is eight hundred leagues from the capital, the Spaniards maintain themselves in a small number, under the command of a governor, among a multitude of enemy nations without taking sides beyond asking the conquering nation to pardon the remnants of the defeated army that sought their protection. With this maxim they make themselves feared and loved by those barbarians who are less crude than those of the pampas and inhabitants of the Chaco."

"From all of this I take it that you regard the Indians as civil people" [remarked Concolorcorvo].

"If you are speaking of the Indians subject to the emperors of Mexico and Peru and their laws, whether good or bad, I say that they have been and are civil, that they are the most obedient nation to their superiors that exists in the world. From the Chichas to the Piuranos, I observed their way of governing. They are assiduously obedient, whether to the regidor, who assumes the duties of constable, up to the corregidor. They live from their plantings and livestock without aspirations to wealth even if they have had some opportunities through the discoveries of mines and tombs. They are content with a little assistance for their fiestas and drinking parties. Some attribute this timidity to concern that the Spaniards will despoil them of those treasures, which usually are imaginary or depend, as in the silver and gold mines, on the industry of many men and great expense. The Spaniards would be delighted if the Indians were rich so they could trade with them and enjoy part of their wealth. But the sad fact is that in the greatest Indian market, which is that of Cocharcas [in highland Bolivia], where over two thousand Indians gather from various provinces, one does not see anyone buying even a real's worth of goods from a Spaniard because they do not like their stinginess. So they go to the Indian women merchants who have the patience to sell them a muleteer's need for a quarter of a real, a bit of string, and so on. The Spaniards' commerce is made among themselves, including the fluctuating numbers of Mestizos and other Castas who are outside the sphere of the Indians. The rare Indian who gathers some wealth is esteemed by the Spaniards, who offer him their goods and gladly offer terms, and do not disdain trade with them and invite them to their tables.

"No Spaniard is capable of deceiving an Indian, and if a Spaniard takes something from an Indian by force, he is pursued in the courts until his dying day. This does not lead me to say (as I have already noted) that there are no tyrannies among them, that they [Spaniards] cannot be regarded as tyrants—since [tyrannies] have a reciprocal basis—because of the bad foundation laid by the first conquerors, who governed themselves according to the custom of the land."

45

Taming the Wilderness, Minas Gerais, Brazil
(1769)

There was nothing at all remarkable about the expedition Field Officer Inácio Correia Pamplona mounted in 1769, except the detailed recording of it. Heading out from his ranch on August 18, his company included fifty-eight of his own slaves, armed as if for war, another seven slave musicians with one White man, a chaplain, a scribe and mapmaker, and some fifty-two pack mules together with a core of about eighty White colonists who included Pamplona's son and two women from the family. White people of status rode on horseback; slaves marched on foot. Two days out a surgeon and some others joined them. And so it was over the next three months as they rested for the night at scattered hamlets or ranches along the way; a man or two showed up keen to ride with them until, by the end of the three-month march, some 150 settlers in all claimed their reward in land either as participants or providers of shelter.

Such expeditions were familiar in the late eighteenth-century captaincy of Minas Gerais in both the eastern and western wilderness zones that flanked either side of what had been the spectacularly rich mining area of such towns as Vila Rica, São João del Rei, Sabará, Diamantina. By mid-century, however, the gold and diamond deposits neared depletion, the sources of the vast wealth being shipped to Portugal began to run dry, and men looked for other means. Portugal's brilliant and ruthlessly ambitious prime minister, Sebastião José de Carvalho e Melo, the Marques of Pombal, urged a policy of settlement to turn wilderness into harnessed productivity. And while these quasi-military expeditions, or *bandeiras*, never abandoned the search for new gold discoveries, their assignment, especially on the eastern frontier, was to exterminate nomadic Indians such as the Botocudo, who refused subjugation and were seen as an impediment to settlement and the prosperity of the colony. Between 1760 and the beginning of the nineteenth century, governors sent out dozens of such bandeiras, and in the space of only five years—between 1768 and 1773—one governor ordered at least thirteen expeditions to the eastern area alone.

Pamplona made his fortune running such expeditions. Born in 1731 in the Portuguese islands of the Azores, Pamplona, then a migrant to colonial Brazil, traded goods from Rio de Janeiro to the mining towns, including São João del Rei, where he lived with his wife, a former slave, Eugênia Luísa da Silva. By the early 1760s, in the wake of the mining bust, Pamplona was exterminating Indians, flushing runaway slaves from their *quilombos*, or refuges, and searching for gold near the head-waters of the São Francisco River. The king rewarded Pamplona generously for his services with eight *sesmarias*, or royal land grants each covering nine square leagues, making him the regional potentate. He had both the wealth and the influence necessary to organize, outfit, and lead the expeditions that made him famous. After 1765 he conducted five more, including the one described in this selection, as well as one in 1782 that attacked the Caiapó Indians. Although Pamploma's were exceptional in number and extent, such grants formed a regular part of royal policy to promote settlement of the backlands. A man or woman with slaves to work the land qualified, so that during the course of the eighteenth century between 6,000 and 7,000 grants went to settlers, while in some single years the governor conceded as many as 300 or 400, expansion being especially vigorous in the period between 1740 and 1770. Free land did not eliminate bitter disputes among Whites, as this document reveals, and it undeniably drove up the violence between settlers and Indians. As a result of this expedition alone, Pamplona heard requests for more than 200 royal grants and, as the governor's representative who in turn acted for the king, he distributed lands to those whose charters were in order.

In the late 1780s, Pamplona's notoriety took on dangerously political hues. In reaction against the tightened, centralizing policies of Pombal's successor, Martinho de Melo e Castro, and in particular against the threat of reviving a head tax, a group of conspirators in Vila Rica secretly plotted the overthrow of royal government in Minas Gerais, including the governor's assassination, and the declaration of an independent republic. Their plans failed, possibly because of an informer. The tax, rather than being imposed, was canceled; the main conspirators were tried and their sentences commuted, except for one (the only one without wealth or social standing) who was hanged. Pamplona appears in these events as a wealthy merchant and landowner who at first joined the conspiracy, was promised the profits from supplying military forces to be sent from the coast, and then, possibly as the governor's spy, denounced it, apparently gaining little in exchange except protection. He left Vila Rica immediately following the suspicious death of one conspirator. Conveniently away on a search for diamonds, he was never called to give testimony. He emerges as a man scrambling for a toehold on the winning side, however that might turn out, and in this document as boastful and self-promoting.

Who did his boasting for him in this account of the 1769 expedition? Although never officially named, the author was possibly the scribe, Jolião da Costa Resende, listed at the end of the journal among those from the small village of Nossa Senhora da Conceição Conquista do Campo Grande who took possession of land grants in November of that year, just before the expedition dispersed. And was the scribe in turn related to the expedition's chaplain, Gabriel da Costa Resende? Whatever his name and connections, he had the important job of making maps as well as recording pertinent information about the region and its inhabitants. This laudatory journal was clearly meant as a report for the governor, with its deeds explained and applauded, the men rewarded, and Pamplona himself further celebrated as a man of unerring judgment and decisive action. Yet it is remarkable that in this remote place, among generally illiterate or barely literate people, any record at all was made. Missing from this edited translation are many of the repetitions that convey the measured pace of the march marked by daily Masses as well as numerous sonnets, referred to by the scribe as the "dessert" with which they finished many meals. It is worth noting that the sonnets were spoken, not read from written texts, and belong to an oral culture easily carried with the marchers.

The expedition's surface objectives were clear enough. They extended the settled world by opening roads and building bridges to give access to new villages and landholdings and at the same time drove Indians farther into the forests or forced them into subjugation. Along the way they kept a lookout for runaway slaves and took detours to search for gold in the stream beds. But seen from another angle this long procession into the wilderness was a civilizing ritual designed to order an untamed region. How did these men, and the few women, understand the difference between wilderness and non-wilderness? What dangers threatened them, and what fears did they carry with them? What elements of civilization did they bring to this landscape, and how were they expressed? And what code of honor or personal conduct can be inferred from this openly slanted account?

∼ Daily Notice of the Marches and Most Noteworthy Happenings in the Expedition Made by Field Officer Regent Inácio Correia Pamplona

On the 18th of August [of 1769] the Field Officer Regent left this Capote Ranch, accompanied by thirteen horsemen, some of whom would go with him to the *Sertão*, or Wilderness, and others [only] a certain distance, out of friendship. And on this day he traveled three leagues and rested at a ranch called Cataguases.

His retinue-train included fifty-eight of his slaves, armed with muskets, carbines, machetes, ammunition-pouches, powder, lead, and bullets.

The musicians who accompanied him consisted of seven of his slaves, beyond those already mentioned, and a White man, totaling eight—with small guitars, fiddles, horns, and transverse flutes—and two Black drummers with their drums covered with oilcloth.

The equipment was carried by fifty-two pack mules with food and drink of various kinds, some from this land, some from Portugal. They also carried a well-stocked pharmacy. . . .

On the 19th of August the Field Officer Regent set out with everything and spent the night at the house of the Reverend Father João da Costa Resende, brother of the expedition's chaplain, Father Gabriel da Costa Resende. The officer and his entourage were received and lodged with all care and preparation.

At this same place on the 20th, before traveling, we were joined by some other persons to accompany us into the Wilderness, enlarging the retinue, including one who became its surgeon. As well, the most enlightened persons of that area came to our table to greet us, the most distinguished of whom were the Reverend Vicar of Prados, two [militia] captains, and José Antônio and Severino Ribeiro, along with some other priests. . . .

On the 22d an hour before dawn the drums signalled reveille and then the musicians at the sound of their sonorous instruments sang their songs until the sun came up. They then sang the Ave Maria and the Reverend Chaplain offered the Holy Sacrifice of the Mass, which was heard by those of our troop as well as by many people who had come there in order to request [land grants]. . . .

On the 25th [of August] . . . we slept at a place called Barbosa, or rather Manoel Barbosa, who came to await us along with others a league before arriving at his house, where we arrived in mid-afternoon, having advanced five leagues.

Here we were joined by a lieutenant, son of the Secretary, and a soldier, both of whom had been ordered to Jacoí. About an hour later there also arrived [militia] Lieutenant José da Serra, along with others to wait on the Field Officer. The Field Officer assigned some lands here with his customary rectitude.

At this place many complaints were made in private to the Field Officer regarding the said lieutenant José da Serra Caldeira, and the Field Officer took them under advisement until better informed.

On the 26th, an hour before sunrise, with drummers and musicians playing, the Holy Sacrifice of the Mass was celebrated. All those poor persons there considered it a miracle from Heaven, for years had gone by since they had heard Mass. Then we mounted our horses, along with the owner of the ranch, the lieutenant who was going to Jacoí, and other persons who had come from Piuí to await the Field Officer and in whose company we went to Piuí. We traveled four leagues and rested at the house of Lieutenant Serra. There in private many complaints were repeated of unjust decisions by this Serra which he practiced as absolute lord, without fear of any punishment.

Here the Field Officer went to see the location of the chapel and found it a cattle corral. He became disgusted with such barbarous and untamed people who abused God and His saints by not preserving a temple and said they should demand from this man the requisite services. The inhabitants defended themselves, saying that Serra had sold off the church ornaments, as if to say they would never hear Mass said there. So the Field Officer gave Lieutenant Serra a written order in the best form to raise a church within three months, saying also that anyone who refused to cooperate in the project would be subject to arbitrary punishment. There resided here a man named Valentim, a master tailor, dirty as a pig, who, they say, administered the last sacraments to the dying. Our Reverend Chaplain baptized two children of the neighborhood who were [already] teething. . . .

On September 3d the Field Officer ordered a soldier and three other men arrested, along with a Black criminal and a woman, his mistress, as accomplices in a crime, for they had killed their respective master and husband.

On September 6th these persons were brought in and on the 7th they were sent, along with the officially hired slave catcher, to Vila Rica to the Most Illustrious and Excellent Count and General.

On September 8th the Reverend Vicar of Santa Ana de Bamboí [that is, Bambuí] celebrated a sung Mass with the Field Officer's slave musicians singing plainsong and Father José Bernardes, coadjutor of Tamandoá, our preacher in these days. The Field Officer dispatched two *bandeiras*, or forces, to the Wilderness with all necessary and sufficient preparation, naming Lieutenant José da Serra [Caldeira] as head of one bandeira and José Cardoso as head of the other. . . .

On the 11th [September] we left this place, not following a road or track, but with another guide. Lots of slaves went in front with bill-hooks, axes, and hoes to push through the forests, open trails, and make bridges over streams and small rivers, through which the troop could pass. And on this day, trail-blazing and pushing through the forest with much work, we reached the edge of the São Francisco River. All of us were on foot, without any horses, while over half our troop and all our horses and train, pack mules, everything, were scattered across fields and woods, as they could not overcome the obstacles of several streams, woods, and swamps. So we were all badly lodged [that night].

On this day the Field Officer became annoyed with some men who displayed little zeal and, dismounting, went forward on foot with the other workers who were in the front. By his unrelenting diligence he reached the edge of the river, being the first to see it along with a few men who kept up with him in this arduous endeavor.

On the 12th, two hours before dawn, the Field Officer rose, ordered reveille, and sent a message to the Reverend Chaplain to celebrate the holy office of the Mass. With that done, he distributed the work, assigning some men to cut trails and straighten pathways, others to open a cart road, others to cut lumber, others to fix the road so the rest of the baggage that had been left in the fields and woods could arrive. Nothing else happened until the 21st except continuous work toward building a bridge and [getting] lumber for the anticipated scaffolding to be placed in the river in order to build the intended structure with greater ease. . . .

[On the 1st of October] because a supporting post had been sunk into the river at the wrong place, it was necessary to pull it out. Once it had been raised it turned upside down, falling on top of the scaffolding and killing more than fifty people who were struggling with the beam. The Field Officer rushed to this danger, throwing himself [into the river] from a very high embankment and, reaching a canoe that was there, rowed to where the beam was becoming loose from the scaffolding to fall with its entire weight. One end was already touching the water and the beam was rolling on the scaffolding, so everyone would die. But he drove the canoe [toward it] and, putting his shoulder to the beam, he held it until four slaves who swam toward him were able to assist in such a tight moment. His act was so timely, prompt, forceful, and valiant that, before God, it saved many lives. It left everyone agape, admiring his valor and speed and the way he fearlessly acted, paying no attention to his own danger in order to free and save so many souls.

On the 2d of October, as the Field Officer and others working on the bridge looked on, a good Black fell from the bridge, at first striking his right thigh on a pointed stick that tore it to the bone, and then tumbling a second time, to lie on the bank of the river. Others immediately carried him in their arms to his campsite where the expedition's surgeon went to treat him with all care and diligence, as the occasion demanded.

No sooner had he finished than a shout went up from the bridge and a new misfortune was revealed: the work supervisor himself had fallen in the same way, from all that height, hitting the scaffolding and landing on the river's edge, with half his body in the water and the other half on land. Without hesitation the Field Officer leapt down the embankment followed by the Reverend Chaplain to aid the unfortunate man, whom they found in a faint. Fearing he was dead, they brought him up in their arms. With the immediate ministration of medicines and the use of spirits he soon showed signs of life, although bathed in blood from some injuries to his head and scratches on his face. He was soon treated with the most efficient diligence, as the case required, attended by the Field Officer with as much care and generosity as could be [given] in such a place, in order for these ministrations to be applied truly and well.

In six days the injured man was totally well, by virtue of the promises the Field Officer made to Our Lady of the Conception and to Saint Francis of Sales. On the very day before his fall the work's supervisor had helped raise the posts for the chapel to Saint Francis of Sales, planning the effort and directing the job of raising them into place. And also, as has been said, nothing was left wanting in the application of temporal remedies. For the same reason the slave with the punctured thigh became healthy and well, without even a scar. . . .

On the 7th of October at the Ave Maria [tolling of the angelus at sundown], they finished laying the last boards for the bridge decking. Just at that moment, when the Field Officer looked to the other side of the river, he saw his pack train arriving at the bridge, having come along the newly completed road. It had come from his Capote Ranch laden with provisions and aid for some things that were almost depleted.

This sudden happening caused well-founded satisfaction, because everyone saw that a pack train that came to supply them with necessities could, without wetting any feet, cross such a mighty river. So the Field Officer immediately ordered a solemn procession, with a crucifix of Our Lord in front, along with Our Lady of the Conception. For a thanksgiving service attended by all sorts of people who were around there, a procession was organized and all passed over the bridge, singing a Te Deum Laudamus, going directly to the chapel of Saint Francis of Sales. There, an altar was raised on which Our Lord and Our Lady were placed, everyone singing a litany-chant with music. When this service was finished, we all returned to our lodgings singing the most devout prayers to Our Lady.

On the 8th [of October] the Field Officer rose before dawn, and ordered reveille to be played, to which sounds all came to work on the embankment. So by one o'clock it was all done and finished.

The Field Officer then arranged all the men in military order, and, marching two by two with the said Officer and Reverend Chaplain at the front, with drums, horns, and flutes playing a march, we marched across the bridge in this disciplined unity to the Saint Francis of Sales chapel. There the Reverend Chaplain celebrated the Holy Sacrifice of the Mass, at the end of which were repeated many devoted prayers in praise of Our Lady, to the sound of instruments.

At the conclusion of this act we marched once again in the same unvarying order, crossing the bridge a second time and retiring to our lodgings after placing the most sacred images in their correct place. Then we all gathered before the bridge and lifted into place before it a most holy Cross, fairly high up, to be reverenced by all who pass that place, as a sign of our redemption.

When this was done, a table was set for dinner with a splendid banquet at which we counted sixty-five White men. . . .

Afterwards various people arrived to make requests for land . . . and they each asked for three leagues of land. The Field Officer inquired of each one, since they had not sent any slave to help build the bridge, how many [slaves] they would send for the extension of the new road or for building the main chapel for the Church of Our Lady of Bamboí. Each one replied that he had only one or two little Blacks and even then that one was sick and only one well. To this the Field Officer would nod and [seem to] agree. Then he would change the subject of the conversation to a very different matter and after a good while, when they were engaged in the new subject, suddenly the Field Officer would ask each one whether he had the wherewithal to develop the said three leagues of land they were requesting. Having forgotten what they said before, they replied: one that he had eight Blacks, another ten, and another twelve. The Field Officer thus came to perceive the refined cunning which they all uniformly used: to help with these works for the common good that were so needed at the beginning, all were reluctant to cooperate with aid destined for a goal that everyone perceived to be of manifest utility. Notwithstanding his observing this reluctance, he would always grant their requests with maturity and prudence in such terms that it followed that they understood his intention.

On the 9th we left the river after hearing Mass and, after going four or five leagues, we arrived at the parish to which the Field Officer had some days earlier dispatched a number of men to open cart roads in the nearby forests, cut post timbers, and trim lumber for the raising of the main chapel of the said parish's church. Without dismounting, the Field Officer went to the woods with some who accompanied him, to see, observe, and examine the work they had done on this matter. He dismounted at the edge of the woods and, after a minute examination, he returned, mounted, and, with the others, wandered through the savanna to choose the most appropriate place to raise the chapel. After making his firm decision, he ordered the holes marked for the posts. By this time the carts were arriving with the posts and he returned to the woods to order the beginning of carting lumber. He ordered his baggage train that was arriving on the neighboring plain to camp next to the location of the chapel. On this day we lost two pack mules, besides the three we lost . . . on our way to the Wilderness. . . .

On the 10th [of October] an hour before sunrise the musicians and drummers played their ordinary and daily routine and we heard Mass as we always did without failing a single day. The Field Officer ordered all the people, regardless of quality, to gather, and, going in front, at the sound of instruments he went to the chapel. There with untiring diligence and zealous care he began assigning people to their respective tasks. He joined the largest group working that day to open holes and raise up posts, a very tiring job because of their great weight: the first one broke two carts when being brought.

On that same afternoon Lieutenant José da Serra Caldeira arrived where we were. Before speaking to the Field Officer he began to complain publicly and to murmur, blaspheming against him, saying that the said officer had taken away not only his credibility but his land. At that point a friend of the Field Officer objected, asking Serra why he so dissolutely complained about his superior officer with such injurious words that could demolish and scatter his prestige, honor, decorum, and regard, demanding that he should specify the motives for such a harmful and odious excess. To which Serra answered, in the presence of Casemiro de Morais, José Antônio, and others who were there, that the Field Officer had dressed him down in a letter, lessening his prestige, and that in his absence he had given part of his lands to a João Pereira.

The man who defended the Field Officer replied, saying, "This complaint is far from the truth, most frivolous, and improperly uttered against so worthy a person and is a most dissolute and prejudicial excess, considering that you lack cause for such harmful hatefulness and excessively strong words, words that may discredit and injure a man who has done nothing to offend you. The letter that the Field Officer wrote did nothing more than express surprise at the half-heartedness, lack of energy, and carelessness with which you behaved in not energetically carrying out the orders given. [These orders] were directly extracted from those issued by the Most Illustrious and Excellent Count and General to the Field Officer, in view of which, all the injurious calumny proffered in this complaint is unjust. [For the Field Officer] to have acted differently would have been to betray the trust and confidence placed in him by that Most Excellent Sir and, in view of what has been said, you would do well to restrain yourself from discrediting him who has not injured you.

"And as to the lands about which you complain there is a like parallel to the above, because someone he had never known or seen before asked for them to cultivate them. It is his duty to make such grants in keeping with the orders of the Most Illustrious and Excellent Count and General, especially since the Field Officer did not know what you now allege. What is certain is that you have not yet made a request or presented your loss, because, had you done so, you would see whether he acted with rectitude or injustice in this case, and then you could have relied on reality and not on airy bases. Certainly there is antipathy when the complaints come before the experience."

In view of this argument, Serra went to speak to the Field Officer with greater serenity, and there they discussed Serra's failures in the Wilderness. He spent the night with us.

On the 11th, after hearing Mass before sunrise, the Field Officer stressed to the Reverend Vicar of the Church of Our Lady of Santa Ana the careful diligence with which he should continue the work for the said Lady's chapel, taking advantage of this occasion because another one might not occur later on. He also advised him on how he should proceed, and gave him the necessary authorizations regarding any lack or need that might come up. Then, at the sound of drums, he ordered all the people to gather, selecting those who seemed best to him to stay and continue the work on the chapel. He admonished and warned them to offer willing obedience in executing the commandments that the Reverend Vicar might determine, for, if they did not, they would know [about it] when he returned from the Wilderness.

With this done, we mounted our horses along with the others who would accompany us to the Wilderness and that day we slept at São Simão, three leagues away. There we rearranged our baggage for the trip to the Wilderness.

On the 12th we stayed in São Simão because of the heavy rain that day. All we could do was prepare our weapons, do target practice, and distribute the powder, lead, and bullets that seemed necessary for our supply and the protection of the travelers....

On the 16th [of October] we left this coppice-wood and headed for the Quilombo do Ambrósio [runaway slave settlement] and we reached a wide stream where the Misericórdia Ranch ends. There we spent some time digging into the embankments on each side so we could get the horses and pack mules across. We did so successfully at the cost of much work on the part of the Field Officer, who became hoarse with so much shouting to the workers.

At this point two local field men reported that they had found tracks of Blacks who were spying on us. From this rumor there arose among the people a good deal of fear, each one murmuring according to the valor or cowardice that graced him.

This crisis gone, we traveled on until we reached the Quilombo do Ambrósio. There we wondered at the ruined buildings and the multiple camouflaged trenches studded with spikes that characterized the Quilombo. We will not provide a more specific and detailed description because it is in the diary and accompanying map where its arrangement is truly pictured.

On this same day we camped alongside a stream that is near the Quilombo. The murmuring, provoked by the fear of Blacks that had begun at the wide stream, as mentioned above, now began to increase. As the Tapejaras Indians of the Wilderness were the most fearful and timorous, their fear and dread easily spread. So much so that the Field Officer became aware of the whispered anxiety or labyrinths of fright. He became furious at all, even at his trusted friends who had never given him the least trouble, and lumped them together with the other transgressors. The blameless cried out in protest, but it is true that he quickly undid the intrigue that the fearful ones had woven.

An hour before sunrise on the 17th the drummers and musicians continued their accustomed practice and our Reverend Chaplain celebrated Mass, which we all heard. The Field Officer then divided the people of his entourage. Half were to carry out, in all the streams and rivulets around us, a detailed examination of caves and holes to the center of the gravel and shale to discover any signs of gold. With them went soldier José Francisco Serra to observe whether or not they did this assigned task. The other half went with the Field Officer to clear, burn, and till the land to plant corn. He spent all day in the hot sun, working and laboring alongside them, making the others work, in which violent exercise he sweated three shirts. At night they all retired, worn out; but those who went to look for gold came back with the disappointment of not finding any. . . .

On the 20th [of October] the Field Officer along with the Reverend Chaplain and others joined in the search for gold, from which effort nothing resulted. That night the workers at the streams slept where they worked, returning to their lodgings on the 21st, it being Saturday. But the news of gold was always as before.

On this the 21st the Field Officer went to the clearing to plant corn with the others who worked on this. But in the afternoon, a bit before sunset, he left the clearing alone, having spotted a deer. He went after it to kill it. While following the deer that with slow steps meandered off, and concentrating on this task, he lost track of the direction of the encampment. Then, the more he looked for it, the farther he got from it. In the meantime, night fell with a closed-in darkness, without his being able to find the direction he should take. After everybody [else] was back in camp and seeing that only he was missing, we began to consider why he was absent. Those who had been working at the clearing declared at what time he had left there, indicating the direction he had taken and that he had gone alone. Then the Tapejara Indians of the Wilderness became convinced that the Field Officer had become lost in the savanna. As we did not know whether he had encountered some danger posed by Blacks, heathen Indians, or some beast, everyone was uniformly saddened, giving vent to their grief according to the degree of their love for him. We divided ourselves into various groups, each firing many shots in a certain direction, beating drums so the said gentleman could find the direction of the drums and the shots which we continually fired, and of these there were so many and so close together that someone unacquainted with our purpose would think that it was a pitched battle. We lit bonfires at the top of the highest hills to see whether the said gentleman, seeing the great flames, might direct himself to them to rejoin our loving company. We were all anxious, confused, and perturbed, like cattle without a herdsman. But God deigned to allow that around midnight, from about a league away from our camp, he heard the shots and was restored to our company at midnight more or less. His arrival caused great joy to all, happiness and satisfaction. As we had bemoaned his absence, so repeatedly we exaggerated in demonstrating our joy at his restitution. After greeting us all and thanking us for our affection, he paid us in the same coin, [declaring that], when he had become convinced he was lost, the only thing he thought of was the sorrow that his faithful friends would feel. . . .

On the 25th [of October] after the drummers did their job and our hearing the customary Mass, the Field Officer mounted his horse and accompanied by twenty-five horsemen and twenty persons on foot set off toward a part of the Wilderness to explore the streams and rivulets to see if there were gold. He spent all day on this enterprise and at night, because he was far off, they camped out at the foot of the Escalvada Serra. There they saw, quite close to them and in different directions, three fires. The Tapejaras of the Wilderness, judging that many Blacks were near our entourage, feared to go and discover them or scout them out, no matter how much the Field Officer tried to persuade them to do so. They replied every time by pointing to the great danger, saying the quilombos were many in that direction as evidenced by the signs of those very fires and that it was well known that there was a quilombo there composed of more than two hundred Blacks.

On the 26th the Field Officer sent for all the baggage and other people who had remained behind to join those he had with him in order to increase the number of people and weapons and go see whether the areas in which the fires burned were truly infested with Blacks. While he waited for them to arrive [from the previous encampment], he occupied his time doing a minute inspection of the most likely areas in which to find gold. But, having done so, nothing resulted, for he found no signs of what he searched for with so much energy.

It was after nightfall before the gold prospectors, the baggage train, and its guard arrived. After singing their litanies to Our Lady and making some devout prayers as was their ordinary custom, the Field Officer ordered that there be picked out from among them all those considered most reliable and ready for the intended enterprise, and he found that forty-two had been chosen according to his criteria. To them he issued powder, lead, and bullets as well as weapons for hand-to-hand combat [such as knives and daggers] and put José Cardoso in charge. He ordered that on the following day they should march out to examine the areas that seemed most suspect where Blacks could be hiding. If he [Cardoso] found any believable signs that indicated the existence of Blacks, he should promptly send word so that he [the Field Officer] could go speedily with the rest of the people to reinforce him.

On the 27th the above-mentioned people left, numbering forty-two, to search the areas mentioned in the above paragraph. Meanwhile the Field Officer ordered the rest of the people to continue searching [for gold], but the results were the same as before because they did not find any gold. On this day they killed six partridges and a deer.

On the 28th the Field Officer continued the repeated and detailed search of the area that seemed most propitious for bearing gold, but despite excellent arrangements, no gold or shadow of gold was found. Working at this, already near nightfall, he saw part of the bandeira he had sent out the previous day. As they were still far away, and he was desirous of knowing what had happened in their effort, he mounted his horse along with others and went to meet them. They began immediately to tell him that they were arriving worn out and famished, that they had walked for two whole days breaking through forests and rugged mountain ranges, carrying out their scouting work to see if they could find some signs, but that they had found nothing except their own exhaustion and weariness. They said, yes, there was, by the evidence of fires, a clear sign of the presence of Blacks nearby, but that they must be connected more closely to the Wilderness either in one direction or another. Since they did not have a guide to take them to the location and living-place of the Blacks, all such initiatives would be frustrated, in vain, and dangerous.

In light of what they said the Field Officer returned to his lodging along with those who were there as it was already night, and the others came in groups until all had joined.

On this same day a pack train arrived here loaded with supplies, for we were needing them and we had no more than enough for two days. After praying a chaplet we retired. . . .

On the 30th, after Mass, we mounted our horses and traveled until two o'clock and we reached the foot of a mountain range. The Field Officer dismounted, and forty of us, including the said Gentleman, all on foot and well armed, entered the coppices of the woods and into high mountains, rugged and thick, heading toward a quilombo called Corisco. And having ordered all the others and the baggage train to go to the same destination by a more circuitous route, by four o'clock we arrived there with utmost caution. But our effort was in vain because the Blacks, perhaps having seen us by virtue of their spies, had deserted [the place]. . . .

The Field Officer arrived dripping with sweat, allowing his clothes to dry on his body because the baggage train was delayed; as a result, he was not well for a few days.

On the 31st of October, after hearing Mass, half the people were put to planting a field of corn of which they planted three *alqueires* [or between 39 and 108 liters of seed], and they also planted some beans, squash, castor-bean plants, manioc, lima beans, and much cotton. The other half were assigned to examine and dig in the stream beds but they found nothing all day, except a bit of emory.

On this same day there arrived at this place the Field Officer has named Santos Fortes, three men who came by way of the new road the Field Officer has been opening to this location at Santos Fortes. One is called José Teixeira Aranha, another José Gonçalves, and the third Alexandre Pereira Brandão.

The first came to request lands for his home, the second because of a dispute he has with José Pinto, and the third because of a dispute that he said he had with the Field Officer [himself], and he put forth his request orally in the following manner:

That he, the supplicant, was owner of a ranch called Perdizes, but now he finds it measured and demarcated in the name of the Field Officer, with improvements, cattle, and people living on it. He had spent four hundred and some *mil-réis* in two expeditions that he had led, the first one six years ago and the second three. In light of this he had come to see if the Field Officer would give him his ranch and, if not, give him permission to complain of this to the Most Illustrious and Excellent Count and General.

To which the Field Officer differed, saying that all the soil of this land belonged to His Most Faithful Majesty as Grand Master of the three Orders of Christ, and that only those may claim dominion of any part of it who have received a true concession from the said Lord or from whoever does his bidding. Without this circumstance no person could call himself legitimate master of a single foot of land and even less allege dominion over such. For indeed no individual could obtain true dominion without the said circumstance, for to do so would be to deprive His Most Faithful Majesty of the rights of a lawful owner. This is the law of this land at the present time as practiced by the Most Illustrious and Excellent Sirs who represent the Most Noble Person of the King Our Lord. And the courts of Justice, whether high or low, have made this clear with unbroken rectitude. In the light of which the supplicant should give up, for he [the Field Officer] was no schoolboy to be persuaded by such reckless abuses and had given the supplicant all the satisfaction that he merited. The Field Officer knew that the supplicant was also of that number who, with a bit of manioc flour in his knapsack, would clear a few trees from the banks of three streams and then, having done as little as possible, will say, "This ranch is mine." They then sell it as if they were owners of the royal treasury, because, having sold it, they go and in the same way do it again. Such a practice was contrary to applicable law and he could not, therefore, understand it.

The Field Officer then asked him if he had a *sesmaria*, or royal grant, for the said lands that he claimed as his. He responded that he did not. So the Field Officer repeated, saying, "So you came there once six years ago and then again three years ago and therefore you claim these lands are yours without ever keeping there a pig or an ox or a cow or a mare or a horse or any person, not having planted one grain of corn, nor even putting up a small floorless, thatch-roof hut, nor a path, nor a road, nor anything.

"The others, even though not following the rules, call something theirs because they at least live on the land and harvest from it and populate it, but you, on the contrary, call something yours without a land grant, without populating it, nor harvesting from it, nor possessing it in any way. Even if you had a royal land grant you would always be obliged to people it and cultivate said lands, for those are the orders of the King Our Lord, so how can you call it yours when you do not have a royal land grant nor have ever possessed it nor harvested from it?"

In the light of which Brandão said that the Field Officer was right, that he, Brandão, had no right to the said lands unless he, the Field Officer, would give them to him, for he had children who would inherit from him. The Field Officer replied that he also had children who would inherit in the same way and that was why he had surveyed and marked off his royal land grant, and had populated it with improvements, with people, with corrals, and cattle. Nevertheless, if he wanted half that land he would give it to him, to settle the matter, keeping the other half. To which Brandão replied, "Either all or nothing."

So the Field Officer responded, "Since you do not make use of an action that is so politic and born of my urbanity, and have rejected my offer of what was mine alone and never yours, now I say to you: 'Not half, nor a little, nor a lot, nor anything!'

"And for you to know to whom you speak—who it was agreed to give you half of that which by any measure and by law was mine—know that those whom you hired to place signs of your possession on that land, they themselves say that it is true you ordered them to do so, but they did not know it was called Perdizes Ranch and only now learned of it. For them it was clear that that ranch belonged to Sergeant-Major So-and-So from São Paulo who lived in Piuí, because he had lived on that land in a house, with a small manioc flour mill and an establishment of slaves, with fields, clearings, corrals, and cattle. He had moved away some twenty years ago because runaway slaves had killed five of his slaves.

"In view of which, Senhor Brandão," said the Field Officer, "which of us is ahead in verifying and researching the present case? And for you to know even more, I'll show you this: Here you see this sales contract signed before many witnesses that shows that I bought said ranch from that Sergeant-Major and that it became mine ever since the day on which he sold it to me, transferring to me all the rights and dominion he might have.

"You see I offered you half of what was mine as much by royal grant as by so-called squatters' rights just so I could keep the good name I have always had. But because you exploited me and scorned the favor I was doing you, now I say to you that I no longer want to do it, given that you did not know how to make use of the courtesy and regard with which I treated you."

On this day they killed some partridges.

On November first the musicians and drummers worked hard at their task and, after we heard Mass, we mounted our horses [and rode on], sleeping by the side of a small river called Salitre. For many years there was a quilombo there and recently it has been rebuilt; it is called Catiguá, and has more than 150 wooden cots. It is certain that it was a quilombo of much strength and power, which is clearly shown because, there being in this area many woods, all those near the quilombo are destroyed and worn out by the many and repeated plantings that the Blacks made there. They left recently, for fear of our bandeiras. We harvested some of the corn that they had left, and it served us to feed some horses that were less energetic.

Here we set up an outpost or hamlet of grass huts, well laid out, because the locale is itself attractive and pleasant. We hunted and killed a number of deer, partridges, and guans. On the night we arrived, Simão Rodrigues went fishing in the river and in a short while caught thirteen fish called *tabaranas* [tubaranas], which are quite large....

On the 4th [of November] the Field Officer got up very early and after the musicians and drummers did as they usually did, he sent a message to the Reverend Chaplain, who was still sleeping, to get up and say Mass. After we had all heard it, the Field Officer had the drummers beat their drums again, to gather any who were missing, and he told us to get ready with our horses to go and conduct a formal act to found a village or outpost and claim the area.... With much gaiety we mounted our horses ... and went two leagues until we encountered a grass fire along our way. The lively wind raised notable flames and we split up, galloping our horses, each one in a different direction, taking care not to get burnt.

Going on until well after noon, we neared a ridge at a delightful and attractive place. The Field Officer and all of us dismounted there, and he had the drummers beat their drums. Summoning a council of those he deemed most worthy of deciding, he asked them what they thought of the place. He said he thought it was a good place for founding a hamlet or outpost, but that to claim the land it would be better to do so at the top of the nearby ridge, to be able to take in all that could be seen, lands destined for the new arrivals who would follow him or had come with him. All agreed. When we reached the top of the ridge it also seemed like a good place to erect a hamlet or outpost. The Field Officer then ordered us all to dismount and, having the drummers beat their drums, gathered us all. From a sucupira tree they hewed four crosses at the foot of which the Field Officer had them set up an altar. After the most holy images of Our Lord and Our Lady were placed on it, the Reverend Chaplain had us all kneel and pray a Hail-Mary and a Salve Regina to Our Lady asking her to grant us much success. And this we did with all devotion.

Once this was done, the Field Officer had them play the horns, flutes, small guitars, and fiddles while at the sound of these instruments other musicians sang. Then he said to soldier José Francisco Serra in a loud voice that he, the Field Officer, took possession of that place to which he had come by order of the Most Illustrious and Excellent Count of Valadares, Governor and Captain General of this Captaincy of Minas Gerais, to divide those lands among those who asked for them; that those who so desired should request them, for he was ready to grant their requests with evenhandedness.

Those who had land-grant authorizations ready requested them first and named the places they wanted. Then came those who had had their petitions certified, then some who made their requests orally, and finally all those who carried with them powers-of-attorney to petition on behalf of those who were absent.

The Field Officer responded to all with equal integrity and rectitude. He stated that by this act he recognized all as now in possession of the sites they had requested and went on to advise them that they should take care to populate what they had requested, because the Most Illustrious and Excellent Count and General did not want these lands left empty. Anyone who failed to carry out this charge should not complain if these lands were [later] given to another who asked for them.

And he also said that all of us were running short, that many were without clothes, and that he was among them because he had divided his among those who most needed them, as they had witnessed with their own eyes. So no farther advance into the Wilderness would be possible without first populating this place so that those who did go farther would have access to supplies among those from this place and thus might more easily establish themselves. This would not be possible unless they followed the above requirements.

When we had concluded all this, we returned to the quilombo of Catiguá and the hamlet or outpost we had left that morning. . . .

On the 6th [of November] after the drummers and musicians did their duty and after Mass, we mounted our horses. Along the way a mulatto and two Blacks who had stayed behind with a sick stallion at the Santos Fortes Quilombo caught up with us. They said that runaway slaves had been spying on them at night, as they knew by the growling of two puppies that had stayed with them and by the tracks of three Blacks that they had found in the morning. This had happened every night they were there. But the horse was now well.

On this day, as we traversed the savanna, we gathered a quantity of cashews, an excellent fruit. We saw [the smoke of] fires on our left toward the Wilderness that all of us judged to be of runaway slaves because, since no one else lives in the Wilderness, the fires must be of such Blacks. That day we slept beside a small river which the Field Officer named Santa Eriá. We arrived after dark, for this day our trip was long and we covered seven leagues. Along the way we killed some [wild] pigs and partridges. . . .

On the 11th [of November] the Field Officer ordered reveille very early, the instruments were played very early and after that he ordered the drums beaten to summon the people. When they were gathered, he said farewell to all those in that place with a brief talk, saying that he was very grateful for their good and faithful company. He also said they should not forget to populate their ranches as soon as possible, because it was much more preferable to possess them there for free than to get them somewhere else, as was the usual custom, by paying many thousand *cruzados*, which they would have to work their entire life to pay off and never succeed in doing so and in the end find themselves always in debt, leaving their families in extreme poverty as they well knew. The land of the Wilderness is very fertile, abundant, and healthy. He invited them by this gift to rely on this assistance, even those who were already wealthy and much more so the distressed. He begged them to forgive him if he had offended anyone in any way during this trip, as his intention had only been to carry out, as a faithful vassal, the instructions of the Most Illustrious and Excellent Count and General, to honor all of them, and not to offend anyone. They could count on the São Simão ranch, where they could rest and allow their horses to recover [their strength] with some sustenance, and he was ready to serve them with whatever else there was at that ranch. He said they should not keep him company any longer because he was going to Santo Estêvão, where he would spend some time on necessary errands and important business.

Everyone much thanked the Field Officer for the good way, courteous benevolence, and affability with which he bid everyone farewell, and said they would accept his kind offer in case they needed [such help]. With that they said farewell, and the Field Officer mounted his horse and, along with his trusted slaves and other baggage, set off in a different direction headed for the top of the Desempinhado Hill and, from there, headed in the direction of Santo Estêvão.

We travelled all day, knocking down embankments of streams so the troop could pass, but all in vain, because Simão Rodrigues, who was our guide, was an errant guide, and the farther we went the more lost we became. The Field Officer, recognizing near nightfall that the guide had certainly lost his way, became much annoyed with him and, suddenly giving the horse its head, set off in a different direction than that followed by the other. The rest of us followed him at some distance, not getting too close because he was still annoyed. And it was a good route because while he was knocking down an embankment at a small river in order to cross it, the field hands of the ranch where we were headed, seeing our entourage from afar, began to signal with repeated shots. A Castilian peon, a slave of the Field Officer, most quickly approached us and with his arrival we cheered up; he led us and we were presently conducted to the Santo Estêvão ranch, which we reached after dark.

On the 12th, very early, reveille was ordered and the musicians, with much happiness and pleasure for having reached the Santo Estêvão ranch, played beautiful minuets which were much admired, not by us who had heard them on most days but by some families of the Field Officer, I mean, by the families of the dependents of the Field Officer. These were already settled there to be transferred, little by little, to the Wilderness, where they have been assigned to ranches received in the distribution.

Around eight o'clock Mass was said. Then the Field Officer ordered that all the pregnant mares be gathered in one corral where he could go see them in the afternoon, and all those with foals in another, as that separation is the present custom among breeders. After dinner we went to see these mares and we were surprised, for we had seen them earlier and they had come here very thin, and now, as they say, they were fat as cows—that's why we were surprised. In another separate corral there were sixteen *achiote* burros, which are the male ones that cover the mares, and they were also very fat, strong, and glistening. The obvious health of these animals pleased and satisfied not only the Field Officer but all of us, because it served as a believable indication of the quality of pastures in the Wilderness.

After this pleasureful recreation, the Field Officer ordered the animals freed to their respective pastures and we returned to the house, never ceasing to praise the good choice he had made in introducing such a lucrative breeding activity. For certainly, with God's favor, he would realize a very considerable and continuous reward. We also praised him for deciding to establish ranches in the Wilderness, because only its broad spaces could support the weight of so numerous a quantity [of livestock].

When we reached the house we found there our friend and companion José Antônio de Sousa Pinto, who had stayed in São Simão because of illness. At the same time the Field Officer received three bundles of letters from Rio de Janeiro and Minas [Gerais], forwarded from the São Simão ranch. Also, they summoned our Expedition's surgeon to go treat Casemiro de Morais, who was ill at that ranch. . . .

On the 16th [of November] there arrived at the Santo Estêvão ranch twelve people to collect the gold which the Field Officer owed [them] in that region for the provisions that his overseer had bought there to supply the present Expedition. He paid them, ordering that to each one should be weighed out the amount of his share, which totaled, according to the count made by the Expedition's surgeon, 517 and 5/8ths ounces. The nearby places had become depleted of supplies. . . .

On the 21st [of November], after Mass, we marched to Tamandoá, about two and one-half leagues away. Along the way we met the Reverend Vicar of that hamlet, his coadjutor, the Commander, the Cavalry Ensign, and many others who had come to meet the Field Officer. After greeting him and the others who traveled with him, we marched to the hamlet in good order, two by two. As soon as we were within sight, the people of Tamandoá began to play trumpets as a sign of their welcome and their happiness in receiving the Field Officer. We went directly to the house of the Reverend Vicar where rooms had been readied for us; as we neared [his house], the cavalry formed two rows up to the vicar's doorway with only the Field Officer moving between them, mounted on a superb black horse very well groomed and equipped with richly decorated saddle and reins. He dismounted at the door of the Reverend Vicar, bowed to everyone, and entered along with the priests and the other distinguished persons named [above], who then visited with him.

Now the requests began to boil up, as did the squabbles, the complaints, and the controversies in such variety that they seemed a labyrinth, and in the next twenty-four hours he hardly had time to eat a hurried bite or sleep two hours. For the people were many and the issues even more, and the Field Officer found himself perplexed, for he wanted to satisfy everyone, to calm everyone and put them at peace, but the strength of their hatred and ill will was almost inflexible. For this reason it took much, much effort to pacify them and restore them to a domestic and peaceful consonance, yet he nevertheless achieved this glory, except among two or three.

Then the Field Officer had brought to him one of the Blacks who had been captured by a bandeira at a quilombo and demanded from him that he should confess publicly who had murdered the married man who had been killed there. The Black, in the presence of all, said that it was the Blacks of the Quilombo Sambabaia who had killed that man and that his things, which were delivered to his widow, had come from the same quilombo. He said he had seen it all, for he had been captured at the said quilombo.

To which the Field Officer added, before all, that those were the deeds carried out by the Blacks of Campo Grande; and that while he was engaged in extinguishing them in order to create the *res publica* and establish its wellbeing—a service of great utility to relieve them of such prejudicial and damaging fears—the reward he got for such sustained zeal and penitential self-discipline was the ordinary calumny with which people spoke ill of him. But they could be sure that he had done nothing to counter those who murmured [against him], but everything in pure obedience to the only one who could make him undo [what he had done], and that was only the Most Illustrious and Excellent Count of Valadares, Governor and Captain General of this Captaincy. . . .

On the 27th [of November] the drummers played at dawn and the musicians worked with zeal, since this was the last day of our trip. The Holy Sacrifice of the Mass was celebrated and while we were halfway through it, five horsemen arrived to accompany the Field Officer. When Mass was over we mounted our horses and came to a place that he called Tapera, where he ordered the sheep he had there to be gathered, and they were so numerous that they covered a great expanse of the fields there. And when he had seen enough, he ordered gathered just the ones that had lambs with them, and they too were a great number.

Then he ordered the female burros that had young brought and there were ten; and after having inspected them, he ordered the ones who were single brought and there were thirty-six of these. Having seen everything in detail he reprimanded the slaves who worked at that task about some defect he had found. Then we mounted our horses and left to go to another ranch of the same master called Cataguases.

We arrived at Cataguases and found three corrals full of mules, all raised on his ranches, and he remained there more than an hour, inspecting and re-inspecting. When he had finished seeing the mules at the Cataguases ranch, we came toward Capote and in its fields he spent time seeing the mares that had given birth to mules. The slaves had gathered them for this purpose. And there he delighted even more in seeing those young animals. From afar we saw the mares that had already given birth, and in another direction those that were pregnant and had not yet given birth, but we could not inspect them because it was late and the Field Officer longed to see his home and his noble family.

When we neared his house we once again ran into so many sheep that they covered the fields and were more numerous than we had seen at the Tapera ranch. Then we entered his patio and dismounted, with the Field Officer safe and sound.

Here they saluted him with more than 300 shots, and played various instruments; in short, there was much happiness, as he retired to his home.

This is the faithful account of all the events worthy of being noted along the entire course of the trip and what happened to us.

46

Thanking Saint Anne–An Ex-voto from Brazil
(1755)

How does one thank a saint? Colonial Brazilians thanked theirs with votive offerings in the form of small paintings, such as the one in this selection dedicated to Saint Anne. Each story-painting recalled how a favorite saint, when urgently called upon to intervene, had miraculously rescued the donor from a grave but familiar danger: a fall from a horse, into a river, or out of a tree; illness or fever; a boat capsizing in a sudden storm, a child nearly crushed under a wagon wheel, escape from a burning house, a difficult childbirth. The person saved was obligated to offer thanks to the saint. A local artist was hired to make the painting, which the donor then placed in a chapel or at a shrine, typically one devoted to that saint, or hung in a special place such as the Sala dos Milagres, or Room of Miracles, at the pilgrims' Sanctuary of the Bom Jesus de Matosinhos in Congonhas do Campo, Minas Gerais.

Especially numerous in the coastal and mining regions of Brazil in the eighteenth century, the tradition of votive offerings of thanks, or ex-votos as they are called, came to Brazil and Spanish America from Portugal and Spain and was already well developed by the fifteenth century in Italy. In Brazil the artist's materials were typically oil paint on small wooden panels, rectangular in shape and never longer than about eighteen inches. Sometimes canvas or tile was used instead of wood. More often in Minas Gerais than in other places, the pictures were framed, but only rarely were they as richly decorated as the red and gold painted frame shown here. The artists were local craftsmen without academic training who, over time, nonetheless adopted similar techniques of color and perspective. Yet no artist could merely copy another: each miracle was unique and required its own rendering, and each artist interpreted a client's story according to his degree of skill. Few of them signed their pictures; the important relationship was between client and saint whose names, along with the date of the miraculous event, were allowed to shine.

Space within the picture was typically divided into three horizontal planes: in the upper, celestial sphere, indicated by clouds, floats the saint; human figures occupy the middle, earthly zone, usually at the moment of crisis just as the miracle is about to happen; and the bottom layer is text, a brief narrative and testimonial to the miracle. Those found in Minas Gerais frequently differed by dividing the middle and upper space vertically: the left side portrays the crisis, while clouds and the holy figure fill the right side.

Figure 32. "Thanking Saint Anne," an ex-voto offering, artist unknown, Brazil, 1755.
Courtesy of José Mindlin, São Paulo, Brazil.
⤳ SEE PLATE 12 ⤳

In eighteenth-century Minas Gerais, Saint Anne was a favorite, along with the Black Saint Benedict; Saint Luzia was addressed in times of eye injuries or diseases, and Saint Barbara and Saint Jeronimo were sought for protection against lightning and storms. So, too, was the Virgin Mary in any of her many personas. But the divine was not always a saint; the crucified Christ or the Holy Spirit might be chosen as the surest access to God.

The recipient of the miracle might be depicted kneeling in prayer, facing the saint and establishing a link between the heavenly and human spheres or else facing the viewer. Often only the key person is portrayed, while in more complex (and expensive) scenes family members and their Black servants encircle the sickbed, or several persons, united by a shared catastrophe, are tossed about in floodwaters or engulfed in a landslide. Fine furnishings or fancy clothes elevated a person's actual circumstances, such as those of the Black woman, Tiadozia da Costa (her last

name indicated she was African), in an ex-voto painted in 1798. She lies perilously ill in a big four-poster bed complete with red canopy and side curtains, fluffy pillows, and a dark blue cover decorated with white flowers. Chairs, a domestic comfort reserved for the rich and important, seldom appear in these paintings. Maladies were graphically shown: Silvéria Maria da Conceição, bitten by an insect, was portrayed with blood dripping from her lip; another woman prayed to the Most Holy Trinity to cure an abscess in her lower chest; and a man described a tumor on his leg.

Ex-votos were an authentic form of popular religion. Just as the art was free from academic rules, the devotion expressed in the art was similarly free from Church rules. Although, at the Council of Trent in the mid-sixteenth century, the Catholic Church had defended and encouraged veneration of the saints, votive offerings were practiced without doctrinal instruction and without official monitoring by the Church or its clergy. The sequence of actions—appeal to a holy being for a favor, the favor granted, gratitude offered —established a direct connection between the victim-donor and the divine, an intimacy forged in moments of grave and uncertain danger. Dependence on divine favor and the obligation to reply with gratitude extended and affirmed the patronage of everyday relationships—all without a priest as intermediary. Attention focused firmly on the dangers of this world, not on salvation or the condition of one's soul. And the small miracles, although matters of life or death to those concerned, were not ones formally recognized by the Church.

Why trouble to make these popular devotions public when thanks could be offered privately? A miracle known only to one person is scarcely a miracle at all. A picture, however, that hangs permanently on a church wall or beside a shrine announces and confirms the miracle. It was not just the offering of thanks that counted, but the recording of thanks that spread a saint's fame and efficacy. It also publicized the donor's worthiness as the recipient of holy favor and intercession. After all, illness might suddenly strike anyone down; why should this person be cured and not others in need? Here was evidence of selection as one of the specially protected.

Yet the writing, an essential element upon the surface of these images, was directly available only to those literate enough to read both the handwriting and the words. At first this seems a convincing clue to the identity of those who commissioned ex-votos as not coming from among the poor—the free poor, slaves, and former slaves who generally were illiterate. With ex-votos, experience of the miracle gave the maker of the offering authority to dictate her or his story, which was set in motion with the standard phrase, "The miracle that Saint So-and-So made." Whether the artist doubled as scribe or a second person was called on varied according to the circumstances. Dictation meant that any among the poor who were able to pay the fee could record a miracle.

The votive offering in this selection is painted in strong colors and confident lines. Saint Anne, seated on a throne, holds Mary on her lap and is teaching her to read—a book being Saint Anne's standard iconographic prop—a model of caring but practical motherhood. An accessible and sympathetic figure who was childless for the first twenty years of her marriage, Saint Anne was not divinely born herself, yet she marks the entry of the divine into the human sphere. Two angels, supporting the substantial cloud on which Anne and Mary sit, point to still higher celestial realms.

The center portion of the picture is puzzling. Where is the danger? Despite the reference to illnesses in the text, the three persons (and two donkeys) in the picture appear hearty. The river, which they have somehow managed to cross, does not threaten; indeed, it is a place to fish. Their lean-to looks sturdy; one animal grazes, the other is harnessed and loaded for travel. Does the Black man, a slave or former slave, wearing pants tucked into his boots, jacket, and hat, also carry a stick or a gun with powder in a pouch at his side? The man kneeling in prayer has deferentially removed his hat. A tranquil, bucolic scene.

The text is similarly ambiguous. A translation of the narrative reads: "Miracle that Senhora Saint Anne made for Manuel Fernandez Paredes [as he was] going to Goiás with his troop, freeing him and his people from illnesses [while they were] halted beside the river called Saint Matthew—in the year 1755." Perhaps stopping at the river was an unwelcome and imposed delay that exposed them to illness; or perhaps this scene represents the journey's safe end, the danger past.

47

Jeremiah in the Stocks–Baroque Art from the Gold Fields of Minas Gerais, Brazil
(ca. 1770s)

The religious art of Antônio Francisco Lisboa, one of Brazil's most celebrated artists and certainly the most celebrated of the colonial period, adorns all the principal churches of Minas Gerais, the mining district from which, in the eighteenth century, poured the vast wealth in gold and diamonds that sustained Portugal's overseas empire and financed nascent British industries. Not civil architecture, but churches—cathedrals, parish and convent churches, and chapels belonging to the confraternities—dominated the skylines of colonial towns both in scale and number. Sponsored by Jesuit, Benedictine, Franciscan, and Carmelite orders as well as by parishes, the churches were designed, built, and decorated by locally resident artists and craftsmen who had immigrated from Portugal, the Azore Islands, or Italy or who had been born in the mining towns—sometimes Mulattoes such as Antônio Francisco, who later came to be known as Aleijadinho, or "Little Cripple."

The great variety of Aleijadinho's work ranges from design to woodcarving and sculpting in stone, especially in the regionally quarried soapstone. He began in 1760 by carving the wooden altars dedicated to Saint Anthony and Saint Francis of Paula for the church of Nossa Senhora do Bom Sucesso. A year later he sculpted a stone fountain in his home town of Ouro Prêto, or Vila Rica do Ouro Prêto ("rich town of black gold"), followed by work on the stone facade and bell towers for Saint John the Baptist church in Barão de Cocais. In 1764 he drew the architectural designs for the Saint Francis of Assisi church in Ouro Prêto. A few years later he completed this church by sculpting the intricate portal decoration that rises to a circular carved stone medallion, which in turn lifts the viewer's eyes to a central cross and the twin bell towers with their celestial-pointing spires, and by carving the lavish and delicately worked ceiling and arch of the apse. Besides other fountains, portals, and facades in stone as well as carved wood interiors, Aleijadinho designed the high altar of the church of the Brotherhood of the Blacks of Saint Joseph in 1772. He carved a statue of Saint Michael, two pulpits for the Nossa Senhora do Carmo church in Sabará, and the ornate stone lavabo in the sacristy of the church by the same name in Ouro Prêto, work that carried into the 1780s.

The style is Baroque combined with the later Rococo, elaborate and soaring in its curving lines that ascend Heavenward. Images of saints, winged angels, the Holy Ghost represented as rays of light, the crucified Christ, faith portrayed as a blindfolded Franciscan friar, parables from the Bible—this is the imagery with which Aleijadinho embellished his churches. Unlike the famous Baroque churches of Salvador, Rio de Janeiro, and Recife, churches with glittering interiors "entirely of gold," here there is more stone, and spaces are opened up in which a painted white background provides further contrast to intricately carved bas-reliefs. Instead of the monochromatic gold, paint of various colors is added. Exterior facades are more decorated, interiors less densely covered. The effect is one of greater light and of graceful, enchanting movement in which the structural lines—columns, moldings, arches, domes—remain defined. With the Saint Francis church in Ouro Prêto, Aleijadinho brought curved lines into the design by forming the central nave from two overlapping ellipses, giving to the outer shell and bell towers a rounded shape.

Aleijadinho learned his art not by any formal schooling but by seeing and doing. His father, Manuel Francisco Lisboa, who emigrated from Lisbon to the mining fields in 1724, worked first as a licensed carpenter, reaching the highest rank in the carpenters' guild by 1757; he was also consulted as an expert on architectural design. From building bridges and laying pipe, he increasingly worked on churches. Aleijadinho probably accompanied his father to the sites, learning as he watched and doing small jobs. His uncle, Francisco Antônio Pombal, also a carpenter and architect, is credited with the innovative design for the upper reaches of the nave in the Pilar church in Ouro Prêto, where for the first time he imposed a frame to contain the confusion of carving and thus set the style for religious architecture as it developed in Minas Gerais. Illustrated Bibles, engravings, and other books imported from Europe instructed Aleijadinho, who knew Latin, in examples of art and design beyond his immediate experience. By 1766, Manuel Francisco Lisboa had designed and begun construction on the church of Nossa Senhora do Carmo in Ouro Prêto, a project that Aleijadinho took over from him four years later, modifying his father's plans in basic ways.

At about the age of forty, Aleijadinho became afflicted with a debilitating disease (probably a form of leprosy) that crippled his feet and hands and eventually contorted the muscles of his face. After his toes were amputated, he went about on padded knees or was carried by one of his three slaves. As his hands became progressively deadened by the disease, he continued to work by strapping hammer and chisel to his wrists; he was lifted on and off the tall ladders by a slave assistant. Late in his life he created the two complex works for which he is most famous. In six small chapels on the slope leading up to the Sanctuary of the Senhor Bom Jesus de Matosinhos in Congonhas do Campo are his scenes from the Passion. The life-size wooden figures, carved between 1796 and 1799, portray the Last Supper, Prayer in the Garden of Gethsemane, the Capture of Jesus, the Flagellation and Crowning of Thorns, the Road to Calvary, and the Crucifixion. Still more dramatic are the Twelve Prophets sculpted in stone that lead up the double staircase to the open terrace and then to the Sanctuary of the Bom Jesus, done between 1800 and 1804. They appear as sentinels silhouetted against church and sky, gesturing silently to each other and to God as pilgrims slowly make their way up the hill past the Passion scenes. Scholars point to roughness in the carving of the wooden figures and to unevenness in the stonework as evidence either of Aleijadinho's inability to command his damaged hands or of less skilled artists working under his instructions. Heads, faces, and hands are unmistakably Aleijadinho's, distortion and exaggeration being techniques he had long employed. But the figures' robes and the scrolls that bear identifying inscriptions from the Bible for each Prophet were likely completed by other artists from his workshop.

Like many aspects of Aleijadinho's life, his Mulatto birth is caught up in a swirl of controversy and uncertainty. Some say, basing their

Figure 33. "Jeremiah in the Stocks" by Aleijadinho, Ouro Prêto, Brazil, ca. 1770s.
∽ SEE PLATE 13 ∽

claim on an inconclusive 1730 baptismal certificate, that he was born a slave to a slave woman, Izabel, and freed by his father, Izabel's owner, at baptism. Although unpersuasive, the myth has followed him. A death certificate fixes his death in 1814, at the age of seventy-six. That would make 1738 the probable year of Aleijadinho's birth, the same year that his father married Antônia Maria de São Pedro from the Azores. Together they had four children, the family in which the illegitimate Aleijadinho grew up. His mother was probably not Izabel but one of the several women of color with whom his father is known to have had relationships. Aleijadinho himself never married in the Church, but he had a son, with freedwoman Narcissa

Rodrigues da Conceição, a Brazilian-born Mulatta, whom he named after his father. Narcissa left him and took her son to Rio de Janeiro, where he later became a cabinetmaker.

Despite family ties to Black or Mulatta women who were once slaves, there is nothing to suggest that Aleijadinho was influenced in his art by Black culture or experience, with one possible exception—the small but striking carving of Jeremiah, done sometime around 1770 for the side altar of Saint John the Baptist at the Nossa Senhora do Carmo church in Ouro Prêto, on which he worked with his father before taking over the project. In the Bible, Jeremiah, judged a traitor, was imprisoned in a man's house as punishment for having warned the Jews to flee a besieged

Jerusalem. Aleijadinho instead chose a form of imprisonment familiar to Brazilians, especially to slaves: the stocks. Carved in dark, unpainted wood, Jeremiah's face easily becomes that of a Black man, his arms raised imploring God against his unjust punishment.

Aleijadinho knew fame in his lifetime. Confraternities in the important towns throughout the region vied with each other for his sculptures, altars, pulpits, ornaments, and chapels. He was well paid. Then, for more than a century following his death, silence surrounded him until, in the 1920s, modernists in search of the roots of an authentically Brazilian art rediscovered him. They saw in the exaggerated facial expressions and hands of saints and Prophets the elements of a Brazilian expressionism. Aleijadinho began to be studied: Brazilian and European critics debated his work, biographers pieced together the uncertain facts of his life, and conferences were held. Today he is recalled not only as an artist of outstanding (albeit uneven) talent but also as a national symbol of Mulatto—that is, Brazilian—creativity and originality.

～ 48

Two Castas *Paintings from Eighteenth-Century Mexico*

Through most of the eighteenth and into the early nineteenth century a number of artists in New Spain produced sets of portraits collectively known as "*castas* paintings." These sets sought to portray different racial combinations in late colonial Mexico. The term "castas" referred specifically to those people thought to be of "mixed race" and excluded Spaniards (*españoles*) and other Europeans, Blacks (*negros*), and Indians (*indios*) even if, in the eighteenth century, it was common enough for anyone who was not Spanish to be considered a casta. Many of these canvases were not signed or dated, but the bulk of the works on the castas theme appears to date between 1750 and 1800, with the earliest series currently believed to have been painted about 1725.

Some of the painters of castas were obscure and anonymous, and some created series that were copied (at times crudely) from earlier castas groups. But the theme also attracted the likes of the master Miguel Cabrera (1695–1768), a Mestizo from Oaxaca who had moved to Mexico City in 1719 and was painting at the viceregal court by mid-century. Between 1761 and 1766, Cabrera produced portraits of a number of the most powerful secular and religious personalities in Mexico. And it was roughly at this time that he executed a striking series of castas portraits (not all of which have been found) from live models. Other known artists of castas include Ignacio de Castro, Luis de Mena, José de Páez, Ignacio María Barreda, and two painters whose work is featured here: José Joaquín Magón (Figure 34) and Andrés de Islas (Figure 35).

In idealized ways, the castas paintings depict people in a variety of trades and occupations, in their homes and customary dress. A few of the pictures consist of a single canvas or panel on which the different racial combinations were compartmentalized and classified. Many others are separate compositions, commonly showing a mixed-race couple with at least one child, within a series of paintings (usually about sixteen) meant to be viewed in succession. Some, but not all, castas series included a final painting depicting not racial mixture at all but "savage" Indians, sometimes identified as Mecos (Chichimeca) or Apaches from northern Mexico. It became customary to inscribe a number and an identifying explanation on each canvas. The inscription described the racial mixture being portrayed and sometimes (as in Figure 34) included a short descriptive phrase.

Many sets of castas paintings have been found in Europe. Others have been discovered in Mexico, with their frames removed and rolled up in preparation for shipment. These castas were commissioned as souvenirs by Spaniards returning home after a time in America. Other Europeans who had never crossed the Atlantic sought them as exotic curiosities, both decorative and in some sense descriptive of the many racially mixed people of Mexico. Still other sets appear to have been undertaken for members of the Spanish and Creole elite within New Spain. The paintings can be viewed in part as another dimension of the increased regard for scientific inquiry in an "enlightened" and order-seeking Bourbon era, a general interest in descriptive classification and rationalization here delivered with a blunt message of Spanish racial superiority. The urge to classify seems particularly pronounced in images such as Figure 35, in which the castas vignette with its careful description is accompanied by American fruits and vegetables similarly indicated and labeled.

The first image (Figure 34; Plate 14), without a precise date but from the second half of the eighteenth century, was painted by José Joaquín Magón, an artist from Puebla, Mexico, who approaches the level of Cabrera in his skills. This is the first of sixteen canvases, and an inscription at the top of the painting introduces the series: "In America are born people of diverse colors, customs, temperaments, and languages." The painting offers a peaceful and sentimental domestic scene in a household of some means. A bright red bird perched on the back of a chair to the far left is

Figure 34. Castas painting featuring the Mestizo, child of a Spanish man and an Indian woman, by José Joaquín Magón, Mexico (second half of the eighteenth century).

∼ SEE PLATE 14 ∼

the American marker, reminding the viewer that this locale is an exotic place. A young Mestizo boy, dressed as elegantly as any contemporary adult in his French-style coat and white shirt, exhibits the results of a recent lesson in letters to his father. His expression is expectant and proud as he receives his father's praise.

Light falls on the white paper that the boy is holding, on which he has written the word *parco* (meaning temperate and moderate), and on his father, an extraordinarily pink-cheeked, doe-eyed Spaniard seated at a desk on the left. The man wears an unbuttoned cutaway coat over a richly embroidered vest. His clothing and demeanor suggest that he is a professional man of some standing. He is at home; and thus in place of the white wig he would wear in public, he sports a cloth cap of the kind commonly worn by nobles and professional men to keep their heads warm when their wigs were off. The father is shown just closing Miguel de Cervantes's masterpiece, *Don Quixote de la Mancha*—further emphasizing the benefits of the education that his son is beginning to receive. (In another painting in this series, a Spanish father sits within reach of bookshelves upon which the labeled works of Virgil are prominently displayed.) Figure 34 seems to suggest that literacy in the Spanish language is the key to civility and refinement for the Mestizo (as it is for the Indian in the opinion of many of Magón's contemporaries in Spanish America, not least Alonso Carrió de la Vandera; see Selection 44). The father is only too pleased to receive his son and looks affectionately into his eyes. The boy's mother, a demure Indian woman to the right, dressed in a delicately embroidered garment and with glittering earrings and a necklace, regards the boy's exhibition with a tender smile as she points out a practice page of repeated letters. But the moment occurs mostly between Mestizo son and Spanish father. The Indian mother is painted in a shadow, framing the main action with her smile.

Here is a picture of a harmonious union, a successful fusion of European and Indian

resulting in a new "American" racial type, the Mestizo. A second inscription beneath a Roman numeral "I" (for the first class of race mixture) reads: "From a Spaniard and an Indian woman issues a Mestizo, who is commonly meek, tranquil, and straightforward." The Mestizo might be found wanting in a number of the qualities possessed so effortlessly by his Spanish father, the painting seems to say, but he is sober, obedient, and well-meaning. And, within certain limits, he is able to learn. There are worse qualities for a colonial subject to have. The Mestizo is imagined as an ideal servant.

Magón's portrayal of the Mestizo is a determined step away from the ways in which Mestizos and many other castas were usually described in contemporary literature, drama, and chroniclers' accounts. Especially in the sixteenth century, Mestizos were often the offspring of illicit unions. This illegitimacy contributed to their negative image among privileged Spaniards as rootless and disruptive figures. Like the Zambos (people said to be of Indian and African ancestry and often identified as "Mulatto" in seventeenth-century Mexico), Mestizos by their very existence demonstrated that official attempts to keep Europeans, Africans, and castas out of the Indian communities had failed, and failed rather spectacularly.

Mestizos were perceived as floating uncertainly between Spanish and Indian cultures, the very agents of chaos within a cultural and racial framework that colonial law defined in simple terms that did not go far beyond the idea of the "two republics" of Spaniards and Indians. Mestizos were said by their detractors to make cruel use of their acquaintance with the Spanish language and ways to victimize gullible Indians. Not that Mestizos could be much trusted by anyone else, either. The caricature of the Mestizo serves up a rash and absurd upstart who brags incessantly, a pretentious and uneducated half-breed, anything but "parco." By keeping such derogatory stereotypes out of this picture, Magón paints a new world in which Spaniards and Indians marry and live in peace and in which Mestizos are accepted, tutored, and supported—even if, in an imaginary world as in the real one, there were limits to what a person supposed to be "meek, tranquil, and straightforward" would be judged capable of achieving.

The second castas portrait (Figure 35; Plate 15) was painted by Andrés de Islas about 1774.

It is the fourth picture in a series of sixteen. This work departs sharply from the realm of domestic bliss and literacy of Figure 34. Life for this family is seen as closer to basic matters of food, clothing, and shelter, with less room for luxuries and refinements. Whereas the Spanish father in Figure 34 seems to preside over a productive calm, the Spaniard in Figure 35

Figure 35. Castas painting featuring the Mulatta, child of a Spanish man
and an African woman, by Andrés de Islas, Mexico, ca. 1774.
Courtesy of the Museo de América, Madrid.
⁓ SEE PLATE 15 ⁓

has no control and the family threesome is embroiled in a fierce quarrel. An African woman, gritting her teeth, has flown into a rage and grabs her Spanish partner by the hair. With her free hand she is about to strike him with a cooking utensil. The man's eyes are wide open as he tries to restrain her. The child of their union, a Mulatta, looks up and screams in fear as she grabs her mother's skirts.

At the foot of this domestic strife, fourteen carefully numbered "fruits from this country" seem an absurdity to the modern eye, except that the results of scientific classification fold into this painting's message and distance the scene from its presumably European audience. The painter and his patron have a negative view of Blacks, and the image warns Whites against unions with them. The African woman is portrayed as violent, and her union with a Spaniard has descended into an unhappy mess for both parents and the child. (Another canvas from the same series, not reproduced here, seems to underscore the point. In it, an industrious Mulatta is seen participating in a peaceful and shared task with her Spanish male partner, while their Morisco boy, lighter-skinned than his mother, looks on. The tension felt in Figure 35 is lifted as the artist seems to say that a further stage of miscegenation in the right, or White, direction is a good thing, altering a person of part-African extraction for the better.) Considering Figure 35 with Figure 34 (not to mention other depictions in the castas genre), the viewer is informed that Spaniards do not fare as well in their relationships with Africans as with Indians.

In making such statements or in taking on such commissions, Islas and Magón confirmed general opinions. In many learned as well as popular circles, *mestizaje*—miscegenation or racial mixture—was perceived as detrimental, bringing about the deterioration of human character, ability, and intelligence. Yet segregation laws and official warnings did not prevent it, nor did they eliminate miscegenation anxiety. And by the time most of the castas paintings were executed in the second half of the eighteenth century, the old racial

classifications of early colonial times—Spaniard, Indian, Black, Mestizo, Mulatto, Zambo, Castizo (offspring of Spaniard and Mestizo), and Morisco (offspring of Spaniard and Mulatto)—no longer sufficed to identify and order society. Most supposed "Mestizos" and "Mulattoes" were themselves the children of casta parents. Thus the categories grew considerably more elaborate, as the contemporary castas series and classification lists show. The more elaborate they became, the more impossible they became to distinguish visually.

A *tente en el aire*—a localized Mexican expression meaning "suspended in air"—was the offspring of six possible racial mixtures (a *torno-atrás* man and a Spanish woman, a *cambujo* man and an Indian woman, a *salto-atrás* man and an *albarazado* woman, a *jíbaro* man and a Mulatto woman, an albarazado man and a jíbaro woman, or a cambujo man and a *calpamulo* woman). Most of these castas themselves were the products of a comparable number of alternative unions. To consider only one of the parents of a tente en el aire for the purposes of illustration, a cambujo man (derived from the name of a reddish-black stallion) might himself be the offspring of some nine possible parental combinations.

Most of the elaborated classifications amounted to mental puzzles, exhibitions of pseudoscientific precision. They tell far more about an eighteenth-century elite's refined sense of racial privilege and order in society than about social realities. For people in Mexico and other parts of Latin America had long been spilling beyond, and defying, the bounds of even the extended ideals of race and privilege. And many racial categories (cambujo, for instance) effectively referred to a dark-skinned person who, in practice, might have sought and been identified by other terms—and perhaps by even more than one in the course of his life.

The castas paintings offer insight into the eighteenth-century elaboration of attitudes and prejudices toward miscegenation which, to some extent and from different points of view, would have been shared by painters and patrons. Racial categories were more than abstractions, and they mattered to and for people beyond the various officialdoms and before the eighteenth century. The compartmentalized renderings and imaginings within the castas paintings capture only parts of these colonial realities—parts that might seem strange or simply amusing on a wall in Spain. As a number of selections in this book demonstrate, individuals and their actions could usu- ally be depended upon not to conform perfectly to their officially designated categories, such as the image of the passive and dutiful Mestizo boy in Figure 34. People from among the so-called castas were sometimes able to live beyond the limits set on their activities, whether in separate communities, through their intelligence and charm, or by "passing" as Spaniards thanks to wealth, education, and personal connections.

49

Juan Francisco Domínguez's Discourses on the Ten Commandments, Mexico

(1805)

Catholicism remained the state religion of Spanish America throughout the colonial period, but there were notable changes both in the place of the Church as an institution in public life and in the religion promoted from Spain and cathedral cities in the colonies. Especially during the eighteenth century, these changes had at least as much to do with developments in Europe as with American circumstances.

Many of the late colonial changes gave the appearance of a lighter, gentler Christianity. The old metaphor of fear and love as the two wings of flight toward Heaven fell out of favor in Church teachings, replaced by a heavy emphasis on love. The bishops' pastoral letters and urban religious art presented God less as a remote and stern judge than as a loving Father, and the crucified Christ less as a wounded figure in agony than as a sublime human form anticipating the Resurrection. The sky in fashionable paintings of the Virgin Mary grew pink with the backsides of frolicking baby angels. There were fewer references in learned theological treatises to the Seven Deadly Sins, less preoccupation with the Devil, Adam and Eve's Fall, and the innate sinfulness of humanity; less of the somber solemnity, mystical strivings, and endless war

between body and soul that pervaded seventeenth-century beliefs and practices (see Selections 30, 31, and 32). With the glass half full rather than half empty, a more optimistic view of human nature pointed toward education for salvation and the potential for growth in "la felicidad pública" (public happiness and welfare). The Ten Commandments and the epistles of Saint Paul grew in prominence as positive guides to improvement through love, charity, and sociability. And, as in the sixteenth century, the early centuries of the Church were recalled as a model of Christian values in practice.

This apparently softer, more loving religion did not emerge in a vacuum, nor did it capture the imagination of most Church members. The late eighteenth-century redefinition of the parish priest's role in public life as the loving teacher and spiritual specialist had less to do with a sea change in religious sensibility than with the politics of religion. Bourbon policymakers were intent upon enhancing the power and prestige of royal governors by removing priests from their customary position as moral judges who oversaw the family life and public affairs of communities in their parishes. With a more forgiving and approachable God, there should have followed—as there apparently did in Spain—a decline in the veneration of saints as intercessors. But no such decline seems to have occurred in the old centers of colonial Spanish America. On the contrary, the growing veneration of Mary there in the eighteenth century suggests that her intercession was needed more than ever.

A lighter version of Christianity was preferred especially by educated city people, colonial administrators, bishops, and other Spanish immigrants. It could be used to reduce religion to an individual matter in a realm of its own, and relegate the Church to a subordinate bureau of the state instead of a partner (even instead of the wife and mother in the old family metaphor for the political hierarchy and social order). It tended to root more deeply in emerging regions such as Argentina, Venezuela, and Cuba than in rural areas of the old centers in Peru and central Mexico.

This selection by a prominent Mexico City priest is in keeping with these changes, but it also expresses deep worries about their ramifications for the Church, public virtue, and political order. When it appeared in 1805 in the opening pages of a lengthy treatise on the Ten Commandments, the author, Juan Francisco Domínguez, was an eighty-year-old senior pastor of the cathedral parish who had served eighteen years in Indian parishes of central Mexico. Before his death in 1813 he produced a small string of publications on devotional subjects and moral issues including the virtues of the Virgin Mary, the renowned image of Our Lady of Guadalupe, and sermons on pure love and proper relations with women.

The emphasis on love, charity, the teachings of Saint Paul (the "Apostle" whom Domínguez keeps mentioning), and a loving God who is the essence of generosity and goodness are here in abundance, along with an optimistic view of human potential for virtuous conduct, "felicidad pública" in this world, and salvation in the next. In this passage, as in several others within the treatise, Domínguez turned the negative injunctions of

particular commandments into positive statements about Christian virtues. Even the Fifth Commandment, "Thou shalt not kill," is presented as an affirmation of God's love for humanity by forbidding acts of hatred and violence against others. This view follows Christ's positive reflections on the Ten Commandments in Matthew 19, more than that of the thundering Old Testament God in Exodus 20, but Domínguez balanced his optimism about the potential for virtuous behavior with stress on the prohibitions embedded in each of the commandments and the rampant selfishness he saw around him. He did not forget "the terrible sting of the Almighty's hand" or the Virgin's gift of forgiveness when she might well have "raise[d] the lash of her justice."

Despite his disclaimer that the treatise was not directed toward Bourbon governors and councillors, it is hard to avoid the conclusion that they were his intended audience, the group whom he wanted most to persuade. The title itself—"Religion and the State Conjoined"—and the way that Domínguez developed the political implications of reducing religion to a separate, secondary place in public life make this clear. He sees religion being removed from the center of human affairs and replaced by the "happiness of the state" ("la felicidad del estado"). Yet how could the two be made distinct in this way, he asks, when the irreplaceable foundation of a just and happy state is the divine law embodied in the Ten Commandments? The state cannot achieve maximum peace, order, and happiness unless it actively supports religion (and its priests), he keeps saying. There is more than a subdued warning in his repeated thought that justice and the common good are the state's only purposes, and that "in God dwells all justice and truth." True to form, he ends on a positive and loyal note, with a ringing endorsement of common cause between state and religion in order to breathe life into the Ten Commandments, "which will bestow upon us honor, peace, and glory."

From the first discourse [on the First Commandment: You shall love God above all else, and your neighbor as yourself.]

The point of my discourses will be to persuade with evidence that if we yearn for good order, the exceedingly useful harmony of souls, innocence in our customs, peace with everyone and victory over foreign enemies, help for the unfortunate, the blessings of God over the fruits of the Earth, abundance and equity in trade and commerce, [and] essential provisions—in a word, a reasonably abundant fulfillment of needs, made up of the foregoing, which make for a fortunate state— we must obey the commandments of God.

By "the state" we mean consonant harmony between the principality and the people for a political government that establishes kingdoms with good customs, preventing the divisions that have desolated many kingdoms. From such harmony, true peace springs. By "religion" we mean that first among moral virtues, which has as its object the worship of God, not only in sacrifices and offerings or the furnishing and magnificence of its churches or awe for these buildings and their altars and ministers. Although religion has especially to do with the [officials] of the Church, [we mean] also the wholehearted observance of its commandments. Each of the commandments reflects on some special virtue: almost all of the Ten Commandments have to do with charity and justice. But they all share the injunction to do what God commands, which is the object of religion.

The words of Ecclesiastes 12:13, which I have chosen to give spirit to my own [words], say it concisely: Fear God, and obey His commandments. This applies to all people, as if the passage said: the entire being of a contented person, and his entire well-being consists of obeying the commandments, animated by the holy fear of God. Everyone is obliged to do this. No vassal, king, great person or small, poor person or from the high reaches [of society], or even the lowliest of the low, no one is human who has not absorbed this respect for what God commands. For the very destiny and purpose of human creation was to serve God. Thus, if the sun no longer shone, it would cease being the sun; and humans would cease to be human if they did not serve God because they would no longer be taken for humans, but for donkeys. All this the wise Ecclesiastes wished to tell us in this pithy warning, with which he closed his loving and salubrious sermon. I infer from this: if every person by his very being should keep the commandments, he who does not observe divine law lives outside human society. And with such a multitude (for the number of stupid people is infinite) living outside the law, how can there be a society? And without society, how can the state exist? Let us go on to reflect on each of the commandments, and it will be lucidly clear that the observance of all those [commandments] that religion prescribes is utterly necessary for the well-being of the state. And if it [the state] is not based on religion and religion is not called upon by the state, if they do not come together, everything will be ruin and desolation for the kingdoms. . . .

Section 3

This commandment [You shall love God above all else, and your neighbor as yourself] is not two separate commandments, but one that the Divine Master subdivided in two because of its distinct objects, God and one's neighbor (in which

the Supreme Legislator orders us to love the neighbor as we love ourselves).
Even though the beloved objects are infinitely distinct and distant from each
other, the motive force of love is the same. Let us love God through God and the
neighbor through God. So our standard theology teaches, according to Saint
Thomas Aquinas.

This powerful motive force softens the inclusion of love for one's neighbor in
this commandment, without which [neighborly love] would seem extremely hard.
Considering the vices, bad tempers, perverse opinions, and ingratitude of people
that make them unworthy of love of any kind, to love them as ourselves even if they
were lovable would seem an impossible thing. Self-regard ranks high in our hearts
as we covet our own well-being, preferring our own welfare above all that can be
done for others. But with God in the picture, what God wants and commands must
be fulfilled even at some personal sacrifice. This is a commandment that Jesus
Christ took as His own, so that it is not only from a God who, being God, must be
obeyed, but from a God become human, from a God who became human and died
for us in order to give us the supernatural state of grace. That He gave His life for us
obliges us, as the Apostle [Saint Paul] says, to give our lives for others.

Taken all together, not much is required of us. Our self-regard is left intact
when we are ordered to love our neighbor as we do ourselves. This does not require
us to love others as much as we love ourselves, only [that we love them] in the same
way as we do ourselves. This amounts to wanting the good things for others that
we want for ourselves, and not wanting the misfortunes for others that we would
not want for ourselves, as in the advice that Tobias gave to his son. But we shall not
fulfill our duty simply by wishing others well and causing them no harm in a
detached way, as if we did not really love them. Beyond not doing harm to anyone,
we must seek out the opportunities to influence and contribute to their well-being.
This is not simply a negative precept not to hate or wish misfortune upon others,
but a positive one to love and do well. Of course, it does forbid hatred, envy,
pretense, the scandals that cause spiritual ruin, and the hardness of heart that keeps
us from helping those in great need.

Section 4 [the final section in Discourse 1]

There is no need to reflect deeply to be convinced that nothing suits the
happiness of the state so much as the love of God above all else and [the love] of
our neighbors as ourselves. This is one of those truths that is evident in its very
terms. If we love God above all things, we shall never violate justice because of
selfish motives of honor, life, or property. This is the moral fiber of the Republic.
With its observance alone good Order is preserved, rights are respected, and good
government operates. Justice gives to each what is his, not only in material terms
but also in personal rights. Justice requires that the constituted authorities be
obeyed, that they govern with equity, that they do not lack humanity either in
guiding or collaborating toward what is just, that crimes are punished and merits
are rewarded. Justice directs the tribunals, arranges business transactions, and
attends to the public interest. The only thing that threatens it is self-interest, which
causes merit to be ignored in public officeholding, the worthy and best-suited to be
left out of these offices, [and] subjects to disparage the public authority granted by

God to those who govern us. It [self-interest] causes the impious to prevail against the just, leading to perverse judgments, as Jeremiah lamented. In short, iniquity upsets everything, confuses everything, ruins everything. Therefore, justice is the epitome of the law, and our law in the Ten Commandments is, as Saint Thomas teaches, the law of justice. Everything is maintained and fortified by the love of God alone, above all things, and everything can be lost if it is neglected.

The state is strengthened just as much by mutual love among ourselves. Just as a building cannot stand if the stones are not well joined, the Republic cannot last without the bond of charity uniting its people. If everyone only wants to live for oneself, against the maxim of the Philosopher [Saint Thomas Aquinas], not caring for one's neighbor, no one will contribute to the common good and everyone will perish for lack of assistance. Some may help others because they fear the governor's authority, but [they serve] badly and not for long if they do not help because of love. With chains of gold, love binds subjects to their prince, servants to their lords, [and] children to their parents. Under the soft and efficacious influence of love, elders and superiors look out for the well-being of minors and inferiors. Through love, difficulties that stand in the way of the welfare of others are surmounted because love conquers all. No doubt the entire foundation of a happy Republic depends on peace. But how can there be peace where there is conflict? And how can there be harmony where mutual charity is lacking?

The Apostle calls charity the bond, because it ties people to each other. With this charity everyone moves with equality toward the target of universal happiness. The unfortunate person, because of illness or unemployment, cannot support his poor family. He has many companions in his misery, and they cast a shadow over the happiness of the people. You who have an abundance, give them a hand, relieve their poverty with your abundance. Do the same for other unfortunates who are worthy of equal compassion and they will no longer live in misery.

Husbands and wives are not working together under the yoke of matrimony. They live in continual disagreement. Despite being yoked together, one goes off in one direction, the other in another. The result is furious arguments, which is scandalous for their children. This family falls apart and, since there are many in this unfortunate situation, many homes do not contribute to the beauty of this city [Mexico City]; that is, many [do not contribute to] the beautiful edifice of the Republic. The [family of the] Church was never better governed than in the first centuries when all believers formed a single spirit and heart, according to the accounts of the Apostles.

And how does religion influence this reciprocal charity? Beyond its role in the observance of all law, as already said, it directly inspires charity among brothers and sisters. Such is the character of Christians, and consequently the spirit of religion, that in the first centuries when persecution prevented them from congregating and communicating among themselves, they were known for this [reciprocal charity]. Look (said the pagans) how they love each other, how they are quick to give up their lives for others. Religion has joined us in a baptism in which we were remade as children of God; a single Father unites us in a single faith, at one table where we eat of the same bread, the bread that Our Father sent us from Heaven, the bread that gives us life. Christ dwells within us, and thus we are animated by His spirit. How can we not declare ourselves Christians and, through our religion, be united by love? This is characteristic of Christianity. Those who do not love, who put their vile self-interest before the preciousness of their character [as Christians], do not belong.

We are in urgent need (I say again with the Apostle) of the charity of Christ. Can we be Christians if we do not follow Christ? Of course not. If we are to follow Christ, who loved us all, we must love each other. Religion inspires this love, and by this love (for the reasons mentioned) the Republic lives and the happiness of the state is preserved.

50

Brazilian Slaves Who Marry

(1811)

When in 1563 the Council of Trent concluded nearly twenty years of deliberations, the Church had (among its many reforms) elevated marriage to the status of a holy sacrament capable of bestowing grace on those who "worthily receive it." Those who wanted to marry should not only have confessed and been absolved of their sins, but they also must marry freely by their own consent and without impediments.

The Brazilian Church also urged marriage as a remedy for mundane ills such as desire among those who found abstinence impossible, although chastity remained a more holy state than matrimony. A settled married life, said the Church, offered the way to spread order through a scattered, inherently disorderly and unruly population. It accused vagabonds who roamed from place to place of living "licentiously in the vice of lust and concubinage," feigning marriage with women whom they brought with them and many times leaving behind their legitimate wives (or husbands). Speaking through the *Constituições primeiras* of 1707, a codified version of the diocesan laws as they were to govern the Brazil archdiocese, the Church instructed priests to notify all vagabonds living in their parishes that within a month they must certify that they were legitimately mar-

ried and in what place. To stop all the comings and goings from parish to parish, the Church directed their congregants to live a married life in a fixed place, or at the very least to take their spouses with them and live in decency.

Church authorities worried, too, about slaves, warning that they could marry either with free persons or other captives and that their masters could not deny them marriage or their practice of it. Masters, although they might decide what was "an appropriate time and place," were cautioned against putting obstacles in the way of their slaves or against selling a slave husband to a faraway place where his wife could not follow. As encouragement to owners, the Church reminded them that married slaves remained slaves still fully obligated to their masters' service.

The following selection offers a glimpse into the making of marriage patterns that followed from the Church's prescriptions, drawing somewhat closer to the slaves' points of view. This small story shows how courtship proceeded between one young slave woman and her partner. It records a slave mother's change in preference of a husband for her daughter and, taking the petitioner at his word, the daughter's defiant response. The outcome of the petition remains a mystery.

And we know next to nothing about the protagonists—only that the mother came from the Mina coast of Africa or at least was transported from there, and that they all lived in the parish of São Pedro do Rio Fundo in Bahia.

Status as a slave or freed person, ethnic identity, and place of birth all counted here. West African Yorubas, or Nagôs as they were called in Bahia, figured increasingly among African Blacks in Bahia from the end of the eighteenth century into the early decades of the nineteenth. Among slaves buried by the Santa Casa da Misericórdia (assuming the buried dead were roughly representative of the living), Mina Blacks outnumbered both Fon-speaking Gêges and Nagôs, but all these were in turn outnumbered by Bantu-speaking Angolans. By the 1830s, Nagôs dominated among African slaves, a reflection of where the slave trading was most lucrative, and their numbers more or less equaled the often Muslim Hausas among freed Africans. Although Nagôs, Hausas, Gêges, and Angolans each sought to preserve their ethnic differences, for example, by maintaining separate religious brotherhoods, at times they found compelling reasons to form alliances. A rebellion in 1809 and, later, the 1835 Malê revolt by freed and slave Africans against Whites demonstrated how ethnic differences could be subordinated to strategic requirements. The far more insurmountable split was between Africans and Creoles. Regardless of whether they were slaves or freed persons, Creoles were excluded from participating in the revolt; in 1835, Africans had even killed two Creoles in the one long night of fighting.

In this situation of competing ethnic origins and African religions, the Catholic Church might insist on a couple's consent to validate their marriage, but a Nagô mother acted according to different understandings. And if the daughter had not yet reached majority, as seems to be the case here, then civil law further directed that the mother could disinherit her daughter if she married without permission.

The proposed marriage of Joaquina Maria do Sacramento was not unusual among plantation slaves. As more and more research accumulates from various regions of Brazil, evidence shows that it was not uncommon for at least one-third or more of all adult slaves on a coffee or sugar plantation to be married, especially on substantial holdings where the pool of eligible slaves was larger and they might marry without having to choose partners from other plantations, a practice seen by owners as disruptive and which they tried to prevent. Sometimes two or three generations of a family survived intact, in extended families of brothers, sisters, aunts, or uncles and their children. But continuity was rare. Even when slaves were not sold, sooner or later the death of the owners required that the property be divided and distributed among the heirs, breaking apart whatever slave families were established there. On most of the prosperous colonial plantations, new Africans were regularly purchased and the cycle of forming families began again.

A Slave Mother Opposes Her Daughter's Choice of a Husband (Bahia, 1811)

Alexandre Francisco, a freed Creole, resident on the Jacuipe do Brito Sugar Mill, says that on the same lands lives a Black slave woman by the name of Ana, who has a Creole daughter, Joaquina Maria do Sacramento, of whom the petitioner is fond. He asked the mother [for permission] to marry and she did not hesitate, expressing appreciation for the favor he did her. And the alliance they planned thus being agreed upon and contracted, the petitioner frequently visited her house where she fed him and washed his clothes, as well as other things. The banns having been ordered, the mother then raised an impediment. Being of the Nagô Nation, she allowed herself to be persuaded by those of her Nation; she now wants her daughter to marry a Nagô Black slave, arguing that the petitioner is a slave and married, which is entirely false because he is a freed man and a widower as the two attached documents reveal [attached in the original but since lost], and with which all the mother's suspicions are dispelled. [He says], moreover, that the said daughter wants to marry only the petitioner, and is together with him in that she has left her mother's house; she sought and was given shelter at the house of Dona Joaquina, owner of the Mill where the petitioner is supplying her necessities, such that (with all due respect) he has deprived her of her honor. For all these reasons the petitioner, received at the benign feet of Your Most Reverend Excellency, comes to beseech you through the depths of your mercy, that, if the impediment be as related, you order that they may be received in matrimony and [if] there be another cause it may be sent to the Archiepiscopal Chamber quickly without a loss of time and there its terms be dealt with, because the daughter of the petitioned says publicly that she wants to marry only the petitioner and not the other one, a Black Nagô slave. Hence he [the petitioner] asks that Your Most Reverend Excellency should deign to aid the petitioner in his intention in view of the related [facts].

51

Two Brazilian Wills
(1793, 1823)

While the Church officiated over the sacred aspects of marriage, issuing banns and performing the rites by which a couple became indissolubly joined before God in holy matrimony, the profane matter of a couple's conjugal property and its inheritance by appropriate heirs remained for civil law to resolve. In colonial Brazil, and continuing into the empire when Brazil became an independent nation in 1822, the body of law that regulated civil questions was known as the *Código Philippino*, also referred to as the *Ordenações*, promulgated in 1603 during the reign of King Philip III of Spain when the once-separate kingdom of Portugal was annexed to Spain and for sixty years (1580–1640) ruled by Spanish monarchs. Although during the empire Brazilians found it necessary to replace parts of the *Código Philippino* with their own, newly written commercial and criminal codes, those sections pertaining to inheritance and property remained in force (with modifications in interpretation and practice) until the promulgation of a new civil code in 1916.

Civil law decided how conjugal property was to be distributed. The law directed that two-thirds of a couple's property pass in equal shares to their children as the prescribed heirs. No primogeniture existed, and the oldest male child was favored only in the exceptional case of entailed estates, or *morgados*, which were eliminated in 1835; thus, female children inherited equally with their brothers. Further, a couple could dispose freely, through the terms set out in a last will and testament, of only one-third of their property. From this third they made bequests to other family members or to non-kin such as a lay brotherhood, the Church, or their slaves. One spouse could will his or her share to the other spouse or to any of the children as an additional legacy. Unless a prenuptial agreement specified otherwise, their property was understood to be communal, with each spouse owning one-half. At the death of either spouse, one-half of the property could be distributed to the heirs, but it was frequently kept intact until the surviving spouse also died.

Actual families seldom arranged themselves so neatly, and the law had to be flexible enough to cover variations. Property was reserved for the direct line within the family: descendant heirs, that is, children or grandchildren, inherited first, but if there were none, then property reverted to ascendant heirs, parents or grandparents. In their absence, property then might be assigned to collateral kin, brothers or sisters, but this was a matter of choice and not something decreed by law.

Without direct heirs, a couple enjoyed complete testamentary freedom over their conjugal property and could assign it to whomever, and in whatever proportions, they chose. Forced inheritance presumed marriage and legitimate children, or children legally recognized as future heirs.

Sometimes parents made gifts to one or another of their children during their lifetimes, especially to daughters in the form of marriage dowries. Were gifts merely a way to disguise favoring one child over the others? Not legally. In the final distribution of a couple's property, children were required to bring the value of any dowry, gift, or loan back into the accounting, a process described as *colação*. If a daughter, for example, had received a dowry in excess of her share of the estate, then she owed the difference to her siblings; similarly, if she had received less, then the estate owed her the difference. In this way, a couple's wealth was preserved for their children, not simply as it existed at the time of their deaths but as it was accumulated over the course of the family's lifetime.

What about persons who never married or were prevented from marrying—a single mother or father, for example, or a priest? The law ignored them unless they went to the trouble of instructing in a last will and testament how their property was to be distributed. And many did. A particularly rich source for insight into the lives of poor Blacks, both freeborn and former slaves, in nineteenth-century Bahia are their wills, which parcel out a small house or shed, cooking pots, clothes, pieces of jewelry, or slaves. The appointed heir might be a lifelong companion, a natural child, or someone remembered for having given care during a long and dangerous illness. In a reversal of roles, former slaves not infrequently gave alms for Masses to be said for a master's soul. Unmarried persons without legally recognized children did as they chose with their property.

The following are two such wills, one belonging to a priest, the other to an African woman, a freed slave who had never married and who had borne five children. It is telling to compare their property, those they named as their heirs, and their religious and secular connections. The wills reveal how differently they anticipated death and presented themselves in this life in preparation for the next, and to whom they prayed for their soul's protection and intercession before God.

◠ Last Will and Testament of Padre Felippe de Santiago Xavier, Santa Anna de Parnaíba, São Paulo, *1793*

Jesus, Mary, and Joseph. In the name of the most Holy Trinity, Father, Son, and Holy Spirit, three persons and one true God.

Know, all those who will see this document, that in the year of Our Lord Jesus Christ one thousand seven hundred and ninety-three [1793], in this town of Santa Anna de Parnaíba on the fifteenth day of May of the said year, I, Father Felippe de Santiago Xavier, being of sound mind and judgment, which God Our Lord gave me, sick in bed and fearing death, and wishing to put my soul on the path to salvation, not knowing what God Our Lord wants to do with me, nor when it will serve Him to take me to Him, I make this will in the following way.

First, I commend my soul to the Most Holy Trinity, which created it, and I beseech the Eternal Father by the death and passion of His only begotten son to receive it as He received His when He was dying on the tree of the True Cross. I ask my Lord Jesus Christ, by His divine wounds, that since He has already granted me the mercy of His precious blood in this life and [through] the worthiness of His works, to give me also in the life we await the reward of Glory. I ask and beseech the Virgin Mary, Our Lady, Mother of God, and all the saints of the celestial court, especially my guardian angel and my patron saint, the apostles Saint Philip and Saint James and the princes of the apostles, Saint Peter and Saint Paul, for whom I have devotion, that they intercede and beseech my Lord Jesus Christ now and when my soul leaves this body because, as a true Christian, I profess that I live and die in the Holy Catholic Faith, and believe what the Holy Mother Church of Rome believes, and in this faith I hope to save my soul, not by my worthiness, but by the Most Holy Passion of the only begotten Son of God.

I request my brother and *compadre*, Antonio Bernardino de Sena, Captain-Major Bartolomeu da Rocha Franco, my compadres Lieutenant Antonio Francisco de Andrade and Ensign Francisco Antonio de Andrade that they be willing, as a service to God and as a favor to me, to be my executors.

I declare that I am a secular priest, a native of this town of Parnaíba, the son of unknown parents, an orphan in the house of Maria Thomaz, and I have no heirs, either ascendant or descendant.

My body will be shrouded in priestly vestments and buried in this town in the main parish church in grave number two for the alms of fifteen *patacas* [silver coin worth 320 *réis*] if the church wants to receive it and, if not, beneath the altar of Our Lady of Sorrows, and accompanied by the Reverend Vicar and the other reverend priests who find themselves in this town on that occasion, whom I wish to say the Mass of the *corpo presente* [that is, preferably before burial and certainly before the transmigration of the soul from the body was believed to be complete], [and] for everything the customary alms will be paid.

For my soul I want fifty Masses said for the usual alms of three hundred and twenty réis each, and that burial rites be said, paid for at the usual [rate in] alms.

I declare that I possess more than two hundred and fifty *mil-réis* in money, credits, written obligations, [and] coins.

I possess another fifty-one thousand and two hundred réis in four-*vintem* silver coins; these will be delivered to the Reverend Vicar for him to distribute among the poor children of this town, giving to each one a half pataca.

I declare that I further have three *dobras* of twelve thousand and eight hundred réis each, in small gold coins of ten and five patacas.

I declare that I possess several houses of two eaves below the main parish church, which I assign to be given to Our Lady of Sorrows.

I declare that between me and my brother Antonio Bernardino, we own a row of small houses on the rua Direita of this town, bordering on one side with the large houses and on the other with those of Dona Izabel de Almeida, widow of the deceased Captain Antonio Barboza Fagundes.

I declare that I possess a farm at the place called Itaquires, with 600 *braças* [one braça measured approximately seven feet] of frontage and one-half league deep into the wilderness, which once belonged to the deceased Jozé da Costa Ferreira, and which I [want] auctioned and the cash applied to my debt.

I declare that I possess two silver spoons and their matching forks, a tin jug with its plate, those plates both shallow and deep that are found, one medium-sized copper vat, a small copper cauldron, and one copper kettle, also small.

I declare that I possess two wooden footstools in my parlor, and several carved wooden benches.

I declare that the houses which above I say are to be given to Our Lady of Sorrows are in payment of the amount of one hundred mil-réis which I owe in interest by virtue of a contract which I have in my possession.

I declare that at present I own ten slaves, that is, Mattheus, Maximiano [*sic*], Anna, Floriano, Caetano, Luciano, João, Maria, Gonçalo, and Eugenia.

I declare that a long time ago I gave to Mattheus de Santiago his brother Francisco, and I also gave to him, Mattheus de Santiago, the back part of my yard to build a house for his lodging, with the condition that he serve Our Lady of Sorrows, caring for her altar in the way he has cared for it until now.

I declare that I leave thirty mil-réis to my nephew, I mean, to Francisco das Chagas.

I declare that I owe sixteen thousand and eight hundred réis to my compadre Ignacio Gonçalves do Prado, resident on the Couros River on the Mogi road, which were given to me to deliver to him.

I declare that after my funeral is paid, my debts satisfied, and my legacies fulfilled, I name and institute my soul and the children of Antonio Bernardino as the heir [*sic*] of my estate.

I declare that Anna, my slave, with her five children with the condition that they serve in the company of Antonio Bernardino de Sena, I mean, I declare that I free of any and all slavery the five little Mulattoes, that is, Floriano, Caetano, Luciano, João, and Maria, with the condition that they serve Antonio Bernardino or some of his heirs.

I declare that I leave Anna, their mother, to the said little Mulattoes her children, so that she can finish raising them, as she has done until now.

I declare that I possess some mules, and some cows with their calves on the farm at Itaquires.

I declare that I leave the slave Efigenia as a dowry to the first daughter of my compadre Lieutenant Antonio Manoel who marries.

I leave ten mil-réis to my goddaughter, Anna Caetana de Jezus, daughter of my compadre Luiz Mendes Vieira.

I declare that I have in the possession of the Reverend Father João Gonsalves Lima a certain amount of money for him to distribute in the way I explained to him in the confessional.

I leave a further forty mil-réis to my same goddaughter, Anna Caetana de Jezus, to help with her marriage dowry.

I leave that from my estate should be given another forty mil-réis, twenty to my goddaughter Maria, daughter of Antonio de Medeiros da Costa, and another twenty to my goddaughter Anna, daughter of Manoel Correa Pedrozo.

I declare that a slave by the name of Efigenia, whom I own and whom I forgot to make mention of when I named the ten above, I leave to a daughter of Lieutenant Antonio Manoel as I say above.

I leave thirty mil-réis to be given, that is, fifteen to Mattheus, and another fifteen to Anna.

To satisfy my legacies, the charitable works declared here, and to expedite the rest of what I order in this my will, I once again ask those gentlemen named at the beginning that they agree to be my executors as a service to God Our Lord and as a favor to me. As in the beginning of this will, I ask each one and all as a whole, [and] I give them all the power that in law I can and that if necessary, that they may take my goods and sell what is necessary for my funeral and fulfillment of my legacies and payment of my debts.

I declare that to satisfy these I do not want a judicial accounting, nor that they should be sold at public auction, [but rather] their estimate of the just value of my goods.

And as this is my last will in the way I have said, I sign. Parnaíba, fifteenth of May of the year one thousand seven hundred and ninety six, I mean, ninety three.

[signature of] Felippe de Santiago Xavier

∿ *Last Will and Testament of Anna de São Jozé da Trindade, Salvador, Bahia, 1823*

In the name of God, amen.

I, Anna de São Jozé da Trindade, Roman Catholic since baptism, always firm in the faith of the Catholic religion that I profess, and in this way I will be saved through the worthiness of Christ, and of the Virgin Mary, Our Lady, in the mystery of her most pure conception, whom I invoke, and, although ill, being of sound mind and judgment to make a will, for this reason I declare the present Will in the following manner:

I declare that I was born on the Coast of Africa from where I was transported to the states of Brazil and the city of Bahia where I have lived until the present. I was the slave of Theodozia Maria da Cruz, who bought me as part of a parcel of slaves, and who freed me for the amount of one hundred *mil-réis* [the equivalent at the time of about U.S.$103.00], which I gave her in cash, and a new slave, for which she handed me the respective letter of manumission which I keep in my power. And as a freed woman I have enjoyed this same freedom without the least opposition until the present time.

When my body dies, it will be wrapped in the habit of the patriarch Saint Francis, and placed in a coffin, and then commended [to God] by my reverend parish priest, and sixteen priests, who will accompany my coffin as it is conducted from the Irmandade of the Glorious Saint Benedict of the Monastery of Saint Francis, of which I am an unworthy and redeemed lay sister and was an office-holder, paying to the reverend parish priest his altar dues, giving him a pound of wax and to the other reverend priests the customary alms and wax, and then being buried at the foot of the altar of the same Glorious Saint Benedict.

The other irmandades to which I belong will also be advised so that they may accompany my body to the grave. They include the sodalities of Good Lord Jesus of the Redemption of the Holy Body, Our Lady of the Rosary, Saint Benedict da Conceição da Praia, the irmandade of Jesus, Mary, and Joseph of Carmel, those of

Our Lady of the Rosary, Saint Benedict, and Saint Anthony of Catagerona on the Baixa dos Sapateiros, and Saint Ifigenia of San Francisco so that, as sisters, they may accompany my body and carry out their prayers for the dead. If I am owing annual dues, I order that they be paid.

On the day following my death or the next day, I request that twenty-five Masses be celebrated for my soul with the body present, that is, ten in my parish church and fifteen in the Monastery of São Francisco, for alms of three hundred and twenty *réis*.

And later my executor will request that the following Masses be celebrated in the same Monastery of São Francisco: sixteen for the souls in Purgatory, eight as my recognition for the soul of my deceased mistress, ten for the souls and devotion of the persons with whom I had accounts and did business, and sixteen for the souls of my recently deceased slaves, twelve for the souls of my children for whom I have already prayed sufficiently, an offering of three hundred and twenty réis being made for each of these Masses. And I recommend that these prayers for the dead be carried out soon for the benefit of these souls.

I declare that I was never married and always remained single. And in this state I had five children, three sons deceased, and two daughters who are still alive, that is, Joanna Maria de Santa Justa, married to Captain Jozé Ferreira da Silva Feio, and another unmarried daughter who lives in my company, Jozefa Maria da Conceição. As well there exists a grandson, the legitimate son of my son Jozé de Souza, and because this son is dead, this grandson represents his father as my heir together with my two daughters. And I name them and institute them as my universal heirs of two-thirds of my goods.

I declare that the goods I possess are the following: a slave by the name of Maria, whom I leave conditionally freed for the amount of sixty mil-réis to be paid to my granddaughter Matildes, married to Professor Felipe Carlos Madeira; Anna, whom I free; Maria Victoria, whose value I include in my third and whom I leave to my daughter Jozefa Maria da Conceição; and Roza, who is mad, I free.

I declare that I have three slaves born into my household: a little Creole, Domingos, whom I gave to my daughter Joanna, married to Captain Jozé Ferreira da Silva Feio; a little Creole girl, Joanna, whom I gave to my other daughter, Jozefa Maria da Conceição; and another little Creole boy named Manoel, whom I took for myself and have given his letter of manumission.

I further possess several gold scapular medals with thick cords; a rosary of thick gold; another scapular medal also of gold with gold cords that wind around four times; some red coral strung on gold cords which I leave to my granddaughter Maria, together with a silver spoon and fork; a crucifix also of gold with three lengths of gold chain; other gold scapular medals with finer cords which I leave to my granddaughter Matildes; and two pairs of gold buttons.

I also possess a group of two-storey houses with shops at street level and a basement below with lodgings, located on the Ladeira do Carmo, where I live on land belonging to me. And I leave no money at all.

I declare that when my daughter Joanna Maria de Santa Justa married, I gave her a slave named Roza, valued at eighty-five mil-réis, a gold reliquary with four loops of chain and, later, the little Creole, Domingos.

I declare that [I gave] to my daughter Jozefa a gold crucifix with four loops of gold cord, a gold rosary with seven Our-Fathers and seventy Hail-Marys, two lengths of fine cord and a pair of diamond tear-drop earrings, and a topaz ring.

I declare that before the death of my son Jozé de Souza, he, wanting to go to the Coast of Mina [on the west coast of Africa], I lent him thirty-two mil-réis to prepare for the trip, and because he did not repay me, this amount should be accounted as part of the inheritance of his son, my grandson, as should the amount of sixty mil-réis which I spent on the rite for the body present and the [other] Masses I had celebrated for his soul, just as my two daughters and heirs will discount from their inheritance what each has already received.

I declare that when alive Francisco Xavier de Figueiredo pawned to me, for the amount of four hundred mil-réis on which he promised to pay interest, a silver jar and plate, a pair of gold shoe buckles, a rosary with the image of Saint Anthony, a necklace with four gold strands, a pair of gold buttons, all of which are in my power because he never repaid me in his lifetime, nor has his widow since his death.

I declare that possessing two slave women, Maria Angelica Angola, and another Gêge [a West African ethnic group from Dahomey, now Benin] by the name of Joaquina, I turned them over to the same Francisco Manoel de Figueiredo, his true name and not Xavier as was written by mistake in the clause above, for him to sell. Both were sold for one hundred and sixty mil-réis, which he did not turn over to me. But later I bought a new slave from him for one hundred and thirty mil-réis which, deducted from the price of the two slaves he had gotten rid of, left him owing me thirty mil-réis, which I order be collected together with the four hundred mil-réis loaned against the items pawned.

I owe nothing to anybody.

Twenty-five paupers will accompany my body to the grave, and to each one will be given alms of eighty réis.

The executor, who agrees to administer this my will, will hand to each of the two female slaves whom I free her letter of manumission and, if it is not given, this clause will serve as proof of the freedom which I freely grant them.

As my executors I name and institute in first place my daughter, Jozefa Maria da Conceição; in second place my son-in-law, Captain Jozé Ferreira da Silva Feio; and third, Professor Felippe Carlos Madeira. I beseech each one, in the order named, to accept this my will, executing all my dispositions as I have ordered, with full powers. And, it being necessary, I consitutute them as my attorneys on my account. And for settling the accounts [of my estate], I set a period of three years, and if this is difficult, in this case the Judge of Accounts will extend the time as necessary. I permit [the executor] the twentieth [part of one-third of the estate, a standard fee paid to an executor] for her or his work, which I order to be paid.

In this way I have declared and concluded this my testament which I want fulfilled as it is, being my last and final wishes. And if for its greater validity it lacks any legal clauses required by law to be expressed and declared, [I wish it to be obeyed] as if each one of them were expressed and declared in the best form and according to law. And not knowing how to read or write, I ordered this written by

Manoel Goncalves Pereira, who also signed for me at my request in this city of
Bahia on the sixteenth of January one thousand eight hundred and twenty three. I
sign at the request of the testator, Anna de São Jozé da Trindade

[signature of Manoel Goncalves Pereira]

Ratification

May all know who see this public instrument of ratification that in the year of
Our Lord Jesus Christ one thousand eight hundred and twenty-three, on the
sixteenth day of the month of January in this City of São Salvador of the Bay of All
Saints on the Ladeira do Carmo, in the house of the testator Anna de São Jozé,
where I, the Notary, came [and] found her ill but of sound mind and good
judgment, in the opinion of me the Notary and of the witnesses signed below, by
the replies she gave to the questions I put to her; in her presence, from her hands to
mine, this paper was given me saying that it was her solemn last will and testament
which, after being made, was hereby delivered to me and which revokes any other
will made before this one because she wishes that only this one should be valid and
have force and power. She implores that His Majesty's Justices enforce it and fulfill
it as it is comprised and declared, and if for its greater validity are lacking any
clause or clauses necessary in law to be expressed and declared, [she wishes it to be
fulfilled] as if each one of them were expressed and declared. And taking the said
will, I ran my eye over it and finding it clean without blanks, blots, or additions
between the lines nor any reason to cause doubt, I stamped it with my stamp which
says "Soares," and having carried out all the solemnities practiced in similar acts,
and after this will having been read in the presence of the said witnesses, the
testator said she accepted it [as] correct and, all being well, I accepted and accept it
insofar as I should and can and by reason of my office am obliged. Being present to
everything as witnesses, Manoel Jozé Loubato, Manoel dos Passos, Antonio da
Silva, Manoel Domingos, Bernardo da Cruz Romalho, Antonio Jozé de Santa Ritta,
and Antonio Narcizo who all signed and along with the testator who, because she
does not know how to write, at her request Joze Pereira dos Passos signed for her,
and I Manoel Soares de Albergaria, Notary, who wrote it, in witness of the truth,
(here there is a public seal)

[here follow the ten signatures]

The testator declared in the presence of the same witnesses that this last will
and testament was made at her order by Manoel Goncalves Pereira, and I the above
named Notary declared it "approved": The solemn will of Anna de São Jozé,
stitched through five holes with dark thread and sealed with drops of red wax
along the spine, [dated] Bahia, seventeenth of January one thousand eight hundred
and twenty-three

Manoel Soares de Albergaria

The Opening

I opened it; carry it out except for any nullity or damage to a third party. Bahia,
eighth of March one thousand eight hundred and twenty three. [signature of] Basto

Let it be registered and only in this court give an account of the profane as the law instructs, under pain of nullification. Bahia, eighth of March one thousand eight hundred and twenty three. [signature of] Basto

Acceptance

I accept the executorship of [the will of] my mother Anna de São Jozé with the compensation of the twentieth as the will mentions and, not knowing how to write, I requested Aleixo Custodio de Souza to sign for me. At Bahia on tenth of March one thousand eight hundred and twenty three, I sign at the request of Senhora Jozefa Maria da Conceição [signature of Aleixo Custodio de Souza]

Entered in the second book, page seventy-seven verso. Bahia, fifteenth of March one thousand eight hundred and twenty three. [signed] Almeida

Stamp

Number 198. Paid, two hundred and forty réis stamp tax, Bahia, fifteenth of March one thousand eight hundred and twenty three. [signed] Chaves Junior Sepulveda

Distribution

To the scribe, Souza. Bahia, eighteenth of March one thousand eight hundred and twenty three. [signed] Ribeiro

Registration

Registered in Book number 129, on page 77. Bahia, eighteenth of March one thousand eight hundred and twenty three. Paid two thousand and eighty-one réis.

Certification

I certify that fifteen Masses were said by the religious of this monastery for the alms of three hundred and twenty [réis] each for the soul of the deceased Anna de São Jozé da Trindade which her daughter and executrix, Senhora Jozefa, ordered said. And being true and having received the said amount, I wrote this in my own hand and seal, the San Francisco Monastery of Bahia, eleventh of March one thousand eight hundred and twenty three. [signed] Frei Manoel de Santa Anna.

52

Late Eighteenth-Century Inscriptions
on Fountains and Monuments in Mexico City

Some important changes in politics and culture were promoted from the top of Spanish and colonial American society after the War of the Spanish Succession (1700–1713), when a French Bourbon dynasty replaced the Hapsburgs on the Spanish throne. Administrative and economic reforms were introduced, aimed at material improvement and a more centralized authority for an "enlightened" monarch and his *peninsular* advisers, but these reforms were not often achieved in lasting ways or with the intended results. "Fixed rules," strict obedience to law, reason, and applied science became the new watchwords, while customary practices of Baroque Catholicism were often discredited as irrational and dangerously tangled in confusion. Bourbon administrators hoped to restrain the elaborate, high-spirited, and costly religious festivities of virtually every community in the old heartlands of the empire, and channel that energy and wealth into more sober, productive activity. For the new Spanish monarchy, ancient Rome became, again, a revered model of greatness and order.

These aspirations and values of Bourbon leaders—a somewhat pale, top-down version of the great Enlightenment changes becoming evident elsewhere in western Europe by the late seventeenth century—were expressed in some ordinary, overlooked ways. By the reign of Charles III (1759–1788), the kingdoms of Spain were more conspicuously personified in the current occupant of the throne. The king's visage now appeared on silver coins of the realm in place of the royal coat of arms, his head in profile with a laurel wreath, like some Roman emperor. The point was driven home in a larger-than-life equestrian statue of the reigning monarch Charles IV commissioned for Mexico City at the turn of the nineteenth century. The king, again, appears in the dress and posture of a Roman emperor. The cool, restrained monumentality of the neoclassical style of art and architecture, also inspired by Roman models, appealed to the Spanish Bourbons' obsession with orderly, rational grandeur (which often meant massive, symmetrical, and austere). An official academy of art in its own neoclassical building was established in Mexico City during the 1780s to teach the properly "regal" aesthetic.

The many public works undertaken during the late eighteenth century—bridges, paved roads, waterworks, parks, fountains, municipal buildings, jails, and the like—were characteristic of the Bourbon program.

And, unlike earlier construction initiatives, every new work seemed to merit an inscription for the public's edification. Here are three examples from late eighteenth-century Mexico City that convey more about their time and sponsors than just names and dates. But even dates on buildings were not "just" dates. The vogue of dating the beginning and completion of new works and of commemorating centennials and other anniversaries with inscriptions on buildings in the late colonial period suggests a heightened historical consciousness that was more alert to change.

Figure 36. The Salto del Agua, Mexico City, 1779.

Figure 37. Inscription on the Salto del Agua, Mexico City, 1779.

Translation of the inscription on one side of the Salto del Agua (Figure 37), the great fountain at the terminus of the newly built aqueduct that brought water to the city from springs at Chapultepec:

> From the reservoir to this receiving station
> is a distance of 4,663 *varas* [13,056 feet, or about
> two and one-half miles], and from the Chapultepec
> bridge there are 904 arches [in the aqueduct].
> And having made various experiments to achieve
> the greatest elevation and water pressure, the
> height of this new aqueduct was raised another
> one and three-quarters varas [nearly 5 feet],
> while the previous governors had raised the
> water channel by just over one vara [2.8 feet].
> The results of this new construction are clear:
> a height of two and three-quarters varas [7.7 feet]
> over the original aqueduct has been achieved
> by (as already stated) various prolix and
> exquisite experiments.

On the opposite side of the Salto del Agua is another inscription in an identical frame (not illustrated here), translated as follows:

This aqueduct and receiving station were
completed on March 20, 1779, in the reign of His
Catholic Majesty Charles III (may God protect him);
being Viceroy, Governor, and Captain General of
this New Spain and President of its Royal Audiencia
the Most Excellent Baylio Frey Antonio María Bucareli
y Urive, Knight-General, Descendant of Military Leaders,
Commander in the Order of Saint John, Gentleman of His
Majesty's Council, soon-to-be Lt. General of the Royal
Armies; being Judge-Conservator of Ways and Means of
this Most Noble City Don Miguel de Acedo, member of
His Majesty's Council and Audiencia judge in the city
of Mexico; and being the magistrate in charge Don
Antonio de Mier y Terán, perpetual alderman of this
Most Noble City.

Figure 38. Monument for the New Roadway to San Agustín de las Cuevas, Mexico City, 1787.
Courtesy of the Archivo General de la Nación, Mexico City.

Translation of the inscription on the Monument for the New Roadway from Mexico City to San Agustín de las Cuevas, Mexico City, 1787 (Figure 38):

> Stay a moment, Traveler, and listen carefully
> To the Great Conde de Gálvez about the care
> Taken by this Royal Mexican consulado [the powerful merchant guild],
> Their concern for [American] development.
> For the greater embellishment of Mexico
> And to ease the lives of beggars and the needy
> They have built this beautiful roadway,
> Emulating the splendor of Rome:
> The Via Stabiana, the beautiful Via Cornelia
> The famous Via Salaria of Sabinius [and]
> The one that goes between Capua and Rome.
> Claudius built the Via Appia for the traveler;
> All others acknowledge the glory of this famous road.
> Now continue on your way, Traveler.
> This roadway, which begins here, ends
> at the town of San Agustín de las Cuevas.
> It is four leagues and 1,141 *varas* long
> [about fifteen miles], partly with a crushed
> stone embankment and partly paved; and along
> its course three bridges have been restored,
> seven new ones have been added, plus six
> underground drainage channels. The work was
> begun on April 29, 1786, and completed on
> December 31, 1787.

Translations of the inscriptions on the four fountains of the Plaza Mayor, Mexico City, 1794 (not illustrated here):

On the fountain in front of the cathedral:

> In the glorious reign of Charles IV, being Viceroy
> the Most Excellent Juan Vicente de Güemes Pacheco
> de Padilla, Count of Revillagigedo, this plaza was
> lowered in the years 1790 to 1793 and its four
> fountains were erected. The atrium of the Holy
> Cathedral Church also was lowered and redecorated,
> and its façade was completed and beautified.

On the fountain in front of the main entrance to the viceregal palace:

> In 1790, during the glorious
> reign of Charles IV, being Viceroy the Most Excellent
> Juan Vicente de Güemes Pacheco de Padilla, Count of
> Revillagigedo, public lighting in the streets of this
> city was introduced, as were the most useful lantern-
> keepers who attend to them and to the public safety.

On the fountain in front of the entrance known as that of the viceroy:

> In the reign of Charles IV,
> in the viceregency of the Most Excellent Juan Vicente
> de Güemes Pacheco de Padilla, Count of Revillagigedo,
> the street plan of the city was laid out, glazed tiles
> to mark the name of every street and plaza were set in
> place, the houses were numbered, annexes were marked,
> the façades of many buildings were painted, and a
> regimen of general cleanliness was undertaken.

On the fountain in front of the municipal offices:

> In the glorious reign of Charles IV, being Viceroy the
> Most Excellent Juan Vicente de Güemes Pacheco de Padilla,
> Count of Revillagigedo, between 1790 and 1794 the principal
> streets of this city were paved: 545,039 square *varas*
> [4,273,106 square feet] of paving were laid, 16,535
> square varas [129,634 square feet] of drainage canals,
> and 27,317 square varas [214,165 square feet] of sidewalk
> with piping underneath; and the plazas for markets were
> formed and arranged.

53

Túpac Amaru I, Remembered

(eighteenth century)

This painting by an unknown artist in the eighteenth century carries on a colonial tradition of idealized Inka kings' portraits and an interest in portraying Inka history. Yet the person depicted here is not one of the line of pre-Hispanic Inkas whose Tawantinsuyu was invaded by the Spaniards in 1531–32. Rather, this is a depiction of Túpac Amaru (d. 1572), the last from the dynastic line of Inkas which established a royal court and government in defiance of the Spaniards from a mountain fortress in the region of Vilcabamba, north of Cusco, between 1537 and 1572.

Manco Capac was a son of Huayna Capac, the last Inka to rule over a united realm. In 1534, after one half-brother, Atahuallpa Inka, had been garroted and another half-brother, Topa Gualpa (the first of the Spaniards' puppet Inkas), had died, Manco Capac was crowned Manco Inka by a hopeful Francisco Pizarro. However, Manco soon defected and led Indian forces in rebellion in 1536. After a siege of Cusco that lasted over a year and nearly culminated in his retaking the imperial city from the Spaniards and their Andean allies, Manco Inka retreated with an entourage to Vilcabamba. Here the group, dubbed the "neo-Inkas" by George Kubler, built their capital-in-exile (in counterpoint to Manco's rival younger brother, Paullu [d. ca. 1550],

who became the Pizarros' next Inka in Cusco). The early Quechua interpreter and chronicler Juan de Betanzos, who accompanied a Spanish embassy to Manco Inka's young successor, Sayri Túpac (or Saire Topa, d. 1560) in 1556–57, wrote of a "town in the image of Cusco" that had emerged in the "wilds," a rugged country of mountain passes where horses soon became useless, where "even the Indians go up arm in arm on ropes and tree roots and vines." In 1610, Captain Baltasar de Ocampo wrote a narrative of the events surrounding Túpac Amaru's capture and execution, at a remove of almost thirty years and at a time when this aged eyewitness was seeking recognition and favors for the settlers in the region where he was now an official. He said that the fortress-city in Vilcabamba possessed "an extensive level space, with very sumptuous and majestic buildings, erected with great skill and art." Manco and his successors exacted tribute from loyal groups in the region and organized raids against areas under Spanish rule.

After a succession of entreaties and promises, the Spanish embassy to Sayri Túpac persuaded the Inka to leave Vilcabamba and accept extremely advantageous terms in Cusco. Sayri Túpac's elder brother Titu Cusi Yupanqui Inka (d. 1571) spurned the palaces and an Inkaic noble's life in conquered Cusco, however—and he knew something of what he was rejecting. As a young child, Titu Cusi had been captured by Spanish troops and taken for three or four years to live in the home of the Spanish noble Fernando de Oñate, until 1541 when Manco bargained for his return to Vilcabamba. Titu Cusi remained in Vilcabamba, usurping power from a legitimate heir and younger half-brother, Túpac Amaru, in about 1558–1560. Titu Cusi's strategy of hostilities and negotiation, along with his professions of interest in Christianity, were increasingly suspect in Lima and Cusco.

The newly arrived viceroy of Peru, Francisco de Toledo (1569–1581), abandoned the luring and negotiating tack of his predecessors and acted decisively and swiftly in the matter of the rebel Inkas. He ordered an assault on Vilcabamba from Cusco in 1571–72. For the expedition, he augmented Spanish troops with some two thousand Indian auxiliaries, among whom were a large contingent of pacified Inkas and a company of Cañari guardsmen (the same native Andean allies discussed in Selection 38). By this time, Titu Cusi had died; and his Mestizo secretary, Martín Pando, and an Augustinian friar named Diego de Ortiz had been killed at court in Vilcabamba, on the suspicion that they had poisoned him. The assault led by Toledo's captains proceeded as planned, and perhaps with even greater purpose once this intelligence was known. On October 4, 1571, after a battle and a chase, the youthful new Inka, Túpac Amaru, was seized along with his elite guard.

Túpac Amaru had been a largely neutralized younger half-brother after Titu Cusi's assumption of power by 1560. He appears to have kept up hostilities against "pacified" regions and to have repulsed Spanish efforts to communicate with Vilcabamba in 1571. But his reign as rebel king was above all short and tragic; he took power as if only to preside over the dissolution of early colonial hopes for the survival of an independent Inka state. After Túpac Amaru Inka was captured and marched off to Cusco, the Vilcabamba over which he ruled so briefly was officially transformed: it was reconsecrated in memory not of thirty-five years of heroic Inka resistance but of conquest and domination achieved. The Spanish town of San Francisco of the Victory of Vilcabamba was founded with much pomp and fitted with a Spanish garrison, just in case.

According to Ocampo's narrative of events, the triumphal party stopped at the entrance to the city at the archway of Karmenka (in the parish of Santa Ana, again see Selection 38) to put the troops in order and chain together Túpac Amaru and the members of his court and guard. The Inka was said to have been wearing a brilliant crimson tunic and the fringed headpiece, or *masca paycha* (see Selection 2). He was marched through the streets, presented before Viceroy Toledo, and then imprisoned in a palace. The Inka's "captains" were sentenced to hang, although, according to Ocampo, after much mistreatment only two made it to the gallows. As if in reenactment of what had happened before Atahuallpa's judicial murder forty years earlier, Túpac Amaru was instructed in the tenets of Christianity for "two or three days" and was said to have been baptized in his prison by two Quechua-speaking Mercedarian friars. Túpac Amaru was then led from his prison to a scaffold erected in the central square in front of the cathedral and beheaded by a Cañari executioner before a crowd of thousands who filled two plazas and the streets and watched from balconies, windows, and rooftops. The Inka's head was put on a high spike in the main plaza, intended as an example to anyone contemplating defiance of the Spanish will. However, the head was removed when, it is said, Indians were observed in what appeared to be nocturnal worship of it.

Figure 39 is no great work of portraiture, yet the rather wooden image is strikingly deliberate with its storytelling. What does one make of the expression and the stance of the young prince in the painting? With a serious expression, gazing upward as if awaiting a higher justice, he wears links of chain around his neck and arms, but the bonds appear more like reminders or props—the symbolic

Figure 39. "Don Felipe Tupa Amaru," artist unknown (eighteenth century).
Courtesy of the Museo Nacional de Bellas Artes, Buenos Aires.

attributes of a hero or martyred saint—than devices of restraint. He stands erect and dignified with his arms crossed in front, seemingly more out of choice than because the chains hold them thus. The plaque in the lower left corner, amid its basic identifying information, gives a reason for his stoical attitude to any viewer who cared to read it. This is "Don Felipe Tupa Amaru, last Inka of the Pagan Kings of Peru," it announces, proceeding to tell of his royal marriages and children, his public decapitation on the orders of Viceroy Toledo, and the burial of his body. The plaque carefully notes that Toledo's summary action was disapproved of by King Philip II, a piece of information perhaps gleaned from the claim by Mestizo humanist and historian El Inca Garcilaso de la Vega (1539–1616), whose *First Part of the Royal Commentaries* (Lisbon, 1609) and *General History of Peru* (Córdoba, 1617) were widely read. Garcilaso had written that, upon the viceroy's return to Spain, the monarch rebuked Toledo for his actions in the case of Túpac Amaru and banished him from favor.

What were the expectations and needs of the late colonial audience of the painting? What kind of past is being drawn, and then drawn upon, and why? Why, some two centuries later, the survival, and even mounting, of concern over the treatment of a rebel and obstacle to Spanish dominion? Why the preoccupation with the justice of Toledo's decision?

Remarkably little is known of Túpac Amaru. Yet this short-term rebel was the last Inka of Vilcabamba, and, in being so and in dying as he did, he has become as evocative a symbol as one is likely to find in Andean Peru—with time, often merging in the collective Andean imagination, as Alberto Flores Galindo has shown, with Atahuallpa, the last Inka executed by Pizarro at Cajamarca. The many local revolts, uprisings, and conspiracies in the Andes through the eighteenth and early nineteenth centuries frequently played upon the "Inka's head" and on the theme of beheadings, along with the transforming memory of Túpac Amaru and the expectation of an Inka's resumption of power. For some,

natural catastrophes such as floods and earthquakes seemed to herald an overturning of a corrupt order in Andean Peru.

Critical reflections on the way that Túpac Amaru died in Cusco in 1572 were popular among late seventeenth- and eighteenth-century Peruvian Creoles and well-to-do Mestizos, the people who would have formed this painting's principal audience. At least until the great rebellion of 1780–1782 dampened many Creoles' enthusiasm for things Inkaic and "Indian," members of the eighteenth-century elite in Cusco even allowed spoken Quechua and the chewing of coca leaves in their intellectual gatherings. And they commissioned and collected paintings that featured indigenous themes and motifs, paintings like this one and the earlier examples from the Corpus Christi series (Figures 27 and 28 in Selection 38). José Gabriel Condorcanqui, the *kuraka* (regional native governor) from the south-central Andes who adopted the name Túpac Amaru II (d. 1781), became the most memorable, but not the first, Andean rebel leader to present himself successfully to a multi-ethnic audience as a disinherited descendant of the Inka Túpac Amaru I and to reclaim rightful authority in the land. Critiques such as those which seem to appear in this image could merge with hopes and plans for the coronation of a late colonial Inka who might rule over a new confederation, a reborn Tawantinsuyu, which might remedy any number of abuses that people perceived as embodied in the practice of Bourbon rule.

The prisoner in the painting seems to touch his viewers' discomfort and their dreams. He wears a glittering crown adorned with feathers and a tapestry tunic with a circular design (a stylized sun?) on his chest. His dress and accoutrements, his dignity, suggest royalty, yet now in a vague and patterned way. The details of a post-Conquest Inkaic tunic and a distinctive masca paycha, so carefully rendered in many earlier paintings and chroniclers' accounts, seem to have grown either less important or more dangerous. This Túpac Amaru seems depicted more as a legendary hero than as an actual Inka rebel. Artists and viewers deemphasized certain details and recast the rebel, and events from the sixteenth century, for their own purposes. The painting's message about *peninsular* outrages in America seems clear. Viewers might attach this image of the heroic rebel Túpac Amaru, wronged and murdered without a proper trial by a peninsular viceroy, not only to similar depictions of the death of the Inka Atahuallpa but also to a general brutality that, according to some views, characterized Spanish treatment of their American subjects, not least the Creoles.

The colonial memory of this sacrifice in Cusco in 1572 did not depend on a sense of grievance about Bourbon reforms. And it was well remembered by a wider set of observers and subsequent tellers than the early generations of disgruntled Creoles or native Andean eyewitnesses within the crowd in Cusco's center (who are said to have wailed and groaned at the sight of Túpac Amaru's death). Both Garcilaso's and Ocampo's early seventeenth-century descriptions of the execution of Túpac Amaru precede the messages in this eighteenth-century canvas with similar feelings. In particular, they treat the subject as Toledo's serious, criminal blunder. A higher verdict seems required and awaited. Ocampo lists the heads of the religious orders in Cusco by name and claims that before the execution each of them pleaded with the viceroy to spare the Inka and send him to Spain to be properly tried by the king. El Inca Garcilaso, whose projections on the Inka past inspired a multi-ethnic elite readership in the eighteenth century that perhaps included Túpac Amaru II, implied even more about justice and legitimacy—explosive messages to many late colonial readers who reflected on his account of the death in Cusco's central square in 1572: "So ended the Inka," wrote Garcilaso, "the legitimate heir to the empire by the direct male line from the first Inka Manco Capac to himself."

54

"America Nursing Spanish Noble Boys," Peru
(ca. 1770s)

Art historians George Kubler and Martin Soria identify this as a painting from the central Andes (perhaps Lima) in the late eighteenth century. They write, "Toward the end of the century, perhaps during the rebellion of Túpac Amaru II (1780), an anonymous painter showed America nursing Spanish noble boys. Negroes and Mestizos are pressing around her throne, while naked Indian children weep, abandoned. Two richly dressed Indian couples present their gifts in a beautiful park crowded with different animals."

The sense of movement of the figures, the informal posture of the Inka lord with crossed legs, and the swooping lines of the decoration around the inscription place the painting well into the eighteenth century. But perhaps it was done shortly before the Túpac Amaru rebellion rather than during that violent and complex Andean struggle of the early 1780s, which pitted Indian communities against each other or against their leaders in alliance with Creole (American-born Spanish) elites, as well as Indians against colonial elites of all kinds. The painting expresses a popular Creole elite identity and a standard lament during the Bourbon reforms of the second half of the

eighteenth century: invoking their American-ness through a glorious Indian past, and de-crying the privileges of *peninsular* appointees at the expense of sons of America. Judging by their costumes and complexions, the children looking on as the two peninsular boys in fashionable European outfits nurse at America's breasts are Creoles as well as Mestizos and Afromestizos.

These sentiments of indignation and Americanness were expressed with parti-cular vehemence by Creoles in Spanish America during periods of *visita*—the inspec-tion tours carried out by high peninsular offi-cials appointed by the king to raise revenues and otherwise reform administrative proce-dures in the name of good order and effi-ciency, largely to the Crown's advantage. Criticism of this kind and scattered rebellions accompanied the visitas to New Spain in the 1760s and to New Granada in 1780–81. The notorious visita to the Viceroyalty of Peru headed by José Antonio de Areche during this period began in 1777, thus making 1777–1780 a likely date for this painting— before Peruvian Creoles were jolted from their comfortable association of America with the Indian past.

Figure 40. "America Nursing Spanish Noble Boys," artist unknown, Peru, ca. 1770s.
The inscription at the bottom reads in part:
"Where in the world has one seen what one sees here. . . .
Her own sons lie groaning and she suckles strangers."

∼ SEE PLATE 16 ∼

~ 55

José María Morelos's "Sentiments of the Nation," Chilpancingo, Mexico

(1813)

The two great leaders of the early, unsuccessful struggle for Mexican independence in 1810–1815 were parish priests from the Diocese of Michoacán: Miguel Hidalgo and José María Morelos. Hidalgo, a Creole Spaniard, held a doctorate in theology and was a leading figure in the cathedral city of Valladolid (modern Morelia) before running afoul of ecclesiastical authorities. He was charged with mismanaging funds of his diocesan seminary and was mistrusted for his eclectic intellectual life; there was some suspicion that he held unorthodox views about Christian doctrine. On the eve of the struggle he served the prosperous parish of Dolores in the modern state of Guanajuato. Morelos, the priest of a poor parish in the hot country of lowland Michoacán, had studied briefly with Hidalgo in Valladolid but was not as well educated— less well read and less bold in his ideas. His baptismal record identifies him as a Creole Spaniard, but he was evidently a Mestizo, or perhaps an Afromestizo. In any case, he came from more modest roots and relied on experience and studies of moral theology and pastoral manuals for his sense of political ethics.

Hidalgo's insurrection in 1810 did not openly declare for independence, but it was clearly opposed to colonial government and the immigrant Spanish elite (*peninsulares*) in Mexico. He was captured and executed in 1811. Morelos had joined Hidalgo's forces some weeks after the insurrection began; and, after Hidalgo's death, he became the outstanding military leader in the first years of struggle against colonial rule and privileged Spaniards. But he did not succeed in overthrowing Spanish rule, and, unable to hold any important provincial cities for long, he operated mostly on the edges of the heartland of colonial Mexico—in lowland Michoacán, Guerrero, Oaxaca, and Puebla. He, too, was captured and executed in 1815.

Nonetheless, under Morelos's nominal leadership, a declaration of independence was finally issued and a congress was convened to plan for a new national government in 1813. Morelos was not a political philosopher, and his ideas for an independent nation emerged slowly. They are most clearly expressed in the following document known as "Sentiments of the Nation," presented to the opening session of the Chilpancingo Congress on September 14, 1813. Usually regarded as a homegrown "liberal" document enshrining popular sovereignty, liberty, and equality, the "Sentiments of the Nation" offer Morelos's growing belief in liberty and elements of equality without giving up a preference for hierarchy, precedence, status, and religious exclusivism. And he did not lightly refer to his words as *sentiments*. For Morelos, ideas expressed passions, longings, and frustrations, not just Enlightenment rationality. Religious sentiments and the social values behind them pervade the document, giving it the character of a pastoral lesson and a connection to the past, while critiquing the present and breaking with colonial rule and its hereditary inequalities.

Morelos's thinking in this text can seem contradictory. He opens with a clear call for national independence from any other sovereign power, but the second, third, and fourth of the original twenty-two articles turn immediately to religion in ways that seem to confuse the liberal cast of the document: Article 2 declares Catholicism to be "the only [religion], without tolerance for any other"; Article 3 provides for the financial support of the priesthood; and Article 4 affirms the responsibility of the Church hierarchy to keep Catholic dogma pure.

Yet, to simultaneously affirm hierarchy, religious intolerance, popular sovereignty, and equality before the law would not have been a contradiction to Morelos, the parish priest. A unifying idea behind this mixture of apparent opposites was the old regard for moderation and balance. Morelos could speak of liberty and equality among Americans without accepting these principles as absolutes or abandoning his conviction that hierarchy was essential to social order, that the poor and humble—like Indians in the colonial conception—required parental care, and that salvation was the highest purpose of human activity. Liberty for Morelos still centered on the freedom to fulfill a Catholic Christian destiny, and it still centered more on freedom from unjust restraint than on freedom as an absolute good in its own right. It was not freedom to practice false religion. Nor was it, in J. H. Parry's words, "freedom to be idle, to be left to one's own devices, to refrain from making any contribution to the well-being of society."

---

1. That America is free and independent of Spain and every other nation, government, or monarchy, and thus it shall be proclaimed, informing the world why.

2. That the Catholic religion shall be the only one, without tolerance for any other.

3. That the ministers of the Church shall live only from the tithes and first fruits, and the people shall not be required to pay for services, except as true offerings and expressions of their devotion.

4. That the dogma of the religion shall be upheld by the Church hierarchy, consisting of the Pope, the bishops, and the parish priests, because *every plant that God did not plant should be weeded out*. . . . Matthew 15.

5. That sovereignty flows directly from the people, and they wish it to be lodged only in the Supremo Congreso Nacional Americano, composed of representatives of the provinces in equal numbers.

6. That the legislative, executive, and judicial powers shall be divided among those bodies that are established to exercise them.

7. That the representatives shall serve for four years in rotation, the old ones leaving office so the newly elected can take their places.

8. The representatives shall be paid a sufficient but not excessive salary. For now, it shall not be more than 8,000 pesos.

9. Government posts shall be held only by Americans.

10. Foreigners shall not be allowed to enter the country unless they are artisans who can instruct others and are free of all suspicion.

11. States alter the customs of the people; therefore, the Fatherland will not be completely free and ours until the government is reformed, replacing the tyrannical with the liberal, and also expelling from our soil the enemy Spaniard who has so greatly opposed our Fatherland.

12. Since the good law is superior to any man, those [laws] that our Congreso issues shall be so, and shall promote constancy and patriotism, and moderate opulence and poverty so that the daily wage of the poor man is raised, his customs improved, and ignorance, preying upon others, and thievery removed.

13. That the general laws shall apply to everyone, including privileged corporations except as applies directly to their duties.

14. To draw up a law, there shall be a gathering of the greatest number of wise men possible, so that the deliberations may proceed with greater certainty. [These men] shall be exempt from some of the duties that might otherwise be demanded of them.

15. Slavery shall be forever forbidden, as shall caste distinctions, leaving everyone equal. One American shall be distinguished from another only by his vices and virtues.

16. That our ports may admit [the ships of] friendly foreign nations, but they cannot be based in the kingdom no matter how friendly they are. And only designated ports—ten percent of those that exist—shall be used for this purpose. Disembarkation in any other is forbidden.

17. The property of every individual shall be protected, and their homes respected as if they were a sacred asylum. Penalties shall be assigned for violators.

18. That the new legislation shall not allow torture.

19. That the new legislation shall establish by constitutional law the celebration of December 12 in every community of the land in honor of Our Most Holy Lady of Guadalupe, patroness of our liberty, and every community is to practice monthly devotions to her.

20. That foreign troops or those from any other [Spanish] kingdom shall not set foot on our soil unless it is to come to our aid, and then only with the authorization of the Suprema Junta.

21. That no expeditions outside the limits of the kingdom shall be made, especially not overseas expeditions; but others not of this kind are to be encouraged in order to propagate the faith among our brothers in the interior [*tierradentro*, or northern Mexico and the American Southwest].

22. That the plethora of tributes, fees, and taxes that weigh us down shall be eliminated. A five percent charge on grains and other produce, or a similarly light tax, shall be levied on every individual. It shall not oppress us like the alcabala, the tobacco monopoly, the tribute, and others. With this light contribution and good administration of property confiscated from the enemy, the cost of the war and the salaries of employees can be paid.

Chilpancingo, 14 September 1813.

[appended Article] 23. That September 16 also shall be solemnized each year as the anniversary of the beginning of our struggle for Independence and our holy Freedom, for on that date the Nation spoke, demanding its rights with sword in hand so as to be heard. Thus the distinction of the great hero, Señor Don Miguel Hidalgo, and his companion, Don Ignacio Allende, will be remembered forever.

56

The Argentine Declaration of Independence, San Miguel de Tucumán

(1816)

Several great areas of South America that had been on the margins of Spanish colonial history in the sixteenth and seventeenth centuries, with smaller populations and a weaker colonial administrative presence, developed rapidly in the eighteenth century. Modern Venezuela and Argentina are the most striking examples. It was from these two areas in which the centralizing institutions of the Catholic Church and the imperial state developed late that the movements for liberation from Spain gained an early hold and spread. Priests and ideas from moral theology (Christian principles applied to everyday life) were less evident in the independence movements of Argentina and Venezuela than in Mexico. Insurgent leaders there expressed themselves more clearly in the modern language of the eighteenth-century revolutions in France and the United States: individual rights and freedoms, popular elections, the will of the people, representative government, separation of powers, and other democratic institutions. The brief Argentine declaration printed below hailed democracy and representative government as natural rights of American peoples that the Spanish monarchy arbitrarily cancelled; it condemned as artificial such a forced connection between American peoples and Spanish kings. These words of political liberation from Argentina differ from Morelos's "Sentiments of the Nation" for Mexico (Selection 55) in their debt to the United States' Declaration of Independence, their vision of democracy, and their way of invoking God and religion. But this Argentine document is not in all ways a clean break from traditional Spanish American ideas about political rights and organization.

Decreed in the meritorious and very worthy city of San Miguel de Tucumán on July 9, 1816. Having terminated its ordinary session, the Congress of the United Provinces continued its earlier discussions on the great and august subject of the independence of the peoples that form it. The clamor of the entire territory was universal, constant, and decided for a solemn emancipation from the despotic power of the kings of Spain. The representatives nevertheless dedicated to this crucial issue all the profundity of their talents, the rectitude of their intentions, and the interest that requires the sanction of their destiny, their represented peoples, and their posterity. Finally they were asked if they wished the United Provinces to be a nation free and independent of the kings of Spain and the metropolis. Filled with the holy ardor of justice, they first acclaimed, and one by one successively repeated, the unanimous and spontaneous vote for the independence of the country, setting forth accordingly the following determination:

Declaration: We the representatives of the United Provinces in South America, reassembled in General Congress, invoking the Eternal One who presides over the universe, in the name of and by the authority of the towns that we represent, protesting to Heaven and to all nations and men of the globe the justice that governs our votes, declare on the face of the Earth that it is the unanimous and unquestioned will of these provinces to break the forced chains that have linked them to the kings of Spain, to recover the rights of which they were despoiled, and to invest themselves with the high character of a nation free and independent from Ferdinand VII as well as from his successors and metropolis. In consequence they remain in fact and by right in possession of full and ample power to provide themselves with the forms which justice requires and which the sum of their present circumstances demands. All and each one of them thus publishes, declares, and ratifies it, and we thus commit ourselves to the fulfillment and preservation of this our will, under the security and guaranty of our lives, our property, and our reputation. Let this be communicated to the appropriate persons for publication, and in recognition of the respect owed to the nations, enumerating in a manifesto the very serious and basic motivations of this solemn declaration. Given in the Legislative Chamber, signed by our hand, sealed with the seal of Congress, and authenticated by our official notaries.

57

The Brazilian Constitution and the Church
(1824)

Brazil arrived at its independence from Portugal by peculiar circumstances. When in 1807 Napoleon ordered Portugal's prince regent, Dom João, to close its ports to British ships and trade, imprison British residents in Portugal, and confiscate their property or face French invasion, the king, deeply dependent on British trade, had no choice. He refused. But with only a modest army and navy to defend itself, Portugal clearly could not hope to repel invading French forces. By a secret convention Britain offered its protection if the prince regent decided to "withdraw" to Brazil. Dom João learned on November 23 that Napoleon and an army of 23,000 men had arrived at the border with Spain, leaving the Portuguese four days until French forces would reach Lisbon. In those few hectic days the elite scrambled to leave: members of the royal family; the highest officials of government, including members of the Council of State, ministers and advisers, justices of the High Court, and Treasury officials; the highest ranking officers of the army and navy; the Church hierarchy as well as members of the aristocracy, bureaucrats, professionals and businessmen, and several hundred courtiers with their servants and hangers-on. At least 10,000 persons, and perhaps as many as 15,000, managed to secure passage and

embarked on the flagship *Principe Real*, eight other ships-of-the-line, eight lesser warships, and thirty merchant vessels. Besides the confusion of their personal baggage, they carried with them the hastily gathered contents of the Treasury, the files of the government, the furnishings of the Royal Chapel, the collections of several libraries, and what was to be Brazil's first printing press. They sailed for Bahia under escort by four British warships.

What at first appeared an ignominious and disorderly flight proved later to have been a well-planned and savvy political move, albeit one for which Britain expected to be reimbursed, not solely from trade through Brazilian ports but in treaties that restricted, and eventually shut down, the slave trade from Africa to Brazil. Portuguese-born merchants in Bahia reacted early and loudly against escalating British influence. They warned Dom João against Britain's trading practices and painted the British as undermining religion—the bulwark, in their view, of a colonial system that relied on slavery. Religion, they wrote to the prince upon his arrival in Bahia in 1808, has not only justified the "sincere intentions of the discoverers of the New World," but also "it has made just the captivity of Africans," enabling them to be nourished with the "sacred milk" of the

Gospel. Their argument, transparently self-interested, was made seriously, and in it can be heard distant echoes of the pope's bull of 1455 (see Selection 6).

Meanwhile, in a dazzling reversal of power, the head of a European state had fled with his government and court to the country's most important colony, suddenly turning the colony into the seat of the empire from which the royal family would rule until 1822. By 1821, with the Napoleonic threat removed, the Portuguese in Portugal wanted their power and their king to reside again in Lisbon, and Brazil again to be their colony, not the separate kingdom that Dom João had made it in 1815. Dom João VI responded to political discontent in Portugal by finally returning to Lisbon and leaving his son Pedro in Brazil as regent. But by this late date neither side could be satisfied. When the Lisbon parliament demanded Pedro's return as well, intending that Brazil should be demoted to its former colonial status and once again be answerable to Portugal, Pedro refused. Instead, in 1822 he declared Brazil independent with himself as emperor, a plan that almost certainly had been worked out earlier with his father.

The legal basis for the independent monarchy was the constitution ratified in 1824, which authorized a parliamentary government. In this liberal, post-Enlightenment era, Brazilians might have separated Church and state but, instead, in spelling out its powers this new government retained the old relationship with the Catholic Church as the state religion. Although not referred to in the constitution and negotiated separately with Rome, the privileges of ecclesiastical patronage, the *padroado*, exercised by the Portuguese Crown since the fifteenth century, were extended to Brazil's emperor, empowering him to appoint bishops on the pope's behalf, collect tithes, and pay the clergy. Non-Catholic religions were tolerated as long as they remained discreetly invisible, but marrying and dying were still Catholic affairs. The state recognized only Catholic-officiated marriages, and all cemeteries and burials were Catholic, except for the few cemeteries permitted the British community for their Protestant dead. Complete separation from a weakened Church came with the end of the empire and was confirmed by a new Republican constitution in 1891.

◞ *Constitution of the Brazilian Empire, Title I, Article 5 (1824)*

The Roman Apostolic Catholic religion will continue to be the religion of the Empire. All other religions will be permitted to hold domestic or private worship in buildings designated for this purpose without any exterior indication of being a temple.

GLOSSARY

Afromestizo—in the Spanish language, person of mixed African, Indian, and European ancestry; a term not used in the colonial period.

Albaicín—sector of Granada, Spain, in which many Moriscos lived.

alcabala—sales tax.

alcalde—community official, member of the *cabildo*; a secondary officer in a head town but often the chief local officer of a subordinate town.

alcalde mayor—district governor appointed by the Crown; also *corregidor.*

alcalde ordinario—community official, member of the *cabildo* exercising judicial authority.

aldeia—mission village established by Jesuits in sixteenth- and seventeenth-century Brazil as a place to resettle Indians for the purpose of converting them.

algarabía—local dialect of the Arabic language spoken in Granada.

Angolans—Bantu-speaking people from the Congo and Angola regions of West Central Africa.

arancel—schedule of fees; here, payable to a parish priest.

atrio—atrium or church courtyard.

audiencia—colonial high court, consisting of a president and judges; also refers to this court's jurisdiction. There were ten Audiencias situated in provincial cities, including Lima and Mexico City, by the end of the sixteenth century; two more were added in the eighteenth century.

auto-da-fé—public ceremony at which sentences of the Inquisition were announced and where processions of the repentant and condemned took place.

ayllu—Andean social, ritual, and territorial unit.

Aztec—common term for the Tenocha-Mexica people of the island city of Tenochtitlan (now Mexico City), who embarked on territorial expansion outside the Valley of Mexico in the decades before the Spaniards arrived.

Bahia—refers to both the captaincy and its principal city, Salvador; the capital of Portuguese America until 1763, when the seat of colonial government was moved to Rio de Janeiro.

bandeira—quasi-military expedition for exploration or Indian slave-raiding in Brazil.

Baroque—term from the art history of Catholic Europe from the late sixteenth century. It suggests religious devotion radically separated from the workaday world, engaged less with the intellect than direct, emotional experience of the heavenly realm through dazzling displays of holy objects and the fine arts.

beata—lay holy woman.

bull—edict issued by the pope as head of the Catholic Church in Rome.

cabecera—head town of a region or parish.

cabildo—annually elected town council.

cacao—chocolate, or the bean or plant from which it comes.

cacique—hereditary Indian leader. The term is Hispanicized Arawak used generically by the Spaniards to refer to a local ruler of an Indian polity.

Cañaris—a resettled Andean people originally from the region of modern Ecuador, south of Quito. The Cañaris had been noted guards and fighters in the service of the Inkas, a set of roles they continued in privileged alliance with Spaniards in the Cusco of colonial times.

candomblé—originally a Bantu word introduced into Portuguese that refers both to the place of worship and to the Afro-Brazilian religious practices devoted to African divinities or *orixás*; today used especially in Bahia.

captaincy—in Brazil, the principal political and administrative division, each with its own captain-general who, in turn, reported either to a governor-general or viceroy (the title varied) or directly to the Portuguese Crown.

caravel—developed by the Portuguese in the fifteenth century, this two-masted, lanteen-rigged sailing ship was smaller, lighter, faster, and hence easier to maneuver than other ships; important in the exploration of the African coast and Atlantic islands.

casta—person thought to be of mixed Indian, African, and European descent and hence not pure-blooded; in late colonial records the term more often distinguishes a non-Indian from an Indian than a non-European from a European. The plural *castas* refers to a genre of late colonial Mexican painting featuring racial mixture.

cédula—written authorization; here, usually short for *real cédula*, or royal decree.

Cercado—walled district of colonial Lima in which many native Andeans lived.

chacra—Quechua term for a plot of cultivable land.

chicha—fermented beverage made from maize; the most common alcoholic drink in the colonial Andes.

Chichimec—term of Nahuatl origin for barbarous invader and looter. It was used by Aztecs and colonial subjects of New Spain to identify enemies in the Chichimeca region, a floating zone defined mainly by rainfall belts separating sparse, semi-nomadic groups of part-time farmers and hunter-gatherers from denser, stable farming communities to the south.

coca—low tropical bush, the leaves of which are among the common offerings to Andean divinities and which are chewed as a stimulant during work and travel.

cochineal—small insect that thrives on the native nopal cactus of central and southern Mexico. The females were collected, dried, and crushed into a deep red dyestuff coveted by Europeans.

cofradía—lay religious association or confraternity established to promote a particular devotion; *irmandade* in the Portuguese language.

colegio—residential college; here, established and run by a religious order; c*olégio* in Portuguese.

coloquio—dialogue; exchange of speeches.

compadre—the relationship established by Catholic baptism between the parents and godparents of the baptized child.

conopa—personal divinity and source of fecundity in the central Andes, the natural or sculpted form of which often depicted its creative function.

converso—"new convert" to Christianity from Judaism.

convivencia—"coexistence," or the living together of Muslims, Christians, and Jews within medieval Iberian society. The term has often stressed creative interaction and intercultural borrowing.

Corpus Christi—term for a principal feast of the Roman Catholic Church in honor of the Holy Eucharist, the body of Christ, His living presence in the consecrated Host, celebrated in the period between late May to mid-June. The Corpus Christi procession, in which the Host in its special vessel is carried through the streets before the whole community, became a prominent part of the feast days in western Europe from at least the middle of the fourteenth century.

corregidor—district governor appointed by the Crown; also *alcalde mayor*.

Council of the Indies—royal tribunal that governed Spanish American affairs and advised the monarch from Seville.

Council of Trent—the nineteenth ecumenical council of the Roman Catholic Church held between 1545 and 1563 in Trento, Italy, the principal purpose of which was to order and clarify Catholic doctrine in the face of the challenges raised by Protestant reformers. The twenty-five sessions brought compromises between radical and more traditional delegates, much legislative reform of discipline and bishops' duties and powers, and the strengthening of seminary education and papal authority. The reform decrees of the Council became the centerpiece of a Catholic revival in the sixteenth century (usually referred to as the Counter-Reformation, or Catholic Reformation) that saw, among other things, the renewal of piety, prayer, mysticism, and the emergence of a Baroque art and culture in Catholic Europe.

Creole—or *criollo* in Spanish America: an American-born person of, or claiming, Spanish ancestry. Or *crioulo* in Portuguese America: a slave born in Brazil, as distinct from an African transported to Brazil as a slave.

cruzado—Portuguese gold coin, later struck in silver, of variable worth.

cura—pastor; parish priest.

cuy, cuyes—Andean guinea pigs raised in homes, important for blood offerings to divinities and for healing rituals.

demonio—demon or the Devil. The term was often applied to indigenous gods themselves in colonial times, and/or to the evil force said to be behind them.

dobra—gold coin, minted in both Portugal and Brazil, of variable worth.

doctrina—elementary Christian dogma that parishioners were to be taught repeatedly and expected to commit to memory. The term may also refer to a parish of Indians, technically a temporary or proto-parish administered by regular clergy in which the newly converted were to receive indoctrination.

dogmatizer—literal translation of *dogmatizador*, a Spanish term for an Andean teacher, guardian, and teller of sacred histories as well as a minister and ritual adept.

Dom—honorific title in Portugal, reserved for a king, his descendants, and the highest officials of the Catholic Church.

Dominicans—common name for the Order of the Friars Preacher, a religious order of the Catholic Church founded especially to preach against heretics in the early thirteenth century by Saint Dominic. The Dominicans became known for their devotion to preaching and study, and in Spanish America they sought to combine the contemplative life with their apostolic endeavors and the administration of Indian *doctrinas*.

Don—an honorific title indicating high status, used sparingly in the early colonial period but more widely in the eighteenth century as a term of respect or standing as a Spaniard or Indian notable.

encomendero—the possessor of an *encomienda*; a Spaniard to whom a group or groups of Indians have been "entrusted." He might demand manual labor and tribute from the Indians in exchange for payment, protection, and religious instruction.

encomienda—a grant of labor and tribute rights from the Crown to an *encomendero* over a specified group of Indians.

escribano—notary; scribe.

español—Spaniard, whether born in Spain or America.

fanega—unit of dry measure, about 1.5 bushels.

fazenda—in Brazil, a large landed estate engaged in farming or ranching; sugar estates are usually referred to as *engenhos*, or mills, where sugarcane was not only grown but also processed.

fiesta—community feast-day celebration.

fiscal—lay assistant to a parish priest; chief legal counsel to an *audiencia*.

forastero—*indio forastero*, an itinerant or migrant Indian who lives away from his place of origin.

Franciscans—common name for the Order of the Friars Minor, a religious order of the Catholic Church founded in the early thirteenth century by Saint Francis of Assisi. The Franciscans pursued an ideal of complete poverty, but successive reforms led to the development of distinct branches within the order. In the early fifteenth century, a division hardened especially in the Spanish kingdoms and in France between a reformed (Observant) branch committed to extreme poverty and missions, and a more moderate one (Conventual) that did not adhere to the reform. The friars who arrived in Mexico in 1524 at the request of Hernán Cortés were from a reformed group within the Observant ranks.

Gêges—also Jejes; the Aja-Fon-Ewe ethnic and language group from the Mina Coast of West Africa, today the country of Benin; rivals of the Nagôs in Bahia.

hacendado—owner of a *hacienda*, a large landed estate.

hacienda—large landed estate engaged in farming and ranching.

Hausas—West Africans from the region of what is now northern Nigeria, many of whom were Muslims.

huaca—local or regional sacred place and divinity in the Andes; sometimes a physical object; often, but not exclusively, conceived of as an ancestor being and "founder" in the landscape surrounding a community, regularly nourished with offerings and given reverence.

humanist—a classical scholar, devoted to the study of the literature or "humanities" associated with the mostly fifteenth- and sixteenth-century revival of interest in ancient Rome and Greece.

idolatry—literally, the worship of a false god represented by an idol; in Christian terms, a grave sin in violation of the First Commandment. Here, idolatry is a judgmental term or charge applied by Spanish and Portuguese Christian authorities and commentators to the most serious religious errors, especially those of Indians. It refers to surviving pre-Iberian beliefs and practices but also to the many aspects of colonial Indian culture, including alleged perversions of Christianity, believed to be subversive to genuine conversion and Christian life. *See* superstition

Indian—*indio*; a major social and ethnic category in Spanish colonial law; a blanket term for descendants of the indigenous population living under either Spanish or Portuguese rule. In Spanish America, Indians were tribute payers, legal minors, and usually associated with a home community or *pueblo*. In Portuguese America, *indio* often referred to Christianized Indians in contrast to *gentios*, who continued to live in their own villages and were regarded by the Portuguese as heathens. The term derives from Columbus's mistaken belief that he had reached India or east Asia in 1492.

infante—any younger son or daughter (*infanta*) of a Portuguese or Spanish king not in line to inherit the throne.

infidel—from a Christian point of view, a non-believer, a heathen; an adherent of a religion opposed to Christianity; here, a Saracen or Muslim.

Inka—or Inca, the common term for the people from the Valley of Cusco in the south-central Andes whose rapid conquests mostly in the course of the fifteenth century extended their power over much of western South America. The Inkas referred to their "empire," which comprised many peoples, as Tawantinsuyu, Land of the Four Quarters. The usage of Inka derives from the Spaniards' mistaken assumption that the Quechua term for the supreme ruler or king applied to an entire people.

irmandade—lay sodality or confraternity, often associated with a parish church and organized around devotion to a chosen saint; it offered its members certain benefits, such as loans or dowries, the purchase of a slave's freedom, or Catholic burial; membership might be limited to a specific group—women, slaves, persons of color, those of similar ethnic background, those who could demonstrate purity of blood, or certain artisans and professions. *Cofradía* in the Spanish language.

Jesuits—common name for the Society of Jesus, a religious order of the Catholic Church founded in 1540 by Saint Ignatius of Loyola. The Jesuits began as a missionary order embodying the discipline and ideals of the Counter-Reformation and soon emerged as leading teachers, scholars, and spiritual directors in Catholic Christendom. After earlier missions, and a number of martyrdoms in Brazil and Florida, the Jesuits established themselves in Peru (1568) and Mexico (1570) and the rest of Spanish America. Jesuits were known not only for their schools, seminaries, and urban ministries (among slaves and in prisons), but also for their missions and "reductions" among indigenous peoples such as the Guaraní.

kuraka—or *curaca*, hereditary native governor in the Andes. *See also cacique*

league—variable measure of traveling distance in colonial times, about 3.5 miles, or 5.57 kilometers.

llactas—small Andean settlements.

malqui—Andean ancestor whose body has been mummified; a divinity of regional significance, and, like the *huaca*, regularly nourished with offerings and commemorative, festive attention.

Mameluco—person of mixed Portuguese and Indian ancestry and culture.

masca paycha—Inka ornamental headpiece.

Mass—"the holiest of holy things," the ritual event performed by an ordained Catholic priest in which the bread and wine of the ceremony become Christ's body and blood.

mayordomo—overseer, or chief steward; here, a rotating position as chief attendant of a religious association.

mendicant—member of one of the religious orders in the Catholic Church committed to living without possessions through work and alms alone; here, especially a Franciscan, Dominican, or Augustinian.

Mestiço—person of mixed racial background, Portuguese and Indian or Portuguese and African or Afro-Brazilian. *See* Mestizo *mestizaje*—racial, but here also cultural, mixture; miscegenation.

Mestizo—person of mixed Spanish and Indian ancestry, sometimes applied more generally to a person of mixed race. *See Mestiço*

Mexican—term used by Spaniards for Aztecs; also a colonial term for people from Mexico City, thus not "Mexican" in the modern national sense.

mita—Spanish adaptation of a labor rotation system employed by the Inkas, the *m'ita*, to gain workers for large projects. An Indian away from his home area for purposes of work was known as a *mitayo*.

Morisco—a new convert to Christianity from Islam in the Spanish kingdoms.

Mulatto—or Mulato, and the feminine Mulata: a person of mixed, but part African, ancestry, often taken to be of roughly equal European and African descent, but a term that in the Spanish language might also refer to a person of Indian and African ancestry.

Nagôs—term used in Bahia for the Yoruba people from the Mina Coast of West Africa, what is now Nigeria; some were Muslims; rivals of the Gêges in Bahia.

Nahuatl—the language of much of central Mexico at the time of the Spanish occupation.

neoclassicism—art style promoted by the Crowns of both Spain and Portugal in the late colonial period, inspired by the buildings and sculpture of ancient Rome. Austere, massive, and symmetrical, it promoted a vision of rational grandeur.

New Spain—the viceroyalty of northern Spanish America with its capital at Mexico City. It included modern Mexico, the American Southwest, and much of Central America and the Caribbean islands.

notarial records—legal documents recorded by, or certified as authentic by, licensed public notaries. Much of the voluminous written record for colonial Spanish and Portuguese America was officially taken down by notaries for courts and governors. A notary's archive (in contrast to a court's or governor's archive) consisted especially of records of wills, property transfers, and other legal agreements.

pacarina—place of origin, venerated by native Andeans, to which one also returns.

padroado—ecclesiastical patronage extended by the pope to the kings of Portugal and then, in an independent Brazil, to the emperor, allowing them to act in place of the pope in such matters as the appointment of Church officials and collection of the tithe.

palenque—protected refuge for runaway slaves.

peça—literally, piece, but in Brazil it referred to a unit of merchandise, and particularly to a prime male slave; old slaves, women, and children each counted for less than a full *peça*.

peninsular—person born in the Iberian Peninsula who has come to America.

Peru—the viceroyalty of southern Spanish America with its capital at Lima. Until the creation of the viceroyalties of New Granada and La Plata in late colonial times, the Viceroyalty of Peru included most of South America with the exception of Portuguese-controlled Brazil.

pintura—literally, a painting, but in colonial usage a map or picture.

plaza mayor—central square of a town.

posa—"stopping place," the chapels sometimes built at the corners of a church courtyard.

presidio—fortified garrison on the frontiers of colonial settlement.

principal—local notable or important person; headman; here, often a member of an hereditary Indian elite in a community.

pueblo—town.

pueblo viejo—old town; Spanish term for the settlement of Andean ancestors before the colonial resettlement of peoples into towns and villages, frequently within walking distance of the resettlements. *See reducción*

pulque—fermented beverage made from the maguey plant, the most widely consumed intoxicating drink in Mexico during the colonial period.

Quechua—the language (or group of related languages) of the Inkas and many of their subjects in the Andean highlands at the time of the Spanish arrival.

quilombo—runaway slave settlement, encampment, or refuge; sometimes temporary, sometimes lasting years or, in the case of Palmares, for decades.

real—one-eighth of a silver peso.

reconquista—the centuries of war by Christian kingdoms against Islam in the Iberian Peninsula; in fact, a time when many tactical alliances and political arrangements were pursued across religious lines.

reducción—town resulting from the forced resettlement of groups of Indians in colonial times; also, a mission community among indigenous peoples established by the Jesuits.

regidor—community official; a secondary member of the *cabildo*.

regular—from *regula* (rule or law), referring to regular clergy, the special groups of Catholic priests, nuns, and aspirants who live by a separate set of rules, for example, Jesuits, Franciscans, and Carmelites. *See* secular

religious—member of a regular order of the Catholic Church; also, a devout person. *See* secular

repartimiento—distribution of anything; here, a labor draft from Indian pueblos.

reparto—*reparto de mercancías*, or *repartimiento de mercancías*, a monopoly trading privilege of a *corregidor* or *alcalde mayor* within his territory.

secular—from *saecularis*, referring to a member of the secular or diocesan clergy living in the world (*saeculum*) under the authority of a bishop, as opposed to living according to the rule of a religious community; also, more generally, a person or thing that is worldly or non-religious. *See* regular; religious

sertão—from the point of view of Europeans, the backlands, an unsettled wilderness region in Portuguese America.

sesmaria—large grant of land given by, or in the name of, the Crown, which carried certain rights and obligations.

Supay—native Andean force with good and evil properties, sometimes described as the flying soul of a relative. Appropriated by some Spanish missionaries and lexicographers as a gloss for the Christian idea of the Devil.

superstition—broad term applied, here, by Christians to religious behaviors and attitudes believed to be contemptible and inherently irrational, the result of ignorance, misinformation, the inventions of sinful people, and fear of the unknown. Like "idolatry," superstition was an impediment to "true religion," yet, by the sixteenth and seventeenth centuries, superstition came to signify an abject, less serious, and thus more easily surmountable kind of error. *See* idolatry

Tawantinsuyu—"Land of the Four Quarters"; the Inkaic term for the Inka empire.

teniente—deputy or assistant.

Tlaxcalans—people of Tlaxcala. A central Mexican people who had maintained a measure of independence in the face of Aztec expansion, the Tlaxcalans became the Spaniards' valuable allies in their military takeover of Tenochtitlan. The leaders and communities of early colonial Tlaxcala successfully argued for a privileged place in the colonial order on the basis of their people's alliance, early embrace of Christianity, and participation in various Spanish colonizing expeditions on the frontiers of New Spain.

tradición—tradition; here, the common colonial gloss for an Andean sacred history regularly told by a native minister-dogmatizer and sometimes performed in dance and song.

tratado—treatise.

Tupi—part of the Tupi-Guaraní family of indigenous languages spoken by people of the northern and eastern coasts of Brazil.

Tupinambá—one of the Tupi-speaking indigenous groups in the area around what became Bahia; in some areas, in the early sixteenth century, they allied with the French against their enemies, the Tupinikin, who, in turn, allied with the Portuguese.

vara—short for *vara de justicia*, or staff of office, especially of an Indian official; also, a unit of measurement or distance of about 33 inches.

vicario—assistant to a parish priest.

viceroy—the Spanish monarch's chief representative with extensive executive and judicial authority and more limited authority to issue laws. The capitals of the two viceroyalties—territories governed by viceroys—in the sixteenth and seventeenth centuries were Lima and Mexico City. Two more viceroyalties were added in the eighteenth century, New Granada and La Plata, with capitals at Bogotá and Buenos Aires. In Portuguese America, viceroy was a title of rank more than authority. Several administrators held this rank in the seventeenth and eighteenth centuries but not continuously; they served as governors of captaincies rather than with general authority over all Brazil.

villca—demigod-like human in native Andean traditions; a favorite of a *huaca*.

Vira Cocha—a principal creator-divinity in the pre-Hispanic Andes. It became a term applied to White people in colonial Peru.

visita—a general tour of inspection, often of a viceroy's or *alcalde mayor*'s administration, commissioned by the Crown.

visitador—a commissioned inspector; an administrative official conducting a tour of inspection (*visita general*). Here, also an inspector periodically sent to Brazil by the Inquisition in Portugal to investigate possible heresies and other errors against the Catholic faith, and a *visitador general de idolatría*, an idolatry inspector and judge who is a priest commissioned to investigate "suspect" Indian religiosity. Also a postal inspector.

Yoruba—language and ethnic group from the Mina Coast of West Africa, today the country of Nigeria; called Nagôs in Bahia.

Zambo—person of African and native Andean descent.

NOTES ON SELECTIONS AND SOURCES

1. Selection 1 is excerpted from *The Huarochirí Manuscript: A Testament of Ancient and Colonial Andean Religion*, edited and translated from the Quechua by Frank Salomon and George L. Urioste, © 1991 (Austin, 1991), pp. 41–54. Courtesy of the University of Texas Press. Readers wanting more of this source are encouraged to consult the paperback edition noted above and Salomon's fine introductory essay, which informs the present introduction. On the context out of which the document derives, see especially Karen Spalding, *Huarochirí: An Andean Society under Inca and Spanish Rule* (Stanford, 1984); and the interpretation of Antonio Acosta Rodríguez, "Francisco de Avila, Cusco 1573(?)–Lima 1647," in *Ritos y tradiciones de Huarochirí: Manuscrito quechua de comienzos del siglo XVII*, edited and translated by Gerald Taylor (Lima, 1987), pp. 551–616.

2. Our opening to discussion of the two tunics in Figures 1 and 2 is indebted to an essay by R. Tom Zuidema, "Guaman Poma and the Art of Empire: Toward an Iconography of Inca Royal Dress," in *Transatlantic Encounters: Europeans and Andeans in the Sixteenth Century*, edited by Kenneth J. Andrien and Rolena Adorno (Berkeley and Los Angeles, 1991), pp. 151–202; and to pioneering work by John H. Rowe, "Standardization in Inca Tapestry Tunics," in *The Junius B. Bird Pre-Columbian Textile Conference*, edited by Ann Pollard Rowe, Elizabeth P. Benson, and Anne-Louise Schaffer (Washington, DC, 1979), pp. 239–64, and Ann P. Rowe, "Technical Features of Inca Tapestry Tunics," *Textile Museum Journal* 17 (1978): 5–28. The Inka key checkerboard tunic (Figure 1; Plate 1) is in the collection of the Textile Museum in Washington, DC (no. 91.147) (Andrien and Adorno, 173, 9d). Courtesy of the Textile Museum. Figure 2 is an uncu from a private collection in Lima, Peru. (The black-and-white image is from Andrien and Adorno, 176, 10b. The color version [Plate 2] is from José Miguel Oviedo, ed., *La edad de oro* [Barcelona: 1986], 233.)

3. This selection is translated from Bernardino de Sahagún, *Coloquios y doctrina cristiana*, edited by Miguel León-Portilla (Mexico, 1986), fols. 34r, 35r, 36r, and 37r (facsimile), pp. 86–89 (Spanish transcription). Courtesy of the Universidad Nacional Autónoma de México.

4. Much of the discussion for Selection 4 is adapted from Richard F. Townsend, *State and Cosmos in the Art of Tenochtitlan* (Washington, DC, 1979), pp. 63–70. The photograph of the stone (Figure 3) comes from Jay A. Levenson, editor, *Circa 1492: Art in the Age of Exploration* (Washington, DC, and New Haven, 1991), p. 503. Courtesy of the Coordinación Nacional de Asuntos Jurídicos, Mexico City. The drawing of the stone (Figure 4) is taken from Antonio de León y Gama, *Descripción histórica y cronológica de las dos piedras . . .* , 2d ed. (Mexico, 1832), plate 2.

5. Selection 5 is excerpted from *Christians and Moors in Spain* (Warminster, Eng., 1992), vol. 3, *Arabic Sources (711–1501),* edited and translated from the Arabic by Charles Melville and Ahmad Ubaydli, pp. 28–31, 52–55, and 110–15. Courtesy of Aris and Phillips, Warminster, Wiltshire, England. Melville's and Ubaydli's short introductions to these texts inform our own, as does their glossary on religious and legal terminology. Also of particular help has been the approach to *convivencia* in the work of Thomas F. Glick, as well as recent formulations on the interdependence of violence and tolerance in related settings by David Nirenberg in *Communities of Violence: Persecution of Minorities in the Middle Ages* (Princeton, 1996). Américo Castro's *España en su historia: Cristianos, moros y judíos* (Buenos Aires, 1948), with modifications and additions, exists in an English translation by Edmund L. King, *The Structure of Spanish History* (Princeton, 1954).

6. The Papal Bull, *Romanus Pontifex,* of Nicholas V, January 8, 1455, is translated by Frances Gardiner Davenport, ed., *European Treaties bearing on the History of the United States and Its Dependencies to 1648* (Washington, DC, 1917), pp. 9–26, translation, pp. 20–26. In dating papal bulls before 1691–1700, the pontificate of Innocent XII, March 25 was usually taken as the beginning of the year, hence the year 1454 in the text becomes 1455 by our reckoning. This introduction draws from C. R. Boxer, *The Portuguese Seaborne Empire, 1415–1825* (New York, 1969), especially pp. 4–37, and for his attribution of the "Green Sea of Darkness" to Arab geographers, see p. 26; and A. C. de C. M. Saunders, *A Social History of Black Slaves and Freedmen in Portugal, 1441–1555* (Cambridge, Eng., 1982), especially pp. 4–46. More recently John Thorton, *Africa and Africans in the Making of the Atlantic World, 1400–1680* (Cambridge, Eng., 1998), pp. 1–125, has radically shifted perceptions regarding African participation in the Atlantic slave trade; David Eltis, although writing about a later period and about English and Dutch traders, similarly argues vigorously and provocatively against any simple African-as-victim interpretation in *The Rise of African Slavery in the Americas* (Cambridge, Eng., 2000), see pp. 57–84, 137–92, 224–57. The opening quote is from Gomes Eanes de Zurara, *Crónica dos feitos notavéis que se passaram na conquista de Guiné por mandado do Infante D. Henrique,* ed. Torquato de Souza Soares, 2 vols. (Lisbon, 1978–1981), 2:145–48; the quote from the 1456 bull, *Inter caetera,* is from Davenport, *European Treaties,* p. 32.

7. The letter of Pedro Vaz de Caminha to King Manuel I, May 1, 1500, is translated, introduced, and edited by William Brooks Greenlee, *The Voyage of Pedro Alvares Cabral to Brazil and India, From Contemporary Documents and Narratives* (London, 1938), pp. 5–33, footnotes omitted. Courtesy of the Hakluyt Society. This introduction relies on Greenlee, especially pp. xvii–xxxi, 4, and Appendix, "Ships and Personnel," pp. 191–202; on C. R. Boxer, *The Portuguese Seaborne Empire, 1415–1825* (New York, 1969), especially pp. 229, 261–62, and the map of Indian trade routes, pp. 54–55; and Anthony Pagden's useful categories of analysis, *European Encounters with the New World: From Renaissance to Romanticism* (New Haven, 1993), especially pp. 51–87. For an excellent account of sixteenth-century native peoples, see John Monteiro, "The Crises and Transformations of Invaded Societies: Coastal Brazil in the Sixteenth Century," in *The Cambridge History of the Native Peoples of the Americas,* vol. 3, pt. 1, *South America,* ed. Frank Salomon and Stuart B. Schwartz (Cambridge, Eng., 1999), pp. 973–1023.

8. This translation first appeared as the first part of Appendix 1 in *The Oroz Codex: The Oroz Relación, or Relation of the Description of the Holy Gospel Province in New Spain, and the Lives of the Founders and Other Noteworthy Men of Said Province, Composed by Fray Pedro Oroz* [1584–1586], translated and edited by Angélico Chávez, O.F.M. (Washington, DC, 1972), pp. 347–53. Courtesy of the Academy of American Franciscan History.

9. Selection 9, an extract from an anonymous original manuscript in the collection of the Biblioteca de Palacio in Madrid, is excerpted from Francisco de Vitoria, *Political Writings,* edited by Anthony Pagden and translated by Jeremy Lawrance (Cambridge, Eng., 1991), Appendix B, "Lecture on the Evangelization of Unbelievers," pp. 341–51. Courtesy of Cambridge University Press. Our introduction to this reading is assisted especially by Pagden's "Introduction," pp. xiii–xxviii; Lawrance's "Biographical Notes" and "Glossary," pp. 353–81; and Quentin Skinner, *The Foundations of Modern Political Thought,* vol. 2, *The Age of Reformation* (Cambridge, Eng., 1978), pp. 135–73.

10. Figures 5 and 6 are from Hugh Honour, *The New Golden Land* (New York, 1975), p. 10. Numerous editions and translations of Vespucci's letters on his voyages exist. An original of the Strassburg

edition of 1509, the German translation that includes Figures 5 and 6, is in the collections of the British Library in London. The letter is reproduced in facsimile in Americus Vespucius, *The First Four Voyages of Americus Vespucius: A Reprint in Exact Facsimile of the German Edition Printed at Strassburg, by John Grüninger, in 1509,* with a prefatory note by Luther S. Livingston (New York, 1902). Among numerous English translations are *The First Four Voyages of Amerigo Vespucci translated from the rare original edition (Florence, 1505–6); with some Preliminary Notices, by M. K.,* edited and translated by Michael Kerney (London, 1885); and *Letters from a New World: Amerigo Vespucci's Discovery of America,* edited and translated by Luciano Formisano (New York, 1992), pp. 57–97.

The circuitous path of Vespucci's letter to Soderini, even within the confines of the five years after it was written, tells us something of the diffusion and reproduction of documents and books of great interest in contemporary western Europe. The original Italian "Lettera di Amerigo Vespucci delle isole nuovamente trovate in quattro suoi viaggi" was written by Vespucci in Portugal on September 4, 1504. It was carried to Soderini in Florence by one of Vespucci's fellow seamen and published there. The publication bears no date, but it was probably printed in 1505 or 1506. The letter found its way to France and was first translated into French by an unknown hand in Saint-Dié in Lorraine, and this version has never been found. But from it, Jean Basin de Sendacour, a member of the college at Saint-Dié and one of a group who had just set up a printing press, made a Latin translation. The letter from "Vespucius" was published in 1507 at Saint-Dié as an appendix to the *Cosmographiœ Introductio* by Martin Waldseemüller (1470–1521?), and it was in Waldseemüller's book that "America" was suggested as the proper name for the new lands beyond the Ocean Sea. The German translation of the Grüninger edition, of which these two images were a part, was thus made from a Latin edition, which itself was translated from a lost French translation of the Italian original.

11. Figure 7 is from Christoph Weiditz, *Authentic Everyday Dress of the Renaissance: All 154 Plates from the "Trachtenbuch"* (New York, 1994), plate XVIII (sheet 1). Weiditz's manuscript is held in the German National Museum in Nuremberg. It was published in a trilingual (German, English, and Spanish) edition by Theodor Hampe as *Das Trachtenbuch des Christoph Weiditz von seinen Reisen nach Spanien (1529) und den Niederlanden (1531/32)* (Berlin and Leipzig, 1927), with forty-one of the plates in color. Dover Publications has printed a paperback edition of the *Trachtenbuch,* retaining Hampe's introduction and contextualizing first chapter along with a slightly revised version of the 1927 work's English text. The plates are in black and white, collected two to a page.

12. Figure 8 is from Christoph Weiditz, *Authentic Everyday Dress of the Renaissance* (New York, 1994), plate LXXX (sheet 100). See note to Selection 11 above.

13. The letters by Nóbrega and the bishop are translated from the Portuguese transcriptions of "Padre Manoel da Nóbrega to Padre Simão Rodrigues, Bahia, July 1552," in Serafim Leite, compiler and editor, *Novas cartas jesuíticas (de Nóbrega à Vieira)* (São Paulo, 1940), pp. 29–33; and "Bishop Pedro Fernandes Sardinha to Padre Simão Rodrigues, Bahia, July 1552," in Serafim Leite, compiler and editor, *Monumenta Brasiliae,* vol. 1 (1538–1553) (Rome, 1956), pp. 357–66, with the note from Leite that this letter was not sent until a year later together with a second letter dated October 1553; and "Bishop Pedro Fernandes Sardinha to Rector, College of San Antão, Bahia, October 1553," in Serafim Leite, compiler and editor, *Monumenta Brasiliae,* vol. 2 (1553–1558) (Rome, 1957), pp. 11–13. For insight into early Jesuit organization, thought, and practice, see Serafim Leite, *História da Companhia de Jesus no Brasil* (Rio de Janeiro, 1938), II, especially pp. 100–103, 336–39, 520; John W. O'Malley, *The First Jesuits* (Cambridge, MA, 1993), especially pp. 77, 87–90, 121–22, 134, 135–36, 157, 159, 267, 330, 342–43. On Bishop Pedro Fernandes Sardinha, see Moreira de Azevedo, "O primeiro bispo do Brasil," *Anais da Biblioteca Nacional* (Rio de Janeiro) 23 (1901): 59–67. For the additional letters of Padre Manoel da Nóbrega quoted and referred to here, see Manoel da Nóbrega, *Cartas do Brasil* (Belo Horizonte; São Paulo, 1988), especially numbers 1, pp. 71–75; 3, pp. 79, 81, 83, 86; 4, pp. 91–93; 6, p. 108; 7, pp. 115, 116; 9, p. 124; 10, p. 128; 11, p. 136; 12, pp. 140–43; 20, pp. 193–200. See also Antonio de Nebrija, *Gramática de la lengua castellana,* intro. and ed. Antonio Quilis (1492; Madrid, 1980), p. 97.

14. Gante's letter is translated from *Cartas de Indias (publícalas por primera vez el Ministerio de Fomento),* editor unknown (Madrid, 1877), pp. 92–102.

15. This selection was published as "The Evils of Cochineal: March 3, 1553," in *The Tlaxcalan Actas: A Compendium of the Records of the Cabildo of Tlaxcala (1545–1627),* edited by James Lockhart, Frances Berdan, and Arthur J. O. Anderson (Salt Lake City, 1986), pp. 80–84. Courtesy of the University of Utah Press.

16. The text in this selection and the image in Figure 9 come from *Papeles de Nueva España* (Madrid, 1905), 4:53–57 (relación), between 52 and 53 (map). Plate 3 is a photograph by Juan Jiménez Salmarón and is courtesy of the Real Academia de Historia, Madrid. Thanks also to Barbara Mundy. Both images in Figure 10 are from John M. D. Pohl and Bruce E. Byland, "Mixtec Landscape Perception and Archaeological Settlement Patterns," *Ancient America* 1 (1990): 120. Courtesy of Cambridge University Press. For Dana Leibsohn's interpretation of indigenous maps, see "Colony and Cartography: Shifting Signs on Indigenous Maps of New Spain," in *Reframing the Renaissance: Visual Culture in Europe and Latin America, 1450–1650,* edited by Claire Farago (New Haven, 1995), pp. 264–81, on the Texupa map especially pp. 278–79.

17. Selection 17 is translated from Enrique Otte, editor (with the collaboration of Guadalupe Albi), *Cartas privadas de emigrantes de Indias, 1540–1616* (Seville, 1988), p. 81.

18. Selection 18 is excerpted and translated from Archivum Romanum Societatis Iesu (Rome), *Epistolae Hispaniae* 104, fols. 129–129v: Hieronymo de Benarcama to Francisco de Borja, Granada, September 25, 1566. Helpful to our introduction and suggestive on Benarcama is Nigel Griffin, "'Un muro invisible': Moriscos and Cristianos Viejos in Granada," in *Medieval and Renaissance Studies on Spain and Portugal in Honour of P. E. Russell,* edited by F. W. Hodcroft, D. G. Pattison, R. D. F. Pring-Mill, and R. W. Truman (Oxford, 1981), pp. 133–54. On the early Society see John W. O'Malley, *The First Jesuits* (Cambridge, MA, 1993), and the first section of essays by Terence O'Reilly in *From Ignatius Loyola to John of the Cross: Spirituality and Literature in Sixteenth-Century Spain* (Aldershot, Eng., 1995). A concise and up-to-date introduction to the experiences of Nahua collegians in New Spain appears in Louise Burkhart, *Holy Wednesday: A Nahua Drama from Early Colonial Mexico* (Philadelphia, 1996), chap. 2, esp. pp. 55–73.

19. Selection 19 is excerpted and translated from José de Acosta, *De Procuranda Indorum Salute,* edited and translated by Luciano Pereña et al. (Madrid, 1984), vol. 1, *Pacificación y colonización,* chaps. 14, 15, and 18, pp. 199–209 and 231–43.

20. Figures 11 and 12 are from *Pintura del gobernador, alcaldes y regidores de México. Códice en gerolíficos mexicanos y en lenguas castellana y azteca, existente en la Biblioteca del Duque de Osuna* (Madrid, 1878), fols. 501v, 470v.

21. Figures 13 and 14 are from the *Códice Sierra. Fragmento de una nómina de gastos del pueblo de Santa Catarina Texupan,* facsimile edition (Mexico, 1906), pp. 16 (Saint Peter, 1555) and 42 (the arm, 1561). Courtesy of the Marquand Library of Art and Archaeology, Department of Rare Books and Special Collections, Princeton University Libraries.

22. Figure 15 is from Diego Valadés, *Rhetorica Christiana* (Perugia, 1579), facing p. 206 (misprinted as "106"). Courtesy of the John Carter Brown Library at Brown University.

23. Figure 16 is a photograph of the Huejotzingo altarpiece from *Retablos mexicanos,* Artes de México series, no. 106 (Mexico, 1966), preceding p. 21. Courtesy of the Coordinación Nacional de Asuntos Jurídicos, Mexico City. The schematic drawing (Figure 17) is adapted from *Retablos,* p. 27. On pp. 26–27 this source has a helpful short essay on the symbolism of the altarpiece by Francisco de la Maza.

24. This painting by Andrés Sánchez Gallque, Figure 18 (also Plate 4), is courtesy of the Museo de América, Madrid. The 1606 document comes from the archive of the Duque de Infantado, Madrid, on microfilm in the E. William Jowdy Microfilm Collection of the Montesclaros Papers, DeGolyer Library, Southern Methodist University.

25. "Blacks Dancing" (Figure 19 and Plate 5) is from Zacharias Wagener, "Tanzende Negersklaven," in "Thier Buch" [1640], Staatlichen Kunstsammlungen, Dresden, No. 105, Ca 226a, and reproduced with the museum's kind permission. For a reprinted edition of the image and accompanying text, see *Dutch Brazil,* ed. Cristina Ferrão [Monteiro Soares] and José Paulo Monteiro Soares, vol. 2,

Zacharias Wagener, "Thier Buch" (Rio de Janeiro, 1997), plate 105 [untitled] and p. 194. On Dutch painting in Brazil, see *O Brasil e os holandeses, 1630–1654,* ed. Paulo Herkenoff (Rio de Janeiro, 1999). The standard history for the period is Charles R. Boxer, *The Dutch in Brazil, 1624–1654* (Oxford, 1957). On African religions, see João José Reis, *Slave Rebellion in Brazil: The Muslim Uprising of 1835 in Bahia,* trans. Arthur Brakel (Baltimore, 1993).

26. The letter is translated from Alonso Ramos Gavilán, *Historia del célebre santuario de Nuestra Señora de Copacabana* [1621], ed. Ignacio Prado Pastor (Lima, 1988), Bk. 2, Ch. 6, pp. 234–38. On this Augustinian friar's life and writings, Waldemar Espinosa Soriano's "Alonso Ramos Gavilán: Vida y obra del cronista de Copacabana," *Historia y Cultura* 6 (1972): 121–94 is without peer. Valuable orientations on the sanctuary and image of Our Lady of Copacabana in English are offered by Sabine MacCormack, "From the Sun of the Incas to the Virgin of Copacabana," *Representations* 8 (1984): 30–60; Carolyn Dean, "The Renewal of Old World Images and the Creation of Colonial Peruvian Visual Culture," in *Converging Cultures: Art and Identity in Spanish America,* ed. Diana Fane (New York, 1996), esp. pp. 175–76 within pp. 171–82; Verónica Salles-Reese, *From Viracocha to the Virgin of Copacabana: Representations of the Sacred at Lake Titicaca* (Austin, 1997); and Michael J. Sallnow, *Pilgrims of the Andes: Regional Cults in Cusco* (Washington, DC, 1987), p. 65. On the contexts in which the earliest official shrine histories came into print, see William A. Christian Jr.'s durable pioneer twins: *Apparitions in Late Medieval and Renaissance Spain* (Princeton, 1981) and *Local Religion in Sixteenth-Century Spain* (Princeton, 1981). On contemporary image-making, the investigations of Susan Verdi Webster offer a useful point of entry: *Art and Ritual in Golden-Age Spain: Sevillian Confraternities and the Processional Sculpture of Holy Week* (Princeton, 1998), esp. pp. 103–10.

27. Felipe Guaman Poma de Ayala left his *Nueva corónica* with a viceregal official in Lima on the understanding that it would be read and viewed by Philip III. Although the manuscript was taken to Spain, there is no evidence that the work received the attention of the king or the Council of the Indies. A Danish ambassador to Spain is thought to have purchased it, thus explaining its eventual home in the Royal Library in Copenhagen. It was found there by Richard Pietschmann in 1908. The two excerpts forming the text in Selection 27 are translated from Felipe Guaman Poma de Ayala, *El primer nueva corónica y buen gobierno,* critical edition by John V. Murra and Rolena Adorno, with Quechua translations by Jorge L. Urioste (Mexico, 1980), 2: 533–39, 570–73. Within vol. 2, Figure 20 appears at p. 602, and Figure 21 at p. 571. Courtesy of Siglo Veintiuno Editores, Mexico City.

28. This selection is excerpted and translated from *Descripción del virreinato del Perú. Crónica inédita de comienzos del siglo XVII,* edited by Boleslao Lewin (Rosario, Argentina, 1958), pp. 55–63. We have not been able to include the marginal titles from the original manuscript of the "Discriçión general del Reyno del Pirú, em [*sic*] particular de Lima" (Bibliothèque Nationale de France, Paris), which Lewin included. For contemporary population figures and other information, we are informed especially by Buenaventura de Salinas y Córdova, *Memorial de las historias del nuevo mundo, Piru: Meritos, y excelencias de la Ciudad de Lima, Cabeça de sus ricos, y estendidos Reynos, y el estado presente en que se hallan, para inclinar a la magestad de su Católica Monarca Don Felipe IV, rey poderoso de España, y de las Indias, a que pida a Su Santidad la canonización de su patrón Solano* (Lima, 1630), and by Frederick P. Bowser, *The African Slave in Colonial Peru, 1524–1650* (Stanford, 1974), Appendix A: The Colored Population of Lima, pp. 337–41. On the author of the "Description" we are indebted to Guillermo Lohmann Villena's deductions in "Una incógnita despejada: La identidad del judío portugués autor de la 'Discriçión general del Pirú,' " *Revista de Indias* 30 (1970): 315–87; on Don Nicolás Vargas (or Corso), see Manuel de Mendiburu, *Diccionario histórico-biográfico del Perú,* 2d ed. (Lima, 1932), 4: 228–29. Figure 22 is reprinted from *Chronicle of Colonial Lima: The Diary of Joseph and Francisco Mugaburu, 1640–1697,* translated and edited by Robert Ryal Miller (Norman, 1975), p. 184. Courtesy of the University of Oklahoma Press.

29. Figure 23 is from Fray Miguel Suárez de Figueroa, *Templo de N. Grande Patriarca San Francisco de la Provincia de los doze Apostoles de el Perú en la Ciudad de los Reyes arruinado, y engrandecido de la providencia Divina. En panegyrico historial, y poetico certamen* (Lima, 1675), foldout page preceding fol. 1. Courtesy of the John Carter Brown Library at Brown University.

30. This reading is excerpted and translated from "Declaración de don Gonzalo de la Maza (o de la Masa) año 1617. Procesos de beatificación y canonización de Santa Rosa de Lima," published in *Una partecita del cielo. La vida de Santa Rosa de Lima narrada por Don Gonzalo de la Maza a quien ella llamaba padre,* edited by Luis Millones (Lima, 1993), from the answers to questions 4, 6, 7, and 29 at pp. 149–52, 153–56, 156–59, 207–8.

Recent essays that inform our introduction and a deepening understanding of Rosa and her historical context include Ramón Mujica Pinilla, "El ancla de Rosa de Lima: Mística y política en torno a la patrona de América," in *Santa Rosa de Lima y su tiempo,* edited by José Flores Araoz, Ramón Mujica Pinilla, Luis Eduardo Wuffarden, and Pedro Guibovich Pérez (Lima, 1995), pp. 53–211; the chapters by Luis Millones and Fernando Iwasaki Cauti in *Una partecita del cielo* (with Iwasaki's also appearing in *Hispanic American Historical Review* 73:4 [1993]: 581–613); Luis Miguel Glave, "Santa Rosa de Lima y sus espinas: La emergencia de mentalidades urbanas de crisis y la sociedad andina (1600–1630)," in *Manifestaciones religiosas en el mundo colonial americano,* edited by Clara García Ayluardo and Manuel Ramos Medina (Mexico, 1993), pp. 53–70; and Teodoro Hampe Martínez, "Los testigos de Santa Rosa (Una aproximación social a la identidad criolla en el Perú colonial)," *Revista del Archivo General de la Nación* 13 (1996): 151–71, which includes a catalog of the witnesses heard at both stages in the determination of Rosa's sanctity. Our thanks to Jodi Bilinkoff for her comments.

31. Sor Juana's letter is taken from her *The Answer/La Respuesta,* critical edition and translation by Electa Arenal and Amanda Powell (New York, 1994), lines 98–123, 210–346, 723–795, 825–844, 861–884, and 1368–1397. Translation ©1994, Electa Arenal and Amanda Powell. Courtesy of The Feminist Press at The City University of New York.

32. Figure 24 (also Plate 6) is a painting of Santa Rosa of Lima with silver decoration whose artist and date are unknown. From Bertha Kitchell Whyte, *Seven Treasure Cities of Latin America* (New York, 1964), p. 229. Figure 25 (also Plate 7) is a posthumous portrait of Sor Juana Inés de la Cruz, also by an unknown artist, from the Robert H. Lamborn Collection of the Philadelphia Museum of Art. Courtesy of the Philadelphia Museum of Art.

33. Padre Antônio Vieira, "Twenty-seventh Sermon, with the Most Holy Sacrament Present," preached at Salvador, Bahia, [ca. 1633], is translated from "Sermão vigésimo sétimo, com o Santíssimo Sacramento exposto, pregado na Baía em data incerta"; and "Sermon on the First Sunday of Lent," preached in the city of São Luís, Maranhão, 1653, is translated from "Sermão da primeira dominga da quaresma, pregado na cidade de S. Luís do Maranhão, no ano de 1653," both in *Padre Antônio Vieira: Obras Escolhidas,* ed. Antônio Sérgio and Hernâni Cidade, Vol. 11, *Sermões (2)* (Lisbon, 1954), pp. 47–95, and 96–123. Sor Juana Inés de la Cruz is quoted in Thomas M. Cohen, *The Fire of Tongues: Antônio Vieira and the Missionary Church in Brazil and Portugal* (Stanford, 1998), p. 87. Details on Vieira's life and understanding of his missionary enterprise are from Cohen, *The Fire of Tongues;* Richard Graham, *Antônio Vieira and the Economic Rehabilitation of Portugal* (São Paulo, 1978); John Hemming, *Red Gold: The Conquest of the Brazilian Indians, 1500–1760* (London, 1978), especially pp. 312–44; and Dauril Alden, *The Making of an Enterprise: The Society of Jesus in Portugal, Its Empire, and Beyond, 1549–1750* (Stanford, 1996), especially p. 113.

34. The confessions are translated from: *Primeira visitação do Santo Officio ás partes do Brasil, pelo licenciado Heitor Furtado de Mendo[n]ça. Confissões da Bahia, 1591–92,* preface by J[oão] Capistrano de Abreu (Rio de Janeiro, 1935), pp. 167–73 and 173–74; and "Segunda visitação do Santo Ofício ás partes do Brasil pelo inquisidor e visitador, o licenciado Marcos Teixeira, livro das confissões e ratificações da Bahia, 1618–1620," intro. Eduardo D'Oliveira França and Sonia A. Siqueira, *Anais do Museu Paulista* 17 (1963): 451–53 and 453–55; the cardinal's rebuke of Mendonça is quoted on p. 23, n. 42. For context on the Portuguese Inquisition and the Brazilian visitations, see J[oão] Capistrano de Abreu, "Preface," *Primeira visitação do Santo Officio ás partes do Brasil, pelo licenciado Heitor Furtado de Mendo[n]ça. Confissões da Bahia, 1591–92* (Rio de Janeiro, 1935), pp. 1–21; A. H. de Oliveira Marques, *History of Portugal,* 2d ed., 2 vols. in 1 (New York, 1976), I:206–7, 287–93, 302–3, 399, 402, 477, II:21; especially useful is Ronaldo Vainfas, "Introduction," in *Confissões da Bahia,* ed. Ronaldo Vainfas (São Paulo, 1997), pp. 5–33, from

which the detail of Mendonça's arrival is drawn; on the Pernambuco visitation, see José Antônio Gonsalves de Mello, *Gente da nação: Cristãos-novos e judeus em Pernambuco* (Recife, 1989), pp. ix–x. For comparisons, see Francisco Bethencourt, *La inquisición en la época moderna: España, Portugal e Italia, siglos XV–XIX*, trad. Federico Palomo (Madrid, 1997). On property confiscated from New Christians in Brazil, see Anita Novinsky, *Cristãos novos na Bahia: 1624–1654* (São Paulo, 1972), and *Inquisição: Inventários de bens confiscados a cristãos novos (Brasil-Século XVIII)* [Lisbon, 1977?]. On Pará, see *Livro da visitação do Santo Ofício da inquisição ao estado do Grão-Pará, 1763–1769*, ed. J. R. Amaral Lapa (Petrópolis, 1978). Ronaldo Vainfas discusses the Domingos Fernandes Nobre case in *A heresia dos índios: Catolicismo e rebeldia no Brasil colonial* (São Paulo, 1995), pp. 143–46, 183–86, 214. For studies of popular religion based on Inquisition records, see Laura de Mello e Souza, *O diabo e a terra de Santa Cruz: Feitiçaria e religiosidade popular no Brasil colonial* (São Paulo, 1987); and *Inferno atlântico: Demonologia e colonização, séculos XVI–XVIII* (São Paulo, 1993).

35. Selection 35 is excerpted and translated from Francisco de Avila, *Tratado de los evangelios que nuestra Madre la Yglesia nos propone en todo el año. Desde la primera dominica de Adviento hasta la última Missa de Difuntos. Explicase el Evangelio, y en cada uno se pone un sermón en lengua castellana y la General de los Indios deste Reyno del Perú, y donde conviene da lugar la materia se refutan los errores de idolatría* (Lima, 1646–1648), "En la Vigilia de la Natividad del Señor," fols. 45–53. This sermon comes from the first part of the *Tratado* and was published in 1646. A shorter second part was published in 1648, the year after Avila's death, by his executor Florián Sarmiento Rendón. The principal biblical text for Avila's sermon is Matthew 1:18–25.

The comment by Pierre Duviols is from *La Lutte contre les réligions autochtones dans le Pérou colonial* (Lima, 1971), pp. 43–44. Informative recent interpretations of Avila's life, intellectual influences, and aspects of his preaching, respectively, are the essay by Antonio Acosta Rodríguez noted above in our reference for Selection 1; Teodoro Hampe Martínez, *Cultura barroca y extirpación de idolatrías: La biblioteca de Francisco de Avila (1648)* (Cusco, 1996); and Juan Carlos Estenssoro Fuchs, "Les Pouvoirs de la Parole: La prédication au Pérou de l'évangelisation à l'utopie," *Annales HSS* 6 (November–December 1996): 1225–57.

36. Selection 36 is translated from the "Denuncia que hace don Juan Tocas principal y fiscal de la dicha visita contra Hernando Hacas, Cristóbal Poma Libiac y muchos indios del pueblo de San Pedro de Hacas, 15 agosto 1656–11 enero 1658," in *Cultura andina y represión: Procesos y visitas de idolatrías y hechicerías, Cajatambo, siglo XVII*, edited by Pierre Duviols (Cusco, 1986), pp. 182–91. Pablo José de Arriaga's 1621 work, *La extirpación de la idolatría en el Perú*, in *Colección de libros y documentos referentes a la historia del Perú*, series 2, vol. 1, edited by Horacio H. Urteaga (Lima, 1920), has been translated into English by L. Clark Keating: *The Extirpation of Idolatry in Peru* (Lexington, KY, 1968).

37. Figure 26 (also Plate 8) is a photograph of the Rosary chapel by James Early. Courtesy of James Early. The description of the dome draws from Early's *The Colonial Architecture of Mexico* (Albuquerque, 1994), pp. 79–88.

38. Reproductions of some of the Corpus Christi series, and much else on the Cuzco School of artistic and cultural production, can be seen in José de Mesa and Teresa Gisbert, *Historia de la pintura cuzqueña*, 2d ed., 2 vols. (Lima, 1982), esp. 1: 177–80; and 2: plates 229–42. Figures 27 and 28 (also, respectively, Plates 9 and 10) are from the Museo del Arte Religioso in Cusco, Peru. Our thanks to Carolyn S. Dean.

Our introduction is informed especially by Dean's *Inka Bodies and the Body of Christ* (Durham and London, 1999); and by the same author, "Who's Naughty and Nice: Childish Behavior in the Paintings of Cuzco's Corpus Christi Procession," in *Native Artists and Patrons in Colonial Latin America*, edited by Emily Umberger and Tom Cummins, a special issue of *Phœbus—A Journal of Art History* (Arizona State University) 7 (1995): 107–26, and "Ethnic Conflict and Corpus Christi in Colonial Cuzco," *Colonial Latin American Review* 2:1–2 (1993): 93–120. See further instruction taken from two essays by David Cahill, especially "Popular Religion and Appropriation: The Example of Corpus Christi in Eighteenth-Century Cuzco," *Latin American Research Review* 31:2 (1996): 67–110; and "Etnología e historia: Los danzantes rituales del Cuzco a fines de la colonia," *Boletín del Archivo Departamental del Cuzco* 2 (1986): 48–54; also Thomas B. F. Cummins, "We Are the Other: Peruvian Portraits of Colonial *Kurakakuna*," in *Transatlantic Encounters: Europeans and Andeans in the Sixteenth Century,* edited by Kenneth J. Andrien and Rolena Adorno (Berkeley, 1991), pp. 203–31; and Juan Carlos Estenssoro Fuchs, "Los bailes de los indios y el proyecto colonial," *Revista Andina* 20 (1992): 353–89.

39. This translation of the "Compromisso da Irmandade de S. Antonio de Catagerona, Cita na Matris de S. Pedro desta Cidade da Bahya, Que Seus Devotos Hão de Guardar, Feito no Ano de 1699," and the image of Santo António de Catagerona (Figure 29 and Plate 11) are both reproduced courtesy of The Catholic University of America, Oliveira Lima Library, Washington, DC (Códices, 16). The letter criticizing the brotherhood of Espírito Santo is Arcebispo eleito da Bahia [Fr. Manuel de Santa Inês], [Juiz] José Carvalho de Andrade, and [Coronel] Gonçalo Xavier de Barros e Alvim to Conde de Oeiras, Bahia, June 15, 1765, Arquivo do Instituto Histórico e Geográfico Brasileiro, Conselho Ultramarino, Bahia, 1751–1782, 1-1-19, fls. 169v–174. A. J. R. Russell-Wood generously supplied information on Saint Anthony of Catagerona in a private communication. The single most-nuanced interpretation of Black brotherhoods in Bahia is João José Reis, *A morte é uma festa: Ritos fúnebres e revolta popular no Brasil do século XIX* (São Paulo, 1991), pp. 49–72, 144–62, 205–12. On irmandades, including Black irmandades, in Portugal, see A. C. de C. M. Saunders, *A Social History of Black Slaves and Freedmen in Portugal, 1441–1555*, pp. 2–3, 151–56. See also Manoel S. Cardozo, "The Lay Brotherhoods of Colonial Bahia," *Catholic Historical Review* 33 (1947): 12–30; Julita Scarano, *Devoção e escravidão: A irmandade de Nossa Senhora do Rosário dos Pretos no distrito diamantino no século XVIII* (São Paulo, 1976); and Kathleen J. Higgins, *"Licentious Liberty" in a Brazilian Gold-Mining Region: Slavery, Gender, and Social Control in Eighteenth-Century Sabará, Minas Gerais* (University Park, PA, 1999), pp. 94, 100–107. For important recent work on the Catholic Church in Africa and the influence of irmandades and devotion to Saint Anthony of Padua in Afro-Brazilian religious culture, see John K. Thornton, *The Kongolese Saint Anthony: Dona Beatriz Kimpa Vita and the Antonian Movement, 1684–1706* (Cambridge, Eng., 1998); and Linda M. Heywood, "The Angolan-Afro-Brazilian Cultural Connections," *Slavery and Abolition* 20:1 (April 1999): 9–23.

40. The letter from Fathers Domingo García and Manuel del Santo to the Padre Comisario of the Missions to the Infidels of the Cerro de la Sal, Father José Gil Muñoz, from Pichana, June 2, 1742, and its postscript are preserved in the Archivo General de Indias, Audiencia de Lima, legajo 541. Our translation is from the document published in Francisco A. Loayza, ed., *Juan Santos, el invencible (manuscritos del año de 1742 al año de 1755)* (Lima, 1942), pp. 1–8. The declaration of Pedro de Torres before the Marqués de Cassatorres, heard and recorded in Concepción de Jauja on August 11, 1752, is preserved in the Archivo General de Indias, Audiencia de Lima, legajo 988 and also is printed in Loayza, ed., *Juan Santos,* pp. 206–8.

Interested readers can complement their study of these documents with others published in Loayza's collection and in Bernardino Izaguirre, *Misiones franciscanas* (Lima, 1923), as well as with the synthesizing point of view of the preacher and chronicler from the heart of the great eighteenth-century Franciscan mission effort at Santa Rosa de Ocopa, Father José Amich, in his *Compendio histórico de los trabajos, fatigas, sudores y muertes que los ministros evangélicos de la seráfica religión han padecido por la conversión de las almas de los gentiles, en la montaña de los Andes, pertenecientes a las provincias del Perú* (Paris, 1854), also published as the *Historia de las misiones del convento de Santa Rosa de Ocopa,* ed. Julián Heras, Monumenta Amazónica series (Putumayo, Peru, 1988).

The modern historiography that concentrates on the rebellion of Juan Santos Atahualpa is not extensive; beyond the brief discussion in Alberto Flores Galindo's *Buscando un Inca: identidad y utopia en los Andes* (3d ed., Lima, 1988 [1986]), pp. 101–17, see the historical discussion by Stefano Varese in *La sal de los cerros: notas etnográficas e históricas sobre los campa de la selva del Perú* (Lima, 1968), esp. pp. 60–85, and the valuable treatment of Juan Santos within the wider context of various eighteenth-century Andean insurrections by John H. Rowe, "El movimiento nacional Inca del siglo XVIII," *Revista Universitaria* (Cusco) 43, no. 107 (segundo semestre, 1954): 17–47.

A basic orientation in English, and an argument against seeing Juan Santos as primarily the spearhead of a local indigenous revolt, can be considered in an untidily edited essay by Jay Lehnertz, "Juan Santos: Primitive Rebel on the Campa Frontier (1742–1752)," *Actas y memorias del XXXIX Congreso Internacional de Americanistas* (Lima, 1970), vol. 4, *Historia, etnohistoria y etnología de la selva sudamericana* (Lima, 1972), pp. 111–25.

While not discussing Juan Santos per se, Scarlett O'Phelan Godoy's *Rebellions and Revolts in Eighteenth-Century Peru and Upper Peru* (Cologne, 1985) offers an English-language study of wider late colonial economic relationships and the minor revolts and atmosphere of reforms, tribute, and tax schemes that set the stage for the rebellion of Túpac Amaru in the early 1780s. The same author explores the "parallel discourse" of a number of Andean rebels from Juan Santos to Túpac Amaru (1742–1782), a shared argument that, most centrally, called for a restored Tawantinsuyu without Spaniards: see Scarlett O'Phelan Godoy, "L'Utopie andine: Discours parallèle à la fin de l'époque coloniale," *Annales* 49: 2 (1994): 471–95. Focusing on Juan Santos's synthetic blend of Catholic and Andean messianism, see Alonso Zarzar, *"Apo Capac Huayna, Jesús Sacramentado": mito, utopía y milenarismo en el pensamiento de Juan Santos Atahualpa* (Lima, 1989). We want, finally, to acknowledge Karin Vélez, whose essay on José Amich's chronicle (written for Kenneth Mills's spring seminar in 2001) has led to this selection by sending us after ways of stimulating discussion of Juan Santos Atahualpa and his context.

41. Selection 41 is translated from Martin Lienhard, editor, *Testimonios, cartas y manifiestos indígenas (Desde la conquista hasta comienzos del siglo XX)* (Caracas, 1992), pp. 332–35. Courtesy of Biblioteca Ayacucho, Caracas. The plan of La Concepción, Figure 30, is from *Documentos de arte argentino, Cuaderno XIX: Las misiones guaraníes* (Buenos Aires, 1946), illustration "E." Courtesy of the Academia Nacional de Bellas Artes, Buenos Aires. See Barbara Ganson, " 'Like Children under Wise Parental Sway': Passive Portrayals of the Guaraní Indians in European Literature and *The Mission*," *Colonial Latin American Historical Review* 3:4 (1994): 399–422; James Schofield Saeger, "*The Mission* and Historical Missions: Film and the Writing of History," *The Americas* 51:3 (1995): 393–415; and Philip Caraman, *The Lost Paradise: The Jesuit Republic in South America* (New York, 1975).

42. The first decree was published in Charles Gibson, editor, *The Spanish Tradition in America* (New York, 1966), pp. 231–33. Courtesy of HarperCollins Publishers. The second is translated from Richard Konetzke, editor, *Colección de documentos para la historia de la formación social en Hispanoamérica* (Madrid, 1953–1962), 3:434–35. Courtesy of the Consejo Superior de Investigaciones Científicas, Madrid.

43. Archivo General de la Nación, Mexico City, Ramo de Tributos, vol. 43, expediente 9, folio 8r. According to this count, free Blacks and Mulattoes were distributed in the following numbers by intendancy district: Guadalajara, 63,009; Zacatecas, 58,317; Potosí, 49,140; Valladolid, 48,768; México, 46,813; Guanajuato, 42,868; Mérida, 29,036; Oaxaca, 17,767; Puebla, 11,304; Arispe, 10,070; and Veracruz, 5,849. "Mulatto" is often thought to identify people of mixed African and European descent, but it was regularly used in the colonial period for people of mixed African and Indian descent (see also Selection 24). Selection 43 was originally published with a different introduction in William B. Taylor, "The Foundation of Nuestra Señora de Guadalupe de los Morenos de Amapa," *The Americas* 26 (1970): 439–46. Courtesy of *The Americas*.

The map in Figure 31 is located in the Archivo General de la Nación, Ilustración num. 2455; originally in Ramo de Tierras, vol. 3543, exp. 2, from which additional information was drawn for our introduction. Courtesy of the Archivo General de la Nación.

44. This selection is translated from the first edition of *El Lazarillo de ciegos caminantes desde Buenos-Ayres, hasta Lima con sus Itinerarios según la más puntual observación, con algunas noticias útiles a los nuevos comerciantes que tratan en mulas; y otras históricas. Sacado de las memorias que hizo Don Alonso Carrió de la Vandera en este dilatado viage . . .* ("Gijón: Imprenta de la Rovada, 1773" [Lima, 1776]), unnumbered pp. 16–39 of the 58-page Tercera Acusación.

45. This translation is made from a published version of the document, "Notícia diária e individual das marchas e acontecimentos mais condignos da jornada que fez o senhor mestre-de-campo regente e guarda-mor Inácio Correia Pamplona, desde que saiu de sua casa e Fazenda do Capote

às conquistas do Sertão, até se tornar a recolher à mesma sua dita Fazenda do Capote, etc., etc.," in Biblioteca Nacional do Rio de Janeiro, *Anais* 108 (1988): 47–113. Laura de Mello e Souza first interpreted this account with her reading of it, "Violência e práticas culturais no cotidiano de uma expedição contra quilombolas, Minas Gerais, 1769," in *Liberdade por um fio: História dos quilombos no Brasil*, ed. João José Reis and Flávio dos Santos Gomes (São Paulo, 1996), pp. 193–212. For an understanding of some of the larger events surrounding this expedition, see Harold Langfur, "The Forbidden Lands: Frontier Settlers, Slaves, and Indians in Minas Gerais, Brazil, 1760–1830" (Ph.D. diss., University of Texas at Austin, 1999), especially pp. 8–9, 15, 88–91, 111, 129, 131, 160–70. On the Minas conspiracy, see Kenneth R. Maxwell, *Conflicts and Conspiracies: Brazil and Portugal, 1750–1808* (Cambridge, Eng., 1973).

46. Ex-voto, eighteenth century, is from the collection of José Mindlin, São Paulo, Brazil, and reproduced here as Figure 32 and Plate 12 with his generous permission. Examples of pictures and texts are drawn from Márcia de Moura Castro, *Ex-votos mineiros: As tábuas votives no ciclo do ouro* (Rio de Janeiro, 1994). A recent and provocative study of Brazilian ex-votos is Guilherme Pereira das Neves, "Uma prática votiva popular no coração do Brasil? A propósito da coleção de ex-votos pintados de Congonhas do Campo, Minas Gerais," *Anais da Sociedade Brasileira de Pesquisa Histórica* (1996): 169–72. An earlier starting point is Maria Augusta Machado da Silva, "Ex-votos brasileiros," *Cultura Internacional* 1:2 (April–June 1971): 22–30. On fifteenth-century Italian votive paintings, see Arnoldo Ciarrocchi and Ermanno Mori, *Le tavolette votive italiane* (Udine, 1960). For useful comparisons with the Mexican tradition, see Gloria Fraser Giffords, *Mexican Folk Retablos* (1974; Albuquerque, 1992); and Solange Alberro, "Retablos and Popular Religion in Nineteenth-Century Mexico," and Elin Luque Agraz and Michele Beltrán, "Powerful Images: Mexican Ex-votos," both in *Retablos y ex-votos*, Colección, Uso y Estilo (Mexico City, 2000), pp. 72–77, and 77–81.

47. "Jeremiah in the Stocks" (Figure 33 and Plate 13) is from Germain Bazin, *Aleijadinho et la sculpture baroque au Brésil* (Paris, 1963), p. 138. Bazin is the most thorough, scholarly, and critically reflective discussion of Aleijadinho's work. Our introduction also draws from *The Art of Brazil*, ed. Carlos Lemos, José Roberto Teixeira Leite, and Pedro Manuel Gismonti (New York, 1983), pp. 54–147; J. B. Bury, "The Architecture and Art of Colonial Brazil," in *The Cambridge History of Latin America*, ed. Leslie Bethell, vol. 2, *Colonial Latin America* (Cambridge, Eng., 1984), pp. 747–69; Fernando Jorge, *O Aleijadinho: Sua vida, sua obra, seu gênio*, 6th revised ed. (São Paulo, 1984); and Heliodoro Pires, *Mestre Aleijadinho: Vida e obra de Antônio Francisco Lisboa, gigante da arte no Brasil* (Rio de Janeiro, 1961).

48. For Figures 34 and 35 (also, respectively, Plates 14 and 15), featured in this selection, see María Concepción García Sáiz, editor, *Las castas mexicanas: Un género pictórico americano/ The Castes: A Genre of Mexican Painting* (Milan, 1989). The series by José Joaquín Magón (in a private collection in Mexico) is no. XI, pp. 102–11; and that by Andrés de Islas (in the Museo de América, Madrid) is no. XV, pp. 124–33. Figure 34 is at p. 103 (a), while Figure 35 is at p. 127 (d). Figure 35 (Plate 15) is reproduced courtesy of the Museo de América, Madrid.

Helpful on the *castas* genre are García Sáiz's "Introduction" to *Las castas mexicanas,* and the illustrations and short essays within a special issue of *Artes de México* 8 (nueva época) (Summer 1990) on "La pintura de castas." García Sáiz identifies over fifty surviving groups of *castas* paintings. The series thought to date from 1725 hangs in Breamore House in Wiltshire, England. Other groups are in the Museo de Monterrey, Monterrey, Mexico, and in private collections in Mexico, the Museo de América in Madrid, and the Musée de l'Homme in Paris.

49. The discourses are excerpted and translated from the Princeton Theological Seminary Rare Books Library's copy of Juan Francisco Domínguez, *Conveniencia de la Religión y el Estado. En diez discursos sobre los Mandamientos de Dios* (Mexico, 1805), pp. 3–7, 16–27.

50. The translation of the Petition, Alexandre Francisco, Salvador, Bahia, 1811, Arquivo da Cúria Metropolitana, Salvador, Bahia, Dispensas Matrimoniais, no. 31, is based on the transcription made and commented on by Luiz Mott, "Revendo à história da escravidão no Brasil," *MAN* (*Mensário do Arquivo Nacional,* Rio de Janeiro) 11:7 (July 1980): 21–25. On Church rules, see Sebastião Monteiro da Vide, *Constituições primeiras do Arcebispado da Bahia. Feitas e ordenadas*

pelo . . . 5º Arcebispo do dito Arcebispado e do Conselho de Sua Magestade: Propostas e aceitas em o synodo Diocesano que o dito Senhor celebrou em 12 de junho do anno de 1707. Impressas em Lisboa no anno 1719 e em Coimbra em 1720. . . . (São Paulo, 1853), nos. 259, 260, 300, 301, 302, 303; and Candido Mendes de Almeida, ed., *Código Philippino; ou Ordenações e leis do reino do Portugal, recopiladas por mandado d'el-rey D. Philippe I. 14 ed. segundo a primeira de 1603 e a nona de Coimbra de 1824. Addicionada com diversas notas . . .* (Rio de Janeiro, 1870), Liv. 4, Tit. 88, Para. 928. On Nagôs in Bahia, see João José Reis, *Slave Rebellion in Brazil: The Muslim Uprising of 1835 in Bahia,* trans. Arthur Brakel (Baltimore, 1993), especially pp. 44, 140–42, 152–53; and Carlos Ott, *Formação e evolução étnica da cidade do Salvador,* vol. 1 (Salvador, 1957), Appendix 3, "Negros," pp. 91–93.

51. Translations are made from: Testamento, Padre Felippe de Santiago Xavier, Santa Anna de Parnaíba, São Paulo, 1793, Arquivo do Estado de São Paulo, 456-2, "Registros de Testamentos," Livro 6, fls. 2-8; and Inventário, Anna de São Jozé da Trindade, Salvador, Bahia, 1823, Arquivo Público do Estado da Bahia, Seção Judiciária, 04/1840/2311/02, fls. 4v-12. For Brazilian civil law, see Candido Mendes de Almeida, ed., *Código Philippino; ou Ordenações e leis do reino do Portugal, recopiladas por mandado d'el-rey D. Philippe I. 14 ed. segundo a primeira de 1603 e a nona de Coimbra de 1824. Addicionada com diversas notas . . .* (Rio de Janeiro, 1870), Liv. 4, Tit. 46, 82, 96. Although in colonial Brazil coins were struck in gold, silver, and copper, their value was expressed in terms of the *real* or, in the plural, *réis*. One thousand réis was written 1$000. For a brief history of colonial coinage, see A. J. R. Russell-Wood, *Fidalgos and Philanthropists: The Santa Casa da Misericórdia of Bahia, 1550–1755* (Berkeley, 1968), Appendix 3a, "Currency in Circulation in Brazil, 1550–1750," pp. 376–79, and Appendix 3b, "The Price of Labor, 1680–1750," p. 380. Alida Metcalf, *Family and Frontier in Colonial Brazil: Santana de Parnaíba, 1580–1822* (Berkeley, 1992), p. xvi, notes that in eighteenth-century São Paulo a strong young slave either male or female was worth between 100 and 150 mil-réis.

52. The photographs and transcriptions for the Salto del Agua (Figures 36 and 37) are by William B. Taylor. The roadside monument drawing (Figure 38) is in the Archivo General de la Nación, Mexico City, Ilustración num. 268, removed from Ramo de Historia, vol. 118, exp. 5. Courtesy of the Archivo General de la Nación. Inscriptions on the four fountains in the Plaza Mayor were published in Francisco Sedano, *Noticias de México desde el año de 1756 . . .* (Mexico, 1880), 1:138–40.

53. The painting shown in Figure 39 hangs in the Museo Nacional de Bellas Artes in Buenos Aires, Argentina. From Carmen Bernand, *The Incas: People of the Sun* (New York, 1994), p. 53. Courtesy of the Museo Nacional de Bellas Artes. A number of key sources for Inka history, and on the Inkas of Vilcabamba and the figure of Túpac Amaru in particular, are now available in English translation. Informing and pertaining to our discussion are Juan de Betanzos, *Narrative of the Incas* [1557], translated and edited from the Palma de Mallorca manuscript by Roland Hamilton and Dana Buchanan (Austin, 1996), pp. 276ff.; Baltasar de Ocampo, "Account of the Province of Vilcapampa and a Narrative of the Execution of the Inca Túpac Amaru" [1610] in *History of the Incas by Pedro Sarmiento de Gamboa and the Execution of the Inca Túpac Amaru by Captain Baltasar de Ocampo,* translated and edited by Sir Clements Markham (Hakluyt Society, second series no. XXII, 1907) (Millwood, NY, 1967), pp. 203–47; and El Inca Garcilaso de la Vega, *Royal Commentaries of the Incas, and General History of Peru* [1609; 1617], translated and edited by Harold V. Livermore (Austin, 1966). See also Alberto Flores Galindo, *Buscando un Inca: Identidad y utopía en los Andes* (Havana, 1986); and George Kubler, "The Neo-Inca State (1537–1572)," *Hispanic American Historical Review* 27 (1947): 189–203.

54. Figure 40 is from George Kubler and Martin Soria, *Art and Architecture of Spain and Portugal and Their American Dominions, 1500–1800,* Pelican History of Art (Baltimore, 1959), plate 179(b). Its color reproduction as Plate 16 is courtesy of an anonymous collector.

55. The "Sentiments of the Nation" is translated from Ernesto Lemoine Villicaña, editor, *Morelos: Su vida revolucionaria a través de sus escritos y de otros testimonios de la época* (Mexico, 1965), Document 110, pp. 370–73. Courtesy of the Universidad Nacional Autónoma de México. The quotation from J. H. Parry is found in his *The Spanish Theory of Empire in the Sixteenth Century* (Cambridge, Eng., 1940), pp. 174–75.

56. Selection 56 was originally published in Charles Gibson, editor, *The Spanish Tradition in America* (New York, 1966), pp. 239–40. Courtesy of HarperCollins Publishers.

57. *Constituição do Império do Brasil*, March 25, 1824, Título I, Artigo 5. See Alan K. Manchester's vividly detailed account, "The Transfer of the Portuguese Court to Rio de Janeiro," in *Conflict and Continuity in Brazilian Society*, ed. Henry H. Keith and S. F. Edwards (Columbia, SC, 1969), pp. 148–83. John Lynch provides a useful account of Church-state relations, "The Catholic Church in Latin America, 1830–1930," in *Cambridge History of Latin America*, ed. Leslie Bethell, vol. 4, *c. 1870 to 1930*, pp. 562–66; on ecclesiastical patronage, see João Dornas Filho, *O padroado e a igreja brasileira*, Brasiliana, Serie 5a, vol. 125 (São Paulo, 1938), pp. 15–17, 43–44. Opposition to the British is from Corpo do Comércio da Bahia to Prince João, Salvador, Bahia, [January 1808], Biblioteca Nacional, Rio de Janeiro, Seção de Manuscritos, I-31, 28, 26.

✐ INDEX

References to definitions and identifications found in the Glossary are printed in boldface type.

Abedaño, Fernando de, 262
Academia de San Carlos (Mexico City), 316
Acosta, José de, 66, 127; on architecture and art in Lima, 188; on evangelizing Indians, 134–43, 200; on Spanish Christian responsibility, 176
Adorno, Antônio Dias, 237
Afonso V, 35, 37, 38, 39, 40, 41
Africa: Angola, 35, 164; Angolans from, 281, 373; Bight of Benin, 35; Congo, 35; El Mina, 36; Gêges from, 281, 373; Gold Coast, 35, 36; Hausas from, 373; Mozambique, 35; Nagôs from, 373, 374; North Africa, 35, 36, 37; Sierra Leone, 35; slaves for Portuguese trade, 34, 35–37; Sudan, 36; West Africa, 35; Yorubas from, 281, 373
Age of Reason, 207–8
Albaicín, 127–28, **405**
Al-Bakri, 29
Al-Hakam II, 29
Al-Jarsifi, 'Umar, 29
Al-Laithi, Yahya b. Yahya, 30
Al-Tamili, Abu'l-Asbagh 'Isa b. Muhammad, 28, 29
Al-Turtushi, Ibrahim b. Ya'qub al-Isra'ili, 29, 31
Albergaria, Manoel Soares, 382
Albornoz, Cristóbal de, 173
Albotodo, Juan de, 130, 131, 137
Alcalde, 123, **405**
Alcalde mayor, 320, 321, 323, **405**
Alcalde ordinario, 114, **405**
Alcoforada, Ana, confession of, 236, 241–42
Alcoforado, Antonio, 241
Aldeia, 95, 218, **405**

Aleijadinho, 356–59
Alexander VI, Pope, 65
Alfonso X, 213
Alhambra, 127
Allende, Ignacio, 400
Almeida, Izabel de, 377
Aluadán, Juan Bautista, 174
Alvares, Diogo, 96
Ambrose, Saint, 156, 157
"America Nursing Spanish Noble Boys," 395–96
Amerindians: exploitation by priests, 176, 177; impact of disease on populations, 113, 117, 144, 219; as slaves by nature *(natura servus)*, 67; used as labor, 104, 105, 106, 107–12; woodcuts accompanying "Letter to Soderini," 80–83. *See also specific tribe*
Amrique, Frei, 49, 56
Amuesha Indians, 305
Anansaya, 167, 168
Anchieta, José de, 94
Andrade, Antonio Francisco de, 377
Andrade, Francisco Antonio de, 377
Angelorum, Francisco, 64
Angola, Maria Angelica, 381
Angolans, 281, 373, **405**
Angulo, Domingo de, 114
Anne, Saint, ex-voto offering to, 353–55
Anthony, Abbot, Saint, 156, 158
Anthony of Catagerona, Saint, 281, 282
Anthony of Padua, Saint, 156, 157, 356
Antônio, José, 337, 341

Antunes, Heitor, 241
Antunes, Isabel, 241
Apache Indians, 360
Areche, José Antonio de, 395
Argentina: Declaration of Independence, 401–2; role
   of Catholic Church, 367, 401; San Miguel de
   Tucumán, 401–2
Arguim, 36
Arobe, Francisco de, 159, 160, 161
Arobe, Pedro de, 159, 160, 161
Arriaga, Pablo José de, 189, 250, 260
Atahuallpa, 67, 185, 300, 390, 393
Atayde, Vasco d', 45
Augustine, Saint, 156, 157
Augustinian Order, work in Peru, 188
Autos-da-fé, 187, **405**
Avendaño, Diego de, 121
Avendaño, Fernando de, 247, 263, 264
Aveyro, Duchess of, 213
Avila, Francisco de: behavior of, 176, 247–48;
   Christmas Eve sermon of, 246–54; contemporary
   of, 260; notations in Huarochirí Manuscript, 5, 6;
   trilingual sermons of, 246
Ayllus, 5, 256, 259, 260, **405**
Aymara, 135, 246
Azambujo, Balthesar Dias, 241
Aztec Stone of the Five Eras, 23–26, 121, 157
Aztecs, **405**; "Calendar Stone" of, 23–26; *coloquio* of
   holy men with Franciscans, 19–22; Earth
   Monster, Tlaltecuhtli, 23, 24, 25; Florentine
   Codex about, 19; sacred places of, 22; "Sun Stone"
   of, 23–26; Templo Mayor, 23, 25; Tlalocan, 22;
   Tonatiuh of, 23

Bandeiras, 310, 335, **405**
Barbara, Saint, 354
Barbosa, Gaspar, 99
Barbosa, Manoel, 337
Barboza Fagundes, Antonio, 377
Barreda, Ignacio María, 360
Barriga, Bartolomé, 248
Barrio de Sepúlveda, Juan del, 159, 161
Barthes, Roland, 18
Batuques, 164
Beati, 199; *beata*, **406**
Bedón, Pedro, 161
Beliaga, Isabel, 236
Benarcama, Jerónimo de, 127, 130–33
Benavente, Toribio de, 60, 61
Benedict, Saint, 281, 354
Bernardes, José, 338
Bernard of Clairvaux, Saint, 156, 158
Bernardine of Siena, Saint, 156, 158
Betanzos, Juan de, 390
Bisabequí, 299, 300, 302
Black Brotherhood of Our Lady of the Rosary, 219
Blacks: *casta* painting of, 363–64; *cimarrones* (run-
   away slaves), 320–27; and civil law and division of

property, 376–83; in *irmandade* in Bahia, 280–96;
   in Mina Gerais region, 335–52. *See also* Africa;
   Mulattoes; Slaves/slavery
"Blacks Dancing," painting of, 162–64
Bojador, Cape, 35
Bolivia: Lake Titicaca, 174; Potosí, 185
Bonaventure, Saint, 156, 157
Book of Animals, 162
Borja, Francisco de, 127, 130–33
Botocudo, 335
Bowser, Frederick P., 186
Brandão, Alexandre Pereira, 346, 347
Brazil: "Blacks Dancing" painting, 162–64; Black
   irmandade in Bahia, 280–96; Caminha's letter to
   king of Portugal, 43–48; civil law and division of
   property in, 375–83; *Código Philippino* of, 375;
   confessions to Holy Office of the Inquisition,
   234–45; *Constitution of the Brazilian Empire,
   Title 1, Article 5*, 403–4; "crypto-Jews" in, 235;
   Jesuit work in, 93–103, 218–19; Mina Gerais
   region of, 335–52, 356–59; *Ordenações* of, 375;
   Pernambuco, 162, 164; Porto Seguro, 44; slaves
   who marry, 372–74; slavery in, 36, 219–33;
   Tupinambá of, 93–103; Tupinikins in, 44, 45,
   46–49, 50, 51–58; wilderness of Arabo, 237
Brendan, Saint, 79
Brito, Luis de, 237
Brito d'Almeida, João de, 237
Brotherhood of the Blacks of Saint Joseph, 356
Bulls, papal, 36, 65, **406**
Byland, Bruce, 119, 120

Cabanes, José, 305
Cabildo, 113, 115, 116, 171, 311, **406**
Cabral, Pedro Alvares, 43, 44
Cabral de Taide, Fernão, 239, 240
Cabrera, Miguel, 360
Cacao, 114, 115, 116, **406**
Caciques, 122, 265, 308, 311, **406**
Caeté Indians, 96
Cahill, David, 273, 279
Caiapó Indians, 336
Caico, Pedro, 264, 265, 266, 267
Calvino, Italo, 174
Camacho, Domingos, 239
Caminha, Pedro Vaz de, 44, 45–58
Campa Indians, 300, 305, 307
Cañari Indians, 272, 276, 391, **406**
Canary Islands, 44, 45, 128
Candomblé, 164, **406**
Cannibalism, by native populations, 80, 81, 96
Capara, Francisco Affonso, 237
Capcha Yauri, Pedro, 260, 263, 268
Cape Verde Islands, 36, 45
Carabajal, Alonso de, 194
Caraman, Philip, 310
Caratupaico (*malqui*), 268
Cardenel, Miguel, 114

Cardoso, José, 338, 345
Carrillo, Julián, 308
Carrió de la Vandera, Alonso, on Indian affairs, 328–34
Caruatarquivrauc (idol), 264
Carvalho e Melo, Sebastião José de, 335
Carvaxal Castillo de Altra, Nicolás, 323
Cassatorres, Marqués de, 306, 307, 308
Castas, 360, **406**
Castizo, 364
Castro, Américo, 27
Castro, Ignacio, 360
Catechism for the Instruction of Indians (Acosta), 135
Catherine of Siena, Saint, 200, 203, 206, 215
Catholic Church: role in Argentina, 401; role in Brazil, 403–4; role in Cuba, 367; role in Venezuela, 401. *See also* Christians/Christianity; *specific country or region*
Caui Llaca (*huaca*), 8–9, 11
Cervantes, Miguel de, 362
Charles II, 277
Charles III, 329, 384
Charles IV, 384
Charles V, 20; allegations against Cortés, 84; on evangelization of unbelievers, 65, 66, 68, 69; *junta* in Granada, 88; Pedro de Gante's letter to, 104–12, 144; Zumárraga's letter to, 129
Chauchisac, Cristóbal, 263
Chaupi Ñamca (*huaca*), 4, 248
Chaupis, Alonso, 260, 262, 265, 266, 268
Chaupis, Domingo, 266
Chaupis, Isabel, 268
Chaupis, Pedro, 263
Chaupis Condor, Hernando, 260, 262, 263, 265, 266, 268
Chaupis Maiguai, Chatalina, 265
Chaupis Yauri, Domingo, 262, 264, 265
Checa Indians: oral tradition of, 3; recorders of Huarochirí Manuscript, 3–13
Chicha, 261, 262, 265, 268, **406**
Chichimec Indians, 22, 150, 360, **406**
Chocho language, 122
Choque Casa, Cristóbal, 248
Christian Doctrine (Acosta), 135
Christians/Christianity: Aztec response to arrival of, 19–22; capture of Muslim kingdoms on Iberian Peninsula, 27; coexistence with Muslims and Jews on medieval Iberian Peninsula, 27–33; crusades against Muslims, 36; Mozárabes, 28, 29; possible influences in Huarochirí Manuscript, 5, 6; redefinition in eighteenth century, 366–67; rules in twelfth-century Iberian Peninsula, 31–32; symbols of prestige and lineage, 17; Ten Commandments, Domínguez's treatise on, 367–71
Chuchu Condor, Bartolomé, 262, 266
Church of Santo Domingo, Puebla, Mexico, 269–71
Cieza de León, Pedro, 17, 39

Cimarrones (runaway Black slaves), 320–27
Cisneros, García de, 61
Ciudad Rodrigo, Antonio de, 61
Civil law, division of property in Brazil, 375–83
Clement VII, Pope, 84
Clendinnen, Inga, 6
Cobo, Bernabé, 186
Coca, 304, **406**
Cochineal, 113–16, 115, **406**
Codex Osuna, 144–47
Codex Sierra, 148–49
Codex Vindobonensis, 119, 120
Código Philippino, 375
Coelho, Nicolau, 44, 46, 47, 48, 57
Cofradías, 167, 168, 277, 279, **406**
Colação, 376
Colqui, Inés, 265, 266
Colqui Conopa (idol), 262
Colqui Maiguai, Inés, 262
Columbus, Christopher, encounters with New World native population, 78, 79, 80, 81, 83
Conceição, Jozefa Maria da, 380, 381, 383
Conceição, Narcissa Rodrigues da, 358
Conceição, Silvéria Maria da, 354
Concolorcorvo (Calixto Bustamante Carlos Inca), 79, 273, 328
Condorcanqui, José Gabriel, 300, 393
Confraternity of the Rosary, 161
Conopas, 260, **407**
Constituições primeiras, 372
Contrarios, 187
Conversos, 187, 301, **407**
Convivencia, 27, **407**
Copacabana, Our Lady of, 167–72
Cordeira, Caterina, 241
Córdoba, 27
Córdoba, Andrés de, 61
Cornide, Diego, 324
Corpus Christi, 272–79, **407**
Correa, Aires, 47
Correa, Antonio, 194
Correa, Diogo, 239
Correa, Paulo, 243, 244
Correa Pedrozo, Manoel, 378
Corregidors, **407**; in Mexico, 113, 117, 119; in Paraguay, 310; in Peru, 171, 274, 275, 299, 306
Cortés, Baltasar, 114
Cortés, Hernán, 61, 84; conquest commemorated in artwork, 274; return to Spain with human specimens, 84, 86; Tlaxcalan allies against Aztecs, 113
Coruña, José de la, 61
Coruña, Martín de la, 61
Cosio, Apolinar de, 324
Costa, Tiadozia da, 354
Costa Ferreira, Jozé da, 377
Costa Resende, Gabriel da, 336, 337
Costa Resende, João da, 337
Costa Resende, Jolião da, 336

Council of Trent, **407**; acts and decrees composed by
    Acosta, 135; Catholic Christian response to
    Spanish Inquisition, 235; delegate at, 66; on edu-
    cation to become good Christians, 129; marriage
    elevated to holy sacrament status, 372; on preach-
    ing to Indians, 246; promoting saints and images,
    153; on saint-making practices, 198; on venera-
    tion and ex-votos, 354
Counter-Reformation Catholicism, 200
Creoles, 186, **407**
Crockaert, Peter, 65
Croix, Marqués de, 317, 324, 326
Cruillas, Marqués de, 324
Cruz, Sor Juana Inés de la: critique of Padre Vieira's
    sermons, 218; letter of, 207–14; portrait of, 215,
    217
Cruz, Theodozia Maria da, 379
Cruz Romalho, Bernardo da, 382
Cuba, role of Catholic Church, 367
Cubillos, Santiago, 324
Cucana, Francisco, 244
Cuenca, Juan de, 144
Cuni Raya Vira Cocha (*huaca*), 4, 7–11
Cunibo Indians, 307
Cushma, 299

Dean, Carolyn, 274, 275
De la Anunciación, Pasqual, 121
De la Maza, Gonzalo, 199–206, 215
De la Parra, Leonis, 125
De la Rosa, Julián, 114
De la Serna, Antonio, 121
De la Torre, Bernardino, 61
De los Angeles, Francisco, 59, 60, 61, 64, 104
Dias, Bartolomeu, 44, 48, 49, 50, 52
Dias, Diogo, 52, 53, 54, 55
Dias, Hieronima, 244
Dias, Paulo, 99, 102
Diaz, Domingos, 241
Díaz, Pedro, 114, 116
Domingos, Manoel, 382
Domínguez, Juan Francisco, 68, 367–71
Dominic, Saint, 60, 156, 158, 202
Dominican Order, **407**; determining Santa Rosa's
    sanctity, 199, 200; devotion to Our Lady of the
    Rosary, 269; doctrinal preaching of, 60; in north-
    ern Spain, 65; Order of Saint Augustine, 168; in
    residence in Texupa, 122; work in Peru, 167
Don Quixote de la Mancha (Cervantes), 361, 362
Dos Passos, Manoel, 382
Dutch West India Company, 162
Duviols, Pierre, 247, 255

Eckhout, Albert, 162
Efigenia, Saint, 281
El Congo (slave), 301, 302
El Corso, 190, 192
El lazarillo de ciegos caminantes, 328

El Mina, 36
Encomienda system/*encomenderos*, 66, 309, **408**
Enríquez, Martín, 121
Erasmus, Desiderius, 198
Escolar, Pero, 44, 45
Escudo de monja, 215
Esmeraldas, Ecuador, 159, 160, 161
Espírito Santo *irmandade*, 280–96
"Extirpation of idolatry," 246, 247, 255–68
Ex-voto, offering to Saint Anne, 353–55

Fabián y Fuero, Francisco, 324, 326
Fazendas, 239, 240, 241, **408**
Ferdinand V of Castile, 65, 79
Ferdinand VII of Spain, 402
Fernandes, Miguel, 236
Fernandes, Pedro, 99–103
Fernández de Otañes, Andrés, 326
Fernández de Santa Cruz, Manuel de, 208
Fernandez Paredes, Manuel, 355
Figueiredo, Francisco Manoel de, 381
Figueiredo, Francisco Xavier de, 381
Florentine Codex, 19
Flores de Oliva, Isabel. *See* Rosa of Lima, Santa
Flores Galindo, Alberto, 393
Francis of Assisi, Saint, 60, 61, 157, 356
Francis of Paula, Saint, 356
Franciscan Order, **408**; Barefoot, or Discalced order
    of, 60; Capuchins, order of, 60; chronicles of
    indigenous uprisings, 301–8; *coloquio* of holy
    men with Franciscans, 19–22; first Mestizo friar,
    150; Friars Minor, order of, 60; "Observants" *ver-*
    sus "Conventuals," 60, 150; Recollects, order of,
    60; Somoza, Antonio de, 196; "the Twelve," 19–22,
    59–64, 104, 105, 128, 136, 137, 150; work in Peru,
    188
Francisco, Alexandre, 373
Francisco, Antônio, 356
Francisco (priest), 100
Francisco (slave), 301, 302
Frederick III, 104
Freire, Paul Antunes, 244, 245
Freitas, André de, 243
Fuensalida, Louis de, 61
Fuentes, Carlos, 316

Galdós, Alonso de, 113, 114
Galicia, Pablo de, 114, 116
Gallardo, Mauricio, 308
Gálvez, José de, decrees of, 316–19
Gama, Vasco da, 35, 43, 44
Ganson, Barbara, 310
Gante, Pedro de, 59; assisted by Frey Valadés, 150; in
    Codex Osuna, 146, 147; concerns about Indian
    labor, 144; and Franciscan efforts in New World,
    128, 129; in illustration in *Rhetorica Christiana*,
    151, 152; letter to Charles V, 104–12, 136; on
    Spanish Christian responsibility, 176

García, Domingo, letter of, 301, 302–4, 305, 306
García, Lucas, 114
Garcilaso de la Vega, El Inca, 17, 300, 393, 394
Gêges people, 281, 373, **408**
General History of Peru (Garcilaso de la Vega), 393
Gibson, Charles, 316
Gigedo, Revilla, 323
Gobernador, 159
Gomes, Aires, 56
Gómez, Alonso, 114, 116
Gonçalves, José, 346
Goncalves Pereira, Manoel, 382
Gonsalves Lima, João, 378
González, Juan, 325
González, Leonor, 124
González de Ozerín, Ignacio, 263
González de Santa Cruz, Roque, 312
Good Hope, Cape of, 43
Granada, 27, 69, 88, 127
Gregory, Saint, 156, 157
Grüninger, Johannes, 79, 83
Guadalupe, Our Lady of, 367
Guaillapaico, Andrés, 266, 268
Guaman Bilca, Pedro, 265, 268
Guaman Capacha, 260
Guaman Pilpi, Andrés, 265, 268
Guaman Poma de Ayala, Felipe, 5; on architecture
    and art in Lima, 188; concerning priests in Peru,
    173–84; on Spanish abuses of Indians, 186,
    328–29
Guamancama (*malqui*), 265
Guaraní Indians, 81, 176, 309–15
Guaras, Domingo, 265
Guardiola, Marqués de, 323
Guerrero, Pedro de, 127
Guzmán, Diego de, 114

Hacac (*malqui*), 263
Hacas Malqui, Cristóbal, 260, 265
Hacas Poma, Hernando, 259, 263–64, 265, 266, 267,
    268
Hasto Paucar, Francisco, 262, 265
Hausa people, 373, **408**
Henry the Navigator, 35, 36, 37, 38, 39, 40, 41
Hermanos, 127
Herodotus, 79
Hidalgo, Miguel, 397, 400
*History of the Celebrated Sanctuary of Our Lady of
    Copacabana* (Ramos Gavilán), 169
History of the Foundation of Lima (Cobo), 186
Holy Office of the Inquisition (Bahia, Brazil), con-
    fessions to, 234–45
How to Provide for the Salvation of the Indians
    (Acosta), 135, 136, 137
Huacas, 3–4, 174, 248, 256, 257, 258, 260, 267, **408**
Huallallo Caruincho (*huaca*), 7
Huari Indians, 268
Huarochirí, 256

Huarochirí Manuscript, 3–13, 24, 247, 248
Huatya Curi, 13
Huayna Capac, 299, 300, 308, 390
Huejotzingo Altarpiece (Mexico), 153–58, 271, 274

Iberian Peninsula: Aragón-Catalonia kingdom, 27;
    Aragón kingdom, 69; Braga, 31; coexistence of
    medieval Spanish kingdoms, 27–33; *convivencia*
    in medieval times, 27–28; Córdoba kingdom, 27;
    Granada kingdom, 27, 69; León-Castile kingdom,
    27, 31; Portugal kingdom, 27; Saltes, 29; Seville
    kingdom, 27; territory of al-Andalus, 27, 28, 29;
    Toledo kingdom, 27; Valencia kingdom, 27
Ibn 'Abd al-Ra'uf, 29
Ibn 'Abdun, 29, 31
Idolatry, 257, **408**
India, Portuguese trade and production in, 43, 44
Indians, **408**–9; "Inquisition for Indians," 255–68;
    opinion of Peruvian postal inspector on Indian
    affairs, 328–34. *See also* Amerindians; *specific tribe*
Inkas, 299–301, **409**; Capacocha festival, 273;
    Chachapoyas, 272; *huacas* of, 3–4; in Huarochirí
    province, 3–6; "Inka key" pattern, 15; Inti Raymi,
    273; *malquis* of, 4–5; *mitmaqkuna*, 272; "Mr.
    Inca," 328, 329, 331; *raymi* of, 16, 17; Sapa Inka,
    14, 16, 277; Tawantinsuyu (Land of the Four
    Quarters), 3; textiles of, 14–18; themes in Corpus
    Christi procession paintings, 277, 279; *villcas*
    of, 4; "written garments" of, 14–18; Yauyos
    province, 3
"Inquisition for Indians," 255–68
Irmandade, 280–96, **409**; Bahian memberships of,
    281; Black *irmandade* in Bahia, Brazil, 280–96;
    charitable functions of, 281, 283; covenant of
    Santo Antônio de Catagerona, 283–96; origins in
    Portugal, 281
Isabella I, 65, 213
Islam. *See* Muslims
Islas, Andrés de, 360, 363–64
Izabel (slave), 358

James I of Aragon, 87
"Jeremiah in the Stocks," 356–59
Jerome, Saint, 156, 157, 214
Jeronimo, Saint, 354
Jeronymite Order, in Mexico, 207
Jesuit Order (Society of Jesus), **409**; Carrió's opinion
    of, 329, 330; educating indigenous children in
    New Spain, 128–29; expulsion from Brazil, 93;
    Guaman Poma's description of, 174; La
    Concepción mission, 310, 311, 312; missions in
    Paraguay, 310; Morisco Jesuits, 129–30; work in
    Brazil, 218–19; work in Peru, 167, 186, 188, 189;
    work with Moriscos in Spain, 127–29; work with
    the Tupinambá in Brazil, 93–103
Jews: "crypto-Jews" in Brazil, 235; expulsion from
    Iberian Peninsula, 60; mentioned in confessions,
    244, 245; rules in twelfth-century Iberian

Peninsula, 31–32; secret emigration to New World, 187; during Spanish Inquisition, 187, 188
Jezus, Ann Caetana de, 378
João I, 35, 37
João IV, 218
João VI, 403, 404
John the Baptist, Saint, 156, 158
Julca, Pedro, 268
Julca Guaman, Diego, 268

Kubler, George, 390, 395
Kurakas, 277, 302, 393, **409**. *See also Caciques*

La Candelaria, 167, 168
"La felicidad del estado," 367
"La felicidad pública," 366, 367
"La Linda" (Virgin of Cusco), 277, 278, 279
Lara, Gregorio de, 123
Las Casas, Bartolomé de, 66, 105, 136, 137
Lawrence, Saint, 156, 158
Legos, 104
Leiba Esparragoza, Miguel de, 323
Leo X, Pope, 60
León, Felipe de, 169, 170
León-Castile, 27, 31
León-Portilla, Miguel, 19
León Portocarrero, Pedro de, description of Lima, 185–95, 196
León y Gama, Antonio de, 23
"Letter to Soderini," 78–83
Life and Death, and Miracles of Sor Rosa de Santa María (Loayza), 200
Lima: census and description of, 185–95; Church and Monastery of San Francisco, 196–97; postal inspector's letter on Indian affairs, 328–34; Santa Rosa of Lima, 198–206, 215, 216, 277, 278; *Temple of Our Great Patriarch, San Francisco* (Figueroa), 196
Lisboa, Manuel Francisco, 357
Llacsa Tanta, Leonor, 266
Llactas, 256, **409**
Loayza, Pedro de, 200
Lockhart, James, 113
Lohmann Villena, Guillermo, 187
Lombard, Peter, 65, 67
Lopes de Carualho, Andre, 244, 245
Lopez, Affonso, 46
Lorenzana, Maestro, 201
Loubato, Manoel Jozé, 382
Loyola, Ignatius de, 93, 98, 127
Luzia, Saint, 354

Macacayan (idol), 262
Macías, Juan, 199
Macute, Captain, 323, 324
Madeira, 36
Madeira, Felipe Carlos, 380, 381
Madrid, Treaty of, 310

Magón, José Joaquín, 360–62
Malik b. Anas, 28
Malquis, 4–5, 256, 257, **409**
Mamelucos, 100, 241, **409**
Manco Capac, 390, 394
Mandeville, Sir John, 79
Manoel, Antonio, 378
Manuel I, 43
Manuel, Fernando, 321, 323, 324
Marañón, Gerónimo del, 171–72
Marinho, Manoel, 244, 245
Marticorena, Manuel de, 308
Martínez, Diego, 201
Martyr, Peter, 78
Maurits, Johan, 162
Maximilian I, 104
Maxixcatzin, Juan, 114
Mayordomo, 267, **409**
Medeiros da Costa, Antonio de, 378
Medici, Lorenzo di Pier Francesco de, 78, 79
Mejía, Félix, 114
Melo e Castro, Martinho de, 336
Mena, Luis de, 360
Mendes, Antonio, 245
Mendes Vieira, Luiz, 378
Mendieta, Gerónimo, 156
Mendoça, Gabriel de, 123
Mendonça, Heitor Furtado de, 234–35, 236
Mendoza, Antonio de, 108, 111
Mendoza, Francisco de, 114
Mendoza, Juan de, 188, 259, 264, 265
Menéndez Pidal, Ramón, 27
Mercedarian Order: in Mexico, 59; work in Ecuador, 159; work in Peru, 193
Messa Valera, Juan de, 308
Mestizaje, 364, **410**
Mestizos, 129, 176, **410**; *casta* paintings of, 360–65; first Franciscan friar, 150; population in Lima, 186
Mexico: Antequera, 117; *castas* paintings, 360–65; Church of Santo Domingo, Puebla, 269–71; Codex Sierra, Oaxaca, 148–49; Colegio de los Niños, 111; Cuestlavaca pueblo, 122; finding of Aztec Stone of the Five Eras, 23–26; Huejotzingo Altarpiece, 153–58; Mexico City fountains and monuments, 384–89; Mixteca glyph records, 119, 120, 121; Puebla, 117, 269–71; Rosary of Our Lady, 269; San José de los Naturales, 104, 150; Santiago Tlatelolco, 19; Tamaçulapa, 119, 122; Tenochtitlan, 19–22, 84; Teposcolula pueblo, 122; Texupa, 117–23; Tilantongo, 119; Tlaxcala, 113–16; Tonaltepeque pueblo, 122; treatment of slaves, 320; Yanguitlan pueblo, 122
Mexico City: Academia de San Carlos, 316; churches in, 144, 146; Codex Osuna, 144–47; eighteenth-century inscriptions on public works, 384–89; monument for new roadway to San Agustín de las Cuevas, 387–88; Plaza Mayor, inscriptions on, 388–89; Salto del Agua, 385–87

Michael, Saint, 157, 356
Micui Conopa (idol), 262
Minas Gerais: expedition to, 335–52; ex-voto offering to Saint Anne, 353–55; "Jeremiah in the Stocks," 356–59
Minorites, 60
Miranda, Simam de, 47, 56
Mitmaqkuna, 272
Mixtec Indians, 119, 120, 121, 122
Moctezuma, 104
Mogrovejo, Toribio Alfonso de, 135, 199
Mollinedo y Angulo, Manuel de, 276
Monis Telex, Anrique, 241
Montesclaros, Marquis of, 188
Montoro, Bachiller, 170
Montúfar, Alonso de, 104
Morelos, José María, "Sentiments of the Nation" of, 397–400
Moreno, Bachiller, 144
Morenos, 321
Morgados, 375
Moriscos, **410**; drawing of, 87–90; Franciscan preaching missions to, 60, 69, 70; as subjects of Charles V, 87–90
Motecçuma, 122
Motolinía, Julián, 114
Motolinía, Toribia de Benavente, 60
Moura, Pero de, confession of, 243, 244–45
Mozárabes, 28, 29
Mudéjares, 69
"The Mulatto Gentlemen of Esmeraldas," 159–61
Mulattoes, 199, 362, **410**; artist Aleijadinho, 356; Black *irmandade* in Bahia, Brazil, 280–96; family history of Padre Vieira, 218; group portrait of, 159–61; Guaman Poma's depiction of, 176, 177, 178; Jesuits of Mulatto descent, 129, 130; population in Lima, 186; Porras, Martín de, 199
Mundus Novus (Vespucci), 79
Murúa, Martín de, 17
Muslims: Almohads, 27; Almoravids, 27; conquest of, 60; *dhimmis*, 29, 32, 33; intellectual achievements in medieval Spain, 29, 32; Islamic festivals for, 28; Maliki law, 28, 30, 32, 33; Mudéjares, 69; *muhtasib*, 29; observance and participation in Christian holidays, 28; Prophet Muhammad, 28, 29; Qur'an, 28; Ramadan, 28; rules in twelfth-century Iberian Peninsula, 31–32; secret emigration to New World, 187; Sunna, 28. *See also* Islam

Nabin Carua, Leonor, 262, 265
Nahuatl language, 104, **410**; in exchange between Tenochtitlan holy men with Franciscans, 19–22; at time of Conquest, 113; used in Codex Sierra, 148–49; used in Codex Osuna, 144
Narcizo, Antonio, 382
Nassau-Siegen, Count of, 162
Natural and Moral History of the Indies (Acosta), 135
Naturales, 136

Navarro, João de Azpilcueta, 94, 95
Navarro, Joseph Antonio, letter of, 320, 322–26
Navarro, Pedro, 128
Nebrija, Antonio de, 93
Negros, 186
Ñenguirú, Nicolás, 176, 309–15
Netherlands, colonization in Brazil, 162
New Chronicle and [Treatise on] Good Government (Guaman Poma), 173, 174, 176, 178
Nicholas V, Pope, 37–42
Niza, Tadeo de, 114
Nobre, Domingos Fernandes, confession of, 236–41
Nóbrega, Manoel da, 93–101, 102
Novoa, Bernardo de, 255, 256
Nugueira, Francisco, confession of, 242–44
Ñundaa. *See* Mexico, Texupa

Ocampo, Baltasar de, 390, 394
Oliva, María de, 201
Olmedo, Bartolomé de, 59
O'Malley, John, 131
"On the Evangelization of Unbelievers" (Vitoria), 65–77
Oñate, Buenaventura, 114
Oñate, Fernando de, 391
Ordenações, 375
Orixá, 164
Ortiz, Alonso, 124–26
Ortiz, Diego de, 170, 391
Otañes, Andrés de, 323, 324, 325, 326
Our Lady of Copacabana, 167–72
Our Lady of Guadalupe, 367
Our Lady of the Rosary, 168, 219

Padilla, José de, 323
Padres, 127, 128, 174
Padroado, 404, **410**
Páez, José de, 360
Pagden, Anthony, 66, 68
Palenques, 322, **410**
Pampa Condor, Cristóbal, 264, 265
Pamplona, Inácio Correia, expedition into Mina Gerais, 335–52
Pando, Martín, 391
Paraguay, 309; bilingual society of, 309; Guaraní Indians of, 309–15; Guaraní War in, 310
Parco, 362
Paredes, Diego de, 114
Paria Caca (*huaca*), 4, 7, 8, 13, 248
Pastoral Letter (Villagómez), 247, 248
Paul, Saint, 61, 367
Paul III, Pope, 127
Paullu, 390
Paz, Juan de, 114
Pedroso, Antonio del, 114, 116
Peninsulares, 318, 384, 394, 395, 397, **410**
Pereira, João, 341
Pereira dos Passos, Joze, 382

Pereyns, Simon, 156
Pérez de Guzmán, Alonso, 274, 275
Peru, **410**; Acas of, 255, 256, 258, 259, 264, 265;
　Anansaya kin group, 167, 168; Cajatambo, 4–5;
　Cañaris of, 272; Chachapoyas of, 272; Chuquiabo,
　171; Chuquisaca, 171; Colegio of San Francisco
　de Borja, 299; College of San Pablo, 134; Corpus
　Christi procession, Cusco paintings of, 272–79;
　Cusco School, 272; Cusco Valley, 3, 16, 185;
　description of Lima, 185–95; execution of
　Atahuallpa, 67; festival of Vecosina, 259, 267;
　Hayohayo, 171; Huarochirí (Huaro Cheri)
　province, 3–6; Huarochirí of, 256–57; Inka tunics
　from, 14–18, 277; La Chaupiguaranga de Lampas
　region, 264; "La Linda," 277, 278, 279; Lake
　Titicaca, 167, 168, 174, 256; Llacuazes, 256, 257;
　Order of Saint Augustine, 168; Our Lady of
　Copacabana, 167–72; Paracas peoples of, 14;
　Pernambuco, 234; port of Callao, 187, 188;
　Potosí, 185; Santa Ana de Copacabana, 167;
　Santa Rosa of Lima, 198–206, 215, 216, 277, 278;
　Urinsaya kin group, 167. *See also* Lima
Peter Damian, Saint, 156, 157
Philip II, 117, 393
Philip III, 173, 375
Pinto, José, 346
Pinturas, 117, **410**
Piro Indians, 305, 307
Pius V, Pope, 235
Pizarro, Francisco, 185, 390
Pohl, John, 119, 120
Politics (Aristotle), 67
Polo, Marco, 79
Polo de Ondegardo, Juan, 134, 260
Poma Libia, Cristóbal, 264, 266
Poma Lloclla, Gonzalo, 262, 266
Poma Quillai, Hernando, 266
Poma y Altas Caldeas, Francisco, 255–68
Pombal, Francisco Antônio, 357
Pombal, Marques of, 335, 336
Porras, Martín de, 130
Portugal, 27; Caminha's letter from Brazil, 43–48;
　naval expedition to Brazil, 43–58; slave traders of,
　34, 35–37
Post, Frans, 164
Prado, Ignacio Gonçalves do, 378
Prados, Vicar of, 337
Presidios, 329, **410**
Principe Real (ship), 403
Proceso apostólico, 199
Proceso ordinario, 199
Pulque, 114, 115, **410**
Purum Runa people, 13

Quechua language, 135, 246, 257, **411**
Quespo, Pedro, 260
Quilombo do Ambrósio, 342, 343
Quilombos, 335–36, **411**

Quispi Guaman, Alonso, 265
Qur'an, 69

Race/racial classes: *castas* in, 364; classifications of,
　360–65; "passing" as Spaniards, 365; possible
　racial mixtures, 364
Ramos Gavilán, Alonso, 168
Raura, Juan, 265
Reco-reco, 164
Reducción, 321, **411**
Relaciones geográficas, 117; of Texupa, 121–23, 148,
　149
Remirão, João de, 238
Rhetorica Christiana (Valadés), 129, 150
Ribas, Juan de, 61
Ribeiro, Affonso, 48, 53, 55
Ribeiro, Pantaliam, 239
Ribeiro, Severino, 337
Ribera, Domingo, 265
Rivadeneyra, Fernando Carlos de, 324
Rocha, Cristovão da, 240, 241
Rocha Franco, Bartolomeu da, 377
Rodrigues, Ana, 241
Rodrigues, Simão, 95, 96, 99–102, 348, 350
Rodríguez, Fabián, 114, 116
Rodríguez, Gabriel, 123
Rodríguez, Manuela, 325
Rodríguez de la Vega, Miguel, 325
Rodríguez Valero, José Antonio, 322
Romanus Pontifex, 36, 37–42
Rosa of Lima, Santa, 198–206, 215, 216, 277, 278
Rosary, Our Lady of the, 168
Rosary chapel (Puebla, Mexico), 269–71
Rowe, John Howland, 15, 17, 300
Royal Commentaries (Garcilaso de la Vega), 300, 393
Rozas, Sancho de, 114, 116
Runcato, 307

Sá, João de, 44
Sacramento, Joaquina Maria do, 373
Saeger, James, 310
Sáez de Bustamante, Pablo, 307
Sahagún, Bernardino de, 19, 59, 249
Salinas y Córdova, Buenaventura de, 186, 187, 188,
　189
Salomon, Frank, 4, 5
Sambenito, 187
San Antonio, Joseph de, 306, 307
Sanches Carilho, Fernão, 241
Sánchez, Alonso, 191
Sánchez, Francisco, 123
Sánchez Gallque, Andrés, 159, 161
Sandoval, Joseph de, 123
Santa Anna, Manoel de, 383
Santa Casa da Misericórdia, 281
Santa Cruz, Basilio de, 273
Santa Justa, Joanna Maria de, 380
Santa María, Rosa de, 200

Santa Ritta, Antonio Jozé, 382
Santabancori, 300, 304
Santiago, Mattheus de, 378
Santiago Xavier, Felippe de, last will and testament of, 376–79
Santidade, 238, 239
Santo, Manuel del, 302, 303, 304
Santos Atahualpa, Juan, 299–302, 305–7
São Jorge da Mina, 36
São Jozé da Trindade, Anna de, last will and testament of, 379–83
São Pedro, Antônia Maria de, 358
Saracens, 69
Sardinha, Fernandes, 95
Sarmiento, Pedro, 260, 265
Sayago, Juan López, 125
Sayri Túpac, 390
Sebastian, Saint, 156, 158, 167–68
Segura, Gabriel de, 323
Sena, Antonio Bernardino de, 377, 378
Sentences (Lombard), 65, 67
"Sentiments of the Nation" (Morelos), 397–400
Sepúlveda, Juan Ginés de, 67
Sermons on the Mysteries of Our Holy Catholic Faith (Avendaño), 247
Serra, José Francisco, 343, 348
Serra Caldeira, José da, 338, 341, 342
Sesmaria, 336, 346, **411**
Setebo Indians, 307
Seville, 27
Shipibo Indians, 307
Silva, Antonio da, 382
Silva, Domingo de, 114
Silva, Eugênia Luísa da, 335
Silva Feio, Jozé Ferreira da, 380, 381
Slaves/slavery: from Africa, 34, 35–37, 281, 373; "Blacks Dancing," painting of, 162–64; in Brazil, 218–33, 378; Brazilian slaves who marry, 372–74; *cimarrones* (runaway Black slaves), 320–27; civil law and division of property, 376–83; El Congo, 301, 302; Francisco, 301, 302; Izabel, 358; last will and testament of freed slave, 379–83; in Lima, 192; Malê revolt of, 373; Padre Vieira's sermons on, 218–33; in Peru, 186, 192; Portuguese trade in, 34, 35–37; settlement at Amapa, 320–27
Society of Jesus. *See* Jesuits
Soderini, Pietro, 78–83
Soiro, Jorge do, 58
Solano, Francisco, 199
Solórzano, Juana, 268
Somoza, Antonio de, 196
"Sor Filotea," letter of, 208–14, 215
Soria, Martin, 395
Soto, Diego de, 114, 116
Soto, Domingo de, 66
Soto, Francisco de, 61
Sousa Pinto, José Antônio de, 351
Souza, Aleixo Custodio, 383

Souza, Jozé de, 380, 381
Spain: Albaicín, 127–28, **405**; Archivo General de Indias, 117; *auto-da-fé*, 187; College of Granada, 127; Granada kingdom, 127; Inquisition, 187, 188; Laws of Burgos, 66; Medina del Campo, 134; Salamanca, 65–77; "School of Salamanca," 66; "Second Thomism" movement in, 66; Toledo kingdom, 27; University of Alcalá, 132
Suárez, Francisco, 66, 68
Suárez de Figueroa, Miguel, 196
Summa (Crockaert and Vitoria), 66
Summary of Theology (Saint Thomas Aquinas), 65, 67
Sun Stone (Mexico), 23–26

Talavera, Hernando de, 128
Tamoancham, 22
Tanquis, Cristóbal, 266
Tantayana, Domingo, 264, 266
Tapejaras Indians, 343, 344
Tapia, Vicente, 323
Tatcachi, Domingo, 266
Tawantinsuyu (Land of the Four Quarters), 3, 15, 272, 300, 393, **411**
Tecepotzin, Hernando, 114
Teixeira, Marcos, 242, 244, 245
Teixeira Aranha, José, 346
Telles Barreto, Manoel, 238, 239
Téllez, Antonio, 114
Tello, Joham, 48
Temple of Our Great Patriarch, San Francisco (Figueroa), 196
Ten Commandments, Domínguez's treatise on, 367–71
Tenochtitlan: *coloquio* of holy men with Franciscans, 19–22; conquered by Cortés, 84; finding of Aztec Stone of the Five Eras, 23–26
Tente en el aire, 364
Tepanecas, 22
Teta, Juan de, 105
Teutiuacam, 22
Texupa, *relación geográfica* and *pintura* of, 117–23, 148, 149
"Thanking Saint Anne" (1755), 353–55
Third Catechism and Exposition of the Christian Doctrine in Sermons (Avila), 246, 247
Thomas Aquinas, Saint, 65, 66, 67
Thomaz, Maria, 377
Tito Yupanqui, Francisco, 167, 168, 169–72
Tlalocan, 22
Tlaxcala, early colonial residents of, 113–16
Toar, Sancho de, 47, 55
Toledo, Francisco de, 134, 135, 391, 393
Topa Gualpa, 390
Tordesillas, Treaty of, 65
Torres, Diego de, 159
Torres, Pedro de, 306, 307–8
Torres Tuñón, Luis de, 319
Torres y Ayala, Laureano José de, 306

Townsend, Richard, 23, 25
Trachtenbuch (Weiditz), 84
Treatise on the Gospels (Avila), 246
Tulan Vapalcalco, 22
Tulanos, 22
Tupa Puma, Baltazar, 277
Túpac Amaru, 300, 329, 390–94, 395
Túpac Amaru II, 395
Tuta Ñamca (*huaca*), 7

Unamuno, Miguel de, 149, 208
Uncus (tunics), 14–18
Upiai, Inés, 265
Urban II, Pope, 198
Urinsaya, 167
Urpay Huachac, 11
Uruguay, 309
Usátegui, María de, 200, 201, 204, 205

Valadares, Count of, 348
Valadés, Diego, 249; as indigenous assistant, 137;
    composing *Rhetorica Christiana*, 129, 150; illus-
    tration in *Rhetorica Christiana*, 151; on Indian
    human rights, 150–52
Valencia, 27
Valencia, Martín de, 59, 60, 61, 63, 104, 150
Valera, Blas, 129
Vargas, Nicolás, 190, 192
Vasconcelos, Nicolao Faleiro de, 241
Veiga, Lourenço da, 240
Velarde C., Juan Antonio, 324
Velasco, Luis de, 116
Venezuela, role of Catholic Church, 367, 401
Vespucci, Amerigo, "Letter to Soderini," 78–83
Vespucci, Giorgio Antonio, 78
Viegas, Manoel, 244
Vieira, Antônio, sermons on slavery, 218–33
"The View from the Red and White Bundle," 119, 120
Villagómez, Pedro de, 246, 247, 248, 256

Villaumbrosa, Countess of, 213
Viracocha, 303, 304, **412**
Viracocha Inka, Alonso, 167, 170
Visitador, 234, 242, 255, 316, 318, **412**
Visitador general de idolatría, 255
Visitas, 144, 395, **412**
Vitoria, Francisco de, 65–77, 137, 176

Wage labor, decrees of, 316–19
Wagener, Zacharias, 162–64
War of the Spanish Succession, 384
Weiditz, Christoph: drawing of Morisco Woman and
    Her Daughter, 87–90; drawing of Indian Woman,
    84–86

Xavier, Francisco, 127
Xavier, Saint Francis, 136
Xicotencatl, Juan, 114
Ximénez, Francisco, 61
Xuárez, Juan, 61
Xuchatlapan, 22

Yaanicuin, 122
Yaguizi, 122
Yana Ñamca (*huaca*), 7
Yana Pintor, Domingo, 265
Yanacuu, 122
Yanatarquivrauc, 264
Yanaurau (idol), 265
Yesa Huyya, 122
Yoalliycham, 22
Yoruba people, 164, **412**
Yucatán, 63

Zambo people, 362, **412**
Zapaca Inga, Juan, 273
Zeballos, Bernardo de, 323
Zuidema, R. Tom, 17, 18
Zumárraga, Juan de, 129